Teaching Content to All

Evidence-Based Inclusive Practices
in Middle and Secondary Schools

B. Keith Lenz
University of Kansas

Donald D. Deshler
University of Kansas

with **Brenda R. Kissam**

PEARSON

Boston   New York   San Francisco   Mexico City
Montreal   Toronto   London   Madrid   Munich   Paris
Hong Kong   Singapore   Tokyo   Cape Town   Sydney

This book is dedicated to all the content-area teachers out there who struggle—many times doggedly— in their efforts to help students understand and use information that can shape their lives. It is also dedicated to the teachers, students, parents, and administrators in the Shawnee Mission and Lawrence, Kansas, school districts, as well as those in many other school districts across the country, who helped us think about, develop, and test ideas related to teacher planning and instruction that really do work.

Executive editor: Virginia Lanigan
Editorial assistant: Robert Champagne
Executive marketing manager: Amy Cronin Jordan
Manufacturing buyer: Andrew Turso
Production coordinator: Pat Torelli Publishing Services
Cover designer: Suzanne Harbison
Editorial-production service: Stratford Publishing Services, Inc.
Electronic composition: Stratford Publishing Services, Inc.

For related titles and support materials, visit our online catalog at www.ablongman.com.

Cover and chapter art: David Rossman

Library of Congress Cataloging-in-Publication Data

Teaching content to all : evidence-based inclusive practices in middle and secondary
   schools / [edited by] B. Keith Lenz, Donald D. Deshler with Brenda R. Kissam.
       p.   cm.
   Includes bibliographical references and index.
   ISBN 0-205-39224-5
   1. Middle school education--Curricula--United States.   2. Education,
Secondary--Curricula--United States.   3. Inclusive education--United States.   I. Lenz, B.
Keith.   II. Deshler, Donald D.   III. Kissam, Brenda R.

LB1628.5.T43 2004
373.19--dc21   2003043667

Printed in the United States of America

10 9 8 7 6 5 4 3 2 1   07 06 05 04 03

Contents

The Contributors

Lillie R. Albert
Boston College

Jerome J. Ammer
University of San Diego

Gwen Berry
Minnesota State University

Janis A. Bulgren
University of Kansas

Jeffrey W. Cornett
University of Central Florida

Patricia G. Gildroy
Portland State University

Deborah D. Hall
Madison Area Technical College

Margaret E. King-Sears
Johns Hopkins University

Earle Knowlton
University of Kansas

Sharon Lynch
George Washington University

Jean Mooney
Boston College

Jennifer C. Platt
University of Central Florida

Suzanne Robinson
University of Kansas

David Scanlon
Boston College

Juliana Taymans
George Washington University

Preface

The goal of this book is to help prepare teachers to respond to the demands of academic diversity found among students and teachers in middle schools and high schools. In the midst of standards-based school reform, a pressing issue for teachers and reformers is how to ensure that all students have access to the curriculum and effective instruction. All students must be supported in ways that will enable them to meet the standards set by states and local school districts.

This text is designed to provide secondary teachers with effective planning and teaching routines to help them address the learning needs of all students and create a truly inclusive classroom environment. While this text supports inclusive instruction in many respects, it does not, as most inclusion texts do, deal only with inclusion of students with special needs, such as English language learners or students with high-incidence disabilities. This text deals with academic diversity and with planning and teaching for a diverse class. It is what all secondary teachers need to know when they have students with many different types of learning needs. So, for example, the text does not discuss specific adaptations for students with hearing impairments; however, it does deal with the dilemma of *what content is important* if you are going to make adaptations for someone who is hearing impaired when you have 30 other students in your history class.

The traditional approach to inclusion is to list many methods and many adaptations appropriate for different types of disabilities. However, it is clear that implementing and sustaining a wide variety of individualized adaptations is impossible for most secondary teachers, who may teach as many as 150 students each day. Furthermore, teachers might adapt some unimportant content if they have not thought through what content students need to learn. Therefore, focusing only on how individual needs should be met is insufficient.

The methods presented here are effective for instruction of students in middle schools, junior high schools, and high schools, primarily covering grades 4 to 12. Concepts, strategies, and classroom-based activities are provided that can be used by teachers to understand differences among learners and then to plan and teach in ways that respond to learning needs arising from those differences. The book also includes a broad set of materials based on research conducted in hundreds of classrooms by researchers from the University of Kansas Center for Research on Learning. These materials include *Pedagogies for Diversity in Secondary Schools: A Preservice*

Curriculum (1994) and the teaching routines in the *Content Enhancement Series* (see Appendix C).

This book is appropriate for both preservice and inservice teachers. Instructors can adapt the book to fit the level of need for a particular audience or course because the book revolves around a set of underlying principles and strategies. The content and approaches described have been used successfully for preservice and inservice teaching for both middle school teachers as well as high school teachers. This text may also serve as a supplemental text on planning for diversity in any secondary methods course.

PURPOSES OF THIS TEXT

While much of teaching involves spontaneous decision making, that process as well as all instruction should be based on knowledge, experience, and planning. Effective teachers learn what works and incorporate that knowledge into their teaching repertoires. But teachers often teach as they were taught, and for many teachers today that means using primarily teacher-centered methods. While this approach is sufficient for many of today's students, for many other students, it is not.

Today's teachers must face new instructional questions as their classrooms become filled with students from many different cultural backgrounds, from many different socio-economic circumstances, and having special learning needs. This text is designed to help teachers think in new ways about instruction in academically diverse classes by (1) selecting critical content to teach, (2) making connections in learning communities, (3) enhancing content instruction, and (4) teaching students how to learn.

First, we ask teachers to consider their role as curriculum makers. As curriculum makers, teachers need to think carefully about what they want to teach and what they want students to learn. This text provides research-based methods for thinking about and planning a course, a unit, and a lesson.

Second, we describe how teachers can organize their classrooms as learning communities and get to know their students to guide learning. Learning communities provide a way for teachers to establish an environment where connections are made between teacher and students, between students and students, and between students and the content. Learning communities can foster among students a feeling of being supported in their learning. Specific methods are described for establishing a learning community and for maintaining communication with students to more effectively guide their learning.

Third, this text describes teaching methods that allow teachers to *enhance* content in ways that make it more accessible for students to learn. Using methods that enhance content instruction allows teachers to compensate for limitations in students' prior learning or skills development.

Fourth, this text describes learning strategies and why it is important to help students learn how to learn. Specific strategies are presented, as well as methods to help teachers develop their own strategies.

The perspectives and teaching tools in this text can give secondary teachers more ways to address effectively the learning needs of all the many different students in classrooms today.

REFERENCE

Kissam, B., & Lenz, K. (Eds.). (1994). *Pedagogies for diversity in secondary schools: A preservice curriculum.* Lawrence, KS: Center for Research on Learning.

ACKNOWLEDGMENTS

We wish to acknowledge the contributions of Stephanie Carpenter, Ph.D., at Johns Hopkins University, and Helen Sachs Chaset, Ed.D., a school-based administrator in the Montgomery County, Maryland, public schools, for their contributions to early versions of Chapter 4 on course planning. In addition, Mary Vance and Joe Fisher made significant contributions to the development of ideas and materials in Chapters 5 and 6. Thanks are due also to our colleagues at the University of Kansas Center for Research on Learning who enable the work of the Center to go forth, and in doing so have provided important support for this project over the past eight years, especially Jean B. Schumaker, Janet Roth, David Gnojek, and Belinda Schuman.

Introduction

The wide range of academic diversity present in public schools today presents both a challenge and an opportunity to all teachers. It presents a particularly great challenge to secondary content teachers who face increased pressure to "cover the content" as the amount of content grows with additional thinking and research in many academic fields.

Because the challenge is so great and the need to accommodate all students so urgent, we tried to think about the problem of planning and teaching to include all learners in a new way. Inclusive instruction has typically focused on a variety of adaptations to meet a variety of learning needs. However, as academic diversity and expectations for inclusion increase, teaching efficiently and effectively may require a new paradigm.

As teachers prepare to teach a class, they usually think about instructional goals, teaching strategies, instructional activities, assessment, and classroom management. These are the fundamentals of the teaching methods that all prospective teachers learn in teacher education. This book differs from most preservice texts about planning and teaching in that these issues will be looked at from the perspective of better accommodating the different learning needs of all students in academically diverse classrooms, from normally achieving students to those struggling to make sense of the curriculum. In addition, issues related to establishing classroom climate, most often discussed in classroom management sections of basic methodology texts, will be discussed here within the broader context of establishing a learning community. This context brings classroom management into the realm of asking: What authentic work do you have for your students to do and how will you and they do it?

Inclusive teaching in secondary schools is based on seven principles that have guided the development of this book:

1. Diversity among students in secondary schools represents the norm, rather than the exception.
2. A new way to think about inclusive teaching to accommodate academic diversity among students is for teachers to focus on *making connections* between themselves and students, between students and students and, most importantly, between students and the content they must learn.
3. Making connections can be realized by *building a learning community* in the classroom.

4. Making connections depends on learning about and understanding what students already know.
5. Making connections can be realized by *selecting critical content.*
6. Making connections can be realized by *enhancing instruction* through teaching routines to compensate for the learning problems of students.
7. Making connections can be realized by *teaching students how to learn.*

Diversity as the norm.   Thinking about diversity among students as the norm rather than as something out of the ordinary is important as a first step in building inclusive teaching practices. Diane Ferguson (1995) has noted that "Meaningful change will require nothing less than a joint effort to reinvent schools to be more accommodating to all dimensions of human diversity" (p. 282). She argues that we must change our view of the school's role from one of providing educational services, to one of providing educational supports for learning:

> Valuing diversity and difference, rather than trying to change or diminish it so that everyone fits some ideal of similarity, leads to the realization that we can support students in their efforts to become active members of their communities. . . . Perhaps the most important feature of support as a concept for schooling is that it is grounded in the perspective of the person receiving it, not the person providing it. (p. 287)

This is not to say, however, that differences should be ignored. It is important to *respect* differences and acknowledge them by incorporating them into the life of the classroom, as well as the curriculum, so that learning is grounded in what is familiar to students.

Making connections.   What does it mean to make connections? It means that as a teacher you need to be as concerned about understanding your students and what is important and meaningful to them as you are about understanding your content and how to teach it. Making connections means that students need to believe that what you want to teach is important and relevant to them and that you can and will help them learn. Making connections also means that you as the teacher need to believe it is worthwhile to build a learning community in your classroom, to know and understand your students well enough to make choices about content and instruction so that all students have an opportunity to learn. Every good teacher aspires to these goals and many teachers successfully realize them. But as academic diversity among students grows in secondary schools, teachers need more support and more tools to be effective with all learners. Support can be gained, we believe, by thinking about a classroom as a learning community where teacher and students work together to ensure that everyone is learning. More tools become available with the implementation of teaching routines and learning strategies that make learning more accessible to more learners.

Understanding what students already know.   What students already know, or their "prior knowledge," comes not only from what students have previously learned in school, but also from their lived experiences. Lived experience includes all the differences that students bring with them into the schools, such as culture, language, ethnic backgrounds, as well as previous learning successes or failures. Valuing and using the prior knowledge of students allows teachers to link new knowledge to what students already know, thereby making learning more meaningful for students. It also allows students to construct new knowledge for themselves.

Building a learning community. Making connections and building a learning community in your classroom will establish an environment where learning, cooperation, and respect for differences are all valued. The "work" of this community is learning. Everyday practices and routines are based on cooperation in accomplishing this work, and the interests and learning needs of everyone in the community are taken seriously.

In addition to making connections between yourself and your students and between students and the content, you also need to be concerned about students being connected to other students. This is important, in part, because the world of work is based today on cooperation and teamwork. It is also important because teachers cannot hope to meet all the learning needs of all students unless students help each other. Cooperation in the classroom can nurture lifelong habits of teamwork and cooperation. It can give students the opportunity to learn from peers who may be able to explain new ideas in a way that is more relevant or understandable than teachers. It can also give students the opportunity to learn by helping others learn.

Building a learning community also means getting to know your students well enough to make informed decisions about how best to guide their learning. For example, if you plan to have students learn by reading a textbook, you need to know if all students have the skills to identify what is important when reading information presented in that format. If you plan to have students learn from a lecture, you need to know if students can make sense of information presented that way. Do students need help with structured note taking or from visual displays when information is presented in a lecture?

Knowing your students also means being aware of teaching practices and devices that can promote learning and those that, on occasion, get in the way of learning. For example, teachers often use analogies to help students understand particular concepts. If those analogies are drawn from experiences which students have not had, students not only will not learn but may also feel excluded from instruction. Analogies drawn from sports may exclude students with little experience in sports, or analogies drawn from life in rural communities will have little meaning in urban schools—and vice versa. This is not to say that such analogies may not be used or may not have relevance for some students. Rather, the point is that teachers need to be sensitive to what is meaningful to *all* their students and respectful of the background of their students so that teaching devices incorporate experiences familiar to all.

Selecting critical content. Making connections between students and the content they must learn is facilitated when you as the teacher make choices about what students must learn. Some of these choices are dictated by standards in these times of standards-based school reform. Yet other choices remain in your hands. Selecting content that is important and meaningful to students and being clear with students about your goals can help forge important connections between you and your students, as well as between students and the content.

Enhancing instruction.   Connections are made and strengthened in the learning community when you use teaching methods that compensate for students' learning problems. These methods, which we call teaching routines, can enhance your teaching and, in turn, enhance student learning by making learning goals explicit and clear for students. Organizing information and ideas through the use of teaching routines can make learning more accessible for students. The teaching routines that are developed in this text have been shown to improve learning for middle and high school students. New and experienced teachers have found them to be very useful and effective with all students.

Teaching routines discussed in this book can enhance your instruction by helping you plan for instruction using graphic organizers. These organizers allow you to create a picture or map of the big ideas in the content you want to teach and not only make learning goals more explicit for students, but also can help you make careful decisions about what you want students to learn—what the critical outcomes are of your course. Other kinds of teaching routines can help you "frame" what students need to learn within a context that has meaning for them. For example, routines can help you think about ways to compare and contrast concepts you want to teach, comparing what students need to learn to something with which they are already familiar.

Teaching learning strategies.   Finally, students are more likely to make connections in learning the content in your class if they know how to learn. All good learners use strategies to learn new things. Some students are better than others at developing strategies to learn. Inclusive teaching means that you have to take into account whether all your students are good strategic learners. Most likely many are not. This is why it is important to help students become strategic learners, and the only way to do this is to teach them—explicitly—how to use and develop learning strategies.

These seven principles describe the new paradigm we propose to guide inclusive instruction. While this paradigm does not provide particular adaptations to address every particular learning need of every student who may come into your classroom, it does provide an instructional approach that, on the one hand, is realistic and useable for every teacher and, on the other hand, can make learning accessible for all students.

ORGANIZATION OF THE TEXT

In Section One, **Framing Pedagogies for Diversity**, we "frame," or provide a context for, talking about inclusive teaching practices. "Pedagogies for Diversity" refers to the art of teaching students from diverse backgrounds with diverse learning needs. Chapter 1 examines the relationship between diversity among secondary students, on the one hand, and how students learn, on the other hand. This chapter explores how learning differences may lead to learning problems and surveys some of the ways teachers in the past have tried to accommodate individual differences. Also discussed are factors present in today's classrooms that complicate the effectiveness of those methods. The chapter concludes with an introduction to the development of the goals and skills needed for inclusive teaching. Chapter 2 describes the diversity found in secondary classrooms and identifies its sources. Diversity among students in secondary schools has become— and we believe, should be regarded as—the norm rather than the exception. Nevertheless, it can be helpful to new teachers to be aware of the overall features of this diversity nationwide. This awareness can contribute to a better understanding of both the need to develop more inclusive teaching practices, as well as the kinds of problems and issues those practices should address. Chapter 2 also discusses standards-based school reform efforts and how those efforts have an impact on and are themselves affected by the academic diversity in secondary schools.

In Section Two, **Conceptualizing Pedagogies for Academic Diversity**, we move on from describing diversity to looking in more detail at the implications of that diversity for teaching and learning. Chapter 3 discusses the role of teachers in making curricular decisions and introduces the SMARTER planning process based on the idea of selecting critical content that all students must learn. The idea of selecting critical content is basic to inclusive teaching practices because it focuses learning on what is important and helps teachers be clear and explicit with themselves and with students about what is to be taught and learned.

In Section Three, **Routines for Designing Instruction and Learning**, we talk about making connections by selecting critical content and enhancing instruction through planning and teaching routines. Teaching routines are sets of instructional procedures that can help guide the delivery of large chunks of content in a lesson and structure information so that potential learning difficulties are anticipated and addressed. Chapters 4, 7, and 8 describe teaching routines for planning a course, a unit, and a lesson. These routines can help teachers think through exactly what it is they want to teach and ways to structure what they will teach, so that it is meaningful and accessible for all students.

In Chapter 5, we extend ideas about course planning as we discuss building a learning community as a way to make connections between teachers and learners and between learners and the content. A learning community develops as you and your students agree on valued classroom principles, learning rituals, and performance options. A basic building block of a learning community is cooperation, and this chapter looks carefully at the principles underlying cooperative learning. The chapter also stresses the importance of developing social skills for cooperative learning and the need to match cooperative learning methods to appropriate kinds of tasks.

Chapter 6 discusses making connections by establishing good communication in the classroom. Good communication between students and teachers can help teachers know and understand what students already know. This knowledge is a key element in planning for learning that is meaningful to students. This chapter also discusses ways that teachers can examine their own beliefs about learning. This is an exercise that is vital for teachers if they are to be ready to learn about and accept different ways of knowing and learning among their students. It is also important that teachers understand how their own backgrounds and learning habits and preferences have an impact on how they teach. Teachers often teach as they were taught, and it is natural that we teach based on our own knowledge and experiences. However, teaching the way they were taught may no longer be effective for teachers in the classrooms of today.

In Section Four, **Teaching Your Course**, we talk about ways to teach a course so that all learners are brought along on the learning journey. Chapter 9 discusses ways to enhance instruction by using teaching routines to transform the content to compensate for student learning problems. Chapter 10 focuses on learning strategies, or teaching students how to learn. Students who may not have developed good learning strategies on their own can be taught to be strategic learners.

In Section Five, **Inclusion and Special Education**, we recognize that general education teachers increasingly have students with special needs in their classrooms. In Chapter 11 we discuss policies and procedures related to special education, including the development of Special Education law, the identification of students with special needs, and the Individual Education Program. In Chapter 12, *Linking to Other Professionals*, we describe the professional as well as collaborative arrangements available in many school districts to support general education teachers in their efforts to reach all students.

The Conclusion, **Models of Integrated Organizers**, ties together the pedagogies for diversity presented in the book. Appendix A provides the full text for the Learner-Centered Principles of the American Psychological Association, discussed in Chapter 1. Appendix B provides extended scenarios illustrating the use of the SMARTER planning process in secondary core content courses. Appendix C surveys learning strategies and concept enhancements developed by the Center for Research on Learning of the University of Kansas. Appendix D presents tools for compensating for inconsiderate textbooks. A glossary at the back of the book defines terms that may be unfamiliar to readers.

FORMAT

Each chapter has been structured and written to incorporate and model the basic elements of pedagogies for diversity. For example, graphic organizers are provided to structure the information presented; graphic organizers and a set of critical questions alert the reader to the important ideas and information in each chapter; analogies, examples, and other teaching devices representative of a range of experiences, are included to enhance the material presented in each chapter so that it is meaningful to all readers. Questions, exercises, and discussion questions are provided as "Focus and Reflect" activities to help readers extend their learning.

Each chapter has:

1. **Critical Self-Test Questions.** Each chapter opens with a set of critical self-test questions that highlight the important ideas of the chapter and reflect the process of selecting critical content to be taught and learned. This is a process that is emphasized in the planning routines discussed throughout the book.

2. **Graphic Organizer**. A graphic organizer highlights the major topics of the chapter. Each chapter also concludes with an expanded graphic organizer for readers to review in greater detail the big ideas and information presented in the chapter.

3. **Scenario**. After Chapters 1 and 2, which each have a single scenario, each chapter opens with a scenario or vignette to illustrate a problem or challenge faced by teachers as they plan for instruction in their academically diverse classrooms. The scenario is revisited throughout the chapter to show how the methods and ideas presented can help teachers address the challenges of planning and teaching and become more inclusive in their planning and instruction.

4. **Foundations and Principles.** Each chapter has a section linking the content of the chapter to research in the field. This section is designed to help connect the new information in this textbook to the basic methodologies of secondary teaching.

5. **Knowing and Doing**. This section comprises the heart of each chapter. With the exception of Chapter 2, which is descriptive of school diversity, the basic ideas and methodologies of pedagogies for diversity are presented in this section. Examples are provided to illustrate the ideas and methods presented. Activities and exercises are included to provide an opportunity for readers to process the information presented and practice the new methods. Where appropriate, there is a section on assessment to illustrate how teachers can connect the new methods with ways to assess student understanding.

6. **Scenario Revisited**. Each chapter includes a "final installment" of the scenario introduced at the beginning of the chapter. The problem or dilemma posed in the initial scenario is resolved, using the methods introduced in the chapter.

7. **Summary.** The conclusion of each chapter ties together the ideas presented and includes an **Expanded Graphic Organizer** to summarize and show the relationships between the major topics of the chapter.

8. **Making Connections: Implementing**. In this section, included at the ends of Chapters 3 through 12, readers are invited to think about which ideas presented in the chapter would be particularly helpful to them in their teaching. It is unrealistic to try to implement at once all the ideas in this text; it takes even experienced teachers awhile to adapt new methods to their particular needs and circumstances. What this section provides is an opportunity for you to reflect on what you would like to try to implement in your teaching and then to consider ways to do it. It is an opportunity to get a head start on planning for more inclusive teaching.

9. **Web Sites, Suggested Readings, References**. At the end of each chapter, there is a list of web sites that provides further resources for readers. There is also a brief annotated bibliography of suggested readings to extend the knowledge of readers and a complete list of references for the chapter.

REFERENCE

Ferguson, D. L. (1995). The real challenge of inclusion: Confessions of a "rabid inclusionist." *Phi Delta Kappan,* 77 (4), 281–287.

1

Teaching and Academic Diversity

B. Keith Lenz
Donald D. Deshler

Critical Self-Test Questions

- What do we mean by diversity?
- How does diversity among students affect student learning?
- How does teacher knowledge of diversity affect student learning?
- How have teachers traditionally responded to diversity and the challenge of individualization?
- What are the "big ideas" that lead to more inclusive teaching?

Diversity cannot just be acknowledged and understood. The teacher must teach and change teaching in ways that facilitate more learning in a heterogeneous group than would otherwise occur if students were taught as a homogeneous group.

Every class is characterized by academic diversity; students learn differently because they are different. From a teaching perspective, the advantage of the heterogeneous class is that there is more human experience to draw on to make learning interesting. On the other hand, as classes become more heterogeneous, it takes more time and resources to accommodate differences between students. No matter how much we might want to celebrate diversity, it does increase the demands placed on a teacher when a class contains students who have excellent reading skills and students who are poor readers, students who are fluent in English as well as students with limited English proficiency, or students who have the social skills to work cooperatively with others and students who have not developed those skills. Indeed, it is not the presence of diversity but the extremes of diversity that seem to daunt even the most seasoned teachers.

Understanding and acknowledging differences is important and needs to be taken into account in shaping curriculum, instruction, and learning activities. But just acknowledging differences is not sufficient. Therefore, the emphasis of this book is not on the *presence* of diversity, but rather on the *variability* in academic performance that is associated with diversity and the fact that teaching must not only change to accommodate variability in academic performance but also take advantage of it. Teachers need to be concerned about the *academic diversity* in a classroom that results when different people come together to learn. Accordingly, teachers must teach and change their teaching in ways that facilitate more learning in a heterogeneous group than would otherwise occur if students were taught as a homogeneous group.

The following definition of academic diversity illustrates the types of differences that teachers may find among students or between themselves

FIGURE 1.1
Graphic Organizer

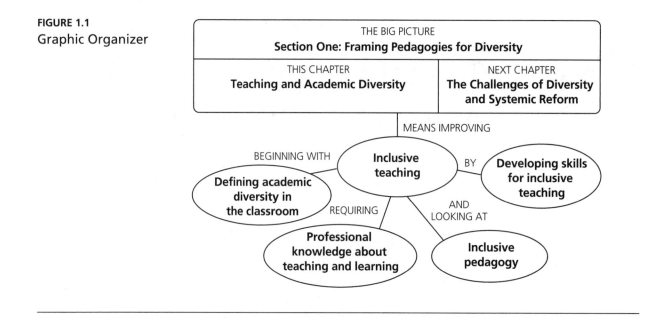

and students and focuses on the range of achievement that may be present in an academically diverse class:

> A class with significant academic diversity is characterized by students achieving in the average, above-average, and below-average range of academic performance as measured by teacher, school district, or state academic standards. This diversity in performance may be attributed to the interaction between individual differences among teachers and students in, but not limited to, learning needs, emotional needs, culture, gender, life experiences, life situations, age, sexual orientation, physical abilities, cognitive abilities, behavior, skills, strategies, language proficiency, beliefs, goals, personal characteristics, and values.

The primary demand faced by the teacher of an academically diverse class is to make the content accessible to all learners and build good solid connections between the content—the ways of thinking and the ideas and information of a discipline—and the learner. It is important to keep in mind that diversity notwithstanding, school achievement is the one variable for which teachers are held accountable. This places pressure on teachers to teach content in ways that are sensitive to individual differences, but are broad enough to be used with the group. Teaching content this way requires more thoughtful content planning, more knowledge of students, more class time devoted to helping students learn how to learn, and more reflection about how to put all of this together in courses, units, and lessons.

FOUNDATIONS AND PRINCIPLES

Most courses in educational psychology and teaching methods focus on helping teachers acquire knowledge of learning and how to promote learning. Research has generated a knowledge base on how learning occurs and is aided by teachers. Each teacher must then translate this information into personal teaching practices and procedures suitable for group instruction, sensitive to the diversity in the classroom, and durable enough to persist in the school environment. Each teacher develops a mindset about what works. The question is how well this mindset stacks up with what research tells us about learning.

There are three types of knowledge related to understanding diversity and learning: (1) knowledge of learning, or what a teacher knows about learning and how learning can be mediated or remediated; (2) knowledge of learning differences, or recognizing that students may not all learn the same way; and (3) knowledge of self, or what we know about our own personal learning needs and how that influences our teaching decisions.

Knowledge of Learning

The Learner-Centered Principles Work Group of the American Psychological Association's Board of Educational Affairs (American Psychological Association, 1997) has blended learning theory with efforts to reform and redesign schools and developed a set of psychological principles that influence learners and learning. These principles encompass (a) cognitive and metacognitive factors, (b) motivational and affective factors, (c) developmental and social factors, and (d) individual differences. They represent one of the best efforts to summarize some of the more critical aspects of our knowledge of learning. By looking at these principles, summarized in the following pages, we can develop a better understanding of how learning occurs and also how learning differences arise. (The Principles are reprinted in full in Appendix A.)

Cognitive and Metacognitive Factors   Learning is most effective when students can connect new information with previous experience. As students encounter new information, they must be able to link it to what they already know. If new knowledge is not integrated with prior knowledge and understanding, it will not be remembered, used, or integrated into new learning situations. Success in learning also depends on having a repertoire of strategies or methods to approach and master new learning. Successful learners know how to learn, either with learning strategies they already use or by creating new strategies to address learning challenges. Successful learners also can monitor how their strategies are working and whether they need to generate alternate methods to meet their needs and goals.

Learning is influenced by context or environment, including the environment in which the student lives, as well as the environment in which learning is to occur. The environment in which a student lives can affect many learning variables, such as motivation and attitudes toward learning. The classroom environment affects learning in the quality of instruction that is provided, as well as its appropriateness—Is instruction at the right level and is it relevant to the experiences of students? Classroom environment also affects learning and the extent to which it is nurturing and supportive.

Motivational and Affective Factors   Motivation affects both what is learned and how much is learned. Without coercion—and sometimes even with coercion—we cannot make someone learn. The extent to which students are motivated to learn is affected by their goals, beliefs, interests, ways of thinking, and positive or negative emotional states. Motivation to learn is also affected by the degree of difference between new learning and prior learning or experience, that is, the degree to which material to be learned is sufficiently new to be interesting but not so new and strange that an individual is uncertain about their ability to master it. Successful learning requires effort, and effort comes from wanting to learn—or wanting to reach the goals that learning offers. This is *intrinsic motivation.* Activating intrinsic motivation is a key to developing effective teaching strategies.

Developmental and Social Factors   Learning is influenced by each student's physical, intellectual, emotional, and social development. It is also influenced by social interactions, interpersonal relations, and communication with others. Learning is enhanced when students have or have had opportunities for positive interactions with others, in their families, in their social lives, and in their classroom experiences. Constructive social experiences in and out of the classroom can promote stability, a sense of security, and self esteem, all of which have an effect on a student's readiness for learning.

Individual Differences Factors   Each student brings a different set of life experiences to the task of learning. These experiences, along with social, cultural, and linguistic background, will influence how a particular student goes about learning. Some students will have developed effective strategies for mastering new learning, while other students may not have developed such strategies yet. Some students may learn best when new information is presented orally, while other students may learn best when the new information is presented in text form. Some students may need more time than others to process and learn new information. These are all differences in the way students approach and master learning, and they should be taken into account in teacher planning and instruction.

Focus and Reflect

- Review the list of Learner-Centered Psychological Principles in Appendix A. Can you relate these principles to your own learning experiences? Can you relate them to experiences of your students or students you have observed? Describe at least three instances where you have seen these principles at work.
- Identify two or more strategies you use when faced with new learning tasks or challenges.
- What motivates you to learn? List as many factors as you can.
- Identify one positive or one negative learning experience you have had and describe its impact on your attitude toward learning.
- How do you learn best?

Knowledge of Learning Differences

Every classroom is characterized by diversity, but some classes are more diverse than others. Knowledge of learning differences comes from being aware of the sources of differences between students, understanding how these differences affect learning, and recognizing how learning differences sometimes result in learning difficulties. Teachers are often aware of the overt kinds of differences that affect student learning needs, particularly differences in cognitive ability, skills, and the use of strategies. Students vary in the development of their natural mental skills and talents and how quickly they learn. But cultural differences and life experiences and situations may also affect cognitive and metacognitive factors, because an individual processes new information according to what he or she already knows. Therefore, information that is inconsistent with what a person has experienced in everyday life may be judged as insignificant or irrelevant. Instruction derived from or based only on the dominant culture, or that is insensitive to other cultures or subcultures, may lead students who are members of a different culture or subculture to disconnect from learning and from others in the classroom.

Life experiences, or the variety of experiences of an individual from birth, are used as a reference for understanding and responding to new experiences. Some students have had a wider range of experiences than others. For example, some students will have traveled outside their community or been included in lively conversations over the dinner table or been avid readers, while others may not have had such experiences. As a result, some students will more readily make connections when faced with new learning experiences.

Less overt but still important are differences in motivation and affective factors. Emotional needs can have an impact on learning. Learning is difficult when an individual is preoccupied with feelings, such as fear, despair, loneliness, or abandonment. Similarly, personal characteristics can affect learning. Personal characteristics refer to the unique traits of a person that set them apart from others or from a group. If students do not feel accepted because they consider themselves unattractive, or because they are overweight, or have habits or other personal characteristics that others feel are undesirable, and if they are not able to overcome these feelings of rejection, it is unlikely that they will devote their full attention to learning.

Beliefs, values, and goals held by students may affect their learning needs, because they may not believe that what you want to teach them will make any difference in their lives. Or they may have religious beliefs that seem to them at odds with what is being taught in your class. Some students may not value school learning because it seems so distant from their lived experience or because teachers or other students in their school do not look like them or talk like them.

Focus and Reflect
Describe a personal experience of being different in some way that made you feel alone or not fully accepted by others. Did you experience accepting as well as nonaccepting behaviors from others? Discuss those behaviors and your reaction to them.

Developmental and social factors also give rise to differences among learners. Students vary in language proficiency or their level of success in communicating with others in a given language. Language fluency affects the speed of learning, storing, and expressing information in the less fluent language. Students also vary in behavior, or the extent to which they have learned to follow rules, control their actions, and make acceptable judgments in social situations. The degree to which an individual controls social behavior influences how much attention he or she can devote to learning. Finally, physical abilities affect learning when students are given tasks they are physically unable to complete when adaptations or alternatives are not provided. Conversely, students may be denied important learning opportunities if they are excluded from certain tasks because of limited physical abilities.

Life situations also can have an impact on learning. These situations, or conditions under which a student is living, may include socioeconomic status, relationships to others in a family, and both long-term or short-term periods of change, stress, or trauma that a student may be experiencing or has experienced. These situations may affect how others think of a student or how a student perceives others. Students who are isolated or feel isolated because of life situations may disconnect from learning experiences.

In a diverse society, there will always be diverse groups of students in the schools. And differences between people—where they come from, what they value, the families and cultures they grew up in—will have an impact on how they learn. Even though this diversity makes teaching more challenging, it can enrich classrooms if teachers remember that

> It is . . . not our job to take [students] from their place to ours. Rather we need to help them pack their baggage for a very special journey among the world's languages and cultures. We need to learn to value and celebrate our differences, which don't amount to much compared to our vast commonalities. (Gullingsrud, 1999, p. 60)

Knowledge of Self

Knowledge of self is based on knowing how our personal learning experiences influence how we teach. It means being aware of how aspects of our individual identities—our cultural background, gender, life experiences, age, beliefs, goals, and values—influence our views of learning and teaching. Our first efforts in teaching are commonly based on the way we ourselves learn best. If we were successful learning in classrooms where instruction consisted primarily of "teacher talk" or lecturing, we may believe that others can be successful learning that way too. However, if, over time, you teach only through your own window of knowledge and experience, you may not be effective in teaching increasingly diverse groups of students. Recognizing that diversity creates learning differences, you may need to alter your teaching methods in order to be effective with the greatest number of students.

How Do We Acquire Knowledge of Self? Knowledge of self is acquired through reflection about personal beliefs, personal history, personal experiences (especially in school), personal biases, and past actions based on these beliefs and experiences. All these elements form our personal identity. Some of these areas are tough to look at, because it often means acknowledging that we may have prejudices about particular individuals or groups. However, it is important to recognize that we all absorb various biases as we grow up. The goal is to be aware of attitudes and beliefs that are prejudicial, to work at eliminating them, and to try to avoid letting prejudice influence how we treat others. York-Barr, Sommers, Ghere, and Montie (2001) advocate "reflective practice" that takes a "deliberate pause" to examine "values, visions, biases and paradigms to gain new or deeper understandings that lead to actions that improve learning for students" (p. 6). To begin the process of gaining knowledge of self, consider the sources of your personal identity. Table 1.1 can prompt you to consider some possible sources. Which ones are particularly important to you? How do these identities define you and how you approach learning? Do they get in the way of understanding others who are different? Does this lead to misunderstandings?

How Can Our Personal Identity Affect Our Teaching? Personal characteristics, experiences, and biases can influence teaching in positive and negative ways. Whether they are aware of it or not, teachers bring to instruction "their own experiences based on race, class, gender, and culture, and these

TABLE 1.1   Sources of Personal Identity

learning needs	culture/subculture	subculture
emotional needs	life experiences	skills
school experiences	age	cognitive abilities
goals	language proficiency	beliefs
values	personal characteristics	sexual orientation
life situation	strategies	gender
physical abilities	behavior	religious belief

Focus and Reflect

- Consider the sources of personal identity in Table 1.1. Select three that are most meaningful or interesting to you and describe how they have shaped who you are.
- Consider how your personal identity might affect how you teach.
- Are there other sources of personal identity that could be listed in Table 1.1?

are both a resource and liability in relating to students" (Ball & Cohen, 1999, p. 9). The examples that a teacher uses to teach certain concepts can reflect the teacher's background but ignore that of his or her students. For example, the concept of capitalism can be taught using an analogy to a lemonade stand business. However, the analogy may miss the mark if students cannot identify with the experience of running a curbside lemonade stand because it is a predominantly white, suburban, middle-class experience. The analogy may be very powerful for students who can identify with the experience but other students may not get the point.

The learning activities that teachers choose, the examples and stories they offer students, and the types of interactions they require in class are all affected by their own experiences which may be dramatically different from those of their students. Therefore, teachers must recognize the potential for such mismatches and understand what can occur when they teach *only* from their own personal perspectives. This kind of awareness should encourage teachers to commit their energies to communicating with and getting to know their students as a way to provide meaningful instruction.

KNOWING AND DOING

Building Inclusive Pedagogy

Knowledge of learning, knowledge of learning differences, and knowledge of self can help create a foundation on which teachers can develop an inclusive pedagogy, or teaching methods that are responsive to a range of learning needs. But aren't teachers using inclusive teaching methods already? Many teachers certainly are. So the next question becomes, what practices are common now, and how well are they working? To answer this question, we review some of the inclusive practices which teachers already use or are expected to be using. We will also examine what influences the effectiveness of commonly used inclusive practices and how we might improve the chances for success with such practices.

Expectations Placed on Teachers   Teachers are asked to respond to diversity among their students in a variety of ways. In general, teachers are typically expected to individualize or accommodate learning difficulties by: (1) planning for variety in teaching presentations, (2) providing students with alternate options to demonstrate learning, (3) making adjustments in practice opportunities, (4) giving individual checks and feedback, and (5) basing instruction on shared background knowledge. These can all be effective tools in individualizing instruction and, indeed, most will be discussed throughout this text.

PRESENTATION VARIETY. Presentation variety means teachers are expected to present important information in a number of ways to accommodate different learning needs and styles. In traditional content-area classes, teachers are expected to use variety in how they present content in order to offer students a variety of opportunities to acquire information. Although it is often assumed that students have the skills and strategies to read a textbook or listen and take notes in class, many students do not have the skills to accomplish all these tasks effectively and efficiently. This is especially true in secondary classrooms where the amount of information covered and the rate at which it is covered are greater than at the elementary level. Consequently, teachers may need to present information verbally for those who cannot read well, or direct students to appropriate text pages if they cannot listen and take notes well. Teachers may provide concrete and participatory experiences for students who have difficulty understanding abstract concepts, or visually represent and organize information for students who have difficulty understanding relationships between pieces of information.

ALTERNATE METHODS TO DEMONSTRATE COMPETENCE. Teachers are expected to develop alternate ways to evaluate student progress, because many students may understand the content but have difficulty demonstrating their knowledge through traditional forms of evaluation, such as tests and quizzes. For example, teachers may be asked to schedule private oral tests for some students, allow someone to read a test to a student, offer alternatives to essay items for students who have difficulty with written language, develop portfolio systems that document progress in learning, or allow demonstrations or projects in lieu of traditional tests. In addition, teachers may be expected to lengthen the amount of time allowed students to take a test or to make arrangements for alternate testing conditions.

ADJUSTMENTS IN ASSIGNMENTS OR PRACTICE OPPORTUNITIES. Teachers may also be expected to make adjustments in assignments in the same way that adjustments might be expected in evaluation activities. Since assignments and practice opportunities are intended to be instructional, modifications usually require teachers to offer students additional guidance, support, and individual explanations. Teachers may also be asked to break assignments into parts to focus student attention and to provide more practice opportunities.

INDIVIDUAL CHECKS AND FEEDBACK. Academic diversity in a classroom increases the likelihood that students perceive and remember information in different ways. Therefore, teachers are expected to increase the degree to which they monitor how both the group and individuals in the group are processing information. When students do not understand the important information or do not learn the appropriate skill, teachers are expected to explain what the student has done correctly, what is wrong with the response, how to correct the information, and then make sure that the student corrects the mistake and understands how to avoid making the same mistake in the future.

INSTRUCTION BASED ON SHARED BACKGROUND KNOWLEDGE. Because diversity means that students bring different levels of knowledge into the classroom, teachers are expected to explore what students already know based on their previous learning and life experiences. With this knowledge, teachers can then construct examples and explanations from a shared knowledge base. Teachers are expected to provide examples and explanations that all students can relate to, not just students who are achieving or who are part of certain subgroups in the class.

Approaches to Individualization   While teachers are expected to individualize instruction to accommodate individual differences, most teachers feel they must still address the needs of the group, even while being sensitive to the needs of individuals. As a result, secondary teachers most frequently respond to expectations to individualize through planning for the group by arranging peer-assisted activities that include choices in work, and by making creative presentations.

ARRANGING PEER-ASSISTED ACTIVITIES. While peer-assisted learning experiences may be structured as formal cooperative learning group activities, most peer-assisted experiences can be described as students being asked to work together on a task or on some type of classwide demonstration or activity. Having students work together seems to satisfy several criteria important to secondary teachers' understanding of how to accommodate individuals in the context of the group. Specifically, group work allows students to explain concepts to each other, using familiar examples and language, and increase the number and variety of explanations that might be simultaneously provided to all the students in a classroom. Group work also increases student involvement in learning tasks.

On the other hand, assigning group work can sometimes inhibit individualization. This can happen, for example, when students do not have the appropriate social skills to participate in group work, do not know how to work effectively in a group, or do not value the process of working in a group. When these conditions are present, one or two individuals may end up doing all the work in the group, either because other students do not know how to participate in the task or because they are unwilling or unable to take responsibility for their part in the work. Sometimes work in a group is taken over by assertive students who are impatient with others or who do not know how to involve everyone in the task. In all these cases, students do not understand that their job is to help each other learn. When this happens, individual learning needs are unlikely to be addressed, and group work might hinder rather than help address individualization.

INCLUDING CHOICES IN WORK. Another way of trying to accommodate individual learning needs in the context of the group is to offer students choices. Choices may involve options in assignment topics, or how a task is to be completed. For example, students might be given choices in topics to research or in how they want to present their work, whether in written form, in a poster display, or in an oral report. Students could also be given choices about whether they want to work in a group, in pairs, or on their own to complete a task.

Providing students with choices can allow them to focus on their strengths and avoid their weaknesses in skills or strategies. It can allow students to shape tasks around their interests and build on what they already know and have experienced. However, providing choices to students may inhibit individual accommodations if they are not aware of their strengths and weaknesses or have difficulty connecting self-knowledge about interests and experiences to classroom tasks. Students do not benefit from choices when they do not have the skills and strategies for making choices and decisions that will benefit them and their learning.

MAKING CREATIVE PRESENTATIONS. Many teachers believe they accommodate the needs of most students by making creative or entertaining presentations. They might build a lesson around a novel approach to presenting content to students, for example, by dressing up and assuming the character of a famous historical figure or mathematician, scientist, artist, musician, poet, and so on, to present a more compelling lecture about the person or his or her ideas or innovations. Similarly, in science classes, a lab demonstration producing amazing or impressive results might better gain students' attention.

Creative or entertaining presentations can include demonstrations, simulations, role-plays, stories, analogies, participatory activities, films, and so forth. The idea is to depart from traditional modes of presentation and increase student motivation to understand and distinguish a concept or information that is difficult but important. However, these efforts to engage all learners can go awry if students focus only on the creative or entertainment qualities of the presentation and do not have the strategies and skills to distinguish the important from the less important elements of the presentation. And whether a presentation or lecture is creative or not, students still remain passive participants during lecture-type presentations.

Focus and Reflect

- Can you identify additional expectations that teachers face to individualize instruction, beyond those listed above?
- In what ways do teachers respond to these expectations?
- What are the barriers to building an inclusive pedagogy? What are the solutions? Given the current structure of schools, what can be done?
- What changes need to be made in schools to promote more inclusive planning?

Complicating Factors Developing instructional methods that are sensitive to diversity is complicated by many factors. Many teachers report it is not diversity that presents the challenge, but rather the amount and extremes of diversity within a group of students that push the limits of being able to teach effectively (Lenz, Schumaker, & Deshler, 1991). The amount of time available for instructional planning during the school day is almost always insufficient, and the nature of the time available is not conducive to the reflective process required for planning for academically diverse classes. Furthermore, teachers report they often feel they do not have the necessary knowledge and skills to plan for inclusive teaching, including information about which instructional techniques, activities, and materials have proved effective with different groups of students (Roach, 1995). Teachers also report that student indifference to school and learning is the biggest barrier to success in teaching and that they do not understand why some students care so little about learning (Lenz et al., 1991).

At the secondary school level, teachers may be faced with teaching well over 100 students each day. In addition, government agencies, administrators, and peers often promote policies that place pressure on teachers to teach more information and to teach it more quickly, causing many teachers to leave some students outside the learning loop. Activities that are not directly related to learning content but which might help teachers understand students and the issues in their lives are often not planned because they would take time away from teaching more content.

Attempts to learn about students not only require time and effort, but such efforts will only make a difference if instruction is altered to take this new information into consideration. Many believe that learning about students and altering instruction based on what has been learned are impossible challenges to which they simply cannot devote precious time and energy. Given these realities, teachers often have mixed feelings about their ability to respond to the needs of academically diverse groups of students.

Focus and Reflect

- How does teaching more content in less time affect our ability to respond to diversity?
- Which of the complicating factors listed above seems most daunting to you in terms of accommodating learning differences in a classroom? Which have you heard expressed by teachers in secondary schools?
- Are there other complicating factors to building an inclusive pedagogy?

Developing the Goals and Skills for Inclusive Teaching

In order to develop skills for inclusive teaching you must believe that responding to diversity by teaching differently is an important goal. Part of teaching differently involves being prepared to alter plans and try new methods if students are not learning. You need to adopt a mind-set that diversity is, in most ways, an advantage to be nurtured and celebrated. This mind-set provides an opportunity for you to prepare students for the future by helping them appreciate the contributions of different views, experiences, and ways of learning. Without such an attitude, teaching in an academically diverse class is likely to be frustrating and unsuccessful.

Achieving the appropriate mind-set must be followed by developing a plan of action with clear goals and related instructional skills and activities. There are at least six goals in a plan of action for inclusive teaching: (1) be smarter about curriculum and curriculum planning; (2) develop an inclusive learning community; (3) create classroom communication systems; (4) enhance critical content; (5) teach learning strategies; and (6) work collaboratively and use support personnel effectively.

You will note that these goals are not merely extensions of, or enhancements to, the inclusive practices typically used by teachers and described earlier in this chapter. Rather, they represent a new approach to inclusive planning and teaching. In this new approach, we propose that, in addition to using methods that provide variety and make adaptations, you plan, up front, to teach in ways that will compensate for the limited prior knowledge and absence of learning strategies among your students. We believe you can plan to select, structure, and present important content so that it is accessible to all students. Further, we believe that when this approach is used explicitly—showing and telling students the purpose and relevance of learning the big ideas of the content and how you will help them learn—you can show students how to become better learners. This is what we believe effective inclusive teaching should be.

As you undertake the challenge of inclusive teaching, remember and take to heart the old adage that "Rome wasn't built in a day." Building inclusive practice will take time. It may be helpful to think about it as a process of building on a foundation of thoughtful planning and adding methods and techniques as you gain experience and knowledge about your craft and about the students in your classrooms. Another way to think about the process is to view it in terms of moving along a continuum of supportive teaching practices. As you learn more about your subject matter, effective teaching practices, and the students in your classroom, you will develop more and better ways to help students learn. Begin by implementing what seems manageable or most meaningful to you in your current circumstances. Later, you can refine methods and add new techniques. You must always be ready, however, to ask what is working and what is not working. Since "teaching occurs in particulars—particular students interacting with particular teachers over particular ideas in particular circumstances" (Ball & Cohen, 1999, p. 10), you may need to ask, what do my students need *now* to help them learn this material?

Be Smarter about Planning Learning may be thought of as a journey. Inclusive planning for that journey starts with a vision of destinations and the broader routes for the journey—the goals and means for reaching them—and moves on to examine how a class or course can be organized into meaningful units and experiences that take the form of "lessons learned." As a result, more time needs to be spent on conceptualizing the "big ideas" of a course and how these "big ideas" are supported in units and played out in lessons on a daily basis.

The key to instruction that is sensitive to different types and levels of background knowledge among students is understanding the big ideas or far-reaching concepts that hold a body of knowledge together. It means knowing "meanings and connections, not just procedures and information" (Ball & Cohen, 1999, p. 7). Ideas or concepts that transcend details and examples define why the details and examples are worth studying. In reality, the details and examples of a discipline simply prove and justify the big ideas and concepts, but too often it is facts rather than ideas that are taught and tested (Goodlad, 1984).

Being smarter about planning requires that teachers think deeply about the content, select what is truly critical for students to learn, and then transform that content in ways that all students find meaningful. Chapters 3, 4, 7, and 8 present an approach to planning that builds on what we know about ways to increase student understanding of critical content in the context of academically diverse classes.

Focus and Reflect

- How can understanding the big ideas of a course help students learn content?
- How would you go about teaching big ideas like democracy, plot, photosynthesis, negative numbers, or harmony? Identify one or two big ideas in your content area and outline how you would approach planning to teach those ideas.

Develop an Inclusive Learning Community An inclusive learning community is an instructional environment where teachers and learners share the view that learning is important and everyone should be included in it, working and learning together. To create such a community, there must be trust and mutual understanding about what matters in the classroom. Sometimes it is helpful to think of building community as building partnerships. In a partnership, each partner assumes responsibilities and roles. Similarly, in the classroom, teachers guide students in what and how to learn and include them as partners in making decisions about their learning. When there is community among teachers and students, covering the curriculum is never as important as ensuring that all students and teachers are working in partnership in a supportive setting to learn what is considered critical about the curriculum and for their lives. Chapter 5 will discuss factors that need to be put in place to create an inclusive learning community.

Creating community involves committing the necessary energy and resources to develop connections among and between all members of the class. Ultimately, a feeling of community requires that students feel connected to each other, the teacher, and to the content. When these connections do not develop, a learning community does not form. The result is a "disconnected" classroom where only some students feel accepted, safe, successful, and are able to meet expectations. In many disconnected classrooms, the most important goal is to cover the curriculum before the end of the year, whether all students are learning or not. Unfortunately, many classrooms, especially at the secondary level, are disconnected classrooms where learning is not occurring for all students.

Focus and Reflect

- How does a teacher communicate expectations to students?
- How can a teacher show respect for one source of diversity and inadvertently show disrespect for another source of diversity?
- Many class discussions revolve around personal values. For example, in a discussion about Democrats, Republicans, and Libertarians, values may be discussed and students may indicate a specific party orientation or affiliation. Students may find it "intolerable" that other students favor an opposing political party. How would you guide students to accept the idea that it is appropriate, expected, and healthy for people to have different political beliefs and that differences should be respected? What guidelines could be established for exploring ideas and specific instances of opposing ideas without attacking individuals or groups? Based on your thinking about how you would guide students to deal with differences in politics, religion, and various kinds of preferences, discuss how you would lead students to deal with other sources of differences. What is and what is not to be regarded with tolerance? In a discussion of tolerance and intolerance, how does a teacher handle the valuing of gang involvement, which, some students may argue, should be respected or tolerated?

Create Classroom Communication Systems   The learning activities you choose, the examples and stories you offer students, and the types of interactions you require in class are influenced by your own preferences, beliefs, and learning experiences. Since these may be dramatically different from those of your students, you need to commit your energies to getting to know students in your classes so you may be more aware of their preferences, beliefs, and prior learning experiences as you plan for instruction. Grant and Sleeter (1996) make the obvious but important observation that "All people want to think and learn about things of concern and interest to them, but may appear lazy or 'slow' when asked to think about things they have no interest in" (p. 232). Of course all students will face the need to think about and learn material they may not think interests them. The challenge for teachers is to connect what must be learned to that which *is* of interest. This is indeed a challenge but becomes less of one when teachers know their students and their interests.

Some teachers like to gather information from school records before school starts. This helps them understand the educational histories and abilities of their students. Other teachers like to have their students fill out a questionnaire and respond to questions regarding their lives, families, knowledge, and interests. Still others use both ways to collect information. Whatever methods you use, the goal is to develop ways to get to know students well enough to develop connections between students, teachers, and the content.

Developing such connections can also help you adjust instruction when students are not learning. These adjustments are an important part of inclusive teaching. While it may seem obvious that teachers would adjust instruction as needed, in fact they often do not but rather continue to teach as they have always taught (Grant & Sleeter, 1996). In Chapter 6, we discuss ways to increase classroom communication and understanding to better inform instructional planning and decision making.

Enhance Critical Content   Each person uses specific strategies and skills for learning. However, there is a great range in the level and type of skills and strategies individuals have and can use successfully to learn. This means that many students have difficulties with various kinds of learning. Some of these difficulties may include:

- Distinguishing important from unimportant information
- Knowing how to organize information meaningfully
- Relating new information to background experiences
- Remembering large quantities of information
- Breaking down complex concepts for learning
- Discovering ways to understand abstract concepts
- Analyzing information to arrive at conclusions and solve problems
- Being aware of teaching devices when they are used
- Using effective and efficient learning strategies

In addition, some students have difficulties because they simply do not believe it is important to learn the information taught in school, or they do not value the process of learning how to learn.

It is an inadequate response to academic diversity to simply decide that students *should* have learned the skills elsewhere and then go on to teach in a manner that assumes students have skills and strategies which they do not. When encountering these kinds of learning difficulties among students, teachers have two choices: One is to teach students the skills and strategies required for learning the content; the other is to teach in a manner that compensates for a lack of skills and strategies among students.

One of the ways to compensate for a lack of strategies and skills among students is to transform critical content in ways that help students understand, organize, and remember information, as well as respond to expectations to use it. This must be done in a way that maintains the integrity of the content, if we value setting high standards for learning. Integrity is maintained when the content is not watered down and when the critical information remains the central message of instruction. This is why it is so important to differentiate critical information from less critical information and build instruction around the important ideas of a course. You can enhance instruction about those ideas with methods, such as using analogies that cut across the different backgrounds of students in your classes. Once the big ideas of a discipline are identified, they must be transformed and taught, taking into consideration the experiences of students. Chapter 9 describes how we can use a variety of teaching methods and create teaching routines that enhance content so that more students can understand and remember it.

Teach Learning Strategies   In elementary schools, the skills and strategies needed for learning content are taught. An unfortunate characteristic of our secondary schools is their failure to continue that instruction. While we are responsible for teaching content, we must also be responsible for teaching students how to learn the content. We need to help all students in our schools develop and use learning strategies. These strategies must be woven into the daily routines of group instruction across all core curriculum subjects. Simultaneously, we must build support structures to ensure that students who need more instruction, practice, feedback, and support

---

Focus and Reflect

- What does the following statement mean to you? "Curriculum frameworks and textbooks are only resources; the true curriculum is actually constructed by the teacher and students each day in class."
- What role does a teacher play in defining curriculum?
- How does academic diversity affect how a teacher might need to transform information for learning?

receive this type of instruction when it cannot be provided in the activities offered in core curriculum courses. Chapter 10 will discuss learning strategies and how they can be incorporated into the curriculum.

Work Collaboratively and Use Support Personnel Effectively Just as teachers should not let themselves be overwhelmed by trying to master more methods than they can manage, so, too, should they be able to recognize when students have exceptional needs. Exceptional needs may require that teachers work collaboratively with other professionals in their building or seek the counsel of others to better address student learning needs. There are times and situations when the challenge is too great for one person working alone. An important part of inclusive practice is understanding when you need help and what resources are available to you and your students. In Chapters 11 and 12 we discuss special education policies and procedures for students with exceptional learning needs and some of the ways teachers can link to other professionals.

■ *Scenario*

TEACHING AND ACADEMIC DIVERSITY

"Hello, Mr. Crandall. I am Corretta Washington, the principal here, and I understand you would like to transfer your teaching assignment to Columbia Beach High School."

"It's a pleasure to meet you, Ms. Washington," said Mr. Crandall. "I have been teaching for the last 15 years at Jefferson High School and I would like to move to a teaching assignment closer to where my wife works."

"I can understand that, Mr. Crandall," said the principal. "I am eager to find out more about you. I understand that your area is science, and that you have been teaching biology for most of your teaching career. We really need a biology teacher. So, to start, why don't you tell me what you think is most important about teaching."

Mr. Crandall smiled and leaned forward on his chair as he spoke. "Ms. Washington, I take teaching biology very seriously. I set high standards for students, and I hold students to those standards. I expect that students work hard in and out of class. When students try, they do well in my classes. If students do not try, they fail. I am not afraid of giving 'A's', and I'm not afraid of giving 'F's' either. I find that sends a serious message to students, and I get results."

Ms. Washington smiled back. "What do you do when students struggle in biology?"

"Well," Mr. Crandall sighed, as he leaned back into the chair, "I have a lot of patience for students who come to class, listen, take notes, and complete assigned work. If students are doing all these things and are still struggling, my door is always open for them to come see me, get extra help, and in some cases, they can do extra credit to improve their grades. Students always have a chance in my classes when they try. I give students choices in what kinds of projects they can do; I put students in groups to work; and I try to entertain them to keep them interested. Teaching is harder these days because the diversity among students causes instructional problems. I have taken the district's diversity awareness class, so I am more aware of the problems that can arise because of cultural and racial differences. I also allow students with disabilities to have the test read to them when they need it. I would say that I do a lot for struggling students."

Ms. Washington slowly stood up, walked to the window, and looked out at students getting on the buses in front of the school. Finally, she

(continued)

TEACHING AND ACADEMIC
DIVERSITY (continued)

turned to face Mr. Crandall. "I guess I am not hearing what I want to hear from you. If you are going to teach in this school, you are going to have to think differently about teaching. I, too, believe in having standards and holding students to these standards. But you have to make sure that you teach in ways that help students meet these standards. Almost half of the students in this school read significantly below grade level. If you make successful performance in your courses contingent on reading material in or outside of your class you are going to condemn a significant number of students to failure. In addition, we have many other students who are going to need your help and attention in ways that are more substantial than just telling them to try harder. Many of our students have tried and have failed; they have failed so often that it is hard for them to believe that trying will make any difference. I assure you, giving them choices when they have not learned how to make good choices will do little without some guidance. Putting students in groups when they have not learned—or have not been taught—to trust, respect, or work with other students will not work either. You can entertain students, but your performance better lead them to master the critical information in the standards you expect them to meet. I have seen many teachers who entertain without teaching. And allowing students with disabilities to have the test read to them will not help if they have difficulty learning the information to begin with.

"Mr. Crandall, if your definition of diversity is limited to race, culture, and disability, then you have an incomplete idea about the kind of student population we have. Yes, these types of differences are significant in our school. But 20 percent of our students are in some type of foster or kinship care, and many of these youth are there because they have been removed from their families or have been abandoned. The very fact that they are here is a miracle, and we are trying to do more for these young people. Some of our students come from gay and lesbian families or are gay or lesbian themselves, and we are currently dealing with problems of harassment of sexual minorities. We have students who come from wealthy families, from extremely poor families, and from families where many different languages are spoken.

"If you teach here, Mr. Crandall, you will not only teach biology, you will also teach students how to learn biology. Your attendance at the district's diversity class is only a start; no class can prepare you for the full range of differences among our students. I want to know how you are going to get to know every student and change your teaching as you get to know them and how they learn. If you don't know them, then you can't teach them.

"If you are going to teach in this school, you can't look at diversity as a problem, Mr. Crandall. Diversity is the greatest asset we have; it is our world. Having a mind-set to appreciate the diversity here depends, perhaps, on whether you approach the challenge as teaching biology or teaching students. I don't expect you to be able to do all of these things immediately, because our whole faculty is still learning and growing. But I do need to know that you are prepared to learn and grow with us and think differently about teaching."

Mr. Crandall sat silently for a minute. He looked up at the principal and past her, at the students milling around in front of the school. "Ms. Washington, I believe I have already started to think differently."

SUMMARY

Recognizing and respecting differences is important to both teachers and students. To recognize those differences, teachers must plan and teach in ways that are sensitive to *individuals* who are different from others in the classroom, while *simultaneously* meeting the needs of the group. Teaching that addresses academic diversity is most effective when it begins with a comprehensive planning process that specifies what students should learn. This process should identify not only important and authentic content, but also the way that content is tied together by overarching themes or ideas. This kind of planning can lead to instruction that is explicit and therefore more accessible to students.

Inclusive teaching means being smarter about planning, working to develop a learning community in your classroom, getting to know students, enhancing critical content for them, teaching learning strategies, and working collaboratively with other professionals. As teachers develop course, unit, and lesson plans, they may consider and select ways to enhance content so that it is accessible to the greatest range of students. Making content accessible for students may mean that teachers need to teach in ways that compensate for underdeveloped skills among students. And, in addition to teaching content to students, they may also need to teach students how to learn. Taking on the responsibilities of compensating for

FIGURE 1.2

Expanded Graphic Organizer

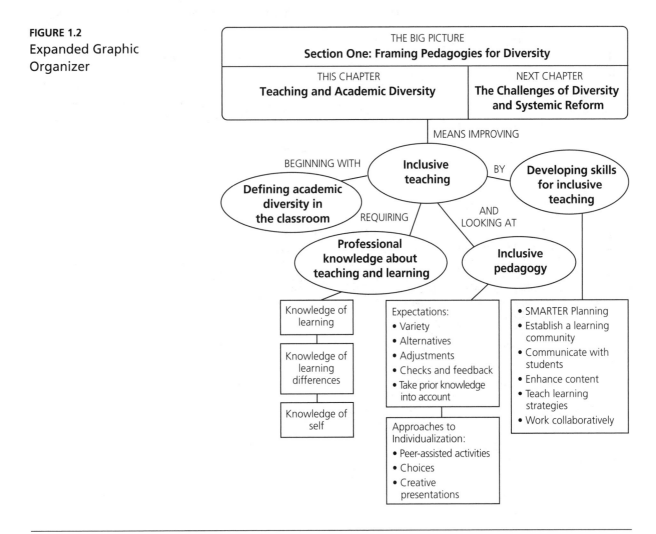

poor learning skills among students and explicitly teaching them how to learn may seem daunting to new and even experienced teachers. However, teaching techniques and practices that respond only to a few types of diversity are insufficient. As teachers learn and master new ways to support the learning of students, they can continue to build their repertoire of inclusive practices. Given the conditions of teaching, we may never be able to be totally inclusive, but we must always strive toward the goal of being as inclusive as possible for all learners.

SUGGESTED READINGS

Grant, C. A. (1991). Culture and teaching: What do teachers need to know? In M. M. Kennedy (Ed.), *Teaching academic subjects to diverse learners* (pp. 237–256). New York: Teachers College Press. Grant points out that there is no "cultural recipe" for responding to diversity among students. He suggests that teachers raise questions about why some students are not successful, beginning with questions about themselves as teachers and how differences between themselves and their students may get in the way of learning.

Kohl, H. (1994). *"I won't learn from you"—and other thoughts on creative maladjustment*. New York: The New Press. In this essay, Kohl relates his experiences as both a learner influenced by special teachers and as a teacher. Of particular relevance is his discussion of the responsibility he feels to see the strengths in people and students and build on those strengths.

Paley, V. G. (1989). *White teacher*. Cambridge, MA: Harvard University Press. Although this book focuses on the work of a kindergarten teacher, the themes about understanding and respecting differences are not bound by education levels. Paley's account of her efforts to better understand all her students and provide the best educational opportunities for them is warm, thoughtful, and engaging.

WEB SITE

http://www.apa.org/ed/lcp.html American Psychological Association—Learner-Centered Principles.

REFERENCES

American Psychological Association (1997). Learner-centered psychological principles: A framework for school redesign and reform. Prepared by the Learner-Centered Principles Work Group of the American Psychological Association's Board of Educational Affairs.

Ball, D. L., & Cohen, D. K. (1999). Developing practice, developing practitioners: Toward a practice-based theory of professional education. In L. Darling-Hammond & G. Sykes (Eds.), *Teaching as the learning profession: Handbook of policy and practice* (pp. 3–32). San Francisco: Jossey-Bass.

Goodlad, J. I. (1984). *A place called school*. New York: McGraw-Hill.

Grant, C. A. (1991). Culture and teaching: What do teachers need to know? In M. M. Kennedy (Ed.), *Teaching academic subjects to diverse learners* (pp. 237–256). New York: Teachers College Press.

Grant, C. A., & Sleeter, C. E. (1996). *After the school bell rings*. Washington, DC: Falmer Press.

Gullingsrud, M. (1999). I am the immigrant in my classroom. In National Council of Teachers of English, *Trends and Issues in Secondary English: Trends and Issues in English Language Arts* (pp. 51–62). Urbana, IL: NCTE.

Kohl, H. (1994). *"I won't learn from you"—and other thoughts on creative maladjustment*. New York: The New Press.

Lenz, B. K., Schumaker, J. B., & Deshler, D. D. (1991). *Planning in the face of academic diversity: Whose questions should we be answering?* Paper presented at the American Educational Research Association Conference, Chicago, IL.

Roach, V. (1995). Supporting inclusion: Beyond the rhetoric. *Phi Delta Kappan, 77*(4), 295–299.

York-Barr, J., Sommers, W. A., Ghere, G. S., & Montie, J. (2001). *Reflective practice to improve schools: An action guide for educators*. Thousand Oaks, CA: Corwin Press.

CHAPTER

2

The Challenges of Diversity and Systemic Reform

Sharon Lynch
Juliana Taymans

Critical Self-Test Questions

- Why is there concern about the quality of education in the United States?
- Why is there concern about the equity of education in the United States?
- What are the sources of diversity that have an impact on academic achievement in schools?
- What is standards-based reform, and what are the reasons for it?
- What are the major goals of standards-based reform for student achievement? How feasible are these goals?
- What are the characteristics of effective teachers of diverse learners in a climate of systemic reform?

You can watch people align themselves when trouble is in the air. Some prefer to be close to those at the top. Others want to be close to those at the bottom. It's a question of who frightens them more and whom they want to be like.

J. Holzer, untitled, from *The Living Series* (1989), Cincinnati Art Museum

A first step in developing skills for inclusive teaching is to explore how diversity manifests itself in the classroom. The diversity in our schools reflects that of society. What is the impact of diversity on teaching and learning? In this chapter we identify and discuss some of the social, cultural, and linguistic differences among students in order to understand how teachers can use the strategies in this book to improve achievement for all.

While diversity can be defined in many ways, it is dangerous and limiting to thoughtlessly lump students into groups and assign labels. Human identity is a complex of many factors. However, because achievement results and school successes are not randomly distributed across groups, it is important to examine group differences with the goal of understanding their causes and working within school communities to mitigate, if not eliminate them. Social justice demands this and the needs of the twenty-first century workplace require it. If educators are to respond effectively to the increasing diversity of the student population, paradoxically, we must attend to group differences in order to eliminate them. The trick is to do this without stereotyping.

We will look at diversity from some of the commonly used and measured perspectives, including gender, ethnicity, socioeconomic status, presence of a disability, or status as a learner of English. We will describe some of the differences that exist in academic achievement among groups of students, differences that have led to a growing awareness of educational inequities in our schools. These inequities become apparent in achievement gaps found between rich and poor children, and between students of different ethnic/racial groups.

FIGURE 2.1

Graphic Organizer

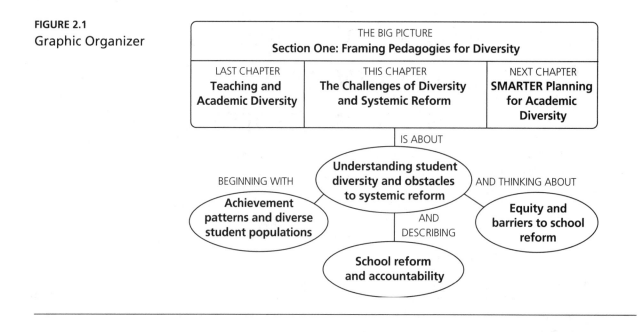

In the last decade, there has been an increase in accountability systems at the national, state, and local levels in order to improve teaching and learning. We will discuss systemic and standards-based school reform and their role in evaluating student performance. Two important principles that guide these reform efforts are (a) alignment of the various parts of the system toward common goals—high standards for all—and (b) teaching for understanding. Both of these principles challenge the U.S. educational system, which, because of its highly decentralized structure and overloaded curricula, results in a tendency among teachers to merely "cover" large amounts of subject matter, rather than guide students to develop a deep understanding of important concepts.

Standards-based reform cannot succeed unless it is implemented by teachers who know their subjects well and how to teach them, and who understand reform goals. Successful teachers of academically diverse groups of learners must be able to develop specific strategies to help all students reach the standards, in order to open doors for further successes in school and beyond. Developing these strategies begins with understanding the differences among students in classrooms today and the effects of standards-based reform on various groups of students.

FOUNDATIONS AND PRINCIPLES

Trends in U.S. Education and School Reform

In 1983, the National Commission on Excellence in Education published *A Nation at Risk.* This report reflected the growing sense that the United States, for all its wealth, power, and prestige, did not have a K–12 education system capable of producing graduates who were sufficiently well prepared

---

▪ *Scenario*

More than half of Virginia's public high school students flunked in at least one basic subject on the new state exams given in the spring and would have fallen short of the requirement for the diploma if penalties had been in effect. . . . There was a 60 percent failure rate on the high school Algebra 1 exam, a 69 percent failure rate on Algebra II. . . . On the three high school social studies tests, failure rates ranged from 38 to 70 percent. Test results were just as poor among elementary and middle school students, as the statewide failure rate on those exams ranged from 28 to 67 percent. (Benning, 1998, p. B1)

---

for the workplaces of the future, which would increasingly depend on well-developed cognitive skills. One reason for the concern was a decline in scores on standardized achievement tests, as well as persistent complaints from employers, policymakers, college professors, and even students about the performance levels of recent high school graduates. In addition, international comparisons of student achievement, especially in science and mathematics, showed that the United States ranked low compared to other highly industrialized countries, despite similar, large per-pupil expenditures on education.

The Third International Mathematics and Science Study (TIMSS) in 1994–1995 compared educational systems in 50 countries (National Science Board, 1998). The TIMSS results showed that U.S. students' achievement scores were in the midrange for science, and lower for mathematics. In the TIMSS 1999 report with results from 38 countries, the United States remained about in the middle of the achievement distribution.

In addition to mediocre results in international comparisons, there has been a growing awareness of educational inequities within the United States. Jeanne Oakes, in *Keeping Track* (1985), has shown how unequal treatment occurs in schools when the practice of tracking is used to group students for instruction, limiting opportunity to learn for many students. Books like Jonathan Kozol's *Savage Inequalities* (1991) have made it clear that U.S. students may have vastly unequal educational experiences from state to state, school district to school district, and sometimes even within school districts. And, the equity of state education funding formulas has been under attack from the courts in the states of New Jersey, Texas, and Kentucky; from the state in Wisconsin, Ohio, and Illinois; and from federal agencies in Massachusetts, Maryland, and the District of Columbia (Henig, 1997).

The basic goal of reform is clear: In order to remain competitive in the global economy, have a better educated citizenry, and attend to a delayed agenda for social justice, a far larger proportion of American students needs to receive the substantive, challenging education that once was reserved for those bound for college and challenging careers. Now all children must be better prepared for the information age workplace, which relies on literacy, but also, to a large extent, on the kind of reasoning traditionally associated with science and mathematics. Students must be able to work together to solve complex problems. They must also have the flexibility to learn new skills to keep pace with changing job requirements and advances in technology.

TABLE 2.1 Average Achievement on the Grade 8 Third International Math and Science Study (TIMSS): 1999 Benchmarking Study, by Country

MATHEMATICS ACHIEVEMENT		SCIENCE ACHIEVEMENT	
Singapore	604	Chinese Taipei	569
Korea	587	Singapore	568
Chinese Taipei	585	Hungary	552
Hong Kong	582	Japan	550
Japan	579	Korea	549
Belgium (FL)	558	Netherlands	545
Netherlands	540	Australia	540
Slovak Republic	534	Czech Republic	539
Hungary	532	England	538
Canada	531	Belgium (FL)	535
Slovenia	530	Finland	535
Russian Federation	526	Slovak Republic	535
Australia	525	Canada	533
Czech Republic	520	Slovenia	533
Finland	520	Hong Kong	530
Malaysia	519	Russian Federation	529
Bulgaria	511	Bulgaria	518
Latvia	505	United States	515
United States	502	New Zealand	510
England	496	Latvia	503
New Zealand	491	Italy	493
International Average	**487**	Malaysia	492
Lithuania	482	**International Average**	**488**
Italy	479	Lithuania	488
Cyprus	476	Thailand	482
Romania	472	Romania	472
Moldova	469	Israel	468
Thailand	467	Cyprus	460
Israel	466	Moldova	459
Tunisia	448	Macedonia, Rep. of	458
Macedonia, Rep. of	447	Jordan	450
Turkey	429	Iran, Islamic Rep.	448
Jordan	428	Indonesia	435
Iran, Islamic Rep.	422	Turkey	433
Indonesia	403	Tunisia	430
Chile	392	Chile	420
Philippines	345	Philippines	345
Morocco	337	Morocco	323
South Africa	275	South Africa	243

Source: International Study Center of Boston College, Lynch School of Education (2001). TIMSS 1999 Benchmarking Highlights—A Bridge to School Improvement.

Achievement Patterns and Diverse Student Populations

Raising achievement for all by identifying and teaching to higher standards presupposes having accepted measures of achievement for students. Unlike other highly developed countries, however, the United States has neither a mandated national curriculum nor consensus about how or what to assess at the national level or among states. The National Assessment for Educational Progress (NAEP) is the K–12 assessment system that best provides a national overview. This assessment compares achievement among states in science, mathematics, reading, writing, history, and geography. States may choose not to participate, and, in fact, eight states and the District of Columbia decided not to participate in the 1992 mathematics assessment (National Science Foundation, 1996). Still, NAEP is our most widely used indicator and is a generally respected test. It provides long-term trends as well as a cross-sectional view of achievement, is given to children at ages 9, 13, and 17, and reports achievement at different levels of proficiency. Consequently, we will discuss diversity and achievement by examining NAEP scores.

Ethnicity/Race   Race is said to be the American preoccupation. There is no denying that racism still exists in the United States. Ironically, although race is often treated as a biological fact, it has been an obsolete concept among anthropologists for at least 50 years (Wright, 1994). There has never been agreement about how to determine racial group membership, or how many groups exist—three, ten, a hundred? As "interracial" marriages become increasingly common, it is harder for many Americans to respond in simple terms to questions about racial identity. Anthropologist Ashley Montagu provides a way to talk about racial identity with the term "ethnic group"—self-perceived group membership in a population. No matter what term is used, two things are apparent: People from different ancestral backgrounds may have different behaviors based on their cultures, and they may be discriminated against because of other people's perceptions about who they are and how they should be treated (Wright, 1994).

It can be awkward to talk about the members of the diverse ethnic groups that constitute the population of the United States, because as diversity increases, we lack accurate and respectful terminology. For example, the term "minority group" is troubling because it gives offense to some, and can be clumsy or inaccurate, as in "the school was majority minority." Other commonly used terms, such as "nondominant," "at risk," "nonmainstream," and "disadvantaged" have pejorative connotations that make assumptions about ethnicity and advantage that are not true. In the past, students in some ethnic groups have been labeled "at risk for failure," when clearly some may be and some may not. These "covering terms" tend to put the onus on the students, rather than on the system that places them at risk, by failing to meet their needs. The English language does not provide a word that means "various-diverse-ethnic-and-other-groups-that-may-or-may-not-be-White" (Lynch, 2000, p. 29). The term "people of color" is respectful but incorrect, because about 25 percent of the White population is darker in color than the lightest quarter of the Black population, an insight that casual observation will easily verify (Hodgkinson, 1995). Consequently, this chapter will use the terms "diverse learners" or "underrepresented groups" as a somewhat awkward compromise to talk about students of various ethnicities or students representing other types of diversity based on differences, such as language spoken in the home, gender, socioeconomic status, or presence of a disability. In addition, sexual orientation can be included as an aspect of "diversity," as well as geographic location or religious affiliation. All have implications for educational opportunities, or their denial.

BLACK/AFRICAN AMERICANS. While the word "African American" typically applies to the large number of people who were brought to the United States from Africa under conditions of slavery hundreds of years ago, the large number of recent immigrants from Africa and the Caribbean suggests the need for a more inclusive term. Atwater (1995) suggests using the term "Black Americans." There are tremendous cultural and linguistic differences within this group of Americans, including distinctions based on nationality, ethnicity, tribal affiliations, religion, second-language use (for instance, Anglo- or Francophone), or socioeconomic or educational status.

Black Americans make up 12 percent of the U.S. population and are more likely to live in poverty than any other group. These statistics can be misleading, however, and leave the impression that all Black Americans are poor. In fact, about 40 percent of Black households in the United States fall in the middle income range, and 25 percent of Black households have higher incomes than the average White households (Hodgkinson, 1995). For the first time, African Americans are graduating from high school at the same rate as Whites (Sanchez, 1996). However, the graduates include a large number of adults who return to school for equivalency degrees, demonstrating that many Black American students do not fare well in the typical American high school. About one out of three Blacks attends a central city public school, the most notoriously weak link in our system of K–12 education. Black American students are less likely to take "gateway courses," such as geometry, algebra II, or chemistry, which limits their access to other upper-level courses and the high-status knowledge that prepares students for higher education (National Science Board, 1998). In the 1980s, achievement gaps narrowed gradually as Black Americans made large achievement gains, but more recent trends in reading and math show that the gaps have widened between Black students and White students (see Figures 2.2 and 2.3).

In summary, while Black Americans have made great strides educationally in the last 30 years, there is no question that Black American children born to poverty or attending educationally impoverished urban schools are a central concern of education reform. These children could stand to gain the most from the push for high standards for all. But unless the standards

FIGURE 2.2 National Assessment of Educational Progress Trends in Reading Scores by Race/Ethnicity

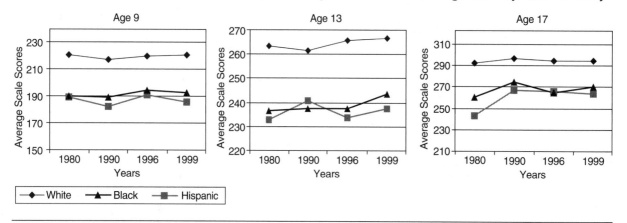

Source: U.S. Department of Education (2000). *NAEP 1999 Trends in Academic Progress,* Chapter 2, p. 33.

FIGURE 2.3   National Assessment of Educational Progress Trends in Mathematics Scores by Race/Ethnicity

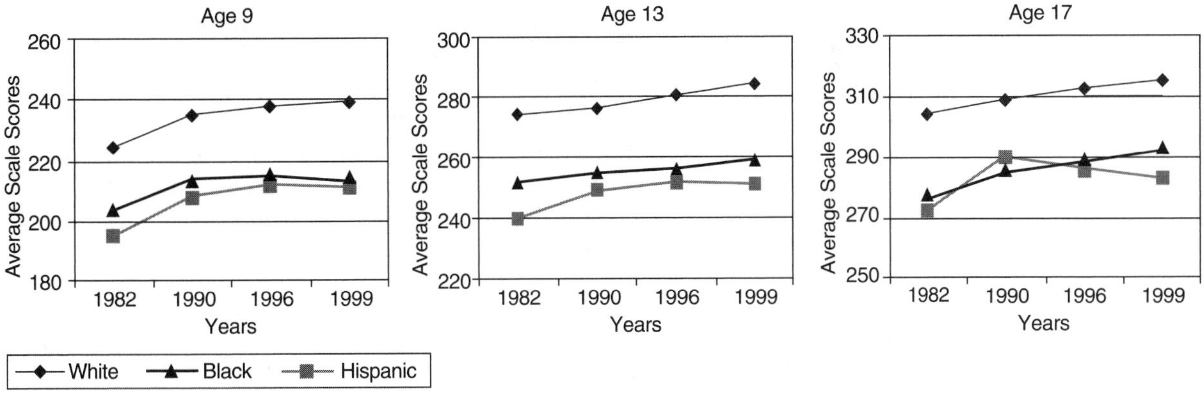

Source: U.S. Department of Education (2000). *NAEP 1999 Trends in Academic Progress,* Chapter 2, p. 33.

are accompanied by sufficient resources to boost achievement, many of these students could lose ground educationally and, ultimately, socially and economically.

HISPANICS. The term "Hispanic" was coined recently and is somewhat artificial. However, since census and achievement data are collected using this term, we will use it, recognizing that "Latino/Latina" is preferable to some. "Hispanics" include peoples from across the Americas, ranging from Mexican Americans whose families have lived in the United States for centuries and who speak only English, to recent immigrants from war-torn Central American countries, who speak no English and have had little formal schooling. "Hispanic" includes people who speak Spanish or Portuguese, including those of European, African, and Central and South American ancestry. They make up about 12.5 percent of the current population, and, according to projections, the Hispanic population of American children is the fastest growing ethnic group (Lewin, 2001).

Overall, Hispanic children have improved their scores on national tests such as the NAEP, but there continue to be serious and stubborn achievement gaps (see, for instance, Figures 2.2 and 2.3). On average, only 57 percent of Hispanics received a high school diploma in the 1990s, trailing behind other groups in graduation rates (Sanchez, 1996), and resulting in lower participation rates in higher education.

NATIVE AMERICANS/ALASKAN NATIVES. A small and extremely diverse group of peoples has been lumped together under the title "Indian" since the time of Columbus. The number of different Native American and Alaskan Native groups represents 50 percent of the number of ethnic groups in the United States. Yet, overall, Native American and Alaskan Natives make up only 1 percent of the population. While traditions vary and over 100 languages are used among Native American nations and people, there are common worldviews and collective experiences that sustain them as a unique indigenous people of American society (Educational Equity Project, 1989). Although there are over 300 tribes in existence, more than half the population are members of 10 tribes (Cherokee, Navajo, Sioux, Chippewa,

Choctaw, Pueblo, Iroquois Confederation, Apache, Lumbee, and Creek) and are concentrated in 10 states (California, Oklahoma, Arizona, New Mexico, North Carolina, Washington, Texas, South Dakota, Michigan, and New York). Most of the Eskimos and Aleuts live in Alaska (Vetter, 1995). Over half the Native American community lives in multitribal, multicultural urban situations (Hampton, 1991). Most Native American and Alaskan Native students—85 percent—attend public schools, with the rest going to Bureau of Indian Affairs or private schools. About 9 percent of these students have limited English and about 40 percent are bilingual, but the majority speak only English (Hodgkinson, 1995).

Native American/Alaskan Native students have a school dropout rate that is high, and they are more likely than any other group to attend disadvantaged schools in rural areas. There is also a high incidence of poverty and the concomitant health problems among this group (Vetter, 1995). Increasing the participation and success of Native American students in education requires finding a balance between maintaining traditional cultures and setting high standards for all students.

ASIAN AMERICANS. In 2000, the U.S. Census Bureau created the categories "Asian" and "Native Hawaiian and Other Pacific Islander," and federal statistics reflect these groupings. The 2000 Census reported that 3.6 percent of the U.S. population are Asian and 0.1 percent are Native Hawaiian and Other Pacific Islander (U.S. Census Bureau, 2000). The terms encompass two extremely diverse groups of peoples with distinctly different ethnic backgrounds. "Asian American" includes Chinese, Filipino, Korean, Japanese, Asian Indian, Vietnamese, and Other Asian. "Hawaiian and Other Pacific Islander" includes Native Hawaiian, Samoan, Gaumanian, and Other Pacific Islander. Rather than having a common cultural bond, each of these groups has a unique historical, social, religious, and linguistic background and their geographic origins cover a large area of the globe.

Asian Americans consistently score high on the NAEP, especially older students. For instance, on the 2000 math NAEP, Asian American fourth graders scored lower than Whites (who had the highest group scores). But by 12th grade, Asian Americans outscored all groups on average, with 34 percent scoring at or above the proficient achievement levels of the NAEP (see Figure 2.4). Asian Americans take more upper-level courses in science and mathematics than other groups. Although Asian Americans are often thought of as the "model minority," the use of such an encompassing term ignores the fact that the successes of some mask the problems of others; many Asian Americans struggle to learn to speak English and suffer from the residual effects of traumas of war in their homelands (Lee, 1995).

In summary, in a climate of standards-based educational reform for all, where the goals are to raise standards as well as close achievement gaps, the disparities between achievement, course-taking patterns, and educational quality for students of different ethnic groups should be a major concern at all levels of our education system. Discrepancies in achievement between groups should prompt us to set instructional goals to close gaps. However, that is not simple in an educational, social, and political system as complex as ours. Various groups with different access to power compete for finite education resources. Moreover, educational research and practice lag behind the needs of many learners, and no one is quite sure exactly how to reach our national educational goals, no matter how lofty the rhetoric and well-intentioned the efforts.

FIGURE 2.4   NAEP: National Achievement Level Results by Race/Ethnicity: 2000 Percentage of Students at or above Proficient Level

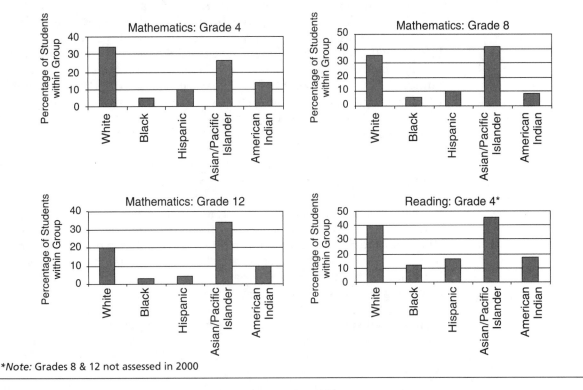

Note: Grades 8 & 12 not assessed in 2000

Source: National Center for Education Statistics, 1990–2000, 1992–2000.

The practice of breaking down data by ethnic group allows us to identify differences in educational achievements and set goals, but ethnicity alone fails to capture other traits that can contribute to problems—or successes—in school. For example, problems may arise for students of any ethnicity if they have working parents with little time to assist them with homework. Similarly, students of any ethnic background may be very successful in school if they have a natural curiosity, or drive, or have access to books and have developed the habit of reading everything in sight. Put another way, a child might see herself as a pretty athlete from El Salvador with a large family and a talent for mathematics, rather than primarily as Hispanic. Certainly, ethnicity can be trumped by any number of other characteristics more salient to an individual student's school success and unique identity. These factors, which we discuss in the following sections, may have more influence than ethnic group membership on school success and access to opportunities.

Socioeconomic Status   Newspaper articles about school achievement data often lead us to associate the urban poor with Black American and Hispanic students who disproportionately occupy central-city schools. However, this association ignores the growing, thriving middle class of people of color, and fails to take into account the poor White children whose opportunities to learn are thwarted by poverty. In raw numbers, the largest segment of the U.S. population that is poor is White.

Given our discussion of achievement gaps and reform goals, it is reasonable to ask whether ethnicity or socioeconomic status (SES) is more important in determining success in K–12 education. Research on large samples of students and U.S. census figures show that poverty has replaced ethnicity/race as the most pervasive index of social disadvantage (Burbridge, 1991; Hodgkinson, 1995). The United States has the highest poverty rate among industrialized nations—in 1999, 16 percent of children lived in families below the poverty line, and many economists predict a worsening trend as the gap grows between the haves and have-nots. But poverty is not evenly distributed among ethnic groups, as Table 2.2 shows. While it is difficult to unravel the effects of ethnic group membership from social class, it appears that social class has trumped ethnicity when it comes to determining who succeeds in American schools (Kahlenberg, 1995a, 1995b). For example, a middle-class Black child in a good school has a better chance for success than any poor student in a poor school.

How does SES (determined by annual income, type of job held by parents, and parents' educational level) influence school success? One national study showed that the top three variables associated with high achievement in science were parents' expectations about educational attainment, learning materials made available by parents, and level of parents' education—all clearly related to SES (National Science Foundation, 1994). So if parents are well educated and affluent, the expectations they hold for their children, their implicit knowledge about how to get the best possible school program for their children, the out-of-school enrichment experiences they provide, and their ability to provide direct help with school work, will all promote school achievement.

However, the picture is complicated by the affluence of a school itself, and the level of resources available. Poor children tend to go to disadvantaged schools, which are defined as schools where at least 50 percent of the children participate in free and reduced-cost lunch programs. Often, such schools are also characterized by low teacher morale, fewer certified teachers, deteriorating facilities, and fewer resources. These factors seem to explain achievement differences in schools more than the ethnicity or SES of

TABLE 2.2 Percentage of U.S. Children under 18 in Families Living in Poverty by Race/Ethnicity, 1999

	NUMBER OF RELATED CHILDREN UNDER 18	NUMBER OF RELATED CHILDREN UNDER 18 IN FAMILIES IN POVERTY	PERCENT
White, not Hispanic	44,527,000	3,921,000	8.8%
Black	11,132,000	3,644,000	32.7
Asian and Pacific Islander	3,026,000	348,000	11.5
Hispanic Origin	11,300,000	3,382,000	29.9
TOTAL	70,480,000	11,510,000	16.3

Source: U.S. Census Bureau, *People and Families in Poverty by Selected Characteristics: 1998 and 1999.*

As a result of rounding, some differences may appear to be slightly higher or lower than the difference of the reported rates. Data for Native Americans, Eskimos, and Aleuts are not shown separately. Data for this population group should not be tabulated from the Current Population Survey (CPS) because of its small sample size.

People of Hispanic origin may be of any race.

the students within them. Once again, though, Black and Hispanic students are more likely to attend these demoralized and demoralizing schools than are White or Asian American children (National Science Foundation, 1994). Still, research suggests that a middle-class student who attends a "low-SES school" is at a greater disadvantage than a poor student who attends a middle-class school, but Black students are more disadvantaged at low-SES schools than White students (Kahlenberg, 1995a; Kohr, Masters, Coldiron, Blust, & Skiffington, 1991; National Science Foundation, 1994; Reyes & Stanic, 1988).

Despite this complex mix of factors, which includes ethnicity, SES, and the affluence of the school, three points are important when considering group differences in achievement (Lynch, 2000):

1. Ethnic group membership should not be confused with social class. While a disproportionate number of Black American, Hispanic, and Native American children are from low-SES backgrounds, it is poverty, not ethnicity, that most inhibits school success.
2. A distinction must be made between a student's home background and the character of the school, because resources are not distributed equally across schools. Some suggest that integration based on social class may be more helpful in raising achievement than integration based on ethnicity (Hodgkinson, 1995; Kahlenberg, 1995a).
3. Achievement levels of students are determined by the kinds of courses available—students cannot learn what is not taught. Poor schools often have few resources, low expectations, and a narrow range of course offerings.

Students with Disabilities During the 1998–99 school year, 5,536,600 students, ages 6 through 21, received special education services (U.S. Department of Education, 1999). This is about 11 percent of the student population in the United States. Within the 13 disability categories recognized by the Individuals with Disabilities Act, the largest percentages of these students have identified learning disabilities (51 percent), speech and language impairments (19 percent), mental retardation (11 percent), and emotional disturbance (8 percent). The statistics for all forms of reported disabilities may be found in Table 2.3.

From 1988 to 1998, the number of students with identified disabilities increased about 29 percent, while school enrollment increased only about 14 percent. These increases resulted, in part, from the introduction of new categories and the reclassification of students who had been reported in other categories. This is especially true for children with autism. The largest increases have been in the categories of autism and traumatic brain injury, categories that were first reported in 1992–93. There have also been increases of more than 20 percent in categories of specific learning disabilities, emotional disturbance, multiple disabilities, orthopedic impairments and "other health impairments." The latter category includes students with attention deficit disorder (ADD) and attention deficit hyperactivity disorder (ADHD).

Demographic factors seem to influence the identification of disabilities. Although males and females are equally present within our school systems, two-thirds of students receiving special education services are male. Research reveals a complex array of factors that appear to influence who is

TABLE 2.3 Percent of Children with Disabilities Served under IDEA by Disability and Age Group during the 1998–99 School Year

Disability	AGE GROUPS 6–21
	Percent
Specific Learning Disabilities	50.8%
Speech and Language Impairments	19.4
Mental Retardation	11.03
Emotional Disturbance	8.37
Multiple Disabilities	1.94
Hearing Impairments	1.28
Orthopedic Impairments	1.25
Other Health Impairments	3.99
Visual Impairments	0.47
Autism	0.97
Deaf-Blindness	0.03
Traumatic Brain Injury	0.23
Developmental Delay	0.21

Source: U.S. Department of Education (1999). Office of Special Education Programs, Data Analysis System (DANS). Data based on the December 1, 1998 count, updated as of November 1, 1999.

identified as disabled. Poverty, English language learner status, inner-city residence, and ethnicity/race combine to increase the likelihood that a student will be identified as needing special education services.

Some students with disabilities, such as those with physical disabilities but no cognitive impairments, will experience education reform in much the same way as students with no identified disabilities. In addition, new technological innovations are increasingly and more effectively compensating for many disabilities.

The educational reform movement has affected students with disabilities in a number of ways. Specifically, setting high standards for *all* students, accompanied by high-stakes testing, has pressured local schools to align individualized education program (IEP) goals with standards. On the one hand, school systems may seek to hire teachers with dual certification in special education and general education or pair special education teachers with general education specialists to teach the general education curriculum in mainstream classes that include students with disabilities. On the other hand, it seems that special education classroom instruction has become more focused on passing state proficiency exams for graduation, with all that implies, both positive and negative. National tests, such as the NAEP, have encouraged the inclusion of more students with disabilities in the assessment system by offering a variety of accommodations (O'Sullivan, Reese, & Mazzeo, 1997). This trend is echoed in state assessment systems.

Still, the development of standards-based, field-tested curriculum materials and instructional methods for students with disabilities has not kept pace with the creation of standards, curriculum frameworks, and assessments. This presents a formidable problem for students with disabilities and the teachers who instruct them. The planning and teaching methods presented in this book can help address these challenges. However, we must acknowledge that no one is completely sure how to raise standards for all, assess student mastery for these higher standards, and get *all* students, including those with disabilities, over these hurdles. On the other hand, if reform leads to more focused goals and improved approaches to instruction, many students with disabilities will benefit.

English Language Learners   In contrast to school systems in other countries, U.S. schools tend to label a child learning to speak English as a second language as "limited English proficient" (LEP), rather than some other euphemism that more positively connotes the incipient accomplishment of facility in two languages (Lynch, 2000). We prefer the term "English language learners" to describe such students (Lacelle-Peterson & Rivera, 1993). Nonetheless, such children are at a disadvantage when they make the transition from the English as a second language (ESL) or bilingual classroom into the mainstream classroom where they must rely exclusively on their developing English skills to cope with the heavy demands of academic English. Courses that are loaded with vocabulary and abstract concepts are especially challenging (Lee, Fradd, & Sutman, 1995). In 1999, the number of children ages 5 to 17 who spoke a language other than English at home and had difficulty speaking English was 2.6 million. This represented an increase in the percentage of students who were English language learners from 2.8 percent to 5 percent of the total school population between 1979 and 1999 (Federal Interagency Forum on Child and Family Statistics, 2001).

Sometimes ethnic/cultural differences are conflated with linguistic differences, and many teachers are not adequately prepared to work with students who are learning English (Bernhardt, 1995); often the discussion of the education of immigrants focuses only on low SES, health problems, differences in background knowledge and experience, or bias in classroom practice. For educators, being aware of and respecting cultural differences is necessary, but not sufficient, to bring English language learners into mainstream education. Teachers need to understand second-language acquisition and how to use this knowledge to teach English language learners. Disregarding, for a moment, the political skirmishing surrounding immersion (sink or swim) approaches to English language learning, English as a second language (ESL) programs, or bilingual education, three things are clear about English language learners (Bernhardt, 1995):

1. Children who exit from English language support programs—despite their functional proficiency (street or conversational English)—do not speak "academic English" well enough to succeed in the typical classroom.
2. It takes an average of five to eight years to build English skills equivalent to those of native speakers, and while this is occurring, students will probably have to learn academic subject matter in English language classrooms.
3. English language learners who have made the transition into mainstream classrooms may be ignored or asked to do busy work by teachers who don't know how to work with them. About 35 percent of these students are placed in classes below grade level and are more likely to drop out than native speakers of English (Spurlin, 1995).

Gender Women constitute slightly more than half of the population of the United States and made up about 46 percent of the labor force in 1997. Tremendous progress has been made in women's participation rates in many different professional areas. The differences between males and females in K–12 science and mathematics achievement, as measured by NAEP scores, have narrowed substantially from 1977 to 1999 as females have made significant gains in math and science scores overall (Zernike, 2000; National Education Goals Panel, 1997). But a gap in the NAEP science scores of 12th grade males and females persists, and is especially evident at the highest level of science proficiency (National Education Goals Panel, 1997). In math, females have made consistent gains in test scores. They are now taking gateway courses, such as geometry and algebra 2, at higher rates than males and have caught up to males in participation in calculus courses (National Science Board, 1998). Despite these gains, however, women are underrepresented in many careers. For instance, in 1997, the percentage of women engaged in careers in the natural sciences, social sciences, mathematics, engineering, and technology was about 22 percent, and while more than half of social scientists are female, less than 10 percent of engineers are women (National Science Board, 2000).

The American Association of University Women report, *How Schools Shortchange Girls* (1992), discussed how the classroom climate may lead to differential achievement. Females may be treated in ways that disadvantage them, particularly in fields related to science, mathematics, and technology. However, even if overt gender bias by teachers is eliminated, other factors impinge on girls' opportunity to learn (Eccles, 1995). In many math and science classrooms, a few students, usually White males, dominate teacher-student interactions and assume the leadership roles in laboratory activities. These same students often monopolize laboratory equipment and computers, effectively denying females the opportunity to use these tools and develop confidence in their ability to master the skills involved in laboratory sciences. Under such conditions, females tend to withdraw and become observers rather than active participants. Girls participate more frequently and achieve more when teachers: (a) use noncompetitive teaching strategies; (b) give extended examples of applications from medicine, engineering, and so on; (c) stress the creative components of math and science along with facts and word problem sets; (d) provide extensive hands-on learning experiences; and (e) are actively committed to nonsexist education (Eccles, 1995).

Gender patterns in achievement, attitudes, and participation in careers may differ according to membership in ethnic group, socioeconomic status, or geographic location. Many urban educators seem to consider Black American males as the group most at risk in school, and especially out of school. More boys than girls are identified as having disabilities. Consequently, while we are well aware of the factors that hurt girls' opportunities to learn in K–12 education overall, it is also apparent that in some situations, males are increasingly disadvantaged. We urge you to consider the advantages and disadvantages conferred by gender in your unique school settings. Equity demands that the responsible adults attend to how gender, ethnicity, and other factors affect students' opportunities and choices.

PRINCIPLES OF STANDARDS-BASED EDUCATION REFORM

Education reform at the national, state, and local levels has increasingly come to be seen as an accountability system, where standards are established and resources are directed toward achieving these standards, with frequent student assessments of achievement administered in order to evaluate progress. This "systems approach" to educational improvement is often called "standards-based reform" or "systemic school reform." There are two central ideas behind this approach to education reform: (1) alignment of classroom practices with goals of high standards for all, and (2) reforms that lead to teaching for understanding (Clune, 1993; Smith & O'Day, 1991).

Alignment of Standards with Classroom Practices

A central idea driving reform principles is that greater coherence is needed between the various parts of America's vast educational system. One way to achieve more coherence is to develop national standards. These standards, which are voluntary for state and local school systems but nonetheless influential, are consensus documents written primarily by scholars in the various disciplines, as well as university educators and teachers. The documents were developed taking into account principles of child development theory and best practice. Such standards are well established in K–12 mathematics in the *Curriculum and Evaluation Standards for School Mathematics* (National Council of Teachers of Mathematics, 1989), and for science in *Benchmarks for Science Literacy* (American Association for the Advancement of Science, 1992) and in *National Science Education Standards* (National Research Council, 1995). In other content areas, such as social studies, national standards have been developed or are under development but have been less influential than the science and mathematics standards, either because they are more recent or more controversial.

The national standards documents are reinterpreted by each of the states, which, according to the U.S. Constitution, are sovereign in most educational matters. State curriculum frameworks form the basis of the grade-level K–12 curriculum and instruction programs within local school districts and schools. The United States has a long tradition of local school autonomy, so there is considerable latitude for local interpretations of standards. Because of this highly decentralized education system (atypical of educational systems in other well-developed countries, according to TIMSS), the effective adoption of standards and the development of consensus on curricular issues has been a huge challenge in the United States. Consistency between the national standards documents and state and local interpretations varies greatly, as the national standards are translated into curricula in local school districts, schools, and classrooms.

The many levels of authority driving education in the United States can result in a distorted message about standards (Schmidt, McKnight, & Raizen, 1997). There are problems in aligning standards with state or national assessments, and with the instruction that goes on in classrooms from day to day. While standard setting should logically precede the construction of assessments, in some states this has not been the case. The development of assessment systems has lagged behind the development of standards. Some state assessment systems are old and borrowed from bygone eras, bearing little relationship to the goals of current reforms (Consortium for Policy Research in Education, 1995; Land, 1997). Some states have developed new tests well aligned with their standards while others have created new assessments of dubious quality. Consequently, to achieve standards-based reform, it is important to align the various parts of the educational system, including:

- Instructional and curriculum materials used in classrooms
- Preservice and inservice professional development efforts provided for teachers
- School resources
- Student assessments
- Accountability measures for teachers and schools (Clune, 1993)

At the state level, policymakers have used measures of student achievement to drive reform. Assessment is central to systemic reform and is used as an index for judging its success. The assessment system is intended to stimulate reform by communicating standards and holding schools and students accountable for them (Land, 1997). State-mandated assessment results may be used to bring about reform within a school by dictating future resources available to the school, or even by forcing interventions or state takeovers. Schools and their teachers could be rewarded or punished if students do not meet performance goals. Whole schools could be reconstituted if student performance does not meet certain norms over extended periods (Wycoff & Naples, 1998).

High-stakes testing can also determine whether a student is retained in grade or allowed to receive a diploma and graduate. When high-stakes tests are used, students and their parents have powerful incentives to ensure that schools are providing opportunities to learn so that students can achieve the standards (Lynch, 2000). In 1993–94, about 17 out of 50 states and the District of Columbia had high-stakes assessments in place (Rivera & Vincent, 1997). In a more recent study, Wycoff and Naples (1998) reported that 18 of the 30 states in their study planned to have high-stakes assessments. Just as raising the course requirements for high school graduation has resulted in improvements in student achievement (Chaney, Burdorf, & Atash, 1997), high-stakes assessments are likely to lead to achievement gains for some students (Bishop, Moriarity, & Mane, 1998).

Because this accountability system has become so important to schools for accreditation, to teachers for merit raises and promotions, and to students for passing to the next grade or receiving a diploma, some educational systems have tried to keep low-achieving students out of the picture by sending them on field trips, encouraging them to stay home on test days, or excusing them from the tests altogether (Ysseldyke, in Kantrowitz & Springen, 1997).

In 1997, the Individuals with Disabilities Education Act (IDEA) was reenacted, providing that students with disabilities be given greater access to a general education, including the accountability system. States receiving IDEA funds were to identify performance goals for students with disabilities and include these students in large-scale assessments aligned with standards, to the greatest extent possible. Individual accommodations for students with disabilities were to be provided during assessments and alternative assessment programs administered to students who could not participate in state assessment programs (U.S. Department of Education, 1999). However, individual states have interpreted this directive in different ways (National Center on Educational Outcomes, 2000). For example, there are vast variations in the proportions of students with disabilities who are actually assessed, the type of accommodations provided to them, and the way this information is reported to the public (or not). This creates a troubling dilemma. On the one hand, requiring students with disabilities, English language learners and others to take high-stakes tests seems unreasonable, because it may lead to a loss of confidence or an increase in dropout rates if students perform poorly. It can also create pressures to teach to the test, and in some circumstances, a "dumbing down" of instruction for students with disabilities and others who need more inspiring and developmentally innovative approaches. On the other hand, it could be argued that students with disabilities and English language learners are exactly the ones who already are most likely to receive low-level instruction from teachers who are not certified in the subject area (Lynch, 2000). Thus, in many such classrooms, both the standards and accompanying assessment system could lead to more challenging and appropriate curricula and instruction, if reform can be used to pressure the system to improve opportunities to learn for students who otherwise would just be passed along (Lynch, 2000).

The purpose of reform is to raise standards for all students, relying on an accountability system that should result in better teaching and learning for all. In other words, if students aren't assessed, the system has no information to use for improving itself, thereby hindering reform. While exempting students from assessments can be well-intentioned, if the standards are for all, then the system must have access to information about areas of the curriculum that create difficulties for diverse learners, in order to find ways to help them succeed. Passing students along when they are learning little does not prepare them well for much of anything, and sends a distorted message about their futures.

Higher and more rigid standards, however, are likely to leave more children behind. If a high school diploma is made contingent on passing rigorous tests in specified subjects, some students will not graduate. Will other avenues for further education and decent jobs be open to those who do not receive the high-stakes diploma? In Europe, where such tests have been administered for decades, it is widely understood that students need a variety of ways to demonstrate a range of intellectual competencies and skills for meaningful employment (Madaus, 1994). These assessment systems often include 30 or more subjects, and report on differing levels of attainment, so students can leave high school with some credentials. Given statewide assessment programs, where few schools reach the high standards and the vast majority of students fail tests, it seems inevitable that state education agendas will develop better policies to balance high standards for all with the recognition of individual differences and multiple intelligences (Gardner, 1983).

Systemic Reform and Teaching for Understanding

The second major principle in standards-based reform is teaching for understanding. Rather than relying on the basic skills and minimum competencies that characterized earlier reforms, standards-based reform curricula aim for active learning by students and support teaching for understanding (Clune, 1993). While it is hard to imagine a teacher whose goal would be anything other than teaching for understanding, there is, in fact, a strong research base that suggests otherwise. Students are often required to memorize superficial facts or engage in activities that seem designed more to keep them busy than to learn (Lynch, 2000). By specifying high standards for all students and requiring deeper mastery of important concepts and skills, the system should produce more students who are prepared for postsecondary education, the demands of the information age, and employment in a global economy.

As noted earlier in this chapter (see Table 2.1), international comparison data indicate an achievement gap between U.S. students and those in other countries. The TIMSS data provide clues about the reasons for the gap. While U.S. students had similar patterns of school attendance, homework, computer use, and television viewing, it appears that the U.S. education system is different from those of other countries with higher educational achievement in three important areas: (1) organization of curriculum, (2) instruction, and (3) teacher education.

Curriculum   U.S. science and mathematics curricula have been called "a mile wide and an inch deep" (United States National Research Center for TIMSS, 1996). These curricula are unfocused and deal with many more topics than in other countries with higher achievement, although the total amount of instructional time is about the same (see Figure 2.5). In the United States, many topics are repeated year after year, while others get short shrift in terms of allotted time (United States National Research Center for TIMSS, 1996). U.S. textbooks exacerbate these problems as major textbook companies frequently add more topics over time (Schmidt, McKnight, & Raizen, 1997) in order to meet the standards of many different states and to sell more books.

FIGURE 2.5

Average Number of Topics in General Science Textbooks in Germany, Japan, and the United States, by Grade: 1994–1995

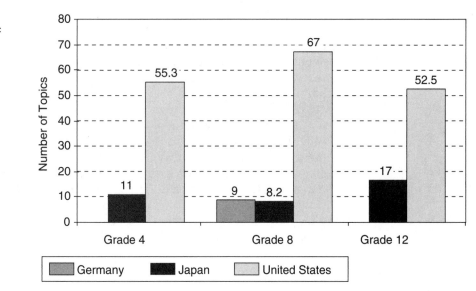

Source: W. H. Schmidt, E. E. McKnight, and S. A. Raizen, *A splintered vision: An investigation of U.S. L. C. Science and Mathematics Education* (Boston: Kluwer Academic Publishing, 1997)

Perhaps most disturbing, TIMSS found that the level of performance set by textbooks is often relatively low. In textbook readings and embedded activities, students are frequently exposed to facts and minutia about a given topic, while understanding of important integrating concepts is not effectively addressed. Textbooks seldom provide students with real-life messy problems or require high-level reasoning, which would help students develop an ability to apply learning in broader contexts. These limitations can have a substantial impact on curriculum and instruction, because the majority of teachers depend on textbooks in selecting the content they teach and the instructional materials they use. In one study, 54 percent of eighth-grade science teachers reported that they rely primarily on textbooks (National Education Goals Panel, 1995).

Instruction   Another important issue in the reform effort is ensuring that students have the opportunity to learn, including access to appropriate instructional strategies, curricula, and tools for assessing student performance as well as the necessary materials, funding, and resources (Darling-Hammond, in National Science Board, 1998). Opportunities to learn may be limited in several ways. Students with disabilities, English language learners, and poor children are most likely to be taught by teachers who are not certified in the content subject matter that they are asked to teach (Oakes, Muir, & Joseph, 2000). These teachers may be least equipped to sort through the unconnected concepts one frequently encounters in commercial textbooks, which cover too much material and often cover it superficially. Only students who enter the classroom with substantial background knowledge are likely to make sense of such texts and the instruction based on them.

Teacher Education   Ensuring that all students have the opportunity to learn also requires that instruction come from fully qualified teachers who are knowledgeable about the subject matter they teach (Darling-Hammond, in National Science Board, 1998). While reform efforts have focused, initially, on standards and tests, it is increasingly clear that the states that have planned for content- and curriculum-focused teacher preparation and professional development seem to be making the most gains in student achievement. For instance, Cohen and Hill (1998) found that fourth- and eighth-grade California mathematics teachers, who participated in professional development activities based on standards-based curriculum materials to be used in their classrooms, were more likely to report using teaching practices that were aligned with reform goals.

How does a teacher begin planning and teaching in the context of standards-based reform? The national standards documents are an obvious place to begin. They contain the "critical content" and provide developmental benchmarks for learning. A close reading provides a teacher with a means to resolve the depth-versus-breadth problem, when considering what to teach. If state and local standards and accompanying testing/accountability systems are well aligned with national standards, then the focus will be on core, essential knowledge and skills. This is the basis of course, unit, and lesson-planning methods introduced later in this text.

In summary, the educational reform movement, as characterized by higher standards for all students, holds a great deal of promise for students in underrepresented groups because of its inclusiveness. Frequent evaluation

Focus and Reflect

- If you don't already have them, obtain a copy of the most recent national, state, and local versions of standard documents in your subject area. Compare and contrast. Are they at all aligned? Which set of standards makes the most sense to you, if the goal is teaching for understanding?
- Using Web sites or print resources, examine the most recent state and local level achievement test scores for your subject area. Does the assessment align with the standards and your curriculum and instructional methods? How are the data disaggregated? Based upon what you know about the system and various groups of students within it, how might the assessment system be improved to more accurately reflect all students' learning?

of the effectiveness of the reforms through high-stakes assessments can draw attention and resources to who is learning and who is not. In some states, education reform provides new financial, human, and administrative resources that increase student opportunity to learn. However, it must also be said that the movement is new, and the U.S. educational system has had little experience with a common and connected system of standards, curricula, and assessments. Perhaps even more revolutionary is the notion that all children, rather than a privileged few, need to have access to high-status knowledge and skills. What must we do in order to achieve these goals?

EQUITY AND BARRIERS TO SYSTEMIC REFORM

Systemic reform considers all the interconnected parts of the educational system. In equitable systemic reform, the goal is equality of outcomes for all students. These outcomes, or achievement results, are based on identified high standards and must be assessed by measures aligned with the standards. This does not mean that we can expect the same test score for all children—that is unrealistic. Instead, test score patterns and averages should be similar for all groups, rather than different, according to ethnic group membership, gender, SES, and so on. This is the goal of the reform: raising standards for all while closing the achievement gaps between groups.

However, if group differences in achievement are found, it is reasonable to examine reasons why those group differences occur. For example:

1. Do all students have access to reasonable supplies of learning materials and decent facilities?
2. Do all students have qualified teachers who know the subjects that they are asked to teach?
3. Have the teachers had extensive professional development experiences aligned with the new standards? Do they understand the standards sufficiently well to develop or adopt appropriate curricula and teaching practices?
4. Is the school management team making decisions consistent with reform goals and analyzing troubling patterns of achievement among groups in order to reprioritize resources?

If the system has not provided these prerequisites, then it is reasonable to question whether students should be held accountable for achieving what they have not had an opportunity to learn. A basic principle of systemic reform is that the system responds to inequities with an infusion of resources at the school level. Administrators and teachers should be given both the opportunity to improve and the means to get there.

However, if the answers to the above questions are in the affirmative, and some individual students or identifiable groups of students are still not experiencing success, we must further examine the system and be willing to make some trade-offs, given a world of finite resources. This includes examining common practices, such as tracking or ability grouping, or assigning the least experienced teacher to students who present the greatest learning challenges. Careful decisions must be made about how discretionary funds are distributed. Systemic reform means that all parts of the system are involved in maintaining healthy, high-achieving schools, and leaving no student ignored and underserved.

Although top-down policy is seen as a driving force for change, it is widely recognized that teachers are at the heart of any reform. While they may not be able to control how decisions are made at the state or school district levels, teachers' voices are heard. Most importantly, they are the instrumental means of raising standards and achievement. The following section discusses the role of the teacher in systemic reform.

Focus and Reflect

Discuss how opportunity to achieve the standards is stratified (provided differentially) to different groups within your school situation.

Successful Teachers of Diverse Learners

Because teachers are the ultimate decision makers about what occurs in their classrooms, active networks of knowledgeable teachers are crucial to the success of school-level responsiveness to standards-based reform. The research on effective teaching in a standards-based environment suggests that secondary school teachers must possess three traits, shown on the left side of Figure 2.6, under "Just Plain Good Teaching" (Lynch, 2000). The first trait they must have is a good command of the subject they are asked to teach. Minimally, this means teachers should be certified and teaching in their fields. Unfortunately, the trend in many U.S. schools is to hire teachers on an emergency certification basis or to ask teachers to teach "out of field." Students in poor urban and rural schools are far more likely to be taught by teachers who are not certified in any of the disciplines, including the humanities (see Figure 2.7). Unfortunately, this may also be true for students in special education and ESL/bilingual classes, or in basic-level or remedial classes in affluent schools (Lynch, 2000).

Second, teachers must possess the pedagogical content knowledge (Shulman, 1986) to get their subjects across to their students, manage classrooms to create productive learning environments, and engage students by connecting the subject matter to students' lives. These skills can be taught in preservice education programs, but they are developed only through direct experience with students over time. Strong, helpful, evaluative feedback, peer support, and access to well-constructed curriculum materials help teachers develop and refine their pedagogical content knowledge. Most important, teachers must be able to reflect on their instruction and be willing to make improvements in it.

Third, a great deal of evidence suggests that in order to successfully teach the deep conceptual understanding, critical thinking, practical applications, and problem solving sought in standards-based reform, many teachers need to change their beliefs about teaching and learning and then change their practice. If this is to occur, teachers must first understand the reform principles. Unfortunately, evidence has shown that this is not so easy (Lynch, 1997). Many teachers tend to teach as they were taught, not taking into account the diverse learning needs of students today. Other

FIGURE 2.6

Successful Science
Teachers of Diverse
Learners

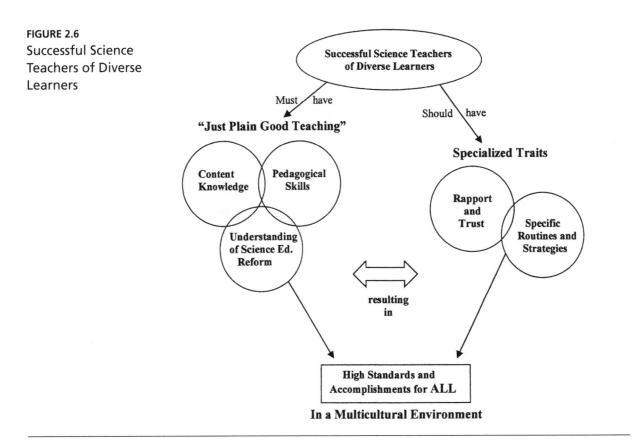

Source: From *Equity and Science Education Reform* (p. 190), by S. Lynch, 2000, Mahwah, NJ: Lawrence Erlbaum & Associates. Copyright 2000 by Lawrence Erlbaum & Associates. Reprinted with permission.

FIGURE 2.7

Percentage of Public
Secondary Students
Taught by Teachers
without at Least a
Minor in the Field,
by School Poverty
Enrollment: 1993–94

Note: In a low-poverty school, 0–5% of students are eligible for free or reduced-price lunch; in a high-poverty school, 41 to 100% of students are eligible for free or reduced-price lunch. The percentages for biology, chemistry, and physics represent students taught by teachers without at least a minor in those particular fields.

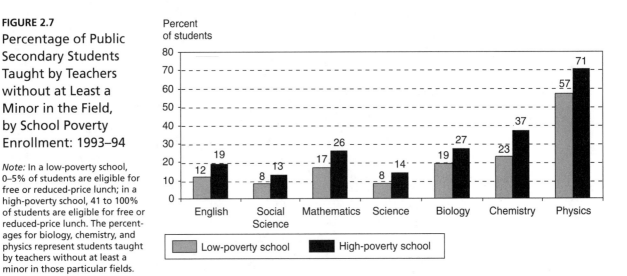

Source: National Center for Education Statistics, 1996, *The Condition of Education 1996. NCES 96–304,* Washington, DC: U.S. Department of Education.

teachers may have developed techniques to cover a bloated curriculum that focuses on facts and details rather than ideas and concepts. Consequently, professional development activities or preservice programs must provide teachers the opportunity to do the serious thinking that allows them to find the pieces necessary to implement the reforms—whether they are new curriculum materials, instructional practice, a hard look at assessment, or myriad other factors that affect teaching and learning.

The research on successful teachers of diverse learners shows two other specialized traits. These are found on the right side of Figure 2.6. The first is rapport and trust. If one watches a good coach teaching children to do something difficult or dangerous (gymnastics, rock-climbing, football), it becomes apparent that even very young children quickly size up the competence of the coach. If he or she is deemed trustworthy and knowledgeable, young people are more willing to take the risks necessary to learn the sport. The same perspective can be applied to teaching diverse students in classrooms. Education reform is built on the premise that all students can achieve high standards. Teachers play a major role in creating, perpetuating, or extinguishing stereotypes about competence; building or tearing down self-perceptions; molding expectations for success or failure; or encouraging students to develop their abilities or sending disheartening messages (Eccles, 1995).

A series of studies about effective urban science teachers reveal the importance of rapport and trust in this environment. For example, one such teacher said, "... it takes a quarter to develop control, cooperativeness, *rapport* to make most kids feel that they can be successful, establish the expectations. ... You have real good warm relationships at the end of the year" (Colburn, 1997 p. 5). Similarly, after spending a year in urban science classrooms, Meadows (1998) cited *teacher warmth* as a key facet of effective pedagogy. In a study by Luft, da Cunha, and Allison (1998), two science teachers identified as successful with Hispanic students and other students of color were described as *valuing* their students and *really wanting to help*. Vasquez (1988) used the term *"warm demanders."* Other researchers mention how effective schools provide a structure for *caring teachers* and counselors (Benedict, as cited in Murphy, 1996). Martin Haberman (1995) described a humane, respectful, caring, and nonviolent form of *"gentle teaching."* (The emphasis in the above paragraph is ours.)

In the literature on effective instruction for females, persons with disabilities, students learning to speak English, and urban students, the attribute of caring comes forth loud and clear: Teachers who care deeply about their students are most *effective*. By building rapport and trust, teachers not only connect with the students but build positive interactions between students as they participate in activities and learn substantive content. As a result, students are more likely to attend classes, have more positive attitudes, and show higher achievement (Van Sickle & Spector, 1996).

The second specialized trait of successful teachers in Figure 2.6 is the use of specific teaching routines and strategies to provide more effective learning experiences. These routines and strategies can include a broad range of approaches, from the trivial but effective (smiley face stickers or dictionaries in students' first languages) to the profound (the critical-questions approach of the Coalition of Essential Schools or the Socratic method). Researchers at the University of Kansas Center for Research on Learning

Focus and Reflect

Who is the best teacher you know in terms of the ability to reach all students? Does this person exhibit the characteristics seen in Figure 2.6? Does he or she have additional characteristics that help students be successful? Discuss.

have developed and tested a series of teaching routines and learning strategies designed to help teachers plan for and implement more effective instruction in academically diverse classrooms. Many of these strategies and methods to enhance instruction in content areas are included in this text.

No one characteristic of effective teachers of diverse learners seems sufficient. Rather, it is the combination of characteristics that creates classrooms where teachers help students attain standards. Such teachers are able to create a community of learners who value and respect what they are accomplishing, leading to a wider range of opportunities in school and in life.

FIGURE 2.8

Expanded Graphic Organizer

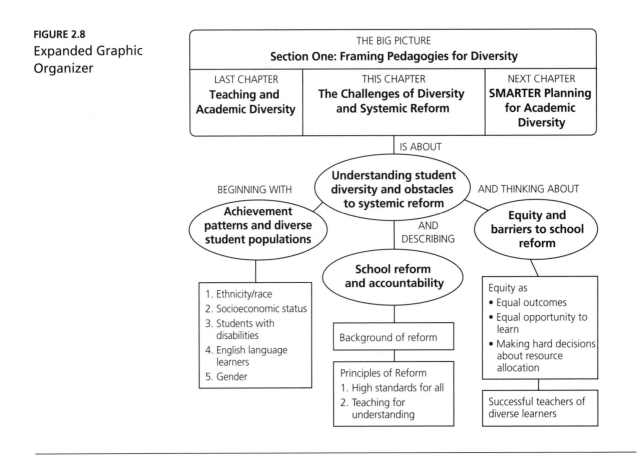

SUMMARY

In this chapter, we have described trends in achievements based on student diversity. We have also discussed the evolution of systemic or standards-based reform in the United States and the forces behind such efforts. Systemic reform holds promise for all students, especially those who have been ignored or underserved because

of low expectations for school success and an educational system that has traditionally set high goals for only some students.

Yet, even as reform proceeds, not all parts of the system are well aligned. Curriculum materials and assessments do not always match national, state, or local standards. In addition, unfocused curricula and textbooks that "cover" too many topics can result in student learning that is, at best, superficial and, at worst, confused or nonexistent. Because a well-aligned and accountable educational system is a relatively new idea in U.S. public education, some students could be caught in a system that holds them responsible for achieving standards without providing the means to do so. This is clearly inequitable and defeats the purpose of reform.

High standards for all means that all students will be expected to learn the concepts, habits of mind (high-level thinking and problem solving), and skills specified by the adopted standards. In order to achieve such learning, students must have an equal opportunity to learn based on access to effective instruction and appropriate materials—a traditional view of equity. However, educators will need to find better ways of reaching students who have been bypassed by the education system in the past, and develop strategic or individualized approaches to improved teaching and learning, a more recent view of equity principles consistent with special education philosophy. In addition, accountability must be determined by assessments aligned with the standards. If standards-based reform is equitable, the result should be a reduction in the achievement gaps between groups of diverse learners.

While resources and clear-headed, goal-oriented management is crucial, teachers are the heart of systemic reform. Well-qualified teachers must help students construct the bridges between their lived experiences and the attainment of standards. To do this, teachers must establish the rapport and trust that encourages students to cross these bridges, and they must provide the effective instruction and strategies to support them in their journey.

WEB SITES

http://www.project2061.org Benchmarks for Science Literacy by AAAS Project 2061.

http://ehr.aaas.org/sera2/website/contents.html Equity and science education reform.

http://www.nsf.gov/sbe/srs/nsf99338/start.htm K–postdoctoral-level statistics, updated every other year, on women, minorities, and persons with disabilities in science and mathematics.

http://www.coled.edu/NCEO/default.html National Center for Education Outcomes posts statistics on outcomes assessed for students, nationally and by state.

http://nctm.org/standards National Council for Teachers of Mathematics Standards.

http://www.ncte.org/standards National Language Arts/English Standards.

http://www.nap.edu/readingroom/books/nses/html National Science Education Standards.

http://www.indiana.edu/~ssdc/stand.htm Social Studies Standards and Curriculum: This is an ERIC Web site that leads to all of the social studies and arts standards documents.

http://www.ed.gov/offices/OERI/statecur State curriculum documents and content standards.

http://timss.enc.org and **http://www.ed.gov/pubs/TIMSSBrief** Third International Mathematics and Science Study.

SUGGESTED READINGS

American Association of University Women. (1992). *How schools shortchange girls.* Washington, DC: Author.

Kozol, J. (1991). *Savage inequalities.* New York: Crown Publishers.

Oakes, J. (1985). *Keeping track.* New Haven, CT: Yale University Press.

Shulman, L. S. (1986). Those who understand: Knowledge growth in teaching. *Educational Research, 15* (2), 4–14.

REFERENCES

American Association for the Advancement of Science. (1992). *Benchmarks for science literacy.* New York: Oxford University Press.

American Association of University Women. (1992). *How schools shortchange girls.* Washington, DC: Author.

Atwater, M. (1995). *Equity for Black Americans in science education.* Background paper prepared for Equity Blueprint Committee. Washington, DC: American Association for the Advancement of Science, Project 2061.

Benning, V. (1998, Nov. 3). Most high school students flunk new Va. exams. *The Washington Post,* pp. B1, B6.

Bernhardt, E. B. (1995, April). *A content analysis of science methods texts: What are we told about the bilingual learner?* Paper presented at the annual meeting of the American Educational Research Association, San Francisco.

Bishop, J. H., Moriarity, J. Y., & Mane, F. (1998). Diplomas for learning not seat time: The impacts of New York Regents Examinations. In *Educational finance to support high learning standards: Final report.* New York: New York State Board of Regents.

Burbridge, L. (1991). *The interaction of race, gender and status in education outcomes.* Wellesley, MA: Center for Research on Women, Wellesley College. (ERIC Document Reproduction Services No. ED 360243).

Chaney, B., Burdorf, K., & Atash, N. (1997, Fall). Influencing achievement through high school graduation requirements. *Educational evaluation and policy analysis, 19*(3), 229–244.

Clune, W. (1993). *2061 and educational equity. Background paper prepared for the Project 2061.* Washington, DC: American Association for the Advancement of Science, Project 2061.

Cohen, D. K., & Hill, H. C. (1998, January). State policy and classroom performance: Mathematics reform in California. *CPRE Policy Briefs,* RB-23-January 1998, 1–13.

Colburn, A. (1997, April). *Beliefs driving the behaviors of an exemplary urban science teacher.* Paper presented at the 1997 Annual Conference of the National Association of Research Science Teaching.

Consortium for Policy Research in Education. (1995, July). Tracking student achievement in science and math: The promise of state assessment programs. *CPRE Policy Briefs,* July, 1–12.

Eccles, J. S. (1995). *Issues related to gender equity.* Background paper prepared for Equity Blueprint Committee. Washington, DC: American Association for the Advancement of Science, Project 2061.

Educational Equity Project. (1989). *Our voices, our vision: American Indians speak out for educational excellence.* New York: The College Board and Boulder, CO: American Indian Science and Engineering Society.

Federal Interagency Forum on Child and Family Statistics (2001). *America's children: Key national indicators of well-being, 2001 (Part I).* Retrieved from http://www.childstats.gov.

Gardner, H. (1983). *Frames of mind.* New York: Basic Books.

Haberman, M. (1995, June). Selecting "star" teachers for children and youth in urban poverty. *Phi Delta Kappan, 76,* 777–781.

Hampton, E. (1991). Toward a redefinition of American Indian/Alaska native education. *Canadian Journal of Native Education, 20,* 261–309.

Henig, J. R. (1997, March). *Building confidence for sustainable school reform in the District of Columbia.* Paper prepared for the seminar on "Education Reform in the District of Columbia: Lessons from Other Cities," organized jointly by the Woodrow Wilson International Center for Scholars' Comparative Urban Studies Project and the George Washington University Center for Washington Area Studies.

Hodgkinson, H. L. (1995). What should we call people? Class, race, and the Census for 2000. *Phi Delta Kappan, 77*(2), 173–179.

Holzer, J. (1989). Untitled. From *The Living Series.* (Medium: Mixed) Cincinnati, OH: Cincinnati Art Museum.

International Study Center of Boston College, Lynch School of Education (April, 2001). *TIMSS 1999 Benchmarking highlights—A bridge to school improvement.* Retrieved from http://www.timss.bc.edu/timss 1999b/pdf/t99b_highlights.pdf.

Kahlenberg, R. (1995a, April 3). Class, not race. *The New Republic,* pp. 21, 24–27.

Kahlenberg, R. (1995b, July 17 & 24). Equal opportunity critics. *The New Republic,* pp. 20, 22, 24–25.

Kantrowitz, B., & Springen, K. (1997, Oct. 6). Why Johnny stayed home. *Newsweek,* p. 60.

Kohr, R. L., Masters, J. R., Coldiron, J. R., Blust, R. S., & Skiffington, E. (1991). The relationship of race, class, and gender with mathematics achievement for fifth-, eighth-, and eleventh-grade students in Pennsylvania schools. *Peabody Journal of Education, 66,* 147–171.

Kozol, J. (1991). *Savage inequalities.* New York: Crown Publishers.

Lacelle-Peterson, M., & Rivera, C. (1993). *Will the national educational goals improve the progress of English language learners?* Washington, DC: Clearinghouse on Language and Linguistics. (ERIC Document Reproduction Services No. ED 362 073).

Land, R. (1997). Moving up to complex assessment systems. *Evaluation Comment, 7* (1), 1–21.

Lee, O. (1995). *Asian American students in science education.* Background paper prepared for Equity Blueprint Committee. Washington, DC: American Association for the Advancement of Science, Project 2061.

Lee, O., Fradd, S. H., & Sutman, F. X. (1995). Science knowledge and cognitive strategy use among culturally and linguistically diverse students. *Journal of Research in Science Teaching, 32,* 797–816.

Lewin, T. (2001, July 19). Children's well-being improves, report says. *The New York Times,* p. A14.

Luft, J., da Cunha, T., & Allison, A. (1998, April). *Increasing the participation of minority students in science: A study of two teachers.* Paper presented at the annual meeting of the National Association for Research in Science Teaching, San Diego, CA.

Lynch, S. (1997). Novice teachers' encounters with national science education reform: Entanglements or intelligent interconnections? *Journal for Research in Science Teaching, 34*(1), 3–17.

Lynch, S. (2000). *Equity and science education reform.* Mahwah, NJ: Lawrence Erlbaum and Associates.

Madaus, G. F. (1994, Spring). A technological and historical consideration of equity issues associated with proposals to change the nation's testing policy. *Harvard Educational Review, 64*(1), 5–30.

Meadows, L. (1998, January). *Effective teaching in an urban middle school.* Paper presented at the annual meeting of the Association for the Education of Teachers in Science, Minneapolis, MN.

Murphy, N. (1996, March). *Multicultural mathematics and science: Effective K–12 practices for equity.* (ERIC Document Reproduction Services Number EDO-SE-96–1).

National Center for Education Statistics. *National mathematics achievement level results by race/ethnicity 1990–2002.* Retrieved December 19, 2002, from http://nces.ed.gov/nationsreportcard/mathematics/results/natachieve-g4re.asp, g8re.asp, and g12re.asp.

National Center for Education Statistics. *National reading achievement level results by race/ ethnicity 1992–2002.* Retrieved November 2, 2001 from http://nces.ed.gov/naep3/reading/results/ethachieve.asp.

National Center for Education Statistics. (1996, July). Increasing the inclusion of students with disabilities and limited English proficient students in NAEP. *Focus on NAEP, 2,* 1–5.

National Center on Educational Outcomes (2000). Accountability for persons with disabilities. http://www.coled.umn.edu/NCEO.

National Commission on Excellence in Education. (1983). *A nation at risk.* Washington, DC: Author.

National Council of Teachers of Mathematics. (1989). *Curriculum and evaluation standards for school mathematics.* Reston, VA: Author.

National Education Goals Panel (1995). *Data for the national education goals report: Volume One: National data.* Washington, DC: U.S. Government Printing Office.

National Educational Goals Panel (1997). *The national education goals report: Building a nation of learners, 1997.* Washington, DC: U.S. Government Printing Office.

National Research Council. (1995). *National science education standards.* Washington, DC: National Academy Press.

National Science Board. (1998). *Science and engineering indicators-1998.* Arlington, VA: National Science Foundation.

National Science Board. (2000). *Science and engineering indicators-2000.* Arlington, VA: National Science Foundation.

National Science Foundation. (1994). *Women, minorities, and persons with disabilities in science and engineering.* Arlington, VA: Author.

National Science Foundation. (1996). *Indicators of science and mathematics education, 1995.* Arlington, VA: Author.

Oakes, J. (1985). *Keeping track.* New Haven, CT: Yale University Press.

Oakes, J., Muir, K., & Joseph, R. (2000, May). *Diversity and coursetaking: Equity concerns in science and mathematics.* Paper presented at the Fifth Annual NISE Forum, Southfield, MI.

O'Sullivan, C. Y., Reese, C. M., & Mazzeo, J. (1997). *NAEP science report card of the nation and the states.* Washington, DC: U.S. Department of Education.

Reyes, L. H., & Stanic, G. M. A. (1988). Race, sex, socioeconomic status and mathematics. *Journal for Research in Mathematics Education, 19,* 26–43.

Rivera, C., & Vincent, C. (1997). High school graduation testing: Policies and practices in the assessment of English language learners. *Educational Assessment, 4*(4), 335–355.

Sanchez, R. (1996, Sept. 6). Blacks, Whites finish high school at same rate. *The Washington Post,* p. A3.

Schmidt, W. H., McKnight, C. C., & Raizen, S. A. (1997). *A splintered vision: An investigation of U.S. science and mathematics education.* Boston: Kluwer Academic Publishers.

Shulman, L. S. (1986). Those who understand: Knowledge growth in teaching. *Educational Researcher, 15* (2), 4–14.

Smith, M. S., & O'Day, J. (1991). Systemic school reform. In S. H. Furman & B. Malen (Eds.), *The politics of curriculum and testing* (pp. 233–267). Philadelphia: Falmer Press.

Spurlin, Q. (1995). Making science comprehensible for language minority students. *Science Teacher Education, 6*(2), 71–78.

U.S. Census Bureau, *People and families in poverty by selected characteristics: 1998 and 1999.* (n.d.) Retrieved September 5, 2001 from http:// www.census.gov.

U.S. Census Bureau (2000). *Profiles of general demographic characteristics: 2000 Census of population and Housing.* Retrieved September 5, 2001 from http://www.census.gov.

U.S. Department of Education (2000). *NAEP 1999 trends in academic progress: Three decades of student performance,* NCES 2000–469, Office of Educational Research and Improvement. National Center for Education Statistics, by J. R. Campbell, C. M. Hombo, & J. Mazzeo. Washington, DC.

U.S. Department of Education (1999). *Number of children ages 6–21 served under IDEA, Part B by disability during the 1998–99 school year.* (Table AA2), Office of Special Education Programs, Data Analysis System. Retrieved from http://nces.ed.gov.

U.S. Department of Education. (1999). *Twenty-first annual report to Congress on the implementation of the Individuals with Disabilities Education Act.* Washington, DC: Author.

United States National Research Center for TIMSS. (1996, September). *A splintered vision: An investigation of U.S. science and mathematics education.* Dordrect, The Netherlands: Kluwer.

Van Sickle, M., & Spector, B. (1996). Caring relationships in science classrooms: A symbolic interaction study. *Journal of Research in Science Teaching, 33*(4), 433–454.

Vasquez, J. A. (1988). Contexts for learning for minority students. *The Educational Forum, 52*(3), 243–253.

Vetter, B. M. (1995). *Status of Native Americans in science and engineering in the United States.* Washington, DC: American Association for the Advancement of Science.

Wright, L. (1994, July 25). One drop of blood. *The New Yorker,* 46–55.

Wyckoff, J. H., & Naples, M. (1998). Educational finance to support high learning standards: A synthesis. In *Educational finance to support high learning standards: Final report.* New York: New York State Board of Regents.

Zernike, K. (2000, August 25). Gap widens again on tests given to Blacks and Whites. *The New York Times,* p. A14.

SMARTER Planning for Academic Diversity

B. Keith Lenz
Janis A. Bulgren
Brenda R. Kissam
Juliana Taymans

Critical Self-Test Questions

- How do teachers decide what to teach?
- What does it mean to select critical outcomes?
- Why is selecting critical outcomes important in academically diverse classrooms?
- How can you go about selecting critical outcomes?
- What is SMARTER planning?
- How will SMARTER planning help teachers address the learning needs of all students?

Planning shapes the broad outlines of what is possible or likely to occur while teaching.

—C. M. Clark and R. J. Yinger, *Teacher Planning* (1987), p. 95

One of the major planning dilemmas you will face as a teacher is deciding what to teach. State and local standards, in addition to school system guidelines, curricula, and textbooks, are all sources that are used. The troubling reality is that there is much more potentially important information to teach than you can feasibly target in a meaningful way. The question of depth versus breadth frames the planning conundrum. As the information base of any course of study grows, the time allotted to a course in secondary schools usually remains the same. Educational reformers plead the case for "less is more" (Sizer, 1996). This means targeting fewer, but the most essential and relevant, concepts and processes for in-depth study, rather than choosing *more,* which means introducing students to more material, which can be processed only superficially.

Research on teacher planning for inclusive classrooms tells us that a reality of teacher planning is that secondary teachers have limited planning time, considering the instructional challenges they face (Joint Committee on Teacher Planning for Students with Disabilities, 1995). Planning time in schools is often taken up with administrative duties, appointments, and unexpected demands. In much of their planning, teachers target activities to engage and motivate students, rather than thinking in terms of larger outcomes, that is, what students need to know and understand. This is why curriculum standards are important: They help us maintain a focus on what students should be learning.

As you begin to think about teaching a course, you might assume that your role in developing curriculum is minimal, that these decisions have already been defined for you in state or local curriculum guidelines. However, teachers can and do make decisions every day that have a major

FIGURE 3.1
Graphic Organizer

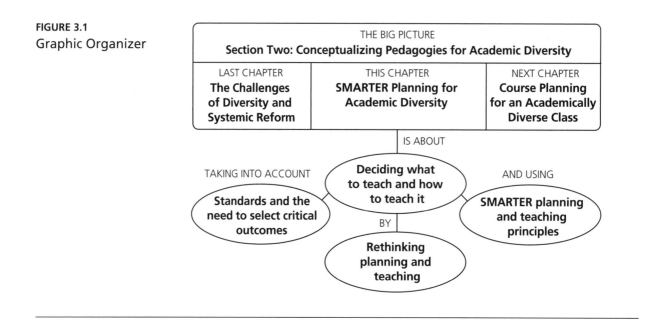

impact on the curriculum their students are taught and learn. Therefore, unless you understand the curriculum process and your role in it, you may not succeed in effectively teaching all students.

FOUNDATIONS AND PRINCIPLES

Researchers have suggested that teacher planning influences both content coverage and students' opportunity to learn (Clark & Yinger, 1987). Teachers translate and adapt the curriculum into instructional activities for many types of students. One of the first planning decisions teachers make that has an impact on *all* student learning is *selecting the critical outcomes*—identifying what it is they want students to learn in their classes. A critical outcome

■ *Scenario*

Mary Cochran and the rest of the social studies faculty from Franklin High School arrived on Friday morning for their weekly department meeting. It was the last month of the school year, and they had agreed to see whether they could get a handle on how to tie the state standards into classroom practice. Expectations about being more responsive to student learning needs were finally reaching the high school. The teachers were concerned about how to meet these expectations and about how their courses would be affected by new district initiatives to increase reading and writing achievement test scores. Some teachers had trouble every year just covering the content they believed they were supposed to teach. American history teachers rarely taught much further than World War II by the end of the school year. All the teachers worried that they would cover even less content if they were required to provide remedial instruction for some students.

for a biology course might be that students understand and be able to describe how groups of organisms are organized. A critical outcome for a U.S. history course might be identifying significant technological advances and describing their impact on American society and the economy.

Many students have difficulty understanding how particular facts are related to broader ideas or concepts and often lack the background knowledge necessary to connect pieces of information. When students have trouble making such connections—and many students do face this problem, even high-achieving students—it is essential that teachers be prepared to support student learning by being very clear about the critical outcomes, or "big ideas," in a course.

Selecting Critical Outcomes

Many teachers appear to think of the process of selecting critical learning outcomes as selecting critical *content*. But the two processes are not the same (Zahorik, 1975). The problem with planning that is based initially on content rather than learning outcomes is that instruction tends to center on discrete topics rather than the broader concepts and ideas that connect topics and give them meaning (Goodlad, 1984). For example, in the study of U.S. history, learning when the cotton gin was invented and by whom are not particularly important pieces of knowledge in and of themselves. What is important is the impact of this invention on the cotton industry, the institution of slavery, and the economy of the South (see, for example, Foner & Garraty, 1991). If the invention of the cotton gin is not discussed within this context and if student learning about this invention is not evaluated on the basis of this connection, learners will not understand the significance of the invention nor, in most cases, are they likely to find it very interesting or memorable.

Too Much Information, Too Little Learning

Focus and Reflect

Try your hand at translating one or more state standards in your content area into course goals and related instructional activities. Do your course goals encompass a focus or overarching idea that ties discrete content topics together? (State standards are accessible from Web sites provided at the end of this chapter.)

Newmann and Associates (1996) argue that for many students, learning isolated bits of information is difficult and does not engage their interest or attention. They suggest that a better approach is to limit the amount of fact-based content and pursue fewer topics in depth. Similarly, Fensham (1992) has reported that in science classrooms, concepts are often taught in a manner similar to the teaching of facts, disconnected from a broader "appreciation of how these concepts originated in the data of science or of their usefulness in applications in the real world" (p. 794). Racing through factual content provides no opportunity for students to think about what they are being asked to learn, nor does it allow students to master the skills and strategies essential to understanding and retaining content information (Good & Brophy, 1994; Parker, 1991). A curriculum structure that has "greater depth and less superficial coverage" helps students better understand and retain new knowledge (Glatthorn & Jailall, 2000, p. 108). In addition, if curriculum goals are to teach thinking and decision-making skills, then, as Parker (1991) observes, these objectives are best achieved by "thoughtful learning on a limited number of topics" (p. 353). Parker argued further that the explicit teaching of learning strategies and thinking skills must be a part of such in-depth study so that students will have the cognitive skills needed to "construct and operate on knowledge" (p. 353).

KNOWING AND DOING

Rethinking Planning and Teaching

The way curriculum is currently conceptualized and implemented is a big obstacle to developing an inclusive learning environment in the secondary setting. Too often the goal has been to promote content coverage rather than learning. Wiggins and McTighe (1998) described this approach as "teaching by mentioning it," or covering topics and ideas by drawing attention to them without developing them with students.

The first step to reaching more students is to dramatically change the way we think about curriculum and what students should know and do as a result of curriculum experiences. Wiggins and McTighe have argued for an approach to curriculum planning called "backward design," whereby teachers rethink their approach to curriculum planning and teaching by deciding what to teach based on sorting information into three levels: "enduring understanding," "important to know and do," and "worth being familiar with" (Wiggins & McTighe, 1998, pp. 9–10). Other educators over the last three decades have made similar suggestions (e.g., Beane, 1995; Blythe & Associates, 1998; Bruner, 1960; Caine & Caine, 1997; Perkins, 1992), and these suggestions are slowly beginning to shape how high schools deliver the core curriculum (see Erikson, 1998).

However, important questions must be answered as we think about implementing this approach. One question is, what happens when secondary teachers move to a more conceptual approach to curriculum design as a framework for making decisions about what to require of all students in their classes? While it is clear that a concept-centered approach can be effective, it is critical that teachers be prepared to guide students with limited background knowledge and skills to profit from this type of teaching. There may be a big difference between the highly conceptual national, state, and professional standards that teachers are expected to teach and the specific day-to-day instructional activities that they plan and implement with students. And, in fact, studies have shown that teachers do not consistently use learning activities and assignments that focus on concepts and skills contained in state standards. In some cases, teachers thought they were using activities to support conceptual learning, but they were not because they had not recognized "the full complexity of the skills being measured on the state assessment" (McDonnell, McLaughlin, & Morison, 1997, p. 43). Certainly, if all students are to meet higher standards that include conceptual learning, teachers must be prepared to help them by planning appropriate learning activities.

Teaching Difficulties Other issues arise as teachers think about curriculum planning. If teachers move to an abstract level of instruction, access to the content becomes even more difficult for some students. This can happen when teachers try to teach critical thinking without a good understanding of how students learn and practice critical thinking. Teachers also may not be prepared for the explicitness, time, and effort required to lead many students to understanding critical ideas. Furthermore, textbooks may not help them organize information around critical ideas. Finally, teachers may not believe that all students can learn all the content of a particular lesson.

(Hence the commonly heard response: "You want us to develop a lesson in which all the students will 'get it?' That never happens; there are always some students who will never get it.")

These difficulties are understandable. As we have watched secondary teachers struggle to teach content to academically diverse groups of students, we have developed a new paradigm for curriculum design that provides guidance on how to plan to teach critical content that all students will learn. This new approach is based on the idea that addressing the diverse learning needs of students begins with the selection of critical learning outcomes—what do you want students to know and be able to do after completing a given lesson, unit, or course? This new approach then provides a structured way to plan for instruction that is organized, explicit, and examined.

Focus and Reflect

- What do you think is meant by the "teaching by mentioning it" approach to content coverage?
- Using a textbook in your content area or a state standard available from one of the many Web sites listed at the end of this chapter, choose a unit topic and develop a list of the important ideas, concepts, or information students should learn in that unit. Then, using Wiggins and McTighe's approach to curriculum planning, classify the unit information as (a) important for students to know in order to have an "enduring understanding" of the topic, (b) important for students to "know and do," or (c) "worth being familiar with."

Exploring the Curriculum

Approaches to promoting more inclusive planning have been proposed by some researchers. For example, Wiggins and McTighe (1998) argued for selecting content that all students should know based on whether or not the information helps students understand an overarching idea or concept in a course. This is consistent with what Carnine (1994) and Woodward (1994) have described as teaching through "big ideas," or the generative principles and concepts that help students develop holistic understandings of content. An example of such an idea or principle might be an examination of economic roles and responsibilities of capitalists in late nineteenth century U.S. history. Should we regard men like John D. Rockefeller and Cornelius Vanderbilt as "captains of industry" or "robber barons?" The different characterizations of these men convey different views of political and economic developments in the United States at that time, and could provide the opportunity to present engaging big ideas, as well as organizing concepts to structure learning.

Building on what we know about curriculum, teaching, and diversity, teachers must approach planning in smarter ways, an approach that is in line with the "backward design" curriculum framework proposed by Wiggins and McTighe (1998). We believe that "smarter" planning involves three components: content, process, and integration. First, it requires us to think differently about how we select *content* to reflect learning expectations specified in state and local standards. Second, smarter planning can be accomplished more efficiently when we develop a *process* for thinking about curriculum planning decisions. In this chapter, we will introduce this planning process and in the next chapter, we will outline the steps used to implement it. This smarter planning process will be revisited in many of the remaining chapters of this book as it is *integrated* in planning at the course, unit, and lesson levels. Chapters 6, 7, and 8 will focus on planning at each of these levels and Chapters 9 and 10 will focus on teaching practices to enhance learning.

FIGURE 3.2
Curriculum Knowledge

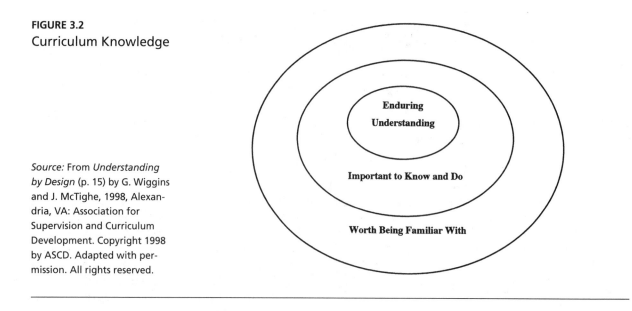

As mentioned, Wiggins and McTighe (1998) proposed that we think of the curriculum as consisting of knowledge that contributes "enduring understanding," is "important to know and do," and/or is "worth being familiar with." They depict this continuum in a visual consisting of three progressively wider circles (see Figure 3.2). This framework helps us think about curriculum in light of the standards movement because it provides a way of sorting information according to its importance to the learner. However, it falls short of helping us understand what should be mastered by all students, given the realties of the secondary classroom. For example, what should *all* students be expected to know and be able to do and what should *most* students be expected to know and be able to do? And is there a part of the content we should not necessarily expect all students to master because it is not critical to an understanding of the important ideas in a course?

We can begin to examine what content to emphasize by thinking about the continuum represented in Figure 3.3. Let's start by considering the body of knowledge that represents the field of social studies. Social studies incorporates a vast amount of information covering the entire development of all the civilizations of the world. Curriculum developers group this information into disciplines, such as history, civics, geography, and so forth, in order to focus learning. Within the discipline of history, courses focusing on the history of the world or on specific countries (e.g., History of the United States or History of Canada) are created. More specialized courses may focus on state history (e.g., Kansas State History). So, for all knowledge related to social studies, decisions are made about what information should be grouped to create courses about history.

The many dots in Figure 3.3 represent all known information about social studies. The outer circle groups information related to the field of history. Moving inward, the next circle represents the set of information that could be grouped as relating primarily to United States history. However, because we cannot teach everything about the history of the United States, the next inner circle represents information about the United States that might be included in a high school history class. A United States history class taught in a middle school would require another inner circle, and a

FIGURE 3.3
Social Studies
Knowledge

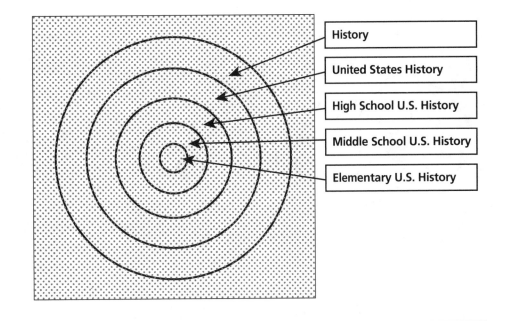

History

United States History

High School U.S. History

Middle School U.S. History

Elementary U.S. History

course taught in an elementary classroom would require yet another, and even smaller, circle. The point is that, because of the sheer quantity of information that exists, we are constantly required to determine what to include in a specific course.

The question for historians and curriculum makers, however, is what makes United States history worth knowing. We create courses to help us teach important sets of information, linked by big ideas, that organize and help us understand a body of knowledge thought to be important. Courses that are considered to be most important are "required," and all students must take them. Elective courses are judged as important for some students, and enrollment is optional or "elective."

Now let's take a look at how we can think about course design. Earlier we described a course as a set of information selected from a larger subject area and targeted at a particular grade level of students. We use a circle (Figure 3.4) to cluster the information that would be included in a course. As we consider the information within this circle, we need to remember that a course is based on or revolves around a set of critical ideas, represented by stars in Figure 3.4, that define how the larger set of information should be organized and understood. Figure 3.5 shows these ideas as a set of stars clustered at the center or core of the circle. These ideas should be drawn from content-area standards set at the national, state, district, school, department, or classroom level. They represent what is essential for all students to learn, and they often represent enduring understandings. However, more important, they must represent what is critical for *all* students to know in our society, and they must provide an anchor for all the other information that is presented in the various units in a course. In addition, decisions related to instruction, activities, and evaluation must revolve around ensuring mastery of this critical information for all students.

Using the image of a circle or pie to represent the curriculum of a course, we can then extend our thinking about curriculum design to the unit level. Figure 3.6 shows the circle or pie sliced into pieces that may be thought of as

FIGURE 3.4
Course Knowledge

FIGURE 3.5
Critical Course Knowledge

FIGURE 3.6
Course Knowledge Divided
into Units

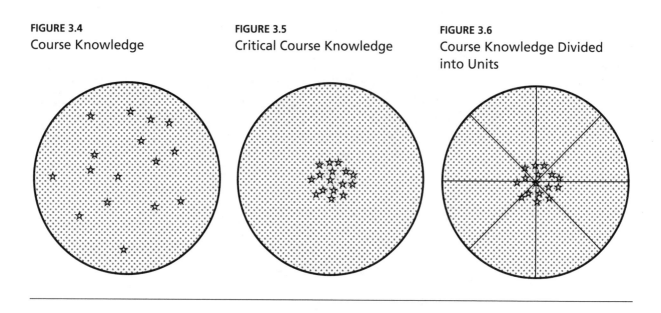

units in a course. Notice the stars at the small end of every slice (unit) of the course pie. The stars represent critical ideas of a unit that anchor the rest of the information in the unit.

The Unit: A Slice of the Course Pie   A slice of the course pie representing a unit is shown in Figures 3.7 and 3.8. At the unit level, we can begin to think in more detail about how we will organize curriculum experiences for students. The point or narrowest part of the slice represents the critical content that all students should be expected to know and demonstrate. At the very center of this narrow area we use a star to indicate that the content in this unit should be selected based on the degree to which it supports understanding of a critical idea, concept, or, as Wiggins and McTighe propose, an "enduring understanding" that rests at the heart of the discipline.

If all students should be able to master this content, what percentage of the content do you think this would be? It is important to remember that as classes become more diverse, it will take us longer to teach the same content. Therefore, it is important to select the set of concepts that helps organize the rest of the information in the unit and then to identify the supporting content that is absolutely critical for unlocking the discipline and the rest of the content included in the unit. Therefore, the critical ideas and content in the narrowest portion of the slice should be thought of as the content that unlocks understanding of the larger body of knowledge at the broader end of the slice that all students must master. As an example, in Figure 3.8, 10 percent of the content may be designated as critical. The part of the content that includes concepts or themes, and supporting ideas and information, designated as critical may be relatively small, because a unit is often constructed around only one or two critical ideas. We could expect student work that demonstrates mastery of the critical ideas and content at this level to be evaluated as "C" work, the average or expected level of performance in a secondary school curriculum.

Focus and Reflect
Using a textbook in your content area or a set of state standards available from one of the many Web sites listed at the end of this chapter, identify a course you might teach. Using Figures 3.4 and 3.7, consider what you believe students should learn in this course. Identify first the Course Knowledge and then the Critical Course Knowledge.

FIGURE 3.7 Units as Slices of the Course Curriculum Pie

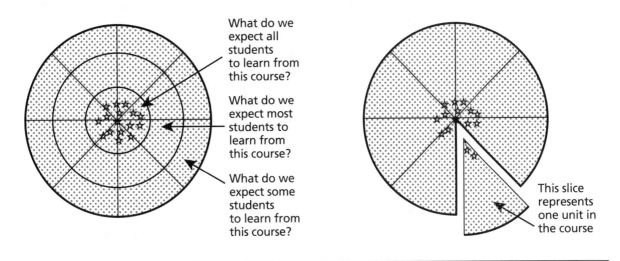

What do we expect all students to learn from this course?

What do we expect most students to learn from this course?

What do we expect some students to learn from this course?

This slice represents one unit in the course

In a unit on the causes of the Civil War, a critical idea that unlocks understanding might be the concept of "sectionalism"—conflicts that arose because of differences between geographical sections of the country. If a teacher believes that "sectionalism" is an important idea that is at the heart of understanding the Civil War, then this is a critical idea that will guide instruction for other content in this unit. Therefore, we must now determine what all students must know about sectionalism as a cause of the Civil War. A teacher might decide that all students must understand how economic, social, and political differences led to sectionalism. Having made this decision, a teacher would then need to make choices about what information is critical to understanding these differences. For example, do students need

FIGURE 3.8
Prioritizing Content for Instruction in High School Core Curriculum Courses

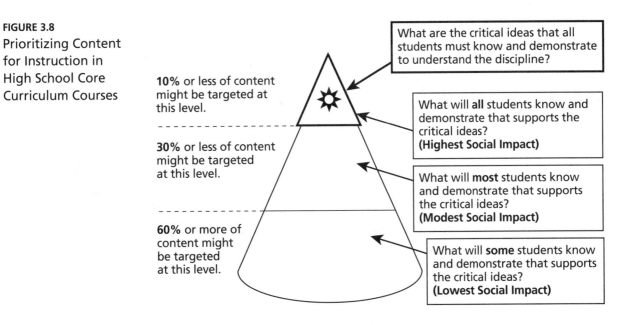

10% or less of content might be targeted at this level.

30% or less of content might be targeted at this level.

60% or more of content might be targeted at this level.

What are the critical ideas that all students must know and demonstrate to understand the discipline?

What will **all** students know and demonstrate that supports the critical ideas? **(Highest Social Impact)**

What will **most** students know and demonstrate that supports the critical ideas? **(Modest Social Impact)**

What will **some** students know and demonstrate that supports the critical ideas? **(Lowest Social Impact)**

to know about the invention of the cotton gin? Do students need to know how the invention of the cotton gin affected the economy of the South? Is this information important in understanding the economic differences noted above? Is this something all students should know?

Because it may be argued that the invention of the cotton gin "revolutionized" the economy of the South and "helped perpetuate slavery" (Foner & Garraty, 1991), it might be considered an important idea in a study of sectional differences in the United States. In order for students to appreciate its significance, it would be critical for them to know that this invention permitted cotton growers in the South to increase cotton production. Students would also need to understand that increased cotton production required more slaves to provide labor, and that the South became ever more dependent on slavery as their growing economic wealth became dependent on the cultivation of cotton.

Figure 3.9 illustrates how content related to a unit on the causes of the Civil War might be sorted out. The middle area of the unit slice represents what *most* students should know and demonstrate about the critical idea represented by the star at the top of the slice. The percentage of information at this level of the pie increases, but it is still limited because we want most students to acquire this information. In other words, we judge it to be important, but not critical. We could expect the work of students that meets the stated mastery criteria for the critical ideas and content at both the top and the middle part of the curriculum pie to be evaluated as "B" work— above average or greater than the expected level of performance in a high school curriculum.

The broadest, lowest area of the pie represents the content in a unit that some students should know and demonstrate. The quantity of information at this level is the most extensive and, to a large degree, is highly personalized. That is, there is more information here than all students need to know in order to understand the big ideas of the unit. What students focus on

FIGURE 3.9

Example of Prioritized Content

Prioritized Content for "Causes of The Civil War"

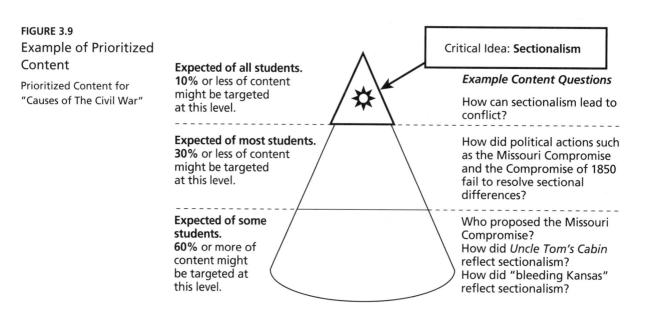

Expected of all students. 10% or less of content might be targeted at this level.

Expected of most students. 30% or less of content might be targeted at this level.

Expected of some students. 60% or more of content might be targeted at this level.

Critical Idea: **Sectionalism**

Example Content Questions

How can sectionalism lead to conflict?

How did political actions such as the Missouri Compromise and the Compromise of 1850 fail to resolve sectional differences?

Who proposed the Missouri Compromise?
How did *Uncle Tom's Cabin* reflect sectionalism?
How did "bleeding Kansas" reflect sectionalism?

may, to some extent, be a function of their interests or curiosity. This area of the pie does not represent information that is unimportant or trivial; it may be interesting information, and it might ignite the imagination of some students. As such, the information here may be helpful to students doing research projects or reports, or for students who want to extend their learning to a more detailed level. However, our expectations as teachers should be that, because this content is not essential for understanding the big ideas and supporting information of a unit, smaller amounts of instructional time should be devoted to it than to the critical ideas and information of the course. Similarly, it should not represent a significant share of the assessment of student mastery of the unit content.

Returning to our example of the economic causes of the Civil War and the invention of the cotton gin, a teacher might decide that information at the lowest, broadest level of the unit slice might include details such as the date when the cotton gin was invented and how it worked. This information is not central to understanding the important role of this invention in the economic development of the South, and therefore we have the least social investment in all, or even most, students being held accountable for this level of detail. We would expect the work of students meeting the stated mastery criteria for the critical ideas and content at all three levels of the pie to be evaluated as "A" work, well above average, or the highest level of expected performance in a high school curriculum.

It is very important to note that while we cannot expect all or even most students to become proficient at this level, *all* students should have access to information here. For example, the information may spark the interest of individual students, prompting them to want to explore topics or ideas further. The information in this area of the pie is worth knowing; however, in terms of planning for instruction and assessment in the real world of limited time and resources, information at this level of the curriculum slice is not critical for understanding the important ideas of a unit. Students should have the opportunity to learn it, but not all students should be held accountable for it in terms of passing or failing.

However you choose to select critical content, it remains an essential step in planning and an essential process for including all students in learning. If choices about critical content are not made at this early stage, you run the risk that instructional time, focus, and energy will evaporate as you try to cover everything. And, in trying to cover everything, you run the risk that instruction and learning will be superficial for all students. This is not an effective way to include all students in learning.

Ways of Thinking In addition to prioritizing content for purposes of instruction and assessment, it is important to think about the different ways students will be expected to think about and use the knowledge they will be learning. These ways of thinking are often discussed in preservice texts in the context of Bloom's taxonomy of cognitive objectives (see, for example, Sadker & Sadker, 1999). We have found in talking to teachers over the years that, in practice, they find the six levels of Bloom's taxonomy cumbersome, and that the levels overlap a great deal. We have reconfigured the taxonomy of cognitive objectives to three levels: acquisition, manipulation, and generalization. Acquisition corresponds to Bloom's levels of knowledge and comprehension; manipulation corresponds to application, analysis, and synthesis; and generalization corresponds to evaluation.

Focus and Reflect
Take the course knowledge you have identified in the previous Focus and Reflect activity and break it down into units. For each unit, identify the critical course knowledge. Look at Figures 3.6 and 3.7 to help you conceptualize this process.

■ *Scenario Revisited*

Mary Cochran and the rest of the social studies faculty from Franklin High School had just spent three days at a workshop on curriculum planning with other department teams from their school. During the workshop, they had worked on planning. The principal had agreed to pay for several days of team planning time over the summer, and to invest in some follow-up training and support in August and throughout the following year. The team agreed to work individually at first and report progress at the weekly department meetings that would be held during the last five weeks of the school year.

Over the weekend, Ms. Cochran spread the materials from the workshop out on her dining room table. The workshop guidelines for planning suggested that she should begin by focusing on curriculum planning. First, she pulled out the list of state standards. She worked to cluster the benchmarks and the ideas that were embedded in them. After digesting what the standards were really getting at, she looked in her textbook to see where and how the standards might be taught and learned. She also thought about whether the standards would help organize or tie together information in the textbook.

Teaching with both the state standards in mind and a goal of reaching all students was clearly going to be a challenge. While Ms. Cochran had always made choices about what she would teach, she had let the textbook be her guide in selecting and organizing topics to teach. As she looked at the textbook in light of the standards, she realized that the textbook did not really set out many good organizing themes or big ideas to tie together the chunks of information. Consequently, she was going to have to think carefully about what she would teach now and how she would teach it.

Figure 3.10 applies these ways of knowing to the unit slice we have been discussing. The white interior area of the slice represents student performances, demonstrating student acquisition of facts and concepts. Moving outward from the center area is the next layer, shaded light gray, which represents student manipulation of information. The outermost layer, shaded darker gray, represents student performances where there is generalization of content knowledge so that it may be applied and used. Note that all three ways of thinking—acquisition, manipulation, and generalization—are addressed in all three content sections of the slice. At the top of the unit slice, the important ideas and information of the unit may comprise a small portion of the total amount of content information to be learned, but all students will be expected to successfully use cognitive processes of acquisition, manipulation, and generalization to process that knowledge. Acquisition of the content knowledge in this top slice, as well as manipulation and generalization in using this content, will result in students attaining a passing grade (commonly associated with a "C" performance).

Assessing Competence   Standards-based reform requires that we think about what we teach (the content standards) and how we want students to demonstrate competence (performance standards). The discussion up to this point has focused on what to teach and how to make decisions about where to focus instructional time and resources. However, we must also think about how we want students to demonstrate what they have learned and how to develop assessment tasks.

Focus and Reflect

Take one of the units you have identified in the previous Focus and Reflect activity and choose one part of the critical content of that unit. Describe the critical content and then outline instructional activities designed to help students acquire, manipulate, and generalize that content, as described above and shown in Figure 3.10.

FIGURE 3.10
Linking Teaching
and Assessment

Assessment Focus Is on the
Type of Outcome Expected

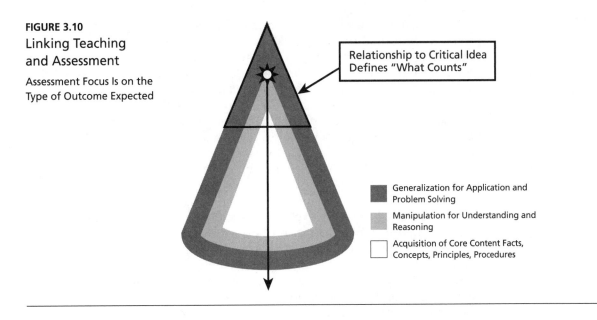

Relationship to Critical Idea
Defines "What Counts"

■ Generalization for Application and
Problem Solving

■ Manipulation for Understanding and
Reasoning

□ Acquisition of Core Content Facts,
Concepts, Principles, Procedures

Let's continue to use the image of a slice of the course pie and the unit as our focus to explore how we can think about competence in terms of both content knowledge and ways of thinking. Figure 3.11, in addition to showing how the slice of the course pie can be divided to show how content is prioritized, may also be divided into layers from the inside out (as in Figure 3.10) to indicate how we can develop expectations about student performance in manipulating content.

FIGURE 3.11
Linking Teaching
and Assessment

Assessment Focus Is on the
Type of Outcome Expected

Relationship to Critical Idea
Defines "What Counts"

Expected of all students.
10% or less of content
might be targeted
at this level.

Expected of most students.
30% or less of content
might be targeted
at this level.

**Expected of some
students.**
60% or more of
content might
be targeted at
this level.

Focus of Assessment

"C" Performance
Assessments emphasize what
all students should know; test
items and tasks are weighted
to reflect this content.

"B" Performance
Students who demonstrate
"C" and "B" level performance
earn a higher grade.

"A" Performance
Students who demonstrate
"C," "B," and "A" level
performance should earn the
highest grades.

■ Generalization for Application
and Problem Solving

■ Manipulation for Understanding
and Reasoning

□ Acquisition of Core Content Facts,
Concepts, Principles, Procedures

The white, innermost area within the top section of the unit slice represents the information that students need to know so other learning can occur (e.g., What is democracy? What is a simple sentence? How do you measure a room? What is a mammal?). At this level, teachers assess whether students have *acquired* knowledge of facts, concepts, principles, and procedures. In assessments of this type, students may be asked to identify, state, define, or summarize the information they have acquired. This allows us to determine whether students know facts and understand concepts, principles, and procedures, and whether they comprehend the information at a level that allows them to explain or summarize the information in their own words.

Moving outward through the layers of performance expectations, the next layer (gray) indicates expectations related to how we want students to manipulate the content core, and how we want them to think about and explore information (e.g., Why do people value democracy? How are simple and compound sentences alike and different? How can measuring wrong affect construction costs? How are mammals different from birds?). In assessments of this type, students may be asked to analyze the characteristics of concepts, compare or contrast information, or cluster information based on similarities of characteristics. They may also be asked to apply information they have learned in the content area.

The outermost layer indicates teacher expectations related to application of information to the real world in the form of novel problem solving and generalization (e.g., How has creating a democracy affected the people of Russia? Write a letter to persuade the mayor about something that is important to you. What kind of apartment can you afford in this neighborhood on the salary that you plan to earn when you graduate? How will recycling affect your taxes and environment over the next ten years?). At this level, teachers may ask students to use the information they have acquired in new situations, that is, to *generalize* their knowledge to new challenges. This may involve creating new solutions or plans, solving ill-defined problems, evaluating materials or methods, making decisions, persuading others of their opinions, or inferring patterns.

To summarize, using Figure 3.11 can help you visualize how to select and prioritize content that students will learn. It can also help you visualize what your expectations are about how students will process content. For each level of content, from the essential ideas and information all students must master to the information and ideas that are less essential, all students will be expected to process information at each of the three levels of acquisition, manipulation, and generalization. Because the information selected for assessment will not be limited to any one type of content information (i.e., from any one level of prioritized content), instruction should result in all students being able to meet performance standards for all three types of knowledge.

SMARTER Planning and Teaching Principles

Content selection is fundamental to planning for inclusive instruction, along with maintaining the integrity of the content. The integrity of the content is maintained when it is not watered down and the critical information remains as the central message of instruction. You, as the teacher, have the primary responsibility for differentiating critical information from less criti-

▪ *Scenario Revisited*

As Mary Cochran developed her plans, she tried to think about assessment as well as critical content. For each critical idea that Ms. Cochran identified in her planning, she thought about different ways to assess student learning. She wanted students to learn some factual information, because they needed a base on which to build more complex understandings of ideas and concepts. This kind of knowledge was easy enough to assess with objective tests, and she could have students practice learning the information through classroom games like Jeopardy—they always enjoyed that!

Ms. Cochran also wanted students to be able to reason about the big ideas of the course. For example, in the unit on exploration of the New World, she had tentatively decided that a critical idea was the importance of technological innovation in spurring exploration. The invention of better instruments and sailing ships could be explored with students, and parallels could be drawn to modern-day inventions that spurred space exploration. In the process of guiding students in learning about these developments, she wanted to structure activities along with assessments that would require students to ask and answer questions such as, Why did European explorers risk everything to sail into the unknown? Why did they risk it at this particular time in history? Perhaps these could be research projects or group projects. She would have to think about that some more.

To help make history come alive for her students, Ms. Cochran also wanted to have students take what they were learning and apply it to different situations to gain insights about current political and social developments. For example, in the unit on exploration, perhaps students could discuss the exploits of Christopher Columbus in light of current views on his accomplishments. What has influenced the attitudes of some today in the United States toward Columbus? This was an interesting idea, but perhaps it is not tied to a critical idea for the course. Perhaps she would incorporate this at a lower level in her prioritizing of content. This was a complicated business, sorting out content and how to guide and challenge students to think about it in different ways. Ms. Cochran recognized that she would never have had the time—or energy!—to do this kind of thinking during the school year.

cal information and building instruction around important ideas. In addition, critical elements must be transformed to meet the needs of the group, as well as individual students. You have the responsibility to transform content in ways that students will be able to understand, organize, remember, and respond to expectations to use the information. As a process that includes all these elements, inclusive planning is indeed a challenge. To meet that challenge we propose a process that can help you select critical content, transform it to make it accessible to students, plan to accommodate the diverse learning styles of students, and use appropriate assessments. In the remainder of this chapter we will discuss the broad outlines of the SMARTER planning process.

As we discuss this planning process, we urge you to tolerate a degree of "cognitive dissonance" which, according to Thompson and Zeuli (1999), is a first requirement for real change in professional practice. The methods described in this text represent a new approach to inclusive planning and teaching. However, if you are unwilling to question old ways—if you cannot tolerate some cognitive dissonance—then you may not implement this new planning process in the manner shown by research to make it effective and instead may merely "tinker" with your practice, say Thompson and Zeuli, rather than transform it.

Although the SMARTER planning process incorporates a new planning paradigm, it also incorporates more traditional ways to teach inclusively. In this chapter we paint the "big picture" of the new planning paradigm with the SMARTER planning process. Then, in later chapters, and especially in Chapter 9, "Teaching Content in an Academically Diverse Classroom," we elaborate on methods that may be incorporated in the SMARTER planning approach, some of which have been used as tools over the years to accommodate differences among learners. The key in transforming practice is that the content planning must be done up front to make traditional techniques and methods most effective.

The SMARTER planning process provides a structure for reflective planning that will help you shape critical questions about your content, organize content in a graphic map, analyze that content for learning difficulties it may pose, reach decisions about how to enhance your teaching to overcome learning difficulties students may have, teach strategically to help students learn how to learn, and then evaluate student mastery of your content and revisit learning outcomes. We discuss all seven parts of the process, but since this chapter is about curriculum planning, we will focus here on curricular issues. Other parts of the process related to teaching methods will be developed in more detail in subsequent chapters.

Just as we will not present all of the SMARTER planning process in this one chapter, so too should you avoid trying to implement all parts of this process in a single "chapter" of your teaching. Be patient with implementation of these new ideas. We suggest—and continue to suggest throughout the book—that you choose a few basic ideas and methods to begin with and then add other parts of the process to your planning and teaching repertoires as you come to understand more fully how the SMARTER planning process works and how it can help you involve more students in learning.

Shape the Critical Questions   Teachers commonly are required to adhere to state-specified standards. Such standards include many sets of objectives or "essential learnings" that have been generated by a state educational agency, the local school district, a professional organization, or the publisher of the textbook or instructional materials used in a classroom. The teacher's task is to know the standards and transform the expectations into a functional and meaningful set of learning goals and activities. To do this, you must stand back and consider the expected outcomes in a way that will help you stay focused and translate learning goals to students. Failing to select and focus on the critical outcomes is likely to result in simply covering a myriad of pieces of information at a surface level.

An effective way to achieve learning goals is to translate the critical outcomes into a small set of "big idea" questions that reflect what is critical in and about the content to be learned. You can shape these critical questions by asking yourself what is really critical for all students to know and understand in whatever course, unit, or lesson you are planning to teach. How can learning outcomes be cast as critical questions that capture the essence of what students need to learn? And, just as importantly, what are the central or big ideas that tie all of this information together?

Critical questions should meet several criteria in order to be considered good questions. In general, they should be broad questions, not objectives or commands, that use words like "how" and "why." (It is easy to make the mistake of writing critical questions the same way you write learning objectives.) They should be in a form that requires an extended verbal explanation. At the course level, the questions should not only be broad but conversational (see examples in sidebar); at the unit level, the questions are targeted at mastery of unit content and need to be more specific; at the lesson level, the questions need to be more concrete and lead to mastery of unit questions. In math or language arts, a final outcome task that requires computing or writing should be accompanied by a "how" or "what" question. For example, a critical question might be, "What is good writing and how can it help you achieve your goals?" While good questions do not always have to begin with these words, it frequently helps if they do. Questions that can be answered by providing one word, a definition, or a list are usually poor questions.

Critical questions should identify ways in which students should understand the information to be learned. Questions must communicate how the teacher wants students to think about content and ideas. If an expected learning outcome is to be able to compare two concepts, then a question simply asking students to define each concept is inadequate. A critical question should prompt the performance level that is expected. An example of this kind of question might be: "What is a democracy and what is a republic and how are they similar and different?"

Course Questions for a Middle School Spanish Course

1. How are Spanish and American cultures alike and different?
2. Why is it important to memorize certain expressions?
3. How is pronunciation the same in English and Spanish?
4. How is pronunciation different in English and Spanish?
5. What are good ways to practice new words and phrases?
6. What are some of the advantages of learning a foreign language?
7. Where is Spanish spoken in the world?
8. How are reading and writing in Spanish and English alike and different?

Well-constructed critical questions can help students think not only about the content but also about how the content is meaningful or important. Questions that are worth discussing usually have some relationship to life other than "the teacher made me learn it." Thus, questions should prompt students to relate learning to life or to other learning. For example, "What are the systems in the body?" is not as good a question as "How do the systems of the body work together to keep us healthy?" Of course, the first question is part of the second, larger question and students need to be able to answer the first question before they can answer the second, broader question. However, the bigger "context" question is the critical question because it communicates context and meaning for learning.

Good critical questions should help students organize information to be learned, because they should be tied to the supporting information and help students make connections. Once the question "How do the systems of the body work together to keep us healthy?" is posed, students should expect that they will be spending a significant amount of learning time understanding different systems, remembering what they are, and then describing how they work together. In other words, all the information to be presented about body systems will be tied to answering this single question. If the question does not help the student tie learning together, make associations, and help them organize, the question is flawed.

Critical questions may include expectations for learning how to learn the content, as well as what content to learn. Outcome questions can address *how* a student should learn, as well as *what* a student should learn. For example, if learning a strategy for developing good writing skills or writing good paragraphs is to be part of an English course, then learning that strategy should be part of a critical course question. Such a question might be: "How do you write a great paragraph using the paragraph writing strategy?" If *how* a student is to learn the content is important, then that should be reflected in the critical questions.

Critical questions should help students identify the critical concepts or ideas to be learned and help them to do well on outcome evaluations. The questions should focus student attention on what is important and communicate to the student where most study time should be spent. Of course, critical questions should be linked to the tests or performance measures that will be used to evaluate learning. If a set of outcome measures have already been selected to evaluate learning, then the tests should be used as a guide in constructing the critical questions.

For course planning, teachers should develop about 10 questions that every student in a class will be able to answer by the end of the year. Once the questions are developed, they are given to students who can use them to guide course progress as the units in the course are taught and learned. (More examples of course questions may be found in Appendix B, in which four scenarios describe teachers using critical questions in their planning.)

Map the Critical Content   While keeping the critical questions in mind, construct a content map to provide a graphic representation of how the content might be organized or sequenced. By constructing such a map, you can help students visualize a way to think about the content. Clear statements of the unit titles, essential points, and key vocabulary set the stage for an overview of the entire course.

Each chapter in this book begins with a content map (graphic organizer) showing the major topics to be discussed and how they are related to one another. In the content map for this chapter, the three major topics are: Standards and the Need to Select Critical Outcomes, Rethinking Planning and Teaching, and SMARTER Planning and Teaching Principles. At the end of each chapter is another, expanded content map showing the main subtopics. For example, in this chapter, under SMARTER Planning, the seven steps of this planning process are set out, both indicating how this fits into the overall plan for this unit of instruction and providing a review sheet of the topics covered. If you look at the critical questions presented at the beginning of this chapter, you will see that the elements of the content map are all related to the critical questions.

Organizing the content of a course for students can provide a scaffold on which they can "hang" newly learned content. Textbooks do not necessarily provide this structure or scaffolding. Studies have found that many students have trouble reading and understanding textbooks, and that textbooks often present information in ways that confuse students (Anrig & Lapointe, 1989; Doyle, 1992). In organizing course content, you need to think not only about how to sequence topics but also what the connections and relationships are between topics, ideas, and concepts. While the critical questions help focus attention on what to learn, it is still necessary to help students think about the content in ways that allow them to answer the critical questions. As the content expert, you have the responsibility to help students think about the content in meaningful ways.

There are several criteria for developing a good content map. In general, a good content map should include the "big idea" paraphrase. It should capture the major point to be learned as the content is taught. For the content map at the beginning of this chapter, for example, the "big idea" paraphrase is "Deciding What to Teach and How to Teach It."

In general, a big idea paraphrase should capture in a few words the main idea or point to be emphasized during instruction. It should be understandable and constructed of vocabulary that can either be understood independently by students, or easily explained, so that all students can understand it. Finally, it should be inclusive so that all learning outcomes can be linked to the paraphrase.

The heart of the content map is a graphic representation of the various elements of the content to be taught and learned. To be effective as a learning guide, the map should be well structured. A good content structure is limiting, connected, linear, hierarchical, labeled, and simple.

1. *Limiting.* The idea of the content map is to show students how to think about and organize the content so they can use the map to recall the information. The map should be limited to help focus student attention on the big ideas that will be used to organize the content. If the map becomes very complex with many parts and connections, you and students will have trouble focusing on the critical ideas of the course. For a unit or lesson, there should be seven or fewer parts. Supporting information can then be organized around these ideas.

2. *Connected.* Each section of the map should be connected with lines to the other sections when an important relationship is to be established. Arrows may be included to show additional relationships.

3. *Linear.* While not all thinking and organizational patterns are linear, the content map should present a linear representation of the order in which the content will be learned or show when the content will be presented and how it is to be mastered. Some content maps may illustrate both. In general, the sections on the left side of the map indicate what will be learned/accomplished first, whereas the sections on the right side show what will be learned/accomplished last.

4. *Hierarchical.* Each section of the map should allow for the development of subtopics and associated details. The connecting lines show the hierarchical relationships between the big idea paraphrase and supporting information. Any subcomponents are linked by lines to the associated topic. Different shapes or colors can be used to show the relationship between a topic and its associated subtopics.

5. *Labeled.* At the unit and lesson level, it is critical to make explicit connections within the content. Consequently, content maps for lessons and units include lines and arrows that are labeled with words to explain the relationship or relationships to be explored during instruction. You can check whether your labels are clear by making sure that a complete sentence can be created by linking the topic, the big idea paraphrase, and each part of the content structure. For example, in the graphic organizer at the beginning of this chapter, the title of the chapter and the big idea paraphrase are connected to the topics of the chapters using labels that make the paraphrase and each of the topics a complete sentence: "SMARTER planning for academic diversity is about deciding what to teach and how to teach it by taking into account standards and the need to select critical outcomes."

6. *Simple.* Think of the K.I.S.S. principle: Keep It Simple for Students. The fewer the parts, the clearer the language and vocabulary, and the fewer the words, the more likely it is that students will be able to use the content map to help organize their ideas as learning progresses.

At the course level, a map of the units in a course helps create a road map for what has been learned and what will be learned. Figure 3.12 shows a map for a U.S. History course. In Figure 3.13 the map focuses on one of the course units—"Expansion," in this case—and illustrates how the mapping process extends identification of the important topics and information at the level of a unit of study. When you are teaching at the unit and lesson levels, a content map can be constructed and shared with students to preview learning, organize instruction as the unit or lesson proceeds, and to review learning at the conclusion of instruction.

Some teachers find that constructing a content map first helps them think about the content in different ways, and then afterward, helps them develop different types of critical questions. Other teachers like to develop the questions first and then construct the content map. Regardless of how you approach the planning task, keep in mind that students should be able to use the content map to answer the course questions you have generated. (Other examples of course maps are included in Chapters 4 and 5 and in the Math Scenario in Appendix B.)

FIGURE 3.12   Course: United States History to 1900

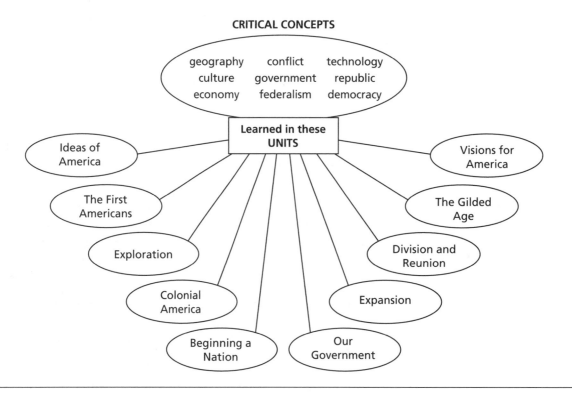

Source: Adapted from *The Course Organizer Routine*, by Lenz, Schumaker, Deshler, & Bulgren, 1998, p. 72.

FIGURE 3.13
Course: United States
History—Expansion

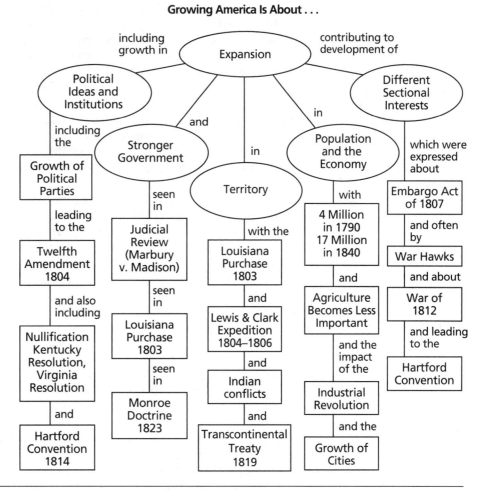

Growing America Is About . . .

Analyze for Learning Difficulties Once you have selected the critical content and organized it in a content map, you will be in a good position to think about whether students will have difficulties learning the information and ideas in your class. Being able to analyze difficulties that some students may have learning the content you have to teach is based on your knowledge of the content and its complexities. It is also based on your previous experiences in teaching the information and the characteristics of the students in your class.

Knowing the characteristics of the students in your class is particularly important as you establish learning outcomes. Will the content be sufficiently relevant to the lives of all students to engage them in learning? Will all students have the background knowledge necessary to learn the new content? Are certain concepts in the course particularly difficult for some or all students to understand? For example, federalism is an abstract concept that is encountered in history and government courses. How would you teach this concept to students? Comparing and contrasting federalism with, say, the roles and responsibilities of administrators, teachers, and students in a school might be a way to help students understand a new concept within the context of a familiar situation.

Is there information that students simply must memorize in order to have the knowledge base upon which to build further learning? Are steps involved that many students frequently have difficulty following? Is there a theme in a textbook that is clearly identified but for which there seems to be little explanation or development? These are all recurrent teaching problems that surface during the year. Since planning at the beginning of the year dictates so much of what teachers are able to attend to in their instruction, it becomes important for teachers to think about and plan for ways to address these learning difficulties early.

Some teachers may plan to incorporate discovery learning in a course. In analyzing the learning difficulties in such an approach, remember that some students may not "discover" underlying themes in content presented to them. If they cannot discover or construct the knowledge, they will be at a disadvantage in organizing and remembering information related to a course, unit, or lesson. You must be the mediator of content learning, manipulating sources of information and explicitly teaching students using techniques to make information accessible and more learning friendly. If learning goals are clear in your mind and explicit in your instruction, all students will benefit. Anticipating students' learning problems early in the planning process is crucial to inclusive instruction, because figuring out how to address such problems may take more thought and time than you will be able to muster during a typically packed school year. Some evidence suggests that planning methods used by teachers before or early in the school year affect the curriculum experienced by their students all year long (Yinger, 1980). Consequently, if you do not plan up front for how you will teach to address learning needs, these needs may not be addressed during instruction.

How to analyze for learning difficulties, as well as how to address those difficulties through reaching teaching-enhancement decisions, will be further developed in Section Four, Teaching Your Course, and also as unit and lesson planning are discussed in Chapters 7 and 8. In addition, scenarios presented in Appendix B provide a snapshot of teachers analyzing learning difficulties in secondary content classrooms.

Reach Enhancement Decisions   Some of the most important planning decisions you will make are about how you can help students learn the content of your class. This is where you decide how to teach in a way that will address the learning problems you have previously identified. Another way to think about this process is to consider how you might compensate for learning skills or background knowledge that some or many of your students may not have developed.

TEACHING DEVICES. As part of an overall instructional plan, review the list of potential learning difficulties and select devices that might be used to guide learning. Teaching devices are techniques to promote learning and are used by good teachers all the time to help students learn. Common devices include using a mnemonic like FACE, to help students remember the notes in the spaces of a musical staff. Another device is using an analogy to relate new information to something students are already familiar with. Graphic organizers, or content maps, that appear in the chapters in this text, are another device used to help the reader see the organization of the ideas and information in the chapter.

Draft, in writing, what devices or other instructional methods you plan to use and what content information they will be used with. If you are going to use devices like graphic organizers, draft what the organizer might look like. Be prepared to modify devices as you learn more about your students' background knowledge and their learning needs. To make the most effective use of teaching devices, plan for and develop procedures to show students how the device can help them learn the new content. Planning for the explicit use of teaching devices is an important step because this is where you "come clean" with students about how to learn, telling them about the "tricks of the trade" used by good learners. For even as you compensate in your teaching for learning skills that your students may lack, you want to help your students become better independent learners.

TEACHING ROUTINES. When you teach students about the devices you are using to help them learn content, you are developing a teaching routine. A teaching routine is a set of integrated instructional procedures used to guide the introduction and learning of large chunks of information in a lesson (Bulgren & Lenz, 1996). Teaching routines can ensure that devices are used effectively. The procedures of a routine are introduced to the whole class explicitly, that is, students' attention is drawn to the fact that learning particular kinds of content can be facilitated when a particular routine is used. For example, a simple kind of teaching routine might consist of teaching students to learn about concepts by comparing and contrasting them. Characteristics of two concepts may be identified and compared and contrasted as a way to develop definitions of each of the concepts. (A concept-comparison teaching routine is described further in Chapter 9, and other teaching routines are briefly summarized in Appendix C.)

Two factors must be considered when teaching routines are prepared: First, students must know how to take advantage of the routine so they can use the device to learn the information. This means that they need to be informed about how the routine works and how they are supposed to use it to facilitate learning. Some routines may be presented to students at the beginning of the school year and used repeatedly throughout the year; others may be presented for a specific unit or lesson and then used regularly thereafter. However, most routines become effective only after students understand them and have had an opportunity to practice learning with them several times.

Second, teachers must provide leadership in helping students use a routine. While a teaching routine can help compensate for students' lack of an effective or efficient learning strategy, you play a critical role in showing students how to use the routine to learn new information. Therefore, you must plan how you will develop a learning partnership with students. This partnership should be based on the goal of working together to co-construct meaning, with both parties bringing something to the learning situation. As the teacher, you bring knowledge of the content, while students bring their prior knowledge, as well as beliefs about the value of the knowledge. When you use teaching routines in partnership with students, you help students construct their own learning.

In later chapters you will learn more about comprehensive teaching routines that can enhance your instruction. These routines can, among other things, help you help students graphically organize information, explore conceptual knowledge in depth, or understand relationships that recur frequently in a content area. Further information about teaching routines is included in Appendix C, which describes routines that are part of the Content Enhancement series developed at the Center for Research on Learning at the University of Kansas. In the context of this chapter, however, it is important to recognize that developing ways to enhance learning is an essential part of inclusive teaching and should be part of your overall curriculum planning.

Teach Strategically Using teaching routines will help guide classroom instruction, but once in the classroom and interacting with students, teachers need to adopt a mind-set for making decisions consistent with the principles of strategic teaching. Strategic teaching is defined as instruction that compensates for the fact that students frequently do not have good skills or strategies for learning, and that simultaneously shows students ways to compensate for their lack of skills or strategies to learn information independently. Strategic teaching uses the processes of: (a) explaining, showing, and modeling for students how information will be taught and learned on an ongoing basis; (b) working with students in partnerships to arrive at learning outcomes; and (c) communicating to students the value of learning how to learn. In strategic teaching, you as the teacher take an active role in involving the student in the learning process. This means being explicit about the way you are teaching and the way students can best learn. Strategic teaching creates a partnership between you and your students so that they see that the way you are teaching is designed to help them learn and that strategies you are teaching them to use can improve their performance.

Strategic teaching requires that teachers emphasize the following in their plans and in their spontaneous interactions with students during instruction:

- *Provide informed instruction.* Informed instruction involves teaching students about the routines or methods you will use to promote their learning. Methods or routines should be thoroughly explained to and demonstrated for students through easily understood examples and familiar information. For example, in teaching students how feedback will be provided, you might explain each step of the feedback routine that you will use throughout the year and then demonstrate the process using a humorous or trumped-up situation by asking a student, another teacher, or the principal to dress out of character in messy clothes. You would then model good feedback on the problem and show students how feedback should be used to alter future performance in this situation and in academic situations.
- *Provide explicit instruction.* This means you must be clear about the goals and expected outcomes of instruction and find ways to share these expectations with students. Some students can readily figure out what is expected of them and can successfully fulfill all expectations. Many other students are not as practiced at figuring out what they are expected to do and need clear and explicit guidelines on what is important and what is expected. Organized and sequenced content instruction and guidance on how to perform critical learning and assessment tasks is a must for many students. Explicit instruc-

tion also involves reminding students when teaching routines are being used and then guiding them to effectively participate in the use of the routines to succeed in learning.

A way to remember what is needed in explicit instruction is to use the **Cue-Do-Review** sequence. This sequence is a process used by a teacher that can promote the explicit instruction needed for strategic teaching. To engage students in learning, **cue** the students about important content, the ways you will be teaching to enhance learning, and your expectations regarding attention, note taking, and participation. Then, teach (**do**) the content using the methods, devices, or teaching routines in a partnership with students. Finally, **review** both the content information and the process involved in teaching.

- *Share plans.* When teachers share their plans with students, they allow students to see what and how learning will occur. You can share your plans with students by developing graphic organizers that help them see how information fits with previously learned information and how they might organize or structure information for learning. Used at the beginning of a course, unit, or lesson, graphic organizers can help you lead students to identify the important relationships, strategies, activities, or standards it will be important to keep in mind as learning progresses.

- *Develop learning partnerships.* A learning partnership is created when the teacher assumes the role of instructional leader and actively seeks the involvement of students in shaping instruction so that it is meaningful and relevant for them. The course of instruction is altered as you get to know your students' background and lives by taking an interest in their prior knowledge and experiences. You show respect for students' experiences, beliefs, and values when you develop lessons that build on what students know, giving them a voice in determining how information will be explored and learned.

- *Communicate the value of using strategies.* Once you become more strategic in your teaching, it is important that your students understand that they are expected to take advantage of this type of instruction and put forth effort themselves to use more effective and efficient strategies for learning. You can help students understand the connection between learning content and using good strategies by making sure they realize that using effective learning strategies can help them be more successful learners. (Developing and teaching learning strategies is discussed more fully in Chapter 10.)

Evaluate Mastery   An important element in planning to meet the learning needs of all students is evaluating whether critical learning outcomes have been achieved. Having identified the desired outcomes, you need to be certain that your methods of instruction and evaluation in fact help students attain desired learning and that they measure attainment of the learning and not that of other, unstated, or unspecified learning outcomes.

For example, if a social studies teacher decides that a curricular goal will be the development of reasoning, then instructional activities requiring problem solving should be used to help students develop and practice using reasoning abilities. Goodlad (1984) has observed that if students are only asked to read a textbook, listen to lectures, fill out worksheets, and take quizzes they will not learn how to reason or think critically. Similarly, tests that require only regurgitating memorized information will not demonstrate whether students have learned any critical thinking or reasoning skills.

Goodlad's observations (1984) underscore the importance of the evaluation step in the planning process. Here, teachers are encouraged to step back and consider what learning has occurred in a completed lesson or unit. Without such reflection, deficits in the instructional process are likely to be repeated, rather than rectified, in succeeding instruction. As you seek to address the learning needs of your students, it is important to reevaluate not only "what worked" and what "didn't work" in your classes, but also, whether it worked for *all* students. Evaluating mastery may help you revise what you are teaching and how you are teaching it so you can more successfully achieve your goals.

Therefore, a critical part of SMARTER planning involves shifting the attention of the evaluation process away from an exclusive focus on students and toward evaluating teacher planning and instruction. Evaluation should focus on assessing the outcomes of planning and teaching to help shape future planning decisions. Ask yourself such questions as: If a device was used, was it effective? If a teaching routine was created, did it work? Did I spend enough time developing the routine? Do I need to redo a routine or use a different one? Did all the students learn what was intended? What do I need to do differently next time?

Evaluation of students may be formal or informal. It can be accomplished through a quiz, an assignment, or an oral question to a specific student. However, as you evaluate students, it is important to remember that your goal is not just to assign grades. In the planning process, evaluation is also conducted to help teachers answer the questions: Am I doing a good job? and What should I do differently?

Revisit Outcomes   At the end of instruction, the outcomes chosen in the planning step, Select Critical Outcomes, must be reviewed. If something is critical, that standard should not be compromised. This means that if students have not learned the critical information, additional instruction should be provided. Abandoning standards may compromise the integrity of the curriculum. The pressure to cover the curriculum should never result in compromising the standards and the integrity of the curriculum for any student. Only if teachers are able to revisit outcomes after a unit and identify where instruction needs to be adapted will they be able to plan ahead to modify instruction in the next unit to enhance the learning of all students.

If there are any outcomes that have not been achieved, then you have only two choices:

Choice 1: Reteach for mastery. Provide additional instruction so the outcome is achieved. If the outcome is critical, the instruction cannot move on until the outcome has been achieved. The word "critical" implies a "life-or-death" outcome for the student in terms of future learning and success. Therefore, the list of critical outcomes or questions becomes the standard for deciding whether to move on or to reteach.

Choice 2: Abandon the outcome. You may choose not to provide additional instruction in an outcome area by admitting that a targeted outcome is not really critical. In essence, by choosing this option, you admit you made a mistake in determining what was critical and that the standards for instruction need to be altered. This is a legitimate choice, because during the process of teaching, teachers constantly reevaluate what is and what is not important. Sometimes the outcomes will change; some outcomes may be dropped while others may be added.

Doyle (1992) noted that teaching is a curriculum process where content is produced and transformed continuously. Looking at curricular decision making in this way may help you develop a keener awareness of your role as a "curriculum maker." This last step in the SMARTER Planning process provides you with an opportunity to evaluate your curricular decisions

▪ *Scenario Revisited*

As Mary Cochran began to plan using the SMARTER planning ideas, she focused first on her course in U.S. history. Pulling out the list of state standards, she thought about what was involved in helping students meet the standards and benchmarks. After digesting what the standards were really getting at, she began to develop a set of 10 critical questions that seemed to capture what she wanted all students to know. For each question, she jotted down subquestions and points to help her remember what was involved with each question.

Next, she began to work on organizing the content. She developed a graphic organizer or content map showing the units she wanted to create. Ms. Cochran quickly realized that the units that captured the critical ideas were not necessarily organized the same way as the textbook for the course. She made notes of the pages of the textbook that seemed to go with the name she had given to each unit. As she developed the map, she listed key ideas and outcomes that supported the course questions and the state benchmarks. At this point she realized that she had spent several hours developing her critical course questions and creating the map of the units in the course. Ms. Cochran knew that the questions were going to change as the summer went on and would probably change throughout the school year as well, but at least she had a running start at selecting what was critical.

The next day, Ms. Cochran reviewed her course map. She made a few changes and notes. Then, she began to think about what would make this content difficult for students. Well,

she knew the organization of the information in the textbook was a problem. She realized that neither she nor the textbook did a very thorough job of identifying important concepts like federalism and nationalism. She also recalled that separation of powers and checks and balances were difficult ideas for some students to understand well. And, because one of her newly identified "critical outcomes" was that students understand how institutions of the U.S. government evolved and continue to evolve, she tried to think about how she could best teach that idea. As she thought about the concepts and ideas that would pose learning difficulties for many students, she realized that she was identifying themes that would resurface throughout the course. Ms. Cochran looked back at her list of critical questions and her course map to see if these ideas and concepts had all been included. She found that most of them had, but she took some time to refashion her questions and her map to reflect her developing ideas about her course.

Ms. Cochran paused to think about what a challenge this SMARTER planning process was! And what a lot of fun it was to think about the big ideas of her course and how they could best be taught. There was always so much to do during the school year that "big picture" planning simply wasn't on the agenda. Even now during the summer, a small part of her wanted to leave school matters behind and get caught up on her personal life. Now, though, this planning was prompting her to think about a lot of interesting issues, and she was grateful for this structured opportunity for making curriculum.

based on your knowledge and expertise about your students and their learning needs. Some have argued that teachers should adopt a "deliberationist perspective" in curriculum development and view the relationship between curriculum and instruction as dynamic rather than static (McCutcheon, 1988; Thornton, 1991). Such a perspective may lead you to become more reflective about what you are trying to teach (McCutcheon, 1988) and how, given your particular students, your particular classrooms, and your own past teaching experiences, you can best teach it.

FIGURE 3.14
Expanded Graphic
Organizer

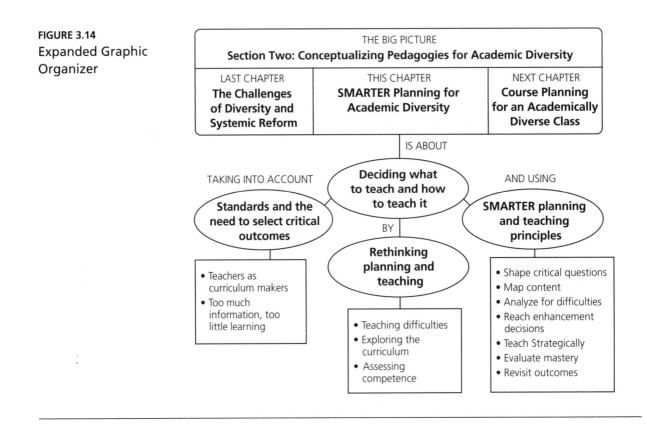

SUMMARY

Teachers play an instrumental role in constructing the curriculum that is taught in classrooms. Standards shape only the broad outlines of what students should learn; it is you, the teacher, who determines the specifics of the content to be covered and how learning will be structured and guided. Planning to structure and guide learning that includes all students requires that you carefully think through what you want to teach and how you plan to teach it, and that you do this thinking well before the school year begins.

Using the SMARTER reflective planning process can be a way to do this kind of planning effectively.

Learning may be thought of as a journey. Planning for including all students on that journey starts with a vision of the broader routes and destinations for the journey—the goals and means of reaching them for a course—and moves on to how the course can be organized into meaningful units and revealing experiences that take the form of "lessons learned." As a result, more time needs to be spent on conceptualizing the big ideas of the course, how they are supported in units, and how students can be helped on a daily basis to understand them.

The curriculum planning process presented in this chapter can be a helpful tool for new and experienced teachers and can help to ensure effective instruction that will accommodate student differences. The course, unit, and lesson-planning routines to follow in Chapters 6, 7, and 8 incorporate the ideas introduced in this chapter. They include planning for instruction that is appropriate for high and low achievers, and that allows teachers to be clear in their own minds and in their plans, about what they want to teach, and what they want and expect students to learn.

MAKING CONNECTIONS:
Implementing SMARTER Planning

SMARTER planning principles are a very effective way to plan to teach. We recognize, however, that the principles and process can be a bit overwhelming, at first. Rather than trying to master and integrate all the principles into your planning at once, you might try to select one principle to implement. Then, as you become comfortable working with that one principle, you can try integrating more of the ideas into your planning and teaching. For example:

1. *Here are the big ideas to get you started:*
   Shape the Critical Questions
   Map the Critical Content
   Analyze for Learning Difficulties
   Reach Enhancement Decisions
   Teach Strategically
   Evaluate Mastery
   Revisit Outcomes

2. *Here's what you need to get started:*
   - A copy of the state standards or local guidelines for the course you will teach or are teaching
   - The textbook for your course

3. *Try this:*
Start by trying to write three of your 10 course questions. Reread the section of this chapter about shaping the critical questions. Remember that the questions should:

- Be broad questions.
- Identify ways in which students should understand the information to be learned.
- Help students identify the critical concepts or ideas to be learned.
- Help students think about the content and how the content fits into other contexts.
- Help students organize information that supports the critical concepts or ideas to be learned.
- Include expectations for learning how to learn the content. If how a student is to learn the content is important, then that should be reflected in the critical questions.
- Lead students to do well on outcome evaluations.

4. *Evaluate your work:*
   - Compare your questions to the state standards for your area. Your questions should provide an umbrella for addressing about a third of your state standards.
   - Compare your questions to unit or chapter headings in your textbook. Does the textbook use meaningful ideas to frame units and chapters?
   - Ask a colleague for feedback on your questions or get together with a fellow teacher and discuss whether your questions capture the big ideas of the course.

5. *Next steps:*
Select *one* of your critical outcome questions. In the chart below, enter the question in the space to the right of "Shape the Critical Questions." Then, for each step of the SMARTER process, record one item in the column on the right. For example, list one topic that would be included in a map of your course, one learning difficulty students might experience trying to answer your course outcome question, one way you might enhance instruction to help students with that learning difficulty, one way you might teach more strategically, one way you would evaluate whether your instruction helped students learn the critical outcome. Under "Revisit Outcomes," you might think back on your experiences in a classroom to describe any instances where not all students learned. Was the critical outcome really critical? How might it have been retaught? Was it retaught?

Shape the Critical Questions	
Map the Critical Content	
Analyze for Learning Difficulties	
Reach Enhancement Decisions	
Teach Strategically	
Evaluate Mastery	
Revisit Outcomes	

SUGGESTED READINGS

Erickson, F., & Shultz, J. (1992). Students' experience of the curriculum. In P. W. Jackson (Ed.). *Handbook of research on curriculum* (pp. 789– 829). New York: Macmillan. Includes a telling metaphor about delivery of the curriculum to students, likening it to school lunch, prepackaged and, on occasion, force fed, chopped up into small, predigested bits. Provides perspectives to prompt reflection about curriculum and the role of teachers in developing and delivering it.

Glatthorn, A. A., & Jailall, J. (2000). Curriculum for the new millennium. In R. S. Brandt (Ed.), *Education in a new era* (pp. 97–121). Alexandria, VA: Association for Supervision and Curriculum Development. This essay provides a thoughtful and succinct summary of curriculum movements and developments over the last 50 years in the United States.

Wiggins, G., & McTighe, J. (1998). *Understanding by design.* Alexandria, VA: Association for Supervision and Curriculum Development.

WEB SITES

http://www.cde.ca.gov/board California State Board of Education. This page lists all the content areas for which the state has established standards. When you click on specific content areas you get an overview of California Frameworks, and then you get specific grade-level standards.

http://standards.nctm.org National Council of Teachers of Mathematics Curriculum and Evaluation Standards for School Mathematics

http://www.mcrel.org/standards-benchmarks Content Knowledge–the McREL Standards Database. This is a compendium of standards and benchmarks for K–12.

http://edstandards.org/standards.html Wappingers Central School District—Developing Education Standards. Includes links to standards by state and subject area.

REFERENCES

Anrig, G. R., & Lapointe, A. E. (1989). What we know about what students don't know. *Educational Leadership, 47*(3), 4–5, 7–9.

Beane, J. (Ed.). (1995). *Toward a coherent curriculum: The 1995 ASCD yearbook.* Alexandria, VA: Association for Supervision and Curriculum Development.

Blythe, T., & Associates (1998). *The teaching for understanding guide.* San Francisco: Jossey-Bass.

Bruner, J. (1960). *The process of education.* Cambridge, MA: Harvard University Press.

Bulgren, J. A., & Lenz, B. K. (1996). Strategic instruction in the content areas. In D. Deshler, E. S. Ellis, & B. K. Lenz (Eds.), *Teaching adolescents with learning disabilities: Strategies and methods* (2nd ed., pp. 409–473). Denver: Love Publishing.

Caine, R. N., & Caine, G. (1997). *Education on the edge of possibility.* Alexandria, VA: Association for Supervision and Curriculum Development.

Carnine, D. (1994). Introduction to the mini-series: Diverse learners and prevailing, emerging, and research-based educational approaches and their tools. *School Psychology Review, 23*(3), 341–350.

Clandinin, D. J., & Connelly, F. M. (1992). Teacher as curriculum maker. In P.W. Jackson (Ed.), *Handbook of research on curriculum* (pp. 789–829). New York: Macmillan.

Clark, C. M., & Elmore, J. L. (1979). *Teacher planning in the first weeks of school.* Institute for Research on Teaching. Research Report 56. East Lansing: Michigan State University.

Clark, C. M., & Yinger, R. J. (1987). Teacher planning. In D. C. Berliner & B. Rosenshine (Eds.), *Talk to teachers* (pp. 342–365). New York: Random House.

Doyle, W. (1992). Curriculum and pedagogy. In P. W. Jackson (Ed.), *Handbook of research on curriculum* (pp. 789–829). New York: Macmillan.

Erickson, L. (1998). *Concept-based curriculum and instruction: Teaching beyond the facts.* Thousand Oaks, CA: Corwin Press.

Erickson, F., & Shultz, J. (1992). Students' experience of the curriculum. In P.W. Jackson (Ed.), *Handbook of research on curriculum* (pp. 789–829). New York: Macmillan.

Fensham, P. J. (1992). Science and technology. In P. W. Jackson (Ed.). *Handbook of research on curriculum* (pp. 789–829). New York: Macmillan.

Foner, E., & Garraty, J. A. (Eds.). (1991). *The reader's companion to American history.* Boston: Houghton Mifflin.

Glatthorn, A. A., & Jailall, J. (2000). Curriculum for the new millennium. In R. S. Brandt (Ed.), *Education in a new era* (pp. 97–121). Alexandria, VA: Association for Supervision and Curriculum Development.

Good, T. L., & Brophy, J. E. (1994). *Looking in classrooms* (6th ed.). New York: HarperCollins.

Goodlad, J. I. (1984). *A place called School—Prospects for the future.* New York: McGraw-Hill.

Joint Committee on Teacher Planning for Students with Disabilities. (1995). *Planning for academic diversity in America's classrooms: Windows on reality, research, change and practice.* Lawrence: University of Kansas, Center for Research on Learning.

Kame'enui, E., & Carnine, D. (1998). *Effective teaching strategies that accommodate diverse learners.* Columbus, OH: Merrill.

McDonnell, L. M., McLaughlin, M. J. & Morison, P. (Eds.) (1997). *Educating one & all: Students with disabilities and standards-based reform.* Washington, DC: National Academy Press.

McCutcheon, G. (1988). How do elementary teachers plan? The nature of planning and influences on it. *Elementary School Journal, 81,* 4–23.

McKee, S. J. (1988). Impediments to implementing critical thinking. *Social Education, 52,* 444–446.

Newmann, F. M., & Associates (1996). *Authentic achievement: Restructuring schools for intellectual quality.* San Francisco: Jossey-Bass.

Parker, W. C. (1991). Achieving thinking and decision-making objectives in social studies. In J. P. Shaver (Ed.), *Handbook of research on social studies teaching and learning* (pp. 345–356). New York: Macmillan.

Perkins, D. (1992). *Smart schools: From training memories to educating minds.* New York: Free Press.

Sadker, M., & Sadker, J. (1999). Questioning skills. In J. M. Cooper (Ed.), *Classroom teaching skills* (pp. 101–146). Boston: Houghton Mifflin.

Schumm, J. S., Vaughn, S., & Leavell, A. G. (1994). Planning pyramid: A framework for planning for diverse student needs during content area instruction. *Reading Teacher, 47*(8), 608–615).

Sizer, T. R. (1996). *Horace's hope.* Boston: Houghton Mifflin.

Thompson, C. L., & Zeuli, J. S. (1999). The frame and the tapestry: Standards-based reform and professional development. In L. Darling-Hammond & G. Sykes, (Eds.), *Teaching as the learning profession: Handbook of Policy and Practice* (pp. 341–375). San Francisco: Jossey-Bass.

Thornton, S. J. (1991). Teacher as curricular instructional gatekeeper in social studies. In J. P. Shaver (Ed.), *Handbook of research on social studies teaching and learning* (pp. 237–248). New York: Macmillan.

Tyler, R. W. (1950). *Basic principles of curriculum and instruction.* Chicago: University of Chicago Press.

Wiggins, G., & McTighe, J. (1998). *Understanding by design.* Alexandria, VA: Association for Supervision and Curriculum Development.

Woodward, J. (1994). The role of models in secondary science instruction. *Remedial & Special Education, 15*(2), 94–104.

Yinger, R. J. (1980). A study of teacher planning. *Elementary School Journal, 80*(3), 107–127.

Zahorik, J. A. (1975). Teachers' planning models. *Educational Leadership, 33*(2) 134–139.

CHAPTER 4

Course Planning for an Academically Diverse Class

B. Keith Lenz
Brenda R. Kissam
David Scanlon

I think that one thing that has been affirmed for me . . . is that strong belief, that what is appropriate for the kids I think of as at-risk . . . is really what's appropriate for all kids. And that maybe what I need to do is some rethinking of the way that I deliver [content] as opposed to wishing I had a different kind of kid in my classroom.

—A high school history teacher, in B. K. Lenz, D. D. Deshler, & J. B. Schumaker (1993).

Critical Self-Test Questions

- Why is course planning important?
- What is the role of course planning in inclusion?
- How can state standards be used to guide course planning?
- How do I create critical course questions?
- How can I use critical course questions with students to help them learn?

Course planning focuses on thinking about how an entire course will be organized and how course ideas will be launched at the beginning of the year, maintained throughout the year, and pulled together at the end of the year. Course planning is the level of planning where teachers work through issues about professional and state standards, overall outcomes, the type of learning community they want to create, the type of systems and routines that will be implemented throughout the year, and the types of skills and strategies that will be emphasized as vehicles to learn content. Teachers' beliefs and mind-set about diversity, individualization, and educational responsibilities to students shape their course plans.

Course-level planning involves more than creating a syllabus with an overview of the content, assignments, and grading criteria for the course. It can provide opportunities to address the overall purpose of the course, the scope and sequence of individual units and lessons, the amount of time to be devoted to each unit, ways to evaluate students' performance, concepts to appear throughout the course, and the specific teaching techniques that will be used consistently to facilitate student mastery. The course planning process described in this chapter is unlike traditional approaches to planning in that it focuses on the students you will teach as much as on the content you plan to teach. The planning process outlined here provides a structure that allows you to plan efficiently to select the content all students need to learn, to assure that your teaching is organized and explicit for students, and to enhance the delivery of content so that you can compensate, through your teaching, for any lack of learning strategies among your students. This planning approach also allows you to build a learning community in your classroom, to mobilize all support services—other school personnel, as well as students in your classroom—and to make sure all learners are included and learning.

FIGURE 4.1
Graphic Organizer

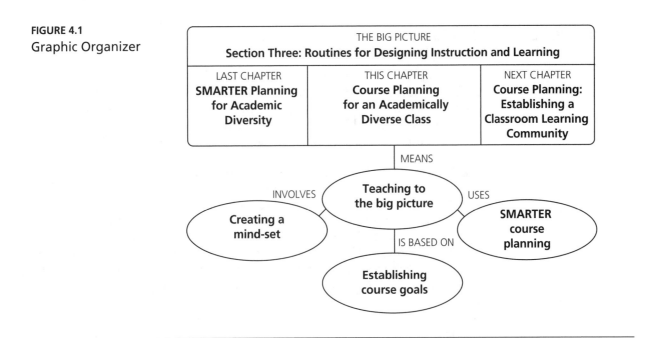

Using a travel metaphor, course planning can provide learners with an "itinerary" for the learning "journey" in a course. A picture or map of how the course is organized can show students where they have been along the route of learning and where they are headed. Teachers may be thought of as "tour guides," pointing out the major sights (concepts) and developing ways to help those on the journey understand the significance of what they have seen and learned. As tour guides, teachers need to plan, ahead of time, how they will present features of the trip in a way that will be meaningful to everyone on the trip. And just as a tour guide must plan ahead if some travelers need special arrangements, so too must teachers plan ahead for the teaching enhancements and adaptations needed for a course to be accessible to all students.

▪ *Scenario*

Ms. Jessel, a high school English teacher with four years of experience, was feeling discouraged about the past year. She had struggled to incorporate the new state standards in her ninth-grade English literature course. As a result, she finished the school year without having completed her course objectives. From the course evaluations she learned that the students felt overwhelmed, confused, and shortchanged. She was frustrated that she hadn't covered the content that she had planned, including having to omit her favorite units. She wanted to approach the new year and her first-semester course planning with a clean slate and a fresh, positive attitude. She knew she could be well organized, and she believed that use of the standards would improve her teaching. Yet, she wanted to teach the course in a way that would involve the students to a greater extent than had been the case in the past. Ms. Jessel didn't know where to begin.

FOUNDATIONS AND PRINCIPLES

Little research has been conducted on course planning. Yet, available studies have indicated that course planning influences all the other types of planning teachers do. For example, Brown (1988) found that decision making by middle-school teachers relied "increasingly on plans set at the preceding (and more general) level as they moved from yearly and unit [planning] to more detailed and specific weekly and daily planning" (p. 74). Clark and Yinger (1987) have also described how classroom routines established early in the year exert a "powerful, if subtle, influence on thought and behavior" during the course of the school year (p. 87).

Course planning reflects a teacher's mind-set about a course. Specifically, the way a teacher thinks about how to approach a course and about course outcomes significantly influences the methods selected to deliver course content. Course planning promotes the development of broad and inclusive teaching routines that are more likely to be responsive to academic diversity in a classroom. Many veteran teachers report that how the first few weeks of a course are organized is critical for establishing a positive tone and clear course expectations. However, few staff development programs help teachers learn about course planning and launching. In addition, beginning teachers may not have had an opportunity to discuss course planning in teacher education programs, and they generally do not have opportunities to work with veteran teachers in planning or launching a course during preservice teaching experiences.

As we noted in Chapter 1, planning for instruction in diverse classrooms has typically included using a variety of instructional methods and activities and/or making adaptations and modifications for some students. Those kinds of accommodations can be effective and useful and will be discussed in depth in Chapter 9. What we are proposing in this chapter is that planning for academic diversity is most effective if it begins at the course planning level. This represents a different way of thinking about accommodating differences among students and individualizing for instruction, because decisions you make in *selecting* and *organizing* course content are as important as decisions about instructional methods and activities—the more traditional focus for addressing diversity. Decisions about classroom teaching and learning routines remain as an important focus of course planning, because the methods and routines selected will help assure that students are supported in learning from the beginning of your course through to its conclusion. However, being clear about what you want students to learn is an essential first step.

Course planning can help allay some of the uncertainties students experience at the beginning of the school year. These uncertainties include understanding the kind of classroom climate the teacher wants to create and how to participate in establishing this climate. Other issues include learning how the teacher approaches teaching the course, feeling comfortable with teaching routines and learning strategies that comprise classroom rituals, and learning what standards will be used to evaluate classroom performance. Attending to classroom practices and procedures at the course level can significantly influence student learning. To be good learners, students need to understand why it is important to learn the information covered in a course. They need to understand how course ideas are related to units and lessons and be able to create ways to organize and categorize what they are learning and integrate new with previous learning. They also need to feel comfortable with teaching routines and learning strategies used in the class and be able to see the progress they have made. Planning for these elements of a course and assuring that students understand them can reduce frustration and help minimize disruptions as instruction proceeds.

In a two-year study of course planning, Lenz (1998) found that several things occurred when teachers used a course-planning routine that prompted them to inform students about course components and regularly connect course content and student learning outcomes. In general, as a result of using the routine, teachers elevated the importance of course planning and reflection, because they realized that course decisions would affect what content would be most important to learn. They also realized that how students were going to learn that content would be an important and regular part of teaching activities.

More specifically, participating teachers changed their teaching in several ways. First, they spent considerably more time introducing major course ideas, concepts, themes, and routines to students than did teachers who did not use the course planning routine. Second, they integrated an average of eight new inclusive teaching practices into their classes, whereas teachers in comparison classes were only able to maintain about two new practices. On a test of major course outcomes, students with learning difficulties answered an average of three questions correctly at the beginning of the course and eight questions correctly at the end of the course, whereas students with disabilities in comparison classes answered an average of three course questions correctly at the beginning of the course and four questions correctly at the end of the course. In addition to the progress made by struggling students, other students in the classroom either improved in learning or maintained steady course progress. Finally, teachers reported that the course planning routine provided a focus for unit and lesson planning and offered guidance in making decisions about content selection. If unit and lesson information did not fit within the framework of course decisions, teachers felt more comfortable not including this content in their instruction.

KNOWING AND DOING

Planning a course begins with establishing course goals. Establishing goals in a course means that teachers know what they want students to learn and that students know what they are expected to learn. Simple as this may sound, it does not always happen. Is the goal of your course to "cover" all the material in a textbook? *some* of the material in a textbook? to get through a district curriculum? to "learn about" history, or biology, or geometry? What content must students know? What skills do you want students to have, coming away from the class? Even when teachers can answer these questions, do students know what they are supposed to be learning? Is there, as some have described it, "a shared detailed understanding between teacher and students of what is going on, what needs to be done and how it will be done" (Boomer, Lester, Onore, & Cook, 1992, p. 288)?

Establishing and Evaluating Course Goals

As mentioned in Chapter 3, explicit learning goals should convey to students the big ideas of the course, its units, and its lessons. For example, in this chapter, the big idea or unifying theme, as conveyed in the opening graphic organizer, is that course planning is about teaching to the big picture. All the topics in this chapter are subsequently connected to that one big idea. Some students, especially those who struggle with learning or emotional difficulties, as well as other students who may be considered at risk for school failure, do not see the relationships among ideas and concepts that they are expected to learn. For them, a course may appear to consist only of discrete and isolated bits of information with little connection:

> Confronted by a succession of . . . encounters with disembodied information that they are expected to remember and reproduce, unengaged learners confirm over and over again their view that school knowledge is an end in itself, unconnected to the world outside school. . . . They learn to expect subject matter knowledge to be boring, disconnected, and meaningless. (McDiarmid, 1991, p. 261)

Structuring learning for "unengaged" learners can begin with developing themes or big ideas in a course. Such big ideas provide a kind of scaffolding for students to "hang" new knowledge on. Identifying big ideas can also provide a rationale for learning, a reason why it is worthwhile to know and understand the bits of information as a means of understanding the big idea.

Establishing course goals requires you to do some hard thinking about your course to clarify learning expectations in your own mind and, ultimately, for your students. What students must learn needs to be made explicit at the beginning of a course. Then content goals may be revisited regularly throughout the year to promote understanding of what they are learning and why. Creating a graphic picture of your course can help make learning goals clear to you and to your students. It is equally important to specify standards, or what you expect students to learn and how they will demonstrate that learning.

What Do You Plan to "Cover" An important planning issue is making choices about what you will cover in a course. In committing to what to cover, it may be most effective for student learning if you adopt the idea that "less is more." That is, put aside the concept of "coverage" and assumptions that you absolutely must cover certain topics and instead, step back from your material and consider what students really need to take with them when they leave your course. Teachers participating in a study of course planning commented that this process was one of their more valuable planning experiences and that, while it was difficult to figure out those "essential learning outcomes," it was well worth the effort (Lenz et al., 1993).

Depending on the course and your personal interests, you may want students to acquire social skills and strategies for learning, in addition to content knowledge. Therefore, your own "essentials" may come from any or all of these areas. Or you might consider selecting the content you want to cover, based on topics you would like your students to get started on in your class, and perhaps pursue later in some other class or context. With what topics might your students get really involved? Or what might excite their imagination, curiosity, or interest? Teachers have found different ways to sift through course content to discover the essentials.

LESS REALLY *IS* MORE. At the end of the year, teachers who taught with this approach to planning said they in no way felt students had missed out or learned less than other students (Lenz et al., 1993). One middle-school social studies teacher commented:

> The concept of "less is more" is really exciting to me. The curricular demands have seemed so extensive in the past that it is not surprising to me that students may have retained or learned little. I am very comfortable with . . . focusing on a few major learnings for the course. (Lenz et al., 1993)

A high school social studies teacher said:

> The notion of less being more taught me that I can give up things and still keep the essence of what I'm trying to teach. It also taught me to go from more teacher-centered classrooms to switching back and forth between student-centered and teacher-centered activities. (Lenz et al., 1993)

STANDARDS AND SCHOOL-DISTRICT GUIDELINES. There may be district curriculum guidelines or state standards that affect what you teach, and state or district textbook-adoption procedures may have an impact on the materials available for you to use. However, these kinds of guidelines often give teachers leeway to make many curricular decisions. If your students must take certain standardized tests to show mastery of topics or skills, you must ensure that whatever specifics you expect your students to learn will also prepare them for such tests. In cases where state or district guidelines are very specific, you may want to consider an approach reported by Perrone (1994): Teachers devoted a specific day or days of the week to do what they called "Caesar's work" or work required by the district or state; on other days they taught the other things they believed it was important for their students to know and understand.

HOW WOULD YOU TEACH YOUR COURSE IF YOU HAD ONLY TWO WEEKS? Planning a two-week, condensed version of a yearlong course is one way to think differently about selecting the content of a course. The idea of teaching your whole course in two weeks can be a framework for selecting the most important content you want to teach—that you want your students to know and understand. A two-week overview of course content might also be a way to launch a course. Teaching the basic concepts early on might provide an advance organizer, or scaffolding, for students, better enabling them to understand not just discrete pieces of information but relationships and connections, as well.

What Is Your Course Really About? How you develop, think about, and implement the big idea (or ideas) of your course will depend on your own teaching style, the course subject matter, the students in your course, and what you're comfortable doing. To develop these ideas, you need to be able to answer the following question in the fewest words possible: "What do I want the learning experience in this course to be about?" This kind of question invites you to consider not only the content of the course, but how you want the students to experience being in your classroom. For example, a high school visual arts teacher, struggling with district standards, developed a "personal guiding statement" that each of her students become "an informed interpreter of art in many forms and also an independent creator

Focus and Reflect

If you had two weeks to teach the most important aspects of your course, what would you teach? What would you expect students to learn? This exercise may help you struggle with the issue of coverage.

of unique and original art" (McDougal, 2002). While this goal did not begin as a course goal, it was easily transformed into one, namely, that the course, Visual Arts, is about learning to become an informed interpreter of art in many forms and an independent creator of unique and original art. Whatever your big idea becomes, it will help guide you and the students from beginning to end in the course. It will also suggest activities, room arrangement, assignments, and assessment. It will become part of your creative process as a teacher.

A THEME. Your big idea may emerge as an overarching theme for the course. As musicians and literature teachers know, themes are recurring or identifying elements that help unify the overall work. For example, a science teacher used the theme "Planet Earth"—with earth symbols on papers, bulletin board designs, group activities, and more—to reinforce the concept of earth as an interactive, interdependent community. This theme also allowed her to emphasize the class as a community with the same characteristics (Lenz et al., 1993).

A METAPHOR. Other teachers develop a course metaphor. A metaphor immediately conveys a likeness between two seemingly dissimilar things. For instance, the metaphor of a course as a "journey" captures many ideas: We are on a trip together, we make stops along the way, the teacher is a guide, the course is an experience in discovery, students are fellow travelers, we will have memories of the trip and tell stories afterwards, and so on.

AN IMAGE, A WORD. The big idea may also emerge as a word, a phrase, or an image. In fact, there are endless ways in which the big picture may take shape. A science teacher could, for example, decide on "relationships" as the big idea. By choosing "relationships," the teacher has decided to link the idea of relationships among life forms with the idea of relationships within the learning community.

Finding the big idea helps us create spaces for inquiry, self-examination, and to help our thinking. Looking for the big idea can help us challenge existing structures and thinking. A high school science teacher commented:

> I think that in the last two years I have done a better job of keeping the big ideas in front of the students. One way is by using the metaphor. Just by introducing the class as I did, I think students got the point about learning science skills. (Lenz et al., 1993)

Another teacher used a metaphor to launch the course and commented: "Working through the idea of using a metaphor is a good way for teachers to discern what is really important and interesting about their course and also how they relate to it personally" (Lenz et al., 1993).

A COURSE PARAPHRASE. Look at the name of the course and ask yourself what the course is really about. What standards need to be addressed in creating this course? How is this course different from other courses? For example, how is the eighth-grade language arts course different from the ninth-grade English course? When you introduce this course to students, what are you going to say it is about? If a student were describing the course to her parents, what would she say it was about?

Based on the course title, write a paraphrase or summary of what your course is about. The paraphrase should convey to students the emphasis or "gist" of the course in a way that distinguishes this course from other courses and clearly and explicitly communicates what students will learn. In essence, the course title paraphrase should: (a) capture the main idea of the course, (b) distinguish the course from other similar courses, (c) clearly and meaningfully communicate course content, and (d) provide a conceptual umbrella for course learning. In the course organizers in Figures 4.2, 4.3, 4.4, and 4.5, a course paraphrase is given in the oval below the name of the course.

USING THE BIG IDEA. Don't rush the process. Let the big idea develop fully before you start to think about how you could translate it into actions. Explore all the possible implications. Decide which parts of the idea, theme, or metaphor do not work. Don't rush into thinking about what students will do. Instead, think through what your course is really about and what kind of learning environment you want to establish.

SMARTER Course Planning

At the course-planning level, teachers not only decide what content must be learned. They must also decide how the course will be delivered and what types of processes should be put in place to make learning happen for all students. A plan should be created for introducing the course to students and for maintaining connections between the big ideas, concepts, and information throughout the year. Finally, plans should be created for evaluating student progress and ensuring opportunities for course revisions. The SMARTER Planning process, introduced in Chapter 3, can help you develop a plan to organize and deliver a course. Let's quickly walk through the SMARTER steps and see how course planning decisions can be addressed.

Shape the Critical Questions
Map the Critical Content
Analyze for Learning Difficulties
Reach Enhancement Decisions
Teach Strategically
Evaluate Mastery
Revisit Outcomes

Examples of Explicit Course Paraphrases

This course is about:

1. Reading to find out how different short stories are written and learning how to write different types of short stories.
2. How the story of America has become the story of civil and human rights.
3. How to apply mathematics to help solve everyday problems.
4. What makes all life forms on earth connected and dependent on each other.

■ *Scenario Revisted*

ESTABLISHING COURSE GOALS

Ms. Jessel discussed her course planning dilemma with the other members of the English Department. Mr. Jardo mentioned that he had attended a workshop on course planning and had started developing a course organizer that he handed out to students. Handing out the organizer and going through it at the beginning of the year and then returning to it at the end of each unit was working really well, he said. The parents of students in his class also liked the organizer.

Ms. Jessel began meeting with Mr. Jardo to learn how to do the organizers. First they worked on developing a course theme or paraphrase.

Mr. Jardo explained that this was a good way to begin thinking about what was really important in a course. Ms. Jessel thought about this for several days and came up with the idea that her ninth-grade literature class was about reading literature as a way for students to learn about themselves and the world. Tackling literature from this perspective might help students see the value and relevance of her course to their lives. Of course, she would need to redouble her efforts to incorporate in the course some of the literature from the cultures represented by students in her class.

FIGURE 4.2

Teacher(s): **Mr. Culbertson**

Time: **10:05-10:57**

Student: **Jean Wojoski**

Course Dates: **9/98-5/99**

The

Course Organizer

① **THIS COURSE:**

United States History to 1900

is about

How the United States was created, grew to be a nation, and led the world into a revolution based on technology.

② **COURSE QUESTIONS:**

1. What ideas have shaped (are shaping) the destiny of the U.S.?

2. How has geography affected the creation and development of the U.S.?

3. How has conflict affected the destiny of the U.S.?

4. How do different sources help us understand the U.S. experience and how do we use these sources?

5. How have we protected our civil rights, and why has this been an important concern in the history of the people of the U.S.?

6. How have art and literature served as windows to U.S. history?

7. How has technology affected U.S. society and history?

8. How can learning and understanding history affect our decisions?

9. What is the culture of the U.S.?

10. How has the "American Dream" affected U.S. culture?

③ **COURSE STANDARDS:**

What? CONTENT:	How?	Value?
1. Understanding Big Ideas	Unit Tests	50 pts.
2. Applying Big Ideas	Unit Projects	10 pts.
3. Providing Examples & Details	Daily Work	10 pts.
		70 pts.
PROCESS:		
1. Using Strategies	Class Demo	20 pts.
2. Participating	Class Demo	5 pts.
3. Following Rules	Class Demo	5 pts.
		30 pts.

COURSE PROGRESS GRAPH

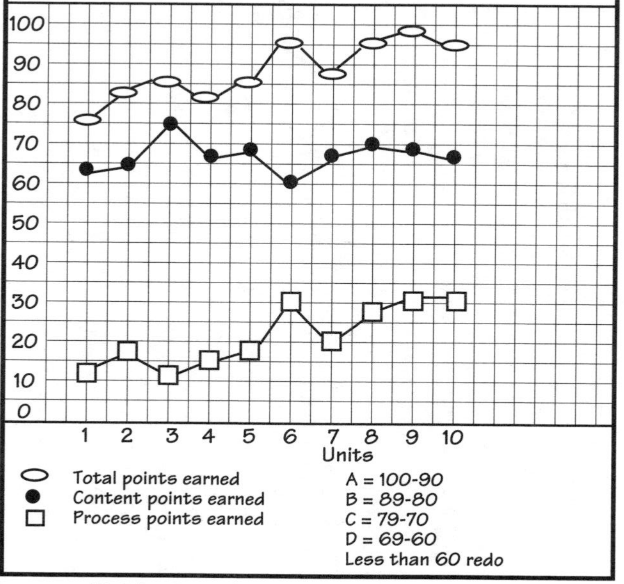

Units

A = 100-90
B = 89-80
C = 79-70
D = 69-60
Less than 60 redo

◯ Total points earned
● Content points earned
☐ Process points earned

Source: From *The Course Organizer Routine* (p. 71) by B. K. Lenz, J. B. Schumaker, D. D. Deshler, & J. A. Bulgren, 1998, Lawrence, KS: Edge Enterprises.

FIGURE 4.3

The

Course Organizer

Teacher(s):	Mr. Sanders	Student:	Nancy Nolder
Time:	8:05-8:57	Course Dates:	9/98-5/99

① THIS COURSE:

Biology

is about

How living things
exist in the world around us.

② COURSE QUESTIONS:

1. How do the forms of matter relate to each other?

2. How are organic macro molecules the basis for life?

3. How does the cell theory relate to life?

4. How are groups of organisms organized?

5. How do molecular characteristics of organisms determine heredity?

6. What is the connection between biological evolution and the classification of organisms?

7. How does the interdependence of organisms affect the world?

8. How do matter, energy, and organisms interact?

9. What defines and/or influences the behavior of animals?

10. Why are natural resources important or not important to living things?

11. How does natural selection provide an explanation for evolution?

③ COURSE STANDARDS:

What?	How?	Value?
CONTENT:		
1. Critical unit concepts	Unit tests	20 pts.
2. Examples of concepts	Unit tests	10 pts.
3. Relationships	Demonstrations	20 pts.
4. Facts	Daily work	10 pts.
		60 pts.
PROCESS:		
4. Paraphrasing	Class demo	20 pts.
5. Teamwork	Class demo	10 pts.
6. Being prepared	Class demo	5 pts.
7. Journalling	Journal	5 pts.
		40 pts.

COURSE PROGRESS GRAPH

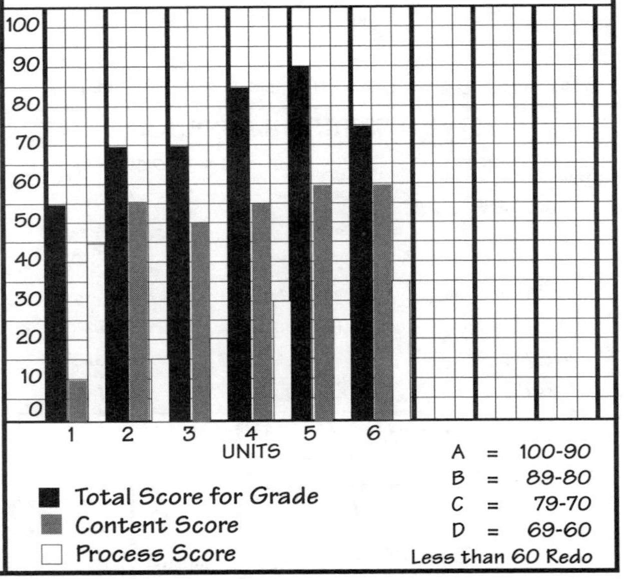

Total Score for Grade (■)
Content Score (▨)
Process Score (□)

UNITS

A = 100-90
B = 89-80
C = 79-70
D = 69-60
Less than 60 Redo

Source: From *The Course Organizer Routine* (p. 73) by B. K. Lenz, J. B. Schumaker, D. D. Deshler, & J. A. Bulgren, 1998, Lawrence, KS: Edge Enterprises.

FIGURE 4.4

Teacher(s): Miss Williamson

Time: 1:05-1:57

The Course Organizer

9th Grade Language Arts

Student: Paul Friedman

Course Dates: 9/98-5/99

① THIS COURSE:

is about

Is about exploring the world and self through writing in different genres and for different purposes.

② COURSE QUESTIONS:

1. How do you write a great paragraph?
2. How can technology and other resources help you communicate?
3. What are the characteristics of a winning essay?
4. How do you use different types of writing strategies to improve your communication?
5. How can you use writing to achieve your goals?
6. How has understanding personal strengths and weaknesses improved your writing?
7. How do you conduct and report research?
8. How do you make sure you can understand and apply what you read?
9. How does reading different types of literature help you understand yourself and the world?
10. How do you use literature to make your point?

③ COURSE STANDARDS:

What?	How?	Value?
1. Ideas	Three writing samples/unit:	3 pts./trait
2. Organization		18 pts./sample
3. Word Choice	1 Narrative	54 pts./unit
4. Voice	1 Expository	
5. Sentence fluency	1 Persuasive	
6. Conventions		

COURSE PROGRESS GRAPH

		Trait 1	Trait 2	Trait 3	Trait 4	Trait 5	Trait 6	Total
Unit 1	A	3	2	2	3	3	3	14
	B	3	2	2	2	3	3	14
	C	3	2	3	3	3	3	16
Unit 2	A	2	1	2	2	3	2	10
	B	2	2	3	3	3	3	15
	C	1	2	2	3	3	3	13
Unit 3	A	1	1	2	2	2	3	10
	B	3	2	2	2	3	3	14
	C	3	2	3	3	3	3	16
Unit 4	A	2	3	3	2	3	3	15
	B	2	2	2	2	3	3	13
	C	2	3	2	2	2	3	14
Unit 5	A	3	2	3	1	3	3	14
	B	3	2	2	2	2	3	14
	C	3	2	3	3	3	3	16
Unit 6	A	2	2	3	1	3	3	13
	B	1	2	3	2	2	3	11
	C	1	2	3	3	3	3	14

0 = Did not meet criteria - redo
1 = Almost met criteria - redo
2 = Met criteria
3 = Creatively met criteria

48-54 points = A
39-47 points = B
30-38 points = C
21-29 points = D

Source: From *The Course Organizer Routine* (p. 75) by B. K. Lenz, J. B. Schumaker, D. D. Deshler, & J. A. Bulgren, 1998, Lawrence, KS: Edge Enterprises.

FIGURE 4.5

The

Course Organizer

| Teacher(s): Mrs. Ramirez | Student: Susan Wilkins |
| Time: 9:00–9:57 | Course Dates: 9/98–5/99 |

① THIS COURSE:

Pre-Algebra

(is about)

The use of numbers, shapes, and letters to solve problems.

② COURSE QUESTIONS:

1. When do you use addition to solve a problem?
2. How do you use addition to solve problems involving whole numbers, integers, fractions, decimals, and/or variable expressions?
3. When do you use subtraction to solve a problem?
4. How do you use subtraction to solve problems involving whole numbers, integers, fractions, decimals, and/or variable expressions?
5. When do you use multiplication to solve problems?
6. How do you use multiplication to solve a problem?
7. When do you use division to solve problems?
8. How do you use division to solve a problem?
9. When do you use percent to solve problems?
10. How do you use percent to solve a problem?
11. When do you use geometry to solve problems?
12. How do you use geometry to solve a problem?

③ COURSE STANDARDS:

What?	How?	Value?
CONTENT:		
1. Concepts	Quizzes	20 pts.
2. Principles	Projects	10 pts.
3. Performance	Daily Assignments	40 pts.
		70 pts.
PROCESS:		
1. Explanation	Math Notebook	10 pts.
2. Paraphrasing	Demonstrations	10 pts.
3. PACE Requirements	Daily Notebook	10 pts.
		30 pts.

COURSE PROGRESS GRAPH

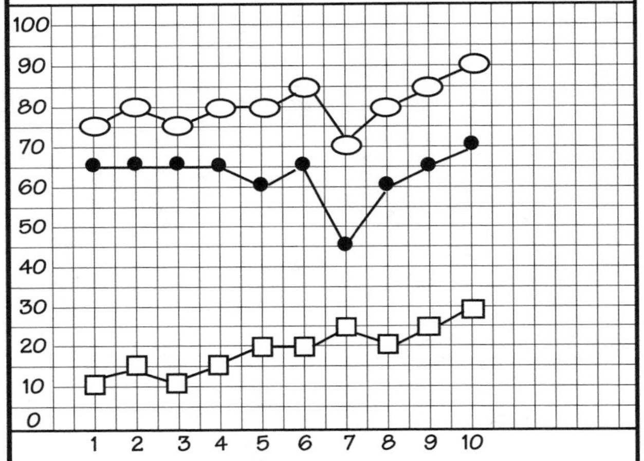

Total points earned ◯
Content points earned ●
Process points earned ☐

A = 100-90
B = 89-80
C = 79-70
D = 69-60
Less than 60 redo

Source: From The Course Organizer Routine (p. 77) by B. K. Lenz, J. B. Schumaker, D. D. Deshler, & J. A. Bulgren, 1998, Lawrence, KS: Edge Enterprises.

Focus and Reflect

- Identify three courses you teach or plan to teach and develop a metaphor for each.
- Identify one course you teach or plan to teach and develop plans for teaching the critical content in two weeks.
- Once you have developed a course vision and course goals, how would you communicate them to students?

Shape the Critical Questions   You will recall from Chapter 3 that a way to identify the "essential learnings" in your course is to distill what you would like your students to learn into 10 or fewer questions. Students should be able to answer these questions at the end of your course. Developing questions can be a useful exercise to help you prioritize what you believe is most important to teach in your class and can also guide course development and student learning. To help you select the most important information for developing your critical questions, ask yourself: What are the underlying ideas and concepts that really capture the essence of the critical content in this course? What are the central or big ideas that tie all of this information together? What standards must be addressed in this course?

As you think about course content, keep in mind the guidelines you are required to follow as a professional educator. These guidelines may include the objectives, standards, outcomes, or "essential learnings" that have been generated by a state educational agency, the school district, a professional organization, or the publisher of the course textbook and instructional materials that have been adopted. Think of these standards as professional guidelines that must be translated into a usable form for your students.

Prioritizing is important in course planning, because researchers have found that the quantity of content secondary teachers believe they must "cover" is becoming unmanageable (Lenz, Kissam, Bulgren, Melvin, & Roth, 1992). In addition, just because you have "covered" a topic does not mean that your students have "learned" it. To learn something, students must have some time to absorb it, become involved with it, manipulate the information, and practice it. If you recognize that there is not the time in one school year to "cover" everything, then you need to make choices and establish priorities.

Another way to think about developing target questions is to imagine that someone (your principal?) is going to interview your students and ask them about the most important "learnings" obtained in your course. How would you want your students to respond? What points would you want them to make? What would you like them to demonstrate as part of their answer? How would you like them to describe what they've learned?

The critical course questions should provide focus for instruction. For students in courses in middle and high school, create only about 10 questions. Once you have created your 10 questions, use them in a flexible manner, allowing student input and revising as needed. The value of the course questions (in fact, of all plans) emerges as you really "live" or experience the reaction of students and are required to revise. Figures 4.2, 4.3, 4.4, and 4.5 show examples of critical questions for four courses.

Teachers have reported incorporating the outcome questions in the quarter final essay test and discussing the outcome questions throughout the course. A middle-school science teacher created a mnemonic, PLANET EARTH, for her 10 questions, and incorporated the mnemonic into the theme she had set for the course for the year (Lenz et al., 1993). The possibilities are endless.

Formulating the target questions is not an easy process. One teacher indicated that it should be an ongoing process, returned to throughout the year and across the years. Other teachers found that initially their questions were "too lofty" and needed to be more specific, both for themselves and for their students. One high school history teacher reported that "It took me [all year] to see the value of focusing on what might be or what you think will be the ten most important questions that you want to answer" (Lenz et al., 1993).

COURSE QUESTIONS FOR A HIGH SCHOOL COURSE IN UNITED STATES HISTORY

1. Why do we study history?
2. What are the key events that have influenced U.S. history?
3. What are the key documents that have shaped the United States?
4. What are the key institutions that have shaped the United States?
5. Who are the key figures who have shaped the United States?
6. What was the role of the frontier in the United States?
7. What were the causes and the consequences of the Civil War?
8. What is the role of reform in U.S. history? When and under what circumstances did it emerge?
9. Is the United States a "melting pot"? Why or why not?
10. How has the international role of the United States in the world changed since colonial times?

COURSE QUESTIONS FOR A MIDDLE SCHOOL COURSE IN SCIENCE

1. What are the steps of the scientific method?
2. How can the scientific method be used to problem-solve?
3. What are two important activities that happen in a cell?
4. Why is it important to know about cells?
5. What are the differences between a virus and bacteria?
6. Think of examples of each to use in explaining your comparison.
7. How are vertebrates and invertebrates alike and different?
8. What are the major characteristics of each category of vertebrates?
9. How does photosynthesis affect our world?
10. How do the systems of the body work together to keep us healthy?

(Adapted from material in Lenz et al., 1993)

By formulating questions (the exact number is not important and will vary from teacher to teacher), you will have set out for yourself useful and important markers to guide your planning and thinking throughout the school year. Additionally, if you present these questions to your students at the beginning of the year, you will be providing them with information about the themes and direction of your course.

Having your students answer course questions at the beginning of the year can provide you with an indication of student background knowledge. Having your students answer the target questions at the end of the year can provide you with an indication of whether students learned what you hoped they would learn. (Appendix B has four scenarios describing teachers using the SMARTER planning process in four different courses. More examples of course questions may be found in each of the scenarios.)

▪ *Scenario Revisited*

Ms. Jessel continued meeting with Mr. Jardo to learn how to do the organizers and developed a set of course questions. As she began to regularly return to the course questions, she realized that her questions were too difficult and that she had to break them down into supporting questions and content reviews. Gradually, she realized that this was helping her become more organized and helping her make content connections for students. Twice she stopped and revised her course questions. She realized that she was beginning to think differently about her units and her unit tests.

What Is a Concept?

A concept is an abstract idea based on and defined by a set of essential characteristics that are always present in examples of the concept.

Map the Critical Content   Once you have decided what topics or ideas are most essential to your course, you need to consider how to organize them. How are the parts of what you want students to learn related? A graphic picture of your course can help highlight the major ideas and topics to be learned. Students then have a visual "map" of where they are headed in a course, as well as where they have been. A good content map of the course includes the critical concepts embedded in the course and a depiction of the structure of the content or units.

To represent the structure of the course, you can create a graphic organizer that identifies the concepts that are critical to course learning and the relationships and flow of units in the course. The course map is comprised of a list of the course concepts and a content map showing all the units of the course. Figure 4.6 shows a course map developed by a teacher for a ninth-grade language arts course.

WHAT CONCEPTS ARE CRITICAL? The course concepts should reflect the important ideas embedded in the content of the course. These concepts may be the basis of specific units or may permeate and run throughout the course. Often the course questions are written with a view toward helping students understand and apply these concepts. To identify the course concepts, examine the course questions that you have developed, as well as the course paraphrase. The course concepts are important for unlocking the key ideas conveyed in your questions and course paraphrase.

HOW WILL LEARNING BE STRUCTURED? The content map provides a representation of how content will be organized across the entire course. The major purpose of the map is to help students see the course units and then, as the units are studied, help them gain a sense of both context and progress. As the map is prepared, remember that each unit included on the course map should lend itself to being expanded in a unit content map. Unit planning and content maps will be discussed in Chapter 7.

Typically, the name of each unit is placed in an oval below the list of concepts. The first unit to be taught in the course is placed in the first position on the left side of the map and the last unit of information to be taught is placed on the last position on the right side of the map (see Figure 4.6). When possible, leave space under or next to each unit oval so key information or vocabulary terms associated with that unit can be added as the course progresses. In some courses, the names of the units can be enhanced by adding a symbol or picture that represents the information being taught.

Focus and Reflect

Identify one course you teach or plan to teach and develop a map of what it is about.

Mapping the content of a course is an opportunity to make explicit the relationships between topics in your course. Even an outline does not always convey to all students the connections between topics. Many students, especially those with learning difficulties or disabilities, do not see the connections between the pieces of information they are learning. Developing a "big picture" or theme for a course, as well as mapping its content, may help students better understand how the parts of a course fit together. Some teachers have even reported that one or both of these exercises has helped *them* better understand what their course was about! One teacher reported visually organizing her course as a road map for a car trip. She reported that this visual map of the course helped her "articulate more clearly how I 'see' the teaching of history" and that it "focuses me on where we are in the lesson" (high school social studies teacher in Lenz et al., 1993).

FIGURE 4.6   Course Map

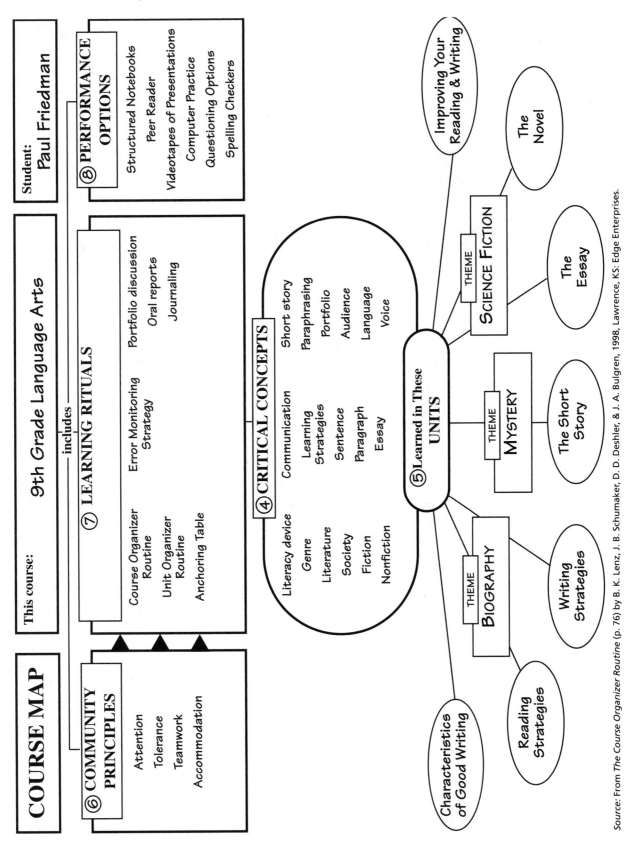

Source: From The Course Organizer Routine (p. 76) by B. K. Lenz, J. B. Schumaker, D. D. Deshler, & J. A. Bulgren, 1998, Lawrence, KS: Edge Enterprises.

■ *Scenario Revisited*

Ms. Jessel continued to use a course organizer, but she implemented its features gradually in her classes, as she found that it could be overwhelming to try to do all these new things at once. So far, she had developed a "big idea" for the course and a set of course questions. Next she tried to make a graphic map of all the units that would be included in the course. This would help students see what they had studied already and what they were going to study. Ms. Jessel also found that reviewing became easier, because the visual device helped students to keep a record of what they had learned from unit to unit.

When Ms. Jessel handed out copies of the course map, the map turned out to be something of a student-feedback mechanism too, providing Ms. Jessel with a bit more information about student interests. For example, several students, after looking over the units to come, exclaimed excitedly about the prospect of reading mysteries. At the same time, several students let her know they were disappointed not to see science fiction included as a unit.

Analyze for Learning Difficulties   Once you have made decisions about the content students will learn, you will need to identify content that might be difficult for students to learn because of the anticipated or known academic diversity among your students. This is an important step in inclusive course planning, because it is where you specifically focus your attention on the potential for exclusion. You should ask questions such as: What has made this course difficult for some students in the past? What caused disconnections between content and students, students and students, and students and the teacher? How did the teaching methods I used lead to problems? What strategies for learning seemed to be missing? How did communication between me and students about learning and progress cause problems? How did the format of presentations, assignments, and tests inhibit learning and performance? How well did students understand course standards and expectations? This step and the next one, Reach Enhancement Decisions, are so important that Chapter 9, "Teaching Content in an Academically Diverse Class," discusses how to identify content that may be difficult for students and ways to enhance your instruction to address those difficulties. Chapter 9 discusses diagnostic tools, as well as teaching devices and routines, that can help you anticipate and compensate for learning skills some students may not have developed yet.

Academic and social diversity among your students is not a problem, it is a given. Failing to plan for diversity is a problem. While teachers sometimes move on when the majority of students seem to grasp the content (Scanlon, Deshler, & Schumaker, 1996), it may be that some students are left behind. Those students did not "get it" for individual reasons and, in truth, not all of the students who "got it" got the same thing and in the same way. Students understand differently because of their background knowledge, skills for learning, and level of engagement on any given day. In some cases, a student's educational disability is related to how she or he uniquely learns. As part of analyzing for learning opportunities and difficulties, teachers need to consider how individual students in a class will benefit from the planned lesson.

Jean Schumaker has suggested a way to monitor and take action to improve the learning and performance of all students in a classroom. She suggests thinking of three different students, with one being representative of high achievers in the class, one of mid-level achievers, and one of low achievers. The acronym "HALO" can be used to capture the idea that learning should occur for **H**igh achievers, **A**verage achievers, **L**ow achievers, and **O**ther achievers. Who are the "other achievers"? They are the individuals who may fall within any "achiever" group but experience barriers to learning either on a short-term or long-term basis. Barriers to learning might include limited prior learning, a learning disability, or English as a second language. The "other" category is not used to suggest marginalization of students but rather that achievement categories of high achiever, average achiever, and low achiever do not adequately describe the pervasive diversity in a classroom.

Reach Enhancement Decisions Enhancement decisions for course planning should focus on creating an overall plan for addressing learning opportunities and potential learning difficulties in an academically diverse class. Previously, we have discussed making decisions about focus, importance, structure, and possible opportunities and challenges in the content to be taught and learned. Having made these decisions, you can use this information to make important course design decisions and prepare instructional activities and materials. At this stage of the course planning process, you must decide what strategy will be used to launch the course with students. For example, will students receive copies of the course questions and course map? How will you preview these organizers with students? How will you assess students' prior knowledge or learning?

Once you have analyzed for learning difficulties and reached decisions about how to enhance instruction, you should be ready to introduce the course content and processes to students. Therefore, you need to develop plans for when and how to revisit the course questions and how to structure the culminating activities at the end of each unit to help students see connections in the content, both within the unit and between units. Procedures need to be developed for students to store the course map and the course questions. Additionally, you need to think through how students will add notes to those documents, or to any other type of course organizer, to help them answer the course questions and keep track of concepts learned.

Of course, in addition to decisions about how you will launch, maintain, and bring closure to a course, you need to consider other ways to make the course content accessible to all students. Again, Chapter 9, "Teaching Content in an Academically Diverse Class," presents a variety of teaching ideas, as well as teaching devices and routines, that suggest ways to enhance your teaching and your students' learning. There are also examples of teachers using this SMARTER step in Appendix B.

POSITIVE BEHAVIORAL SUPPORTS. An example of an enhancement decision you might make is to use a positive-behavioral-supports approach to class management. Some of your students might dislike school, or at least the subjects you teach; other students may like school but accept any opportunity to be distracted or to disrupt instruction or classroom routines. A useful approach to teaching reluctant students is to provide an engaging learning environment.

Positive behavioral supports is a research-based approach to organizing classrooms and lessons for learning. It was first developed for students with significant disabilities but has been found effective for most all learners and classroom situations. The premise of positive behavioral supports is to provide an environment that "supports" student engagement and success in learning. Instead of trying to entertain students to keep them engaged, teachers employ well-established practices that prevent disengagement and disruptions. Students are likely to remain involved if they are interested in the lesson and are having success.

Positive behavioral support begins with setting up environments appropriate for learning by removing any obstacles to engaged learning. Most obstacles are obvious: lower the lights if you want the students to see a movie, do not sit students where they think you cannot see them, do not engage students in noisy activities in one section of the room when others should be reading silently in another section. The environment should not only be nonthreatening to learning, it should be conducive to learning. Let students know by words and deed that you are available to help them complete tasks, and make a classroom where participation and achievement are valued. Established classroom routines will help. But it is not just the physical environment that must be conducive, it is also the curriculum. Lessons should be planned so that they are accessible to all of the students, not just to those most predisposed to learning the subject. Content should be presented in ways that students understand it. Unit and lesson organizers can help them to see its relevancy and previewing key questions can provide students a beginning for understanding. Using "grabbers," or experiences or activities to heighten student interest, can also help students become engaged in learning. The key is to support positive learning behaviors by creating an environment that prevents other behaviors. Instead of punishing students when they disengage, provide them with an environment that first invites appropriate behavior and then rewards it with interested and successful participation.

Using well-established teaching practices can help support positive learning behaviors in the classroom. Munk and Karsh (1999) describe seven instructional practices that have been found by research to support engaged learning: (1) student choice in learning tasks—although the content and menu of choices can still be planned by the teacher; (2) using a variety of learning tasks in place of one long task; (3) using fast pacing between teacher prompts and student responses—in a large class this can mean calling on a variety of students or coming up with ways for all students to *actively* participate in a lesson; (4) teach, giving directions students are likely to follow and asking questions they are likely to answer—this draws them into participating even in more onerous aspects of a lesson, by providing them with opportunities to both comply with the lesson and have success; (5) using preferred learning activities, such as those the class agrees on when drafting the class routine; (6) providing opportunities for student success by graduating the difficulty of tasks; and (7) using predictable lesson and classroom routines, so students know what is expected of them and can engage appropriately.

Of course, not all students like the same kind of learning activities or have the same amount of tolerance for unpleasant responsibilities. Positive behavioral supports can greatly enhance the learning atmosphere, but some student disengagement will still occur. In Chapter 5, functional behavioral assessment is described as a companion approach for identifying causes of disruptions so that positive behavioral supports can be modified when needed.

Teach Strategically As we described in Chapter 3, teaching strategically involves a dynamic interaction between planning and teaching. Students must be kept informed of how instruction is being carried out, and the teacher must be prepared to move to the appropriate level of explicitness to ensure student learning. The concepts of informed and explicit instruction at the course level mean that you must develop plans to share course plans, teach students about coursewide activities, and regularly or routinely return to course ideas throughout the year. Therefore, you should be prepared to share all the decisions and plans developed in SMARTER with students at the beginning of the year.

A way to do this is to develop course notebooks, portfolios, and bulletin boards that highlight course ideas and decisions so that course content and processes can be regularly discussed and monitored throughout the year.

At the end of each unit, return to course questions, concepts, and the course map and discuss the relationship of unit ideas to the course. In addition, return to course processes (i.e., routines and strategies) and discuss their value and any changes that may be needed to help students use them effectively.

Plan end-of-course activities that focus on answering course questions and using course notebooks and portfolios in ways that help students integrate ideas and information. Revise course plans and decisions based on the academic diversity, as well as the learning progress of students in the course.

Evaluate Mastery Teachers who are committed to responding to academic diversity must be committed to evaluating the impact of their teaching. We must ask continuously whether we have made the right course decisions. Regarding our success, we must continuously ask if students are learning what they are supposed to be learning, gaining some personal satisfaction from their learning, and seeing that their learning is reflected in the grades they receive.

To answer these evaluation questions, you might consider regularly discussing with the whole class what they are learning and having them summarize ideas. If you say something is critical at the course level, do the items included on unit tests or performance measures relate to the critical course questions and concepts? If not, you may want to either revise your course questions or revise your assignments and tests.

Regularly review course plans and check to make sure that the questions, concepts, and routines you are using direct students' time and attention toward what they are supposed to be learning. Routinely ask and

---

Focus and Reflect

- Identify three concepts, ideas, or skills in your content area that you believe are difficult for students or that you have seen students struggle with.
- Select one of the items identified above and develop a learning activity to address student learning needs. Describe how your activity helps. For example, does it make instruction more explicit? Does it organize information for students? Does it teach them a process for learning a skill? Does it compensate in some way for lack of prior knowledge?

answer with students the course questions and supporting unit questions. If you find that students can't answer these questions, slow the pace of instruction, consider other ways to enhance the information you are presenting, and focus on helping students answer the questions. Provide multiple opportunities for students to test their knowledge. Provide regular opportunities for students to talk about the value and worth of the information they are learning. Be prepared to provide rationales that are personalized and believable, and that directly affect students. Check to see that students feel they are learning how to learn the content. If they are not learning, identify learning strategies that are important in your content area. Begin to teach students how to learn the content by explicitly teaching these learning strategies on a regular basis. Develop a daily or weekly communication system between you and your students to allow them to ask you privately about the content or the way they are learning the content.

Other ways to evaluate mastery include evaluating the type of tests you give and determining whether the course and unit ideas are appropriately reflected in the tests and are emphasized over less important ideas and information. Evaluate and give students grades for the progress they make in how well they learn and apply strategies to master the content. Base these evaluations on individual progress. That is, high-achieving students, who put forth little energy toward improving how they are learning, may make little progress, while low-achieving students may not be as high achieving but may make tremendous progress. (Examples of teachers using this SMARTER step are described in Appendix B.)

WHAT STANDARDS WILL BE IMPORTANT IN YOUR COURSE? Learners are most likely to increase their performance when they have a clear understanding of the evaluation/grading criteria before completion of performance tasks. Such understanding is created when the relationships between performance and grading criteria are made explicit and when feedback about how well learners are meeting expectations is provided on a regular basis. Course standards include communicating to students what will be emphasized in evaluating whether they have: (a) learned the critical content, (b) learned the processes for learning the critical content, (c) followed the rules of behavior that have been established, and (d) participated in contributing to the learning of others in the classroom community. Course standards involve telling students *what* is important to learn or do, *how* learning or performing will be evaluated, and the *value* that will be attached to each standard. Figures 4.2, 4.3, 4.4, and 4.5 show the course standards set out in four different courses. These figures also illustrate, in the lower right corner, how students could graph their progress in both learning the content and mastering process learning, like using learning strategies or participating effectively in a cooperative group project.

Establishing standards can mean more than assessment. It can mean emphasizing the importance of participation or good classroom citizenship and giving these performances weight by taking them into account in grading. An important part of establishing standards is being explicit about what those standards are. Standards should also be in keeping with the goals, principles, and rituals that have been established in a classroom.

The kind of course standards you set in your classroom, as well the way you involve students in establishing them, will have a great impact on the level of trust that develops between you and your students. When you evaluate students, they will trust you to be consistent and fair. If you have said that certain content and ways to learn that content are important, students will expect that to be incorporated into all aspects of the work of the course. They will also expect you to match assessment to the instruction and learning activities you provide.

While you, as the teacher, must determine how student learning will be assessed, there may be times when you can give students some voice and influence in setting standards in a class. For example, you might ask students, as a class or homework assignment, to write three or more questions for a quiz or test. Students could survey the content in a textbook to construct their questions about what they see as important. Constructing test questions can be a valuable learning exercise for students, but be sure to give them some guidelines for how to construct good questions (e.g., no question that can be answered with just yes or no; questions should cover important ideas and information, not just tricky details, etc.). When students construct test questions, they have an opportunity to show you what they have learned, as well as to tell you what they believe is important about what they have learned. It is up to you to decide what, if any, questions to actually use on an exam or quiz. However, to keep trust with your students, either use some of the questions they have written or spend some time discussing with them how their questions were lacking as assessment tools and therefore were not used.

Another way to involve students in establishing standards is to regularly ask them about their perceptions of what they are learning and how instructional activities have helped or not helped them learn. Extra credit could be awarded to students on quizzes or tests for answering well-framed questions about what and how they have learned in a unit or lesson. For example, you might ask students what they most enjoyed learning in a unit, what they found least interesting, what was hard for them, and so on. Getting students to answer these kinds of questions thoughtfully might require discussion or modeling on your part ("Let's talk about ways one might answer this kind of question. I need more than a one- or two-word answer if your comments are going to help me make instruction clearer, or this test a better measure of what you learned, or the content more interesting to you.")

Just as the course paraphrase or course questions need to be reevaluated periodically, so too do course standards. Out of fairness to students, you cannot change standards in the middle of a grading period, but at the end of each quarter or semester, or at the beginning of a new year, you should reexamine the standards you have set for your course. Keep in mind past student performances, because this may indicate something about your instruction or the design of your tests, as well as the effort or abilities of your students. If many students have not done well on tests or other forms of assessment, you might ask yourself, Did the test match my instruction, and was it written at the appropriate level? Were practice opportunities adequate? What did students learn well, and what instructional activities did I use for the content they learned well? What did students not learn well, and what learning activities were used for the content they did not learn well?

Focus and Reflect
- What standards would you want to establish in your classroom?
- How would you go about including students in developing standards?

▪ *Scenario Revisited*

Ms. Jessel had always given her students a syllabus indicating how their grades would be determined. As she and Mr. Jardo worked together on developing course plans, she learned that perhaps she could help students see their own progress by charting their grades on a graph. This might be an additional incentive for some students—to want to see their graph line go up! It could also provide an opportunity after each unit to talk about what had gone well in this chunk of learning and what students—as a group or as individuals—might do in the next unit to improve their performance.

Revisit Outcomes Finally, be prepared to revise your course. If you have developed a set of course questions that you believe truly reflect what is critical for students to know and do, you must be prepared to change your instruction and instructional plans so that students can answer the course questions. However, sometimes we have simply developed the wrong course questions. In those cases, we may have to revise course questions to more accurately reflect what is important. This is a necessary process. Developing a set of critical questions based on a best guess and then living with these questions with a group of students as the year progresses should result in a meaningful revision of the questions. In many cases, it may take three or four years to develop a good set of course questions. (Examples of teachers using this SMARTER step are described in Appendix B.)

▪ *Scenario Revisited*

As the year progressed, Ms. Jessel decided to enlist her students' help in reevaluating the course paraphrase for the course. She took some time at the beginning of a class and asked her students to brainstorm with her about possible course metaphors or themes. Through this discussion with her students, she was able to discover what students thought about studying literature as well as the "big picture" they had of the subject.

The class came up with six more ideas. Ms. Jessel reworked all the ideas by combining some and eliminating others and got the list down to three. She then asked for volunteers to make a graphic for each of the three themes. Six students worked on this project outside of class time and their art work was much admired by Ms. Jessel and the rest of the class.

Ms. Jessel and the class reconsidered the list each time they began a new chapter in their textbook, and Ms. Jessel thought she (and the class) were getting closer to identifying an overarching theme that helped students appreciate what the course was about and why reading was important. As they reconsidered their course theme and goals, they looked at each new topic within the context of the themes they had identified to see if it "fit." This provided a way to make connections between old and new learning, and previous and current topics.

Ms. Jessel's class regularly returned to the course themes they had set out, connecting what they were currently doing to what they had done before. By the end of the year, every student could answer all of her questions. As a result, some of the students who seemed lost or disinterested at the end of the first semester seemed to be making connections that she had thought they would never make. It finally dawned on her that it was not the students who had changed; she had changed her thinking about the course and had made the content of the course more accessible for more students.

FIGURE 4.7
Chapter Graphic
Organizer–
Expanded

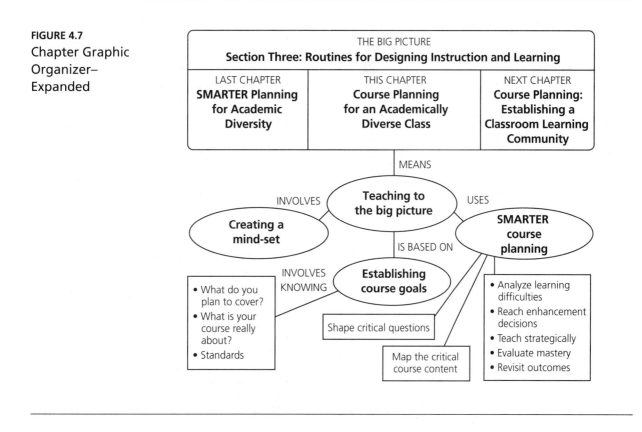

SUMMARY

Planning course goals by developing a course paraphrase and course questions and mapping the course for students is a good beginning for providing the explicit instruction that supports learning for all students. Establishing standards also helps students see how their learning should be focused. Other elements of course planning remain to be discussed: establishing community principles, learning rituals and performance options, and developing and maintaining communication systems with students. These are the elements of a course that set the tone for learning and help establish trust and cooperation in the classroom. Because we believe that establishing a learning community, based on principles, rituals, and performance options, involves more than simply setting out behavior expectations and class rules, we devote the next chapter to that topic. Similarly, we believe developing and maintaining a communication system with students is essential to planning for authentic learning activities, so we devote Chapter 6 to that topic.

MAKING CONNECTIONS:
Implementing Course Planning

1. *Here are the big ideas to get you started:*
  ▪ The first task in course planning is to identify what your course is about and what the important big ideas are. To address these issues, try to develop a course paraphrase, theme, or metaphor that captures the essence of your course.
  ▪ The process of identifying important ideas and information may be undertaken by writing about 10 course questions. Questions should be open-ended ones that, when answered appropriately, encompass

the important learning to be accomplished in your course.

- Course planning continues with the drafting of a course map showing the major units of study of the course. Other important planning to be undertaken at this point includes setting standards for the course—identifying how students are going to demonstrate that they have learned the important ideas and information of the course.

2. *What you need:*
   - A course textbook
   - A copy of standards for your content and grade level
   - Other textbooks or content-area resources to mine for ideas!
   - A syllabus from the course as previously taught, or from a course you have taken

3. *Try this:*
   - Start by developing a course paraphrase. Brainstorm metaphors or themes that help characterize what your course is about. Consider including your students in this process at some point during the school year. Although they begin the course not necessarily knowing what it is about, in the process of engaging in this kind of brainstorming for a course paraphrase, students may give you useful insights into what their expectations are for the course.
   - Try mapping out the units that would be included in your course. Think about connections between the units. Reflecting back on your course paraphrase should help you identify what these connections might be. If your course paraphrase does not help, it may be an indication that the paraphrase is wrong, or that the units you have identified do not contribute all that you hoped they would to the important "learnings" of the course.

4. *Evaluate your work:*
   - A way to evaluate your course paraphrase, course questions, and course map is to identify the concepts you will teach in your course. Be sure to select the important concepts, the ones that are critical to understanding the important ideas and content in your course. Does your course paraphrase

reflect the importance of these concepts? Will you be able to teach these concepts in the units you have included in your course map? Do your course questions incorporate these concepts in some way?

5. *Next steps:*
   - Once you have developed a course paraphrase, a course map, and a set of course questions you are satisfied with, begin to think about the parts of your course that have caused all or some students problems in the past or that you anticipate will cause problems for students. Make a list of these learning challenges and think about how you will address them instructionally.

WEB SITES

http://www.mcrel.org/standards-benchmarks McREL—Compendium of Standards and Benchmarks. A compilation of content standards for K–12 curriculum in both searchable and browsable formats.

http://www.music.org/InfoEdMusic/EleSecon.html The Web site of the College Music Society contains information about and links to the National Standards for Arts Education.

http://www.getty.edu.artsednet The Getty Education Institute for the Arts. Includes lesson plans for arts education.

SUGGESTED READINGS

Meier, D. (1995). *The power of their ideas.* Boston: Beacon Press. In the chapter entitled "It's Academic," Meier questions why some activities and areas of study are considered academic while others are not, and wonders if perhaps we might want to rethink some curriculum choices.

Perrone, V. (1991). *A letter to teachers: Reflections on schooling and the art of teaching.* San Francisco: Jossey-Bass. Chapter Six: "Evaluating and grading student performance" (pp. 55–67) is a reflective piece on evaluation as a means of "informing, guiding and supporting the growth of students" (p. 55) and about the need to find "as many *different* (emphasis in original) ways as possible for students to share with you their understandings of the content under study" (p. 60).

REFERENCES

Boomer, G., Lester, N., Onore, C., & Cook, J. (Eds.). (1992). *Negotiating the curriculum: Educating for the 21st century.* London: Falmer Press.

Brown, D. S. (1988). Twelve middle-school teachers' planning. *The Elementary School Journal, 89*(1), 69–87.

Clark, C. M., & Yinger, R. J. (1987). Teacher planning. In D. C. Berliner & B. Rosenshine (Eds.), *Talk to teachers* (pp. 342–365). New York: Random House.

Lenz, B. K. (1998). *The course organizer routine.* Lawrence, KS: Edge Enterprises.

Lenz, B. K., Deshler, D. D., & Schumaker, J. B. (1993). [The development and validation of planning routines to enhance the delivery of content to students with handicaps in general education settings]. Unpublished raw data.

Lenz, B. K., Kissam, B., Bulgren, J., Melvin, J., & Roth, J. (1992). *Obstacles to teaching in the face of academic diversity: Implications for planning for students with disabilities* (Res. Rep. No. 70). Lawrence, KS: University of Kansas, Center for Research on Learning.

McDiarmid, G. W. (1991). What teachers need to know about cultural diversity: Restoring subject matter to the picture. In M. M. Kennedy (Ed.), *Teaching academic subjects to diverse learners* (pp. 257–269). New York: Teachers College Press.

McDougal, D. W. (2002). Visual arts standards and creativity. In R. Stone (Ed.), *Best practices for high school classrooms: What award-winning secondary teachers do* (pp. 182–188). Thousand Oaks, CA: Corwin Press.

Meier, D. (1995). *The power of their ideas.* Boston: Beacon Press.

Munk, D. D., & Karsh, K. G. (1999). Antecedent curriculum and instructional variables as classwide interventions for preventing or reducing problem behaviors. In A. C. Repp & R. H. Horner (Eds.), *Functional analysis of problem behavior.* London: Wadsworth.

Perrone, V. (1994). How to engage students in learning. *Educational Leadership, 51*(5), 11–13.

Scanlon, D., Deshler, D. D., & Schumaker, J. B. (1996). Can a strategy be taught and learned in secondary inclusive classrooms? *Learning Disabilities Research & Practice, 11*, 41–57.

5

Course Planning

Establishing a Classroom Learning Community

Brenda R. Kissam
B. Keith Lenz
David Scanlon

Critical Self-Test Questions

- How can you go about building an inclusive learning community in a class-room?
- What are classroom principles and what is their role in establishing a learning community in your content class?
- What are learning rituals and how can they help students in an academically diverse class?
- What is the role of cooperative learning in an inclusive learning community?
- What is the relationship between performance options and classroom principles in a learning community?

The most successful class-rooms may be those in which teachers succeed in creating commonly shared goals and individuals cooperate in ensuring each person's success in achieving them.

—J. I. Goodlad, *A Place Called School* (1984), p. 108

This chapter seeks to guide the reader in making the shift from thinking about "teaching a course" to thinking about "establishing a learning community." A learning community is an environment where learning is valued and accessible for all learners and where teachers and students work together to make sure everyone in the community is learning. On the face of it, this sounds like what teachers and students have always done in schools. The reality in many schools, however, is that learning is not valued by or accessible to all students, when they do not understand what they are supposed to learn, how they are supposed to learn it, or why it is important.

In a classroom that is an inclusive learning community, you, as the teacher, commit yourself to engaging all students in learning by building connections. Building connections is central to establishing community: Inherent in the idea of community is the idea of belonging and being accepted. Building connections is also central to the idea of learning because for new learning to occur it must have some connection to something that is known and understood; you can help students see that what they need to learn has a connection to what they already know.

A learning community may involve change that is uncomfortable at first. Building community may mean considering student viewpoints and creating partnerships that involve new perspectives on student and teacher roles. In a seventh-grade math class, for example, a teacher might seek to learn how best to build connections between students and the content by gathering information from students about difficulties they have had in math in the past. When teachers give students opportunities to express their views, they are, in a way, "empowering" students and developing new ways of creating classroom climate (Lincoln, 1995, p. 90).

FIGURE 5.1
Graphic Organizer

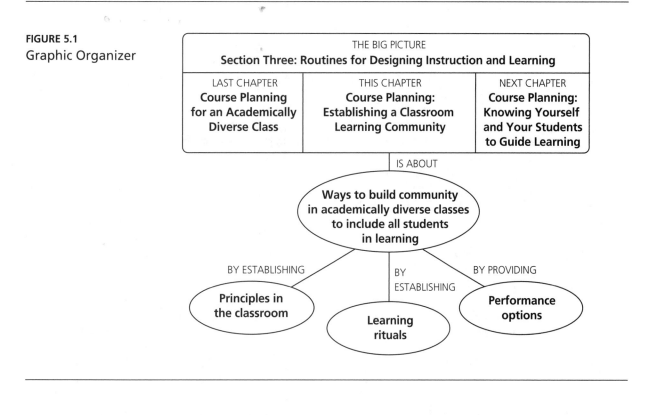

FOUNDATIONS AND PRINCIPLES

Research indicates that secondary teachers, faced with the wide range of skills, knowledge, and abilities among students in their classrooms, believe that engaging reluctant or discouraged students in the learning of a course is a particular obstacle to planning and teaching (Lenz, Kissam, Bulgren, Melvin, & Roth, 1992). Research has also identified some of the reasons why students who are unsuccessful in school are discouraged: these students are often bored with school, tend to give up when they do not understand what is going on in class, and often believe their teachers do not care about them (Schlosser, 1992; Phelan, Davidson, & Cao, 1992). Before you can help students learn, you have to not only get their attention, but also gain their interest and commitment to learning. Engaging reluctant learners can be a huge challenge.

A teacher may say that, of course, they are teaching all students, care about all students, and want and expect all students to succeed. But unless teachers are aware of whether or not students feel included and supported in their classrooms, instructionally as well as socially, they may persist in making choices and behaving in ways that contribute to some students feeling or being excluded. For example, a well-intentioned English teacher might persist in using texts for reading that do not include any material written by authors who might reflect experiences closer to those of many of his or her students. Problems arise when teacher choices and behaviors do not extend beyond what one writer has called "idiosyncratic connections" (Ladson-Billings, 1998) with individual students, or the kind of connections that occur irregularly and only with some students. These kinds of connections do not permit you to know your students' interests and prior experiences

■ Scenario

Elizabeth Haven's fourth-hour math class moves through the curriculum at a steady pace but without enthusiasm or energy. The class is large—27 students, mostly 8th graders with a few 7th and 9th graders mixed in. Even though math classes at her school are tracked, students in this class have a wide range of abilities and experience. Along with students who do A and B work, there are a number of students who struggle with the curriculum and a couple of students who are simply oblivious to what is going on and don't seem to care very much about the class either. One student, who uses a wheelchair, needs to come late to class everyday, and Ms. Haven struggles to catch him up on what he has missed. Another student appears to listen very attentively to all that is going on, yet fails every test miserably. Another student spends most of the hour gazing out the window, coming back to attention only when called upon. And yet another student seems to have few friends in the class, does well when she is in class but is often absent; the accumulation of missed classes is beginning to have an effect on her ability to manage the work. These students represent just a sampling of the diversity Ms. Haven encounters daily—students with varying abilities, attitudes, and preoccupations! Also troubling to Ms. Haven are the two boys who excel in the class but periodically ridicule, under their breath, other students who respond slowly during instruction.

Ms. Haven works with whole-group instruction for part of the period, instructing and then checking for comprehension. When students are practicing individually, she moves quickly about the room, helping as many students as possible. She uses cooperative learning groups frequently but finds that too often one or two students in the group do all the work, because they are too impatient to work through the problems with other group members who don't understand the task. While most of the students in this class are passing the course, Ms. Haven is increasingly concerned about the 10 or so students who struggle, including three who are failing the class. And even though Ms. Haven tries many things to bring energy and enthusiasm to her teaching, she is also concerned about the general lack of engagement of her students in this class.

well enough to understand how to connect new learning to what students already know and care about.

Students say that teachers who are sensitive to their problems in mastering subject matter make a big difference in their feelings about school and their ability to achieve academically (Phelan, Davidson, & Cao, 1992). As a teacher, you can show students you want to help them learn by making your classroom an inclusive learning community. This chapter will address three major elements in building an inclusive learning community: (1) establishing community *principles,* (2) using effective learning *rituals,* and (3) providing students with *performance options.*

KNOWING AND DOING

Creating a Learning Community by Establishing Principles in the Classroom

Valued classroom principles provide a set of explicit norms for how members of the learning community will work together. Principles in a community or classroom set the tone and clarify expectations about how people can best work together to meet individual and community goals. A community principle might be: "Differences among people in the community are to be respected." Respecting differences applies not only to characteristics related to culture, gender, and language, but also to differences in how fast some students learn and the differences in the amount of practice some students need.

While establishing principles has some similarity to the well-established teacher practice of setting rules at the outset of each year or semester, there are two important distinctions between the two processes:

1. Establishing principles goes beyond behavior issues to make explicit which day-to-day practices, behaviors, and attitudes best promote the learning of all members of the community.
2. Principles are shared and co-constructed by teachers and students. Developing principles involves a careful balance between teacher direction and expressed student views. Allowing students to have some voice in developing community principles helps ensure their investment in and adherence to the principles.

If principles are not established and made explicit, the community runs the risk that its goals will not be achieved, because classroom practices may be inconsistent with or working at cross-purposes to those goals. As Sergiovanni (1994) has noted, "Schools cannot become caring communities, for example, unless caring is valued and unless norms are created that point the way toward caring, reward caring behaviors, and frown on noncaring behaviors" (pp. 71–72). Similarly, if teacher and students agree that students should cooperate in helping each other learn, then care must be taken that classroom activities support that norm. If activities are planned where students compete against one another and are rewarded with special privileges for their individual achievement, students may question whether cooperation in learning is really valued in the classroom.

Teachers and students also need to think about what norms will contribute to forging a community to promote the learning of specific content for all learners in a course. For example, researchers observed a middle-school science classroom where "sense-making behavior" was highly valued and "face-saving behavior" was not (Anderson, 1991, p. 11). In this classroom "questions and arguments were perceived as worthwhile and enjoyable, and it was recognized that a cogent defense of an incorrect position might contribute more to the individual and collective sense making of the class than simply knowing the right answer" (Anderson, 1991, p. 11). The teacher and students in this classroom established a norm that was important and useful in helping students learn science.

Establishing and Maintaining Valued Classroom Community Principles
Establishing or negotiating classroom principles is something that should occur at the very beginning of the school year. Ideally, these principles should be negotiated and discussed with students in order to gain their full commitment, and they should represent shared ideas about the purposes of the community, how the members will work together to achieve their goals and relate to one another to assure that everyone is included and engaged in the work of the learning community.

The principles that underlie the work of a classroom community are created through a careful balance between teacher direction and student input.

FIGURE 5.2

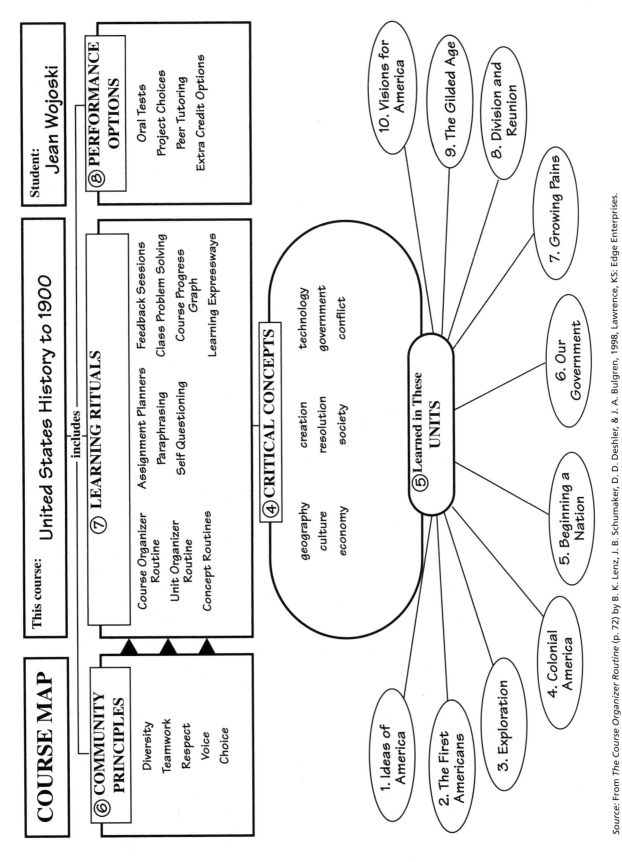

COURSE MAP

This course: United States History to 1900

Student: Jean Wojoski

⑧ **PERFORMANCE OPTIONS**

Oral Tests
Project Choices
Peer Tutoring
Extra Credit Options

⑦ **LEARNING RITUALS**

Course Organizer Routine — Assignment Planners — Feedback Sessions

Unit Organizer Routine — Paraphrasing — Class Problem Solving — Course Progress Graph

Concept Routines — Self Questioning — Learning Expressways

— includes —

⑥ **COMMUNITY PRINCIPLES**

Diversity
Teamwork
Respect
Voice
Choice

④ **CRITICAL CONCEPTS**

geography — creation — technology

culture — resolution — government

economy — society — conflict

⑤ **Learned in These UNITS**

1. Ideas of America
2. The First Americans
3. Exploration
4. Colonial America
5. Beginning a Nation
6. Our Government
7. Growing Pains
8. Division and Reunion
9. The Gilded Age
10. Visions for America

Source: From *The Course Organizer Routine* (p. 72) by B. K. Lenz, J. B. Schumaker, D. D. Deshler, & J. A. Bulgren, 1998, Lawrence, KS: Edge Enterprises.

However, because of your experience and responsibility for content mastery, you must play an important role in shaping the principles that will be used to organize the class. Figure 5.2 provides an example of principles that were identified for a class in U.S. history.

Classroom principles should be identified and developed for making connections between students and learning at both the individual and group level. Group principles foster the learning of the whole group, while individual principles ensure that each individual in the class is benefiting from the learning experiences in a course.

The core principles you select for promoting *group* connections will help determine the types of routines and strategies you will introduce to your class. The principles you select should be ones that

1. You believe are critical for successful teacher and peer interactions.
2. You are willing to revisit and discuss with the class on a regular basis.
3. You can define and for which you can provide examples and non-examples.
4. You are prepared to evaluate and provide feedback.
5. You will enforce with appropriate attention and consequences.

Principles that can define a community include respect for others, tolerance for diversity, teamwork, and consensus. However, simply identifying a principle is not enough. For each principle that you have identified, create a definition and a list of examples and nonexamples. Figure 5.3 shows how to define a principle.

While group principles usually nurture the group's progress, principles that focus on individuals are centered on the teacher's ability and willingness to honor, protect, and assist individuals. Principles can guide your approach to promoting individual connections in presenting course material, selecting learning activities, and offering students different performance options. Principles that can define personal connections include accommodation, choice, attention, and forgiveness. Definitions and positive and negative consequences need to be created for these principles as well. Figure 5.4 shows an example of a definition.

Negotiating Community Principles with Students   To begin the process of establishing connections with students and developing principles in a classroom, a teacher might consider using a student survey or classroom meetings, or both. Various kinds of surveys may be helpful (for examples, see Bailey, 1983; Fraser, 1999). One kind of survey that may provide information about what is important or meaningful to students in their classroom

FIGURE 5.3
Group Principles

PRINCIPLE	DEFINITION	EXAMPLE	NONEXAMPLE
Respect for others	A way of treating people in which your behavior does not negatively affect the rights of others	• Asking permission • Working quietly • Respecting privacy • Putting back • Taking turns	• Name calling • Teasing • Not putting back • Talking out

FIGURE 5.4
Individual Principles

PRINCIPLE	DEFINITION	EXAMPLE	NONEXAMPLE
Accommodation	A way of accepting differences in which people can learn and perform tasks in alternate ways that allow them to avoid their weaknesses and take advantage of their strengths.	• Offering oral tests for those who have trouble reading. • Allowing audio-taped reports on topics for those who have trouble writing. • Allowing students to leave the class-room to work when they are highly distractible.	• Providing alternatives because it would be easier or more fun.

interactions, as well as in their learning, is a **Student Expectation Survey**. See Figure 5.5 for a sample of a student expectation survey. You will notice that this survey gives students an opportunity to let teachers know about particular learning preferences and problems they may have and about their attitudes toward school in general or your course in particular. The survey also lets students express ideas about what they would like to study.

During the research for which the above survey was developed, a young high school history teacher had his students complete a questionnaire similar to the student expectation survey in Figure 5.5. Looking at the results of the survey, he noticed a pattern in the preferences students expressed about what they would like to learn during the course. Noting that a significant number of students wanted to study the Vietnam War era, he adjusted his course plans. For the first time since teaching American history, this teacher covered the 1960s and reported a much greater level of student engagement in the content of the class (Kissam, Lenz & Tinder, 1994).

In a class meeting, students and teachers may brainstorm about what they value in a course, and the group may work together to assemble a list of the principles by which the class will operate. One middle-school science teacher negotiated classroom rules by having students construct them in groups within the context of a metaphor: Expedition–Planet Earth. She asked students to make a list of rules they thought expedition members should live by. Students then worked in small groups, and each group came up with rules. By the end of the first week, they had a set of rules or class-room principles. The students were surprised and pleased when the teacher wrote the principles they had helped develop on a sheet of paper and taped it up (Lenz et al., 1993).

While negotiating classroom principles and rules is important, it is equally important for teachers to promote and model principles they feel strongly about. For example, if you feel strongly that students should feel comfortable asking questions and not be intimidated from doing so, then you might suggest a classroom principle such as "Asking questions is part of learning and is to be respected."

Voice and Choice as Classroom Community Principles   In inclusive learning communities, members must believe that their presence matters to the community, that they have a say in what happens, and feel safe to express

FIGURE 5.5 Student Expectation Survey

> *Here is a sample student survey that teachers have used at the beginning of a course. Using this survey, or some other means to elicit student input, provides students voice and choice. The results of the survey will give you ideas to enhance voice and choice in the learning community. Consider revising this survey and adapting it for your own use.*

I would like to know your thoughts and ideas about this course as we begin the year together. Your answers will influence what happens this year.

1. Please list 3 things you *want* to learn in this course.

_____

_____

_____

2. Please list 3 things that may be worrying you about this course.

_____

_____

_____

3. How would you *like* to be graded in this course? Please rank four of the following kinds of tasks from 1 to 4, with 1 being the task you would **most** like to be graded on, and 4 being the task on which you would **least** like to be graded.

_____ Tests   _____ Class participation
_____ Projects   _____ Cooperative group work
_____ Papers   _____ Class work/Daily assignments
_____ Quizzes   _____ Folders/Portfolios of work
_____ Other (please describe) _____

4. How do you learn best most of the time? Please rank four of the following ways of learning from 1 to 4, with 1 being the way you learn **best** and four being the way you learn the **least well**.

_____ Lecture   _____ Class Activities
_____ Worksheets   _____ Portfolios or Projects
_____ Class Discussion   _____ Reading
_____ Cooperative Learning
_____ Audiovisual (slides, videotapes, etc.)
_____ Other (please describe) _____

5. How often would you like to work with other students in this class? (circle one)

  Never   Once or twice   Sometimes   Often

(continued)

FIGURE 5.5   Student Expectation Survey *(continued)*

6. How important is it to you to get to know other students in classes? (circle one)

Not at all   A little bit   Fairly important   Very important

7. Do you usually feel comfortable asking questions or speaking during class discussions? (circle one)

No   Maybe   Yes

8. List 2 or 3 things teachers have done to help you feel comfortable speaking up in class.

_____

_____

_____

9. Please list 2 or 3 (or more) things teachers have done to help you feel as if they cared about you as a person.

_____

_____

_____

10. Please list 2 or 3 (or more) things teachers have done that bothered you or that interfered with your learning.

_____

_____

_____

11. In general, do you like school? (circle one)   No   Maybe   Yes

Please give 3 reasons you answered the way you did.

1._____

2._____

3._____

12. Please explain how you think this course will be useful to you in the future.

_____

_____

_____

13. Other Comments?

_____

_____

_____

who they are and to try new things. Actually, what fosters a sense of community among the learners in a class is exactly what creates community among neighbors, coworkers, church and synagogue members, or other groups of people. While many qualities contribute to this commitment and sense of belonging to a group, two characteristics seem especially crucial: allowing individuals voice and choice. Many of the ideas presented below for giving students voice and choice were developed with middle- and high-school teachers, based on what the teachers found worked in their classrooms (Lenz, Schumaker, Deshler, & Bulgren, 1998).

CHOICE. One group of writers has noted that "The power of choice in motivating secondary students is great. It is the basis for developing trust, cooperation, and individuality. It is the foundation for developing authentic relationships with teachers" (Retish, Hitchings, Horvath, & Schmalle, 1991, p. 91). Choices can be offered to individuals, as well as the group, by providing opportunities from time to time to choose what to learn, how to learn, how quickly learning will occur, or how learning will be evaluated.

Researchers working with teachers on better ways to do course planning found that an important theme emerged: Teachers came to understand that when students are offered choices about how to practice learning new information, they became more willing and involved participants in learning (Lenz et al., 1993). For example, a middle-school science teacher commented that "My classes seem to be developing . . . community because individuals are able to CHOOSE their routes through this trek! There is less grumbling about chores or work, because each is choosing his or her direction" (Lenz et al., 1993).

Teachers should be careful, however, not to offer student choice about *nonnegotiable* issues. Asking for student feedback and then not attending to it will undermine a trusting relationship with students and building community in the classroom.

VOICE. Giving students "voice" means finding ways to help each student find her or his *unique* voice—what makes her or him an individual. Among the ways a student's unique voice may be expressed are in their ideas, the particular knowledge and talent they bring to class, in cultural background, or in a meaningful past experience. Creating a classroom atmosphere where students feel supported, safe, and even encouraged to speak up and express their ideas and have confidence that their ideas will be heard and respected allows students to have voice.

When students are listened to this can be said to be "honored" voice, which has been defined as "a deep responsiveness in the classroom culture to students' ideas, opinions, feelings, interests, and needs" (Oldfather & McLaughlin, 1993, p. 8). Voice, however, means more than students expressing their ideas. It also means that you and the rest of the classroom community take notice of who students are, respecting the things that are important to them, and taking into account their interests whenever possible. For example, in literature classes, you might use literature that comes from some of the cultures represented by students in your class. Or you might make an effort to identify and recognize women who have made contributions to scientific discoveries, or minorities who have made breakthroughs in understanding mathematics.

It is important for teachers to incorporate in the curriculum and its materials as much of students' backgrounds and interests as possible, as a way to help students see and develop the connections with the content that must be learned. As Herbert Kohl has observed, the "continual informal contact with students that allows them to reveal themselves and show their strengths and aspirations enhances the ability to teach well and reach students in ways that nurture them" (Kohl, 1994, p. 83). In addition, voice and choice are a way for teachers who may or may not share the same background as many of their students, to demonstrate respect for their students.

Research by Oldfather and McLaughlin (1993) has suggested that student learning and motivation may be stimulated and enhanced when students are given "voice and perceived empowerment as knowers within a community of learners" (p. 3). They provide some concrete ideas about how teachers can honor student voice:

> A teacher may well . . . say "I would like to find ways to honor students' voices and to create a community of learners—but how can this be translated to practice in my classroom?" This is a vital question. [Teachers] assess what they are already doing in their classrooms to honor student's voices (and students can be involved in this initial assessment). Then they determine what aspects of the curriculum are non-negotiable, and consider with students how to incorporate increasing levels of student decision-making into the classroom and school. Responsive teachers engage in gradual experimentation (preferably in collaboration with colleagues) to offer students expanded opportunities for self-expression and choice. (Oldfather & McLaughlin, 1993, p. 22)

How might you find ways to provide learners with choice and voice in your course? How could allowing choice and voice enhance your own experience in the classroom? Below are some ways that one teacher responded to student voice in her classroom:

1. Frequently assessing and adjusting to individual and group pacing needs throughout the day;
2. Acting on students' requests about assignments and activities, such as agreeing to discontinue reading log assignments for awhile;
3. Accounting for students' interests by providing individualized resources, allowing individual flexibility of topic, form, and audience for sharing their learnings;
4. Seeking students' ideas, opinions, and leadership for curriculum development;
5. Exhibiting students' projects;
6. Taking time for thoughtful interactions with students about their writing processes;
7. Making clear through body language, dialogic style, and explicit conversation [a respect for] multiple viewpoints. (Oldfather & McLaughlin, 1993, p. 9)

In another example, Onore (1992) reports on a classroom where what students wanted to know about a topic played a central role in the curriculum. Initially, the teacher assigned student groups to make a list of what they knew already about a topic. As students discussed what they knew, the teacher instructed them to keep track of any questions about the topic that arose. Then the students used these questions, during a subsequent discussion in their groups, to indicate what additional information they would like to learn about the topic. The lists of questions guided the topics teacher and students studied for this unit. This teacher had a topic that she wanted her students to study—a nonnegotiable issue—but at least some of what they would study was determined by student interest and curiosity, based on what they already knew about the topic.

To give students voice means first identifying what is meaningful or important to them and then incorporating this into teaching. In thinking about student voice, you may need to consider whether students or groups of students in your classroom value school knowledge. McDiarmid (1991), in talking about "What Teachers Need to Know About Cultural Diversity," observes:

> Some students grow up believing, as an article of faith, that school knowledge is important and that doing well in school will be rewarded. . . . Other students, particularly poor children and those of color, may see little evidence of the value of school knowledge. They may know few people who have done well in school and continued their education. (McDiarmid, 1991, p. 259)

Indeed, as Meier (1995) has observed, "Many kids don't want to be 'well-educated' because they can't even imagine what it is that could be 'wantable' about being well educated" (p. 163). These issues are important to think about because they will affect how you elicit student voice, and they will affect how you structure learning so that students can "make sense of the subject matter within their own realities" (Gollnick & Chinn, 1994, p. 301).

A FINAL THOUGHT:

> Students may not know they have a voice. Or, if they know they have one, they consciously repress it when in the presence of adults in authority. Consequently, patience in the process of letting student voices emerge is essential, as is active listening, probing, and the form of nonjudgmental "brainstorming" that has proven so dynamic and creative in U.S. industry. (Lincoln, 1995, p. 88)

Planning for Classroom Management   Every teacher has planned the perfect lesson only to have it go hopelessly wrong because of the inappropriate behavior of one or more students. Such misbehavior might be as subtle as minimal student engagement (e.g., not actively participating in class discussions, not putting effort into quality writing, following the steps of a science lab but not thinking about the scientific question being researched), or as overt as defiance and disruptions (e.g., refusal to participate, aggression toward others). When inappropriate behavior occurs, teachers react, and suddenly the students are in charge of the lesson. Even when students are

---

Focus and Reflect

- How can knowing about learner expectations in your course help you to plan *what* to teach?
- How can knowing about learner expectations in your course help you to plan *how* to teach?
- Create a student expectation survey appropriate for the level and content area you teach or will teach. What information from students would be helpful to you in planning how to teach your subject matter?
- Identify three ways you would give students voice in your course.
- What classroom principles would be important for you in your classroom?

involved in formulating classroom principles, they may still misbehave, and it often requires a response. However, planning for disruptions can minimize their occurrence and maintain the classroom as a learning community.

As necessary as it is to reprimand students for misbehavior, reacting to disruptions interrupts the lesson. Scolding, taking away options, increasing work demands, shaming students, or removing them from the room all change the mood of the class. Concentration is broken and motivation is decreased; class becomes about appropriate behavior instead of about learning the content.

If you can plan lessons that invite students to *want* to be part of the lesson, they will be too engaged to disrupt. This is the best kind of classroom management. But you may also be able to avoid disruptions by removing their causes. To prevent a disruption you have to see it coming. For example, teachers who plan to have students practice conjugating verbs or solve taxing word problems should anticipate that some students may get bored or frustrated with the task. By anticipating potential disruptive reactions, teachers can break up a task, plan to provide assistance while students work, or offer meaningful incentives for completion of the task. If you can identify the cause of a disruption, you may be able to defuse a situation before it occurs.

FUNCTIONAL BEHAVIORAL ASSESSMENT. Positive behavioral support (PBS), discussed previously in Chapter 4, is an approach to behavior management where disruptive behaviors are prevented by removing their causes (Repp & Horner, 1999). Functional behavioral assessment is a process teachers use, along with PBS, to determine causes of disruptions. When unanticipated problems occur, functional behavioral assessment enables the teacher to determine the cause of a problem instead of just reacting. The first step is to identify the problem behavior, whether it is as simple as students not being engaged in a lesson or a single student acting openly defiant. Then, the teacher needs to carefully assess what happened to cause the behavior. It may have been boredom or fear of failure. Perhaps the cause was a bully on the school bus, or distractions from a noisy hallway. When we learn about these causes, we can stop them; if we don't learn about causes, problems continue and we punish the victim but do not solve the problem. Often the teacher can ask the student in private what caused the disruption. Other times, the teacher must carefully observe what conditions led to the problem. Both task demands (e.g., a difficult or uninteresting assignment) and setting demands (e.g., whole-class versus cooperative group activities, how dark or bright the classroom is) are possible conditions. By taking note of setting and task demands that occurred just before a disruption, you can watch for patterns over time to identify true causes of disruptions. Then, adjustments may be made, and if the disruptions cease, you can confirm the real cause systematically while learning what adjustments are effective and do not violate the integrity of the lesson. Making adjustments in situations that cause disruptions differs from responding to the disruption alone, by removing the source of the problem instead of simply reacting to it.

If students know what is expected of them and agree to it, they have fewer reasons to disrupt a lesson. Individual students who are frustrated or confused are more likely to engage in disruptive behaviors. They may need to revisit the course goals and community principles, because not understanding them, no longer buying into or being able to meet them could all

▪ *Scenario Revisted*

PRINCIPLES FOR AN INCLUSIVE CLASSROOM LEARNING COMMUNITY

Elizabeth Haven decided to develop some classroom principles with her fourth-hour math class to see if it would help her students work together with more energy and purpose. She began by taking a class period to discuss "community" in her class—what the word means, how communities are made up of people with different skills and interests, how every member of a community contributes something unique, and how a class is a community. She and the class also discussed other ideas related to "community," like feeling safe to express one's ideas or to be oneself, acceptance of others, and how personal beliefs about such things as conflict, class, and work may be different.

In an effort to learn why so many students seemed so disinterested in the course, she asked students to complete a student expectation survey, which was modified to ask students about aspects of her course. This survey included questions about what students had expected to learn in the course, what they wanted to learn in the course, how they thought they learned best (lectures, class discussions, group work, individual special projects, group projects, and so on).

After talking about these matters, Ms. Haven and her students worked together to set out the following classroom principles for their class: respect, patience, helping others "get it," being prepared.

Respect others (by not making fun of them).

Be patient (with questions other students need to ask; waiting to get help yourself).

When working with other students, the goal is to make sure everyone "gets it," that everyone knows how to do the assigned problems.

Students will come to class every day prepared with pencils, paper, their completed homework, and their textbook.

Ms. Haven regularly returned to the list of classroom principles with students. She posted the principles on a bulletin board and had them duplicated so students could have them in their notebooks. It became a ritual for the class to revisit the principles regularly after each unit test.

be causes of the problem. This may seem like a daunting task in a crowded and diverse classroom, but it must be done. Functional behavioral assessment provides a method that minimizes guess work and gets at true causes. A teacher who ignores a student having academic difficulties because the rest of the class is ready to move on is not practicing inclusive teaching. Likewise, a teacher who only responds with punishment will never minimize class disruptions, teach appropriate behaviors, or successfully teach that perfect lesson.

INCLUSION AND STUDENTS WITH SPECIAL NEEDS. While positive behavioral support is generally an effective approach to management, it is particularly effective when students participate in determining how they will learn. Research has shown that, not only does positive behavioral support work in classrooms that include students with disabilities (Munk & Karsh, 1999), but also that providing for student choice and work on preferred tasks helps to address common causes of disruption, reflecting the importance of community-developed principles in the classroom. In addition, employing principles of effective instruction supported by research (Swanson & Hoskyn, 2001) also serves to reduce causes for disruption (Munk & Karsh, 1999).

Creating a Learning Community by Establishing Learning Rituals in the Classroom

Learning rituals are the accepted and respected ways that teachers and students work together to promote learning. They include teaching methods and learning activities that are taught, emphasized, repeated, and shared throughout a course. These rituals are usually introduced by the teacher at the beginning of a course and then used and reinforced throughout the course.

In an inclusive learning community, even when curricular topics are chosen carefully to have some connections to students' lives, and even when teachers know their students well, it is also important to understand that student learning must be *supported* with teaching methods and learning activities that help students learn. Students may want to do well but have little confidence in their academic abilities. Moreover, they may have little idea what they need to do—what actions they need to take—to be academically successful (Schlosser, 1992). These students will not be engaged in learning and, out of frustration or confusion, may disrupt the classroom community. Learning rituals can help students understand what they need to do to be successful.

Learning rituals may include the way that a new unit of study is introduced or how content will be reviewed in preparation for a test. Rituals may also be procedures as simple as the way assignments are turned in to the teacher or returned to students by the teacher. The key elements that characterize a learning ritual are that it must always be:

- A set of concrete steps about how an important learning activity is done successfully;
- Explicitly identified in the classroom as a learning ritual;
- Taught to or learned by all students;
- Done essentially the same way whenever used;
- Viewed as valuable and helpful by students and teacher alike.

Rituals can involve familiar ways for students to organize, understand, remember, and believe what they learn, creating "comfort zones" for expectations and participation. We will discuss three kinds of learning rituals: (1) teaching routines, (2) learning or social interaction strategies, and (3) cooperative learning.

Teaching Routines   You will recall that a teaching routine, discussed earlier in Chapter 3, is a set of integrated instructional procedures used to guide the introduction and learning of large chunks of information in a lesson. Teaching routines are based on teaching devices that are used regularly, with consistency, and with the expectation that students will identify and use the device to learn the content. When teaching routines are used, plans should be developed to introduce the routine to students, teach students how to use it, and to work in a partnership with students to help them acquire the targeted content.

Figure 5.6 shows how teaching routines for a biology class were identified. These are identified under "Learning Rituals." Selecting or building a teaching routine for an academically diverse class begins with identifying a teaching device. A teaching device is an instructional tool used by a teacher and students *together* to promote learning. Devices may include stories, analogies, films, graphic organizers, study guides, field trips, lab experiences, projects, and so on.

FIGURE 5.6

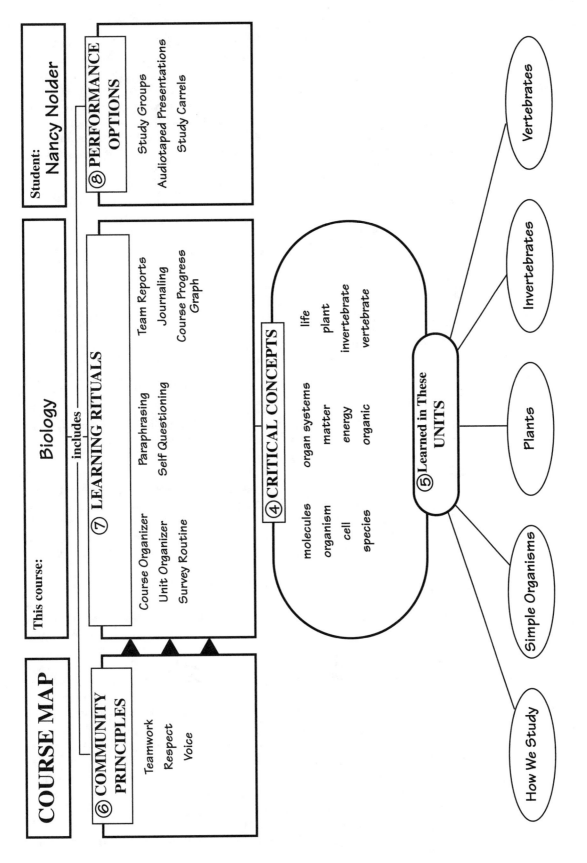

Source: From *The Course Organizer Routine* (p. 74) by B. K. Lenz, J. B. Schumaker, D. D. Deshler, & J. A. Bulgren, 1998, Lawrence, KS: Edge Enterprises.

119

The devices upon which routines are built must be important enough to learning that students are taught about the device and how it will be used to promote learning. As the device is used, the teacher provides explicit guidance to ensure that learning outcomes are achieved. In this process, the teacher cues students when the device is being used, guides learning in a partnership with students, and reviews the use of the device and learning outcomes. Teaching devices and routines are discussed further in Chapter 9, and examples of how they may be implemented in classrooms are included in the SMARTER scenarios in Appendix B.

Learning Strategies   Learning strategies are methods we use to approach learning new skills and content. Good learners are continually devising strategies to help them learn new information. For example, given a list of items to memorize, one strategy might be to develop a mnemonic to help remember the items. While good learners often develop strategies like this on their own, many students do not. These students need to be taught how to develop and use learning strategies.

A learning strategy must help a student meet a demand related to learning or performing a task, and must consist of steps that help the student meet a learning demand. The learning strategy must be directly explained and its application to content learning modeled by the teacher in ways that show how the strategy should be effectively and efficiently applied.

A strategy must be learned through practice, using an authentic learning task or demand in its simplest form. Gradually increase the complexity of the learning demand, while discussing adaptations and extensions of the learning strategy. Progress in learning the strategy should be evaluated and feedback provided to the student. Additional instruction in the strategy should be provided for individuals who are not able to learn the strategy solely through group instruction. Whenever learning strategies are taught to students, they should be discussed, referred to often, practiced regularly, and evaluated on an ongoing basis. In Figure 5.6, you can see that a learning strategy for paraphrasing was identified as a learning ritual in a biology course.

A variation on teaching learning strategies is teaching social interaction strategies. Teaching social interaction strategies can improve learning interactions between students. A social interaction strategy must help students meet a social demand faced during learning. Frequently, instruction in social strategies is needed for students to be successful in cooperative learning activities. Social interaction strategies designed to facilitate cooperative learning group work include *The SCORE Skills: Social Skills for Cooperative Groups* (Vernon, Schumaker, & Deshler, 1993b). Cohen (1986) also describes group-building activities which she calls "Cooperative Training Exercises."

Like learning strategies, social strategies must be taught to students. When social strategies important to course outcomes are identified, they must then be described, modeled, discussed, and continually practiced throughout the course. Also like instruction in learning strategies, social strategies should be evaluated on an ongoing basis.

Learning strategies are more thoroughly discussed in Chapter 10. In addition, Appendix C describes a wide range of learning strategies shown by research to be effective in improving the learning of students at risk for school failure.

Establishing Explicit Learning Rituals   A first step in helping students become full participants in the classroom may be to ensure that all students value and understand the importance of learning and learning rituals. Some students in schools today "don't see a connection between their efforts and school success, don't know what it is they need to practice, can't imagine themselves ever being 'academic,' and have never seen 'academics' played" (Meier, 1995, p. 164). To engage these students in learning may require very structured and very explicit instruction. This does not mean teachers "telling" students what they need to learn. Rather it means that, with whatever instructional activities are implemented, teachers must always share explicitly with students the rituals of the classroom—the familiar ways that learning in the course will be organized, understood, and remembered.

Most important, learning rituals should be understood and valued by students and teachers alike as a way to promote learning and community in the classroom. If students do not understand and value the rituals, the rituals will not promote learning. And, similarly, if teachers do not value them, they are unlikely to be used effectively. If either students or teachers do not value whatever learning rituals have been established or do not participate in them, the wrong rituals may have been selected. Keep in mind the words of an experienced teacher: "The rituals which work for me are the ones which work for the kids. If they don't work for them, they need to be changed" (Lenz et al., 1993).

What kinds of rituals could be useful in an academically diverse classroom? How can you help students feel like real participants in these rituals? You probably have already developed some ideas about teaching techniques and activities that you believe most effectively promote student learning. Experienced and inexperienced teachers have ideas about particular practices, procedures or "rituals" in classrooms that "work," that they have had success with before, or that have helped them as learners. One such ritual is cooperative learning.

An Effective Learning Ritual: Cooperative Learning   A classroom ritual that can be effective in an academically diverse setting is cooperative learning. Cooperative learning encompasses a number of models that all share the objective that students work together to help each other learn (Johnson & Johnson, 1998). Cooperative learning techniques are especially appropriate in establishing a learning community, because they emphasize cooperation and students helping one another. Such cooperation can provide another resource for teachers. Students can translate "teacher talk" for other students or just provide another way to approach a task or understand a concept.

Research has found that cooperative learning methods can help students learn, but only if implemented appropriately (Putnam, 1998). Cooperative learning is not just having students work in groups. Different methods require attention to somewhat different priorities. All methods require five conditions be present: (1) The task must be authentic, worthwhile, and appropriate for students working in groups; (2) small-group learning is the goal; (3) cooperative behavior should be taught to and used by students;

(4) group work should be structured for interdependence, so that students depend on one another to complete a task successfully; and (5) there should be individual accountability, so that everyone has a stake in the success of each individual in the group (Putnam, 1998).

Incorporating all these conditions in cooperative learning structures helps to avoid some common problems that undermine its effectiveness to support learning. Cooperative learning is obviously a poor method when students are not engaged in a task. This is why the learning task must be authentic—something students perceive as worthwhile to work on or learn together, and something that is most effectively done "as a group," rather than by students individually. Even when students are enthusiastic about working together and about the task they are to accomplish as a group, they often need explicit instruction and practice in how to work together. This is a key feature in using this method and one that is often overlooked. Finally, there must be an incentive for students to work together, and there must be accountability to insure cooperation. All the research that has shown cooperative learning to be effective has incorporated interdependence and accountability.

One common situation that develops when group work is poorly structured is that one or two individuals do all the work. This may happen when more assertive individuals, or more experienced students, simply take over the group task. It may also happen when some students are left to do all the work, because one or more students in a group do not participate fully. Some of these problems may be avoided by taking the time and making the effort to instruct students in the social skills needed to work together. Planning to incorporate interdependence and accountability also can help assure that all students are involved.

Cooperative learning methods vary, depending on which cooperative learning approach is followed. To begin thinking about how you might use cooperative learning in your classroom, let us consider two cooperative learning methods: (1) The Teamwork Strategy (Vernon, Deshler, & Schumaker, 1993a), and (2) Student Teams Achievement Divisions (STAD) (Slavin, 1987). In the Teamwork Strategy, students work together to accomplish a task or do a project. In STAD, students work together to teach each other concepts, factual material, or skills previously presented by the teacher and on which students will be tested individually.

THE TEAMWORK STRATEGY. The Teamwork Strategy is used in classrooms when students are expected to produce a product as a group. Vernon, Deshler, & Schumaker (1993a) stress the importance of having students develop the social skills needed to work cooperatively. This format can be especially beneficial to at-risk students. Tasks can be divided up in a group-study format, where individuals in the group contribute their different talents to a project. Students can make contributions to the group effort, drawing on their academic strengths and/or drawing on their experience or knowledge. This cooperative learning structure can provide opportunities for students from diverse backgrounds to enrich the work of a classroom community.

In the Teamwork Strategy, you identify learning assignments that students work on together in groups and that result in one product, like a written report, a presentation, a play, or a display. Such assignments should be designed to include tasks that can be divided among members of a group and that cannot be completed by one or two students working alone in the time allotted (Vernon, Deshler, & Schumaker, 1993a). You should also take responsibility for forming groups of students to work together. As you select student groupings, consider how individual students work with others. Create combinations of students who work well with others with students who work less well with others, students who need a great deal of help with those students who are more independent learners. Also, consider student achievement levels by forming groups that reflect the heterogeneity of your class. However, do not expect students of widely varying achievement levels to work well together. Therefore, do not group the highest achieving student with the lowest achieving one; the disparity may be too great to permit effective group functioning.

Once you have made assignments and formed groups, you will also need to teach groups how to work together. The Teamwork Strategy has steps to guide cooperative learning groups in approaching their task and learning how to work together effectively. The steps of the strategy, which can be remembered with the acronym TEAMS, are: (a) **T**alk about what needs to be done, who in the group will do each task, and when it should be done; (b) **E**ach member of the group does the task they have been assigned or have chosen, and other group members help and support each other in completing tasks; (c) **A**sk for and give feedback to other group members to complete individual jobs; (d) **M**ake changes and revisions, as needed, as the group assembles the individual work products into one project or presentation; and (e) **S**urvey how the group worked together by talking about and completing a written evaluation. The Teamwork Strategy must be taught to students by describing how it works, modeling how it works, and then discussing it with students and practicing and evaluating it on an ongoing basis.

The Teamwork Strategy model for cooperative learning particularly stresses the importance of teaching and having students practice social skills needed to work together effectively in groups. These skills include learning how to share ideas with others, both in terms of knowing how to signal others in the group that you wish to share an idea, and how to listen attentively and receptively to the ideas of others (Vernon, Deshler, & Schumaker, 1993a). Other important skills are: (1) knowing how to compliment others, to aid positive group functioning; and (2) knowing how to offer help or encouragement, how to recommend changes, and how to exercise self-control (Vernon et al., 1993b). Once these skills have been taught to students and modeled for them, and they have practiced them, groups need to continue to monitor their work to assess whether they are all using effective group practices. A cooperative learning evaluation like the one shown in Figure 5.7 can facilitate this process.

STUDENT TEAMS ACHIEVEMENT DIVISIONS (STAD). Cooperative learning tasks must be organized so that the method chosen suits instructional objectives. For example, Student Teams Achievement Divisions (Slavin, 1987) is most effective when used with learning that, when assessed, has a single correct answer. This is a different approach than a group process method, where students work in teams to "divide and conquer" a task and to produce one product or outcome.

In STAD, students are assigned to four-member learning teams that are heterogeneous in academic performance levels, gender, and ethnicity. The teacher presents a lesson, and students work in groups to master the material. Students need to be told explicitly that their task is to learn the material

FIGURE 5.7 Cooperative Learning Evaluation Form

1. Make a check mark next to each social skill your group used:

____ Group members shared ideas.

____ Group members were complimentary about the contributions of others.

____ Group members encouraged each other.

____ Group members gave and received criticism in a positive manner.

____ There was good eye contact between members when discussing work.

2. For this assignment, our best group-work skill was:

3. The best thing that happened in our group today was:

4. We need to improve:

Source: Adapted from *The Teamwork Strategy*, p. 79, by D. S. Vernon, D. D. Deshler, & J. B. Schumaker, 1993, Lawrence, KS: Edge Enterprises. Copyright 1993 by Edge Enterprises. Adapted with permission

and to make sure that each member of their group also learns the material—that is, their job is to teach each other.

Following group work, students are quizzed or tested individually on the lesson material. Benefits accrue to teams through individual improvement scores. Improvement scores are a way to provide "equal opportunity scoring," which allows students to get credit for doing work that shows improvement over previous performances (Slavin, 1987; Putnam, 1998). Students' scores on individual assessments are compared with their own past scores, and points are awarded to teams as group scores, based on the degree to which individual students exceeded their past scores. For example, if a student earned a score of 75 on a previous test and a score of 83 on the next test, that student would contribute 8 points to his or her team's group improvement score. Teams with the highest improvement scores are then recognized, using some tangible reward, extra credit points, or whatever reward the teacher has established ahead of time.

PLANNING FOR COOPERATIVE LEARNING. As with most teaching, careful planning ahead of time will assure the greater effectiveness of cooperative learning as an instructional method. In planning for cooperative learning, you need to decide which method or model to use, identify learning goals, and how you will have students evaluate how they worked together as a group. A planning guide, like the one shown in Figure 5.8, may be used to help you structure cooperative learning in your classroom. You will note that the guide prompts you to consider specifically what cooperative learning

FIGURE 5.8
Cooperative Learning
Planning Guide

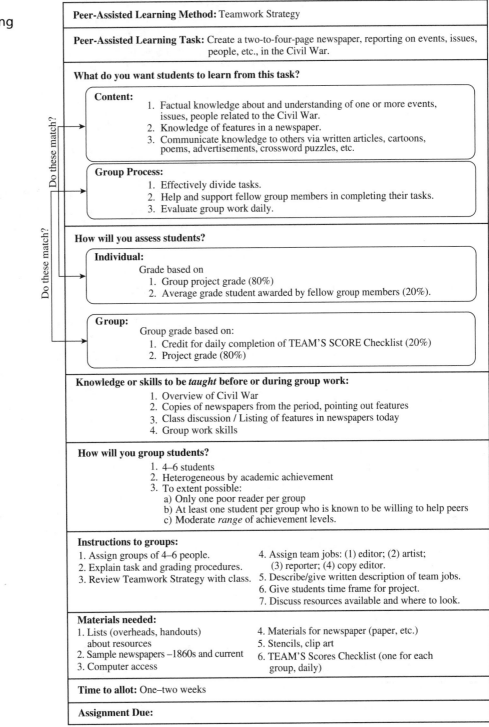

Peer-Assisted Learning Method: Teamwork Strategy

Peer-Assisted Learning Task: Create a two-to-four-page newspaper, reporting on events, issues, people, etc., in the Civil War.

What do you want students to learn from this task?

Content:
1. Factual knowledge about and understanding of one or more events, issues, people related to the Civil War.
2. Knowledge of features in a newspaper.
3. Communicate knowledge to others via written articles, cartoons, poems, advertisements, crossword puzzles, etc.

Group Process:
1. Effectively divide tasks.
2. Help and support fellow group members in completing their tasks.
3. Evaluate group work daily.

How will you assess students?

Individual:
Grade based on
1. Group project grade (80%)
2. Average grade student awarded by fellow group members (20%).

Group:
Group grade based on:
1. Credit for daily completion of TEAM'S SCORE Checklist (20%)
2. Project grade (80%)

Knowledge or skills to be *taught* before or during group work:
1. Overview of Civil War
2. Copies of newspapers from the period, pointing out features
3. Class discussion / Listing of features in newspapers today
4. Group work skills

How will you group students?
1. 4–6 students
2. Heterogeneous by academic achievement
3. To extent possible:
   a) Only one poor reader per group
   b) At least one student per group who is known to be willing to help peers
   c) Moderate *range* of achievement levels.

Instructions to groups:
1. Assign groups of 4–6 people.
2. Explain task and grading procedures.
3. Review Teamwork Strategy with class.
4. Assign team jobs: (1) editor; (2) artist; (3) reporter; (4) copy editor.
5. Describe/give written description of team jobs.
6. Give students time frame for project.
7. Discuss resources available and where to look.

Materials needed:
1. Lists (overheads, handouts) about resources
2. Sample newspapers –1860s and current
3. Computer access
4. Materials for newspaper (paper, etc.)
5. Stencils, clip art
6. TEAM'S Scores Checklist (one for each group, daily)

Time to allot: One–two weeks

Assignment Due:

(Side labels: "Do these match?" appears twice along left margin connecting to the Content/Group Process boxes and the Individual/Group boxes.)

method you will use and what the task will be for students. (As discussed previously, it is important to focus on the match between method and task, because not every method is suited to every task.) Then, the guide prompts you to identify the specific content you want students to work on, as well as how they will work together. Because some methods require that you provide content or skills instruction up front, this is another issue to plan for ahead of time. As you think about the content you want students to work on together, you must also think about whether you will assess students on both content and process, keeping in mind that you need to match assessment to what you want students to learn from the activity. Other matters to plan include how to group students, what your instructions will be to the groups, materials needed, and the time frame.

Teaching students how to work with others in general, and specifically, how group work is to be carried out in the learning community, helps assure the success of cooperative learning activities. In Slavin's Student Teams Achievement Divisions, for example, the objective is for students to help each other learn. To achieve this objective, students must understand that their purpose in working together is to teach each other. **Teachers must be explicit about this goal so that students will focus on helping each other learn.** Just as instruction in academically diverse classes should be explicit, examined, and organized, so too should cooperative learning be explicit, examined, and organized.

Teachers often assume that students already know how to work in groups. In many, if not most, cases, this is not true. Making cooperative learning work in your classroom will depend in large measure on how effectively you *teach* students how to work together. Teamwork is increasingly valued in the workplace today, so these are very valuable skills for all students to learn, in addition to the content they can help each other learn.

For cooperative learning to become a ritual, it must be used in a course with the same frequency and regularity as other instructional methods. Students need to understand that this is a way for them to learn, and they need to know what they will do each time cooperative learning is used. If more than one cooperative learning structure is used, students must be instructed clearly in their roles and responsibilities for each method and reminded of these each time they change structures. Also, the value of cooperative learning must be made explicit, and students should understand what benefits they can expect from participating in this instructional method.

Effective cooperative learning does not happen in a day, a month, or even a year. It takes time to learn how to do it right. To this end, there needs to be ongoing reassessment in the classroom community of how groups are working together. Students and the teacher need to examine and reexamine how groups are functioning. The Cooperative Learning Evaluation Form in Figure 5.7 can help you and your students evaluate whether the ritual of cooperative learning is working in your classroom to effectively guide and promote student learning.

Creating a Learning Community by Providing Performance Options

The academic diversity within a class increases when circumstances outside of the student's control limit the student's ability to interact with the content and demonstrate competence. Teachers can reduce the impact of this academic

Focus and Reflect
- What rituals can I establish in my course that will help students learn?
- What experiences of students do I need to consider in selecting rituals to promote learning in my course?
- How will I establish rituals in my classroom and make sure all students are ready and able to participate fully in them?

▪ Scenario Revisited

Elizabeth Haven decided to restructure the cooperative learning methods she was using in her classroom. Instead of just putting students in groups to work together, she resolved that she would be explicit about the need for students to help each other learn. She also decided that she would provide for individual accountability for students helping each other learn by making grades for the activity contingent on the mastery of the task by each individual in the group.

She decided to use teacher-formed groups of three or four students, balanced according to student learning abilities. Groups would remain together for a quarter. Periodically (once a week? once every two weeks?), a major portion of a class period would be devoted to group-study work.

Ms. Haven explained to her class how the cooperative learning ritual would work:

1. Groups will be given a concept to master.
2. General instruction will be provided to the class.
3. The class will then break up into groups. Each group will have an activity or a set of problems to practice the new concept.
4. It is the responsibility of each group to make sure that each and every member of the group understands the concept and is able to do the problems.
5. Students will then be quizzed individually on the concept.
6. The *extra credit* grade of each student will be *the average of the quiz grades achieved by everyone in the group.* In this way every student has a stake in the learning of every other student in the group; yet, because it is extra credit, no one student's grade is dependent on the ability or diligence of another student.

To help students understand the importance of working together, an important part of the learning ritual was for students to evaluate their group work by completing an evaluation form each time they worked together. Ms. Haven demonstrated to students that she believed how they worked together was very important by reading each group's evaluation, complimenting them on their successes, and helping them find ways to problem-solve when difficulties arose.

diversity by providing specific alternatives or performance options for learning and demonstrating competence. Circumstances over which the student has no control might include having a physical or a learning disability. If it were not for these circumstances, the student would otherwise be able to interact successfully with the content. Teachers are legally required to provide performance options in the form of accommodations for students who have been identified with a disability. Students who have not been taught how to meet classroom demands, or who have disabilities that prevent them from meeting these demands, may require an accommodation. A variety of individual performance options may be provided. Providing accommodations for other students in the class may also be justified if there are circumstances beyond the student's control that indicate such a need.

Policies and procedures for providing group performance options that will maximize the inclusiveness of the classroom should be established at the beginning of the course and evolve as the course progresses. Discussing these options at the beginning of the course can reduce the stigma attached to being given "special rights." However, these options need to be defined, and students should know when they will and will not be used. A discussion of options within the context of "business as usual" helps prepare all students for the acceptance and use of appropriate and legal accommodations in the workplace they will encounter after school.

Developing performance options will often require altering or adapting teaching methods, materials, or the physical environment. A variety of accommodations have been developed for use with special populations. Many of these accommodations can also help other students. Special education staff in a school should be able to provide support and resources in identifying and implementing a wide variety of performance options. For students who qualify for special education services, these options will be part of individualized education programs (IEPs) that identify legally required accommodations, why they are required, how they will be implemented, and who is responsible for implementing them. Such options are required for some students who qualify for special education services, because they may have more difficulty acquiring, storing, expressing, or demonstrating what they have learned because of an identified disability.

Some curricular materials may be designed so poorly that a teacher may seek alternate materials to use, or decide to present information included in instructional materials in different ways. Textbooks, for example, often lack "coherence" which is "exacerbated by digressions, too many subtopics, no explicit overarching organizing concept, and poorly used headings" (Raphael & Hiebert, 1996, p. 176). Consequently, you should evaluate whether the textbook you are using is indeed accessible to your students for independent or any other kind of learning. A number of curriculum researchers have developed guidelines for evaluating the design of instructional programs and materials. For example, Deshler, Schumaker, and McKnight (1997) developed a checklist to identify features of reading materials that are inconsiderate of readers, and an associated list of instructional activities that might be implemented to address these features. This checklist, and an accompanying list of strategies for enhancing text problem areas, are included in this text as Appendix D.

Regardless of whether alternate options are legally required or curricular materials are unsuitable, you must clearly understand whether or not an option being provided should be focused on *content* or *format*. Content options involve changing the nature or amount of what will be learned. For example, instead of acquiring the social studies concept of federalism through a study of the relationships between states and the U.S. government, the learner acquires the concept through a study of the relationships between administrators, teachers, and students in their school. Do you want all students to understand (a) the process, (b) the process plus how it is implemented by one national government, or (c) the process plus how it is implemented in two or more national governments? Do all students need to understand (a) but not necessarily (b) and (c)? Or do all students need to understand (a) and (b) but not necessarily (c)? Content options require that critical learning outcomes be clearly identified. Once identified, those outcomes and the way learning has been structured for learners, and processed and acquired by them, should be reflected in any performance expectations.

Format options refer to changing the way information is presented to students. For example, instead of having students acquire the concept of federalism by assigning them to read about it in a textbook, a teacher might offer students alternative, less complicated reading material. The learner acquires the same content through material presented in an alternative format. Another option might be to have a structured class discussion about the concept of federalism in the context of decision making in school. Whatever content or format options are offered, teachers must be able to articulate what all students should know and how they will demonstrate that knowledge.

Performance options are used to allow students to meet the academic demands of: (1) acquiring information, (2) storing and retrieving information when needed, and (3) expressing and demonstrating competence. Therefore, performance options should be selected, based on the demands placed on students. Figure 5.2 shows how performance options for a class were identified by a teacher. Figure 5.9 presents a variety of group performance options associated with varying academic demands. Teachers need to define and describe options for students when they are presented and provide and discuss examples and nonexamples of appropriate use of the options.

In Figures 5.2 and 5.6, you will note that performance options have been spelled out for students. This lets all students know that they will have opportunities to show what they have learned in a variety of ways. While teachers have legal obligations to provide alternate performance options for students identified with special learning needs, it can be useful to consider offering all students a variety of ways to demonstrate what they have learned. Providing variety in performance options may give you a clearer picture of what some students have actually learned. For example, a student

Focus and Reflect

- Analyze a chapter in a textbook in your content area and grade level according to the Checklist for Considerate Text Characteristics in Appendix D.
- Make a list of problem areas you have identified in item 1 in the checklist and identify strategies that you might use to enhance problem text areas, consulting the TRIMS strategies presented in Appendix D.

▪ Scenario Revisited

At parent-teacher conferences, Ms. Havens learned that one of her students had been complaining to his parents that he never had enough time to finish his math tests. The tests Ms. Havens used were ones that came with the textbook series, and they did not seem overly long. Indeed, some students finished very quickly. However, Ms. Havens recalled her own experiences as a math student, remembering how distracted she had always been when some students finished and turned in their tests in what seemed like 15 minutes into the exam period. (Only later did she learn that many of those students did not do well—some did the problems they knew how to do and simply gave up on the others.)

In thinking over this issue, Ms. Havens tried to think of a way to give students who needed it more time to complete the chapter and unit tests. She decided that she would discuss this matter with students. Perhaps her students would be interested to know, as she had learned after her student days, that just because people handed in tests quickly did not mean the test was easy or that they necessarily did well. She would talk about how some people needed more time than others to finish tests, and the fact that they needed more time did not mean they were less smart or capable. What they needed to work out was some way for the testing period to be extended beyond the half hour usually devoted to it, yet provide other activities for people who did finish early—activities that would not distract those still working on the test. She didn't have an answer for this yet, but she would talk to her colleagues to seek suggestions, and she would discuss it with her students to see if they had suggestions. She felt confident a way could be found to make sure all students had time to show her their best learning.

FIGURE 5.9 Performance Options

PERFORMANCE OPTIONS

These options can be made available to the entire class on a routine basis, to individuals upon request, or to individuals who need specific accommodations. Some of the options are more easily implemented on a class-wide basis while others are easier to implement on an individual basis. In addition, they will need to be modified to individual class and course requirements. For example, instructional aides may be more appropriate for some activities than peers. Also, since this list is not exhaustive, there are many other options that might be considered to improve student performance. As you discover these options, you can add them to the bottom of each list as reminders for future use or to share with others.

GETTING AND ACQUIRING INFORMATION

Extended Work Time. The time given for the completion of any task can be extended (for example, doubled or extended a day) upon request.

Peer Reader/Tutor. Tutors have been trained for reading written materials or for assignment completion and are available upon request.

Audio-Taped Text. Audio tape recordings of major reading assignments have been prepared and are available on request.

Audio-Taped Presentations. Audiotape recordings of class presentations have been made and are available on request.

Copies of Presentation Notes. Outlines and notes of teacher presentations have been organized and copied and are available on request.

Talking Calculators. Calculators that speak calculations have been purchased and are available on request.

Alternate Work Areas. Movement or seating in different areas of the classroom or supervised areas of the school to complete work and improve learning is possible on request.

Visual Importance Cues. Textbooks that have been highlighted and marked to indicate test-related important information have been created and are available on request.

Graphic Organizers. Graphic organizers of information in units and lessons have been created and are available on request.

Structured Reviews. Sessions that focus on reviewing background knowledge with new information can be scheduled on request.

Textbook Study Outlines. Outlines of textbook chapters have been prepared and are available on request.

Repeated Mastery Checks. Opportunities to take ungraded quizzes for you to check your own learning and progress towards mastery of the information are available upon request.

Computer Presentations. Software programs to review important course topics covered in presentations and text are available on request.

Videotapes of Presentations. Videotape recordings of class presentations have been made and are available on request.

Other options to enhance getting and acquiring information (add your own):

STORING AND RETRIEVING INFORMATION

Alternate Notetaking Formats. Examples of different ways to take notes are available that will work in this class and they can be taught and used on request.

Structured Notebooks. A format for organizing course notebooks have been created that matches presentations and text chapters and can be taught and used on request.

Audiotaped Notes. Audiotapes of the important information for each presentation and each unit have been created to check notes and are available on request.

Peer-Study Teams. Matching teams of students for studying can be arranged and is available on request.

Study Partners. Matching two students for studying can be arranged and is available on request.

Structured Review Sessions. Structured review sessions to help prepare for tests can be arranged and are available on request.

Note Checkers. Individuals have been trained to check the accuracy of notes and give feedback and are available on request.

Note Review Sessions. Individuals have been trained to systematically review class notes throughout a unit and sessions can be arranged on request.

Assignments Presented Orally and in Writing. A written form of each assignment has been created and is available on request.

Mnemonic-Device Construction. Memory devices have been created for lists of hard-to-remember information in each unit and are available on request.

Color-Coded Papers. Different colors of paper can be used to indicate a different type of assignment and can be used on request.

Flash Cards. Flash cards of key terms, ideas, problems, and examples have been created for use during studying and are available on request.

Class Test Review. An in-class review of information that will be on the test will be conducted the day before each test and participation is available on request.

Computer Practice. Software programs that provide additional practice opportunities have been purchased and are available on request.

Other options to enhance storing and retrieving information (add your own):

EXPRESSING AND DEMONSTRATING COMPETENCE

Peer Writer. Peers have been trained to write down dictated information and are available on request.

Audiotaped Tests. Tests have been audiotaped and are available on request.

Audiotaped Responding. Audiotape players have been purchased to record answers and talk through calculations and procedures and are available on request.

Computerized Responding. Software programs have been purchased to enhance written responses and are available on request.

Timers for Time Monitoring. Quiet timers have been purchased (audiotapes can be recorded to do this as well) to enhance checking work, staying on task, and monitoring time and are available on request.

Task-Completion Checklists. Checklists have been created for each unit and project to help monitor work completion and are available on request.

Task Goal-Setting Sessions. Sessions to identify goals and plans to complete unit work or projects can be scheduled on request.

Task-Completion Peer Coach. Peers have been taught how to help monitor work progress toward goals and can be assigned on request.

Earphones/Earplugs. Earphones and earplugs have been purchased to reduce noise distractions and are available on request.

Private Study Carrel. Individual study carrels have been purchased to reduce visual distractions and are available on request.

Getting-Started Activities. For each assignment, a getting started activity has been created that provides a model of a correct response and partial completion of one assignment item that must be completed. These activities are available on request.

Self-Control Choices. A list of appropriate alternative activities, some of which can be completed in this class, while others need to be completed out of this class, have been created for completion when involvement in the current activity or situation is not possible. These activities are available on request.

Questioning Options. A list of different ways to ask private questions has been created and is available on request.

Assignment Performance Choices. A list of appropriate options for completing assignments has been created and is available on request.

Team Task Completion. Completion of assignments in teams can be arranged and is available on request.

Spelling Checkers. Spelling checkers have been purchased (and are included in word processing programs) and are available on request.

Other options to enhance expressing and demonstrating information (add your own):

Source: From *The Course Organizer Routine* (pp. 65–66) by B. K. Lenz, J. B. Schumaker, D. D. Deshler, & J. A. Bulgren, 1998, Lawrence, KS: Edge Enterprises.

in a science class who panics at the prospect of a multiple choice test, may, in fact, understand how groups of organisms are organized and be able to describe the relationships in a written answer when plenty of time is provided. Similarly, you might consider occasionally offering students a choice of doing a written report, an oral report, a videotape presentation, or a poster display within one unit of study in the course. You may find that some students, unmotivated or overwhelmed by having to respond to items on an objective test, become more engaged in demonstrating knowledge in other ways.

FIGURE 5.10
Expanded Graphic
Organizer

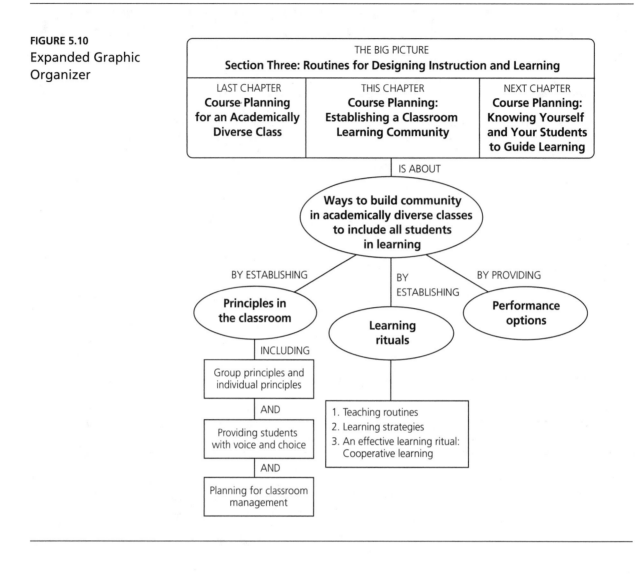

SUMMARY

Creating a classroom learning community where teachers and students successfully work and learn together involves committing the necessary energy to developing connections among and between all members of the class through the establishment of principles and learning rituals. Offering students performance options can also be a way to include all students in learning so that they are able to show what they have learned.

When connections do not develop between students and teachers, between students and students, and between students and the content, a learning community does not form. The result is a disconnected classroom, an instructional envi-ronment where only a portion of the students in the class feel accepted and successful, and are able to meet expectations. Unfortunately, many classrooms, especially at the secondary level, are "disconnected" classrooms that do not facilitate the learning of all students. The most important goal in many disconnected classrooms is to cover the curriculum before the end of the year, whether the students are learning or not. In a learning community, covering the curriculum is never as important as ensuring that all students and the teacher are working together in a sup-portive setting to learn what is considered criti-cal about the curriculum and for their lives.

The ideas in this chapter for building a learning community were developed with middle- and high-school teachers, based on what they found worked in their classrooms (Lenz et al., 1993). It is important to remember, however, that what works during one moment in time does not necessarily work forever. A learning community is not a static enterprise; it is always changing. It is always a work in progress.

Suggested Activities

1. Choose one or more readings from those about "voice" in the list of recommended readings at the end of this chapter and have a discussion about what voice is and why it is important in a classroom or a learning community.
2. Explore the many meanings of the word "community" and discuss how these meanings may contribute to an understanding of the idea of a learning community.
3. Survey class members' prior knowledge about how to address individualized learning needs. Maintain a list of this prior knowledge and come back to it from time to time to compare and contrast new and/or similar ideas in subsequent chapters of this book.

MAKING CONNECTIONS:
How Can I Establish a Learning Community?

1. *Here are the big ideas to get you started:*
   - As you begin to think about how you will teach a course, you may wish to consider establishing effective community *principles, learning rituals*, and *performance options* as a way to build a learning community.
   - Community principles in a course help identify clearly how students will relate to and interact with one another and with the teacher. Learning rituals identify the way you will help students learn and the ways they will help themselves and each other learn. Performance options clarify for everyone the variety of ways students can demonstrate what they have learned.

2. *What you need:*
   - Make a list of techniques, methods, activities—learning rituals—that you have or would like to have in your repertoire of teaching skills and methods.
   - Have at hand the lists of performance options provided in this chapter.
   - Make a list of principles you believe would be important in your classroom. Consult Figures 5.3 and 5.4 in this chapter to begin the process of identifying and defining important principles.

3. *Try this:*
   - The first step in this process is to make some choices about which of the ideas presented in this chapter will work well for you, given your interests and concerns as a teacher, the subject matter you will be teaching, and the students you anticipate having in your classroom. It is important to recognize that it is difficult to effectively incorporate more than a few new techniques into your teaching repertoire at one time. You might consider, now, which of the ideas presented in this chapter you want to try first.
   - Another example of a way to begin thinking about establishing an inclusive classroom community is to examine your own thoughts about valued classroom principles. What kind of classroom environment was most helpful to your learning as a secondary student? Developing a list of your own classroom principles will help prepare you for discussing classroom environment with students.
   - To help you develop your own ideas about what makes a classroom learning community, use the form on the next page to list some possibilities.

Classroom Principles	Consistent With?	Learning Rituals	Consistent With?	Performance Options
1.	—→?		—→?	
2.	—→?		—→?	
3.	—→?		—→?	

4. *Evaluate your work:*

- The arrows and question marks between columns should prompt you to think about the connections between the ideas you include in each category. Will your ideas complement each other or work at cross purposes? For example, cooperation as a valued classroom principle fits very well with cooperative learning as a classroom ritual. On the other hand, having a classroom principle that identifies student voice as valued in the classroom will ring hollow in conjunction with learning rituals that are all teacher-directed.

5. *Next steps:*

- Whatever decisions you make about establishing a learning community, you will need to keep in mind the importance of building trust with your students. Do not offer them choices you do not intend to let them make. Recognize that some things are nonnegotiable. And when you do develop with students principles and rituals that will be used in the classroom, honor the commitments you have made and revisit them regularly to make sure they are working.

WEB SITES

www.mcrel.org/standards-benchmarks McREL—Compendium of Standards and Benchmarks. A compilation of content standards for K–12 curriculum in both searchable and browsable formats.

www.air.org/cecp/safetynet.htm The Web site has links to projects that offer research-based strategies to educate students with emotional/behavioral problems by maximizing resources already present in communities. Projects briefly described in the executive summary entitled "Strengthening the Safety Net" are described in their entirety at this Web site.

www.ku-crl.org This is the Web site for the Center for Research on Learning at the University of Kansas, where there is more information about professional development and materials related to many of the topics discussed in this chapter.

SUGGESTED READINGS

Student Voice and Choice:

Boomer, G., Lester, N., Onore, C., & Cook, J. (Eds.). (1992). *Negotiating the curriculum: Educating for the 21st century.* London: Falmer Press. There are many excellent essays in this volume, but especially recommended is Chapter 6 (pp. 78–90) "An open letter: New York to Adelaide" by Stefanie Siegel and Ellen Skelly, two new teachers in New York City who tried to implement some of Garth Boomer's ideas about negotiation in the classroom. Siegel and Skelly discuss how teachers need to "come clean" with students about choices available and those not available, about how offering choice alone may not be meaningful, because the principles of the learning community will have an impact on choices, as will the intentions of students. The article suggests that "choice without intent means nothing" (p. 83). At a minimum these articles should spark good discussions about the issues involved.

McElroy-Johnson, B. (1993). Giving voice to the voiceless. *Harvard Educational Review, 63*(1), 85–104. A junior high school English teacher writes about her concerns about the development of today's African American students and their need for voice.

Oldfather, P., & McLaughlin, H. J. (1993). Gaining and losing voice: A longitudinal study of students' continuing impulse to learn across elementary and middle-level contexts. *Research in Middle Level Education, 17*, 1–25. An excellent introduction, grounded in school experiences, to the idea of student voice.

Phelan, P., Davidson, A. L., & Cao, H. T. (1992). Speaking up: Students' perspectives on school. *Phi Delta Kappan, 73*(9), 695–704. This study to identify factors that affect students' engagement with schools and learning found that students' "perspectives on school and learning, rather than being at odds with those of teachers, are remarkably similar" (p. 704). The study substantiated that secondary students "want teachers to recognize who they are, to listen to what they have to say, and to respect their efforts" (p. 696).

Student Feedback:

Bailey, G. D. (1983). *Teacher-designed student feedback: A strategy for improving classroom instruction.* Washington, DC: National Education Association. Provides information about how to construct student feedback instruments as well as samples of feedback forms for several school levels.

Fraser, B. J. (1999). Using learning environment assessments to improve classroom and school climates. In H. J. Freiberg (Ed.), *School climate: Measuring, improving and sustaining healthy learning environments* (pp. 65–83). Philadelphia, PA: Falmer Press.

Cooperative Learning:

Cohen, E. G. (1986). *Designing group work—Strategies for the heterogeneous classroom.* New York: Teachers College Press. Cohen includes suggestions for group-building activities which she calls "Cooperative Training Exercises" Cohen also includes a Sample Student Questionnaire that may be used to evaluate group work, including social process skills.

Larson, C. E., & LaFasto, F. M. (1989). *TEAMWORK—What must go right/What can go wrong.* Newbury Park, CA: Sage Publications. May be a source for rationales for teamwork from the business and professional world.

Lyman, L., & Foyle, H. C. (1990). *Cooperative grouping for interactive learning: Students, teachers, and administrators.* Washington, DC: National Education Association. Lyman and Foyle provide a number of ideas for group-building activities as well as assessment forms and observation sheets that may be used to evaluate student use of cooperative social skills.

Slavin, R. E. (1987). *Cooperative learning: Student teams.* Washington, DC: NEA Professional Library.

Vernon, D. S., Deshler, D. D., & Schumaker, J. B. (1993b). *The SCORE Skills: Social skills for cooperative groups.* Lawrence, KS: Edge Enterprises, and Vernon, D. S., Deshler, D. D., & Schumaker, J. B. (1993a). *The Teamwork Strategy.* Lawrence, KS: Edge Enterprises. Published strategies that have been field-tested and validated in classrooms. Training is highly recommended to learn all the procedures for teaching the strategies to students, and training is required in conjunction with purchase of the manuals. For more information about these strategies, contact the Center for Research on Learning, 1122 W. Campus Road, University of Kansas, Lawrence, KS 66045, or http://www.ku-crl.org.

Performance Options

Perrone, V. (1991). *A letter to teachers–Reflections on schooling and the art of teaching.* San Francisco: Jossey-Bass. Chapter Six, "Evaluating and grading student performance" (pp. 55–67), is an excellent reflective piece on evaluation as a means of "informing, guiding and supporting the growth of students" (p. 55) and about the need to find "as many *different* (emphasis in original) ways as possible for students to share with you their understandings of the content under study" (p. 60).

REFERENCES

Anderson, C. W. (1991). Policy implications of research on science teaching and teachers' knowledge. In M. M. Kennedy (Ed.), *Teaching academic subjects to diverse learners* (pp. 5–30). New York: Teachers College Press.

Bailey, G. D. (1983). *Teacher-designed student feedback: A strategy for improving classroom instruction.* Washington, DC: National Education Association.

Boomer, G., Lester, N., Onore, C., & Cook, J. (Eds.). (1992). *Negotiating the curriculum: Educating for the 21st century.* London: Falmer Press.

Cohen, E. G. (1986). *Designing groupwork: Strategies for the heterogeneous classroom.* New York: Teachers College Press.

Deshler, D. D., Schumaker, J. B., & McKnight, P. (1997). *The survey routine.* Lawrence: Center for Research on Learning, University of Kansas.

Fraser, B. J. (1999). Using learning environment assessments to improve classroom and school climates. In H. J. Freiberg (Ed.), *School climate: Measuring, improving and sustaining healthy learning environments* (pp. 65–83). Philadelphia, PA: Falmer Press.

Gollnick, D. M., & Chinn, P. C. (1994). *Multicultural education in a pluralistic society.* (4th Ed.) New York: Merrill.

Goodlad, J. I. (1984). *A place called school.* New York: McGraw Hill.

Johnson, D. W., & Johnson, R. T. (1998). Cultural diversity and cooperative learning. In J. W. Putnam (Ed.), *Cooperative learning and strategies for inclusion: Celebrating diversity in the classroom* (pp. 67–85). Baltimore, MD: Paul H. Brookes Publishing.

Kissam, B. R., Lenz, B. K., & Tinder P. (1994). Inclusive teaching practices in a high school American history class—A case study. (Research Report). Lawrence, KS: University of Kansas. Center for Research on Learning.

Kohl, H. (1994). *"I won't learn from you" and other thoughts on creative maladjustment.* New York: The New Press.

Ladson-Billings, G. (1998). Who will survive America? Pedagogy as cultural preservation. In D. Carlson & M. W. Apple (Eds.), *The meaning of democratic education in unsettling times* (pp. 289–304). Boulder, CO: Westview Press.

Lenz, B. K., Deshler, D. D., & Schumaker, J. B. (1993). [The development and validation of planning routines to enhance the delivery of content to students with handicaps in general education settings]. Unpublished raw data.

Lenz, B. K., Schumaker, J. B., Deshler, D. D., & Bulgren, J. A. (1998). The course organizer routine. Lawrence, KS: Edge Enterprises.

Lenz, B. K., Kissam, B., Bulgren, J., Melvin, J., & Roth, J. (1992). *Obstacles to teaching in the face of academic diversity: Implications for planning for students with disabilities.* (Res. Rep. No. 70). Lawrence, KS: University of Kansas. Center for Research on Learning.

Lincoln, Yvonna S. (1995). In search of students' voices. *Theory Into Practice, 34* (2), 88–93.

Lyman, L., & Foyle, H. C. (1990). *Cooperative grouping for interactive learning: Students, teachers, and administrators.* Washington, DC: National Education Association.

McDiarmid, G. W. (1991). What teachers need to know about cultural diversity: Restoring subject matter to the picture. In M. M. Kennedy (Ed.), *Teaching academic subjects to diverse learners* (pp. 257–269). New York: Teachers College Press.

Meier, D. (1995). *The power of their ideas.* Boston: Beacon Press.

Munk, D. D., & Karsh, K. G. (1999). Antecedent curriculum and instructional variables as classwide interventions for preventing or reducing problem behaviors. In A. C. Repp & R. H. Horner (Eds.), *Functional analysis of problem behavior.* London: Wadsworth.

Oldfather, P., & McLaughlin, H. J. (1993). Gaining and losing voice: A longitudinal study of students' continuing impulse to learn across elementary and middle level contexts. *Research in Middle Level Education, 17,* 1–25.

Onore, C. S. (1992). Negotiation, language, and inquiry: Building knowledge collaboratively in the classroom. In G. Boomer, N. Lester, C. Onore, & J. Cook (Eds.), *Negotiating the curriculum: Educating for the 21st century.* London: Falmer Press.

Phelan, P., Davidson, A. L., & Cao, H. T. (1992). Speaking up: Students' perspectives on school. *Phi Delta Kappan, 73*(9), 695–704.

Putnam, J. W. (1998). The process of cooperative learning. In J. W. Putnam (Ed.), *Cooperative learning and strategies for inclusion: Celebrating diversity in the classroom* (pp.17–47). Baltimore: Paul H. Brookes Publishing.

Raphael, T. E., & Hiebert, E. H. (1996). *Creating an integrated approach to literacy instruction.* Fort Worth, TX: Harcourt Brace.

Repp, A. C., & Horner, R. H. (Eds.) (1999). *Functional analysis of problem behavior.* London: Wadsworth.

Retish, P., Hitchings, W., Horvath, M., & Schmalle, B. (1991). *Students with mild disabilities in the secondary school.* New York: Longman.

Schlosser, L. K. (1992). Teacher distance and student disengagement: School lives on the margin. *Journal of Teacher Education, 43*(2), 128–140.

Sergiovanni, T. J. (1994). *Building community in schools.* San Francisco: Jossey-Bass.

Slavin, R. E. (1987). *Cooperative learning: Student teams.* Washington, DC: NEA Professional Library.

Slavin, R. E. (1991). *Student team learning.* Washington, DC: National Education Association.

Swanson, H. L., & Hoskyn, M. (2001). Instructing adolescents with learning disabilities: A component and composite analysis. *Learning Disabilities Research & Practice, 16,* 109–119.

Vernon, D. S., Deshler, D. D., & Schumaker, J. B. (1993a). *The Teamwork Strategy*. Lawrence, KS: Edge Enterprises.

Vernon, D. S., Schumaker, J. B., & Deshler, D. D. (1993b). *The SCORE skills: Social skills for cooperative groups*. Lawrence, KS: Edge Enterprises.

CHAPTER 6

Course Planning

Knowing Yourself and Your Students to Guide Learning

Jerome J. Ammer
Jennifer C. Platt
Jeffrey W. Cornett

Critical Self-Test Questions

- What are your theories and beliefs about learning and teaching, where do they come from, and how do they affect how you teach?
- What does it mean to "get to know" a student?
- Why is it important to get to know students?
- What methods and tools can be used in an academically diverse classroom to get to know students?
- How can knowledge about students be used to guide teaching and learning?

In order to teach you, I must know you.

—Native Alaskan educator, in L. Delpit (1995), p. 183

In this chapter we discuss ways to get to know students as an important part of planning a course and establishing the rituals that help build a learning community. Knowing and understanding the host of differences students bring to the classroom learning community provides essential information to inform planning and teaching decisions. At the same time, it is important that you understand the differences *you* bring to the learning community as well, so that you do not confuse what worked for you as a student with what will work for your students.

It is not realistic to expect that you can, in advance, learn and understand everything about the many aspects of diversity likely to be represented by students in your classroom. The range of diversity may simply be too broad. This is why it becomes important to get to know the individual students who are in the classes *you* teach. While you may not know everything about every kind of diversity you encounter, you can find ways to let the students in your classes teach you about themselves as learners, about their background knowledge and prior experience, about their academic strengths and weaknesses, and about how they learn best. You are unlikely to get to know your students well in a day or a week; rather, the process should be ongoing. To assure that this process occurs, you should establish some kind of communication system so that your students have a way to let you know when learning is going well or not so well. Having such knowledge enables you to plan for more effective instruction to guide learning.

In this chapter we will be looking at three interrelated aspects of developing effective teacher-student communication: knowing yourself, knowing your students, and guiding learning. In the first section, Knowing Yourself, we discuss the importance of being aware of your own attitudes and beliefs that shape your personal practical theories about teaching.

FIGURE 6.1
Graphic Organizer

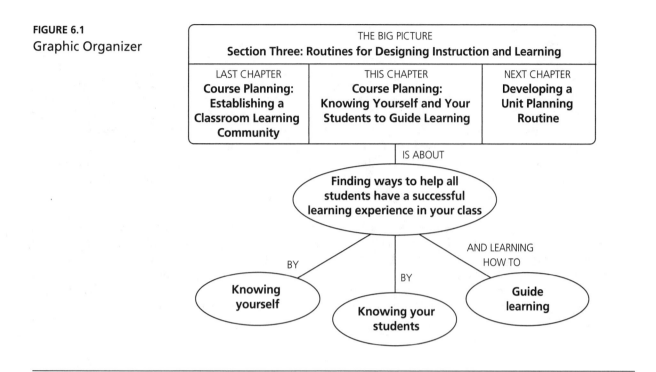

These theories implicitly influence your planning, as well as your teaching, and may either assist you in your ability to understand what students tell you or hinder this communication. In the section on Knowing Your Students, we discuss ways to get to know students and establish communication systems that allow you to monitor the quality of the learning experiences of your students. The focus in this process must always be on information that is important in guiding learning. Teachers must be careful not to pry into students' lives inappropriately. Consequently, it becomes very important to identify the kinds of information about students you need in planning and teaching the particular content of your course to the particular group of students you have. Finally, in the section on Guiding Learning, we discuss ways that you can use your knowledge about your students to plan for and guide their learning.

FOUNDATIONS AND PRINCIPLES

Students must see a classroom setting as a culturally relevant place, rather than a painful assimilation center. Carroll and Taylor (1998) describe the classroom as a "culture under construction" (p. 9). They argue that in a successful learning environment, an emerging common language for communicating is a key element in establishing a classroom culture. Similarly, Ladson-Billings (1994) found that African American children become successful learners when teachers learn to communicate their expectations in a manner that builds trust and an excitement for learning. Establishing a classroom community and culture through effective communication with

■ *Scenario*

KIM'S ISOLATION

At the back of the eighth grade classroom where a history lesson is in progress, Kim Lucchese sits quietly at his desk. While the other 26 students are involved in independent seatwork that requires them to complete the questions at the end of the chapter, Kim is hunched over his work and his arm is covering most of the worksheet.

When approached by a student teacher, Laura Kane, who is observing the class, Kim takes a painfully long time to tell her his name as he mumbles something about the directions for the task at hand. Upon closer inspection, she sees that his paper is almost completely empty except for doodling on the outer edges of the worksheet. When Laura asks if she can help, Kim responds that he is done with the assignment.

Just at that moment the teacher, Bob Daluraya, tells the students to form groups of four to discuss the main ideas in the chapter they are studying. Everyone scrambles into groups. Kim neither attempts to get into a group, nor does any group invite him to join them. Mr. Daluraya barks at Kim to join a group and, getting impatient, tells Robyn and Mikki to let Kim work with them. The girls make room for Kim to join them but make no attempt to draw him into their conversation. Except for Kim, everyone in the classroom seems to be pouring over the textbook or taking notes. Kim just looks at the floor and sits slouched in his chair with his hands folded over his chest.

students can help students feel a greater sense of belonging which, in turn, can help them become more willing to participate in learning activities (Bloom, Perlmutter, & Burrell, 1999).

Garcia (1999) argues that educators must become responsive teachers before a classroom "tapestry" can emerge. Giving students an opportunity to express their views about what they are interested in, what they care about, and what concerns them, can substantially address problems of student motivation, engagement in the curriculum, and even classroom management. One student teacher who sought feedback from students commented on what a difference it made in his relationship with his students:

> The feedback I requested from students was a great help. Not only did it let me know what the students were thinking (which was surprisingly different from what I thought they were thinking), it also let the students know I considered myself and them as a team, working to better my teaching and improve their learning. I requested feedback once in the middle of the placement [for student teaching] and again at the end. The students were not only impressed to be asked for their opinion, but also amazed to see modifications actually made from their suggestions (feelings of empowerment). They were also pleased that their opinions were respected (plus it gave my classroom management a major edge—student responsibility—especially in the general level class who seem to feel, and in fact often are, discounted by the staff). (Featherstone, Munby, & Russell, 1997, p. 50.)

Communicating honestly and openly with students, about what must be learned and how you plan to help them learn it, can go a long way toward building trust with students. In addition, "Creating opportunities to talk and listening to what learners say . . . convey to students respect for them as people whose ideas may be of value to others" (McDiarmid, 1991, p. 267).

While an awareness of student interests and concerns can provide a window for identifying the learning needs of students (Bloom et al., 1999; Carpenter, Bloom, & Boat, 1999), it is difficult to know all the needs and preferences that would engage all students in learning. So, as one educator has proposed: "Teachers must genuinely ask learners to tell what they know, think and hope, so that teacher and learner may together plan for profitable work" (Cook, 1992, pp. 18–19). Teachers and students planning together involves identifying and negotiating those parts of the curriculum that can be changed to accommodate students' interests and those parts that cannot be changed. Some aspects of the curriculum, particularly in an environment of standards-based school reform, are simply nonnegotiable—they must be taught and learned. Establishing effective communication with students means "meeting constraints head on—not by pretending they don't exist, but by admitting them and working around them once they're out in the open for all to see. Too often, teachers know them, but students, like sprouting mushrooms, are kept in the dark" (Cook, 1992, p. 19).

The ultimate result of good communication with students is that teachers and students learn more about themselves and each other and use this information for building a learning community within the classroom. When teachers and students can evaluate the success of a learning experience that just took place, it facilitates the ability to stop and seek additional information or ponder a strategy to improve future classroom experiences. When teachers and students can "talk" with one another through some kind of ongoing communication system, the learning needs of all students are more likely to be addressed.

KNOWING AND DOING

Knowing Yourself

How do you believe students learn? What teaching method do you believe is most effective in helping students learn? Do you really believe that all students can learn? As you teach, you may come to reassess what you once assumed or believed about the best ways to learn and the best ways to teach. Furthermore, you may need to examine whether your ideas about how *you* learn best get in the way of thinking more broadly about how *others* learn best.

We all have what is variously called a filter, a framework, a lens for viewing the world. This filter is influenced by our past experiences, our attitudes, our beliefs. For example, if you have always been successful in school, you may find it difficult to understand why and how some students have difficulty in school. Similarly, if you always found school a challenge but worked hard to be successful, you may believe that if only students would work harder, they could be successful.

There are benefits to exploring our own beliefs, attitudes, and biases and all the influences that contribute to our personal worldview or filter.

Self-awareness can help us avoid making assumptions about other people and their needs, assumptions that can lead to misunderstandings and, in the case of teachers, to less effective teaching. For example, Delpit (1995) found that "When a significant difference exists between the students' culture and the school's culture, teachers can easily misread students' aptitudes, intent, or abilities as a result of the difference in styles of language use and interactional patterns" (p. 176).

Understanding Personal Practical Theories   Cornett et al. (1992) call the systematic theories or beliefs of teachers their personal practical theories (PPTs). These theories are based on experiences that teachers bring from their lives outside the school setting, as well as their experiences in the classroom. Experience as a parent or previous experience as a student may form the foundation of your personal practical theories and filter how you think as a teacher and how you make decisions in your classroom.

Cornett (1990) postulates that your PPTs are theories because they (a) systematically guide your actions, and (b) are based on a lifetime of action, reflection, and reconstruction of experiences. For example, you may have had, at one time in your schooling, a very good (or very bad) experience working as part of a cooperative learning group. You may also have strong views about teacher actions that facilitated or undermined the effectiveness of this learning method. These experiences and attitudes will influence your personal practical theories about the use of cooperative learning. Other examples of beliefs that emerge from PPTs, based on the research of Cornett et al. (1992), are listed in Table 6.1.

Let us consider how some of the examples in the table might influence the curricular and instructional decisions made by teachers. If, for example, a teacher believed that learning should be fun, would that belief contribute to planning lessons that were entertaining for students but not effective in helping students master a difficult concept? Or, to take another example, if a teacher believed that students should always learn the basics first, would that belief hinder planning for challenging lessons that would engage students, even when they might not have fully mastered accompanying skills?

Knowing about and understanding your own personal practical theories can influence your decisions as you think about your course content, plan for a specific class, or consider teaching methods to use in teaching a particular unit. Suppose you have as PPTs that "teaching for understanding is important" and "teachers are the content experts who can help students understand by using the lecture method." In this case, there may be two theories at war with each other; some students may not come to understand a concept simply from listening to your lecture about it. If the method you

TABLE 6.1   Examples of Teaching Beliefs Emerging from Personal Practical Theories

• Learning should be organized and systematic.	• Students should be responsible.
• Learning should be fun.	• Skills are important.
• All students are important.	• Concepts are important.
• Teachers are experts.	• Students should learn the basics.
• Teachers are resources.	• Teachers should be rigorous.
• Working collaboratively increases ideas.	• Everyone deserves a chance to participate.

choose in teaching for understanding does not work, will you be able to step outside your personal practical theory to consider other methods? Being clear about your instructional goals and finding the most effective ways to achieve them are both facilitated when you can clearly identify what your personal practical theories are.

Taking the time to reflect on your personal practical theories also enhances your ability to understand how others perceive you, respond to you, and interact with you. Once you have identified the "lens" of personal practical theories that brings a focus to your thinking and actions about teaching and learning, you may be more ready to reflect about whether and how well each of your theories supports and facilitates the learning potential of the students in your classes.

Knowing Your Students

Understanding Why It May Be Difficult to Get to Know Students There are many reasons why some teachers do not get to know their students well. Secondary teachers usually teach more than 100 students each semester. Some teachers are called upon to teach as many as three to five different courses. Even when a teacher is teaching the same course to two or more classes of students, different preparations may be needed to accommodate the differences among groups of learners. It is important to know what conditions and attitudes make it difficult to get to know students in order to find ways around those blocks.

Although it may be unrealistic to get to know every student equally well, knowing your students should be an ongoing goal. To know students well, it is particularly important for teachers to promote and utilize effective communication in all aspects of teaching and learning. Developing, refining, and perfecting communication skills may enhance many aspects of your performance as a teacher in both the school and community (Platt & Olson, 1997).

Elements That Encourage and Discourage Building Trust with Students
Dialogue and communication within a classroom does not just happen. Teachers who are successful at getting to know their students establish a climate of

Focus and Reflect

Write a short story describing your "educational history," identifying people who had an influence on your education, critical events in that education and your "experience of school, how school felt, and how you best learned and when you felt most valued . . . or least valued" (Bullough & Gitlin, 1995, p. 27). After you have written your story, see if you can identify five or so of your personal practical theories.

TABLE 6.2 Blocks to Getting to Know Students

CONDITIONS THAT MAY KEEP TEACHERS FROM GETTING TO KNOW STUDENTS	ATTITUDES THAT MAY KEEP TEACHERS FROM GETTING TO KNOW STUDENTS
Numbers of students	Lack of student trust in system or teacher
Teacher course load	Students' negative prior experience with adults
Administrative demands on teacher	Teacher belief that it's not important to know students
Lack of time	Teacher belief that everyone learns the same way
Grading and evaluation demands	Teacher belief that diversity has no impact on
Insufficient time to plan for instruction	opportunity to learn
Cultural differences between teacher and	Lack of teacher respect for students
students, leading to problems understanding and communicating effectively with one another	Lack of student respect for teacher

trust and respect in their classrooms. Trust emerges over time as students see their teachers respecting their points of view. From this teacher openness, dialogue emerges. Kissam and Lenz (1994) caution that teacher behaviors can encourage or discourage the trust and openness that facilitate communication. Behaviors that can encourage or discourage dialogue go beyond oral language. Table 6.3 highlights some styles that build or weaken the establishment of trust among students and teachers. As an educator, it is your professional and ethical responsibility to demonstrate encouraging behaviors that model the communication exchanges expected in your community of learners.

As you think about how to get to know students to guide their learning, you will need to keep in mind the diversity present in your classroom, because it may affect the kind of communication system or procedure you select. If many of your students have difficulty expressing themselves in writing, you will not want your communication system to be wholly dependent on written messages. If some of your students do not speak English well, you will need to think about how they can best give you feedback about whether or not they feel included in the learning community. A thoughtful plan of action is vital if communication is to fit both the particular group of students you are teaching, as well as the content you must cover. In the following pages, we discuss a variety of ways you might structure effective regular communication with your students.

Developing Good Communication   Good communication is purposeful, planned, personalized, open, and clear (Lang, Quick, & Johnson, 1981). In purposeful communication, your intention is always clear. "I will open my history class today with an advance organizer to show students what we will accomplish in class." Planned communication leads you to think about what is being communicated. "I want to let students know why today's topic is important." In personalized communication, you relate to the audience's background. "I'll refer to this morning's newspaper and show students how today's topic relates to their lives." Open communication conveys an inquiring, receptive attitude. "I'll ask the students to share their thoughts about what was in the newspaper and about our lesson topic in general." Finally, communication that is clear uses words that can be understood. "I'll remember not to use any acronyms or terms they do not know."

Relationship–Building Skills   An important part of establishing good communication with students is developing good relationship-building skills. Relationships emerge from mutual respect and from sharing things in common. The classroom is both a laboratory for learning and a community for refining relationship-building skills. It is also a setting where lifelong relationships and attitudes toward others are formed, tested, and revised. Researchers investigating variables that help and hinder relationship building in classrooms stress three factors (Grant, 1991; Ogbu, 1992):

1. Teachers model and practice good interactive communication skills.
2. Students are provided with opportunities to interact with all individuals in the classroom.
3. Teachers and students work together to modify and expand each other's interactive behaviors to increase a sense of community and mutual respect.

Focus and Reflect

- What aspects of a teacher's style might get in the way of knowing students?
- What other factors in a teacher's school setting can get in the way of knowing students?
- Which of the conditions or attitudes listed above are under a teacher's control? Which are not?

TABLE 6.3   Examples of Encouraging and Discouraging Trust-Building Behaviors

ENCOURAGING TRUST	DISCOURAGING TRUST
Teacher to Student	**Teacher to Student**
• Treats students with respect. • Conveys real interest in students as people. • Jokes in class are not at anyone's expense. • Connects with students individually (through the use of eye contact, discussions during and outside of class, etc.). • Learns names quickly. • Indicates interest in students as people. • Treats class members equitably while respecting differences.	• Uses sarcastic tone of voice when talking to students. • Makes fun or belittles students. • Has little or no eye contact with individuals. • Fails to have discussions with students in or outside of class. • Does not learn student names. • Plays favorites.
Teaching Style	**Teaching Style**
• Checks students' understanding frequently. • Tests and other evaluation experiences are not surprises. • Delivers on promises made regarding course content, assessment, class routines, etc. • Genuine interest in subject matter. • Competent regarding subject matter. • Zest for teaching. • Flexible regarding "rules."	• Rushes through material. • Does not check to see if students are understanding. • Tests material not covered. • Shows lack of interest in subject matter. • Shows lack of interest in teaching. • Inflexible regarding "rules."

Source: From Kissam, B. R., & Lenz, B. K. (Eds.). (1994). *Pedagogies for diversity in secondary schools: A Preservice Curriculum.* Lawrence, KS: Center for Research on Learning. Adapted with permission.

THE RELATE STRATEGY. RELATE is a strategy that teachers can use to strengthen their relationship-building skills (Vernon, Walther-Thomas, Schumaker, Deshler, & Hazel, 1999). The six components of the strategy are: **R**emain Positive, **E**ncourage Participation, **L**isten Attentively, **A**cknowledge Feelings, **T**ell it in your own words, **E**mpathize. The steps of the strategy are as follows:

Remain Positive
• This step is a reminder to the teacher to make positive statements to a student about a topic or subject that the student has initiated.
   "Yes, I saw your article in the school paper. I thought you did a great job on it."

Encourage Participation
• This step reminds the teacher to ask open-ended questions, avoid close-ended questions, discuss topics that interest the student, and provide connections so that the student can understand the material that is being taught.
   "Good idea. How did you happen to decide to solve the problem that way?"
   "Bev, remember the short story we read last week that you liked so well? How is it similar to this one?"

Listen Attentively

- This step reminds teachers to show students that they are listening attentively and they care about what a student is saying. This may be accomplished with nonverbal communication (eye contact, facial expressions, and posture) and verbal encouragers. *"Hmm, I see."*

Acknowledge Feelings

- This step is a reminder to the teacher to make a reflective statement about what the student has said. The teacher attempts to restate what he or she thinks the student is saying and feeling. *"I sense that you are concerned about what you heard."*

Tell it in your own words

- This step cues the teacher to paraphrase what the student has said. *"Let me see if I understand. You have an outline developed, but can't seem to get started on the writing of the paper. Is that it?"*

Empathize

- This step reminds the teacher to communicate that he or she understands the student's feelings or experiences. This is done with a verbal statement that shows that the teacher has had a similar experience or has been in a similar situation. *"Yes, I think I see how you feel. It reminds me of the time that I was . . ."*

The RELATE strategy is a tool which you can use on a regular basis to help facilitate trust-building within a learning community and also model

---

■ *Scenario Revisited*

After observing Kim's isolation, Laura Kane, a student teacher in Mr. Daluraya's class, resolved to try to learn why Kim was so uninvolved in this class. Laura talked with Mr. Daluraya and learned that he too was concerned about Kim but that he had been unable to find the time or the means to resolve the problem. Kim's parents did not come to parent-teacher conferences, and whenever Mr. Daluraya had tried to talk with Kim, he was met with stony silence.

Laura took a two-pronged approach to getting to know Kim. First she made a point of making at least one observation in her notebook each day about how Kim had interacted with the teacher and other students in class. Second, she proposed to Mr. Daluraya that she be allowed to have the students in his class complete a student survey. In one of her preservice courses, Laura

had had an assignment to develop a student interest questionnaire. She persuaded Mr. Daluraya to let her administer a short questionnaire to the whole class, inviting them to list three things they were interested in learning and three things they had difficulty learning in his class.

Laura's actions helped her learn a bit more about Kim. She discovered in the process of observing him that he became quite animated one day when classroom work involved practicing learning factual information by working puzzles containing terms, names, and events in the course. He was especially good at the letter grid puzzles with hidden terms. Laura suggested to Mr. Daluraya that this activity be done in groups some day so that Kim could shine as the expert on occasion.

good relationship-building skills for your students. Using this strategy will also help ensure that your behaviors encourage rather than discourage good rapport and communication with students.

Knowing Students to Guide Their Learning: Developing a Communication System

As you begin to think about developing ways to stay in touch with students and their learning experiences in your classroom, you need to consider what information you might want to gather. This information will differ, to some extent, depending on the course you are teaching. For example, math stirs fear in the minds of many students, so a math teacher might be particularly interested in learning about students' attitudes toward the subject. In a literature class, you might want to know what kind of fiction your students are interested in or, if their cultural heritage is different from yours, is it represented at all in the materials selected to read in the course?

Whatever communication system you develop and implement, you should be sure it is clear, promotes positive, constructive interactions, and that it is used and valued by all members of the classroom learning community. To assure that you use the system on an ongoing basis, it must be practical for you and personally meaningful for students. To be useful it also must provide quick access to student information. You should create materials and plan a system you can implement with simple modifications for your teaching situation. The ultimate result of a good communication system is that it should help you know and understand your students' learning needs and promote responsiveness on your part to those needs. Therefore a communication system should promote adjustments in instruction and prompt authentic teacher change.

Some options for gathering and processing information about students include:

- **Student questionnaires.** Given several times during the course, questionnaires can ask students about topics related to course content, student interests, or student learning strengths and difficulties. (For example, see the *Student Expectation Survey* [Figure 5.5] in Chapter 5.)
- **Dialogue about the course content.** For each class period, students generate questions about the reading. Three students are selected for each class period to present their questions to start the class discussion of the material. These kinds of student-generated questions can convey to teachers a lot of information about what students understand and do not understand about the content.
- **Student folders.** Create folders for students to use to send messages to you, to turn in drafts, ask questions, or to share information about out-of-school accomplishments or interests. You need to establish regular times when folders will be reviewed and inform students about these times.
- **Journals.** You may ask students to write in journals once a week or every two weeks to record things that are going well or are not going well for them in the course. This can also provide an opportunity for students to inform you about problems or distractions in their lives.

Whatever system you devise to establish and maintain regular communication with all students, you need to decide what is realistic for you—what will work for you in your circumstances and with your habits and preferences. A communication system that is not used regularly will not accomplish much, and telling students you are going to do something and then not doing it may undermine any trust you have established with them.

The Learning Express-Ways Communication Routine The Learning Express-Ways Communication Routine (Lenz, Adams, & Fisher, 1998) is an example of a communication system designed to improve and enhance the way teachers get to know their students. This routine utilizes the Learning Express-Ways Folder as a communication device. The routine can be an effective method for getting to know students at the beginning of the year, as well as to maintain dialogue with them throughout the school year. Lenz, Adams, and Fisher (1998) suggest that this can be a good way for teachers to engage individual students in an ongoing conversation. Students are given a folder that contains preprinted questions, prompting them to provide information helpful to teachers in understanding and planning for their learning needs.

THE ROUTINE. The Learning Express-Ways communication device consists of a four-sided folder. Interestingly, as students complete Learning Express-Ways folders, they can learn more about themselves as learners, at the same time they are helping a teacher to know them better. As shown in Figure 6.2 , the cover of the folder (page one) is divided into three segments. The largest segment (located across the top of the page) is labeled "Schedule." This area could be used to record a student's daily class schedule and after-school activities, giving a teacher a sense of what classes and other activities each student is involved in. Some students also add their club meetings, sports activities, or work schedules. The rectangular box just below the schedule has no specific function and is available for teachers and students to use as they wish. Lenz, Adams, and Fisher (1998) suggest that students might use it to write a brief autobiography, a list of what they want to learn in the class, or a brief statement about why they are taking the class. Teachers who use Learning Express-Ways folders report that students include in this area information they want a teacher to know about them. Some students put down nothing at the beginning of a course, and it is only after they feel comfortable and safe in a classroom that they begin to write information in this area. The third (square) box below the schedule may be used for a photo of the student. Teachers report that they either take pictures for the students or allow them to put their own favorite picture in the box. The growing use of digital cameras allows for a quick and relatively inexpensive means for producing these pictures. Some students even draw a picture of themselves.

A student's interests and goals are the focus of the second page of the folder. This area is designed to provide teachers with background information about each student. Page two of the folder, shown in Figure 6.3a, includes topics such as family, work, activities, education, career goals, and expected outcomes of the class. When using this page, be sure to tell students that they should complete only the information they are comfortable sharing. To build trust with students, it is important that they not feel coerced to provide any personal information they do not want to share. At the same time, it is also important that you explain to students that you are asking for this information as a way to know them better as individuals and

FIGURE 6.2

Page One of Learning Express-Ways Folder

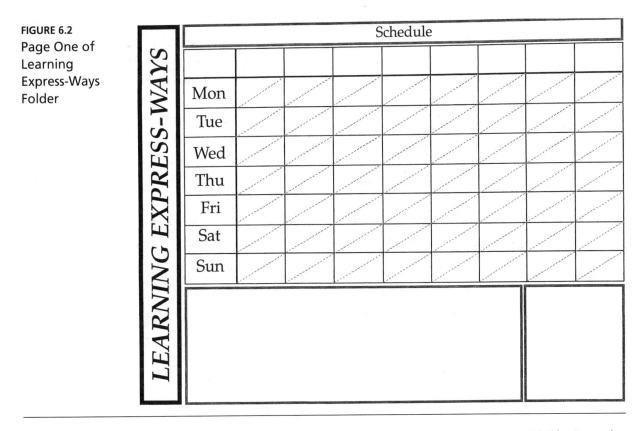

Source: From *Learning Express-Ways Folders* (p. 1), by B. K. Lenz, G. Adams, and J. Fisher, 1998, Lawrence, KS: Edge Enterprises.

as a class so that you can make better decisions about their learning needs. The information students provide on this page may be very helpful to you in connecting learning to student interests and activities, in setting realistic expectations for each student, and in making decisions about the need to modify assignments.

The third page of the Learning Express-Ways consists of two parts: (1) learning preferences and (2) strengths and weaknesses (see Figure 6.3b). The student can write his or her name sideways along the side of this page. A popular request in one teacher's class was for students to put the name they want to be called in the space just to the right of their formal name.

The information on page three of the folder requires self-reflection. Students are asked to think about their learning experiences to date. What helps and what hinders their learning? Students may indicate their assignment preferences (e.g., written reports, lab projects, etc.), instructional preferences (e.g., computer, discussion), grouping preferences (e.g., whole group, small group), and testing preferences (e.g., multiple choice, short answer). Next, students mark their academic strengths (e.g., remembering information) and weaknesses (e.g., performing calculations) and their social strengths (e.g., working in groups) and weaknesses (e.g., talking with teachers). With this information, teachers can take into account the learning, assessment, and social needs of students and help them set appropriate academic and social goals based on their strengths and weaknesses.

FIGURE 6.3a
Page Two of
Learning
Express-Ways
Folder

Personal Interests

Complete the following sections with information you are comfortable sharing

Family   With whom do you live and what is their relation?

( ) ( )
( ) ( )
( ) ( )

Work   If you work, where? _____

How many hours a week? _____

Activities   In what activities are you involved? _____

In what other activities would you like to be involved? _____

Education/Career   How do you plan to continue your education? _____

In what career do you hope to work someday? _____

Outcomes   What do you expect to learn here? _____

What would you like to learn here? _____

Is there anything about you that a teacher should know to help you be more successful learning?

If you were the teacher, what 3 things would you want to do or include? _____

Source: From *Learning Express-Ways Folders* (p. 2), by B. K. Lenz, G. Adams, and J. Fisher, 1998, Lawrence, KS: Edge Enterprises.

The back side of the Learning Express-Ways folder (page four) contains four large blocks that may be used for a variety of purposes (see Figure 6.4). Lenz, Adams, and Fisher (1998) suggest using the space for setting goals, describing plans related to how goals will be achieved, or for monitoring progress. Over several years, teachers in training and inservice teachers have indicated a variety of suggestions for using page one (front of folder) and page four (back of folder). Some of these suggestions are provided in Table 6.4.

FIGURE 6.3b
Page Three of
Learning
Express-Ways
Folder

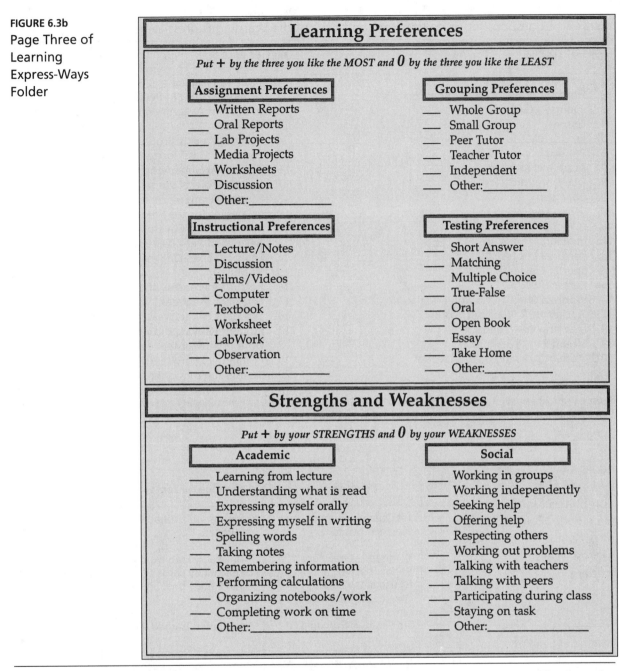

Learning Preferences

*Put **+** by the three you like the MOST and **0** by the three you like the LEAST*

Assignment Preferences

___ Written Reports
___ Oral Reports
___ Lab Projects
___ Media Projects
___ Worksheets
___ Discussion
___ Other:_____

Grouping Preferences

___ Whole Group
___ Small Group
___ Peer Tutor
___ Teacher Tutor
___ Independent
___ Other:_____

Instructional Preferences

___ Lecture/Notes
___ Discussion
___ Films/Videos
___ Computer
___ Textbook
___ Worksheet
___ LabWork
___ Observation
___ Other:_____

Testing Preferences

___ Short Answer
___ Matching
___ Multiple Choice
___ True-False
___ Oral
___ Open Book
___ Essay
___ Take Home
___ Other:_____

Strengths and Weaknesses

*Put **+** by your STRENGTHS and **0** by your WEAKNESSES*

Academic

___ Learning from lecture
___ Understanding what is read
___ Expressing myself orally
___ Expressing myself in writing
___ Spelling words
___ Taking notes
___ Remembering information
___ Performing calculations
___ Organizing notebooks/work
___ Completing work on time
___ Other:_____

Social

___ Working in groups
___ Working independently
___ Seeking help
___ Offering help
___ Respecting others
___ Working out problems
___ Talking with teachers
___ Talking with peers
___ Participating during class
___ Staying on task
___ Other:_____

Source: From *Learning Express-Ways Folders* (p. 3), by B. K. Lenz, G. Adams, and J. Fisher, 1998, Lawrence, KS: Edge Enterprises.

The final part to the Learning Express-Ways Communication Routine is an insert, called a Sample Response Sheet, to be used as a feedback form, giving students and teachers a way to have an ongoing conversation (see Figure 6.5). The insert is a tool for the student and the teacher to use to ask questions, share comments, and air concerns. The insert has two columns with blank spaces on each side. For example, in the first column under "Information about My Learning," the teacher may prompt student comments with questions such as:

TABLE 6.4 Suggestions for Using the Front and Back of the Learning Express-Ways Folder

FRONT OF FOLDER	BACK OF FOLDER
1. Schedule or Calendar	1. Student Progress
2. Homework Assignment Organizer	2. Goal Area with Reflection
3. Events/Activities	3. Important Assignments, Field Trips, & School Activities
4. Grades	4. Daily or Weekly Progress of Behavior
5. Progress Made Towards Semester Goals	5. Family or Class Portrait
6. Projects	6. Seating Arrangement
7. Academic Progress	7. Special Project Dates
8. Due Dates on Tests	8. Monthly Plans
9. Changes	9. Strategies for the Students
10. When They Need to Take Medicine	10. What Is Being Covered
11. A Picture or Photo	11. Records of Periodic Assessment
12. Individual Art Work	12. Learning Likes/Dislikes
13. Personal Interests	13. Hobbies
14. Special Classes	14. Record of Progress on Learning Strategies
15. Personal Logo	15. Goals for the Week
16. Progress Chart to Go Home to Parents	16. "Student of the Week Award" Information
17. Tracker for Completed Work	17. Student Reevaluation Date
18. Learning Preferences	18. Date of a Job Interview
19. Strengths & Weaknesses	19. Communication Board Vocabulary
20. Student Drawing of Class/School	20. Translation of Key Terms to Primary Language

Source: From Kissam, B. R., & Lenz, B. K. (Eds.). (1994). *Pedagogies for diversity in secondary schools: A preservice curriculum.* Lawrence, KS: Center for Research on Learning. Adapted with permission.

FIGURE 6.4

Example of a Completed Block from Page Four of Learning Express-Ways Folder

Source: From *Learning Express-Ways Folders* (p. 4), by B. K. Lenz, G. Adams, and J. Fisher, 1998, Lawrence, KS: Edge Enterprises.

Goal 2	Develop and use a study routine for tests.	
PROGRESS	1st Quarter: Earned D and C on first two tests Y=missed vocabulary Y=poor essay G=use study cards G=use Unit Questions	2nd Quarter: Earned B− on 3rd test Y=missed vocab words G=use study cards G=find study buddy
PROGRESS	3rd Quarter: Earned a B Y=ran out of time G=use PIRATES test-taking strategy	4th Quarter: Earned a B+ Y=lost unit Organizer G=put in notebook for studying

This example shows how a teacher used the blocks to prompt students to record and track goals for each school quarter. The goal is written at the top of the block. In each section, the student records progress toward reaching the goal for the quarter. The teacher prompts the student to evaluate progress by asking "Why did you perform this way?" The "Y" symbol is used to indicate the "why" question. The student answers, using the "G" symbol, to indicate his or her goal for improving performance.

FIGURE 6.5
Sample Response
Sheet

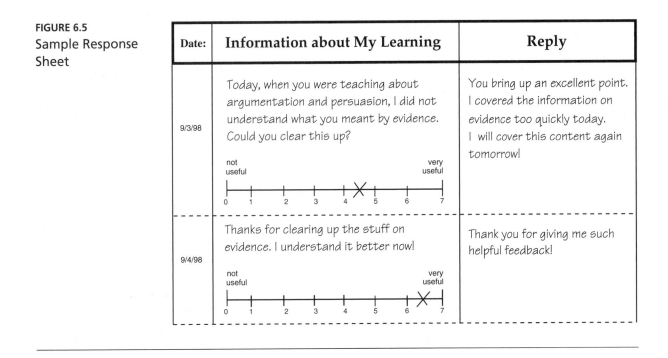

Date:	Information about My Learning	Reply
9/3/98	Today, when you were teaching about argumentation and persuasion, I did not understand what you meant by evidence. Could you clear this up? not useful ————————X——————— very useful 0 1 2 3 4 5 6 7	You bring up an excellent point. I covered the information on evidence too quickly today. I will cover this content again tomorrow!
9/4/98	Thanks for clearing up the stuff on evidence. I understand it better now! not useful ————————————X—— very useful 0 1 2 3 4 5 6 7	Thank you for giving me such helpful feedback!

- "How did you feel about the discussion in class today? I noticed that you didn't join in the way you usually do."
- "How are you doing with the small group project? I remember you said in your folder that you prefer to work independently or with a peer."
- "Did you understand today's lesson? Do you have any questions about how to complete the assignment?"

After the teacher writes comments in the first column, or whenever a teacher has asked students to comment on an assignment or just how things are going, the insert is given to the student for a response. Notice that in each box of the first column, a rating scale is provided. Teachers may want students to rate the quality of the day's lesson or their understanding of the content. In one class, a teacher had students rate each of the comments made on the response sheet in terms of its immediate importance to the student. For example, a "1" might indicate the student is sharing information that is not critical to successful learning for the student at the moment. On the other hand, if a student circled the "7," this might indicate a comment about a matter needing swift attention or that was very important to the student. This is an important self-advocacy skill for students to develop—to communicate with teachers and to make judgments about what is important.

The "Reply" column is used for the teacher to respond to students' comments and questions. The replies are usually short and to the point. If a longer reply is needed, the teacher may suggest to the student that they meet after class. Please note that use of the insert may be initiated by students as well as by teachers. For example, a student may ask a question about a lesson, assignment, or an upcoming test.

- "I didn't understand what you said in class about the difference between ozone depletion and the greenhouse effect, so now I don't know how to do the assignment. Could you help me?"
- "Thanks for looking at my outline. I didn't know if I was on the right track."
- "I don't have a clue how to prepare for next week's test and I have trouble with essay questions. Do you have any suggestions?"

For quicker responses to student feedback, some teachers are turning to the use of e-mail. Students write "feedback" in the subject line on their e-mail so the teacher is alerted to the nature of the message. Using the Learning Express-Ways Routine this way is in keeping with the new era of electronic communication which "is changing how we live, work and learn. Educators need to understand the power of this transformation and apply it to creating schools that meet the needs of today's learners" (Thornburg, 1997, p. 229).

Introducing the Learning Express-Ways Communication Routine to Students The folders should be distributed to students at the beginning of the year. The teacher should describe each section of the folder, giving several concrete examples of ways students might respond to items in the folders and answering any questions that students may have. Make sure to carefully define and give examples of terms such as, "small group," "media projects," and "participating during class" so that students have a clear understanding of what is meant. Distribute copies of the insert and discuss how and when it might be used.

Maintaining the Learning Express-Ways Communication Routine As the year progresses, students may want to change or add information to the folder, as they become more aware of their learning strengths, weaknesses, and preferences. Additionally, if the insert is used on an ongoing basis, the folder becomes a natural part of the classroom routine. You may want to have folders accessible to students as they enter the classroom and have them return them before they leave. After class, you can go through the folders and write comments on the insert to respond to student questions, comments, and concerns. It can take from 5 to 30 minutes to respond to a class of 30 students using the insert.

Teachers who use the folders with several classes may want to distribute them on a different day for each class and return them the next day. In that way, a teacher with five classes can make a personal response to 150 students once a week or every two weeks or once a month. The key to the success of using the folders is in the quality and timeliness of the response from the teacher. If students see that the teacher is responsive, there is a greater likelihood that the student will continue to communicate questions, concerns, and comments, thus enhancing the communication process. Research with secondary school students enrolled at all academic levels in both regular and special education classes confirmed that the use of the Learning Express-Ways System helped students and teachers to communicate more effectively and made students more aware of progress and options for improving performance (Lenz, Graner, & Adams, in press).

Using a Communication System to Plan   Once you learn more about your students, the next question becomes, what to do with this information. While just knowing your students well will help you relate to them in more meaningful ways and will, in many respects, help you teach them more effectively, your instruction will be most effective if you develop ways to incorporate what you know about students in your planning for instruction. As we have seen in earlier chapters, the planning you do at the beginning of the year affects how you and your students operate all year (Clark & Yinger, 1987). Therefore, it is important to examine early on the features of your instructional planning together with what you know about your students. The focus of your planning should include:

- The **content** you have to teach
- What kind of **classroom climate** you believe would best promote learning by your students
- What **teaching methods and routines** you will use
- What **learning strategies** your students will need to use
- How learning will be **assessed**

CONTENT. Because it is helpful to the learning of all students for you to be clear about the "big ideas" of the content you want to teach, you will want to factor in the prior knowledge and the interests of students as you develop your content focus. You will also need to think about how to transform that content so that is it meaningful and accessible to the students you have in your classroom. Asking students what they want to learn and how they think they learn best may help you shape your plans to incorporate student interests as well as curricular requirements in your instructional planning.

CLASSROOM CLIMATE. Having made content decisions, it is important for you to share with students your expectations about what is to be learned in your course. Communicating your expectations is part of the process of developing with students the classroom principles, learning rituals, and performance expectations that are part of course planning and establishing the learning community. This process sets the tone for many things, including student acceptance of others and of different ways of teaching. A good communication system can help you and your students monitor how things are going in the course and the learning community.

TEACHING METHODS AND ROUTINES. As you learned in previous chapters, teaching methods and routines are the means by which you will transform the content to help students learn. You can use the communication system to enlist the help of students in figuring out ways to transform the content and establish learning rituals. A communication system can also help you monitor whether the methods and routines you are using are effective in helping all students learn and whether all students are comfortable with the learning rituals, can understand them, and use them to facilitate classroom participation.

LEARNING STRATEGIES. A communication system can help you assess the strengths and weaknesses of how your students learn. If many students indicate they have trouble memorizing information, that may cue you to the need to teach them a strategy that will help them perform that learning task more effectively and efficiently. If students complain that they have trouble answering essay questions on tests, it may be worth your while to take some instructional time to teach students how to construct a good answer to an essay question and then provide time and content material for them to practice the skill.

ASSESSMENT. As with classroom methods, routines, and procedures, assessment should not be a secret kept from students. Rather, you must be open and up front with students about how they will need to demonstrate their learning. And, as with content and instructional methods and procedures, you may want to offer students some options or choices in how they will be assessed. A good communication system will provide students with an opportunity to express their preferences. Providing choice helps students become involved in and take responsibility for their own learning. The key in providing choice, as noted earlier, is to be honest with students about what parts of curriculum, instruction, and/or assessment may be altered to accommodate student preferences and what parts cannot be changed. Standards-based reform may dictate that some things must be learned by all students and that all students must demonstrate that learning in a prescribed way.

Acting on Knowledge about Students to Guide Learning: **Responding**   If you have established an effective way to communicate regularly with your students, you will learn more about them and their learning needs as the year progresses. The next question becomes, What do you do with that ongoing information? How do you incorporate this additional information into your day-to-day planning and teaching?

Again, the planning decisions you have made at the beginning of the year play a role in how you can use information about students during the year to guide their learning. If you are to be effective in using information about students, you need to establish some routine or practice that both prompts you to inquire of students how their learning is going and also provides you with a way to process the information that emerges. One way to do this is through the Learning Express-Ways folder system, coupled with how you decide to use the folder. How you will actively use the information you gather will be determined by your willingness to develop and establish habits or practices that fit with your planning preferences and procedures. For example, you might decide that you want to have students make comments on folder response sheets at the end of each unit of study. You could then read student comments and perhaps have a short class meeting to discuss any patterns you saw among student comments indicating that some changes might be needed in the course learning rituals, principles, or performance options. Or you might decide to have short individual conferences with students to discuss both how they did on a unit test or project and any comments they may have included in their folders. There are many possibilities for using a communication system like the Learning Express-Ways folder. The important issues for improving learning are to follow through with what you have told students you will do and to use your knowledge about students to make changes in your instruction, or in the learning community, or in your relationship with students.

Another way to maintain communication and dialogue with students is to have students complete a simple questionnaire at the end of each unit to find out what they liked and did not like about instruction, practice opportunities, and/or assessment during that unit. You could then take that information into consideration as you make final plans for the next unit of instruction. Another possibility is just to add a question at the end of a unit exam to provide students with an opportunity to tell you what problems they may have had learning the content in that unit or, in a more positive vein, what they learned that they had wanted to learn or enjoyed learning.

Some teachers have reported using 5 X 7 note cards or half of a sheet of paper to make progress checks on how learning is going for their students. Communicating with students through progress checks enables teachers to monitor the effectiveness of their teaching and the learning environment in the classroom. In this short and simple technique the teacher asks students at the conclusion of a lesson to write down responses to three simple questions about the lesson:

1. Tell me one thing you learned in today's lesson.
2. Tell me one thing that you may be confused about.
3. Tell me one thing that you would like to know more about.

Responses to these questions let teachers know how effective their instructional techniques were in helping students achieve learning objectives. The responses also assist teachers in identifying areas that require follow-up or reteaching either to individual students or to the entire class.

■ *Scenario Revisited*

Laura Kane tried to talk with Kim as he was completing the student interest questionnaire. As before, Kim was reluctant to let anyone see what he was writing—or *not* writing! Laura persevered, however, and Kim mumbled that he sometimes had trouble knowing how to answer questions at the end of chapters in textbooks. After some more attempts to clarify what was difficult for Kim, she learned that he did not find the questions worth answering. Laura told Kim she thought she knew what he meant, because when she had been a middle-school student she too thought sometimes the textbook questions weren't very interesting, and that made it hard to make the effort to do a good job answering them. Kim looked surprised to hear this; Laura surmised that perhaps Kim too thought some of the work he had to do in school wasn't very interesting, and that somehow he must not be a good student to think that. Kim and Laura talked some more, and Laura proposed that perhaps she could help Kim learn an easier strategy for tackling tasks, like answering textbook questions. Laura hoped that perhaps she had opened a door to getting to know Kim better and finding a way to draw him into the classroom community.

FIGURE 6.6
Expanded Graphic
Organizer

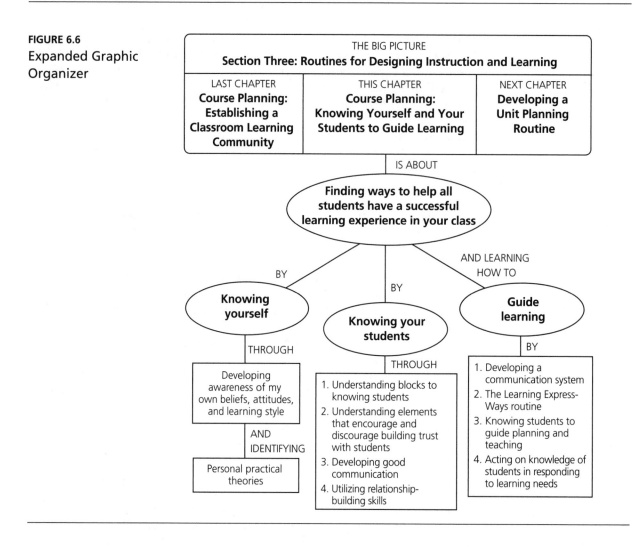

SUMMARY

To meet the challenge of academic diversity, teachers must develop course, unit, and lesson planning, and teaching routines and practices that respond to the greatest range of diversity. Knowing yourself and your students can help in this work. Teaching practices that respond only to a few types of diversity are insufficient and must be expanded to be as inclusive as possible of all the differences among individuals in a learning community.

In this chapter we have talked about the importance of knowing yourself in order to better understand the beliefs and attitudes you bring to the classroom. These beliefs and attitudes, if not examined, may keep you from adequately understanding why learning is difficult for some of your students or what situations or conditions may be preventing students from learning. We all tend to teach as we were taught, believing perhaps that everyone learns the way we do. In our diverse society today, those beliefs simply are not relevant or useful, if they ever were.

In addition to knowing ourselves, we also need to know and understand our students in order to teach them effectively. This requires establishing and maintaining effective ways to communicate with students to monitor their learning. Making sure that you have regular and useful ways to monitor progress and attend to problems that get in the way of individual student learning will require that early in the year

you plan for an effective and useful communication system.

MAKING CONNECTIONS:
Implementing a Communication System

1. *Here are the big ideas to get you started:*

- Establishing a relationship with students that enhances their opportunities to learn in your course may require that you first examine your own beliefs and attitudes about learning. If you find that you think everyone learns the same way you do, you may have to make some adjustments in your thinking and planning.

- Establishing positive relationships with students and getting to know them well can give you insights in ways to make learning both more accessible and meaningful for them. Part of establishing positive relationships with students is finding a way to maintain dialogue with them through some kind of communication system throughout the school year. A communication system allows you to monitor student progress as well as learn about developments or problems that get in the way of student learning.

2. *What you need:*

- Make a list of the options suggested in this chapter for establishing a communication system. Add to the list any options you may have encountered elsewhere or any variations that have occurred to you as you read this chapter.

- Think about the information you would want to have in order to teach your students most effectively. Make a list of what this information might be.

- Consider what features a communication system would have to have for you to use it reliably (e.g., How often could you respond to comments of students? Would you respond to students in writing? Would you prefer to respond in brief one-on-one conferences? Do you find the Learning Express-Ways folder idea attractive because you were already thinking about using folders

for students to turn in their assignments? Is it unrealistic to anticipate you will manage to respond to student comments more than once during a unit?) Make some notes about what features of a communication system are most realistic for you to manage.

3. *Try this:*

- Look at your list of possible options for establishing a communication system. Then look at your notes about what is personally doable for you in a communication system. Cross off items on the list of system options that you think you are unlikely to follow through on.

- Next, look at the list of information about students you constructed. Consider how useful each item on the list would be in the context of the content you have to teach. Make a star or check mark next to the most useful information.

- Try to select one or two communication system possibilities that are doable for you but that also provide the kind of information about students you think you will need to teach them effectively.

- Describe in one page what communication system you would like to establish in your classroom, what students will do in using it, and how often the system will be used. Plan how you will establish a habit or routine of checking in with students about how their learning is progressing and, most importantly, how you will take that information to reevaluate instruction and the learning community. For example, you might anticipate, from the beginning of the year, that after each unit, you will examine what worked and what didn't work instructionally and be prepared to make some changes.

4. *Evaluate your work:*

- Reexamine the communication system you have just described. Does it in fact incorporate what you think you need to know about students to teach them your content effectively? Does it incorporate what is doable for you personally? Have you made sufficiently detailed plans so that when you begin school in September, you have a plan you can pick up and use?

5. *Next steps:*
- Exchange plans with a peer or colleague. Reevaluate what is workable and what is doable in each other's plans. Reconsider what kind of information about students is helpful in the context of the content you have to teach.

WEB SITES

http://communityhigh.org The Web page for Community High School, Ann Arbor, Michigan, describing school programs and principles which are based on cooperation and providing a supportive learning environment.

http://staff.gc.maricopa.edu/~mdinchak/web learn/index.htm Using the World Wide Web to Create a Learner Centered Classroom. Describes the philosophy of the learner-centered college being implemented in The Maricopa Community College District.

www.mcrel.org/standards-benchmarks McREL: Compendium of Standards and Benchmarks. A compilation of content standards for K–12 curriculum in both searchable and browsable formats.

www.air.org/cecp/safetynet.htm This Web site has links to projects that offer research-based strategies to educate students with emotional/behavioral problems by maximizing resources already present in communities. Projects briefly described in the executive summary, entitled "Strengthening the Safety Net," are described in their entirety at this Web site.

www.ku-crl.org This is the Web site for the Center for Research on Learning at the University of Kansas where there is more information about the *Learning Express-Ways Communication Routine.*

SUGGESTED READINGS

Bridging the generation gap between adolescents and teachers requires attention to the culture and mind-set of young adults. The resources listed here can help teachers see things from the perspective of adolescents.

Breeden, T., & Mosley, J. (1992). *The cooperative learning companion.* Nashville, TN: Incentive Publications. This book provides a wealth of resources for organizing groups, creating rules and procedures for

cooperative learning, and reflection on the success and areas where additional structure, direction, or assistance is needed.

Sapon-Shevin, M. (1999). *Because we can change the world: A practical guide to building cooperative, inclusive classroom communities.* Boston: Allyn and Bacon. Excellent book for teachers with ideas for using literature, games, and class activities to create classroom connections with minimal intrusion on instruction time.

REFERENCES

Ammer, J. J. (1998, Oct.). *Meeting the challenge: Providing outcome-based instruction for students with learning disabilities in an inclusive era.* Workshop presented at the Annual California Federation of the Council for Exceptional Children Conference, San Francisco, CA.

Ammer, J. J., & Lawson, E. (1997, Feb.). *Integrated technological approach using scenarios in a bi-coastal teacher training experience.* Paper presented at the joint Technology and Media and California State Federation Conference of the Council for Exceptional Children, "Special Education Technology for the Next Century," San Jose, CA.

Bloom, L. A., Perlmutter, J., & Burrell, L. (1999). The general educator: Applying constructivism to inclusive classrooms. *Intervention in School and Clinic, 34,* 132–136.

Bullough, R. V., & Gitlin, A. (1995). *Becoming a student of teaching—Methodologies for exploring self and school context.* New York: Garland Publishing.

Carpenter C. D., Bloom, L. A., & Boat, M. B. (1999). Guidelines for special educators: Achieving socially valid outcomes. *Intervention in School and Clinic, 34,* 143–149.

Carroll, P. S., & Taylor, A. (1998, Sept.). Understanding the culture of a classroom. *Middle School Journal,* 9–17.

Clark, C. M., & Yinger, R. J. (1987). Teacher planning. In D. C. Berliner and B. Rosenshine (Eds.), *Talk to teachers* (pp. 342–365). New York: Random House.

Cook. J. (1992). Negotiating the curriculum: Programming for learning. In Boomer, G., Lester, N., Onore, C., & Cook, J. (Eds.), *Negotiating the curriculum: Educating for the 21st century.* London: Falmer Press.

Cornett, J. W. (1990). Teacher thinking about curriculum and instruction: A case study of a secondary social studies teacher. *Theory and Research in Social Education, 18* (3), 248–273.

Cornett, J. W., Chase, K. S., Miller, P., Schrock, D., Bennett, B. J., Goins, A., & Hammond, C. (1992). Insights from the analysis of our own theorizing: The viewpoints of seven teachers. In E. W. Ross, J. W. Cornett, and G. McCutcheon (Eds.), *Teacher personal theorizing: Connecting curriculum practice, theory, and research* (pp. 137–157). Albany: State University of New York Press.

Delpit, L. (1995). *Other people's children: Cultural conflict in the classroom.* New York: The New Press.

Featherstone, D., Munby, H., & Russell, T. (1997). *Finding a voice while learning to teach.* London: Falmer Press.

Fosnot, C. T. (Ed.). (1996). *Constructivism: Theory, perspectives, and practice.* New York: Teachers College Press.

Garcia, E. (1999). *Student cultural diversity: Understanding and meeting the challenge* (2nd ed.). Boston: Houghton Mifflin.

Grant, C. A. (1991). Culture and teaching: What do teachers need to know? In M. M. Kennedy (Ed.), *Teaching academic subjects to diverse learners* (pp. 237–256). New York: Teachers College Press.

Kissam, B., & Lenz, B. K. (Eds.). (1994). *Pedagogies for diversity in secondary schools: A preservice curriculum.* Lawrence, KS: University of Kansas.

Ladson-Billings, G. (1994). *The dreamkeepers: Successful teachers of African-American children.* San Francisco: Jossey-Bass.

Lang, D. C., Quick, A. F., & Johnson, J. A. (1981). *A partnership for the supervision of student teachers.* DeKalb, IL: Creative Educational Materials.

Lenz, B. K., Adams, G., & Fisher, J. (1998). *Learning express-ways folders.* Lawrence, KS: Edge Enterprises, Inc.

Lenz, B. K., Graner, P., & Adams, G. (in press). *The Learning Express-Ways Communication System: Building academic relationships between students and teachers.* Lawrence, KS: The Strategic Learning Center & The University of Kansas Center for Research on Learning.

McDiarmid, G. W. (1991). What teachers need to know about cultural diversity: Restoring subject matter to the picture. In M. M. Kennedy (Ed.), *Teaching academic subjects to diverse learners* (pp. 257–269). New York: Teachers College Press.

Ogbu, J. U. (1992). Understanding cultural diversity and learning. *Educational Researcher,* 5–14.

Platt, J., & Olson, J. (1997). *Teaching adolescents with mild disabilities.* Pacific Grove, CA: Brooks/Cole.

Thornburg, D. D. (1997). *Learn and live.* Nicasio, CA: The George Lucas Educational Foundation.

Vernon, S., Walther-Thomas, C., Schumaker, J. B., Deshler, D. D., & Hazel, J. S. (1999). A program for families of children and youth with learning disabilities. In M. J. Fine & R. L. Simpson (Eds.) *Collaboration with parents and families of children and youth with exceptionalities.* Austin, TX: Pro-Ed.

Developing a Unit Planning Routine

<blockquote>Juliana Taymans
Sharon Lynch</blockquote>

Critical Self-Test Questions

- When planning and teaching instructional units, what principles can you follow that will enhance the success of students with diverse learning profiles?
- What is the Unit Organizer, and how does it incorporate research-based practices?
- How can you use the Unit Organizer as a planning and teaching tool?
- What rewards and challenges can you expect when using the Unit Organizer?

*"Cheshire-Puss," she
began rather timidly. . . .
"Would you tell me, please,
which way I ought to go
from here?"
"That depends a good
deal on where you want
to get to," said the Cat.
"I don't much care where—"
said Alice.
"Then it doesn't matter
which way you go,"
said the Cat.
"—so long as I get some-
where," Alice added
as an explanation.
"Oh, you're sure to do that,"
said the Cat, "if you only
walk long enough."
—Alice's Adventures in
Wonderland, Lewis G. Carroll
(pp. 71–72)*

The goal of this chapter is to provide concepts and strategies for unit planning. A unit is a planned learning experience of moderate length (i.e., taking place over a series of days or weeks) that clearly identifies concepts and skills students will be learning. Units incorporate multiple learning objectives and usually include a summative assessment. Earlier chapters have addressed national standards and state-level frameworks that identify what students should be learning within content areas (e.g., math and science) and across grade levels, and in this chapter we acknowledge that unit planning and teaching must be aligned to standards that represent a field's wisdom of what students should know and be able to do. Moreover, we present research about teacher thinking during planning, describing the challenges of planning, as well as direction in planning for students with diverse learning profiles. The final section of this chapter introduces the Unit Organizer, which is a unit planning and teaching tool that incorporates what research tells us is effective for teaching students with a wide range of achievement levels.

CURRENT EDUCATION REFORMS: STANDARDS

As we have noted in earlier chapters, the curriculum in schools today is strongly affected by content and performance standards. Content standards

FIGURE 7.1

Graphic Organizer

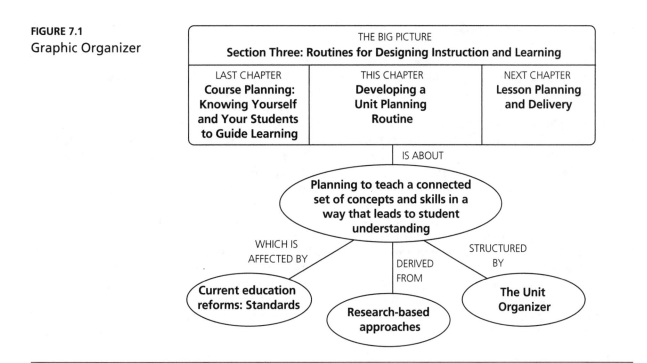

guide what you teach, and performance standards determine how students demonstrate competence. These standards can be important guidelines in choosing concepts and skills that lead students to higher-order thinking and meaningful learning. Yet, these guides must be translated into courses and units of instruction, accessible to the wide spectrum of students attending American schools. As educational systems strive to improve achievement for all students, we must not lose sight of the big picture: A part of healthy adolescent development is a growing self-understanding. One of the building blocks in this process is an increased understanding of and positive connections to an expanding worldview (Keating, 1990). To teach so that *all* students truly grow in their understanding of the world is an exciting and challenging endeavor. This chapter provides some tools to help you do this.

To teach so that students with diverse learning and sociocultural profiles understand the content they are studying demands careful "big picture" planning. To plan and teach for student understanding means that students gain more than textbook knowledge of big concepts like democracy or ecology. True understanding is demonstrated when students use the content they have learned to solve problems, develop a product or performance, and make connections between what they are learning and the world at large. When teachers focus on isolated facts in textbooks they limit the number of students who are going to be successful. Textbook-based learning is difficult for many learners whose experiences, learning styles, reading levels, and motivations are inconsistent with the condensed and didactic form of information presentation (Armbruster & Anderson, 1988). As has been noted in earlier chapters, when teachers use standards to guide their determination of what is most important for students to know and understand, they are on the road to effective planning. This can result in focused learning experiences that help students learn about important concepts and their relationships within and across disciplines and the world at large.

■ *Scenario*

Jerry Uribe is a first-year social studies teacher. He has three ninth-grade American history classes and has observed that many students do not read the textbook assignments he gives. One of the school's special education teachers met with Jerry at the beginning of the school year to inform him that four students with learning disabilities were enrolled in one of his course sections. These students have been successful in previous social studies classes in middle school but read below grade level. Jerry has noticed that many of his students tend to give up easily when given assignments that require writing more than one or two paragraphs. Jerry is having difficulty following the curriculum guide, because it is structured in a very different format from the assigned textbook.

Jerry begins every unit by arranging students in cooperative groups and asking oral questions to ascertain students' prior knowledge. As he begins a unit on World War II, for example, Jerry asks students, "What happened on December 7, 1941?" The answer Jerry receives, to his dismay, is, "Japan attacked the United States because we had dropped a bomb on Hiroshima, which started the Vietnam War."

Jerry feels frustrated and confused about how to help his students learn American history. He reports, "I am struggling with the big picture of what I need to teach. Initially, I made long-term plans, but they seemed unrealistic after the first day. Now I plan day to day. At best, I am two days ahead. I am beginning to realize how much repetition is necessary for many of my students to understand the most basic information."

By the end of this chapter, you will be able to offer Jerry Uribe, a teacher you will meet in the chapter classroom scenario, some informed guidance on how he can more successfully teach important American history concepts to his students.

FOUNDATIONS AND PRINCIPLES

Unit planning should provide a framework that enables all students to be successful in learning important concepts and skills. Since our knowledge base keeps increasing while instructional time does not, it is crucial to identify the most important content to be taught and learned as a first step in helping assure student success. Concept mapping and organizing learning around questions helps make explicit what is important for students to learn. Concept mapping, which is a visual representation of relationships between ideas, can be a useful planning and teaching strategy. Similarly, organizing learning around questions helps teachers think deeply about content as they plan, looking at relationships, and distilling the most important information that students should learn.

Planning for Student Understanding

In the curriculum planning model of Wiggins and McTighe (1998) described in Chapter 3, teachers are invited to be designers of learning. Using this design analogy, we can think about architects or interior decorators who begin their work with a concept of what is to be done. These professionals work from specifications to produce an end result that is functional yet adheres to central architecture or interior design principles. For unit planning the design process can be divided into three phases:

1. *What students should know, understand, and be able to do.* In teaching, the first design phase asks you to think in terms of the desired results of instruction. A self-question for a teacher might be: What should students know, understand, and be able to do? This question asks you to think about the content to be addressed and to determine the most important "enduring understandings" and processes that students should take with them from a particular unit of instruction. For instance, the *Benchmarks for Science Literacy,* consensus documents developed by hundreds of respected scientists and educators, provide a good sense of what these enduring ideas may be (American Association for the Advancement of Science, 1993). Thus, teachers start planning by thinking of conceptual learning rather than activities or information. Enduring understandings or concepts should represent knowledge that all students should be expected to learn. To do this, a teacher must think beyond discrete facts or skills to focus on larger ideas, concepts, principles, and processes. A major tool in doing this is concept mapping, which is discussed in the next section.

2. *What evidence will I collect?* The second planning phase asks you to determine the evidence you will collect to determine whether students have increased their understanding of the concept(s) taught. A teacher's self-question could be: What evidence will I collect that will document that the desired learning has been achieved? Thinking about assessment as a *process* of monitoring students' understanding of key concepts helps you accomplish some important design tasks, such as integrating assessment with instruction and focusing classroom activities and assignments on building conceptual understanding. While the designer's task in phase one is to identify what is important to know and understand, the task in phase two is to design assessments that allow you to monitor the *degree* of student understanding. This is especially important for students with learning challenges. Some students will develop more sophisticated understandings than others, but the evidence should allow a teacher to identify individual student growth. A teacher would expect all students to progress in their understanding of the content and how the content connects with the world at large, but not necessarily to the same degree. When you are teaching for understanding, you must realize that it is not a dichotomous "got it" or not; rather it is a query as to how well a student understands a key concept. It only makes sense that instructional goals and assessments will allow you to monitor student growth and respect the range of starting points for students beginning a unit of instruction. Any group of students will begin a unit with a range of prior experiences with the content. Some students have extensive knowledge that should be expanded and deepened, while others have little or no prior knowledge.

Maintaining high standards means moving all students along to a deeper, more elaborated understanding of key concepts. Although grading is a reality not to be denied, thinking about collecting evidence rather than focusing on grading or assigning points makes it easier to develop flexible ways for students to show what they know and provides the teacher with insights about how well instruction is guiding students in this process. Such flexibility can allow for accommodations needed by students with disabilities, or students who are English language learners. Unit assessments can range from informal to formal. For example, Jerry Uribe began his unit with an informal assessment of student knowledge. More formal checks for understanding, such as quizzes and tests, help monitor students' knowledge base, while curriculum-based projects and problem-solving tasks allow students to show what they know by developing a project, demonstration, or performance.

3. *What "enabling knowledge" and skills are needed?* The third and final stage in the planning process is to develop learning experiences. A teacher's self-question could be: What enabling knowledge and skills are needed to perform effectively and achieve results? Thus, information and skills are linked to helping students learn important ideas and processes. Now that the big picture has been addressed and ways of assessing student understanding have been identified, instructional methods can be matched to them. If a teacher has determined flexible types of assessment evidence that students can produce to demonstrate understanding, this naturally leads to the possibility of more flexible ways of learning. A teacher's job is to make important information meaningful and provocative, and to plan instruction so that students have the time, support, and multiple experiences to learn.

Focus and Reflect

- In the opening scenario, Jerry Uribe commented that he is just beginning to understand how much repetition his students need for new learning to occur. His challenge is to develop activities that give his students the time and practice to build a knowledge base that supports the conceptual learning he wants to target.
- What types of learning activities could Jerry use that would be effective for his reluctant readers and writers?

▪ Scenario Revisited

THE PROBLEM WITH NOT HAVING AN ORGANIZING CONCEPT

Jerry Uribe needed an organizing concept for his unit on World War II. If he had focused on a larger idea, such as *the conflict of ideologies, the drive for world domination,* or perhaps *global conflict,* his students might better understand the importance of World War II in history. Such a unifying idea could help plan the big picture of the unit rather than planning day by day. Jerry seems to be searching for motivating ways to help his students amend their misconceptions. What successes are Jerry and his students going to have if the focus of instruction is only on getting the facts straight? If Jerry uses a big idea like global conflict, his students may have a framework to help organize the information they need to learn and better understand its meaning.

Jerry's opening question was a good probe for background knowledge and certainly revealed students' misconceptions. Rather than feeling discouraged at the answer he received, Jerry could probe further to stimulate students' prior knowledge. Students were able to connect the date of December 7, 1941, to an event of war. How have they learned about that date? What do they know about Hiroshima? And about Vietnam? How far away is Hiroshima from Vietnam? A lively question-answer discussion would help stimulate students' prior learning, identify other common misconceptions, and set the stage for exploring the Japanese-American conflict.

The Dimensions of Unit Planning: Teacher Thinking

We know that lesson and unit planning can feel like a daunting task for prospective and first-year teachers (Kagan, 1992; Reynolds, 1992). Many beginning teachers find classroom management challenging and may dilute instructional demands or try to win students with "fun activities" as a way of controlling student behavior. Experienced teachers, on the other hand, tend to plan in a short-hand form because much of their planning has become automatic, and they may not be explicit about procedures and habits (Clark & Lampert, 1986). In this chapter we describe a well-structured, research-based unit planning and teaching routine that helps teachers develop important reflective and procedural knowledge that can lead to effective teaching. This planning tool was developed with experienced secondary-level teachers, many of whom found it to be an effective means of planning to meet the needs of diverse groups of students (Joint Committee on Teacher Planning for Students with Disabilities, 1995); the tool has also been used successfully by prospective teachers (Taymans & Lynch, 1996).

When teachers plan, they tend to simplify the way they think about their students. This has been characterized as planning for a "meta-student," which is a composite of past experiences with students who achieve reasonably well (Joint Committee on Teacher Planning for Students with Disabilities, 1995). While this way of thinking greatly reduces the burden of considering individual characteristics of students, it eliminates consideration of students who may have difficulty with content and performance expectations. This simplified thinking does not help teachers consider students who may lack some of the skills or prior learning that may be prerequisites to a unit of study. Thus, teachers plan in a way that makes it acceptable that some students with learning challenges will just have to "get what they can" and live with D and F grades (Lenz & Bulgren, 1994). In addition, planning in terms of what works for a "B student" ignores how to significantly engage students who are already very familiar with what will be taught.

Planning for Student Diversity

Many planning and teaching approaches proven to have positive effects for students with learning challenges are also effective for average and high-achieving students (Bulgren & Lenz, 1996; McGregor & Vogelsberg, 1998; Vaughn, 1999). As noted by Vaughn, a well-known researcher in the field of learning disabilities, we do not have to worry about the Robin Hood effect, robbing from the high achievers to give lower-achieving students the experiences they need for success in secondary content classes. That is, good instruction adheres to certain principles that are effective for students across the board.

Up-Front Planning First, planning that takes student diversity into account should be "up front." This planning, which can help identify content and instructional procedures of most benefit to the widest range of learners, is most effectively and efficiently done at the course and unit level of instruction. General education teachers may have opportunities to do some of this planning with gifted and talented resource personnel, teachers of English language learners, speech and language teachers, or special education teachers, if these support personnel have co-planning as part of their responsibilities.

Shared, Explicit Expectations Second, planning that leads to a shared student-teacher understanding and acceptance of clear and attainable goals enhances student performance (Arends, 1991). This means that teachers must be crystal clear about the goals and expected outcomes of a unit of instruction and find meaningful ways to share these expectations with students. Some students can "read" their teachers and, because of their drive, motivation, and active detective work, can successfully fulfill all the expectations. However, many students are not natural detectives; these students need clear and explicit guidelines for what is important and what is expected. Organized, measured, and sequenced presentations of content instruction and guidance on how to perform critical learning and assessment tasks is a must for many students. This is especially true for students who do not receive homework help from adults or who face language and learning challenges. For example, research by Lenz, Alley, and Schumaker (1987) provides evidence that students can benefit from this explicit sharing of expectations and procedures but that it may be necessary to directly teach them how to use the structures teachers share. In this research study, teachers were taught how to deliver an advance organizer that indicated explicitly to students what was important in a lesson. Although all students benefited from this precise introduction, some students needed additional supportive instruction in order to use the information to improve their learning.

Other students will need accommodations because of language and literacy challenges. We cannot assume that students with limited literacy skills also have limited intellectual skills; instead, our charge is to continue to develop students' thinking skills while accommodating their reading and/or writing achievement levels (Ellis, 1998). A clearly focused unit targeted at important ideas can be very accessible to students with literacy needs if the teacher employs cooperative group structures and a variety of experiences aimed at accomplishing unit outcomes.

Integrated Curriculum Third, an integrated curriculum promotes student learning (Pugach & Warger, 1996). We can trace this contention back to John Dewey's (1916) work and find much support for it today (Collins, Brown, & Newman, 1989; Lave, 1988; Pugach & Warger, 1996; Sizer, 1996). An integrated curriculum is structured in a way that helps students connect concepts or skills across disciplines. **Content integration** uses a conceptual focus to create an interdisciplinary or real-life perspective around a common theme, issue, or problem of study. **Process integration** allows students to apply common skills or thinking processes (such as the writing process or using the scientific method to gather data) across subjects (Erikson, 1998).

Thematic instruction across subjects (i.e., math, science, social studies, and English) can emphasize the interrelatedness of knowledge and help students generalize information, which can be critically important for students with learning challenges (Mastropieri & Scruggs, 1996). Thematic units can be taught in the context of contemporary local or global issues, situating school learning in real world situations (Champagne, Newell, &

Goodnough, 1996). For example, using content standards from science, social studies and math, an interdisciplinary team of teachers could develop a thematic unit called The Rainforest—Examining Patterns of Change. In science, students study the contribution of rain forests to the oxygen cycle. In math, they compute and graph the number of acres of rain forests demolished per year to predict oxygen depletion. In social studies, students explore the economic factors contributing to transforming rainforest acreage into farm land, and in English they write a persuasive essay on man's responsibility to the environment. Thematic units across subjects help students apply information, practice new vocabulary and skills, and gain a more indepth understanding of key concepts. Since many students benefit from practice and repetition (Dempster, 1991; Vaughn, 1999), these varied and multiple experiences help students learn new concepts and their application without boring, repetitive exercises.

In addition, curriculum organized around real-world issues holds a number of advantages (Lynch & Harnish, 1998). Specifically, motivation can be increased as students see the relevance of school learning, and the abstract becomes concrete and more personally meaningful (Brophy, 1987; Steinberg, 1997). Real-world applications assist students in transferring their knowledge and skills to out-of-school contexts. Additionally, real-world applications can be centered around solving problems or dilemmas. A problem-solving approach to learning meshes well with cooperative learning, which has a strong research base supporting its effectiveness in helping students with diverse skills and backgrounds work and learn from each other (Putnam, 1998). This format invites students to learn concepts and facts as they engage in higher-order thinking to solve a problem, and it can open the curriculum to meaningful participation by all students.

▪ Scenario Revisited

Jerry decided to rethink his planning for this unit. He looked again at the curriculum guide having to do with World War II. What were the big ideas here? He noted that students would be expected to understand why, how, and when the United States entered World War II.

Jerry recalled that when he had covered World War I in this class, many students never really mastered the geographical information needed to understand what countries were at war and what territory was being contested. Perhaps Jerry should take a more geographical tack now. That would tie in with a "big idea" of *global conflict*—that World War II was the last global conflict. Knowledge of geography would help students clarify that there was a war in Europe and a war in the Pacific. There was a time when Jerry would have assumed students knew this basic information, but the confusion in Friday's class had made it clear that they did not.

There would be a lot of map work, including identifying the countries that were the principal powers in the conflict. But it might also be interesting for students to find out what role other, smaller countries had played in the war. This would be a great opportunity for students to pursue any connections or interests they might have in particular parts of the world. Since some students came from families that had recently immigrated to this country, perhaps this would be an opportunity for them to bring their native history and culture into the U.S. history course.

Jerry was excited about using the "big idea" of global conflict and a focus on geography to provide a structure for learning about World War II.

KNOWING AND DOING

The Unit Organizer

The Unit Organizer is a planning and teaching tool that helps teachers do concept-based planning. The Unit Organizer incorporates key planning and teaching approaches that can help teachers develop units to effectively reach students with diverse learning strengths and needs. The Unit Organizer:

- helps contextualize the unit by relating unit content to previous and future units and to bigger course ideas.
- helps students understand the unit's main ideas through a map that paraphrases the "big idea" of the unit and displays the structure and relationships of key unit concepts.
- is a tool that allows teachers to plan by determining essential questions that can guide student learning. The Unit Organizer also allows students to generate questions to help them focus on and identify the types of thinking they will need to use to answer questions.
- provides a structure for students to track assignments.

Making Connections   New learning does not occur in a vacuum. Cognitive theorists show that a student's existing knowledge base and immediate prior learning is the foundation for future learning and that teacher planning should take this into consideration (Borko & Putnam, 1998). Knowledge is more accessible and useful to students when they are able to make clear connections between prior learning and current instruction. Some students make these connections automatically; others, who are less cognitively active, may need teachers to identify these connections for them. While new learning must connect with what students already know, it should also be presented in a way that makes it meaningful to students within the context of the course of study. One very concrete way to do this is to clearly show how units of instruction are connected to each other and to a course as a whole (Lenz et al., 1998).

Key Concepts and Concept Mapping   All fields of study share one common characteristic: There is much more that can be learned than is possible to accomplish in one course. All disciplines have a knowledge structure of larger, more complex ideas that can be explained through less complex, more specific ideas. This structure can be represented as a concept map (White & Gunstone, 1992), which is a visual representation of relationships between ideas (see Figure 7.2).

Concept mapping is a metacognitive tool that can significantly change the way a teacher plans. By mapping a course or unit, a teacher must determine the most central concepts students should learn. Concept mapping can also help teachers think about how their discipline connects to other content areas and real-world issues and events. This forces thinking about concepts, principles, and processes rather than activities, discrete facts, or skills (Wandersee, 1990).

Concept maps are organized into a hierarchy of "nodes" that are usually enclosed in a shape such as a circle, an ellipse, or a square, as displayed in Figure 7.2. The nodes are connected by lines that are labeled to identify clearly the relationships between the concepts. The linked nodes form propositional networks, which can be read as a series of sentences showing relation-

FIGURE 7.2 A Sample Concept Map

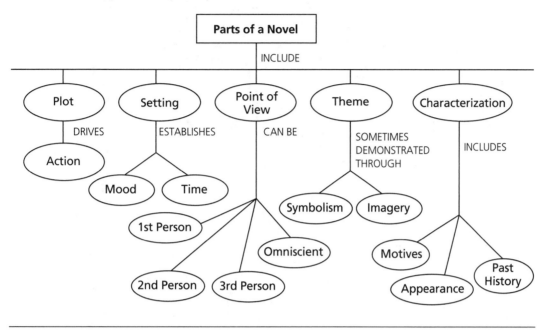

ships. Concept mapping makes the curriculum "conceptually transparent" (Novak, 1990) to the teacher who can then share this visual representation of course content with students. For students, a concept map can be the basis for beginning to make meaning out of abstract concepts by examining relationships and by connecting new concepts with what is previously known.

HOW TO CONSTRUCT A CONCEPT MAP. Concept mapping can be accomplished through a six-step procedure (Zimmaro & Cawley, 1998).

1. Identify the idea or ideas you want to map. In Figure 7.2 the key idea being mapped is the parts of a novel.
2. Arrange concepts in a pattern that best represents the information. In Figure 7.2, a three-level hierarchical structure is used. The main concept, Parts of a Novel, is the first level. The second level names the five parts of a novel, while the third level describes and defines each part.
3. Use a shape such as a rectangle, a circle, an oval, or a triangle to enclose each term or concept. In Figure 7.2 a rectangle encloses the key concept with supporting ideas displayed in ovals.
4. Use straight lines to link related terms. Each line should link only two concepts.
5. Label each line to identify the relationship between the two connected ideas. For example, in Figure 7.2, the line label between plot and action is "drives." This allows you to read the relationship: Plot drives action. In another example of a concept map presented in Figure 7.3, the line label between life and organisms is "composed of." This can be read as: "Life is composed of organisms."
6. Rework the map until it depicts the clearest and most accurate picture of the relationships between key ideas. For example, Figure 7.3 shows the first attempt at mapping the key ideas for a life science course. Figure 7.4 shows the fourth and final reworking of the map.

FIGURE 7.3 First Map Constructed

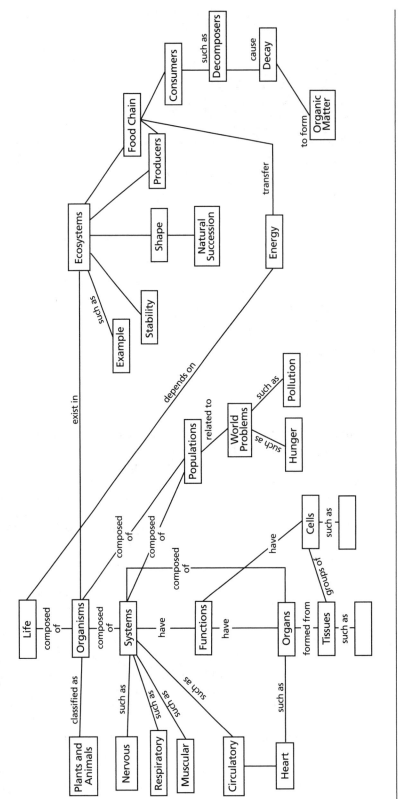

Source: From "Concept Maps as a Heuristic for Science Curriculum Development: Toward Improvement in Process and Product," by M. L. Starr and J. S. Krajcik, 1990, *Journal of Research in Science Teaching, 27,* p. 992. Copyright 1990 by Wiley-Liss, Inc., a subsidiary of John Wiley & Sons. Reprinted with permission.

FIGURE 7.4 Fourth Map Constructed

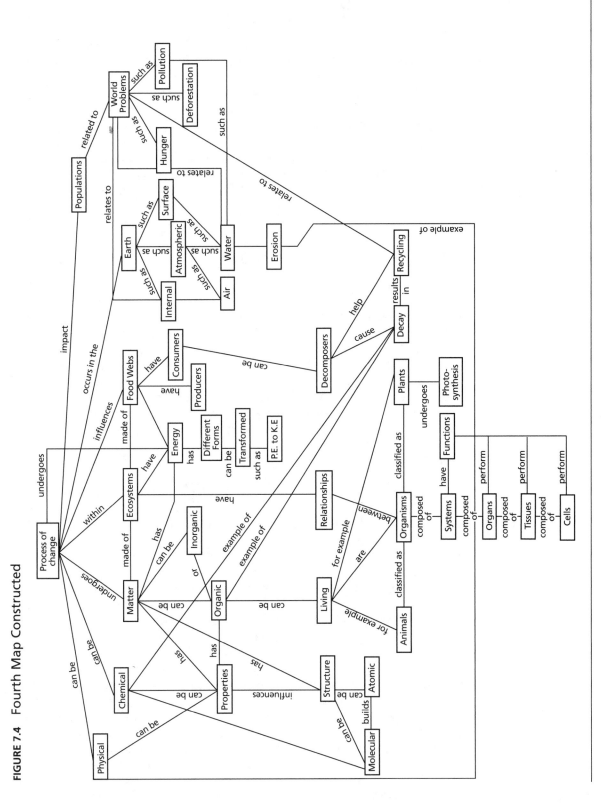

Source: From "Concept Maps as a Heuristic for Science Curriculum Development: Toward Improvement in Process and Product," by M. L. Starr and J. S. Krajcik, 1990, *Journal of Research in Science Teaching, 27,* p. 995. Copyright 1990 by Wiley-Liss, Inc., a subsidiary of John Wiley & Sons. Reprinted with permission.

Let's look at an example of a group of teachers using concept mapping to plan a course. This example is a synopsis of research by Starr and Krajcik (1990), who worked with a group of teachers to plan a life sciences course. The teachers collaborated to conceptually map their curriculum over four planning sessions. Initially, they identified a list of 23 key concepts. From this list they developed an initial concept map for the course. They decided that the concept, *life,* was the overall dominate or superordinate concept supported by 29 nodes. Over the next three planning sessions the super-ordinate concept changed from *life* to *ecosystems* to *change* to the *process of change,* showing that the teachers began to think in more global terms, connecting the life science content to a larger context. With each planning session, the maps grew in complexity, with additional nodes and links adding a more sophisticated view of the course content. Whereas the initial concept list only contained life science concepts, the final map linked life science concepts to earth science and current world problems (hunger, deforestation, pollution).

The benefits of this process for curriculum planning were obvious to both the teachers and the researchers. First, the process of revising the maps forced the teachers to discuss the importance of the concepts they had identified and the connections between them. This increased their knowledge of their own thinking, as well as their understanding of how others thought and how these basic life science concepts could be structured and related. Second, the importance of the revision process was evident. The teachers' first map was much less focused and elaborate than the final version. A course based on this first map would have targeted more superficial understandings than one based on the final map. Third, the map was a good record of their planning work. If a member of the team was absent, the map served as a concise record of the planning work done. Finally, the process laid a solid foundation for anticipating student learning. With the content clearly structured, this group of teachers were now ready to think about how students could engage with these concepts in a meaningful way.

Concept mapping can also be used as an instructional and assessment tool. Instructionally, concept mapping can enhance student learning by providing an organizational strategy that helps students assimilate information into long-term memory. Concept mapping can also serve as a metacognitive strategy that helps learners become more aware of their own thinking. Czerniak and Haney (1998) cite a number of research studies that provide evidence that student-constructed concept maps result in improved student achievement.

Concept mapping can also be used to assess students. Let's look at how this can be done by examining some classroom-based research. Rice, Ryan, and Samson (1998) report using concept mapping first as part of instructional activities and then as an assessment tool in seventh-grade life science. For each unit the teacher/researcher developed his own expert map of the key unit concepts and their relationships as a guide for instruction and assessment (much as the teachers did in the Starr and Krajcik study in Figures 7.3 and 7.4). As a part of classroom instruction, students were taught to make concept maps in a progressive manner over a series of units. In addition, the teacher/researcher incorporated mapping into ongoing demonstrations, lectures, discussions, and reviews. Once the teacher/researcher had thoroughly taught students how to use concept mapping, he phased out the explicit use of concept maps during instruction but continued to stress concepts and their relationships in classroom presentations and activities.

Concept mapping was introduced into the assessment process first as an extra credit option on a unit test. Once concept mapping had been phased out as a classroom activity, it was included as a part of unit tests, with students developing their own individual maps without the benefit of a class map. Tests were constructed so that some multiple-choice questions also addressed relationships that could be displayed in the concept map question. The teacher/researcher discovered some interesting results. First, students performed similarly on concept mapping and multiple-choice items designed to measure similar content. This is an important finding, because it opens the possibility that concept mapping can be used to assess student knowledge. This may be a more flexible and creative way for students to show what they know and understand and lessen the burden of memorizing facts for multiple-choice-type tests. Second, there was no significant evidence of gender and ethnic differences in students' concept map scores. Third, the mapping question allowed the teacher/researcher to easily recognize when a large percentage of students had failed to grasp a relationship, which was the case on one of his tests. This in turn allowed him to reflect on how instruction could be improved; in other words, he was able to see the connection between students' misconceptions and class activities that were ineffective for developing conceptual relationships.

Concept mapping is a tool that both teachers and students can use to identify important concepts and to illustrate hierarchical relationships. The graphic representation of declarative knowledge can reduce the language demands of conceptual learning, directly benefiting students with learning disabilities and English language learners. It can also be helpful to students who learn well visually.

Focus and Reflect

- Examine current textbooks for middle- and high-school students to find concept maps and chapter maps. How might these maps help students identify what is important to learn?
- Identify a familiar concept from your field of study that you might teach (e.g., parts of a novel, pollution, attributes of a polygon, immigration). After reviewing relevant reference materials, develop a concept map that clearly identifies the salient attributes of the concept. Be sure to connect nodes with line labels.

Identifying Unit Questions: Guiding Learning Through Questioning

"Making meaning starts not with answers but with questions" (Hunkins, 1995, p. 7). For the purposes of teacher planning, questions can frame the most important and meaningful outcomes of a unit.

QUESTIONS ARE A WAY TO ORGANIZE AND FOCUS A UNIT. Developing unit questions can help a teacher shrink the amount of information in a unit by focusing on the essential information students will need in order to respond to unit questions. In contrast to instructional objectives written as declarative statements describing specific behaviors and activities, questions give a sharper, more meaningful focus and invite a response. Unit questions should connect the focus of the unit to the larger purposes of the course as a whole, as well as link to the more specific purposes of the particular unit. Figure 7.5 displays an example of course and unit questions.

QUESTIONS ARE A WAY TO STAY TRUE TO THE DISCIPLINE UNDER STUDY. Unit outcomes described in a series of questions can ensure that relevance is couched in experiences that remain true to the discipline under study.

FIGURE 7.5
Course and Unit
Questions

Course: Health
Course Questions: What is healthy eating?
What is a balanced diet?
Unit: Elements of Good Nutrition
Unit Questions: Will an "apple a day" really keep the doctor away?
Why do the foods that are good for you taste bad?
What would happen if you only ate junk food?
What is healthy eating?
What is a balanced diet?

Source: From *Understanding by Design* (pp. 184, 188) by G. Wiggins and J. McTighe, 1998, Alexandria, VA: Association for Supervision and Curriculum Development. Copyright 1998 by ASCD. Adapted with permission. All rights reserved.

Questions that help students explore important conceptual relationships that have been mapped by the teacher should ensure that essential concepts and processes are the central focus of study. The teacher's task is to help students explore "the best of what disciplined minds in the past have sent down to us, but always by displaying yesterday's conclusions fundamentally as questions that always need fresh answers" (Sizer, 1996, p. 78).

Let's examine a set of self-test questions developed for a unit on ecology for a middle-school science course (Taymans & Lynch, 1996):

1. What are biotic and abiotic factors?
2. How do biotic and abiotic factors interact in ecosystems?
3. What kinds of changes occur in ecosystems? Why do population sizes change?
4. How are ecosystems affected by human activity?

The first question asks students to distinguish between biotic (living) and abiotic (nonliving) factors. This is a fundamental biological concept. Research in science education tells us that student understanding of these concepts is developmental and that students need multiple and increasingly complex experiences to help them understand how to answer this fundamental question of biology: What is the difference between living and nonliving things? A question posed later in the unit is, What are some examples of biotic and abiotic factors in your ecosystem? which asks students to construct their understanding of this concept within a familiar context.

Self-test questions 2, 3, and 4 ask students to examine cycles of change in ecosystems, another fundamental biological concept. Students will be exploring a change cycle in a subsequent unit on photosynthesis. Thus, the unit questions are guiding students to think about fundamental biological principles.

QUESTIONS ARE A NATURAL MEANS OF MONITORING PROGRESS AND STRUCTURING LEARNING. Unit questions can guide the types of assessments and teaching-learning activities a teacher uses to gauge and promote student progress.

Likewise, students can use questions to self-assess, thereby removing some guesswork from deciding what is important. A clear congruence between instructional activities and unit questions ensures that activities are both "minds on" and "hands on" (Wiggins & McTighe, 1998). This avoids the all-too-common planning strategy of relying more on engaging activities than activities that build conceptual knowledge. Planning a unit in terms of questions that students will be able to answer can open teachers' minds to creative and flexible ways for students to learn and demonstrate understanding. For example, the question, "What is healthy eating?" (Figure 7.5) could be posed multiple times throughout the unit to help monitor student progress.

QUESTIONS ARE A WAY TO MOTIVATE STUDENTS. Questions that are provocative, puzzling, and connected to students' lives are likely to get their attention and hook them into learning. Questions such as, "How could you improve the human hand?" (Bruner, 1966, p. 98) or "Why do the foods that are good for you taste bad?" (Wiggins & McTighe, 1998, p. 188) are interesting to think about. Allowing students to pose questions they want answered during a unit ensures that the organizing questions are valued by both students and the teacher.

Planning and teaching units focused on answering interesting and challenging questions is a way to offer diverse youth attending secondary schools worthwhile learning experiences. Many students do not easily see the connection between what is presented to them in schools and their present and future lives. The development of relevant and provocative questions first forces us as teachers to make those connections and then to offer students experiences so that they can see that school learning opens the door to life-long learning.

Developing Higher-Order Thinking Skills By Examining Relationships
The purpose of education is to enable students to think. Higher-order thinking is based on the ability to elaborate and manipulate information in relation to conceptual frameworks (Newmann & Wehlage, 1993). Devices such as concept maps and essential questions give students a structure by which they can explore relationships between and among concepts. To develop higher-order thinking skills, students must examine their new learning in relation to what they already know and build connections between the two. Lenz et al. (1998) have developed a framework for identifying types of higher-order thinking students can use to answer important unit questions (see Figure 7.6). These thinking structures can be explicitly identified as students engage in activities to answer course questions. This overt identification of higher-order thinking skills can help students generalize these types of thinking to other less-defined situations. In addition, when teachers clearly understand the type of thinking in which they are asking students to engage, they can provide more support and guidance for students who might need it. For example, for some students determining cause and effect or categorizing information may be a type of thinking they are still learning to perform. If this is the case, they can be offered more structured learning activities (to be described in Chapters 9 and 10) that can guide them through the thinking process.

Specifying Important Assignments
As previously described, there are well-identified ways teachers can plan and teach to promote student success. As students enter secondary and postsecondary settings, they are

FIGURE 7.6   Example Relationships

EXAMPLE RELATIONSHIPS

Information may be structured in one or more ways. The types of structures are not mutually exclusive, and one type of structure may be embedded in another. The various structures are subcategorized by two general types: descriptive and sequential.

Descriptive Structures

Explanation
Clustering: Information grouped by common relationships.
Parts: Arrangement of items that make up a whole.
Characteristics: List of qualities that define an item.
Examples: Representatives of a group or topic (may include nonexamples for contrast).
Hierarchy: Information grouped by levels of specificity, importance, etc.
Categories/Subcategories: Parts of a classification system.
Collection: Items that belong together, but that are not related in any of the above more specific ways.

Comparison
Comparison: Lists of similarities among topics.
Contrasting: Lists of differences among topics.
Comparing and contrasting: Lists of both similarities and differences among topics.
Analogy: Correspondence in some way(s) between items otherwise dissimilar.

Deliberation
Pros and cons: Lists of positive and negative aspects of a topic.
Advantages and disadvantages: Lists of favorable or unfavorable aspects of a topic.

Sequential Structures

Order
Importance: Lists information according to significance.
Rank: Lists information according to some comparative value (e.g., size, priority).
Enumeration: Lists information numerically (e.g., steps).
Descriptive timeline: Lists events that happen in an order but do not influence each other's place in the order.

Process
Timing: Lists events related by time.
Steps: Shows the order of a process.
Cycle: Shows process or series that repeats itself.
Flowchart: Shows the progression of steps, events, etc., in which the order is determined by decisions or outcomes at each step.
Feedback loop: Shows a process or series that may return to the beginning (or some previous step) depending on any one intermediate outcome in the chain of events.

Causality*
Cause & effect: Shows an outcome and what led to that outcome.
Occurrence & consequence: Shows an event and the result of that event.
Cause-effect-consequence: A chain of causality showing a final outcome (consequence), an intermediate force (effect), and the initial reason for the chain (cause).
Causal timeline: A timeline indicating events in the order they influence one another.

Problem and Solution
Problem and solution: Identification of a challenging situation and its resolution (actual or potential).
Problem, solution, and results: Potential or actual challenge(s), resolution(s), and implications of the resolution(s).

* *While these structures are defined in the singular, plural forms are to be expected.*

Source: From *The Unit Organizer Routine* (p. 53) by B. K. Lenz, J. A. Bulgren, J. B. Schumaker, D. D. Deshler, & D. A. Boudah, 1994. Lawrence, KS: Edge Enterprises.

■ *Scenario Revisited*

As Jerry continued to rethink his planning for the unit on World War II, he decided he would have students work in groups to learn about what part countries in different regions of the world played in the global conflict. Each group would focus on a different country or set of countries in a region. These group research projects would tie in nicely with Jerry's practice of talking about current events in class every week. Students could discuss what conflicts were occurring in the world currently, any role the United States had in those conflicts, and whether there were any connections between U.S. foreign relations now and at the time of World War II. Jerry thought about how he might want to develop a set of questions to guide student thinking and analysis in this process.

Learning about the role of the United States in the global conflict of World War II would help students later on in the course as the textbook talked about the changing role of the United States in the Cold War.

Focus and Reflect

Based on Figure 7.6, "Example Relationships," write questions using two descriptive structures and two sequential structures that Jerry could use to help focus his unit.

increasingly expected to be independent learners who know how to organize themselves and manage their time to complete out-of-class assignments and to come prepared for in-class work. Yet many students still need overt instruction and guidance to develop the organization, planning, and self-discipline skills needed to successfully complete high school. Some students come from environments where they have few adult role models or adult guidance in developing these skills. Other students with learning disabilities and attention deficit disorder struggle with these skills as a part of their disability. Teaching students to use organizers, as well as schedules and planning systems, can be one step in helping them plan, manage their time, identify materials needed to complete assignments (Bryan & Sullivan-Burstein, 1997; Patton, 1994), and develop important skills needed for success in postsecondary education and adult life.

Planning with the Unit Organizer

The Unit Organizer teaching routine, based on the concept-based planning described above, was developed as part of a collaborative research project with content teachers who were instructing classes of students with a range of achievement levels. The Unit Organizer tool was developed to help teachers plan and teach units that would explicitly identify the most important content for students to learn (Lenz et al., 1998). In the original research project resulting in the development of the Unit Organizer, teachers received two to three hours of instruction in the routine, had opportunities to discuss the routine with colleagues, spent the necessary time to plan and use the routine with the aim of improving achievement for all students, taught students using explicit instructional procedures, and used the routine regularly over time. The results were that students gained an average of at least 10 to 20 percentage points on tests or tasks that required students to demonstrate learning. Teachers continued using the Unit Organizer routine after the studies were completed. In general, the greatest gains were seen in classes where teachers had the highest expectations for student learning and were consistent in their use of the Unit Organizer over time (University of Kansas, Center for Research on Learning, 1994).

The Unit Organizer helps teachers succinctly and graphically plan and organize units of instruction so that students with a wide range of achievement levels and experiences can successfully engage in conceptual learning. The structure of the Unit Organizer helps teachers think about important concepts and their relationships within and across units of instruction. The Unit Organizer also aids teachers in organizing student learning by posing questions and posting a schedule while introducing the unit that can guide students to focus their learning.

The Unit Organizer is a two-page form comprised of 10 sections. Using Figures 7.7 and 7.8, let's explore the parts of the Unit Organizer by examining how Charmaine Trumbell, a student teacher in science, used this device with her middle-school science students (Taymans & Lynch, 1996).

Course Connections (Sections 1, 2, 3, and 4)   In section 1 of the Unit Organizer (Figure 7.7), the teacher identifies the title of the current unit. In this case, the Ecology unit is part of a life science course. Section 2 identifies the previous unit which was on Evolution, whereas section 3 identifies the next unit, which will be Photosynthesis. Section 4 indicates a theme or idea that connects multiple units, in this case, The Study of Living Things.

Unit Map (Section 5)   In this section, a content map, or visual display of the content of the unit, is constructed. The first part of the section is the unit paraphrase, which, with Ecology in section 1 and the connecting line, summarizes the key concept of the unit in a brief sentence: Ecology is about ecosystems, which are communities of organisms and their environments. The concept of ecosystems is then mapped by graphically depicting how the content will be organized for study within the unit. The map links supporting concepts (biotic factors, abiotic factors, interactions, etc.) to the unit paraphrase by labeled lines that indicate the relationships between supporting concepts and the central concept of the unit. The lines are labeled so that students can read the relationships as complete thoughts. This unit map can be read in several ways: "Ecosystems include biotic factors and abiotic factors," "Ecosystems involve interactions," "Ecosystems undergo changes and can be affected by human activity." This summary unit map represents the important concepts on which the unit is built. To keep it as a manageable, succinct, and memorable organizing summary, the unit map should include no more than seven parts, represented as oval shapes (Lenz et al., 1998). This map conforms to the guideline with its six parts.

Unit Relationships and Self-Test Questions (Sections 6 and 7)   These sections specify the types of thinking teachers want students to do about the key unit concepts (see Figure 7.6). The unit questions in section 7 can help focus students on what is important to learn. This teacher has developed four unit questions, each identified by the type of thinking the students will be asked to do, as shown in the unit relationships box (section 6). For this unit, the teacher wants students to be able to characterize biotic and abiotic factors, so *characteristics* is written in the first box of section 6. For the second question, students are *comparing and contrasting,* and the third and fourth set of questions demand *cause-and-effect* thinking. This specificity in identifying types of thinking can help develop supportive instruction for students who may still be learning higher-order thinking skills.

FIGURE 7.7 The Unit Organizer

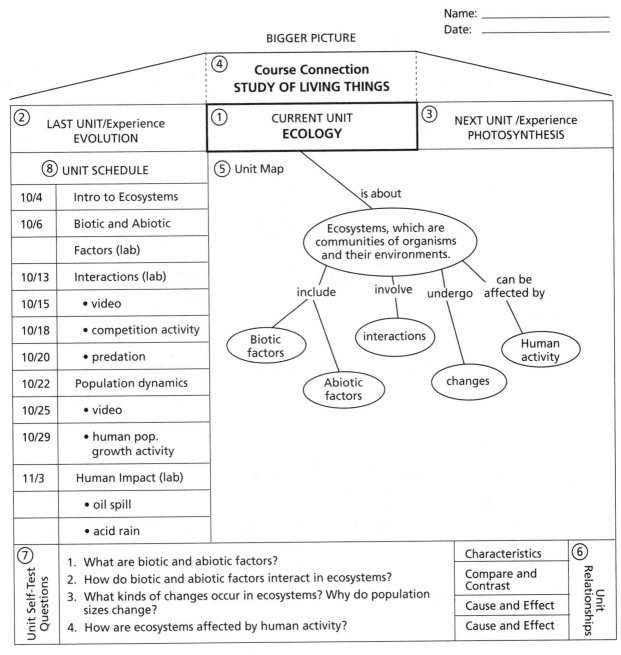

Source: Adapted from Lenz, B. K., with Bulgren, J. A., Schumaker, J. B., Deshler, D. D., & Boudah, D. A. (1994). *The Unit Organizer Routine.* Lawrence, KS: Edge Enterprises

Unit Schedule (Section 8) This section lists the major assignments and activities for the unit, with space to write in the date they are planned. In this ecology unit, students will be working on four labs. Each lab can be

FIGURE 7.8 The Unit Organizer

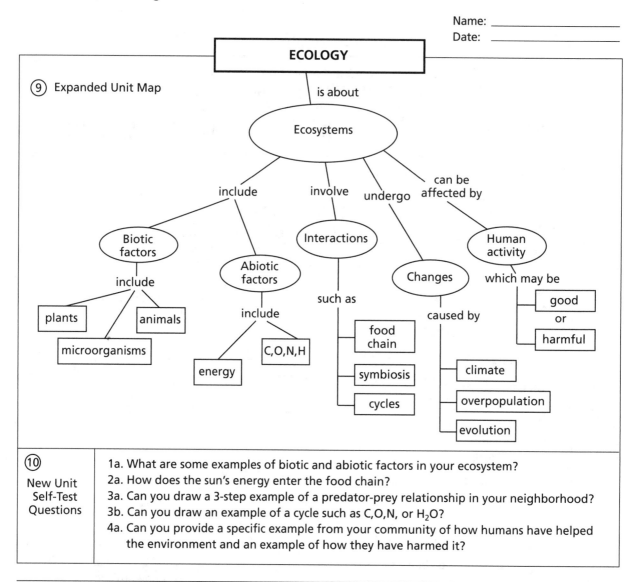

Name: _____
Date: _____

ECOLOGY

⑨ Expanded Unit Map

is about

Ecosystems

include   involve   undergo   can be affected by

Biotic factors   Interactions   Human activity

Abiotic factors   Changes   which may be

include   such as   caused by   good or harmful

plants   animals   include   food chain

microorganisms   C,O,N,H   symbiosis   climate

energy   cycles   overpopulation

evolution

⑩ New Unit Self-Test Questions	1a. What are some examples of biotic and abiotic factors in your ecosystem? 2a. How does the sun's energy enter the food chain? 3a. Can you draw a 3-step example of a predator-prey relationship in your neighborhood? 3b. Can you draw an example of a cycle such as C,O,N, or H_2O? 4a. Can you provide a specific example from your community of how humans have helped the environment and an example of how they have harmed it?

Source: Adapted from Lenz, B. K., with Bulgren, J. A., Schumaker, J. B., Deshler, D. D., & Boudah, D. A. (1994). *The Unit Organizer Routine.* Lawrence, KS: Edge Enterprises

linked to the concepts on the unit map. One lab explores biotic and abiotic factors, one lab investigates interactions, and two labs study changes to ecosystems as a result of human activity. We can also see that information will be presented through viewing two videos. By looking at the beginning and ending dates, we know that this unit will last four and a half weeks.

Expanded Unit Map (Section 9) The expanded map (Figure 7.8) allows for a more detailed view of the unit concepts. The expanded map extends all the nodes, with subtopics indicated as a different geometric shape. The first three nodes (biotic factors, abiotic factors, and interactions) are further elaborated through examples. The "Changes" and "Human Activity" nodes give more information on cause and effect.

Additional Questions (Section 10)   The additional questions address the more specific information added in the expanded unit map, and can deepen students' understanding of the original unit self-test questions. For example, the first question listed under the original unit map is: "What are biotic and abiotic factors?" This question is now personalized by asking students to provide examples from their own lives. Similarly, all the additional questions ask students to extend their thinking, based on the original set of questions used to introduce the unit.

Teaching with the Unit Organizer

The Unit Organizer can also be used as a teaching tool. It is a way for teachers to explicitly share the parameters of an instructional unit with students. Using the Unit Organizer in instruction does not require a lot of time, but it does take a thoughtful, systematic approach to enable students to use it as a tool to guide their own learning. Teaching with the Unit Organizer is designed to enhance student organization, understanding, and memory, as well as the quality of their responses to questions and their belief in the value of learning content (University of Kansas, Center for Research on Learning, 1994).

Cue-Do-Review   The developers of the Unit Organizer recommend that teachers develop a special routine for using it with students. This routine is a set of instructional procedures that are used each time the Unit Organizer is used and may be recalled as the **Cue-Do-Review Sequence** (Lenz et al., 1998). Using the Cue-Do-Review Sequence process is important not only because it provides a foundation for teaching strategically, or explicitly telling students about routines and strategies that can help them learn, but because it can also help students become better independent learners.

Cue: Pointing Out the Important Features of the Unit Organizer   A teacher can introduce the Unit Organizer as a tool that the class will be using to better understand what each unit will be about. The result of this introduction should be that students are able to describe the benefits of using the Unit Organizer and what they will do to make it an effective study tool.

First, students can be introduced to the Unit Organizer form. Some teachers display a blank form and ask students to describe what they see and relate the sections of the Unit Organizer to what they already know (i.e., keeping a schedule, reading a map, asking/answering questions to check their understanding). Students can explore the blank Unit Organizer form by answering questions. For example, the students of Charmaine Sullivan in the scenario, "How a Student Teacher Planned a Unit," had not been introduced to concept mapping. When she introduced the Unit Map section on a blank Unit Organizer form, she asked her students a series of questions, using a map analogy to help them understand the purpose of the Unit Organizer:

- When do people use maps in real life?
- How do maps help us?
- If we were going to draw a map of what we will be doing in science class, what do you think it might look like?

▪ *Scenario*

HOW A STUDENT TEACHER PLANNED A UNIT

As student teacher Charmaine Sullivan prepared to plan her unit using the Unit Organizer, she felt anxious. She believed that she was firmly grounded in *how* she wanted to teach science—in an inductive, activity rich, student-centered fashion, a style that her teacher education program encouraged. But she felt much less sure about *how to plan* for the big picture of unit instruction so that she could develop a unit that was more than just a series of activities. Charmaine reported: "I was actually relieved when I was introduced to the Unit Organizer. I tend to have ideas all over the place, kind of scattered and unorganized. So this has been a great tool to just organize and boil down what's important. Once you have your five or seven main concepts you can always build up."

Charmaine saw the Unit Organizer as a "really good" organizational tool. Her cooperating teachers supplied her with an abundance of books, articles, and laboratory manuals dealing with ecology. They did not have specific lessons or activities in mind because that unit had not been taught at the school in years. So it was up to Charmaine to structure the entire unit. She first developed a concept map on ecology to help her identify key ecology concepts and their relationships.

Then she focused on using the Unit Organizer to plan her specific unit. It took her about 15 hours of advance planning for the unit, which she did over a one-week break in her teaching schedule. While teaching the unit, she did additional daily planning as the unit emerged. The unit stretched over four and a half weeks.

Charmaine's greatest challenge was how to organize the vast amounts of material.

> Ecology is a subject I love, so it was just very difficult . . . first of all to know the level of the students and how much material to cover. I started making the Unit Organizer, trying to figure out what was important, what was related to what the students just did (in the previous unit—evolution) and how to relate that to photosynthesis and respiration . . . so that everything connected well. . . . The first thing I did was to go through the topics of the last and next units—that helped me decide what was important and what kinds of themes I wanted to carry through the whole thing. . . . I worked on the unit map next. That's what helped me decide the individual lessons, assessments, and activities I wanted to use.

Charmaine also pointed out that the Unit Questions were useful, because they helped her to focus on the basic questions she wanted the students to ask of themselves throughout the whole unit.

We can see how the Unit Organizer helped Charmaine plan by first thinking about the concepts to be learned by mapping the bigger picture of ecology and then developing the Unit Organizer map. Once the map had been developed, her learning and assessment activities were developed. She then determined unit questions which linked the unit map to the activities.

Second, a filled-in, or partially filled-in Unit Organizer can be introduced to help students "read" the form. Again, asking questions as students explore the form can help them actively engage in the process.

Teachers can also guide students to think about how they will use the Unit Organizer by asking questions such as: Which section do you think will be most important in helping you be successful in this unit? Which sections can help you study for tests? Taking time to make sure that students can interpret the sections of a filled-in map can help them feel confident with the format.

Finally, students can be introduced to the Unit Organizer that the teacher has developed for a specific unit the class will be studying. This is usually done with a partially or fully filled-in Unit Organizer.

Do: Use the Unit Organizer to Introduce a Unit   Once students are familiar with the Unit Organizer form, the teacher can help them begin to use the Unit Organizer each time a new unit is introduced. The teacher can engage students in writing and discussing the new unit information by handing them already completed Unit Organizers or co-constructing sections of the entire form.

CREATE A CONTEXT (SECTIONS 1–4). First, the teacher discusses how this unit connects with the course as a whole and then specifically with what has been studied previously.

RECOGNIZE CONTENT STRUCTURES (SECTION 5). Using the basic unit map, students are encouraged to examine how concepts are related to each other and how key concepts can be expanded and elaborated. For some students, adding icons and other visual images and color coding information makes the map more meaningful.

ACKNOWLEDGING UNIT RELATIONSHIPS (SECTION 6). Students are asked to do different types of thinking important to the unit of study. For some units sequential structures may be important, such as process relationships when studying government, or comparison thinking when studying types of poetry. Linking the unit map with the types of thinking students will be doing can help strengthen student understanding of the relationships between concepts being studied.

FRAME UNIT QUESTIONS (SECTION 7). Unit questions can be a combination of teacher and student questions. When planning the unit, the teacher should develop questions that can guide student learning. When the unit is presented, students can be invited to suggest other questions that can guide their learning during the unit. When the unit is introduced, these questions can be included in section 7. Important self-test questions that arise during subsequent discussions can be included in section 10 of the Expanded Unit Map.

TIE CONTENT TO TASKS (SECTION 8). The unit schedule (section 8) is introduced as the unit is introduced. This schedule can be revisited to help students monitor their progress and prepare for upcoming activities and assignments.

Review: Using the Unit Organizer throughout the Unit   Once the unit has been introduced, the teacher can use it regularly during instruction to help students monitor progress, review what they have learned, or add concepts or questions to the expanded unit map. For example, Charmaine could display the Unit Organizer periodically during her unit and ask the following questions to help students monitor their progress.

- How does this unit add to our knowledge of living things?
- The Unit Organizer includes a one-sentence summary of ecology. How would you describe ecology?
- What are some important ideas in this unit? Which ideas are the clearest to you?
- Look at the unit map and questions; what is a question you have about what we are studying that you would like answered in this unit?

The Unit Organizer can also be used to review the unit as it is ending. Some teachers display enlarged Unit Organizers throughout the course so students can use them for cumulative reviews.

■ *Scenario*

HOW TWO PROSPECTIVE TEACHERS USED THE UNIT ORGANIZER

The information conveyed in the following scenarios is based on research that investigated the use of the Unit Organizer by a group of prospective teachers (Taymans & Lynch, 1996). The case studies have been revised to be presented in the following conversational form.

DREW BROWN

My name is Drew Brown, and I am beginning a career in teaching. My student teaching in a large urban school system was a challenging, yet rewarding experience. I used the Unit Organizer to teach a civics unit on public policy. My civics classes were like being in the United Nations. I had students from Africa, Colombia, Bolivia, Peru, Korea, and Vietnam, along with diverse students from the United States. My class sizes ranged from 16 to 30 students.

To begin my planning, I used a civics book and a *Newsweek* article, because there was no curriculum guide. Because I was working as part of an eighth-grade middle-school team, I had assistance from a health teacher who had previously used a policy case to help students examine a current health issue, Ritalin use in children. I liked the idea of teaching students by having them examine a current issue by reading and discussing a case. I also had assistance in planning from my cooperating teacher. At this stage in my teaching career, I probably spent one hour of planning for each hour taught, so my unit plan took me about eight hours to complete.

First, I developed the concept map. I wanted to make sure the right concepts were covered. I had read through the chapter several times to make sure I could work things as simply as possible. I knew right away that I was going to use a waste-management case to help students work through the nodes on the concept map. Then I planned the individual class sessions on a separate piece of paper. I planned Monday and Tuesday in detail. Those plans came simultaneously with the map. Then I put down the schedule and wrote the unit questions which were:

1. What is an issue? What is public policy?
2. What are the problems, solutions, and issues in the waste management case?
3. How do I write a persuasive letter to the editor on an issue?

The unit relationships were not difficult to figure out. I knew from the objectives I had developed that **define** and **identify** were low-level objectives that asked students to be able to explain the meaning of the concepts of *issue* and *public policy,* so I wanted one higher-order question that would engage students. It took a while to come up with the main unit question. In thinking about applying information, it seemed that having students examine a problem, describe the issues involved, and suggest a solution would be a good activity. I knew the English teacher had previously taught them how to write a business letter, so I decided to have them write a letter to the editor. Writing Question 3 definitely came last. I figured it was OK to have two lower-order questions if they were supporting my major unit question, which demanded higher-order thinking and a real-world skill.

CARL SCHMITMEYER

My name is Carl Schmitmeyer. People tell me that I am full of ideas, creativity, and energy. While creativity is a strength, organization has always been a problem for me. I know planning with the Unit Organizer helped me focus and gave me a blueprint for translating the big, important science concepts I want students to learn into a coherent and realistic instructional plan.

The first time I used the Unit Organizer was for a unit on environmental science. As I was getting ready to prepare this unit, I met with my cooperating teacher and my special education team teacher to get input. I had a good resource to use for the unit, a popular environmental science video series called *The Voyage of the Mimi.* This is a fictionalized adventure of a group of people on a boat outfitted for marine exploration. I chose a specific episode as the basis for the unit, where the people are trapped on a desert island and they have to learn how to make water. So they figure out how to build solar stills. I took that idea and expanded it to include the concept of the water cycle and the use of water by people.

I used the video to help me draw the concept map. It was a real "aha" experience. I remember watching the video and saying to myself, "Ah! Here they are talking about the earth's water cycle. Ah! They're talking about distillation. Here, they are showing how people use water." The concept map helped me think of activities that could help the kids explore these ideas in more depth, so I worked on the unit schedule so that the activities would match the concepts. I was able to use an activity suggested by the special education teacher, as well as a reading and cooperative learning activity I had used in the past. The unit questions and relationships came last. I found the Unit Organizer to be a good

planning tool. It helped me organize. I got a lot of anxiety out of the way right off the bat; I was able to focus on the most important concepts and then was able to let my creative juices flow.

Introducing the unit by working through the parts of the Unit Organizer took a class period, which was more time than I had anticipated. The best thing about using the Unit Organizer to kick off a unit was its use as a gauge for determining the level of students' prior understanding of the supporting concepts. When we discussed the unit questions, I began to get a picture of their understanding, to see what I was up against during the course of the unit. I found out that they were familiar with the key concepts, so after that first class, I modified some of the activities to meet higher-order objectives. It hadn't occurred to me that the Unit Organizer could be a preassessment tool. But after that introduction, I realized I now had a tool I could use to probe for students' misconceptions that must be addressed during the course of instruction.

ASSESSMENT: IS EVERYONE ON THE JOURNEY?

In this chapter we have described the Unit Organizer as a research-based way of planning and teaching that enables students with diverse learning profiles to achieve within the current educational climate of standards-based instruction. What we have not discussed is how you can define and measure success. This is a crucial variable in the unit planning process.

The structure of the Unit Organizer can help you plan how to assess students. By developing the unit map and the extended map, you will have identified the key content. The self-test questions, additional questions, and unit relationship sections target what is important for students to know and be able to do. Once you have progressed this far in planning, it is possible to decide how students can demonstrate their understanding of the concepts and types of relationships identified during instruction. This connects to the unit schedule where key instructional activities, assessments, and assignments are identified and should enable students to grasp the essential information and skills.

Why Assess Your Students?

First consider what you want the assessment process to tell you. From a design standpoint, the decision on how to collect evidence that students are learning can be sequenced after unit goals are set, but prior to developing instructional activities. We presented this design principle in the section on

Planning for Student Understanding as a way of ensuring that instruction and assessment are appropriately aligned and integrated. Typically, assessments should give a teacher the following information during instruction:

- An indication of gaps in student knowledge and skills that may need to be taught
- The effectiveness of unit content and processes for student learning
- The identification of students who may need extra help

By the end of a unit you should have a class profile of student achievement in relationship to unit goals and identified outcomes.

A well-planned assessment process can help you determine the effectiveness of a unit as it is being taught. Assessing during learning helps target content that is particularly difficult for some or for all students to learn. This allows you to reteach, develop more potent or meaningful learning experiences, or use cooperative learning structures that team higher-achieving students with students who may be having difficulty. Frequent assessment that helps students see that they are being successful enhances both your own and your students' feelings of confidence and success. Ultimately, of course, the assessment process will result in grades, indicating individual student levels of achievement within a unit of instruction.

How Do You Know If Your Students Are Learning?

Wiggins and McTighe (1998) have identified an assessment continuum consisting of:

- Informal interactions
- Observing students and engaging in dialogues
- Tests and quizzes, academic prompts
- Performance tasks and projects

The simplest forms of assessment are informal interactions during instruction that monitor student understanding. Observing students and engaging in dialogues is another method of assessing students. More formal measures that are still relatively efficient and can be easily scored are tests and quizzes that ask focused questions that often have single correct answers. Academic prompts, which are open-ended assessments that require students to think critically and to construct a response, require more judgment on your part to score. The most complex type of assessments on the continuum are performance tasks and projects. In this form of assessment, students solve problems or give performances that are authentic to the field of study.

As you think about your assessment experiences as a student, you may find that you are very familiar with traditional assessments in the form of quizzes and tests. Although the multiple-choice test is alive and well because of its efficiency in administration and grading, many educational researchers and policymakers are calling for open-ended and performance assessments as a more equitable and informative way to assess student achievement. Research supports the contention that certain types of traditional, closed-response tests are more difficult for some students than more open-ended formats. Researchers also warn that standardized tests can be biased against minority students, English language learners, females, and students from low-income families (Neill & Medina, 1989). For example, Hollenbeck and Tindal (1996) studied middle-school students' responses to a unit test comprised of both multiple-choice and essay questions. Students with learning disabilities scored significantly lower than their nondisabled peers on the multiple-choice section of the test, while there were no significant differences on the essay questions, which offered a more flexible format to show what they knew. In science education, Ruiz-Primo and Shavelson (1996) note that females tend to perform more poorly than males when achievement is measured by multiple-choice tests.

Performance assessments offer teachers an alternative to traditional tests. The main attribute of this type of assessment is that the student is performing a task or tasks important to the field of study. In science, this may be lab or inquiry projects. In English, it could be a dramatization or other depiction that demonstrates comprehension and interpretation. By allowing students ways to demonstrate their knowledge that do not rely solely on reading, writing, and test-taking skills, more students are likely to be able to demonstrate achievement. Performance assessments can be ongoing or can be structured to be a summative assessment at the end of a unit.

To determine whether students are learning, a teacher should first know where students are starting out, based on their prior knowledge. In this chapter, we have seen Jerry Uribe and Carl Schmitmeyer using two different formats to find out what students know at the beginning of the unit. Carl was more successful in this process because he had a clear idea of how he would use the information he received from his students. Jerry asked probing questions to check for student understanding at the beginning of his unit, but because he had not identified the concepts he would be teaching, he became lost and discouraged with his students' misconceptions.

The ecology unit developed in the Unit Organizer (see Figures 7.7 and 7.8) contains numerous assessment opportunities. The three labs are examples of performance assessments. In each of the three labs, students have the opportunity to express what they know by charting, graphing, drawing, and writing as they try out their ideas and make conclusions about their findings.

Labs can also be structured to accommodate diverse skill levels. Cooperative labs allow students to work together to try out their ideas and draw conclusions. If the final lab report is an individual product, then a teacher has the opportunity to assess both group and individual performance. During labs, the teacher also has the opportunity to observe students and to engage in informal interactions with them.

Focus and Reflect

Examine the unit schedule in Figure 7.7. What assessment processes is the teacher probably using? What changes would you recommend?

The structure of the Unit Organizer also helps students understand what is important to learn in a unit so that they can monitor their own progress. Further, the Unit Organizer can be a tool for students to self-check and plan ahead. By using the unit map and extended map with the accompanying questions, students have a basic structure to self-assess. Students who are self-motivated and possess metacognitive skills that allow them to evaluate their own learning may do this automatically. Other students, who may be less active learners, may need teacher guidance and monitoring to use the Unit Organizer as a self-assessment tool.

THE UNIT ORGANIZER AND COLLABORATING WITH OTHER PROFESSIONALS

In this chapter, we have offered examples of collaborative planning and teaching. Integrated curriculum, which demands collaborative planning, is seen by many researchers as a way to effectively reach more students. For

▪ *Scenario Revisited*

For assessments, Jerry decided the culminating project would be group projects presenting what students had learned about the role of their selected region or country in World War II and what impact this had on the region's or country's relationship with the United States. Then, in tying the unit together, the class could work together to categorize, list, and locate the major antagonists in the war, and identify which countries the United States was at war with and who their allies were. Jerry thought some kind of chart or map might be helpful in diagramming all these relationships with students. He would have to look around and see if other teachers had some suggestions for how he might organize such information.

example, in the section on concept mapping, we described how a group of middle-school science teachers used concept mapping to plan a course as an example of intradepartmental collaboration. In the chapter scenarios, we offered brief glimpses of interdepartmental collaboration. Drew Brown was a member of a middle-school cross-department team. Because Drew was well acquainted with what the teachers on her team were teaching, she was able to plan a unit that incorporated skills that students had learned in two other courses (analyzing cases in a health class and writing business letters in an English class) to her social studies class.

As the composition of students attending our schools continues to be more diverse, *where* teachers center their conversations about how to reach all students most effectively becomes increasingly important. Standards-based reforms can help teachers center their work around curriculum planning that sets high expectations but is also flexible enough to respect the diverse knowledge, skill, and needs students bring with them to school. Pugach and Warger (1996) have identified the following current reform attributes which make collaborative curriculum development a promising endeavor:

- Covering less material, but covering it in much greater depth
- Focusing on the meaning of what is learned, rather than the facts and figures
- Teaching as the facilitation of student learning
- Linking ideas across subject matter
- Constructing rather than receiving knowledge; beginning where the students are and building on their prior knowledge
- Creating an orientation toward authentic activities for learning to include all students in the work of a classroom community
- Incorporating the acquisition of basic skills into meaningful activities
- Engaging students in cooperative work and problem solving
- Closely aligning curriculum, instruction, and assessment

These conditions, combined with real planning time and administrative support for collaborative planning within and across disciplines, provides a foundation for improved achievement for a wide range of students. As curriculum development teams form at the state, local, and school level, the Unit Organizer should be considered as a valuable tool in developing standards-based units of instruction.

We, the chapter authors, have used the Unit Organizer as a way to structure collaboration in our own teaching at the university level. We have had the opportunity to team teach and have used the Unit Organizer to help us map key course concepts, determine guiding questions, and identify the most important course assignments and activities. As a planning tool, we found that it helped us focus our planning conversations about what was essential to the course, and it helped us come to a common conceptual view of what we planned to accomplish with our students. Although the structure of the Unit Organizer was an invaluable tool to our interdisciplinary planning—Sharon Lynch is a science educator, and Juliana Taymans is a special educator—it did not diminish the great amount of time we spent planning. We discovered that collaborative planning and team teaching is time consuming at first, but each time we taught together thereafter, our common view of what was essential expanded and with it our effectiveness as course instructors. We feel that the Unit Organizer was a significant facilitator in our collaboration.

Focus and Reflect

- Read the SMARTER for Science scenario in Appendix B. This scenario demonstrates how the Unit Organizer can be integrated in the SMARTER planning and teaching process. Identify three to five ways that use of the Unit Organizer benefited Nate and Lelia's collaborative work.
- Read how Charmaine, Carl, and Drew used the Unit Organizer for planning.
    Compare and contrast their approaches.
    How did the Unit Organizer help them engage in planning for big ideas?
    What role did collaboration play in the planning process?
- Now that you have read the chapter, what advice can you give Jerry for more successfully planning and teaching his students?
- Looking back at Chapter 2, consider whether use of the Unit Organizer could fit in with one or more of the devices used by successful teachers of diverse learners. Develop five reasons, not given in this chapter, for using the Unit Organizer.

FIGURE 7.9

Expanded Graphic Organizer

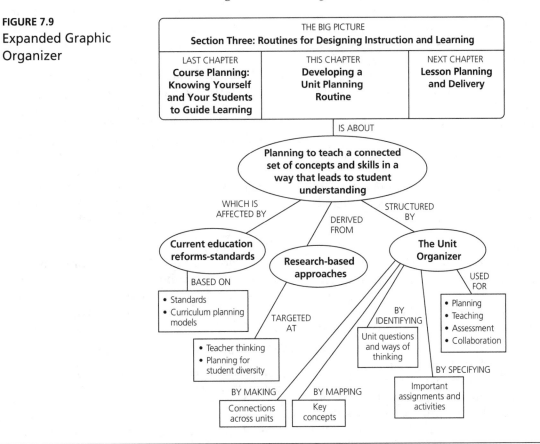

SUMMARY

In this chapter we presented information on planning and teaching at the unit level of instruction. We situated the information on unit planning within current educational reforms that are based on content and performance standards. These reforms are encouraging models of curriculum development that stress integrating teaching and assessment and are aimed at developing students' conceptual abilities. We also examined research on teacher thinking during planning and ways to plan that are effective for reaching students with diverse learning needs. We devoted most of the chapter to describing the Unit Organizer, which is a research-based approach to unit planning and teaching. Specifically, the Unit Organizer helps students make connections across units of instruction, map key unit concepts, identify unit questions and ways of thinking, and see the important activities and assignments to help them plan their time. We concluded with a brief examination of assessment.

The Unit Organizer is a useful tool for the up-front planning we have described as crucial for designing instruction to accommodate students with diverse learning profiles. The Unit Organizer is a tool that any teacher can learn to use, and it can help all teachers design units of instruction that are accessible for all learners.

MAKING CONNECTIONS:
Implementing the Unit Organizer

1. *Here are the big ideas to get you started:*
   - Concept mapping and organizing learning around questions can be useful unit-planning and teaching tools. Organizing the content you want to teach graphically can help you, as well as your students, to be clear about the concepts, ideas, and information to be learned in a unit. Graphic organizers can also help you translate national, state, or local curriculum standards into specific learning goals for your students.
   - The Unit Organizer is a teaching routine based on concept mapping that can help you plan how to teach what is important in a unit of study and can provide context and structure to guide student learning.

2. *What you need:*
   - Copies of national, state, or local standards for courses you teach, or are likely to teach.
   - A textbook or other appropriate materials you are likely to use with students.
   - Examples of concept maps and completed unit organizers.

After having gathered these materials, focus on creating Unit Organizer maps. What's the big idea of the unit? What are the secondary ideas or topics? Be sure to label the linking lines. As you construct maps, think about whether the line labels make sense. Using the map, would students be able to explain to others what the unit is about? Would students be able to identify what the important ideas are?

3. *Evaluate your work:*
   - Consider your unit map within the context of learning goals identified in standards for your content area. Have you identified important concepts and learnings consistent with the standards?
   - Share your map or maps with a colleague. Can he or she readily identify the important concepts and information in the unit, or agree that these are the important ideas and information? Are the learning goals you have identified consistent with the standards? (Remember that reasonable professionals may disagree about what's important, so conversations about this can be useful for both you and your colleagues.)

4. *Next steps:*
   - Develop unit questions to accompany your maps. Remember that the learning goals conveyed in your questions should reflect the topics identified in your map.

WEB SITES

http://www.graphic.org This Web site, with links to many other sites, provides information on the latest publication, software, and projects on graphic representations.

http://www.ascd.org The Association of Supervision and Curriculum development.

SUGGESTED READINGS

White, R., & Gunstone, R. (1992). *Probing understanding.* New York: Falmer Press. This book provides a guide for teachers on how to teach and assess using concepts.

Wiggins, G., & McTighe, J. (1998). *Understanding by design.* Alexandria, VA: Association for Supervision and Curriculum Development. This book is written in a clear, succinct, user-friendly style. It describes how to develop curriculum targeted at conceptual understanding and that integrates assessment and instruction. Also see *http://www.class.org*.

REFERENCES

American Association for the Advancement of Science. (1993). *Benchmarks for science literacy.* New York: Oxford University Press.

Arends, R. I. (1991). *Learning to teach.* New York: McGraw-Hill.

Armbruster, B. B., & Anderson, T. H. (1988). On selecting "considerate content area textbooks." *Remedial and Special Education, 9*(1), 47–52.

Borko, H., & Putnam, R. T. (1998). The role of context in teacher learning and teacher education. In S. J. Sears & S. B. Hersch (Eds.), *Contextual teaching and learning* (pp. 33–65). Columbus, OH & Washington, DC: co-published by ERIC Clearinghouse on Adult, Career, and Vocational Education and ERIC Clearinghouse on Teaching and Teacher Education.

Brophy, J. (1987). Synthesis of research on strategies for motivating students to learn. *Educational Leadership, 45*(2), 40–48.

Bruner, J. S. (1966). *Toward a theory of instruction.* Cambridge, MA: The Belknap Press of Harvard University Press.

Bryan, T., & Sullivan-Burstein, K. (1997). Homework how-to's. *Teaching Exceptional Children, 29*(6), 32–37.

Bulgren, J., & Lenz, K. (1996). Strategic instruction in content areas. In D. D. Deshler, E. S. Ellis, & B. K. Lenz (Eds.), *Teaching adolescents with learning disabilities* (pp. 409–474). Denver: Love Publishing.

Champagne, A. B., Newell, S. T., Goodnough, J. M. (1996). Trends in science education. In M. C. Pugach & C. L. Warger (Eds.), *Curriculum trends, special education, and reform: Refocusing the conversation* (pp. 42–52). New York: Teachers College Press.

Clark, C. M., & Lampert, M. (1986). The study of teacher thinking: Implications for teacher education. *Journal of Teacher Education, 37,* 27–31.

Collins, A., Brown, J. S., & Newman, S. E. (1989). Cognitive apprenticeship: Teaching and the craft of reading, writing and mathematics. In L. B. Resnick (Ed.), *Knowing, learning, and instruction: Essays in honor of Robert Glasser* (pp. 453–494). Hillsdale, NJ: Erlbaum.

Czerniak, C. M., & Haney, J. J. (1998). The effect of collaborative concept mapping on elementary preservice teachers' anxiety, efficacy, and achievement in physical science. *Journal of Science Teacher Education, 9,* 303–320.

Dempster, F. N. (1991). Synthesis of research on reviews and tests. *Educational Leadership, 48,* 71–76.

Dewey, J. (1916). *Democracy and education.* New York: Macmillan.

Ellis, E. (1998). Making real-world connections when teaching major concepts in inclusive classrooms. *LD online.* Available *www.ldonline.org*.

Erikson, H. L. (1998). *Concept-based curriculum and instruction: Teaching beyond the facts.* Thousand Oaks, CA: Corwin Press.

Hollenbeck, K., & Tindal, G. (1996). Teaching law concepts within mainstreamed middle school social studies settings. *Diagnostique, 21*(4), 37–58.

Hunkins, F. B. (1995). *Teaching thinking through effective questioning* (2nd ed). Norwood, MA: Christopher-Gordon Publishers.

Joint Committee on Teacher Planning for Students with Disabilities. (1995). *Planning for academic diversity in America's classrooms: Windows on reality, research, change and practice.* Lawrence: University of Kansas, Center for Research on Learning.

Kagan, D. M. (1992). Professional growth among preservice and beginning teachers. *Review of Educational Research, 62,* (2), 129–169.

Keating, D. P. (1990). Adolescent thinking. In S. Feldman & G. R. Elliott, *At the threshold: The developing adolescent* (pp. 54–89). Cambridge, MA: Harvard University Press.

Lave, J. (1988). *Cognition in practice: Mind, mathematics and culture in everyday life.* Cambridge, MA: Cambridge University Press.

Lenz, B. K., Alley, G. R., & Schumaker, J. B. (1987). Activating the inactive learner: Advance organizers in the secondary content classroom. *Learning Disability Quarterly, 10,* 53–67.

Lenz, B. K., & Bulgren, J. A. (1994). *ReflActive planning: Planning for diversity in secondary schools* (Research Report). Lawrence: University of Kansas, Center for Research on Learning.

Lenz, B. K., with Bulgren, J. A., Schumaker, J. B., Deshler, D. D., & Boudah, D. A. (1994). *The unit organizer routine.* Lawrence, KS: Edge Enterprises.

Lynch, R., & Harnish, D. (1998, March). *Preparing preservice teacher education students to use work-based strategies to improve instruction.* Columbus: Ohio State University College of Education.

Mastropieri, M. A., & Scruggs, T. E. (1996). In M. C. Pugach & C. L. Warger, (Eds.), *Curriculum trends, special education, and reform: Refocusing the conversation* (pp. 42–52). New York: Teachers College Press.

McGregor, G., & Vogelsberg, R. T. (1998, February). *Inclusive schooling practices: Pedagogical and research foundations: A synthesis of the literature that informs best practices about inclusive schooling.* Missoula: The University of Montana, Rural Institute on Disabilities.

Neil, D. M., & Medina, N. J. (1989). Standardized testing: Harmful to educational health. *Phi Delta Kappan, 70*(9), 68–69.

Newmann, F. M., & Wehlage, G. G. (1993). Five standards of authentic instruction. *Educational Leadership, 50,* 8–12.

Novak, J. D. (1990). Concept mapping: A useful tool for science education. *Journal of Research in Science Teaching, 10,* 937–949.

Patton, J. R. (1994). Practical recommendations for using homework with students with disabilities. *Journal of Learning Disabilities, 27,* 570–578.

Pugach, M. C., & Warger, C. L. (Eds.). (1996). *Curriculum trends, special education, and reform: Refocusing the conversation.* New York: Teachers College Press.

Putnam, J. W. (Ed.). (1998). *Cooperative learning and strategies for inclusion: Celebrating diversity in the classroom.* Baltimore: Paul H. Brookes.

Reynolds, A. (1992). What is competent beginning teaching? A review of the literature. *Review of Educational Research, 62*(1), 1–35.

Rice, D. C., Ryan, J. M., & Samson, S. M. (1998). Using concept maps to assess student learning in the science classroom: Must different methods compete? *Journal of Research in Science Teaching, 35,* 1103–1127.

Ruiz-Primo, M. A., & Shavelson, R. J. (1996). Rhetoric and reality in science performance assessments: An update. *Journal of Research in Science Teaching, 33,* 1045–1063.

Sizer, T. R. (1996). *Horace's hope.* Boston: Houghton Mifflin.

Starr, M. L., & Krajcik, J. S. (1990). Concept maps as a heuristic for science curriculum development: Toward improvement in process and product. *Journal of Research in Science Teaching, 27,* 987–1000.

Steinberg, A. (1997, March/April). Making schoolwork more like real work. *The Harvard Letter, 12*(2), 1–6.

Taymans, J. M., & Lynch, S. (1996, Nov.). *Preparing preservice teachers to teach concepts to diverse learners: Four case studies.* Washington, DC: 19th Annual Teacher Education Division, Council for Exceptional Children.

University of Kansas, Center for Research on Learning. (1994). *The unit organizer routine: The content enhancement professional development packet.* Lawrence: Center for Research on Learning.

Vaughn, S. (1999, May). *A synthesis of syntheses.* Presentation given at Keys to Successful Learning: A National Summit on Research in Learning Disabilities. Washington, DC.

Wandersee, J. J. (1990). Concept mapping and the cartography of cognition. *Journal of Research in Science Teaching, 27,* 923–936

White, R., & Gunstone, R. (1992). *Probing understanding.* New York: Falmer Press.

Wiggins, G., & McTighe, J. (1998). *Understanding by design.* Alexandria, VA: Association for Supervision and Curriculum Development.

Zimmaro, D. M., & Cawley, J. M. (1998). Concept map module [online]. Schreyer Institute for Innovation in Learning. The Pennsylvania State University. Available: *http://www.inov8.psu.edu.*

8

Lesson Planning and Delivery

Lillie R. Albert
Jerome J. Ammer

Critical Self-Test Questions

- Why is lesson planning important?
- What lesson planning models have you used or seen used by others?
- How can lesson planning be used to ensure that all students are learning?
- How can the Lesson Organizer Routine promote more effective planning and teaching?
- What formal assessment measures can be used to evaluate student learning on a day-to-day basis?

Students should also be taught how to create their own interpretations of the past and present, as well as how to identify their own positions, interests, ideologies, and assumptions.

—J. A. Banks, 1993, p. 6

In this chapter, we focus on the rationale for constructing and using lesson plans. Lesson planning is the culmination of all the other planning routines. Matching lesson plans with unit and course content helps ensure that teachers incorporate state content standards into curricular goals and objectives. It is where unit plans are played out and where teachers plan for and talk with students about what is to be learned and how they will help students learn it. While unit plans define the overall roadmap for teaching and learning, lesson plans are created to translate and transform the content into experiences that help students organize, understand, and remember key information. Not only does lesson planning focus on what content is to be learned and the activities and tasks students will engage in to learn it, but it is also the level at which teachers interact with students and evaluate how they are reacting to the planned lesson and how their learning is proceeding. Good lesson planning can make instruction responsive to the unique and changing needs of a particular class and its individual students on a daily basis.

The comments made by the teachers in the chapter scenario illustrate the lack of importance many place on lesson planning. Unfortunately, lesson planning is often dismissed as irrelevant and time consuming after student teaching. Instructional planning and decision making are demanding processes that call for a practical understanding of student learning. In addition, a variety of techniques are necessary to meet the diverse needs of students. At the same time, certain curricular goals must be met. These aspects of planning can be overwhelming.

Teachers understand that instructional planning is not simply for their own benefit or convenience, but also for their students. Nevertheless, teachers have traditionally failed to construct or develop lesson plans *with*

FIGURE 8.1
Graphic Organizer

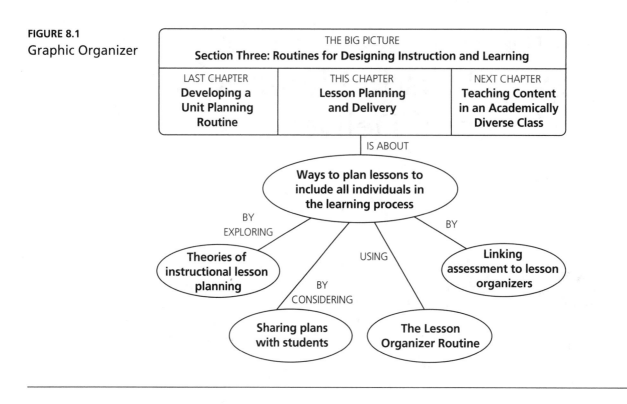

students. Sharing lesson plans with students can be especially helpful in responding to academic diversity and individual differences in secondary classrooms.

The teachers in the following scenario would probably agree that one of their goals is for students to be able to weave concepts and ideas into integrated structures that take into account prior knowledge and experiences. However, they may not be aware of the role that planning can play in accomplishing this goal. In reality, lesson planning is where you make the detailed connections that are critical to mastering the content of a unit. For many students, connections need to be made explicit so that they can understand relationships and connect current learning to prior knowledge and learning.

FOUNDATIONS AND PRINCIPLES

Traditionally, daily instructional planning has reflected the four basic elements of the linear model (Tyler, 1950) or the "mental image" model (Clark & Yinger, 1987), which call for specifying: (1) objectives, (2) materials, (3) procedures, and (4) assessment. Teachers develop daily plans around specific objectives that they have identified, decide on activities or procedures they will use to help students achieve those objectives, and outline how student learning will be assessed. The lesson is developed using a sequence of prescribed steps, which vary in detail. An additional component of a good lesson plan is identification of state, national, and professional standards that are woven into instruction and learning outcomes (see recommended list of resources about standards at the end of the chapter).

■ *Scenario*

Two weeks before the new school year begins at Allen Middle School, the three eighth-grade inter-disciplinary teams and members of the school curriculum committee cluster around tables to discuss instructional planning. The curriculum committee met several times over the summer to talk about planning instruction for academically diverse learners, how to improve student perfor-mance, and ownership and engagement in the curriculum. Another objective was to help the different teams of teachers develop a common format for lesson planning that would make instruction more explicit for students. The group has already identified and created plans for units.

The discussion is being led by Nona Queue, the curriculum coordinator, who has suggested using a graphic lesson organizer. Ms. Queue is arguing that this approach to lesson planning is a way to help students better understand what they need to learn and the relationships between topics in lessons and units. Her proposal causes a buzz among the staff. Bob Smith, an eighth-grade mathematics teacher, remains skeptical. "I don't know about anybody else, but I haven't got the time to make elaborate plans. Too many things cut into our day—and our planning meet-ings—as it is." Several colleagues nod their heads in agreement. The curriculum coordinator pro-ceeds cautiously. "I appreciate your concern, and I have to be truthful; creating lesson organizers will take time, especially at the beginning. It does become easier, though, as you begin to use the format for each lesson." Hardly mollified by this suggestion, Freda Jackson, an English teacher, offers more resistance. "I don't see how a graphic organizer can take the place of my plan book. And why should I share it with the students? It's too soon before classes begin to learn to use something new. I agree with Bob, I don't have the time necessary for this kind of planning either."

In an attempt to engage even one staff mem-ber, the curriculum coordinator cajoles, "I under-stand what you are saying, but the curriculum committee and I believe we must find a better way to help all our students become more involved with the content we teach. We believe that using lesson organizers will help us provide students with better opportunities to learn. It will also build our students' abilities to think divergently; I know most of us are in agreement about strengthening our pupils' higher-order thinking skills. I believe we can do this with graphic organizers, because they will help students see connections between ideas and information in a lesson. I'm convinced that graphic organizers will improve learning opportunities for all stu-dents—those with well-developed skills, as well as those with less-developed skills. The committee and I propose that you try the graphic organizer for one marking period." A silence falls over the room. Freda Jackson continues: "Why can't we continue to plan as we currently are doing, using our weekly plan books? What's wrong with just noting objectives, textbook pages, and proce-dures in plan books?"

On the heels of Freda Jackson's questions, a voice calls out, "Yes, you know the old saying, 'If it isn't broken, don't fix it!'" The status quo appeared to triumph for the moment.

Focus and Reflect

This is both an individual and a group activity.

- Begin by reviewing the conversation that you just read in the scenario. Make a list of what you know about lesson planning.
- What approaches have you seen teachers use to orchestrate their daily planning?
- How effective do you think their lesson-organizing behaviors have been in terms of engaging students in learning? In terms of student achievement?
- Get together in small teams and review your reflections. Revisit the scenario and ponder how the attitudes expressed support or undermine planning for instruc-tion that assists all students in learning.

The Linear Planning Model

The theory that informs this model is that planning requires that content be developed and presented in a logical and hierarchical sequence. The teacher selects learning strategies and presents the lesson to the students, followed by either guided or independent practice; later, student learning is assessed. Scope-and-sequence maps identifying content and the order in which it should be taught are easily adapted to this model; each lesson matches elements from the text or district grade-appropriate scope-and-sequence chart. This model is frequently associated with curriculum and instructional decisions based on the structure and content of a textbook. This is also a model that readily accommodates traditional objective assessment techniques associated with state and national testing.

There are several variations on the steps, or stages, that are included in a lesson plan. Callahan, Clark, and Kellough (1998) suggest seven basic elements that should be found in any lesson plan: "descriptive course data, goals and objectives, rationale, procedure, assignments and assignment reminders, materials and equipment, and a section for assessment, reflection and revision" (p. 154). Although not all teachers or methods course instructors use these seven elements, the idea of a linear frame for instruction can be identified in most lesson plans (Clark & Yinger, 1987).

The lesson plan illustrated in Figure 8.2 is an example of one type of organizer frequently found in classrooms. This is also the format that is appearing on many Web sites that provide lesson plans in a variety of content areas. A computer search on lesson plans is encouraged to explore the richness of examples that incorporate the key elements of a linear lesson plan.

While most commonly used methods texts discuss instructional planning, few provide a template or research base for using lesson plans (Ammer, Hansen, & Alexandrowicz, 1999). Historically, experienced teachers have resisted the rational-linear approach to daily planning (Arends, 1998). Although they were introduced to the method in teacher preparation programs and were required to write detailed plans for student-teaching practica, many teachers abandoned the linear model, unless they were required to use it by the school district in which they worked.

Clark and Yinger (1987) found that practitioners, rather than developing detailed lesson plans, form mental images about how they expect a specific lesson or activity to develop. They suggest that teachers often plan by drawing on past experiences and the learning outcomes they anticipate, as well as the length of time available for instruction, the content to be covered, materials needed to cover that content, and classroom management issues. In contrast to the rational-linear model, Clark and Yinger argue that the process is cyclical in nature, in that it does not proceed in a continuous, direct manner. Yet other theorists, such as Weick (1979), propose that practitioners organize instruction primarily around activities that have worked well in the past or that promise to engage students, and consider goals or objectives later.

Why Make Lesson Plans?

There are several good reasons why teachers should plan lessons in detail. Having a developed lesson plan can help teachers think carefully about what learning outcomes they expect and the ways in which they will help students achieve those outcomes. In addition, detailed lesson plans help

FIGURE 8.2   Lesson Planner: Rational-Linear Model

Lesson Title:_____ Grade Level:_____

Overall Goal:_____

_____

Specific Objectives:

1._____

2._____

Materials:

_____   _____

_____   _____

_____   _____

Procedures:

1._____

2._____

3._____

4._____

Assessment:

_____

_____

_____

_____

Source: Adapted from R. I. Arends, 1998, *Learning to Teach,* Boston: McGraw-Hill.

▪ *Scenario Revisited*

Back in her office, Nona Queue thought about the meeting she had just had with teachers. How could she persuade her colleagues that lesson planning with graphic organizers was worth the additional time it would take? And how could she persuade or show them that it could really help students become more engaged with lessons and improve their understanding of important ideas and information in a lesson?

Nona thought about a divide-and-conquer strategy: Perhaps she could persuade one or two teachers to try using lesson organizers. She remembered that Ed Reese, the science teacher, had been complaining in the teacher's lounge last year about student inattentiveness. "The students have no attention span! They act as if

they never heard anything about this information!" he had exclaimed one day. Perhaps Ed could be persuaded to try using the organizers, because the one Nona had in mind included specific provisions for recording and reminding students about previous and subsequent lessons, as well as connecting individual lessons to the content "big picture" in a course. And maybe she could persuade Lisa Canaille, the special needs coordinator, to work with Ed. This would give him some extra support as he tried something new and, depending on how the relationship worked out, it might give Lisa an opportunity to share with a colleague more of her expertise about individualized instruction.

teachers be clear, in their own minds, about exactly what they want students to learn; these explicit goals can be shared with students to help structure their learning. A lesson plan also provides a concrete way to match instruction and learning outcomes with content standards established by state and professional organizations. No matter how lesson planning has been done in the past, we may need to reassess how to do it in light of curriculum reform that has stressed the need to use pedagogical practices that help all students develop meaningful understanding of course content (for example, see the National Council of Teachers of Mathematics, 1989; 1991; 1995).

KNOWING AND DOING

A New Paradigm for Improved Pedagogy: Sharing Plans with Students

In the previous chapters on course and unit planning, you learned about the importance of setting the stage for learning. Guidelines were presented for using critical questions and content maps with students to provide a context for learning. The lessons of a unit, lasting a single day or several days, provide even more opportunities to "scaffold" or support learning. At the lesson-planning level, the information you collect about students as you get to know them is used to guide daily decisions and interactions with students. The principles, rituals, and performance options discussed in course planning are put in place in the lessons. Indeed, most of the instructional and assessment practices emphasized in preservice methods classes are designed to be embedded in lesson plans. Later, in the chapters on teaching routines and learning strategies, we will further explore how you can enhance learning and make instruction more explicit for students to increase rates of learning in daily lessons. However, in this chapter, we will continue to reinforce many of the principles presented in earlier chapters and provide even more opportunities to focus on how to involve students more fully in the learning process on a daily basis.

As we think about ways to make lesson planning and delivery more learner-centered, we must once again emphasize the idea of involving students in the unfolding or unpacking of a lesson. Some educators advocate including the learner as a participant during the design and delivery of instruction. Active involvement of students in classroom instruction has been encouraged by many educators throughout the past century (Dewey, 1960; Goodlad, 1983; Kohl & Pepper, 2000). Such involvement may better reveal what students already know and may help you incorporate this information in lesson plans. This may be done during an "anticipatory set" or advance organizer.

Anticipatory Set   A common practice for introducing a new lesson is the use of an anticipatory set. Anticipatory set is a "hook" to gain students' attention, giving them an opportunity to think about their previous learning, as well as their personal knowledge, as a way to set the stage for new or expanded knowledge development. Through the use of an anticipatory set, teachers can provide students with opportunities to reveal not only what they know about lesson topics but also how their life experiences relate (or do not relate) to what you will be asking them to learn.

A popular anticipatory set strategy designed by Ogle (1986) is commonly referred to as the KWL learning device. In this approach teachers engage learners as they conduct a quick informal assessment of students' prior knowledge. The three prompts in this technique are: (1) What do I **K**now? (2) What do I **W**ant to learn?, and (3) What have I **L**earned? What students already know or understand can be written down on a chart. This chart, in addition to informing you about what your students already know, may also be referred to as new knowledge is connected to old.

Another way to engage students in learning is to share your instructional plans with them. Creating a graphic organizer for a lesson is an effective way to do this. By constructing an organized lesson diagram with students, you give them more ownership of the learning process, both by sharing the purposes and direction of instruction and by providing opportunities, during the diagram construction process, for students to express their perceptions (or misperceptions!) about the lesson content. The visual nature of a graphic organizer also provides a way to integrate an additional learning modality into instruction. When teachers share plans with students, it can help structure learning and provide a framework that illustrates the flow of lessons and course activities and provides a visual representation of how the content and its concepts, topics, and supporting information are organized and connected.

Developing detailed lesson plans and sharing them with students encourages you to integrate content knowledge and teaching actions (Bulgren & Lenz, 1996; Hyerle, 1996; Lenz, Marrs, Schumaker, & Deshler, 1993). It can help you be more self-conscious as a planner, to examine more carefully what it is you want to teach and what you want students to learn. This kind of self-conscious planning is a constructive way for you to represent a

▪ *Scenario Revisited*

Nona Queue talked with Ed Reese and Lisa Canaille about using a lesson organizer routine in Ed's class. She told them about how lesson organizers could provide a vehicle for active student involvement and interaction with course content. She also explained that a lesson organizer could help students organize information so they could see what they had learned already and how the new information and ideas fit with the old. Making these kinds of connections also provided opportunities for students to share with peers and teachers some of their perspectives on the course content—whether it related or did not relate to anything in their lives, whether they knew people, or had had experiences that gave them insights into information or ideas to

be discussed in a lesson. This would be a good way to address diversity in their classrooms and also include more students in the learning community. Nona was up front with Ed and Lisa about the fact that using this routine would take extra time at first. But she also argued that the effort would be worth it if the routine helped students learn and become more involved in their learning.

Ed's interdisciplinary team at the middle school was scheduled to have practicum students in the first two quarters of the school year, so Ed figured this, along with Lisa's help, would provide some extra help to work on implementing the lesson organizers. He and Lisa agreed to try the Lesson Organizer Routine.

sense of self in your teaching: "Teachers' values and perspectives mediate and interact with what they teach and influence the way that their messages are communicated to and perceived by students" (Banks, 1997, p. 107).

The Lesson Organizer Routine

Prospective and practicing teachers can plan lessons using the graphic organizer approach, called "The Lesson Organizer Routine" (Lenz, Marrs, Schumaker, & Deshler, 1993). The Lesson Organizer Routine is a culmination of the course and unit planning routines presented in earlier chapters. Like those routines, it uses a visual device that graphically frames and organizes the content of a lesson so that students may see the main ideas of the lesson and how the main ideas relate to each other and to prior content knowledge. Content is more meaningful when students are able to see its relevance and purpose in the discipline (Albert, 2000a; Ladson-Billings, 1994). In addition, the lesson organizer, a developmental framework, serves as a schema that helps students focus not only on the lesson's main ideas, but also on the activities, tasks, or procedures they will experience as they grapple with the ideas of the lesson.

Specifically, the Lesson Organizer Routine can help students experiencing learning difficulties because it organizes and explains what is to be learned. It also helps such students by offering them a voice in the development of the lesson, which also helps to make the purpose of the lesson explicit (Albert, 2000b). Learning objectives and processes are made transparent as teacher and students discuss instructional practices, activities, and experiences necessary to encourage and promote learning and understanding for all students.

Based on extensive research (Lenz, Marrs, Schumaker, & Deshler, 1993), the Lesson Organizer Routine facilitates quality delivery of lessons that meet state and professional mandates in a way that helps focus teacher and students on the instructional journey. Successful use of the Lesson Organizer Routine is based on introducing the lesson graphic organizer to students in a clear and explicit way, facilitating active student involvement in its use, using the organizer frequently to help students become familiar and comfortable with it, and shaping concepts and ideas to meet student needs and a teacher's own personal teaching style.

When to Use the Lesson Organizer Routine   Not every lesson to be taught may require explicit written plans. The Lesson Organizer Routine becomes most useful for lessons where the content is particularly difficult for students to master. It may also be used in conjunction with the Unit Organizer Routine discussed in Chapter 7, or it may be used independently of that routine. In deciding whether or not to use the Lesson Organizer Routine, you need to identify what content is difficult for the particular students you are teaching and then organize and structure it for them with the lesson organizer. As with the other graphic organizers in this book, the lesson organizer allows you to order, for yourself and for your students, the relative importance of different sets of information and to show the relationships between and among those pieces of information. In addition, the lesson organizer provides a concrete model to use in presenting new information to students and connecting that knowledge to what students already know. Prior knowledge can be called upon more readily by a visual stimulus, such as a lesson map, which assists students as they integrate new knowledge into an already existing schema.

Preparing to Use the Routine   While you will be using the Lesson Organizer Routine interactively with students, it is important that you plan lesson goals and procedures ahead of time. You are the content expert; it is up to you to identify critical concepts to be learned and how you can best support students in learning them. This means that you will need to specify and paraphrase the lesson topics, identify and map the unit or background knowledge upon which the lesson is based, and identify and prepare a draft of a map of the critical lesson content. You will also need to specify important relationships, generate a list of self-test questions, learning tasks, and work assignments, and specify task-related learning strategies (Lenz, Marrs, Schumaker, & Deshler, 1993). Shaping the broad outlines of the lesson will prepare you to structure new knowledge for your students. At the same time, having a graphic organizer that you and students fill in together provides opportunities for students to be involved in how the lesson unfolds: They may have examples or analogies of their own to illustrate concepts being discussed, or they may raise questions that make you more aware of their confusion or lack of understanding.

As you and your students become more comfortable with the routine, and perhaps after you have taught a particular lesson several times, you may find that you and students can construct a lesson map spontaneously. At times, you may also invite students to work in groups or individually to draft a lesson organizer on their own, after reading a textbook chapter or listening to a lecture presentation.

Creating and Maintaining Learning Communities   The Lesson Organizer Routine, when used with other teaching strategies to enhance instruction, assists teachers in creating and maintaining learning communities. One of the biggest challenges for teachers in fostering learning communities is designing instruction aimed at helping students become active participants in a community so they form connections among and between their classroom peers. "When these connections do not develop, a learning community does not form. The result is a 'disconnected' classroom and instructional environment where only a portion of the students of the class feel accepted, connected, successful, and meet expectations" (Lenz, Marrs, Schumaker, & Deshler, 1993, p. 2). A disconnected classroom is the reality for students in many secondary schools. Too often, lessons may be abstract and questions, directions, and tasks are lost on students. However, in a supported learning environment, lessons, topics, and activities are explicitly connected with previous learning, providing context that contributes to understanding.

Using The Routine   As with the course and unit organizers, the Lesson Organizer Routine incorporates the Cue-Do-Review Process. It also uses Linking Steps. The Linking Steps guide implementation of the routine, assuring that students are involved in its implementation. They are also designed to promote the broad goals of acquiring, remembering, and demonstrating learning. As indicated in earlier chapters on planning, it is important to cue students explicitly about the fact that an organizer is being used as a way to help them learn. In addition, students need to be informed about how you plan to use the organizer and about your expectations regarding their use of the organizer. Will you expect them to fill in the organizer as it is constructed in class? Should they take all or only some notes on the organizer? Should they use the organizer to prepare for tests? How should they "read" the organizer, and how does it show relationships? Until students become very familiar with the use of the organizer, you will need to discuss with them how to use it most effectively.

The Linking Steps for the Lesson Organizer Routine may be remembered by the acronym CRADLE: **C**onsolidate goals, **R**eview knowledge, **A**ssemble anchors, **D**escribe and map content, **L**ink content to anchors, and **E**xplore questions and tasks. Using the Linking Steps, the routine is implemented interactively with students. A lesson centered on Harriet Tubman and Sojourner Truth, within a unit on famous women in American history, may serve as an example of how to use the Lesson Organizer Routine (see Figure 8.3).

CUE USE OF THE LESSON ORGANIZER ROUTINE. Susan Jordan teaches an eighth-grade social studies class. She has decided to combine history, sociology, and language arts in a multidisciplinary unit that celebrates the racial and cultural diversity of famous women of color in American history. Ms. Jordan is concerned that the students in this predominantly white, middle-class environment lack an awareness of racial and cultural differences, so she has decided to construct a unit with her students, the main purpose of which is to promote such awareness and to explore the ways in which students perceive race, gender, and social class.

She began by cueing her students that they would be using a lesson organizer as a way to organize information and also as a way to think together about the contributions and achievements of women of color in American history. She also explained that whenever they used a lesson organizer, she would give them copies of the organizer, which they were to keep in their notebooks, using it as a place to take notes, on occasion. She

FIGURE 8.3 Shared Planning Lesson Organizer: Women in History

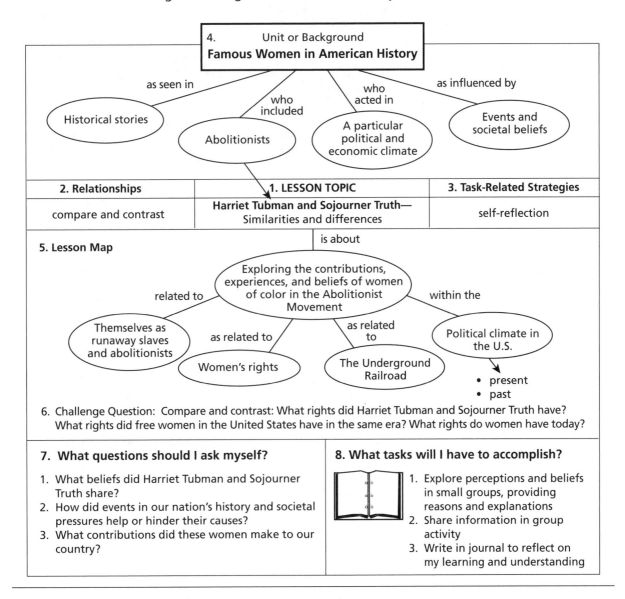

Source: Adapted from Lenz, Marrs, Schumaker, & Deshler, 1993, *The Lesson Organizer Routine,* Lawrence, KS: Edge Enterprises.

told her students that the lesson organizer would help them understand how today's lesson related to our past and present history. Finally, she told them they would be participating actively in the discussion, as they helped construct several parts of the organizer.

DO THE ROUTINE WITH STUDENTS. Actually doing the routine involves the following six steps.

Step 1: Consolidate goals. The purpose of this step is to give students a simple way of thinking about the whole lesson by (a) naming the topic of the lesson, (b) paraphrasing the topic in words the students understand,

(c) identifying important relationships that students need to be looking for within the lesson content, and (d) naming the strategy or strategies students will be using to achieve learning outcomes.

Ms. Jordan began the lesson by introducing a drawing of Harriet Tubman. Rather than identify the woman in the drawing for her students, she elicited guesses from her audience. To do so, Ms. Jordan distributed copies of the lesson organizer with the unit or background section completed. She told students: "We're going to be looking at women in American history, using particular individuals as examples of women who fought for social change. Do you recall the name of the woman in this picture?" Only three hands went up. Ms. Jordan called on two students before somebody gave the correct answer.

Ms. Jordan continued: "That's correct. Harriet Tubman. Today we will be reviewing her contributions before, during, and after the Civil War, as part of our unit on Famous American Women in History. We will be talking about Harriet Tubman and another famous woman in American history, Isabella Baumfree—otherwise known as Sojourner Truth. We will be exploring who these women were and what they accomplished.

"Let's begin by looking at our lesson organizers. (Ms. Jordan uses the overhead projector.) In box 1, we will fill in the *lesson topic,* which, in just one or two words, tells us the main idea of the lesson. It is designed to help you and me focus on the main idea of the lesson. In today's lesson we will talk about some of the contributions made by these two women of color, Harriet Tubman and Sojourner Truth, so you should write that in box 1. (Ms. Jordan and students fill in box 1.)

"How can we learn about these women? That's right, one way is to look at their contributions to the movement to abolish slavery. What else? Yes, we can also talk about any similarities and differences in their beliefs about other issues of their day, including women's rights. When we talk about similarities and differences, we are talking about a relationship called 'compare and contrast,' so we want to write that relationship in box 2. This identifies for us the most important *relationships* to be included in the lesson's content.

"Next we want to identify on our organizer how we are going to explore and learn about the lesson topic. First, we will want to review what we know about the two women. As we discuss similarities and differences between these two women, we can also talk about how they were perceived during the time they lived, and we can talk about the role of women and women of color in our society today. We can also explore our own thoughts and feelings about the contributions of these women. So we will use a process of self-reflection to compare our beliefs and attitudes to those of U. S. society—past and present." Ms. Jordan and students fill in box 3, *Task-Related Strategies,* which identifies how students will gain, store, or express information throughout the lesson. Having framed the lesson with the students, Ms. Jordan decided they were ready to move on to the second of the Routine's Linking Steps.

Step 2: Review knowledge. In the second step, background knowledge that relates to the lesson is discussed by reviewing topics of previous lessons, student background knowledge or experiences, and checking students' understanding of major course, unit, and/or chapter concepts that relate to the lesson. Ms. Jordan reviewed with students what they had already learned in this unit:

Ms. JORDAN: Let's review what we already know about society, politics, and women's roles during this period in history. In what types of activities did women typically engage in the mid-1800s?

SARAH: They cooked, sewed, and took care of their families.

Ms. JORDAN: All women? What about those who were slaves?

SARAH: It was even worse for them. They had to take care of their families *and* the families they worked for.

Ms. JORDAN: Was that all?

SARAH: No, they did the hardest chores.

Ms. JORDAN: How did society perceive women?

JONATHAN: They didn't have any rights.

Ms. JORDAN: What do you mean by "rights"?

JONATHAN: Well, they couldn't vote or make important decisions.

Step 3: Assemble a visual anchor. In this step, the new information to be learned in the lesson is "anchored" (or connected) to previously learned information by graphically depicting the organization of previously learned knowledge in section 4 of the Lesson Organizer. How the new information is connected to or fits within the unit or the background knowledge is demonstrated by drawing an arrow between information in sections 4 and 1.

Ms. Jordan helped her students assemble a visual anchor by helping them to focus on the Unit Map in section 4 of their organizers.

Ms. JORDAN: As you can see, we've already talked about some of the information in the Unit Map in section 4 on our organizers, when we talked yesterday about societal beliefs toward women who challenged traditional attitudes. Which part of the Unit Map are we focusing on today?

TRISTAN: Abolitionists?

Ms. JORDAN: Right, we'll be focusing on the way Harriet Tubman and Sojourner Truth became heroines to the abolitionists, that is, Northern antislavery leaders. (Ms. Jordan helps the students recall what an abolitionist is). She continues, "We know they were both against slavery. What else can we say they had in common?"

SAM: They both spoke out for the rights of women.

JUSTINE: And, they were both runaway slaves and abolitionists.

Ms. JORDAN: Yes, we discussed this in yesterday's lesson. This arrow shows where our lesson fits in the bigger picture of our unit. (Arrow is drawn).

Step 4: Describe and map the content. In the fourth step, the main ideas and information to be covered in the lesson are communicated to the students by naming and explaining them and visually depicting the relationships among these concepts in Section 5 of the Lesson Organizer.

Ms. JORDAN: Let's map what we know so far. In the "is about," or main lesson oval, we can write that this lesson is about "exploring the contributions of women of color in the Abolitionist Movement." We also want to talk about their experiences as slaves and their beliefs about other social causes, such as women's rights. So, let's add "experiences and beliefs" to "contributions" in the main lesson oval. Then, we can identify the subtopics of abolition and women's rights in the ovals below. Okay, what do we know about the experiences of Sojourner Truth and Harriet Tubman?

SARAH: Sojourner Truth was born a slave in New York in 1797, and Harriet Tubman was born in Maryland in 1820.

TAYLOR: Sojourner Truth was not part of the Underground Railroad system.

The class continues to list the information they know about each of the women, and students record important facts under the relevant headings on the organizer. Then Ms. Jordan leads the class in comparing and contrasting the lives and experiences of the two women.

Ms. JORDAN: As you can see, there were many similarities and differences between these two women. Both spoke out against slavery, as well as for women rights, and worked to lead Blacks out of slavery. Harriet Tubman lived in Canada a few months before the start of the Civil War because there was a very large ransom of $40,000 offered for her capture. After the Civil War started, she came back to America and served as a scout and nurse for the Union Army. On the other hand Sojourner Truth, a remarkable speaker, spent most of her time traveling and lecturing.

The rest of section 5 is filled in as students decide that tracking similarities and differences between Harriet Tubman and Sojourner Truth will be a way for them to look at the experiences of these women with slavery, the Underground Railroad, and women's rights during the nineteenth century.

Step 5: Link to students' lives. In this step, students' understanding of why they are learning the information is bolstered by linking the content of the lesson to their background knowledge through additional stories, examples, and analogies and explaining how the content of the lesson relates to the students' lives, using a "Challenge Question" in section 6 of the Lesson Organizer.

Ms. Jordan is interested in getting her students to think about how the lesson might relate to their lives. She engages her students in a discussion about Harriet Tubman and Sojourner Truth and how perceptions and beliefs about roles of women affected them when they lived and affect our views, now, of their lives.

Ms. JORDAN: Is it important to compare and contrast past views with current views of these women? Have perceptions about women's roles really changed all that much in the past century? What do you think? With all the freedom women have claimed over the past century, is it still important to consider societal beliefs today?

SARAH: Yes, because I think they've changed a lot.

TRISTAN: Not in all areas, though.

Ms. JORDAN: Tristan, tell us what you mean—explain to us in greater detail.

TRISTAN: I don't think the way we look at women's roles is very different today. A woman is still considered the person who should take care of the children and do most household chores.

Ms. Jordan: Is this true? Does anyone have a different perspective? (A number of hands fly up.)

Meghan: I don't agree. I know of many families where the mother works outside the home and the dad is raising the children at home. I think women have more opportunities to be anything they want to be—lawyers, doctors, engineers, and carpenters—anything!

Ms. Jordan: OK, so it's important for us to think about societal beliefs as part of thinking about roles of women. How can we accomplish this? Does having two examples to compare and contrast help us explore our perceptions about nontraditional roles for women? What do you think? What comparisons can we make between famous women in American history—past and present? Why is this important to consider? What events or conditions in our nation contribute to our societal beliefs? How are the accomplishments of Harriet Tubman different from those of, let's say, Secretary of State Madeleine Albright? How did (and does) society view the roles these women have taken on? What obstacles did (and does) either face? What tensions or stigmas continue to exist for famous women? What attributes—physical, racial, and cultural—enhance or inhibit their efforts? Understanding today's lesson and how famous women in American history, past and present, carried out their missions amidst public acclaim or criticism might help us understand how women can become a more visible force in the political shaping of our nation.

Step 6: Explore questions and tasks. In the sixth step, the specific lesson outcomes are communicated to students by specifying questions they should be able to answer at the end of the lesson and listing them in section 7 of the Lesson Organizer. The tasks associated with the lesson are listed in Section 8 of the organizer, describing expectations the students must meet.

Ms. Jordan now leads her students in brainstorming about some of the questions they would like to be able to answer at the end of today's lesson. Together they will write these down in section 7 of their Lesson Map.

Ms. Jordan: What questions do we have about nontraditional roles for women and societal beliefs during the nineteenth and twentieth centuries? What are some of the understandings we would like to come away with as a result of today's lesson?

Justine: I'd like to learn about whether negative societal beliefs actually helped famous women achieve greatness.

Toby: That's just what I was going to say! Maybe negative beliefs made these women stronger.

Sarah: I'd like to know how societal beliefs changed the way men viewed women's roles.

Jonathan: I could tell you how my dad feels about that!

Ms. Jordan: Please enlighten us, Jonathan. How does your father feel about traditional and nontraditional roles for women?

Jonathan: Well, he's a nurse, so . . .

Ms. Jordan and her students continued their discussion of similarities and differences between Harriet Tubman and Sojourner Truth. They decided to relate what they were learning about these two women to traditional and nontraditional roles for women—past and present. Their Challenge Question was to answer the question, "Compare and contrast: What rights did Harriet Tubman and Sojourner Truth have? What rights did free women in the United States have in the same era? What rights do women have today?" Ms. Jordan let the students discuss these issues in groups. Then she asked each student to record their views in their reflective journals.

REVIEW THE ROUTINE WITH STUDENTS. Using the Cue-Do-Review sequence, Ms. Jordan reviews and clarifies what she and her students have decided about the context, structure, strategies, questions, and tasks of the lesson.

> Ms. JORDAN: So, who can tell me what today's lesson is about? How does it relate to the unit we've been studying? How does it relate to current societal beliefs about women's roles? How does it relate to our concept of what constitutes an influential woman? Why is this important information for us to understand? As we proceed through the rest of the lesson, take notes on your lesson organizers. For each section, list the ways women's roles are viewed—past and present. Keep your Lesson Organizer in your notebook behind the Unit Organizer for this unit.

As Ms. Jordan and her students implement the Lesson Organizer Routine, the pedagogical focus shifts from the practitioner's teaching to the student's learning. Instead of Ms. Jordan lecturing about Sojourner Truth and Harriet Tubman, she leads students in acquiring and processing new information. In this process, she can not only check for student mastery but also provide opportunities for students to express their own unique understanding of the content.

While unit planning focuses on key concepts and ideas, lesson planning helps students make connections between unit concepts and the specific content knowledge that describes, defines, or characterizes unit concepts. Lesson planning is not only the culmination of course and unit planning; it is a cognitive template that can make concepts more understandable for students. Connecting prior knowledge to new knowledge is an essential step in the learning process, and lesson organizers can provide a schema, or visual way, to make the connections.

Focus and Reflect

- Consider a topic or lesson you would like to teach or are currently teaching.
- Sketch out the lesson like a webbing activity. In your map you should identify: (a) what your lesson is mainly about, (b) underlying theories or assumptions, (c) your lesson's major attributes, and (d) the context within which your lesson is set. Do not try to describe specific instructional techniques, but do determine your overall goal for the lesson and the "branches" that support it.
- When you have finished, share your map with a colleague. Analyze the content of your "main bubble" to see that your lesson goal is compatible with your lesson topic and main unit.
- Consider how you might share the construction of this web with your students.

Basic to the use of the Lesson Organizer Routine is the assumption that while teachers influence student thinking, students also influence teacher thinking. It is in the interaction between teacher and learner that decisions about context, structures, strategies, questions, and tasks are shared and clarified. The narrative about Ms. Jordan and her students illustrates some of the ways that the Lesson Organizer routine can be used as a vehicle for bringing these decisions together. When students are invited to suggest questions they want

■ *Scenario Revisited*

The second quarter of the school year at Allen Middle School has passed and the curriculum coordinator, members of the curriculum school committee, and the three eighth-grade inter-disciplinary teams are having a second meeting about using graphic organizers to plan and implement learning experiences for their students. One interdisciplinary team, including the special educator for that team, volunteered to pilot the Lesson Organizer Routine for two quarters. They have been asked to make a presentation to the other two teams with the hope that it would encourage those teams to also try the Unit and Lesson Organizers. Ed Reese, the science teacher, is addressing the group:

"As you know, my colleagues and I agreed to pilot lesson organizers through the end of the second quarter. We were able to collaborate with our practicum students who, fortunately, had learned about graphic organizers in their methods courses. I know that I speak for members of our team when I say that we found them extremely useful in assisting us in organizing our lessons. For example, the organizers helped students understand what the important parts of the lesson were. It was really useful to have a picture in front of us all at all times to keep us focused on the important information. And I have to admit that the organizer helped me too. I realized that I have probably tried to squeeze too many details into my course. When the organizer made me take all those details and show their relationship to the big ideas and important information, I discovered that some of the details just didn't fit very well."

"But, Ed, how about the workload?" interrupted a member from a third team. "You can't possibly suggest that this was an easy process?"

"Judy," Ed Reese responded, "you are right; it was not easy. But it *was* worthwhile. I saw an engagement on the part of my students that I haven't seen for a long time, as they contributed examples of concepts and questions we could ask. They felt truly 'connected' to the content—especially my verbally gifted students. Some students actually helped clarify my ideas for their classmates. These kids really welcome being part of the process."

"What about your students with special needs?" asked another team member.

"Well," Ed continued, "that was another surprising outcome. Lisa, our special needs liaison, and I co-planned our lessons, which enabled her to work with a variety of different students with varying abilities in our class. That turned out to be very beneficial to me and my students. It helped me to see where I needed to be more explicit for some students, and it helped all students in the class see that a special needs teacher knew the content and could help any student."

"Not to mention how it made *me* feel, Ed," Lisa Canaille chimed in. "Co-planning with the team made me feel like part of the solution. This is the first time I have co-taught with a general education teacher, and I didn't feel like a visitor, or an interloper! It gave me a real sense of empowerment. It empowered our students, also. I got a chance to work with all the students in the class. I actually saw students learn to organize their thinking and see connections and relationships in the lesson concepts and information. They absolutely loved sharing ideas and information with one another."

answered about the lesson topic as well as ideas they want to explore further, learning becomes a community effort. When students can express their misunderstandings as well as understandings as a lesson unfolds, they can see that you are there not just to share your expert knowledge but to help them understand that knowledge.

Lesson Organizers and Improving Professional Practice and Collaboration
Using lesson organizers can fuel reflective practice and be an impetus for transforming teaching and learning in the classroom, for teachers and students. A critical aspect of the process of using lesson organizers is self-assessment, because effective instructional planning with the graphic organizers is an unfolding dynamic process. Creating a graphic organizer and identifying critical questions about the content can be a way for you to see more clearly the connections, relationships, and significance in the content. Creating a lesson organizer can be a way to bring all the pieces together to create a synergy, as opposed to fragmentation, of instruction.

The scenario on the previous page highlights an additional benefit: A lesson organizer can make planning transparent not only for students but also for other professional staff, whose responsibility is to support learning for all students in general education classrooms. As expectations increase for meeting the learning needs of all students, teachers increasingly need to look to the help that may be provided by special education teachers and other support staff to assure that all students are learning. (This topic will be addressed in more detail in Chapter 12.) You and other teachers who can "make the biggest difference in education today are those who are committed to a process of continual professional growth and development. . . . The key to addressing these challenges lies, in large measure, in teachers who are willing to try new ways of teaching and reaching students" (Lenz, Marrs, Schumaker, & Deshler, 1993, p. 26).

Focus and Reflect

- Imagine that you are in the school environment mentioned above. From your perspective as a general or special educator, what questions would you have for Ed Reese about using the Lesson Organizers?
- Compile a list of questions or concerns based on what you already know about Lesson Organizers.
- What part of the process, if any, most attracts you?
- Do you think the scenarios present a realistic portrayal of teachers' concerns? Why or why not?

Linking Assessment to Lesson Organizers

Assessment should be the primary means of providing both constructive responses to students about their performance and information to teachers that will lead to changes in curricular decisions and teaching practices. If assessment practices are to reflect instructional practices, and, in particular, day-to-day planning, a variety of approaches are needed to assess student learning. Assessment is a mechanism that allows teachers to make judgments about student progress, thinking, and accomplishments. It is also a process that teachers use to consider and evaluate their curricular and instructional practices. Several assessment alternatives that work well with lesson organizers are performance assessment, portfolio assessment, and open-ended response items.

Performance Assessment   Performance-based assessment provides students with meaningful and high-quality tasks that have value beyond that of documenting mastery, such as giving an oral report or a dramatic or musical performance. Performance tasks are designed to promote student growth and enhance student learning. They measure how students construct and apply their understanding of course content and conceptual knowledge. Performance-based assessment also provides opportunities for teachers to improve instruction and modify curriculum if necessary. For example, after observing students complete a task and after looking over the completed tasks, you can decide to go on to the next topic, concept, or activity. You may also make a decision to reteach the topic using another approach, or come back to the topic later.

Portfolio Assessment   People in other professions (e.g., artists) commonly use portfolios to display a range of their skills and accomplishments. A portfolio is a systematic collection of student work that documents progress toward learning goals or expectations and demonstrates students' efforts and achievement (Alter, 1992). Portfolio assessment, like performance assessment, can also provide information that allows you to change instruction or adjust curriculum according to student needs.

Open-Ended Response Items   Open-ended response items are questions or tasks that can be used with a variety of writing activities and with lesson organizers. The items are designed to engage students in a process by which they illustrate or express understanding of content area knowledge, integrate concepts or ideas, and solve complex problems. Students are called upon to use critical thinking skills and writing to demonstrate their thinking and thought processes.

When planning open-ended response items, it is important to provide clear information to students about what they need to accomplish to successfully complete an item. More importantly, the assessment item should be relevant to students and closely connected to their learning. Thus, the idea is to design and to develop assessment tasks that measure how students apply and construct their knowledge and conceptual understanding. Open-ended questions provide a medium that allows students an opportunity to expand on their ideas.

For examples of how assessment may be linked to lesson organizers, consider the eighth-grade team at Peterson Middle School, which has been involved in an interdisciplinary team unit titled, "Famous Women in American History." You will recall that Susan Jordan's lesson, described earlier, was part of this unit. Students in social studies classes at the school have been examining, defining, and discussing the roles of such historical figures as Susan B. Anthony, Harriet Tubman, and Sojourner Truth. They have also researched other significant figures in history who fought for the rights of oppressed groups. In their mathematics class, they have developed timelines and graphs that relate to some of the historical events that took place during that period. Moreover, in their science class, they researched inventions developed by women inventors and studied the careers of women scientists and mathematicians.

In their language arts class, they have been reading literature about famous and influential women. For instance, they read a selection from Virginia Hamilton's (1992) *Many Thousand Gone: African Americans from Slavery to Freedom*. The selection, "Her Name Was Truth," gave background information about Sojourner Truth and the period in which she lived. One of the team activities for the unit involved an interpretive dramatization of an excerpt from Sojourner Truth's speech, "Ain't I a Woman?" Social studies and language arts teachers collaborated on the activity. As an introduction, the social studies teacher led a discussion of Virginia Hamilton's story about

Sojourner Truth. The language arts teacher, dressed in costume, presented a dramatic interpretation of the speech. And at the end of the speech, the special educator sang a verse of a traditional spiritual. Following the presentation, students were asked to reflect with a partner on several questions presented to them:

> Taking into consideration the period in which Sojourner Truth spoke, for what right(s) do you think she was speaking? Think about the "flawed grammar" that Sojourner used. Do you think it took away from the effectiveness of her message? Why or why not?

This activity was followed by a whole-class discussion. The final assessment was an open-ended question that students responded to in their reflective writing journals. The following question is an example of the open-ended item posed to students.

> Write a clear reflective statement that explains what you learned from the presentation. Considering the period in which Sojourner Truth lived, do you think she was given the same rights that she was demanding for women of other races? Why or why not?

Figure 8.4 is an excerpt from a journal illustrating how one student responded to the question. This open-ended item was structured in such a way that it encouraged students to grapple with the ideas presented to them. Learning activities like this illustrate to students that their thinking, decisions, and explanations are valued and meaningful.

The teachers all shared in the assessment process, discussing how they would assess the open-ended item. Specifically, the social studies teacher assessed students on their ability to answer the question above, communicating what they had learned about Sojourner Truth within the historical context of the presentation and articulating a clear, concise statement responding to the second part of the item. The language arts teacher's assessment focused on the clarity and coherence of students' written answers to the questions posed.

These assessment activities reflected the decisions of one group of teachers; other teachers may assess students differently. The idea is to design and to develop assessment tasks that measure how students apply and construct their knowledge and conceptual understanding.

When you make a decision to use this type of assessment, keep in mind students' needs (social and academic) and the time allotted for the particular task. Engaging adolescents in activities that require critical reflection supports and facilitates student thinking and problem-solving abilities. This is central to the graphic organizer construct. Thus, using these types of tasks to assess student learning further enhances or, in some instances, maximizes student development of conceptual knowledge because of the social interaction that occurs first between students and later through discussion activities. Students are involved in the doing, finding out, and sharing what they are learning or have learned with their peers. Such student learning is powerful when practical activities speak to the needs of students to be heard and ensure their ideas and views are valued. Careful instructional planning with lesson organizers in tandem with course and unit planning can effectively promote this kind of learning when accompanied by an ongoing program of authentic assessment of student learning.

Focus and Reflect

In order to include all students in the learning journey, it is necessary to clearly delineate not only learning goals but outcomes as well. Consistent with the lesson map that you constructed in a previous activity, discuss some open-ended approaches to assessment that would not only reflect academic goals, but also enhance teacher/learner and teacher/teacher interaction.

FIGURE 8.4
Student Reflective
Journal Entry

I feel that Sojourner was speaking for the right to allow women to have equal opportunities like men, who were considered inferior or dominant. She felt that she and many other women were capable to be whomever they wanted to be, and not what men wanted them to be.

I believe that the approach Sojourner took wasn't the best approach to take, but I understand the reason she spoke the way she did during her speech. She wanted to reach more women. Seeing where men held women in lower classes back from getting a good --or any --education, she had to speak the way uneducated women would understand her best. So, I feel that this didn't diminish the effectiveness of the message.

My opinion is that Sojourner was trying to fight for the people of her time, but people were still prejudiced against African Americans, so she was really helping the white upper-class women and black upper-class women.

Brianna B.

Source: Used with permission.

In the following vignette, the Lesson Organizer Routine comes full circle as general and special educators discuss their use of the graphic organizers. The vignette illustrates the importance of assessment, not just as a gauge for what students are learning but also for evaluating practitioners' effectiveness. How well general and special educators use the lesson organizer construct in their classrooms can be reflected in the assessment they choose.

▪ *Scenario Revisited*

As the school year draws to a close, a third and final curriculum planning meeting is held. Ed Reese and his eighth-grade team are presenting their final evaluation of the graphic organizers to the curriculum committee and the other eighth-grade teams.

Lisa Canaille, the special education teacher who co-teaches with Ed Reese, spoke first: "We have had great success with planning and organizing lessons for all our students using graphic organizers, particularly with our lower achievers. We have faced some challenges, like finding the time for all of us to meet, but the experience has been very worthwhile. I think we've learned to tap the skills and insights of each team member. Working collaboratively means we not only contribute to the discussion, but also provide insights to our fellow co-teachers—insights they might not have realized working on their own."

"Exactly," adds Ed Reese. "Also, with Lisa's help, we've developed some incredible assessment measures that help us understand just what our students are really learning. Using graphic organizers is meaningful not only to the students, but to us as well. Many perspectives

are crucial to the success of our efforts. In fact, I think our team has produced our best lessons, not only in collaboration with each other, but also in collaboration with Lisa. Tapping her expertise has enabled us to create lessons that address the learning needs of more students.

Ed continued: "In response to those of you who were concerned about the time you thought all this extra planning would take, I can say that we have learned that we did not need to use the lesson organizer for every lesson. Not every idea or concept lends itself to this format. We found that we only used it when we believed the content we wanted to present was difficult or complicated or was particularly in need of visual organization for students so they wouldn't lose sight of the big ideas."

In conclusion, Ed and Lisa recommended that their fellow teachers develop at least one lesson for the following year using the Lesson Organizer Routine. They felt confident that most teachers, after working through the routine thoughtfully, would find it to be as useful a planning and teaching tool as they had.

SUMMARY

A teacher's role in the instructional process includes motivating students to want to learn. This is a big challenge. Formerly, educators believed that the teacher's role was to instruct and that responsibility for learning lay exclusively with the students. This perspective on learning and teaching has changed. Students in today's secondary classrooms bring with them many different learning needs. Teachers are responsible for providing the most effective instruction and learning experiences necessary to help students learn and understand course content. To accomplish this, teaching and learning must be viewed as a shared, interactive responsibility, involving both teachers and their students.

The challenge for both prospective and practicing teachers is to craft instruction that aims to help students understand subject matter, rather

than simply compute answers and memorize facts and concepts. The perspective of learning for understanding rejects the view that knowledge is a collection of facts and ideas implemented in rote procedures, with students functioning as passive learners.

The use of course, unit, and lesson organizers offers vital alternatives to the traditional instructional planning approach. This alternative is worth considering, especially if the goal is to better understand learners and the teaching process. Effective instructional planning needs to focus not only on the "product of development, but on the very process by which higher forms are established" (Vygotsky, 1978, p. 64), by teachers as well as their students. This understanding, in turn, will open windows of opportunity for all learners.

FIGURE 8.5
Expanded Graphic
Organizer

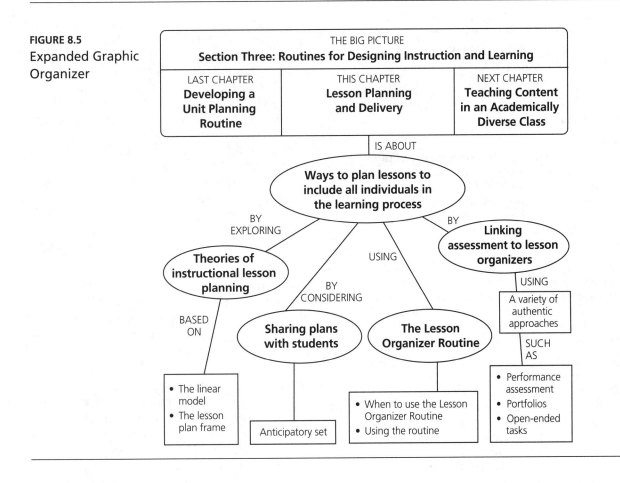

MAKING CONNECTIONS:
Implementing the Lesson Organizer Routine

1. *Here are the big ideas to get you started:*
   ▪ Lesson planning is where instructional planning becomes most detailed. This is where you decide exactly what you hope students will learn and how it is best organized so they can learn it. This is where you decide what concepts or ideas will be difficult for students and plan the instructional methods, learning strategies, and activities that you and your students will use to master difficult content. This is also where you identify how student learning will be assessed.
   ▪ Sometimes daily lesson planning does not require this much detail. At other times it does, as a way to: (a) organize content to help students understand it, (b) connect prior knowledge to new knowledge, and (c) engage students more actively in constructing knowledge for themselves.

2. *Here's what you need to get started:*
   ▪ A topic for a lesson you want to plan using the Lesson Organizer Routine.
   ▪ A textbook or other appropriate materials you are likely to use with students for the lesson.
   ▪ Copies of state or local standards, or those of a professional organization (such as the National Council of Teachers of Mathematics [NCTM]).
   ▪ A good overview of the highlights of the Lesson Organizer Routine (next page).
   ▪ The relevant text pages in this chapter about how the routine is most effectively implemented.

<hr>

The CUE-DO-REVIEW Sequence for the Lesson Organizer Routine

This sequence ensures that, as the routine is implemented, students are involved and engaged in the process.

CUE:

Students' attention is drawn to the use of the Lesson Organizer Routine and what they need to do by naming the lesson organizer routine or the lesson organizer, explaining how it will help them learn, and specifying what they need to do to participate in the routine.

DO:

Using the Linking Steps, the routine is implemented in an interactive way with the students. Depending on the presentation option chosen, the teacher and students construct the lesson organizer, or parts of it, as they proceed through the Linking Steps. This phase is accomplished by:

- **C**onsolidating the lesson goals (Sections 1, 2, 3 of the lesson organizer)
- **R**eviewing background knowledge
- **A**ssembling a visual anchor (and completing Section 4 of the lesson organizer)
- **D**escribing and mapping the content of the lesson (completing Section 5)
- **L**inking the lesson to anchors (Section 6 of the lesson organizer)
- **E**xploring questions and tasks (Sections 7 & 8 of the lesson organizer)

REVIEW:

Students' understanding of the lesson organizer and the related information is checked by asking questions related to the organization of the lesson, the lesson's relationship to the unit and to background knowledge, key concepts, and so on, clarifying any misunderstandings and describing how the students are to use the lesson organizer during the rest of the lesson.

3. *Try this:*

Start by making a list of three lesson topics that (a) you are interested in teaching, (b) you believe involve difficult concepts or ideas or collections of information for students to master and/or (c) you have yourself taught ineffectively in the past or seen other teachers teach ineffectively. Choose one. Then:

- Identify relationships (like cause and effect, compare and contrast, pros and cons, timelines, problem and solution, advantages and disadvantages, etc.) that students will need to understand and use to learn the information.
- Identify task-related strategies (like recognizing, rephrasing, ordering, comparing, evaluating, etc.) students will use to learn or practice the information.
- Map the content of the lesson so that the lesson topic—a statement of what the lesson "is about"—and each subtopic identified below the "is about" statement, make a coherent statement conveying information or ideas students need to learn.

As you can see, you will not have completed all the steps of the Lesson Organizer Routine at this point. But this is a good point to stop and evaluate what you have done before elaborating on the plan any further.

4. *Evaluate your work:*

- Look back at the state or local standards you assembled for your lesson. Does your lesson address any elements of these standards? If so, identify which ones and record this information for future reference.
- Show your planning up to this point to a colleague and discuss with him or her whether the lesson topic and supporting structure are clear.

5. *Next steps:*

- Make a copy of the blank lesson organizer included in this chapter. Finish drafting your lesson plans by following the Linking Steps, completing all sections of the organizer.
- Next, think about how you would use your lesson organizer with students. How would you tell students about the organizer? How would you explain to them how it can help them learn? How would you involve students in filling out the organizer? How will you find out what students already know about the lesson topic? How would you find out whether the topic is interesting or meaningful to students? How would you convince students that it is important that they learn what the lesson is designed to help them learn?

It is important to think about these issues before you teach using the Lesson Organizer Routine, because a basic premise of the routine is that students be informed about its use, understand why it is being used, and participate in the use of it. Presenting students with a completed organizer will not work to make learning more effective (though it may help you as a planner to be clearer about what you plan to teach!).

SUGGESTED READINGS

Campbell, L. Campbell, B., & Dickinson, D. (1999). *Teaching and learning through multiple intelligences* (2nd ed.). Boston: Allyn & Bacon. This book considers the cultural and learning diversity found among students in a classroom and provides ideas for taking multiple intelligence theories into account in lesson planning and instructional assessment.

Chase, M., & Jensen, R. (1999). *Meeting standards with Inspiration: Core curriculum lesson plans.* Portland, OR: Inspiration Software. This spiral-bound book contains a wealth of samples of how the graphic organizer software *Inspiration* can be used to create lesson plans that address specific content standards. Although cross-grade-level graphic organizers are created with the software, a teacher can use the models to create and implement the lesson plans using paper and pencil.

Ellison, J., & Hayes, C. (2000). *Implementing standards-based education.* Philadelphia: Association for Supervision and Curriculum Development. This professional inquiry kit by ASCD is a comprehensive presentation of standards-based instruction from the perspectives of teachers, principals, and parents. The kit includes many charts and recommendations that a teacher might integrate into a lesson plan to ensure that all students are learning and mastering the curriculum content.

Glatthorn, A. A., & Craft-Tripp, M. (2000). *Standards-based learning for students with disabilities.* Larchmont, NY: Eye on Education. The book contains many tables linking standards, lesson objectives, and individual education plans for students with disabilities. The format provides for a comprehensive view of how student assessment, matching objectives to student needs, and building standards into lessons result in more authentic lesson planning.

Gibb, G. S., & Taylor Dyches, T. (2000). *Guide to writing quality individualized education programs: What's best for students with disabilities?* Boston: Allyn & Bacon. This is a quick guide that provides a framework for identifying ways to integrate student IEPs into lesson plans.

Gose, M. D. (1999). *Creating a winning game plan: The secondary teacher's playbook.* Thousand Oaks, CA: Corwin Press. Using the sports playbook metaphor, this is an excellent resource, not only for building the lesson plan but also for planning the operational details that accompany instruction.

Howell, J. H., & Dunnivant, S. W. (2000). *Technology for teachers: Mastering new media and portfolio development.* Boston: McGraw-Hill. This spiral-bound book is full of ideas that a teacher can integrate into lesson plans to provide a vehicle for students to create authentic performance products and to assess the outcome of lesson objectives.

Lazear, D. (1999). *Multiple intelligence approaches to assessment: Solving the assessment conundrum.* Tucson, AZ: Zephyr Press. This resourceful guide helps teachers think about how theories of multiple intelligence can be integrated into performance outcome strategies accompanying lesson plans.

McTighe, J., & Wiggins, G. (1999). *The understanding by design handbook.* Alexandria, VA: Association for Supervision and Curriculum Development. This book provides ideas and strategies for integrating ways to meet the learning needs of a diverse classroom population into lesson plan design.

Paul, R. W. (1987). *Lesson plan remodeling: A strategy for critical thinking staff development, K–12* [Video]. (Available from Center for Critical Thinking and Moral Critique, Sonoma State University, CA). This video investigates how rethinking how lesson plans are created helps build critical thinking into the learning and instruction process.

Tucker, M. S., & Codding, J. B. (1998). *Standards for our schools: How to set them, measure them, and reach them.* San Francisco, CA: Jossey-Bass. Matching the importance of standards to instructional practices, the authors provide a framework for understanding and implementing standards-based objectives into lesson planning.

WEB SITES

http://ercir.syr.edu   Site includes resources on a variety of educational issues. The collection includes Internet sites, educational organizers, and electronic discussion groups.

http://galaxy.einet.net/galaxy/Science/Biology. html   A searchable Internet directory compiled and organized by Internet librarians and providing links to sites on topics related to biology.

http://forum.swarthmore.edu/mathmagic MathMagic, a K-12 project developed in El Paso, Texas, by Alan A. Hodson, was designed to motivate students to use computer technology while increasing problem-solving strategies and communications skills. MathMagic posted challenges in each of four categories (K-3, 4-6, 7-9 and 10-12) which are now archived and available to download in MS Word file format.

http://www.csun.edu/~hcbio027/k12standards California State Board of Education Web site providing access to content area standards by specific grade level.

http://standards.nctm.org National Council of Teachers of Mathematics electronic edition of Principles and Standards. Includes related materials and activities.

http://www.mcrel.org/standards-benchmarks The McREL Standards Database. This is a compendium of Standards and Benchmarks for K-12 content knowledge.

http://www.nap.edu/readingroom/books/nses National Science Education Standards for teachers and students across grade levels.

REFERENCES

Albert, L. R. (2000a). Lessons learned from the five-men crew: Teaching culturally relevant mathematics. In M. Strutchens, M. Johnson, & W. Tate (Eds.), pp. 81–88. *Changing the Faces of Mathematics: Perspectives on African Americans.* Reston, VA: National Council of Teachers of Mathematics.

Albert, L. R. (2000b). Outside in, inside out: Seventh grade students' mathematical thought processes. *Educational Studies in Mathematics, 41*(2), 109–142.

Alter, J. (1992, Spring). Using portfolios of student work in instruction and assessment. *Educational Measurement: Issues and Practice, 11,* 36–44.

Ammer, J. J., Hansen, C. B., & Alexandrowicz, V. F. (1999, Oct.). *Lesson plans—Forgotten link in inclusive instruction.* Paper presented at the 49th Annual California State Federation/Council for Exceptional Children, Costa Mesa, CA.

Arends, R. I. (1998). *Learning to teach.* Boston: McGraw-Hill.

Banks, J. A. (1993). The canon debate, knowledge construction, and multicultural education. *Educational Researcher, 22,* 4–14.

Banks, J. A. (1997). *Educating citizens in a multicultural society.* New York: Teachers College Press.

Barber, L. (1990). Self-assessment. In J. Millman & L. Darling-Hammond (Eds.), *The new handbook of teacher evaluation: Assessing elementary and secondary school teachers* (pp. 216–228). Newbury Park, CA: Sage.

Bulgren, J., & Lenz, B. K. (1996). Strategic instruction in the content areas. *Teaching adolescents with learning disabilities: Strategies and methods.* Denver: Love Publishing.

Callahan, J. F., Clark, L. H., & Kellough, R. D. (1998). *Teaching in the middle and secondary schools* (6th ed.). Upper Saddle River, NJ: Merrill/Prentice-Hall.

Clark, C. M., & Yinger, R. J. (1987). Teacher planning. In D. C. Berliner and B. Rosenshine (Eds.), *Talk to teachers* (pp. 342–365). New York: Random House.

Cooper, J. M. (Ed.). (1994). *Classroom teaching skills* (5th ed.). Lexington, MA: D. C. Heath.

Dewey, J. (1960). *The child and the curriculum.* Chicago: University of Chicago Press.

Goodlad, J. (1983). *A place called school.* New York: McGraw-Hill.

Hamilton, V. (1992). *Many thousand gone: African Americans from slavery to freedom.* New York: Knopf.

Hobson, D. (1996). Beginning with self: Using autobiography and journal writing in teacher research. In *Teachers doing research: Practical possibilities.* Nahway, NJ: Lawrence Erlbaum Associates.

Hyerle, D. (1996). *Visual tools for constructing knowledge.* Alexandria, VA: Association for Supervision and Curriculum Development.

Kohl, J., & Pepper, D. (Eds.). (2000). *Ordinary resurrections.* New York: Crown.

Ladson-Billings, G. (1994). *The dreamkeepers.* San Francisco: Jossey-Bass.

Lenz, B. K., Alley, G. R., & Schumaker, J. B. (1993). Activating the inactive learner: Advance organizers in the secondary content classroom. *Learning Disability Quarterly, 10,* 53–67.

Lenz, B. K., Marrs, R. W., Schumaker, J., & Deshler, D. (1993). *The lesson organizer routine.* Lawrence, KS: Edge Enterprises.

National Council of Teachers of Mathematics. (1989). *Curriculum and evaluation standards for school mathematics.* Reston, VA: Author.

National Council of Teachers of Mathematics. (1991). *Professional standards for teaching mathematics.* Reston, VA: Author.

National Council of Teachers of Mathematics. (1995). *Assessment standards for school mathematics.* Reston, VA: Author.

Ogle, D. M. (1986). KWL: A teaching model that develops active reading of expository text. *The Reading Teacher, 39*(6) 64–70.

Robert, P. L., & Kellough, R. D. (1996). *A guide for developing an interdisciplinary thematic unit.* Upper Saddle River, NJ: Merrill-Prentice Hall.

Tyler, R. W. (1950). *Basic principles of curriculum and instruction.* Chicago: University of Chicago Press.

Vygotsky, L. (1978). *Mind and society: The development of higher psychological process.* Cambridge, MA: Harvard University Press.

Weick, K. E. (1979). *The social psychology of organizing.* Reading, MA: Addison.

Wertsch, J. V. (1985). *Vygotsky and the social formation of mind.* Cambridge, MA: Harvard University Press.

Teaching Content in an Academically Diverse Class

Margaret E. King-Sears
Jean F. Mooney

Critical Self-Test Questions

- What methods have teachers traditionally used to address differing student learning needs?
- How can structured and varied teaching techniques and routines benefit teachers and students?
- How do you analyze student learning characteristics and match them to appropriate teaching strategies?
- How do you figure out what students know prior to instruction, during instruction, and at the end of instruction?
- What is a teaching device? What is a teaching routine?
- How can a device be made into a teaching routine?
- Describe ways student learning may be monitored to determine whether teaching enhancements are working.

Pedagogical content knowledge . . . consists of an understanding of how to represent specific topics and issues in ways that are appropriate to the diverse abilities and interests of learners.

—H. Borko, M. Eisenhart, C. A. Brown, R. G. Underhill, D. Jones, & P. C. Agard, 1992, p. 196

Successfully teaching students in schools today requires exceptional skill, remarkable knowledge, and insightful problem-solving abilities. This chapter extends themes and methods described in previous chapters and travels even further into classrooms, illustrating how content is reshaped and presented—not just *to* students, but *with* students. It is a challenge for teachers to transform content from textbooks and curriculum guides so that students can be successful. Accepting such a challenge requires that teachers have a mind-set that values student diversity and uses it in ways that enrich learning and teaching in classrooms.

In order to effectively respond to student academic diversity, teachers need an extensive repertoire of techniques that they not only know but can use when needed. Teachers constantly make decisions about whether to try another technique, use another analogy, fill in a graphic organizer, or explain something in a different way. Teachers grow into these skills; effective teachers are risk-takers who are not afraid to try alternative methods and learn from their experiences. Teachers' reflections about their experiences spur insightful hindsight that guides future actions.

Teachers strengthen the value of on-the-spot decisions by working from a strong master plan for instruction. If a strong master plan has not been developed, the result may be unconnected, fragmented activities instead of flexible and responsive dialogues and actions with students. Monitoring student progress is an essential part of this process and is accomplished

FIGURE 9.1
Graphic Organizer

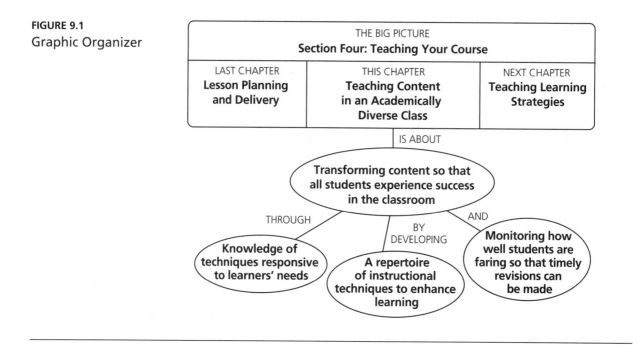

both informally (e.g., observing how and what students are saying during teamwork) and formally (e.g., through projects, assignments).

Teachers are not in this process alone. Effective teachers collaborate with students, families, other staff in schools (e.g., through co-teaching), and sometimes personnel outside of schools (e.g., social workers). Is it hard to be an effective teacher? Yes. Is it worth it? Absolutely. Effective teachers feel a sense of accomplishment when they engage students and see that their actions have enabled students to learn.

▪ *Scenario*

At the end of the first week of school in September, Liz Jackson, a seventh-grade math teacher in a middle school in a low-to-middle-income community, knew she was in for a challenging year. Her third-period math class was comprised of students with varied levels of motivation, organization, attention, and socialization, and she anticipated varied prerequisite skills in math. When she talked to the seventh-grade guidance counselor, she discovered that she had three students from a language-based program in special education, four students with diagnosed attention problems, including hyperactivity (one student was eligible for special education services), two bilingual students from Eastern Europe, and four students with learning disabilities whose IEPs did not call for support in math, and three students (all bilingual) with histories of chronic truancy. The other five students were described as "good kids but turned off to math." The class had been put together by the guidance staff in consultation with the chair of the math department, based on the rationale that all these students needed a strong teacher and an opportunity to be successful in math.

FOUNDATIONS AND PRINCIPLES

Diversity in today's classrooms provides teachers with opportunities to transform and expand on static content by knowing their students and actively involving them in learning activities that make the content more dynamic and relevant. To involve students in the teaching and learning process, deep understanding of content must be coupled with a repertoire of teaching methods that enable the teacher to effectively convey the content to students. Teachers then make decisions about how well students are progressing by monitoring performance during instruction, which provides critical feedback to help shape decisions about when to maintain or change techniques.

Static content becomes dynamic when teachers use their knowledge of students' backgrounds, academic skill levels, adeptness with teamwork and socialization skills, and previous experiences to transform content to "fit" the students. For example, in a static presentation of content, a teacher would simply give directions to students to memorize certain terms and definitions for a quiz, or to read the chapter and respond to questions at the end. In a dynamic presentation of content, by contrast, a teacher would try to enliven student learning of terms and definitions by connecting new terms to terms and experiences more familiar to students, or perhaps identifying critical information or using analogies or comparisons to frame the information in a context that is more familiar to students.

Focus and Reflect

Recall courses you have taken that either seemed very engaging or very dull. Consider:

- How did the teacher make the content meaningful for you and your peers?
- Were analogies used that helped you make an association with something that was already familiar to you?
- What kinds of techniques were used—or could have been used (reflect on content presentations already described in this text)—to enhance and advance learning and teaching?

Knowing What Skills Students Have

Finding out what students already know about the content to be taught is critical. Educators use a variety of sources to figure out what students already know. Standardized assessment scores, previous grades in school, previous course grades, and general content-specific test scores provide some information. (See Table 9.1 for a continuum of assessment techniques.) But educators frequently need more specific assessment information in order to determine students' skill levels related to a particular unit or course. Moreover, targeting students' skill levels includes more than academic information; learning strengths and/or preferred modalities for taking in and remembering information also warrants consideration. In addition to academic skill level and learning style preferences, students' proficiency with functioning independently and interacting with others needs to be considered. Consider actively involving students in providing information about themselves (see Table 9.2 for an example that one middle-school math teacher uses). Asking students can be more efficient, sometimes, than "putting the picture together" yourself from multiple sources. Furthermore the process can prompt students to become aware of their learning preferences.

TABLE 9.1 A Continuum for Evaluating and Reevaluating Student Performance

PRIOR TO INSTRUCTION	DURING INSTRUCTION	AFTER INSTRUCTION
• Pretests • Standardized test scores • Error analysis of previous test scores • Report card grades • Conversation and communication with student	• Error analysis of performance • Reflection journals • Direct observation of student performance • Accuracy of homework assignments • Students' demonstration of skills and knowledge levels via multiple types and modes of assignments and projects • Students' facility in identifying, describing, and explaining information on and connections of content on graphic devices • Students' questions and responses about the content	• Unit test • Course test • Quizzes • Standardized test scores • Continued, interspersed assessment on content previously mastered to ensure maintenance of skills and knowledge learned • Student applies previously mastered skills and knowledge to novel and/or new information

Ways in Which Teachers Respond to Learning Differences

Tracking. Traditionally, teachers and school administrators have dealt with classroom challenges by tracking students into different levels of content courses. Tracking students by "ability" leads to more homogeneity in classes. However, emerging evidence on the barriers and benefits of tracking students suggests that students are "pigeon-holed" early on in their school careers, and that the "low-track" students are frequently unchallenged in both the amount and depth of content that is presented to them or expected from them (Oakes & Guiton, 1995; Tomlinson, 1999).

Alternative approaches to tracking or ability grouping are distinguished by two major characteristics. First, the focus switches from what educators perceive students are capable of learning within a given curriculum to an emphasis on how presentation of the curriculum (i.e., instruction) can engage, challenge, and promote all students' acquisition and use of curriculum content. Second, many students, who once might have been tracked into lower-level courses, are now being taught successfully by teachers using alternative techniques such as those described throughout this text. Consequently, more students are meeting the high standards identified in local, state, and national curricula.

Selection of instructional activities governs the quality of students' cognitive processing. That is, the way a teacher structures and organizes the classroom environment strongly influences students' beliefs about themselves

---

Focus and Reflect

- When students are not learning as expected, to what extent is it the teacher's responsibility to "switch channels" and try different techniques?
- Describe situations in which you noticed that a student's "failure to learn" seemed out of a teacher's control. Within that situation, what other resources (e.g., specialists, counselors, social worker) were available and used effectively?
- What should a teacher do when he/she perceives competing messages from the school system regarding raising test scores and teaching for success for all students?

TABLE 9.2   Personal Learning Portrait

IN MATH I GENERALLY . . .	
feel I need a lot of attention.	am well organized.
work hard to do well.	keep working on a task until I finish it.
have problems getting started on work sometimes.	benefit from encouragement and knowing I'm on the right track.
ask questions when I don't understand.	prefer to work alone.
other:	other:

I AM MOST SUCCESSFUL IN MATH WHEN I . . .	
make sure I do enough practice on the type of problems on the test.	do all my homework and other assignments.
am not absent or make up work quickly after I have been absent.	ask for and/or get extra help outside of class.
put in extra effort to really pay attention in class.	ask in class when I need something clarified.
have opportunities for actively participating in _____.	other:

I AM LEAST SUCCESSFUL IN MATH WHEN I . . .	
let students around me distract me.	don't do all my homework and assignments.
think things are going too fast but I don't ask the teacher to slow down.	am absent a lot and do not make up the work quickly.
let other things on my mind interfere with my listening in class.	don't request extra help when I need it.
don't ask for clarification when I don't understand.	other:

MY TEACHER HELPS ME BE SUCCESSFUL IN MATH WHEN HE OR SHE . . .	
provides lots of practice before a test.	has us work alone.
works with me one on one.	has us work in pairs.
allows me to correct the answers I got wrong on a test.	has us work in groups.
uses visual examples of the problems.	explains how the math work can be used in real life.
keeps the class quiet so I can concentrate.	the rules of the class are clearly stated and fairly followed.
makes it clear exactly what we are supposed to do by _____.	other:

I HELP MYSELF DO BETTER IN MATH WHEN I . . .	
make sure I am not sitting next to someone who will distract me.	keep an assignment checklist with a calendar of when they're due.
seek assistance and/or more explanation from the teacher or my peers.	use good self-advocacy skills to request accommodations I know I need, such as _____.
use good study skills such as _____.	ask to learn strategies such as remembering formulas correctly.
other:	other:

Please add any other information that you feel the math teacher needs to know about you that will assist you in achieving success in math:

Source: From "Accommodating Diversity in a General Education Math Class in a Middle School."
Presentation at Boston College, by J. A. Gorman & K. Lysaght, 1996. Printed with permission.

(Anderson, 1989). For example, one group of teachers challenged Latino students by grouping them according to their interests or project activities instead of perceived abilities (Moll, 1988). By tapping into students' interests and varying the grouping arrangements, students were challenged and successful, in spite of what might otherwise have been low expectations for them.

Differentiation of Instruction   Differentiation of instruction evolves from several premises (Armstrong, 1994; Bradley, King-Sears, & Switlick, 1997; Tomlinson, 1999): (a) Students bring different strengths, interests, backgrounds, and learning needs to the classroom; (b) Students acquire and apply basic knowledge and skills at different rates, and perhaps in different ways, when the knowledge and skills to be learned are more complex; and (c) Students learn at different rates, and learn best in different ways or modalities for basic and complex knowledge and skills.

Consequently, teachers who effectively differentiate in their classrooms ensure student progress relative to the individual rather than all students. That is, a student who triples his or her knowledge of terms and definitions from 8 to 24 has demonstrated remarkable success and should not necessarily be compared to students whose entry level was 20 and grows to 24. Other ways to effectively differentiate instruction include employing a range of instructional strategies that are responsive to students' learning strengths and needs and engaging students in the teaching and learning process through methods such as cooperative learning, self-management, goal-setting, and feedback sessions. Differentiated instruction may also challenge students to reach goals that other teachers may have thought unattainable for particular students.

Tomlinson (1999) aptly describes the rationale for differentiation in general education classrooms:

> In differentiated classrooms, teachers provide specific ways for each individual to learn as deeply as possible, without assuming one student's road map for learning is identical to anyone else's. These teachers believe that students should be held to high standards. They work diligently to ensure that struggling, advanced, and in-between students think and work harder than they meant to; achieve more than they thought they could; and come to believe that learning involves effort, risk, and personal triumph. These teachers also work to ensure that each student consistently experiences the reality that success is likely to follow hard work. (p. 2)

Differentiation can occur on several levels, and what shape it takes will vary according to the complexity of the content (remember, complexity is viewed from the student's perspective; a teacher is already proficient with complex content). Differentiation also can occur in a teacher's presentation and practice and will vary according to student characteristics. Accommodations and adaptations are two ways to differentiate instruction.

An **accommodation** is a modification to the delivery of instruction and/or method of assessing student performance that does not significantly change the content (e.g., mathematics) or the conceptual difficulty (e.g., solving multistep word problems using mixed fractions with unlike denominators) of the curriculum standard, or outcome. The term "accommodation" is interpreted in different ways by different school systems. It is used here to designate a way to differentiate instruction, where no change is made in the curriculum standard a student is expected to achieve, but rather in the way the student shows that he or she has achieved the standard. For example, a student with fine-motor skill disabilities might use a computer for written language instead of handwriting the requested information. Another example of accommodation is a student who is allowed to verbally explain the causes and effects of a situation instead of drawing a diagram. In both of these examples, students demonstrate knowledge of the same curriculum standard, but demonstrate their knowledge in different ways.

Some students with disabilities are entitled to accommodations, which are typically noted on their individualized education programs (IEPs). In classrooms where teachers encourage creativity and capitalize on student strengths, the idea of accommodating a student with a disability may be a moot point because they may already be using multiple teaching and assessment methods. However, in many classrooms, teachers present and assess information in only one way. To some teachers an accommodation is perceived as *any* change in how they present content or assess learning and is sometimes perceived as "lowering their standard," when in fact it does not. Rather, an accommodation enables a student to receive learning and express knowledge in ways that may vary from tradition. For example, instead of just being instructed to read a chapter on their own, students might be guided in identifying important ideas through the use of a pre-reading activity. Accommodations might also be devised to capitalize on a student's strengths. For example, a student who is better at drawing might be allowed to make diagrams or graphic illustrations of important chapter information instead of outlining the chapter.

An **adaptation** is a modification to the delivery of instruction and/or method of assessing student performance that does not change the content, although there may be minor changes in the conceptual difficulty of the curriculum standard.

Another term used to indicate accommodations and adaptations is "tiered" instruction (Tomlinson & Kiernan, 1997), in which teachers may present problem-solving steps to the whole group of students (and/or have students co-construct varied ways to solve problems), yet have different groups of students practice using problems of varying difficulty. For example, students characterized as gifted may be working on problem solving with more complex numbers and more elaborate solutions, students in another group may be working on multistep word problems with mixed fractions with unlike denominators, yet another group may be making up word problems encompassing their choice of numerical indicators and solving them.

In another example, the content of science does not change when an adaptation is allowed, but the standard changes in a minor way (you may need to refer to a student's IEP for guidance about whether an adaptation is needed; some school districts use the terms "accommodation" and "adaptation" interchangeably). Consider a ninth-grade science class: There is a student with a learning disability who has memory problems, so instead of writing definitions of science terms from memory, the student's IEP notes that she may be provided with prompts. So on a portion of a quiz given to all the ninth-grade students, the teacher adapts the definition portion for this student so that she can match terms to definitions. This changes the difficulty level for this student; memorizing information is different from selecting the correct answer from a list. This is an adaptation because the content remains the same (science) but the difficulty level for this student is changed (the student does not have to struggle with what, for her, is a diffi-cult memorization challenge, but can select from choices).

Teachers are realizing that methodologies and individualization tech-niques that were traditionally viewed as useful only for special educators or only for ESL teachers, and so on, are now acknowledged as techniques that all teachers can—and should—use.

Experienced teachers accustomed to traditional "teacher-centered" tech-niques of instruction view differen-tiation as more "student-centered." Indeed, the examples provided above are student-centered, with the accom-modation or adaptation focused on what the student will do. Some teachers resist differentiating instruc-tion, no matter what; others use only simple and quick types of differentia-tion that do not require significant effort or change on their part. Yet other teachers undergo an incremental "paradigm shift" in the way they view

---

Focus and Reflect

- What do you recall from your own experiences about how teach-ers differentiated for you and your peers?
- Were students allowed to demonstrate they had "met the stan-dard" in different ways? If so, what different ways were used? If not, what ways could have been used while still maintaining the integrity of the standard?
- How do you distinguish between a student's need for an accom-modation or adaptation versus an unnecessary "watering down" of a curriculum standard, outcome, or expectation?

■ Scenario Revisited

Given the diversity in her class, Ms. Jackson decided to advocate for the students and herself, so she asked the coordinator of special services to find a special education teacher willing to help. Vicki Contos, who had minored in math, was pleased to volunteer. When Mrs. Contos checked the cumulative folders of the students in Ms. Jackson's class, she recognized a wide range of differences, making a note of the particular characteristics and instructional needs of the 21 students in the class.

Mrs. Contos knew students with attention problems would most likely be slower in retriev-ing facts for calculation, would struggle with the reading demands of complex problems, and would require immediate feedback and reason-able pacing (Zentall, 1990; 1993; Zentall & Smith, 1993; Zentall, Smith, Lee, & Wieczorek, 1994). To help students from the language-based program be successful would mean that their teachers would have to use instructional activities to help students become proficient with the language of mathematics. They would also have to use instructional methods that helped students understand abstract concepts, basic operations, and problem solving (Wallach & Butler, 1994). For these students, and some of their peers, the

teachers knew it would be important to use many concrete examples and nonexamples when teaching concepts. They also knew they would need to provide additional and relevant practice activities, monitor accuracy carefully, and establish predictable routines in the classroom.

The speech/language pathologist could help by including math vocabulary and concept rein-forcement in her sessions with the three students she served. Three of the bilingual students were recent immigrants who had experienced inter-rupted schooling in their home countries because of armed conflicts. They would need extra attention to fill in skill gaps and instructional approaches and accommodations similar to those required for the students with language impair-ments (Igoa, 1995; McCaleb, 1994).

Mrs. Contos knew she and Ms. Jackson would need to be well-organized and creative in order to keep the attention of some students who could grasp the content more quickly, while providing other students sufficient time to acquire the concepts and develop mastery of computation and problem-solving skills. Ms. Jackson and Mrs. Contos were confident they could do many things to accommodate the full range of diversity in the class.

teaching and learning toward using more complex and powerful differentiation techniques.

It is important to acknowledge that all types of educators may fall into one of these categories, even special educators and other specialists who perceive that they already know and do the best of what is available. All educators, when learning new techniques, need sufficient initial training, ongoing support and technical assistance, and reinforcers to learn, maintain, and sustain effective use of new practices.

Using Variety   Teachers often try to provide for individual differences in learner style, ability, and needs by incorporating variety into the learning activities and assignments they plan. While effective teachers should have a variety of instructional methods in their repertoire, it is important to select and use a particular method that is based on the learning needs of the particular students in the classroom. Simply using a variety of methods may not address student learning needs.

KNOWING AND DOING

The difference between a student's current skill levels and the outcomes they are to achieve is the starting and ending point for instruction. Students who have not yet developed effective ways to learn on their own need *support* from teaching methods that compensate for their underdeveloped abilities to learn independently. Selecting critical content and mapping or organizing it for students—the first two steps of the SMARTER planning process—are ways to provide that support through curriculum planning. This chapter presents the "ARTER" part of SMARTER. This is when learning difficulties with the content are identified and analyzed and content enhancement decisions are reached. Teaching strategically ensures that students are informed about and involved in the enhancement process so that they become better independent learners (Bulgren & Lenz, 1996). Evaluating mastery and revisiting outcomes are also essential parts of the process to ensure that the enhancements you have selected and used are, in fact, working to help students learn.

The **SMARTER** steps capture the linear process of making decisions that lead to more inclusive practice in the classroom:

- **S**hape the Critical Questions
- **M**ap the Critical Content
- **A**nalyze for Learning Difficulties
- **R**each Enhancement Decisions
- **T**each Strategically
- **E**valuate Mastery
- **R**evisit Outcomes

The SMARTER structure applies to all content areas. Appendix B presents scenarios of teachers using the SMARTER process as they teach Social Studies, English, Mathematics, and Science. You will see that, even when the scenarios do not focus on your discipline, "watching" these experienced teachers work through their dilemmas and make instructional and assessment decisions can be extremely helpful. The SMARTER scenarios can help novice teachers move from identifying the SMARTER steps to applying SMARTER to their own content and instruction.

Teachers frequently select fewer instructional methods when they limit themselves to what they are comfortable using (King-Sears & Cummings, 1996). One of the challenges of translating research into practice is to find ways to increase a teacher's comfort level with using a range of techniques and ways to represent knowledge so that when students do not understand content, teachers are comfortable using another technique. Therefore, as you develop and make judgments about instructional representations, your decisions about what you will use to help students understand content should be based on what is to be conveyed to students and what students need instructionally, not on your personal preference (McDiarmid, Ball, & Anderson, 1989). For this reason, you need expansive instructional repertoires so that you are confident and comfortable using a variety of methods when students' understanding and performance indicate they need another mode of representation.

Consider how a proficient gardener tends his or her garden; it is not enough to simply plant the garden—a proficient gardener continues to care for, nurture, and provide ongoing attention so that the garden will flourish. Changing weather patterns inform the gardener about varied care techniques: Water more this week, less tomorrow, or not at all for a few days. What different kinds of care do different plants need? How does a gardener best ensure that all plants in the garden flourish?

Similarly, teachers make decisions about instruction and content. Just as a gardener would not simply plant items and expect them to grow on their own, a teacher cannot simply present new content and expect students to "get it" on their own. The art and craft of skillful teaching involves not only knowing what techniques to use, but when to use them, how to use them, and how to monitor whether the techniques are working for students.

Extending Teaching Repertoires: Enhancing Instruction by Redesigning Instruction and Materials

Curriculum does not come in a "one-size-fits-all" package, and most content materials are not ready to be used "as is." Teachers frequently need to adjust instruction or adapt materials to make them more suitable for the learners they have in their classrooms. For example, textbooks often include questions at the end of chapters or units to provide a way for students to learn the information in the chapter or unit. Some students, however, have not learned to distinguish important from unimportant information or how to analyze information to draw conclusions. These students may (and often do) resort to simply copying parts of chapters to answer such questions. Something more is needed to help these students master the content. When teachers can be flexible and responsive as they plan for and present content, engage students in learning, and assess students' progress, then more learners are likely to acquire, practice, and master the new information.

For example, if a teacher is presenting new content to learners using auditory methods (e.g., talking) and visual aids (e.g., illustrations), more students are likely to "get" the new content than if only a talking presentation occurred. Further, if students practice and apply the new information using hands-on projects or cooperative learning techniques, the students' active engagement in learning is increased. Finally, when teachers develop grading or scoring criteria that clearly delineate what learners must show they know and can do, and when teachers allow students to show their learning in a variety of ways (e.g., written project, illustration), then students, permitted to express their learning in different ways, are more likely to be successful. Regularly providing these types of options for students, based on their strengths and learning preferences or styles, places teachers in a stronger instructional position and provides students with more and better opportunities to learn.

Authors and researchers use different terms to describe how teachers can adjust and adapt curriculum and materials to address the different learning needs of their students. Kameenui and Carnine (1998) and Rose, Sethuraman, and Meo (2000) call this process "universal design for learning." Generally, this process is referred to as the concept of universal design. Instructional and assistive technologies are frequently used as examples of applying universal design concepts to curriculum. For example, a teacher may use computer software with graphics and pictures to present new content to students who are visual learners. Or, teachers may use computers that "read" text for students who cannot access print materials because they have a reading learning disability.

Three Essential Qualities for Universal Design for Learning The Center for Applied Special Technology (Orkwis & McLane, 1998; Rose, Sethuraman, & Meo, 2000) organizes universal design elements around three essential qualities: (1) multiple means of representing content, (2) multiple means of students' expression of content, and (3) flexible means of engagement as students learn (see the Web site for the Center for Applied Special Technology at the end of this chapter).

The first quality is that teachers provide multiple means of representing the content. For example, teachers might use visual devices like graphs, timelines, or pictures, in addition to presenting information orally or in print, so that more than one way of presenting, practicing, or studying new content is used (see Figure 9.2 for more examples of various ways to represent content).

The second quality is that teachers offer students multiple means of expressing what they know and can do with content. For example, teachers might provide options for how students demonstrate what they know about the causes of World War II: Some students might write a paper, some students might construct a pictorial timeline with print and graphic content, some students might illustrate a mural and verbally explain the causes, while other students might select some other format that shows they know the information.

The third essential quality is that teachers are flexible in the ways they seek to engage students while instruction is occurring. Teachers frequently seek to engage student attention by lecturing and having students take notes. More flexible means of engagement would include using videos, software, instructional games, role-playing, peer tutoring, cooperative learning, and a similar variety in presenting, practicing, and remembering content. In the next section, more examples of each of the three essential qualities that teachers should plan for and use during instruction are described. Again, note that most curricula will not have these qualities built into them, so teachers need to evaluate their curriculum and materials to determine what is already there and what they will need to develop. Teachers who develop and use these types of design elements are more likely to "reach and teach" more learners who have varied learning levels and strengths. These universal design elements are essential for some students (e.g., the student with a reading learning disability, who listens to the text on audiotape) and beneficial for others (e.g., a student who prefers to gain information auditorily).

Listed below are examples of techniques and materials that teachers can use (Orkwis & McLane, 1998):

How can the content be presented in different ways to students?
- Use print material.
- Use pictures and illustrations.
- Use books on tape.
- Focus on the essential information (e.g., big ideas).
- Use graphic organizers.
- Use multisensory activities.
- Link new content to familiar situations (e.g., primed background knowledge).
- Use combinations of techniques.

What different ways can students use to demonstrate their knowledge?
- Writing
- Drawing
- Constructing
- Verbally describing
- Role-playing
- Using software that helps with writing
- Developing videotape
- Designing a project using software with graphics

In what ways can students be engaged in learning the content?
- Involved in cooperative learning
- Participating in peer-assisted learning
- Listening to book on tape
- Using the Internet
- Watching a video and answering questions verbally or in writing or by illustrating
- Dialoguing with the teacher (e.g., mediated scaffolding)
- Using and connecting strategies (e.g., conspicuous strategies and strategic integration)
- Reviewing the content in different ways (e.g., judicious review)

Other ways to adapt your curriculum could include using scaffolded instruction, reciprocal questioning, modeling, and providing feedback during instruction. These are teaching techniques that make your instruction more explicit, allow you to represent the content in different ways through the use of different teaching devices, and allow you to more effectively engage students in learning.

Scaffolded Instruction   Teachers find it useful to "scaffold" instruction when they move from explicit, teacher-directed instruction to more implicit, student-constructed learning. "Scaffolded" instruction typically occurs after new content has been presented or demonstrated (i.e., after explicit instruction) or when a problem, solution, or strategy is to be constructed or discovered by students (i.e., implicit instruction). Scaffolded instruction is characterized by building student understanding through dialogue. Teachers query students about their thinking and gradually intensify the teaching/learning process to a level that actively engages students and extends and heightens their learning. Teachers also provide assistance and guidance to students who are having difficulty completing a task or answering a question on their own. The interaction between teachers and students goes beyond simple feedback that indicates a right or wrong response. Teacher questions seek to extend the student's knowledge—or construction of knowledge—toward more highly developed skills (Anderson,1989).

"Guided practice" is similar to scaffolded instruction, but it focuses instead on a specific skill or strategy that has been described and modeled by the teacher. The teacher coaches and edits the learner's attempts to achieve mastery of a particular skill. Guided practice and scaffolded instruction are not mutually exclusive but address different aspects of the learning process. That is, in scaffolded instruction the teacher serves as a guide for the learner, implying shared power and authority; in guided practice, the teacher allows students to develop a skill under supervision to prevent error patterns from developing, to promote fluency and confidence in using the skill, and to allow students to achieve self-regulation (Ellis, Deshler, Lenz, Shumaker, & Clark, 1991).

Modeling   Learning is enhanced when teachers use "think alouds"—or "modeling"—which make learning processes explicit for students (either verbally and/or in writing). Modeling differs from telling students information in that the teacher uses the process to be learned and describes it out loud in front of students, using language such as "I need to first . . . " or "Listen while I model how to . . . " instead of "First *you* need to. . . ." The following portrays the "think aloud" dialogue a teacher has with herself in front of students to model how to select a graphic device:

> OK, I've read the first section of the chapter, and I better stop now and figure out what some of this means so I can make graphics for study cards. I could stop later, but I'm already seeing some patterns for information, and last time I forgot some of the important patterns and information when I waited until the end of the chapter to start on them. All right—patterns—I'm reviewing the text—what were the patterns my social studies teacher said to look for? Cause-effect was one. Time order was another. Compare-contrast was another. What do I have here? Well, the text so far is telling about reasons why the revolution occurred. Maybe I should use a time-order graphic. It also seems as if a cause-effect graphic may be good. Hmmm . . . reasons why the revolution occurred—seems more like a cause-effect, because the revolution was the effect of causes. That makes sense to me—OK—so I need to fill in the "effect" box with "revolution" and look for information for the "cause" boxes in the text I've already read.

Modeling exposes the processes that learners use when they are effective in self-regulation of their thinking. It is how good thinkers think. "Metacognition" is a term used to describe how we think about our own thinking. Some students already think this way, and other students are not even conscious that they can make these types of decisions. Without teacher modeling, some students may not learn how to internalize a process. If you are using computer software featuring "reveal codes" functions, consider that modeling is a way of teachers revealing their thinking codes by making their identification of problems, thinking, consideration of alternatives, decision making, and evaluations of decisions overt for students.

When you use modeling as an instructional technique to enhance learning, you can focus on critical learning issues in the content, such as dealing with misconceptions, solving problems, and recognizing and using text structures to organize information (Ehlinger & Pritchard, 1994). Further, modeling encourages learners to be more active and reflective by gaining their attention, highlighting the thinking process, and encouraging participation. When teachers effectively model and then ask students "why" or "how" questions, students' responses are more elaborate, complete, and correct.

Reciprocal Questioning   Students studying sequences of events (e.g., history) can use a reciprocal questioning strategy in which they question each other about why certain events occurred (Kinder & Bursuck,1991). "Why did . . . ?", "What was the effect of . . . ?", and "Why does it make sense that . . . ?" are the types of questions that prepare students for assessments and promote higher-order thinking. By moving beyond simple listings of time lines into why specific events occur during a particular time frame, students learn to think. Reciprocal questioning can also actively involve students with each other in a meaningful learning activity and provide the teacher with the opportunity to circulate among students and monitor their responses to provide appropriate feedback.

Reciprocal questioning is a joint activity where mutual learning occurs, because the student who asks a question also needs to learn or know the answer to verify the correct response. It also engenders a "give-and-take" cooperative atmosphere, where students can talk among themselves to figure out the answers. Reciprocal questioning can also promote higher-order thinking when students ask "Why?" or "How did you get that answer?" Reciprocal questioning is an excellent way to engage students in learning—one of the qualities of universal design described earlier in this chapter.

Feedback During Instruction   Teachers make multiple, complex, and "on-the-spot" decisions during instruction. Those decisions can be informed by feedback derived from questions they ask themselves about how well they are connecting with students—as a class and as individuals. Questions you should be asking yourself during instruction include: Is the student still confused about the concept? Has the analogy provided a familiar connection for the learning, or is a more concrete analogy needed? This feedback is essential for deciding what your next actions will be during a lesson and afterwards and becomes a reflective process that informs you about instructional decisions for a student, small groups of students, and the larger class. The process never ends, and the insights teachers bring to the process are critical "golden nuggets" that provide a basis for future actions.

This chapter and, indeed, this textbook, supports the process of universal design. In addition to techniques like modeling and scaffolded instruction, devices like graphic organizers can be a way for you to adapt your curriculum to provide students with a way to think about the information

■ *Scenario Revisited*

In order to help the students become more competent in math and more active and efficient in their learning, Ms. Jackson and Mrs. Contos used and adapted a variety of instructional approaches. When teaching rules, concepts, and strategies, direct instruction proved to be extremely effective (Kameenui & Carnine, 1998). Then, guided practice was provided in the classroom. When students made errors, they worked with each other and the teachers to diagnose the error patterns and correct them. Not until students had mastered the work did they proceed to practicing independently. Independent practice was provided through homework and group projects. Students were never assigned homework on concepts or processes they had not mastered. When students were given independent work on material they had not mastered, Ms. Jackson and Mrs. Contos knew that error patterns were likely to develop and would be difficult to correct, particularly in math. Homework was assigned for the purpose of developing fluency and speed, and Ms. Jackson and Mrs. Contos reminded students of this frequently. The teachers did not appreciate the full impact of this practice until the end of the year when students were cleaning out their notebooks and discovered dozens of "Get Out of Homework Free" cards that had never been redeemed. When students CAN do the homework, they DO do it. Early in the school year, the homework completion rate for this class reached 90 percent.

to be learned. In the next two sections, we will discuss teaching devices and teaching routines. These are two more ways for you to incorporate essential qualities of universal design in your planning and teaching.

Extending Teaching Repertoires: Enhancing Instruction with Devices

An instructional device is a simple teaching method for helping students understand ideas, information, or procedures. Examples of devices include using a concrete example (showing students a quart bottle and a liter bottle to clarify the difference in size) or making comparisons (the eye is like a camera) to help characterize something.

Effective teachers have long used simple instructional devices to help students learn. To better accommodate all learners in an academically diverse classroom, however, we suggest that, in addition to *using* devices, teachers become very explicit with students about the fact that a device is being used to facilitate understanding of important content. Simply using an instructional device is not enough. It is equally important to call students' attention to the nature of the device and why it can help them learn new information. By telling students when you are using a device, you can help them develop a better understanding of how they learn and what you are going to do to help them learn. Eventually, many students are able to use these devices independently. In the following pages, we will look at graphic devices, verbal and visual devices, and mnemonics.

Graphic Devices Graphic devices are diagrams or pictures that can help students understand both content and relationships. A graphic device can transform information that may be abstract or complicated into a more concrete format (i.e., visual representations). For example, a time line in a history lesson helps students to order information so that they may more easily remember it. A flow chart can show how a process works. The organizer maps that are used throughout this textbook are a kind of graphic device, used to help you see what information will be presented and the relationships between topics to be discussed. It is important to select graphic devices carefully, using those that are most appropriate for the content being represented (Clarke, Martell, & Willey, 1994).

There are many graphic devices and organizers being used in schools today. Indeed, there are whole books of such devices that have been published (see Resources at end of this chapter.) Not all of these devices have been well-conceived, designed, or researched, however. The selection of a graphic device depends on the nature of the content structure and the importance, accuracy, and usefulness of the information. Teachers must choose these tools very carefully. In the language of SMARTER, presented in Chapter 3, the choice of a graphic device is made in the R step (Reach Enhancement Decisions). In this context, the power of the graphic device is assured when a teacher carries it into a fully developed teaching routine. The Cue step alerts students to the fact that a particular device is appropriate and helpful; the Do step guides the students through the correct use of the device though the Linking Steps; the Review step reinforces the rationale for the device, the specific information and important features and relationships among ideas depicted on the graphic, and how the new information connects to what they already know.

Graphic devices are frequently used to depict important content relationships, such as sequencing of steps in a process, or the unfolding of historical events through a time line. They can also highlight characteristics of a key concept, illustrate if/then flow charts, or identify problem/solution relationships. Venn diagrams, using intersecting circles, are a kind of graphic device that can be used to compare properties or characteristics of concepts or processes, showing shared characteristics in the intersecting region(s).

Figure 9.2 describes sample graphics as well as "cue words" that teachers and textbooks use to indicate important relationships among chunks of content. Relationships are often obscure and unspecified in textbooks, and teaching students to identify cue words and connect the content in graphic form can give them a powerful tool to use in decoding text and understanding relationships. It provides the "gestalt" of key features in information and helps students cut away extraneous details that tend to confuse and distract.

A graphic device can transform abstract, textual, auditory and/or complicated information into more concrete formats (i.e., visual representations) that use and reuse similar processes. Such processes include cause-and-effect structures that may be used in multiple content areas or repeatedly within one content area. An important caution for any teacher to remember, however, is that too many graphic devices may tend to confuse rather than enhance the learning process. Using a limited number of powerful and well-constructed visual devices gives students sufficient practice with each to be able to use them on their own.

Verbal and Visual Devices Verbal and visual devices (i.e., "simple enhancers") can be used routinely. An example of a verbal device is an analogy. Teachers use analogies to explain unfamiliar content to students by providing examples of the content using more familiar contexts. Analogies are powerful

FIGURE 9.2
Information Structures, Cues, and Graphic Organizers

Descriptive Structure	Cue Words	Graphic Organizer
Cause and Effect Shows an outcome and what led to that outcome	Causes Effects Results in If…then	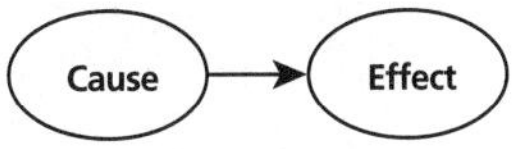 Cause → Effect
Comparison/Contrasting Identification of similarities/differences among topics	Is the same as Is similar to Parallels Is different from Contrasts Versus	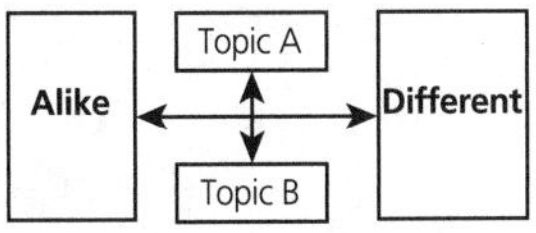 Alike — Topic A / Topic B — Different
Cycle Shows process or series that repeats itself	Returns to become Is once again __leads to__leads to__ __then__then__	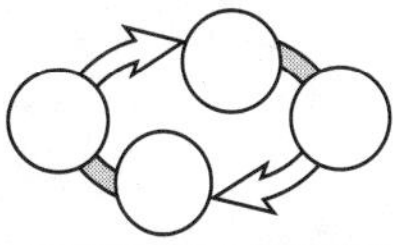
Problem and Solution Identification of a challenging situation and its resolution (actual or potential)	Could be/ is solved by Resolves Problem is	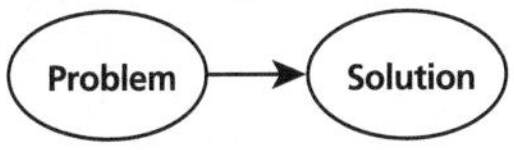 Problem → Solution
Web Starts with a main topic or idea and extends with features, characteristics, examples	For example Including Characteristics Features	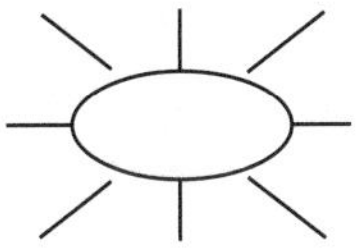
Hierarchy Two or more groups of information categorized by levels of specificity, importance, etc.	Is related to Is categorized with Includes	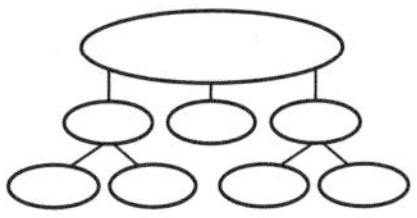
Steps Steps of a process organized according to their occurrence	Initially Finally Beginning with Ending with First, second, third… Next Then	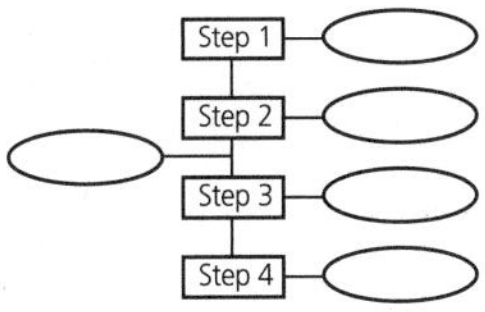 Step 1 Step 2 Step 3 Step 4

Source: B. K. Lenz. (2002). Connectors. *Stratenotes*, 10(5), 4–7.

for promoting students' understanding because background knowledge and previous experiences are used to illustrate new or complex content. For example, a chemistry teacher needing to explain gas chromatography (new information) as part of a chapter on matter and measurement, could compare it to the Boston Marathon (familiar information). This verbal analogy identifies similarities or shared characteristics between familiar information and new information:

BOSTON MARATHON	SIMILARITIES	GAS CHROMATOGRAPHY
Collection of racers	*Participants have different speeds*	*Collection of molecules*
Race course	*Defined path of movement*	*Long sealed tube*
Finish line at Prudential Center	*Place where order of finish is determined*	*Flame ionization detector*

This analogy helps students understand the critical features of a complicated and abstract chemical process by relating it to an analogous and more concrete process, a marathon.

The effectiveness of devices is maximized when they are used in conjunction with the Cue-Do-Review Routine: Cue the students about what device is being used, do the device with students, and review the content using the device. Essential in the Cue-Do-Review Routine is that all parts are used; not using all parts seriously minimizes the chances that all students will "get it." Table 9.3 describes some simple verbal and visual devices.

EXPLICIT TO IMPLICIT CONTINUUM. How information is presented to students, whether using a graphic representation or another type of transformation, can be considered along a continuum of explicit to implicit presentation. **Explicit instruction** consists of a teacher demonstration or presentation of new content, followed by guided practice activities in which students gain up to 80 percent mastery of the new content, and then independent practice activities in which students progress toward 100 percent mastery and fluency. **Implicit instruction** consists of teacher-developed activities that elicit student discovery—or construction—of new content. Although there has been some debate in recent years about whether to use explicit or implicit instructional techniques with learners or for only specific content areas,

TABLE 9.3   Verbal and Visual Devices with Examples

DEVICES	DEFINITION	EXAMPLES
Synonym	A word of similar meaning, more familiar to the student, provided to enhance understanding of an important vocabulary word	"The protest was counterproductive or harmful to their cause." "What is another word for *counterproductive*?"
Simple comparison	A statement(s) expressing the resemblance between two things, one new and one familiar, for the purpose of enhancing understanding of the new concept, object, or person	"The eye is like a camera." "The same thing happened in Vietnam when they were trying to. . . ."
Symbolic example	A statement(s) specifying that a familiar person, object, or event symbolizes an abstract concept	After describing three types of energy, the teacher presents an example by asking, "If I take a bite from a hamburger, what kind of energy is that?"
Graphic depiction	A graphic device that depicts a concept, the relationship of ideas, a series of events, etc.	In history, the teacher asks students to help write a timeline for the major events of the time period 1095–1212 AD. [Students state events with date, and teacher writes on board.]
Concrete object	A 3-dimensional object showing qualities discussed	Showing students a lava rock, the teacher asks students which qualities of igneous rocks they can observe. [Students describe qualities.]

Source: From University of Kansas Center for Research on Learning, 1994. Reprinted with permission.

more recent findings emphatically promote the use of a continuum of explicit (direct instruction of new content to students) to implicit (indirect instruction that invites students to figure out for themselves relationships, meanings, etc., in new learning) instruction (Harris & Graham, 1996; Pressley, Hogan, Wharton-McDonald, Mistretta, & Ettenberger, 1996).

As mentioned earlier, teacher decision making about whether to use explicit or implicit techniques initially depends on students' background knowledge and familiarity with the content. It also depends on the complexity of the content being taught and students' facility with prerequisite skills and strategies (Mercer, Jordan, & Miller, 1996). It is important to note that all students need the range of explicit (more directly taught) to implicit (more student discovery) techniques. And most learners need a combination of explicit and implicit instruction. Furthermore, it is not always the case that high-achieving students respond best to implicit instruction and low-achieving students always need explicit instruction. Learners characterized as gifted and talented need explicit techniques initially when their background knowledge is weak and complex content is being taught. Learners characterized as low achievers can profit from implicit techniques when they have a rich background knowledge of the content and are proficient in problem-solving strategies for a topic.

Memory Devices: Mnemonics   Using mnemonics as remembering tools results in effective acquisition and retention of information (Mastropieri & Scruggs, 1991). Furthermore, students can be taught how to develop mnemonics for themselves instead of relying on teachers to do it for them (King-Sears, Mercer, & Sindelar, 1992). Mnemonics can be used to assist students in recalling definitions of terms though *keyword mnemonics*, in which a familiar word (e.g., "key") is linked to the definition of an unfamiliar or new term (e.g., trachea) along with an interactive illustration to link the keyword to the term's definition (i.e., envision a "key " stuck in the trachea [not a good thing!], the main trunk of the system of tubes by which air passes to and from the lungs). The interactive illustration may be drawn on paper or simply envisioned in one's mind. Mnemonic devices can also be used to help remember lists of information that do not need to be remembered in a particular order (e.g., a mnemonic for remembering the names of the Great Lakes is to envision the HOMES people live in on the lakes: Huron, Ontario, Michigan, Erie, and Superior); or lists of information that need to be remembered in the correct order (e.g., Kind Cats Are Always Sweet and Energetic for remembering Bloom's taxonomy of objectives: Knowledge, Comprehension, Application, Analysis, Synthesis, and Evaluation). For the student who developed this device, using a "cat" sentence was meaningful because she frequently played with her pet cat; for another student, another sentence with different content would be more appropriate.

Some people find developing acronyms, or mnemonics, a very useful technique. However, others become confused by all the mnemonics if they do not use the final step when developing a mnemonic: linking the mnemonic directly back to the term or list. For example, to remember that Bloom's taxonomy goes with the Kind Cats Are Always Sweet and Energetic, the sentence *must* be linked somehow to Bloom's taxonomy—envision that cat smelling the BLOOMing flowers. Without this linkage, a person may remember plenty of acronyms or mnemonics but still not be able to correctly use the mnemonics.

■ *Scenario Revisited*

Because the students in this class were not active or independent in their learning, the teachers taught specific cognitive and metacognitive learning strategies, some published and well-known in math and others invented specifically for the group. Examples included:

Mnemonic for order of operations:
Please Excuse My Dear Aunt Sally

P Parenthesis (Complete all operations inside parentheses.)

E Exponents (Calculate all powers.)

M Multiplication (Multiply or divide in order, left to right.)

D Division

A Addition

S Subtraction

For problem solving, Ms. Jackson and Mrs. Contos developed a mnemonic called USE (Gorman & Lysaght, 1996):

U Understand the question
Ask yourself:
What am I trying to find? Have I solved a problem like this before?

Restate the problem:
Say it out loud. Inflect your voice as you read the question.
Look up words you don't know.

S Select a strategy
Use one you already know.
Draw a picture.
Look for a pattern.
Error-monitor as you go along (step by step).

E Evaluate your answer
Ask yourself:
Does my answer make sense?
Did I use all of the important information?

See also Appendix B where four scenarios using the SMARTER planning process incorporate the use of teaching devices. These scenarios describe a variety of content areas and a wealth of ways to enhance new and/or complex content for students. Note how teachers used their knowledge of students, pedagogy, and content to make decisions before, during, and after instruction.

Extending Teaching Repertoires: Enhancing Instruction with Teaching and Classroom Routines

As was explained in Chapter 3, it is important to be explicit with students when an instructional device is being used about how it can help them learn. Such explicitness helps students see and understand how learning happens. When it is further developed into instructional steps, the device can become a teaching routine. Again, as explained in Chapter 3, a teaching routine is a set of integrated instructional procedures that guides the introduction and learning of large chunks of information in a lesson. It is introduced to the whole class, is used regularly, involves students in the process, and is adapted to meet the needs of the students, as well as the requirements of the content to be learned (Bulgren & Lenz, 1996). A teaching routine can allow a teacher to compensate for students' lack of skills in learning. For example, establishing a set of steps to "walk" students through how to understand a concept or how to tackle reading a chapter in a textbook can help students master content.

A teaching routine can be used to help students understand a difficult concept or to compare and contrast ideas, concepts, events, and so on. A key to using teaching routines is that they become "routine," or such an integral part of classroom work that everyone understands how the process works. While the procedures of the routines should be "routine," care must be taken that they are used appropriately and productively so that students are engaged in learning. Routines should not be used to process trivial knowledge which students see no use in learning, or can easily learn in other ways. (Additional teaching routines, developed as Content Enhancement Routines by the Center for Research on Learning at the University of Kansas, are briefly described in Appendix C.)

The Concept Mastery Routine   A very useful teaching routine is the Concept Mastery Routine (Bulgren, Schumaker, & Deshler, 1993). Bulgren et al. identified characteristics of concepts to consider in deciding which of them would best be taught and learned using the Concept Mastery Routine. These content characteristics are described in Table 9.4.

Questions to ask in considering when and how to enhance instruction about a concept include: Is the concept abstract and difficult for students to understand? Is the concept critical to understanding other concepts? Is understanding the concept critical to understanding what the course is about? If the concept is important and students are likely to have difficulty understanding it, a teaching routine specifically designed to support student learning about concepts can be an important enhancement.

TABLE 9.4   Seven Characteristics of Content That Assist Teachers in Making Decisions about When Content May Need to be Enhanced In Some Way

CHARACTERISTIC	DESCRIPTION OF CHARACTERISTIC
Abstractness	Which concepts are abstract and, therefore, difficult to understand (i.e., ideas, theories, or processes)?
Organization	Which concepts are critical to the understanding of other concepts (e.g., should "economic systems" be taught before "capitalism" or "communism")?
Relevance	Which concepts are so important that the students must understand them if they are to benefit from the course (e.g., if a course is built around the concept of "ecosystems," do the students see the relevance of that concept in their lives)?
Interest	Which concepts do not seem very interesting to students and, therefore, require special attention (e.g., "federalism" may not turn them on, but as citizens, do they need to understand it)?
Assumptions	Which concepts are foundational for terms that I will use later (e.g., to benefit from a civics class, must students understand such concepts as "law," "politics," and "government")?
Complexity	Which concepts are difficult to understand or frequently misunderstood by students (e.g., do students really understand the "electoral college")?
Quantity	Where are there so many concepts mentioned that I must prioritize the key concepts and ignore other less important ones (e.g., is knowledge in science expanding so fast that the students need to understand "problem solving" to help them understand all the new information they will encounter)?

Source: From *The Concept Mastery Routine* (p. 14), by J. A. Bulgren, J. B. Schumaker, & D. D. Deshler, 1993, Lawrence, KS: Edge Enterprises. Copyright 1993 by Edge Enterprises. Reprinted with permission.

The Concept Mastery Routine uses a graphic device or diagram, shown in Figure 9.3, that is constructed in draft form by a teacher, to transform information about a concept into a "learner-friendly" form. Prior to using the routine with students for the first time, the teacher explains the routine and accompanying blank diagram to students, describes how it will be used in class, and specifies what students will be expected to do during and after their co-construction of the target concept using the diagram.

The Concept Mastery Routine has a series of seven linking steps that are completed interactively with students. While the order in which the linking steps are completed is not important, it *is* important that all steps be completed to help students analyze and understand a concept.

The linking steps for this teaching routine may be remembered with the acronym CONCEPT. Initially, the targeted concept is identified along with the larger concept or category to which the targeted concept belongs. This is

FIGURE 9.3   Concept Diagram for Revolutionary War

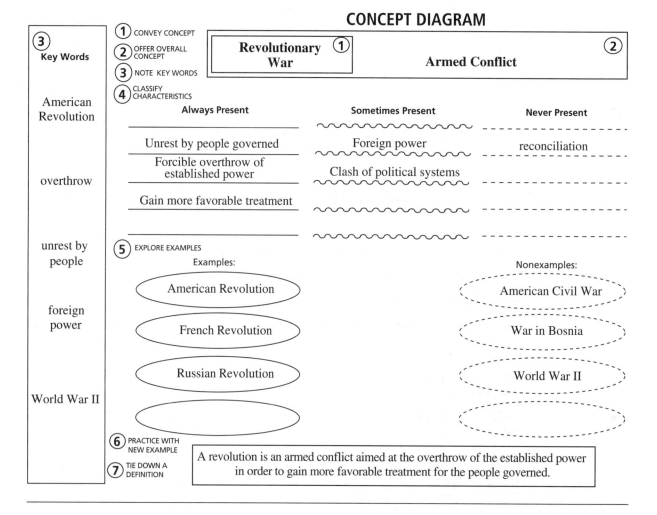

Source: From *The Concept Mastery Routine* by J. A. Bulgren, J. B. Schumaker, & D .D. Deshler, 1993, Lawrence, KS: Edge Enterprises. Reprinted with permission.

1. Convey concept
2. **Offer overall concept**
3. **Note key words**
4. **Clarify characteristics**
5. **Explore examples**
6. **Practice with new example**
7. **Tie down a definition**

an important step because it helps students see that the targeted concept is part of a "bigger picture" of relationships and ideas.

Then, key words related to the concept are identified. These words are generated with students in a brainstorming session, and students will draw some of their responses from assigned readings, previous lessons, or just their background knowledge. This is a good opportunity for teachers to learn more about what students know and do not know about course content. Similarly, in the next step, teacher and students identify and classify characteristics of the concept—characteristics that are always present, sometimes present, and never present. The discussion during this step allows students to reveal what they do or don't understand and allows the teacher, or other students, to correct any misunderstandings.

Next, students explore examples and nonexamples of the concept. Examples and nonexamples can be drawn from information in the Key Word section of the diagram, as well as from previously identified information about characteristics of the concept. Then, learners are prompted to practice with a new example. This practice may be done individually or in small groups. New examples may be checked against the characteristics identified earlier in the routine. The final step is to "tie down a definition" of the concept, using the information in the diagram. The definition is expressed in the form of a complete sentence and should name the targeted concept to be learned, the overall concept, and all of the "always" characteristics that are always true of the targeted concept. As we have noted before, teachers follow the Cue-Do-Review sequence each time the routine is used, cueing students that the device is being used, doing the routine in partnership with students, and reviewing how the device was used, what has been learned, and where the information might be applied.

For an example of how to use the Concept Mastery Routine, look at Figure 9.3 and consider the concept of "Revolutionary War." This concept is foundational and turns up over and over again as students move from American, to European, and to world history. In American history, this concept is essential to understanding the enormity of the commitment and achievement of the early colonists in founding a new nation on principles of self-government. The Revolutionary War was the means to independence from England. In one frequently used textbook in eighth-grade American history, the concept of revolutionary war is not defined anywhere, not even in the glossary at the back of the book. In using this book, therefore, it would be important for a teacher to use the Concept Mastery Routine to focus students' attention on the big idea of Revolutionary War and to make sure all students have an in-depth understanding of the concept's connection to the bigger idea of "armed conflict." By following the linking steps, students are able to identify the characteristics that are always, sometimes, and never present. Listing examples and nonexamples gives students an opportunity to check their own understanding and to clarify misconceptions.

When done correctly, the final definition at the end of the routine is not a rote exercise but is meaningful to everyone in the class. Since the teacher and the students build the diagram together, students become active participants in their own learning and learn to build a solid content schema of an extremely important, recurring concept in the study of historical events and eras.

■ *Scenario Revisited*

As they planned each unit of study, Ms. Jackson and Mrs. Contos identified the particular concepts or processes that are critical to further study in math and (because of their level of abstraction) are difficult for many students to understand. For students with English as a second language and those with specific language disabilities, the language involved in concepts must be explicitly taught and comprehension checked. So Ms. Jackson and Mrs. Contos identified what students needed to know and experience in order to grasp important concepts and where the Concept Mastery Routine could be used to facilitate understanding. For example, the unit on geometry seemed to go very well until Mrs. Contos began to suspect that the students had not grasped the concept of a polygon. She asked for a volunteer to come up to the overhead projector and draw a "funky" polygon. All hands went up. The first student to step up to the projector drew:

The second student drew:

Watching what the students drew, it became apparent to both teachers that the students did not have a clue about the meaning of polygon. At that moment, Mrs. Contos pulled out a blank Concept Mastery Routine graphic, brainstormed key words to elicit students' background knowledge, and led the students through distinguishing characteristics of polygons that were always, sometimes, and never present (see Figure 9.4). The examples drawn above were placed in the nonexample category. Once they clarified the concept of polygon, all students were able to draw correct examples. After that they formulated a definition that had significant meaning to everyone.

When the students showed confusion about the difference between area and perimeter in the unit on measurement, Mrs. Contos used another teaching routine focused on Concept Comparison (Bulgren et al., 1995) to help them compare the characteristics of area and perimeter (see Figure 9.5). The diagram used with the Concept Comparison Routine provides excellent structure for comparing and identifying categories in which concepts are the same and different. Ms. Jackson used content enhancement routines in her other classes as well. Even students in her advanced class occasionally confused concepts, so mediating content area instruction by using teaching routines was important for all her students.

By the end of the year, the students had become very familiar with the devices that helped to clarify the meaning of important concepts. They kept blanks in their notebooks in order to be prepared to contribute to and record the completion of a new concept or comparison diagram.

Later in the course, a logical follow-up would be the use of another teaching routine, the Comparison Routine (Bulgren, Lenz, Deshler, & Schumaker, 1995), to identify the similarities and differences between the concepts of civil and revolutionary wars. When students encounter World Wars I and II at the end of the course, they can enlarge their understanding of armed conflict. Further, when they begin world history in high school, they will have a reliable content scheme related to armed conflict, which should

FIGURE 9.4 Concept Diagram of Polygons

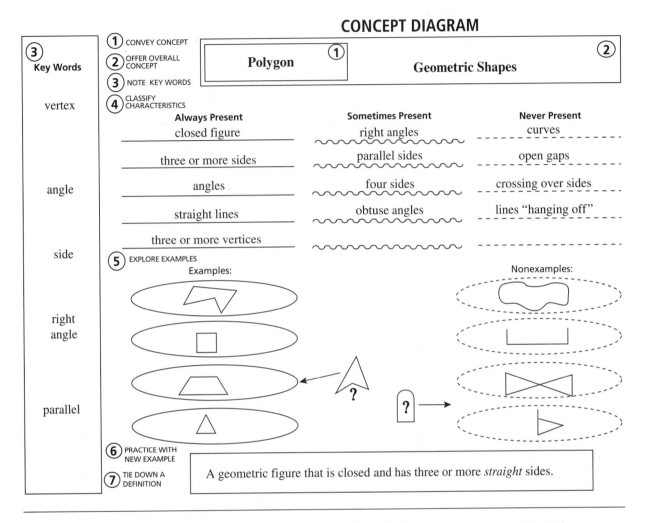

Source: Adapted by J. A. Gorman & K. Lysaght. From *The Concept Mastery Routine* by J. A. Bulgren, J. B. Schumaker, & D .D. Deshler, 1993, Lawrence, KS: Edge Enterprises. Copyright 1993 by Edge Enterprises. Adapted with permission.

serve them well in studying the Boer War in South Africa or the civil war in Cambodia.

Cooperative Learning, Peer Learning, and Structured Small Group Practice
Two models for cooperative learning were introduced in Chapter 5. There are, of course, many other ways to have students learn together and help each other. Students can work with peers to practice new content (e.g., develop fluency with terms and definitions), complete group projects (e.g., each student contributes to the group's project), or discuss content (e.g., focused discussion). Increasingly, employers identify the socialization and problem-solving skills that students can acquire during their school years as among the most desirable characteristics of a successful employee. Consequently, it is important that students have opportunities during courses to acquire proficiency as a productive team member, demonstrate effective interpersonal skills, and successfully solve problems.

FIGURE 9.5 Concept Comparison Diagram for Area and Perimeter

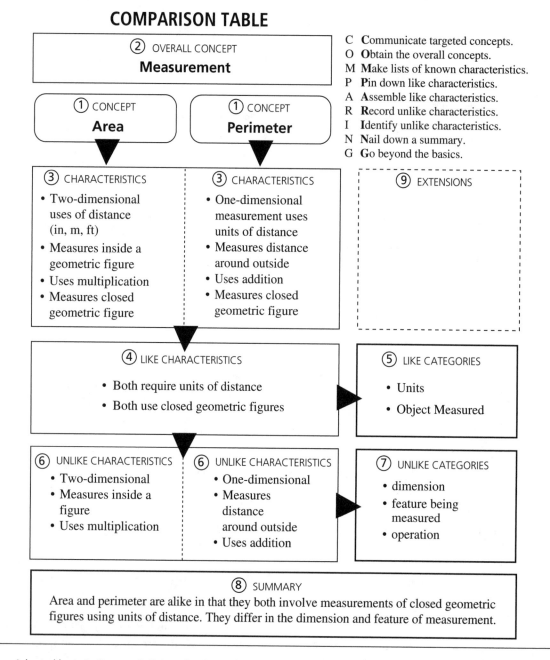

COMPARISON TABLE

② OVERALL CONCEPT
Measurement

① CONCEPT
Area

① CONCEPT
Perimeter

C **C**ommunicate targeted concepts.
O **O**btain the overall concepts.
M **M**ake lists of known characteristics.
P **P**in down like characteristics.
A **A**ssemble like characteristics.
R **R**ecord unlike characteristics.
I **I**dentify unlike characteristics.
N **N**ail down a summary.
G **G**o beyond the basics.

③ CHARACTERISTICS
- Two-dimensional uses of distance (in, m, ft)
- Measures inside a geometric figure
- Uses multiplication
- Measures closed geometric figure

③ CHARACTERISTICS
- One-dimensional measurement uses units of distance
- Measures distance around outside
- Uses addition
- Measures closed geometric figure

⑨ EXTENSIONS

④ LIKE CHARACTERISTICS
- Both require units of distance
- Both use closed geometric figures

⑤ LIKE CATEGORIES
- Units
- Object Measured

⑥ UNLIKE CHARACTERISTICS
- Two-dimensional
- Measures inside a figure
- Uses multiplication

⑥ UNLIKE CHARACTERISTICS
- One-dimensional
- Measures distance around outside
- Uses addition

⑦ UNLIKE CATEGORIES
- dimension
- feature being measured
- operation

⑧ SUMMARY
Area and perimeter are alike in that they both involve measurements of closed geometric figures using units of distance. They differ in the dimension and feature of measurement.

Source: Adapted by J. A. Gorman & K. Lysaght. From *The Concept Mastery Routine* by J. A. Bulgren, J. B. Schumaker, & D .D. Deshler, 1993, Lawrence, KS: Edge Enterprises. Copyright 1993 by Edge Enterprises. Adapted with permission.

Students may work together on an informal cooperative task, such as "think-pair-share" in which students formulate their own view or learning on a topic (*think*), turn to the person next to them (*pair*), and each student explains their position (*share*). Several extensions of this informal cooperative task enhance the process, and if used frequently, it can become a classroom routine. For example, teachers can enhance "think-pair-share" by having students compare and contrast their positions by: (a) identifying similarities and differences of their positions; (b) developing pros and cons for their collective positions and deciding the merits of possible solutions; or (c) explaining why they developed their position.

Another peer learning process is classwide peer tutoring, where each student in the class takes turns as a tutor and tutee practicing specific content. Classwide peer tutoring is a structured format in which the teacher selects specific content (e.g., terms and definitions) for students to practice for a set length of time (e.g., 20 minutes, three days per week). Students involved in classwide peer tutoring are not just paired off to study or practice work together; they are taught how to be a tutor with their peers (including how to provide feedback, how to reward correct answers to earn team points), and they switch roles during each classwide peer tutoring session. Envision a class of 28 students in which 14 peer tutoring pairs are formed: for 10 minutes, one partner is practicing content and delivering team points with a peer, then the pair switches roles so that the tutor becomes the tutee for another 10 minutes. When students practice content using classwide peer tutoring structures, positive academic gains result. (See Fuchs et al. [in press] and Maheady, Harper, and Mallette [in press] for more information on classwide peer tutoring structures and results for heterogeneous middle- and high-school students, including students with mild disabilities, such as learning disabilities and emotional disturbance.)

Maheady, Sacca, and Harper (1987) report the results of ninth- and tenth-grade students (including students with mild disabilities) who used classwide student tutoring teams. Their analyses of group and individual

---

■ *Scenario Revisited*

Because Ms. Jackson and Mrs. Contos wanted to promote active learning, they planned to use cooperative learning and peer tutoring to stimulate problem solving and exploration of math applications in the real world. They felt both of these were important instructional approaches for helping students interact with the content and construct and elaborate on critical concepts. However, many of the students had very little experience with group processes, such as listening to peers' explanations, offering encouragement instead of criticism, and ensuring that each group member contributed equally to the task. Although in September, students suggested that respect, individual differences, and collaboration should be listed as important classroom values on the Course Organizer, most of the group had no idea how to put them into practice. One day

after a completely failed attempt to correct homework in groups, Mrs. Contos wrote in her journal, "Disaster struck! Every day, all over this school kids correct homework together. These kids could not do it" (Gorman, 1996). As a result of this incident, they decided to be more proactive in their approach to socialization and taught SLANT (Ellis, 1991), a social skill strategy focused on the behaviors that contribute to successful participation in the classroom (Sit up straight, Lean toward the speaker, Activate thinking, Note important information, and Track the speaker). They taught SLANT slowly and deliberately. It became routine for a student to step up to the projector to demonstrate the solution to a problem and begin by saying "Would you SLANT this way, please?"

results indicated that a 20 percent average increase on weekly math exam scores occurred, the percentage of students who earned an "A" grade increased above 40 percent, and failing grades were almost eliminated for all classes. Similar results were attained for tenth-grade students in another study that was conducted in social studies classrooms (Maheady, Sacca, & Harper, 1988).

Extending Teaching Repertoires: Monitoring Student Progress

Educators use a variety of informal and formal methods to monitor student progress within units of a course. Effective educators do not wait until the unit test or quiz to find out how students are faring. Instead they employ a variety of techniques to determine how individuals are progressing during instruction. This allows them to better target when alternative instructional techniques are needed, which instructional methods are working well for which groups of students, and when more examples and/or student practice is needed. Experienced teachers make instructional decisions based not only on assessing student performance but also on observing student performance and providing feedback (Housner & Griffey, 1985). To ensure that students are progressing toward the outcome, formative assessments and monitoring during instructional activities can be used (e.g., are the students able to identify new terms, define them, *and* provide explanations to questions in which they use the new terms accurately?). At the end of instruction still other formative assessments may be used (e.g., are the students using the pretest content to study for the unit test?).

Targeting Skills. It is important to target students' skill levels before beginning instruction on the unit or course outcomes. Textbooks may or may not contain necessary and applicable resources for targeting students' skill levels, as well as setting outcomes. Omitting the tasks involved in targeting students' skill levels leaves educators without key information needed to enhance student learning and instruction.

Additional ways to target students' skill levels include formative and summative assessments for teacher and student feedback. Pretests for a current instructional unit could incorporate items related to prerequisite skills, the unit's key content, and brief items on the next unit. These could be tested with multiple choice, fill-in-the-blank, matching, brief response, and essay items. Post-tests could include all of the above, as well as small group projects, class projects with individual accountability, research papers, and projects that involve building a model.

Dialogue with students in the beginning days of class may be used to determine background knowledge, perceptions and misconceptions about the content of the course, and possible variations in the knowledge and skill base among the students. If students have used portfolio assessments in previous courses or units, peruse portfolios and/or have students explain them to you. You could also help students conduct a learning-styles assessment to ascertain how they perceive that they learn best and how they prefer to show what they have learned (see also Learning Express-Ways in Chapter 6). Another option for targeting student skill levels is to check standardized scores from norm-referenced and/or criterion-referenced assessments (note that standardized test scores may provide only limited information about skills related to your specific course content).

Monitoring Student Progress. Monitoring how well students are progressing can occur in subtle, overt, respectful, and insightful ways. Teachers with over 125 students per day may find it overwhelming and unrealistic to get to know well and monitor the progress of all of their students. To overcome this problem, they can target representative students from homogeneous groups within heterogeneous classrooms and monitor their day-to-day progress closely. Some teachers rotate the "target" students, but basically the point is to select a representative student from the following homogeneous groups (HALO students):

- **H**igh achiever (may or may not be labeled as talented or gifted)
- **A**verage achiever (the typical learner in your class)
- **L**ow achiever (sometimes referred to as a student in the "lower quartile" for standardized scores)
- **O**ther student with identified learning challenges (such as a student with an IEP for a learning disability)

Teachers with large numbers of students can become very familiar with the progress, skills, and knowledge areas for representative students, knowing that if the representative student from the group is making progress, the other students within that group are most likely making progress too. Conversely, if the representative student is having problems, other students are probably having problems, as well. The HALO categories should not be perceived as tracking students, nor should students be expected to remain within a fixed group or category or label. The purpose of using HALO is to provide teachers with some benchmarks that are indicative of how students are faring so that instructional decisions can be made more efficiently. These benchmarks can help you focus on how students are responding to basic questions, to note if they are frustrated and in need of another description or presentation in a different way, or to determine how well each student is progressing.

Note the absence of quizzes and tests when we talk about the important parts of monitoring student progress. It is not that quizzes, assignments, tests, and similar types of monitoring do not occur, or are not important. As mentioned, effective teachers attend to how well students are progressing *during* instruction rather than waiting until after instruction is completed and student progress is being measured. Monitoring student progress during instruction can help determine what actions to undertake so that each student is successful on the assignments that count toward the grade in the course.

Readers can refer to the SMARTER scenarios in Appendix B for examples of ways teachers monitor progress. Remember that the "E" in SMARTER refers to "Evaluating mastery" and that teachers evaluate both informally, in the ways noted here, as well as formally, with tests and quizzes and project assignments. The following examples can be used as guides in how to monitor progress in a variety of ways during instruction for groups and individuals.

- Whole-class questioning with individual responses, such as "thumbs up if you think that . . . and thumbs down if you think that."
- Cooperative learning with "think-pair-share" activities where a teacher asks students to consider a question (i.e., think), pair with a peer (i.e., pair), and share their responses (i.e., share). Peers can evaluate each other's responses and provide immediate feedback. This is

most effective when the teacher provides some guidance to assist students in evaluating the accuracy of peer responses.

- Self-management or self-evaluation checklists that students complete periodically about themselves. Checklists can focus on students' knowledge of new content, how well they keep up with their assignments, or a number of other areas where they can help the teacher monitor their progress. The content of self-management checklists can be developed by teachers or by teachers and students. Checklists could also be individualized for students.
- Curriculum-based assessment activities that consist of brief samples (e.g., written responses) gathered periodically across a unit of instruction on key content material.
- Portfolio content that includes student work samples or work in progress that a teacher peruses for feedback sessions with the students.

Grading.   Students often focus more on their grades than on the intended learning. Frequently, students will want to know exactly what teachers want them to know, which sometimes discourages creative and risk-taking thinking (Anderson, 1989). Teachers can proactively address this tendency through developing a course syllabus that clearly delineates course expectations, grading criteria, examples of previous projects, and an emphasis on the use of strategies to solve problems.

Students may try to reduce ambiguity and risk in a variety of ways, such as changing a comprehension task into a memory or procedural task. You can provide students with resources for improving their grades to reduce the risk factors for them, even if the ambiguity remains high, by:

- using teacher modeling,
- including coaching through scaffolded dialogue,
- providing feedback,
- explaining scoring rubrics, and
- drawing frequent conceptual links to clarify to the student the relevant dimensions of the task.

Using different types of assignments and making sure they have relevance for students is essential. For example, one method for enriching students' interest in history and increasing the relevance of history is to have students complete a family oral history (Seixas, 1993). Adolescents can derive several benefits from such an assignment. First, students enjoy having choices about such things as whom they will interview and the topics to be discussed. Second, students are more likely to understand the history they are studying when they can draw relevance from their own family's historical background. Third, class discussions about the students' family histories provide a public forum from which divergent historical experiences may be meaningfully and authentically examined (Seixas, 1993).

As you think about enhancements and assessment, remember to take into account the devices and routines you have used in instruction and the content you have taught using them. Students should have the opportunity to demonstrate that they know how to use a device or the diagram in a routine you have used with them. An important part of strategic teaching is that not only do students learn to use supports like devices and organizers, but that they also understand and value these ways to learn. If students are

---

■ *Scenario Revisited*

Ms. Jackson and Mrs. Contos shared with students the responsibilities for instruction through activities, such as having peers explain the graphics to each other. They also asked students to evaluate their own work through reflection exercises. In these exercises they asked students at the end of each unit to identify three things they had learned in the unit, what they felt good about accomplishing in math in the unit, what they wanted to improve, and what activities, instruction, or assignments had most helped them to understand the content of the unit. In these reflection exercises, the teachers gave the students "voice" in their perceptions of how teaching and learning were progressing. The comments also enabled the teachers to pinpoint activities that worked well, as well as areas where some students needed more practice.

Ms. Jackson and Mrs. Contos also reviewed the effectiveness of the cooperative learning groups at the end of each unit. They noted that some students still had difficulty listening and sharing when they worked in groups. So they decided to ask their administrators for permission to attend workshops or courses to help them learn more about team building, self-management, and social skills so that they could work on developing with students the skills needed for effective cooperative learning.

---

to value devices, they must see that they can make a difference. So it is important that you give students an opportunity to demonstrate what they have learned using the device or routine. For example, if you have used the Concept Mastery Teaching Routine, a variety of formats may be useful to assess student knowledge about a concept. These include having the student:

- reconstruct major elements of a concept map;
- explain a concept map to another student;
- determine whether or not a new term is an example or non-example of the concept;
- provide a full definition of concept;
- given several examples and non-examples, construct a concept map;
- given a novel example, determine if it is an example or non-example by using the bigger picture of the concept map as a guide; or
- identify the concept and tell what characteristics it has.

SUMMARY

Content enhancement is important because not all students understand content the same way. It is important to provide different ways for students to learn so that *all* students have an opportunity to learn. As a teacher, part of your job is to *transform* content so that students without fully developed learning skills can learn it more readily. This is different from the idea of just using variety in your teaching. Transforming content means that you need to have a strong understanding of your content so that you can organize and present it to students in a way that makes it accessible. Making content accessible does not mean making it simple. Rather, it means making it authentic, in the sense of being interesting, engaging, and worth learning about in terms of your students' life experiences. Making content accessible also means organizing it so that there are big ideas to provide students with a frame or context that gives ideas, concepts, as

FIGURE 9.6
Expanded Graphic
Organizer

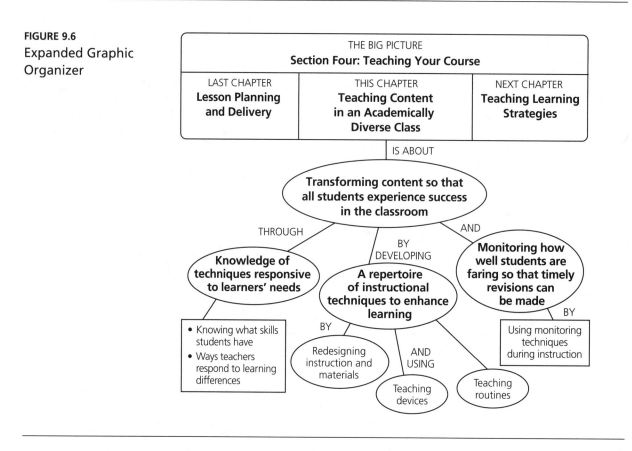

well as bits of information meaning and coherence. Finally, making it accessible means using methods like devices and teaching routines and teaching in ways that help students understand and learn what they need to understand and learn.

Teachers can more effectively respond to academic diversity in schools by using the principles, techniques, and enhancements described throughout this text. The best of what we know is found within these pages. The best of what you can do is found within you. Teachers should be comfortable with feeling uncomfortable as they take risks and enhance their expertise and experience with *becoming* a more effective teacher for all students. People who feel they are there may really have reached a dead end; learning and teaching and learning about how to become a better teacher is a never-ending professional and personal journey. Teachers should never be on that journey alone; students, other teachers, families, and other stakeholders are fellow travelers—use them, work with them, and learn from them—as they do with you.

MAKING CONNECTIONS:
Implementing Content Enhancement

1. *Here are the big ideas to get you started:*
   ▪ To get started on the process of planning to enhance instruction, you may wish to review the five final steps of the SMARTER planning process. It is important, initially, to make the process manageable for yourself by choosing *one* course at *one* grade level. For example, if you are a social studies teacher, you might choose to focus on American history for high school juniors. If you are a math teacher, you may choose to focus on Algebra I and the level of students likely to be enrolled in that course.

2. *Here's what you need to get started:*
   - The textbook and curriculum guidelines or standards for the course you have identified.

3. *Try this:*
   - Bearing in mind your target course and the level of students taking your course, select *one* concept, skill, or other piece of challenging content. Record the difficult content, concept, or skill on the first line of the chart below.
   - For that one content item that you believe will be difficult for a significant number of students, think about what makes the content difficult. Try to identify two or three characteristics of the content that make it difficult. Record those characteristics on the second line of the chart, next to "Analyze for Learning Difficulties."
   - Consider how you might enhance instruction of the identified content by making it more "learner friendly." Another way to think about enhancing difficult content is to consider ways that you might most effectively *support* student learning of the content with methods like a device to help students remember information, or cooperative learning where students help each other to learn. Record your planned enhancements in the chart.
   - For the "Teach Strategically" part of SMARTER, identify at least one way you will inform your students about teaching or learning methods you have planned. Keeping in mind that it is important to make sure students understand that you and they are in a learning partnership, be explicit about how a teaching enhancement can help students learn and how the effectiveness of the enhancement will depend on their participation in the process.

Difficult Content:	Enhancement Decisions
Analyze for Learning Difficulties	
Reach Enhancement Decisions	
Teach Strategically	
Evaluate Mastery	
Revisit Outcomes	

4. *Evaluate your work:*
   - For "Evaluate Mastery," identify one way you will ask students to demonstrate that they understand the challenging content you have identified at the outset of this exercise. If students cannot successfully demonstrate what you believe they should know and understand about the content, you will need to rethink your curricular and instructional decisions.
   - In "Revisiting Outcomes," consider once again, in light of the steps you have followed above, the importance of the content you have identified. As you analyzed the

content for potential learning difficulties and thought about ways to enhance your instruction, did you plan for adequate and appropriate support to help students learn the content? These are all important parts of Revisiting Outcomes, because if students do not learn difficult content, you must either reteach it using different techniques, or reevaluate whether it is really important for students to know and understand.

▪ If you have access to a teacher's edition of the textbook for your course, examine it to see if it identifies the concepts, ideas, or other parts of the content that may be difficult for some students to master. If it does, compare it with what you have identified—does it inventory teaching suggestions and activities related to the difficult content you have identified? Does the teacher's edition have any useful suggestions related to your content? How do its suggestions compare with what you have generated in the chart above?

5. *Next steps:*
  ▪ Make a list of five methods, devices, or routines presented in this chapter that you think would be useful in teaching your content and that you would like to incorporate in your teaching. Sketch out a plan identifying each method, the course you want to use it in, the relevant page numbers for you to refer back to, and a brief sentence about how you think it will enhance your teaching. Put this in your notebook of "Golden Teaching Nuggets."

WEB SITES

http://www.cast.org/udl Center for Applied Special Technology. The CAST Web site supports educators in learning about and practicing Universal Design for Learning (UDL).

http://www.ncss.org/standards/1.1.html Site provides Curriculum Standards for Social Studies from the National Council for Social Studies

http://www.actfl.org Site of the American Council on the Teaching of Foreign Languages provides a link to National Standards in Foreign Language Education accessed under their "Quick Find" menu.

http://www.nctm.org National Council of Teachers of Mathematics.

http://www.menc.org Site of the National Association for Music Education, with access to National Standards for Music Education.

http://www.ncge.org/publications/tutorial/standards The National Council for Geography Education provides The Eighteen National Geography Standards.

http://ericae.net/db/digs/ed380401.htm National Standards for Civics and Government in ERIC Digest.

http://www.sscnet.ucla.edu/nchs/standards National Standards for United States History.

http://www.ash.udel.edu/ash/teacher/standards.html This site has links to National Curriculum Standards in many content areas including the Arts.

http://www.cresst96.cse.ucla.edu/CRESST/pages/Rubrics.htm Provides scoring rubrics from the National Center for Research on Evaluation, Standards, and Student Testing.

http://ssdoo.gsfc.nasa.gov/education/standards.html Standards for Science, Mathematics, Technology and Geography.

http://www.edexcellence.net/standards/best.html Thomas B. Fordham Foundation's appraisal of state standards in English, history, geography, math, and science.

RESOURCES

Graphic Devices

Parks, S. (1990). *Organizing thinking: Graphic organizers.* Pacific Grove, CA: Critical Thinking Press & Software.

Claggett, F., & Brown, J. (1992). *Drawing your own conclusions: Graphic strategies for reading, writing and thinking.* Portsmouth, NH: Heinemann.

Bromley, K. D. (1996). *Webbing with literature.* Boston: Allyn & Bacon.

Other Resources

Friend, M. (1996). *The power of two: Making a difference through co-teaching.* Indiana University. This videotape provides an in-depth look at six different types of co-teaching arrangements by describing and showing what co-teaching actually looks like in elementary through high school classrooms.

Fuchs, L., Fuchs, D., Karns, K., & Phillips, N. (1996). *Peer-assisted learning strategies: Math.* Nashville, TN: Vanderbilt University. A teacher's manual and videotape describe and show in action how peer-assisted learning is used in classrooms.

Greenwood, C. R., Delquadri, J., & Carta, J. J. *Classwide peer tutoring.* Seattle, WA: Educational

Achievement Systems. This kit is complete, from start to finish, with teacher directions, lessons, and handouts for students to use and teachers' instruction for classwide peer tutoring (CWPT). CWPT involves a reciprocal process in which peers take turns in the roles of tutor and tutee, and promotes actively involving students in practice activities.

McDougall, D. (1998). *Teaching students to manage their own behavior.* University of Hawaii, College of Education, 1776 University Avenue, Honolulu, HI 96822. Video vignettes of students learning to use self-management systems are featured, along with an instructor's manual.

SUPPORTS for LRE materials available from Johns Hopkins University, 9601 Medical Center Drive, Rockville, MD 20850. Over 40 materials developed by general educators, special educators, and related service personnel are available. The materials focus on a variety of techniques, including differentiation, curriculum-based assessment, and collaboration.

Tomlinson, C. A. (1999). *The differentiated classroom: Responding to the needs of all learners.* Alexandria, VA: Association for Supervision and Curriculum Development. Ten chapters contain rich information and multiple examples of how to differentiate within classrooms so that all learners' needs are met.

Tomlinson, C. A., & Kiernan, L. J. (1997). *Differentiating instruction.* Alexandria, VA: Association for Supervision and Curriculum Development, 1250 North Pitt Street, Alexandria VA 22314–1453. A facilitator's guide along with activities, overhead masters, activities, and videotapes make up this kit which provides a variety of ways to differentiate in elementary and secondary classrooms.

Vernon, D. S., Deshler, D. D., & Schumaker, J. B. (1993). *The teamwork strategy.* Lawrence, KS: Edge Enterprises, P.O. Box 1304, Lawrence, KS 66044. The teamwork strategy manual provides teachers with a framework for organizing and completing tasks in small work groups. Includes teacher directions, student handouts, and overhead pages.

Vernon, D. S., Schumaker, J. B., & Deshler, D. D. (1993). *The SCORE skills: Social skills for cooperative groups.* Lawrence, KS: Edge Enterprises, P.O. Box 1304, Lawrence, KS 66044. This manual describes the procedures for teaching social skills for effective cooperative group work. Five important social skills are highlighted as prerequisites for more complex cooperative strategies. The manual includes teacher directions, student handouts, and overhead pages.

York, J., Kronberg, R., & Doyle, M. B. (1994). *Creating inclusive school communities.* Baltimore: Brookes. This staff development series for general and special educators is composed of five modules that address specific issues affecting the school community. Materials include overhead pages for instructors, handouts for participants, activities, and videotapes that portray practices described.

SUGGESTED READINGS

Bradley, D. F., King-Sears, M. E., & Switlick, D. M. (1997). *Teaching students in inclusive settings: From theory to practice.* Boston: Allyn & Bacon. This text provides practical information on topics key to successful and supported inclusion.

Cole, C. M., & McLeskey, J. (1997). Secondary inclusion programs for students with mild disabilities. *Focus on Exceptional Children, 29*(6), 1–16. Barriers and solutions for transforming content and developing partnerships within a high school are described in this article. Several brief scenarios depict how teachers initiated and sustained changes in their thinking and practice in ways that benefited all students in this high school.

Kameenui, E. J., & Carnine, D. W. (1998). *Effective teaching strategies that accommodate diverse learners.* Columbus, OH: Merrill. Nine chapters include six content-specific chapters, and one on characteristics of diverse learners in grades K–8, and a chapter on the contextual issues that influence curriculum change and reform. Additionally, an appendix provides more specific information on BIG IDEAS in reading, math, science, and social studies.

King-Sears, M. E. (1994). *Curriculum-based assessment in special education.* San Diego: Singular. This text features the APPLY framework for targeting skills to use for curriculum-based assessment, developing materials and graphs, and many examples of curriculum-based assessment applications across content areas and grade levels.

Parkay, F. W., & Stanford, B. H. (1998). *Becoming a teacher* (4th ed.). Boston: Allyn & Bacon. Fourteen chapters are included in this text, with a range of topics and examples for varied curriculum and content areas.

Thousand, J. S., Villa, R. A., & Nevin, A. (1994). *Creativity and collaborative learning: A practical guide to empowering students and teachers.* Baltimore: Brookes. This book is full of lesson plans, activities, and unique methods that foster instruction as a shared responsibility among teachers and students.

REFERENCES

Anderson, L. M. (1989). Classroom instruction. In M. C. Reynolds (Ed.), *Knowledge base for the beginning teacher* (pp. 101–116). Elmsford, NY: Pergamon Press.

Armstrong, T. (1994). *Multiple intelligences in the classroom.* Alexandria, VA: ASCD.

Borko, H., Eisenhart, M., Brown, C. A., Underhill, R. G., Jones, D., & Agard, P. C. (1992). Learning to teach hard mathematics: Do novice teachers and their instructors give up too easily? *Journal for Research in Mathematics Education, 23,* 194–222.

Bradley, D. F., King-Sears, M. E., & Switlick, D. M. (1997). *Teaching students in inclusive settings: From theory to practice.* Boston: Allyn & Bacon.

Bulgren, J. A., & Lenz, B. K. (1996). Strategic instruction in the content areas. In D. Deshler, E. S. Ellis, & B. K. Lenz (Eds.) *Teaching adolescents with learning disabilities: Strategies and methods* (2nd ed.) (pp. 409–473). Denver: Love Publishing.

Bulgren, J. A., Lenz, B. K., Deshler, D. D., & Schumaker, J. B. (1995). *The concept comparison routine.* Lawrence, KS: Edge Enterprises.

Bulgren, J. A., Schumaker, J. B., & Deshler, D. D. (1993). *The concept mastery routine.* Lawrence, KS: Edge Enterprises.

Clarke, J., Martell, K., & Willey, C. (1994). Sequencing graphic organizers to guide historical research. *The Social Studies, 85,* 70–75.

Ehlinger, J., & Pritchard, R. (1994). Using think alongs in secondary content areas. *Research and Instruction, 33,* 187–206.

Ellis, E. (1991). *SLANT: A starter strategy for class participation.* Lawrence, KS: Edge Enterprise.

Ellis, E., Deshler, D., Lenz, K., Schumaker, J., & Clark, F. (1991). An instructional model for teaching learning strategies. *Focus on Exceptional Children, 23*(6), 1–23.

Fuchs, D., Fuchs, L. W., Thompson, A., Svenson, E., Yen, L., Otaiba, S. A., Yang, N., & Numan, K. (in press). Peer-assisted learning strategies: Extensions downward into kindergarten/first grade and upward into high school. *Remedial and Special Education.*

Gorman, J. A. (1996). *Questioning Cooperative Learning in a Low-track Math Class.* Unpublished teacher's journal, Boston College.

Gorman, J. A., & Lysaght, K. (1996). *Accommodating diversity in a general education math class in a middle school.* Presentation at Boston College, School of Education.

Harris, K. R., & Graham, S. (1996). Constructivism and students with special needs: Issues in the classroom. *Learning Disabilities Research & Practice, 11,* 134–137.

Housner, L. D., & Griffey, D. C. (1985). Teacher cognition: Differences in planning and interactive decision making between experienced and inexperienced teachers. *Research Quarterly for Exercise and Sport, 56*(1), 45–53.

Igoa, C. (1995). *The inner world of the immigrant child.* Mahwah, NJ: Lawrence Erlbaum.

Kameenui, E. J., & Carnine, D. W. (1998). *Effective teaching strategies that accommodate diverse learners.* Columbus, OH: Merrill.

Kameenui, E. J., & Simmons, D. C. (1999). *Toward successful inclusion of students with disabilities: The architecture of instruction.* Alexandria, VA: Council for Exceptional Children.

Kinder, D., & Bursuck, W. (1991). The search for a unified social studies curriculum: Does history really repeat itself? *Journal of Learning Disabilities, 24,* 270–275, 320.

King-Sears, M. E. (1997). Best academic practices for inclusive classrooms. *Focus on Exceptional Children, 29*(7), 1–22.

King-Sears, M. E. (in press). Three steps to gain access to general education curriculum. *Intervention in School and Clinic.*

King-Sears, M. E., & Cummings, C. S. (1996). Inclusive practices of classroom teachers. *Remedial and Special Education, 17,* 217–225.

King-Sears, M. E., Mercer, C. D., & Sindelar, P. (1992). Toward independence with keyword mnemonics: A strategy for science vocabulary instruction. *Remedial and Special Education, 13*(5), 22–33.

Lenz, B. K. (2002). Connectors. *Stratenotes, 10*(5), 4–7.

Lenz, B. K., & Schumaker, J. B. (1999). *Adapting language arts, social studies, and science materials for the inclusive classroom.* Alexandria, VA: Council for Exceptional Children.

Maheady, L., Harper, G. F., & Mallette, B. (in press). Peer-mediated instruction and interventions and students with mild disabilities. *Remedial and Special Education.*

Maheady, L., Sacca, M. K., & Harper, G. F. (1987). Classwide student tutoring teams: The effects of peer-mediated instruction on the academic performance of secondary mainstreamed students. *The Journal of Special Education, 21,* 107–121.

Maheady, L., Sacca, M. K., & Harper, G. F. (1988). Classwide peer tutoring with mildly handicapped high school students. *Exceptional Children, 55,* 52–59.

Mastropieri, M. A., & Scruggs, T. E. (1991). *Teaching students ways to remember: Strategies for learning mnemonically.* Cambridge, MA: Brookline Books.

McCaleb, S. P. (1994). *Building communities of learners: A collaboration among teachers students, families, and community.* New York: St. Martin's Press.

McDiarmid, G. W., Ball, D. L., & Anderson, C. W. (1989). Why staying one chapter ahead doesn't really work: Subject-specific pedagogy. In M. C. Reynolds (Ed.) *Knowledge base for the beginning teacher* (pp. 193–206). Elmsford, NY: Pergamon Press.

Mercer, C. D., Jordan, L., & Miller, S. P. (1996). Constructivistic math instruction for diverse learners. *Learning Disabilities Research & Practice, 11,* 147–156.

Moll, L. C. (1988). Some key issues in teaching Latino students. *Language Arts, 65,* 465–473.

Oakes, J., & Guiton, G. (1995). Matchmaking: The dynamics of high school tracking decisions. *American Educational Research Journal, 32,* 3–33.

Orkwis, R., & McLane, K. (1998). *A curriculum every student can use: Design principles for student access.* Reston, VA: ERIC Clearinghouse on Disabilities and Gifted Education.

Pressley, M., Hogan, K., Wharton-McDonald, R., Mistretta, J., & Ettenberger, S. (1996). The challenges of instructional scaffolding: The challenges of instruction that supports student thinking. *Learning Disabilities Research & Practice, 11,* 138–146.

Rose, D., Sethuraman, S., & Meo, G. (2000). Universal design for learning. *Journal of Special Education Technology, 15*(2), 56–60.

Seixas, P. (1993). Historical understanding among adolescents in a multicultural setting. *Curriculum Inquiry, 23,* 301–327.

Shulman, L. S. (1987). Knowledge and teaching: Foundations of the new reform. *Harvard Educational Review, 57,* 1–22.

Tomlinson, C. A. (1999). *The differentiated classroom: Responding to the needs of all learners.* Alexandria, VA: Association for Supervision and Curriculum Development.

Tomlinson, C. A., & Kiernan, L. J. (1997). *Differentiating instruction.* Alexandria, VA: Association for Supervision and Curriculum Development.

Tompkins, G. E. (1994). *Teaching writing: Balancing process and product.* New York: Merrill, Macmillan College.

Wallach, G. P., & Butler, K. G. (Eds.). (1994). *Language learning disabilities and school-age children and adolescents.* Boston: Allyn & Bacon.

Zentall, S. S. (1990). Fact-retrieval automatization and math problem-solving: Learning disabled, attention disordered and normal adolescents. *Journal of Educational Psychology, 82,* 856–865.

Zentall, S. S. (1993). Research on the educational implications of attention deficit hyperactivity disorder. *Exceptional Children, 60,* 143–153.

Zentall, S. S., & Smith, Y. N. (1993). Mathematical performance and behavior of children with hyperactivity with and without coexisting aggression. *Behavioral Research and Therapy, 31,* 701–710.

Zentall, S. S., Smith, Y. N., Lee, Y. B., & Wieczorek, C. (1994). Mathematical outcomes of attention deficit hyperactivity disorder. *Journal of Learning Disabilities, 27,* 510–519.

10 Teaching Learning Strategies

Gwen Berry
Deborah Hall
Patricia G. Gildroy

A person who has learned how to learn and study in school, how to use sources of information, how to solve problems, and other similar skills, is much better equipped for what awaits him or her after school than is a hypothetical individual who has perfectly memorized everything in the curriculum.

—E. Tulving, *Elements of Episodic Memory*, 1983, p. 52

Critical Self-Test Questions

- What are learning strategies and why are they important to teach?
- How do I choose appropriate learning strategies to teach?
- How do I provide effective strategy instruction?
- How do I evaluate learning strategy instruction?
- How can I work with other teachers to teach and reinforce learning strategy usage?

Many students come to school every day and participate in classroom activities yet never fully engage in the learning process. Often this is not because of a lack of motivation but rather a lack of understanding of the learning process. These students may not use prior knowledge to facilitate understanding, or may be unaware of the thinking processes needed to perform a task, solve a problem, or answer a question. They are not uninterested in learning, nor are they unable to learn. They need classrooms that are responsive to their interests, goals, and abilities, and they need to be taught how to use effective and efficient learning strategies to enable them to become independent learners.

Everyone uses learning strategies. They help us approach learning challenges or tasks. A strategy for memorizing information might be to create a mnemonic to help recall information. For example, school children have long used the acronym HOMES to prompt recall of the Great Lakes: Huron, Ontario, Michigan, Erie, and Superior. Although we all use strategies to learn—and, indeed, to approach many of our daily tasks—some of us are better than others at developing strategies to meet our needs. Similarly, some students are better than others at figuring out ways to learn new information and develop new skills. Some students lack this skill almost altogether; these are the students, for example, who believe that if they read the textbook chapter over and over, they will understand what is in it and be able to pass the test.

Because some students lack skill in developing strategies to tackle learning, they need to be taught how to do this. As you teach and as you get to know your students, be alert to which and how many of your students fail to use or develop strategies to help them learn independently. If you find that you have many such learners in your classroom, you may want to think about setting aside some time to teach your students *how* to learn.

FIGURE 10.1
Graphic Organizer

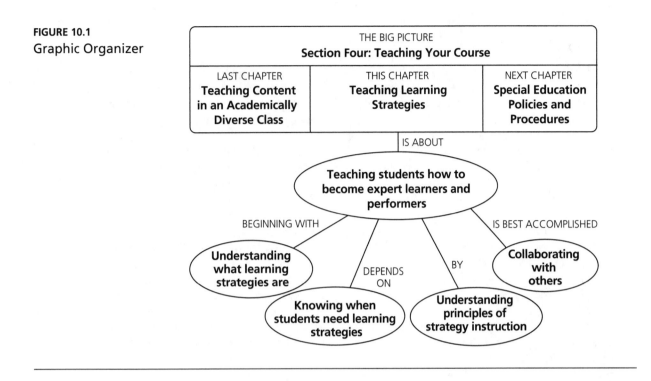

In this book, you have learned how to make your content more accessible to students through the use of planning and teaching routines that can compensate for the absence of good learning strategies among your students. Teachers can also help students become independent, self-regulated, expert learners by teaching them how to develop and use strategies to learn. Or, put another way, we can teach them to become strategic learners.

FOUNDATIONS AND PRINCIPLES

Although not all teachers have an opportunity to work with colleagues in teaching learning strategies as in the chapter scenario, individual teachers face the same types of issues as those described. This chapter addresses some of these issues by providing a rationale and guidelines for teaching learning strategies to students. The chapter also discusses important instructional considerations that have been shown to be essential for effective learning-strategy instruction. Finally, suggestions are made for integrating learning-strategy instruction into content-area instruction as well as collaborating with others to promote students' generalization of learning-strategy use across contexts and settings.

What Are Learning Strategies?

Imagine yourself sitting in a classroom with the final exam in front of you. You see that it is an objective test with one essay question. How would you describe your thinking? (A) Are you hoping that you will do well? Are you afraid that you will fail? Are you looking around the room to see what other

▪ Scenario

Hank Harris, a ninth-grade history teacher, found that his students' overall understanding of the important concepts of the course improved with his use of course, unit, and lesson organizers. However, many of his students experienced difficulty in remembering information they read. For example, when asked to provide written answers to questions at the end of a chapter in the textbook, many students had difficulty. In addition, they frequently just copied information directly from the textbook. When Mr. Harris asked his students to explain or expand on their answers, many were unable to do so. Mr. Harris brought this up at the grade-level meeting and found that the science and English teachers complained about the same types of problems. The special education resource teacher, Rita Sanchez, suggested that the team could work collaboratively to identify the task demands for the different classes and look into developing a plan to teach learning strategies to enable more students to be successful in their respective classes. The team liked this idea and decided that their plan should involve teaching learning strategies that would help their students learn how to: plan and successfully complete their assignments; understand, integrate, and remember what they had read; and produce higher-quality written products.

The ninth-grade teaching team was excited about the possibility of teaching learning strategies to their students. However, they also had a number of concerns. First, they worried about sacrificing instructional time to teach learning strategies, given the curricular demands they faced to "cover the content." Second, they were concerned about how to evaluate students on the learning strategies. Third, they wondered what materials should be used to practice the strategies during the initial stages of instruction. Finally, how could they ensure that their students understood the benefit of using the learning strategies in all of their classes?

students are doing? Or (B) Are you reviewing what you learned and studied? Are you reading over the sections and determining a plan of attack? Do you read the essay before you start answering questions? If you were thinking along the lines described in "B," you were demonstrating an effective strategy that would probably maximize your performance. If you were leaning toward the "A" questions, you were demonstrating an ineffective strategy and you probably would not demonstrate your knowledge well on the test.

Students who use an "A" type approach to tasks will not fare well in schools that expect independent learning. As a result, they would benefit from a strategy that would cue them to approach test taking more systematically. In one published test-taking strategy suitable for objective tests (Hughes, Schumaker, Deshler, & Mercer, 1988), students proceed through seven steps that remind them to do things like survey the test and allot time for each section, read instructions carefully, notice special requirements, and answer items they know first, then return later to those they are uncertain about. This is an example of a learning strategy that will help students be successful when taking tests.

Why Teach Learning Strategies?   Students are asked every day to complete a variety of complex tasks. For example, they are expected to write essays, take tests, memorize information, work cooperatively in groups, and read large amounts of information. As teachers, we often wonder why so many students do not even attempt to complete such tasks. Part of the reason is that many students simply do not know how to get started, and others do not know how to complete a task. As successful adults, we have developed ways to learn and ways to complete tasks. We have learned when we need to read carefully and when we can skim. We have learned how to take notes and when to highlight the text, how to work with others, and how to organize and create a process for task completion. Unfortunately, many students lack the experience or maturity to develop these types of strategies. Instead, they tend to develop *coping* strategies to avoid embarrassment rather than succeed at the task. In the history class scenario above, the students learned how to find the part of the text related to specific questions, but failed to understand the overall purpose of answering the questions and did not understand the writing process as a whole. These students did not have a good repertoire of strategies to help them meet the task demands of learning the content of the course.

To help students become more effective learners, we must teach them the strategies that successful students use. We must help them analyze the task, organize the process, and guide themselves to complete the task. In other words, we can teach learning strategies that provide students with a logical sequence of steps for attacking difficult tasks. These steps make the task at hand manageable and provide students with a place to start.

Focus and Reflect

- As a successful learner, what are the different strategies you use to learn new material?
- How do you go about choosing and modifying strategies you use to meet specific task demands?
- How do you evaluate your own learning?

In short, strategy instruction may be defined simply as instruction in how to learn and perform (Lenz, Clark, Deshler, & Schumaker, 1988). Learning strategies help students learn and perform by providing them with a specific set of steps for: (a) approaching new and difficult tasks, (b) guiding thoughts and actions, (c) completing tasks in a timely and successful manner, and (d) thinking strategically. Students who use strategies on a regular basis begin to think about how they learn best, which is very exciting for both teachers and students. As teachers, if our instructional goals include having students understand the content of our courses so that they can use and apply the information later in life, then the time spent helping students learn must not be seen as a waste of time. In fact, as students become more proficient in using learning strategies, they will become more efficient and independent learners in mastering the content in your class.

KNOWING AND DOING

Knowing When Students Need Instruction in Learning Strategies

There are several ways to know when your students lack appropriate learning strategies. One way is to determine when students are not being successful in learning tasks and activities. Another way is to notice when you are helping individual students and find yourself repeating instructions about how to tackle a particular task. Yet another way is to consult with special education teachers in your school.

Are Students Meeting Task Demands? You may identify critical demands and expectations that your students face every day and determine which of them are not being met by asking two important questions: (1) "What is expected of my students?" and (2) "Where is student performance not meeting my standards?" Researchers at the University of Kansas categorized the demands faced by secondary students into four major areas: academic, social, motivational, and executive (Lenz, Clark, Deshler, & Schumaker, 1988). For example, in the category of academic demands, secondary teachers expect students to gain information from lectures and written material, demonstrate knowledge on tests, and express information in writing. Unfortunately, many students do not know how to read textbooks effectively, so getting information is difficult. Also, many students have never received instruction in how to take notes and have difficulty identifying important ideas and information. Further, many students experience difficulty in spelling, writing complete sentences, constructing paragraphs, and responding to short-answer and essay questions on tests.

In addition to academic demands, secondary students face social demands, such as following rules in and out of school; participating in social activities, discussions, and conversations with peers and adults; accepting criticism and help; recruiting assistance when needed; resisting inappropriate peer pressure; and being pleasant in social interactions. A third demand area for students in secondary schools is motivation. Students are expected to plan for timely task completion and set short-, intermediate-, and long-term goals. Unfortunately, the skills necessary to meet these motivational demands are not explicitly taught to students, and many students fail school as a result. Students in secondary settings also face executive demands that require them to work independently with little feedback, apply knowledge across content areas, solve problems, and organize information and resources. In other words, executive demands require students to think about how they learn best and make decisions about what they will do. Strategies may be used or developed to address all four categories of demands. However, it should be noted that all good strategy use includes components addressing executive demands, because a key feature of any strategy is to think about when to use it, how to modify it, and when it is appropriate to switch to a new strategy. (See Resources at the end of this chapter for a list of published strategies that address academic, social, and motivational demands faced by secondary students.)

Are Many Students Asking for Help As They Experience Similar Difficulties?   Another way to assess when your students need learning strategies is to pay careful attention to extra support you routinely provide students during learning activities. Many teachers use learning strategies in their teaching but may not recognize them as strategies. This happens when teachers are helping students during independent work and explain a process or concept repeatedly to various students. Sometimes the teacher recognizes that a number of students are having the same problem and may pause to clarify a point or process for all students. This process of clarification is itself instruction in a learning strategy. For example, a math teacher may explain how to solve word problems to several individuals during class work time. As the teacher repeats the process, he or she develops a sequence of steps and specific language to describe the thinking and behaviors. The math teacher might say: "First, identify what is being asked for. Then, identify the information that is given. Give a letter, or *variable*, to each unknown quantity. Then, if it helps you, describe the relationship between the known and unknown information using a picture, table, formula or sentence. Finally, write an equation, solve, and check for correctness." In this example, the teacher is basically giving students a strategy for solving word problems.

In another example, a science teacher might tell students that a good way to remember what chlorophyll means is to create a link between the word and the definition. The teacher might say: "Chlorophyll is the chemical in green plants that allows them to generate food from sunlight, minerals, and oxygen. You can remember the word because 'chloro' sounds like 'color' and 'phyll' sounds like 'fill'. So, chlorophyll is the chemical that 'fills' leaves with 'color', in this case green." This teacher is cueing students to use a linking strategy to help them remember the meaning of an important term. Teachers can create strategies for this process and teach them to students. In addition, there are published strategies that teachers may use, such as The LINCS Strategy (Ellis, 1992), which cues students to use visual imagery, prior knowledge, and mnemonic devices to enhance memory of a new concept or vocabulary term.

Are There Colleagues Who Can Help Me Identify Why Some of My Students Are Not Being Successful?   A third way to determine when students might need instruction in effective learning strategies is to consult with the special educators in your school. In the process of providing support for students in resource room settings, special educators often use or create learning strategies to help students to be successful in mainstream classes. These educators may be able to help you determine whether teaching some learning strategies to your students would help them learn the content in your class.

In summary, when deciding whether or not to teach students effective learning strategies, it is important to consider: (a) the demands your students face every day in and out of school; (b) whether you find yourself repeating the same instructions over and over to students; and (c) the results of consultations with resource personnel, like special educators and other teachers.

Focus and Reflect

Have you taught or observed in classrooms where a number of students needed or asked for the same kind of help with a learning task? What kind of help was needed? Could you devise a learning strategy to address the task demand?

Principles of Strategy Instruction

There are three features that should be part of any learning strategy you develop or use. First, the steps in a strategy should cue students to *do* something like read, survey, or examine. Second, the strategy should offer a way to remember the steps to follow in using the strategy. Third, the strategy should address a process that students find difficult. Students need to feel that the strategy will help them meet key demands and expectations. For example, the best time to teach a test-taking strategy may be during freshman year when students start taking objective final exams. This is a time when they may most acutely recognize that they need help figuring out how to approach the task of taking tests.

A learning strategy that incorporates the features noted above is the GRADE strategy, which may be taught to students to help them use their notes to study for a test (Berry, 1999). Students are often perplexed by the task of studying for a test, so the task demand is real. The strategy has steps that direct students to do something, in this case:

- **Gather** missing information from your notes by asking the teacher or a friend for his or her notes.
- **Reread** and highlight notes using different colors to code different levels of information.
- **Ask** yourself questions as you study your notes.

- **Draw** a visual device, like a chart, or graphic to organize the information.
- **Engage** in positive self-talk after studying your notes so you will be mentally prepared when you take the test ("I have studied for this test and I am ready to do my best").

The steps spell the word GRADE, a mnemonic device that helps students remember the strategy, and the steps instruct them on what to do to use their notes to prepare for a test (Berry, 1999).

As the example above demonstrates, learning strategies not only provide a specific set of steps for *approaching* a task, but they also *guide thinking and performance*. As students proceed through each step of GRADE, the strategy guides their approach to a task, as well as their thinking and performance in doing the task. Likewise, learning strategies that teach students how to write a theme, pronounce a word, or solve a linear equation contain a complete plan of action for thinking about and performing a task. Learning strategies can also help students use time efficiently. For example, in the GRADE strategy, the first step of gathering missing information is critical because otherwise students might waste many hours studying incomplete notes.

How Should I Teach Learning Strategies?   In the course of everyday instruction, teachers often cue students to use learning strategies but fail to actually teach them. Once you develop or locate an appropriate strategy, it is important to realize that, although strategies are powerful learning tools, they require explicit instruction, not just casual mention. Students must

---

■ *Scenario Revisited*

THE PARAPHRASING STRATEGY

The students in Mr. Harris's history class would clearly benefit from learning a paraphrasing strategy to help them put information into their own words, which in turn would help them understand and remember information better. One strategy that Mr. Harris chose to teach his students was the Paraphrasing Strategy (Schumaker, Denton, & Deshler, 1984). In this strategy, each letter of the acronym RAP cues students to engage in a specific process aimed at helping him or her understand and remember information. For example, the "R" cues students to "read a paragraph" (or section of information), the "A" cues students to "Ask themselves, 'What are the main idea and details in this paragraph?'" and the "P" cues students to "Put the main idea and details into your own words." Knowledge of these steps helps students understand that there is a process to paraphrasing information. Students then practice applying these steps to different types of information (textbooks, lectures, etc.). As they learn to apply the strategy in different situations, they learn when, where, and how the strategy can be used for maximum benefit. For example, when answering questions at the end of the chapter or essay items on tests, students learn how to state main ideas and corresponding details in their own words. Students also realize that when taking notes, one good system for structuring information is to provide headings for main ideas and subheadings for details. Thus, students begin to think about when, where, and how the Paraphrasing Strategy helps them become better learners.

learn and apply strategies before they will experience any benefits. Consequently, quality instruction is necessary to ensure that students learn how to use a strategy (mastery), use it effectively and regularly (maintenance), and use it appropriately with a variety of tasks (generalization). In addition, teaching learning strategies to your students is accomplished most effectively when (a) students understand the purpose of the strategy, (b) learn how, when, and why to use it, (c) learn different ways to remember the strategy, (d) develop goals for learning the strategy, and (e) see the strategy modeled several times (Lenz, Ellis, & Scanlon, 1996).

Students must understand the purpose for a strategy and how learning it will benefit them personally. If students feel a need for the strategy they will likely understand its purpose. Further, it helps to discuss how the strategy can be applied in other situations so students see a long-term benefit to learning it. For example, the skills developed in the Paraphrasing Strategy will help students listen more effectively to lectures and hone their ability to identify important information.

Students must learn how, when, and why to perform the actions of the strategy—both physical and cognitive actions. Students who can describe the steps performed in the strategy and explain when to use them are more likely to use the strategy independently. In the Paraphrasing Strategy, students must be able to describe the cognitive steps needed to identify the main idea and details. For example, to find the main idea, students should be able to explain that they would look in the first or last sentence of the paragraph, find terms that are repeated, or identify what the details have in common. These cues would help them identify the main idea and details and put the information into their own words. Students should also be able to explain when they would use the strategy—for example, when writing essays on tests, summarizing for a book report, or reading a difficult passage.

Students learn different ways to remember the strategy to enable independent use in the future. Memory devices such as acronyms (e.g., RAP in the Paraphrasing Strategy and GRADE in the strategy described earlier) can help students remember the steps in a strategy. The memory device provides students with an anchor to guide them through a task. Many students, especially those with learning disabilities, have difficulty remembering the

---

The Paraphrasing Strategy (RAP)

Steps for Paraphrasing

Read a paragraph

Ask yourself,

What are the main idea and details in this paragraph?

FINDING THE MAIN IDEA

Questions to Ask:

What is this paragraph about?

This paragraph is about _____.

What does it tell me about _____?

It tells me _____.

Places to Look: Look in the first sentence of the paragraph.

Look for repetitions of the same word or words in the whole paragraph.

Identify what all the details describe or explain.

Put the main idea and details into your own words.

REQUIREMENTS FOR A PARAPHRASE

• Must contain a complete thought, subject—verb
• Must be totally accurate
• Must have new information
• Must make sense
• Must contain useful information
• Must be in your own words
• Only one general statement per paragraph is allowed.

Schumaker, J. B., Denton, P. H., & Deshler, D. D. (1984). *The paraphrasing strategy.* Lawrence: The University of Kansas

sequence of steps in a strategy (Wong, 1996). You should have students verbally rehearse the steps during instruction. There are also other ways to help students remember how to use a strategy: They can make posters or bookmarks with the strategy steps printed on them; they can be encouraged to develop the habit of writing the memory device for a strategy on tests or written assignments to guide them before they begin to recall information or construct written responses to questions.

As instruction progresses, students should monitor their own progress and set short-term goals for learning each step of the strategy. In the initial stages of instruction, you need to be explicit with students about the different stages involved in learning the strategy, and remind them that learning a strategy is like learning a new skill: They will need to practice using it before it becomes fully useful and helpful to them in meeting the demands of a learning task. As with learning any new skill, students can take pride in the steps they have mastered while remaining aware of what they still need to practice.

Students should see the strategy modeled several times and hear how the teacher thinks through the process, using reasoning and problem solving, as the process unfolds. It is important for students to learn how expert learners think about and guide their actions when applying a strategy. You must model the thinking process for students, talking out loud about each of the cognitive and metacognitive processes a strategic learner follows to accomplish a learning task.

Teacher Modeling the Paraphrasing Strategy

T: One of the best ways to learn how to use this strategy is to listen and watch as someone who has used it before demonstrates or *models* how it works. I will be modeling the Paraphrasing Strategy today using the passage entitled "John Fitzgerald Kennedy," which each of you has in front of you. Please notice that as I model, I will be telling you what I am *thinking* as I use this strategy. I will be asking you lots of questions as we work our way through this passage, so be ready with answers.

T: OK, the "R" in "RAP" says to *read* a paragraph, so I will begin by reading the first paragraph: "John Fitzgerald Kennedy, 35th President of the United States, is remembered as an active and eager president. He entered the White House in 1961 at the age of 43, one of our youngest presidents. Even by then, he had lived a full and colorful life. After graduation from Harvard College, he toured Europe and visited Great Britain. In the same year, he published his first book, *Why England Slept*, a study of pre–World War II British politics" (Spargo & Williston, 1980, p. 59). Okay, we have done the "R" step. Now we can go on to the "A" step.

T: The next letter in "RAP" is "A" which reminds me that I should *ask* myself what the main idea and details are. I know that I should try to find the main idea first, and I have a tool that can help me find the main idea: questions! The first question I can ask myself is: "What is this paragraph about?" I know the answer to this question is usually a one-word answer. Let me apply that question to this paragraph. This paragraph is about John Kennedy. Yes, that's the big idea or topic of this paragraph. Now, on to the second question, which will help me refine my topic and create a main idea. The second question I can ask myself is: "What does the paragraph tell me about John Kennedy? Class, what *does* this paragraph tell us about John F. Kennedy?

S: That he was young when he became president.

S: That he graduated from Harvard College.

S: That he wrote a book about England.

T: You're right, the paragraph does tell us all of those things. Would you call each of those statements details or main ideas?

S: Probably details.

T: Why do you think they might be detail statements instead of main ideas?

S: Because they are very specific.

T: Yes. Remember that the main idea of a paragraph or section of information must be broad enough to include all of the details. Let's see if I can give you another hint. Do you remember *where* main ideas are often found?

S: The first or last sentence of a paragraph.

T: Yes. Are they always found in the first or last sentence of a paragraph?

S: No, but that's a good place to check for clues.

T: Thumbs up if you think that the last sentence of the paragraph that I just read is the main idea of this paragraph. Thumbs up if you think that the first sentence of the paragraph that I just read is the main idea of the paragraph.

T: Luis, why do you think that the first sentence is the main idea of this paragraph?

S: Because all of the other sentences in the paragraph show how John Kennedy was active and eager.

T: Excellent. In other words, all of the other sentences in the paragraph provide details about how JFK was an active and eager president. Now, if we were to look away from this passage and put that sentence in our own words, what could we say?

S: That John Kennedy did a lot of stuff at a young age.

T: Great start, but can we find a different word for "stuff"?

S: How about "achievements"?

T: Great! Let's see if we can put those ideas together in one complete statement of the main idea. It might help us to start with the words, "This paragraph is about . . ."

S: "This paragraph is about the early achievements of John F. Kennedy."

T: We've done it! We've got our main idea, which often is much more difficult to find than the details. Let's review the two questions that we ask ourselves to help us find the main idea. The first question is . . .

S: "What is this paragraph about?"

T: And what is this paragraph about?

S: John F. Kennedy.

T: What is the next question we ask ourselves?

S: "What does the paragraph tell us about John F. Kennedy?"

T: Yes. And in our *own words*, what does the paragraph tell us about John F. Kennedy?

S: That he had many early achievements.

T: You're doing great. Now let's turn that last statement into a specific (see if you can get rid of the word "he") and complete the main idea. Remember, you can start with "This paragraph is about . . ." if it helps.

S: This paragraph is about the early achievements of John F. Kennedy.

T: Great work! Let's go back to the steps of the strategy. The "A" in "RAP" says to what?

S: *Ask* yourself "What are the main ideas and the details?"

T: It looks like we need to find two details. How do we find the details in a paragraph?

S: They are what is left over after you've found the main idea.

S: They might be facts.

S: They should support the main idea statement.

T: Wow! You really do know this! So, give me one detail statement that supports the main idea. Remember to use your own words and to make a complete statement.

S: John F. Kennedy became president at the age of 43.

T: Super! How about one more detail?

S: John F. Kennedy graduated from Harvard College.

T: The details seem pretty easy once you have the main ideas, don't they? One thing to think about when you find details is to choose the ones that the teacher might expect you to know for the test. In other words, try to choose the most important details or the ones you think that the teacher will ask you about later.

T: Who remembers what the "P" in "RAP" stands for?

S: Put the main idea and details in your own words.

T: Why do you think this is important?

S: So you know that we did not just copy.

T: Yes, that's one good reason. There's another very important reason to put information in your own words, and that has to do with our ability to remember. Any ideas?

S: We'll remember it better if it's in our own words?

T: You've got it!

T: Let's review the steps again. What does the "R" in "RAP" say to do?

S: Read a paragraph.

T: What does the "A" in "RAP" say to do?

S: Ask yourself, "What are the main ideas and the details?"

T: Which one should we find first?

S: The main idea!

T: What is the first question we should ask ourselves to help find the main idea?

S: What is this paragraph about?

T: About how long will the answer to this question be?

S: One word.

T: What's the next question we ask ourselves?

S: "What does this paragraph tell me about ——?"

T: Great! And how can we find the details?

S: They are what are left after finding the main idea.

S: They might be facts.

S: We should choose details that are important.

T: What does the "P" in "RAP" say to do?

S: Put the main ideas and details in your own words.

T: Why do we put the main ideas and details in our own words?

S: So we remember the information better and so we don't copy someone else's work.

T: OK. Let's move to the second paragraph in this passage. We'll find the main idea together, and then at your tables, each group will find two main idea statements and we'll compare answers. Wanda, will you do us the honor of doing the "R" step?" (teacher and class continue practicing).

This modeling example is just that—an example. You will need to adapt the process for yourself to suit your style and the manner in which you interact with the students you have in your classes. The important thing to remember about modeling is that you need to make your thinking processes transparent for students—they have to be able to see how you approach and do a learning task. Students also have to be actively engaged in the process through responding to specific questions and performing the different steps modeled. Notice in the modeling example above how quickly the teacher engaged the students. Students will not become proficient in using strategies if they remain passive observers.

When you are teaching learning strategies to your students, you may want to use controlled materials initially—that is, materials that are not so difficult that students will be distracted from the task of learning and practicing the new strategy. This will enable students to concentrate on the process of learning the strategy rather than also having to work to decode or understand difficult content. To encourage students in learning this new skill, you should make a point of praising their mastery of the steps of the strategy so that they will be able to monitor their progress in learning the strategy.

Students must be specifically taught to use strategies in other settings so they will understand that the strategies have a use beyond the classroom in which they are taught. No strategy should be taught that is useful in only one setting. Students do not have time in their academic careers to learn something that is not useful beyond their immediate environment. Therefore, goals for strategy use should extend to several contexts and settings.

To appreciate the importance of these principles for teaching learning strategies, think back to the examples given earlier of incidental strategy instruction—the math teacher helping students solve word problems and the science teacher cueing students about how to remember what the word *chlorophyll* meant. The math teacher "told" students about a strategy to solve word problems, but only the very alert and astute students would be able to learn it and apply it across settings and content without further instruction. The science teacher may be successful in helping students learn the word *chlorophyll*, but it is unlikely that many students will take the

The students in Hank Harris's classroom mastered the steps of the Paraphrasing Strategy. His instruction had incorporated important features that made it effective, including addressing the demands of the task and setting, providing steps to guide thinking and performance, presenting the strategy in a format that students could readily learn and apply, and addressing problems that students were experiencing.

Now he decided that the issue of whether the strategy would be used independently across different settings still needed to be addressed. He knew that strategy instruction is successful only to the extent that students internalize the steps, understand when and where to apply it, and realize how it can help them learn and get better grades. After considerable discussion with Ms. Sanchez, the special education resource teacher, he came up with the following plan to promote strategy use in various settings.

Mr. Harris looked for multiple opportunities to model and have students model the strategy. For example, he applied the steps of the Paraphrasing Strategy to reading and analyzing stories in the local newspaper during current events. This demonstrated to his students that he valued the strategy, and they gained a better understanding of when and where to use it.

In each class, he would cue students to use the Paraphrasing Strategy on all reading assignments that required careful reading and comprehension. He used verbal cues prior to giving a reading assignment and often cued use of the strategy on assignments.

He provided performance feedback, including both group and individual feedback, focusing first on the parts of the strategy that students were performing well, and second on the categories or patterns of errors that still needed to be addressed.

Since Mr. Harris integrated the paraphrasing strategy into his daily activities and assignments, he demonstrated to students that they should do the same. One way in which Mr. Harris integrated use of the strategy in daily instruction and assignments was through explicit instruction to use the strategy. For example, he would have students work in cooperative groups to research topics. He instructed students to create paraphrases for what they read and researched and to prepare summaries using their paraphrases of the information as handouts for the class. At other times he had students find a detail that would help them remember each main idea. Mr. Harris also integrated use of the strategy in teaching content when he would provide a quick paraphrase of a difficult reading passage to help students understand relationships within a passage.

strategy and use it to learn other words. These teachers could provide more effective instruction if they explicitly taught the strategies to all students and if opportunities were provided for students to practice the strategy while receiving feedback from the teacher.

Assessment   One of the primary purposes for teaching students learning strategies is to help them master content. Therefore, one of the most important methods for determining if strategies are working is to look at student grades. In some instances, this method of evaluation may be as informal as "eye-balling" student work. For example, if a teacher taught a note-taking strategy to students, simply collecting notes and observing whether or not students are using the strategy may serve as an informative and adequate evaluation.

A major benefit of strategies instruction is to help students improve their grades. The larger purpose, however, is improved learning. A way to impress this larger purpose on students is to assess the *process* of learning how to use a strategy, as well as the outcome. Teachers frequently give students points for the use of other learning processes deemed valuable, like brainstorming, using note cards for research papers, accepting feedback, and working effectively in cooperative groups. Assessing the *process* of learning how to use strategies is no different.

There are a number of ways to encourage and facilitate strategy use in classroom settings through assessment. When students are initially learning a strategy, you might consider testing them on their recall of the steps of the strategy. You might also include a question or two about the strategy in a unit test and ask how they used the strategy to answer question number 5 (for example). Other possibilities for assessing student use of strategies include assigning points when there is evidence that the strategy has been used. In test directions, you could say that students are to use a particular strategy to answer a particular question and specify that they should jot down the steps of the strategy in the margins of their exam paper.

It is important to assess both the process and the outcome of using a learning strategy. By assigning points to the process of learning a strategy, students understand that a teacher places great value on this task. Process assessments also provide students with necessary feedback and reinforcement while learning a strategy. Evaluating the outcome of strategy use—improvement in learning and grades—is critical too. This information provides teachers and students with observable improvement that validates the investment of instructional time in learning strategies.

Collaborating with Others to Provide Strategy Instruction

Successful integration of strategy instruction in secondary classrooms is most effective when teachers work together to identify the strategies that will help students become more successful learners. Content-area teachers have expertise in the particular methods of inquiry for their disciplines, while special educators have expertise in the specific learning needs of students who struggle in school. When these professionals collaborate, strategies instruction can be provided that meets a variety of setting demands and addresses the learning needs of more students.

Individual teachers can provide strategy instruction to their students through the use of careful observation, student interviews, and knowledge of learning processes. They can learn to recognize when students need strategy instruction, and they can find or create strategies to address these

---

■ *Scenario Revisited*

Mr. Harris found many ways to reinforce the use of the Paraphrasing Strategy. Verbal reinforcement ("That was a really good paraphrase.") and written reinforcement ("Good job of finding the main ideas of this chapter!") were effective. Mr. Harris also decided to award bonus points on essay tests when there was evidence that the Paraphrasing Strategy had been used. For some assignments, Mr. Harris considered awarding two grades, one for content mastery and one for strategy use.

needs. However, it is much more efficient, and ultimately more effective, if several teachers collaborate and support one another in teaching strategies.

Teachers who have had the most success in teaching learning strategies have worked to encourage other teachers to teach them as well. When teachers retain samples of student work prior to and after learning strategies, they are often able to use this information to convince other teachers about the power of strategy instruction. Teams of two or more teachers can brainstorm, problem solve, and coach one another as they polish their skills in teaching learning strategies.

The Center on Organization and Restructuring of Schools at the University of Wisconsin found that the most effective schools organize their resources into collective enterprises (Newmann & Wehlage, 1995). These schools are effective because they:

- Reach consensus about the central goals for student learning. To address the requirements of national and state academic standards, teachers and students focus on the process of learning, as well as the content of courses. A critical part of the learning process includes utilizing effective learning strategies to answer questions and solve problems. Therefore, one of the goals that educators must reach consensus on is providing instruction in strategies to all students who can benefit from it.
- Take collective responsibility for student success. Educators can collaborate to identify the strategies needed in particular courses and share methods for instruction. Once learned, strategy use can be cued by other teachers to promote generalization across content, settings, and time.
- Engage in continuous reflection about ways to improve instruction and learning. The responsibility of teachers is to help students learn. However, learning is a complex process that does not occur in a direct, linear fashion. Exploration and experimentation, and false starts and redirection are inherent in the process (Caine & Caine, 1997). Therefore, to meet their responsibility, teachers will need to observe, evaluate, reflect, and dialogue with peers to meet this difficult challenge.

Supports for Learning Strategy Instruction It is important to emphasize that even in the absence of support, individual teachers can provide strategy instruction to students. Such individuals often provide the spark for spreading strategy instruction among teachers and throughout schools. As noted in the previous section, however, it is often much more efficient and effective if several teachers collaborate and support one another. For example, fellow teachers can participate in strategy training together, teach a strategy collaboratively, and engage in reciprocal observing and coaching. Teachers can also help one another come up with ideas about how to practice and assess a particular strategy, as well as share strategies they have developed.

Teachers and researchers cite various sources of support for strategy instruction (Pressley, El-Dinary, Gaskins, Schuder, Bergman, Almasi, & Brown, 1992; Tralli, Colombo, Deshler, & Schumaker, 1996). For example, parents can be enlisted to support strategy instruction in school and at

▪ *Scenario Revisited*

The critical issue of whether the strategy would be used independently across different settings outside Mr. Harris's classroom still needed to be addressed. Mr. Harris and Ms. Sanchez considered this issue carefully, because they understood that strategy instruction is successful only to the extent that students internalize the steps of the strategy, understand when and where to apply it, and realize how it can help them learn and get better grades. After considerable discussion, they came up with the following instructional techniques for all teachers on the team to use to promote strategy use in various settings.

1. *Provide students with cues to use the strategy.* In each class, students should be cued to use the Paraphrasing Strategy on all reading assignments that require careful reading and comprehension. To encourage strategy use across settings, Ms. Sanchez created handouts of each strategy that the team decided to teach. The teachers could use these to help them determine when to cue students to use the various strategies.

2. *Model the strategy.* The importance of modeling was stressed to all teachers, and they practiced the technique in team meetings to assure that all teachers understood how explicit they needed to be to make their thinking process transparent for students.

3. *Provide feedback on how well students are using the strategy.* Performance feedback included both group and individual feedback, focusing on the parts of the strategy that students were performing well and on the categories or patterns of errors that needed to be addressed.

4. *Integrate strategy use with daily instruction and materials.* Once their students had mastered a strategy, teachers were encouraged to use strategies in conjunction with content learning activities.

home by prompting students to use the strategies they have learned in school to complete homework assignments and study for tests. Parents may also volunteer to be trained along with teachers and provide classroom support by giving feedback, grading strategy practice attempts, and developing materials used to practice strategies. Parents can also advocate for strategy instruction across grade levels, programs, and schools.

Enlisting administrative support also fosters strategy use. Administrators can provide professional development opportunities for learning strategies, funds for materials, and release time for teachers to cooperatively plan and coach one another. Administrators can also show their support for teaching learning strategies by attending and actively participating in training sessions. Finally, administrators can play a key role in guiding the creation of a plan for implementing strategy instruction across grade levels and schools.

SUMMARY

Learning strategies help students become effective, efficient, independent learners. Teachers should choose to teach the strategies that students need to address classroom demands and meet teachers' high standards. To ensure that students will use a strategy, teachers must provide explicit instruction about each step of the strategy, including the physical, cognitive, and metacognitive actions that must be performed. Each student should be able to explain the entire strategy and when to use it. Further, students should be able to identify situations in many settings in which strategy use would improve performance.

Students benefit greatly from strategy instruction, even if only one teacher provides it. The most effective strategy instruction, however, takes place in environments in which teachers, students, and parents or guardians all discuss, model, encourage, and guide students in the effective use of strategies—in all settings. It is an environment in which the members are all engaged in active learning activities and in which the process of learning is valued enough to be given time for instruction and practice. The establishment of this kind of environment is supported in standards that have been adopted by most states.

Developing strategic environments involves focusing not only on the completion of tasks but also the processes used to complete the tasks. Therefore, one way to think about integrating strategy instruction into course content is to include *process* in your definition of content. For instance, in nonstrategic environments, a teacher might ask students to read a passage and answer a series of comprehension questions. The teacher

FIGURE 10.2
Expanded Graphic
Organizer

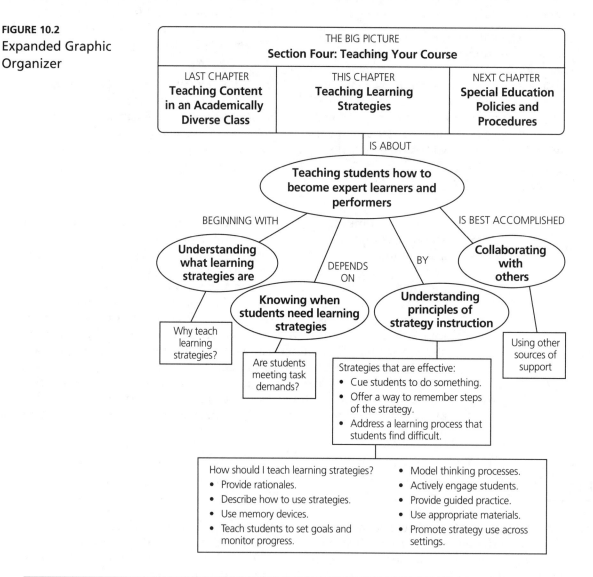

would then determine whether the students gave the correct or incorrect answers. In contrast, teachers in strategic environments would focus on teaching students the processes that are necessary to understand what is read and what is important about it. This would involve explicitly discussing and demonstrating how to determine good questions about what is read, how to link new information to old information, how to evaluate the worth of the information, and how to find or infer answers. In the first example, the students gain only the knowledge that is provided in the passage. In the second example, the students gain knowledge from the passage and also learn how to be strategic readers.

A strategic environment, therefore, not only aids students in meeting the challenges of secondary classrooms but also helps teachers address the goals articulated by state and national educational standards. Strategies can help students meet state academic standards requiring them to use critical thinking skills to solve problems and evaluate information. Strategic selection of content that helps teachers to teach toward application, analysis, and synthesis is critical and is supported by the national academic standards created for each discipline. For example, an evaluation of the geography standards was described in this way:

> Standards that only emphasized knowledge of where things are located—admittedly a vital building block for geographic competency—were judged to have fallen short if they did not also demand that *students ask why things are located where they are and present the knowledge and skills that would enable students to derive reasoned answers to such questions.* [italics added] (Munroe & Smith, 1998)

Strategy instruction encourages students to become experts on how they learn best, with teachers supporting that growth by linking new information to prior knowledge, modeling thought processes, providing guided instruction, using review, and assigning tasks that utilize strategy knowledge. As a result of this process, students develop independent abilities to meet the learning challenges they will face throughout their student and adult lives.

MAKING CONNECTIONS:
Teaching Learning Strategies in the Regular Education Classroom

1. *Here are the big ideas to get you started:*
To be effective and efficient, a learning strategy needs to:
- address the learning demands of the task and setting,
- provide steps to guide thinking and performance,
- present the strategy in a format that students can readily learn and apply, and
- address problems that students are currently experiencing.

2. *What you need:*
- The textbook for your course
- A copy of this chapter or notes listing the features of effective and efficient strategies and the principles of quality strategies instruction.

3. *Try this:*
- Start by trying to identify one learning task or skill demand you have seen students repeatedly have trouble with in learning the content of your course. Do students often have trouble reading the textbook for your course and picking out the most important ideas and information? Do students have trouble learning vocabulary important to an understanding of the content? Have you found that many students do not know how to answer essay questions on tests or have trouble responding to multiple-choice questions on a test? Do students have trouble remembering information that must be memorized to provide a foundation for mastering the content of your course?
- Once you have identified a learning problem, develop a strategy that you can teach your students to help them address the problem. Remember that you need to develop a set of steps that students can follow to

tackle the learning task. There should be *no more than seven steps*, and you will need to develop a device that will help students remember what the steps are.

- Develop a plan for teaching the strategy to your students. You will need to identify content that students can use to practice the strategy. Be prepared to model use of the strategy for students, being very explicit as you "think aloud" in front of students about how to go about using the strategy to address a learning task. Also consider ways you can cue students to use the strategy, through props like bookmarks that highlight features of the strategy, or posters that can be displayed in the classroom to remind students of the steps of the strategy and how and when the strategy is to be used.

4. *Evaluate your work:*
- Look back at the strategy you have developed and your plans for teaching it to your students. Evaluate your strategy in light of the features of effective and efficient strategies set out above and the principles of quality strategy instruction presented in this chapter.
- Be sure to maintain good communication with students as you implement strategies instruction. It is important that students see both the need and the benefits for using a strategy. For the strategy to be beneficial, students need to be able to tell you when they are having problems using the strategy—or even if the strategy is making learning more cumbersome for them. If students find the strategy cumbersome, you may need to reevaluate whether your strategy meets the demands of the learning task and the setting.

5. *Next steps:*
- To fully evaluate the learning strategy you have developed, you need to teach it to students, and your students need to master it and use it. An effective strategy should result in improved performance on a given task. The best way to determine if the strategy improves student performance is to keep records of student performance on a task or test before and after use of the strat-

egy. To get a fair assessment, be sure that students know and use the strategy fluently before doing your "after" assessment.
- Talk to colleagues, administrators, or resource teachers to find out if others are using learning strategies. Explore possibilities for establishing support groups where you and your colleagues can help each other learn more about the most effective way to teach learning strategies. Working with colleagues, administrators, and resource teachers can also be an important way to implement strategy instruction broadly in a school, which will help support your efforts to teach strategies.

WEB SITES

http://www.ldonline.org This site, associated with WETA, the national public broadcast station in Washington, D.C., is devoted to providing information, resources, and updates on issues related to individuals with learning disabilities. Through searching the site, articles related specifically to learning strategies can be found as well as a comprehensive reference list of research articles related to teaching learning strategies across the curriculum. The material is updated on a monthly basis.

http://www.teachingld.org This site is sponsored by the Council for Exceptional Children's Division for Learning Disabilities. It offers recent research-based articles discussing the methods used to teach a range of learning strategies in classrooms, as well as the resulting achievement of students. This Web site is updated on a monthly basis.

http://www.ku-crl.org University of Kansas Center for Research on Learning, providing more information about products, publications, training, and workshops in the Strategic Instruction Model.

http://www.ash.udel.edu/ash/teacher/standards. html National Curriculum Standards, including links to standards in eleven curricular areas and links to other sites with information related to standards.

RESOURCES

Bley, N. S., & Thornton, C. A. (1995). *Teaching mathematics to students with learning disabilities.* Austin, TX: Pro-Ed. The authors provide many teaching strategies that include detailed information about how students learn mathematics most effectively. This information is often presented as a learning strategy, or could easily be adapted to be a learning strategy.

Harmon, J. M. (2000). Assessing and supporting independent word learning strategies of middle-school students. *Journal of Adolescent & Adult Literacy, 43* (6), 518–528. This article describes word learning strategies and the use of "think-alouds" to observe students' strategy use.

Harris, K., & Graham, S. (1996). *Making the writing process work: Strategies for composition and self-regulation.* Cambridge, MA: Brookline. This book presents a variety of validated strategies for planning, revising, and managing the writing process that can be used by students with learning disabilities and others who find writing challenging. The strategies are taught via the Self-Regulated Strategy Development Model, which combines instruction in task-specific strategies, along with procedures for regulating the strategies, the writing process, and student behaviors.

Jones, B. F., Palincsar, A. S., Ogle, D. S., & Carr, E. G. (1987). *Strategic teaching and learning: Cognitive instruction in the content areas.* Alexandria, VA: Association for Supervision and Curriculum Development. The authors have compiled both instructional and learning strategies to help students access, organize, and remember content across the curriculum.

Robinson, F. P. (1961). *Effective study.* New York: Harper and Row. Robinson includes the SQ3R strategy, which teaches students how to survey text to find specific information.

There are other learning strategies that help students meet academic, social, and motivation demands. Strategies developed by the Center for Research on Learning at the University of Kansas are described in Appendix C. These strategies have been field-tested and validated in classrooms. Training is highly recommended to learn all the procedures for teaching the strategies to students, and training is required with purchase of many of the manuals.

SUGGESTED READINGS

Caine, R. N., & Caine, G. (1994). *Making connections.* Menlo Park, CA: Addison-Wesley. This book describes current brain research and how it affects teaching and learning. The authors discuss how we perceive and process information. Included is a list of 12 principles of brain-based learning. The book can serve as an introduction to current research.

Caine, R. N., & Caine, G. (1997). *Education on the edge of possibility.* Alexandria, VA: Association for Supervision and Curriculum Development. The authors describe their experience applying the principles discussed in *Making Connections* in two schools. The resulting volume addresses teachers' "real-world" issues and concerns. In their introduction they state: "Perhaps the most significant thing we have

confirmed for ourselves is that, although actions are important, the thinking that influences and shapes what we do is far more critical. Changing our thinking is the first thing we have to do both individually and collectively, because without that change we cannot possibly change what we really do on a day-to-day basis. Regardless of what new 'method' or latest technique is attempted, the mind/brain will always choose to reduce such practices to fit entrenched assumptions and beliefs. To really restructure anything means to restructure our thinking and shift deep connections in our psyche" (p. vi). This volume provides a theoretical foundation for implementing the innovations recommended in this text.

Lenz, B. K., Ellis, E. S., & Scanlon, D. (1996). *Teaching learning strategies to adolescents and adults with learning disabilities.* Austin, TX: Pro-Ed. The book describes in detail the rationale and procedures for applying the eight stages of strategy instruction that have been validated in the Strategies Instructional Model (SIM). Examples of specific strategies are included, and connections are made for education from elementary-age through adult, for both separate and inclusive instruction.

Mastropieri, M. A., & Scruggs, T. E. (2000). *The inclusive classroom: Strategies for effective instruction.* Columbus, OH: Prentice-Hall/Merrill Education. This text includes ideas and lessons for K–12 teaching strategies in the content areas of math, science, social studies, language and literacy, and the arts.

Mastropieri, M. A., & Scruggs, T. E. (1991). *Teaching students ways to remember: Strategies for learning mnemonically.* Cambridge, MA: Brookline. The first section of this book explains several major mnemonic techniques, how to do them, and what applications they are best suited for. The second section of the book provides examples of applications to various curriculum areas, including social studies, science, mathematics, and other basic skills.

Pressley, M., Burkell, J., Cariglia-Bull, T., Lysynchuk, L., McGoldrick, J., Schneider, B., Snyder, B. L., Symons, S., & Woloshyn, V. E. (1990). *Cognitive strategy instruction that really improves children's academic performance.* Cambridge, MA: Brookline. This book is a compilation of research-validated cognitive strategies for decoding, reading comprehension, vocabulary and spelling development, writing, mathematical problem solving, and science. Additional chapters on memory devices and getting-started teaching strategies help teachers begin the process of teaching cognitive strategies. Designed for elementary- and middle-school teachers.

Wood, E., Woloshyn, V. E., & Willoughby, T. (1995). *Cognitive strategy instruction for middle and high schools.* Cambridge, MA: Brookline. This book identifies and explains empirically validated cognitive strategies and provides explicit examples of their use. Each chapter presents teachers with the concepts underlying the use of strategies in a specific skill or study area followed by appropriate strategies. Topics include mnemonics training, learning from direct teaching, reading comprehension, writing, general problem solving, algebra, science, computer use, second-language learning, and test taking. Designed for middle and high school teachers.

REFERENCES

Berry, G. C. (1999). *Development and validation of an instructional program for teaching postsecondary students with learning disabilities to take and study notes.* (Doctoral dissertation, University of Kansas, 1999).

Caine, R. N., & Caine, G. (1997). *Education on the edge of possibility.* Alexandria, VA: Association for Supervision and Curriculum Development.

Ellis, E. S. (1992). *LINCS: A starter strategy for vocabulary learning.* Lawrence, KS: Edge Enterprises.

Hughes, C., Schumaker, J. B., Deshler, D. D., & Mercer, C. (1988). *The test-taking strategy.* Lawrence, KS: Edge Enterprises.

Lenz, B. K., Clark, F. C., Deshler, D. D., & Schumaker, J. B. (1988). *The strategies instructional approach (Preservice Training Package).* Lawrence, KS: University of Kansas Center for Research on Learning.

Lenz, B. K., Ellis, E. S., & Scanlon, D. (1996). *Teaching learning strategies to adolescents and adults with learning disabilities.* Austin, TX: Pro-Ed.

Macintosh, R., Vaughn, S., & Bennerson, D. (1995). FAST social skills with a SLAM and a RAP. *Teaching Exceptional Children, 27,* 37–41.

Munroe, S., & Smith, T. (1998). State geography standards: An appraisal of geography standards in 38 states and the District of Columbia [Online]. Available: *www.edexcellence.net/standards/geography/geograph.htm# introduction.*

Newmann, F. M., & Wehlage, G. G. (1995). *Successful school restructuring. A report to the public and educators.* Madison, WI: Center for Education Research.

Pressley, M., El-Dinary, P. B., Gaskins, I., Schuder, T., Bergman, J. L., Almasi, J., & Brown, R. (1992). Beyond direct explanation: Transactional instruction of reading comprehension strategies. *The Elementary School Journal, 92*(5), 513–555.

Robinson, F. P. (1961). *Effective study.* New York: Harper and Row.

Schumaker, J. B., Denton, P. H., & Deshler, D. D. (1984). *The paraphrasing strategy.* Lawrence, KS: The University of Kansas Center for Research on Learning.

Spargo, E., & Williston, G. (1980). *Timed readings, Book Three.* Providence, RI: Jamestown Publishers.

Tralli, C., Colombo, B., Deshler, D., & Schumaker, J. B. (1996). The strategies intervention model: A model for supported inclusion at the secondary level. *Remedial and Special Education, 17*(4), 204–216.

Tulving, E. (1983). *Elements of episodic memory.* Oxford: Clarendon Press.

Wong, B. Y. L. (1996). *The ABCs of learning disabilities.* New York: Academic Press.

11 Special Education Policies and Procedures

Earle Knowlton

Critical Self-Test Questions

- What are the major principles of federal special education law and how are they interrelated?
- How did students with disabilities come to be educated in regular education classrooms for all or part of the school day?
- How are students in need of special education services identified?
- Why is it important to understand the heterogeneity of students within the various disability classifications?
- What is the Individualized Education Program?
- Under what conditions are functional assessments and behavior intervention plans developed?
- What is the impact of standards-based reform on the education of students with disabilities?

Students with disabilities are an exceedingly heterogeneous group and, like their nondisabled peers, they have varied learning characteristics and patterns. To meet such a wide variety of learning needs equitably, schools must adhere to policies and procedures that specify what, when, and how special education and related services are to be provided. Both general educators and special educators have specific roles and responsibilities in providing these services and need to be aware of their obligations, why they exist, and how they are designed to promote a free, appropriate education in the least restrictive environment for all students.

Children with disabilities have not always been accorded the opportunity for a public education. As late as the early 1970s, over half of all children with disabilities in the United States were *not* being served by the public schools (McDonnell, McLaughlin, & Morison, 1997). Some of these children resided in institutions and were not educated at all, while others were kept at home by parents who, when they attempted to enroll their children in kindergarten or first grade, were turned away by the very schools their tax dollars helped support (Turnbull & Turnbull, 2000). Paradoxically, there were other children with disabilities who *were* enrolled in public schools during this time but were failing because we did not understand how their disabilities affected how they learned (Reynolds, 1989).

During the last four decades, legislators, litigators, judges, disability advocates, and state and local school officials have turned their attention to

FIGURE 11.1
Graphic Organizer

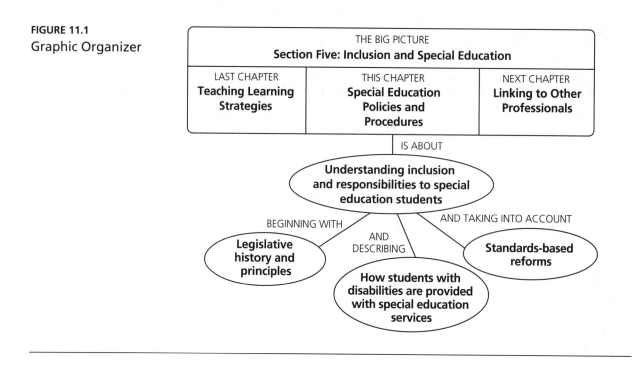

the process of developing the necessary policies and procedures to educate these two disparate groups of children, the unserved and the underserved. Throughout this period, these groups forged a series of legislative acts and regulations, many based in case law, that defined special education for students with disabilities as we know it today. Out of these laws and regulations grew the procedural requirements we, as educators, must meet on behalf of students with disabilities.

FOUNDATIONS AND PRINCIPLES

Legislative History and Principles

By the end of the 1950s, legislation began to appear sporadically at the federal level to fund residential schools for the deaf and for the blind, and teacher education and research in mental retardation (LaVor, 1976). In the 1960s and early 1970s, federal legislation also funded special programs in early childhood education, vocational education, regional resource centers, and the purchase of instructional materials (Turnbull & Turnbull, 2000). Yet, prior to 1973, this legislative patchwork was neither mandatory nor comprehensive but rather discretionary and piecemeal in supporting the education of students with disabilities (Knowlton, 1985). From 1954 on, the courts began to recognize specific rights for equal access to public education for children and youth with disabilities (*Brown v. Topeka Board of Education*, 1954; *Pennsylvania Association for Retarded Children v. Commonwealth of Penn-*

■ Scenario

Suzanne Kiper has had students with disabilities in her seventh-grade math class for many of the 15 years she has been teaching. Sometimes these students had mild disabilities and seemed no more or less capable of mastering the curriculum than many other average or low-achieving students who did not have disabilities. On the other hand, she has had students who experienced great difficulty learning the content of the curriculum or behaving appropriately in class.

Ms. Kiper has always tried her best to help *all* students learn, but each class period seemed to become a frenetic rush to cover the material she needed to cover and give students practice opportunities while she was available to answer questions. There were always many other matters to attend to in any given class period as well: giving assignments, scheduling make-up exams for students who had been absent, getting homework from students who had been absent, announcing the next exam or returning papers

from the last exam, answering student questions about lost papers, pencils, books, and any number of other issues and problems that arose daily.

As each class period flew by, Ms. Kiper did not always manage to work with each student who had special learning needs. That would have to change soon. Ms. Kiper had a number of students with individualized education programs (IEPs) in each of her classes, and her district's inclusion policy now required that all students, including students with disabilities, meet district curriculum standards. This meant that Ms. Kiper would have to try harder to make sure learning goals and instruction for every student were referenced to the basic standards of the curriculum. Ms. Kiper wanted to do this for all her students all of the time, but with more than 120 students coming through her classroom door every day, she was concerned about how she could provide the extra help that many of these students would need.

sylvania, 1972; *Mills v. District of Columbia Board of Education*, 1972), the right to treatment (*Wyatt v. Stickney*, 1974), the right to procedural fairness and unbiased assessment practices (*Diana v. State Board of Education [California]*, 1973; *Larry P. v. Riles*, 1974), and the right to equal protection (*Brown v. Topeka Board of Education*, 1954). Congress, however, had yet to legislate these rights (Turnbull & Turnbull, 2000).

Between 1973 and 1975, Congress moved quickly to ensure that students with disabilities had equal access to an appropriate education in the public schools. In 1973, Congress enacted the *Rehabilitation Act* and, with it, Section 504, which prohibited discriminatory practices on the basis of disability. Any agency receiving federal funds, including public schools, risked losing that funding if it discriminated against those with disabilities. In 1974, Public Law 93–380 established legislative authority for rights earlier recognized by the courts, such as the right to education, the right to treatment, and so on (Zettel & Ballard, 1982). Meanwhile, many states had been enacting statutes and regulations that mirrored those at the federal level. Congress was not satisfied, however, that the appropriate protections were uniformly in place throughout the United States (Turnbull & Turnbull, 2000). Therefore, 15 months after enacting P. L. 93–380, Congress passed P.L. 94–142, *The Education for All Handicapped Children Act.* It mandated that all children from the ages of 5 to 21 receive a free and appropriate education in the least restrictive environment possible, and it assured parents of substantive participation in program planning and educational decision making. The "least restrictive environment" (LRE) in effect meant educating students with disabilities alongside their nondisabled peers whenever possible. P. L. 94–142 also provided that each child with a disability should have an individualized education program (IEP), specifying goals for that student and how attainment of those goals will be assessed. The IEP also must specify the degree to which the student will participate in general education and the special education services to be provided (Schloss, Smith, & Schloss, 1990). In addition, all records and information about students with disabilities are to be kept confidential.

Turnbull and Turnbull (2000) identified six major principles of federal special education policy that emerged from P. L. 94–142: zero-reject, nondiscriminatory evaluation, appropriate education, least restrictive environment, parent participation, and procedural due process. These principles can be conceptualized as three interrelated pairs of features as shown in Figure 11.2. These features are (1) *system entry,* or access to a public school education and a thorough and fair assessment of needs; (2) *system response,* or assuring an appropriate education in the least restrictive environment; and (3) *checks and balances,* or ensuring the child's entry into the public school system and the system's effective response to her or his educational needs (Knowlton, 1985).

System Entry

ZERO-REJECT. In the past, schools rejected the enrollment attempts of certain children, in either overt or de facto fashion, saying to their parents in effect: "We are not equipped to educate your child." Quite simply, many children with disabilities were summarily denied an education. P. L. 94–142 prohibited this practice by guaranteeing *all* children equal access to educational opportunity.

NONDISCRIMINATORY EVALUATION. Congress mandated that the evaluation processes and procedures used to classify children as eligible for special education must be fair and unbiased. Case law established by litigation,

FIGURE 11.2

Major Features of Federal Special Education Policy

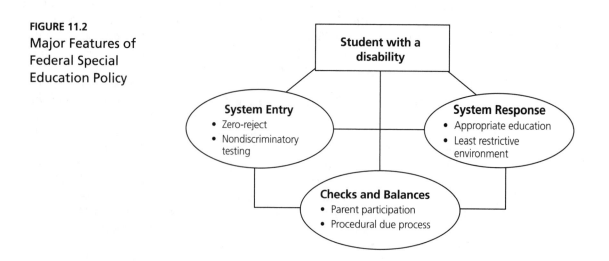

such as *Diana v. State Board of Education (California)* (1973) and *Larry P. v. Riles* (1974), set the stage for this principle's legislative enactment. In each case, children were unfairly discriminated against and labeled when language and cultural differences were ignored by evaluators. In essence, if a child incorrectly defines the word "chandelier," an item on an early version of the *Stanford-Binet Intelligence Scale,* having never eaten under its light or marveled at the prism effect of the sun shining through it, she or he has had no opportunity to learn about a chandelier. Similarly, the child whose language background does not enable her or him to comprehend "chandelier," and the child who cannot hear the word's pronunciation, are treated with bias if such factors are not taken into account. This is a far cry from the child who incorrectly defines "chandelier" after having eaten under its light or otherwise having had opportunities to learn about it. Evaluation for the purposes of classification can be unfair and discriminatory when it fails to account for lack of opportunity, cultural differences, or native language, among other factors.

System Response

APPROPRIATE EDUCATION. Given access and a useful assessment of educational needs, special education and related services must be *appropriate* to those needs. P. L. 94–142 defined special education as providing specially designed instruction, at no cost to parents, that meets the student's unique educational needs [20 U.S.C. § 1401 (25)], as well as related services necessary for the student to benefit from special education [20 U.S.C. § 1401 (22)]. In the *Board of Education v. Rowley* case (1982), Amy Rowley, a student who is deaf, sought but was denied a signing interpreter. Because Amy was found to be benefiting from her special education *without* interpreter services, the court concluded that this education was appropriate. Although the court did not rule in favor of Amy Rowley, it established that an appropriate education is defined in terms of its benefit to the student as a result of an individualized education program, developed on the basis of a nondiscriminatory evaluation of needs, and overseen by parents or guardians who are aware of the student's rights and how to exercise them (Turnbull & Turnbull, 2000).

LEAST RESTRICTIVE ENVIRONMENT. Through the years, there has been a great deal of debate about what constitutes the least restrictive environment (LRE) for individual students (Kauffman & Hallahan, 1995; Lloyd, Singh, & Repp, 1991). Because of the use of the word "environment," LRE is often interpreted strictly in terms of a "place." Instead, it refers to an educational approach that minimizes the degree to which there is a social restriction placed on students with disabilities in order to provide them with an appropriate education. The nature of this social restriction is the presence or absence of nondisabled students without regard, necessarily, to a specific setting. Of course, the general education classroom is obviously "where the action is" with respect to educational setting. Accordingly, "mainstreaming" in the 1970s and "inclusion" in the 1990s, on the surface, were all variations on the theme of placement in a general education setting. Underneath this concern with place, however, was (and still is) the issue of "side-by-side" education and how it should be implemented with respect to curriculum and district and statewide testing, as well as the general education classroom as a setting.

Checks and Balances

PARENT PARTICIPATION. Turnbull and Turnbull (2000) noted that participatory democracy requires shared decision making. That is, persons likely to be affected by a decision ought to have a hand in making that decision. This is the essence of parental participation in special education. Parents not only give or withhold permission to test and to declare their son or daughter eligible for special education services (i.e., affix a categorical label such as learning disabilities or mental retardation), they also have the right to participate in program planning, decisions concerning learning goals, monitoring progress toward those goals, and the like.

PROCEDURAL DUE PROCESS. This principle refers, literally, to the fair procedural process due to a person, under the 14th Amendment to the U.S. Constitution, whenever the state (in the form of a local school district) desires to act on the person's behalf. Not only does a parent have the right to share in educational decision making, but she or he also possesses the right to deny the local district permission to test the child, to place the child in special education, and to keep the child in special education. The school must inform the parent of these rights and of the opportunity to contest the school's proposed actions via mediation and an impartial hearing.

The U.S. Congress has built on these principles through a series of no fewer than six reauthorizations and amendments to P. L. 94–142. Among the more notable amendments was P. L. 99–457 (1986) which extended the rights and safeguards of P. L. 94–142 to all preschool children, ages three to five. In 1990, P. L. 94–142 was reauthorized, amended, and renamed the *Individuals with Disabilities Education Act* (IDEA; P. L. 101–476). IDEA did away with the term "handicap," and used the more precise term, "disability." It also added autism and traumatic brain injury as federal eligibility categories. In addition, IDEA required that transition planning must be done for students age 16 and older to make sure they developed the skills needed to move from school to adult life and work (National Association of State Directors of Special Education, 1990).

In 1997, Congress passed the *Individuals with Disabilities Education Act Amendments* (P. L. 105–17). This legislation has been vital to progress in special education and providing related services to students with disabilities (Turnbull & Turnbull, 2000). These amendments lowered to 14 the age at which transition plans should be made for students with disabilities and required that general education teachers participate in the development and implementation of individualized education programs. They also required teachers to participate in the development and implementation of behavioral plans for students whose behaviors interfere with the provision of special education services (National Association of State Directors of Special Education, 1997). In addition, students, ages three through nine, could now be identified as eligible for special education without reliance on categorical labeling; instead, the noncategorical term, "developmental delay," can be used to establish eligibility (Turnbull & Turnbull, 2000).

Of particular significance is the 1997 IDEA's extension of potential benefits of federal education reforms to students with disabilities. It requires that all students with disabilities participate in state- and district-wide assessments with appropriate accommodations (National Association of State Directors of Special Education, 1997). Consequently, the IEP for each student with disabilities must specify access to the standard general education curriculum (National Association of State Directors of Special Education, 1997). The intent here is to complement other federal reform efforts, notably the *Goals 2000: Educate America Act of 1994* (P. L. 103–227). The message clearly is that students with *and* without disabilities are entitled to benefit from educational reform (Turnbull & Turnbull, 2000).

From Exclusion to Inclusion

The education of children and youth with disabilities has undergone an important transformation since the enactment of P. L. 94–142 in 1975. The legal protections that have evolved in special education policy rest on the assumption that these students *can* learn given the proper supports. This assumption contrasts sharply with the thinking prior to the 1960s and 1970s when it was assumed that children and youth with disabilities were essentially uneducable (McDonnell, McLaughlin, & Morison, 1997). The expectations that these students should, can, and will learn reflect considerable progress throughout the past three decades. Indeed, we have evolved from the initial intent of the principle of zero-reject, which was to assure that previously unserved students with disabilities would at least be assured access to public education, to today's charge to public schools, which is to assure that students with disabilities are not only included in education programs alongside their nondisabled peers, but are entitled to a quality education by means of those programs (Choate, 2000).

Along with advances in legal protections has come a better understanding of the instructional and social supports needed to promote learning. While much has been learned, debate continues regarding what constitutes an appropriate education for individual students. Many professionals and, for that matter, many parents of students with disabilities question the wisdom of assuming that *all* students will benefit from placement in the general education classroom. Some students, they argue, will always need the additional support provided in smaller, more individualized classrooms staffed by highly trained special educators (Russ, Chiang, Rylance, & Bongers, 2001).

The Regular Education Initiative (REI)   For a decade or so after P. L. 94–142, schools struggled with the idea of providing special education services in the least restrictive environment. The term "mainstreaming" was in vogue at that time and referred to putting students with disabilities in classrooms, lunch rooms, and on playgrounds with their nondisabled peers whenever feasible (Reynolds, 1989). The term itself does not appear in the text of P. L. 94–142, though many professionals and parents assumed it did. It was also assumed that "it's the law" to mainstream, but, in fact, it is not. Rather, the law specifies that IEP's must include a statement regarding the extent of any general education classroom placement.

Schools with few resources (mainly in rural and inner-city settings) engaged in a kind of de facto mainstreaming, wherein students with learning disabilities, mild behavior disorders, and mild mental retardation were served in a fashion not dissimilar to how they were served before P. L. 94–142 when they comprised the underserved—enrolled in public schools but otherwise given up on and forgotten, for the most part (Skrtic, Guba, & Knowlton, 1985). In vast, sparsely populated rural districts, for example, one special educator might serve three (and sometimes more) schools and, without paraprofessional support, could work with students for only a very small amount of time each week (Skrtic, Guba, & Knowlton, 1985). Even in wealthier school districts, mainstreaming was essentially for social purposes, with general and special educators preferring the lunch room and the playground as mainstream settings for academic instruction rather than general education classrooms.

In the mid-1980s, in the face of this state-of-practice, the then assistant secretary of education, Madeleine C. Will, proposed what became known as the Regular Education Initiative (REI), which sought to promote the placement of special education students in the least restrictive *learning* environments (Will, 1986). In essence, the message was: Integrating students with disabilities for lunch and recess is not the intent of the least restrictive environment principle. Advocates of the REI have argued that general education teachers can make adaptations to accommodate students with disabilities in their classrooms, while special education personnel provide instructional and social supports either directly to these students or, more often, indirectly, through their general education teachers (Bauwens & Hourcade, 1995).

REI's Evolution into the Inclusion Movement   By 1997–98, 47 percent of students with disabilities, ages 6 through 21, were being served primarily in general education classrooms (U.S. Department of Education, 2000). Moreover, volumes of the professional literature have promoted the concept of inclusion, from Will's Regular Education Initiative in 1986 to many other works published in the 1990s. Despite the exceedingly large number of writings on the topic, inclusion was and continues to be a vexing topic. Generally, those who advocate for children with extremely severe disabilities— children who, only a few decades ago, were excluded from schooling completely—tend to promote *full* inclusion—in other words, full-time general education placement in the student's neighborhood school, with supports brought to the student rather than the reverse (cf. Brown et al., 1991). Those concerned with students who have mild disabilities, particularly learning disabilities, typically promote a more moderate, individualized approach to inclusion, taking into account the student's needs and learning objectives in the context of the school she or he attends. Vaughn and Schumm (1995) called this approach "responsible inclusion" (p. 265), suggesting that a variety of contextual factors, such as the classroom teacher's willingness, resource adequacy, and ongoing professional development must be in place for inclusion to be effective.

Successfully including students with disabilities in general education classrooms requires special educators, general educators, administrators, and related services personnel to share responsibility for providing these students with an appropriate education. It presupposes that general education and special education teachers can readily blend their expertise and collaboratively plan for the learning of all students. Unfortunately, the reality of schooling in the United States is such that its structure allows few opportunities for teachers, especially general educators, to confer with one another (Kozleski, Mainzer, & Deshler, 2000). In middle and secondary schools especially, relationships between general and special educators are even more problematic. Secondary teachers generally see individual students for one class each day. Accordingly, when collaborative work becomes necessary, a special education teacher may need to confer with perhaps a half dozen general education teachers on behalf of any one student who is a part of her or his case load.

Traditionally, special education teachers are taught to focus on individual needs and instruction, and rarely on matters such as curriculum planning or large-group instruction and management (Goodlad & Field, 1993). Some have argued that special education teachers are not prepared for and "are not typically faced with the unusual demands and pressures of the general classroom" (Johnson, Pugach, & Hammitte, 1988, p. 43; Showers, 1990). While special education teachers may feel uncomfortable in the general education whole-class setting, general education teachers may feel insecure about their preparation and expertise to address the special learning needs of students with disabilities (Goodlad, 1984; Goodlad & Lovitt, 1993). Goodlad and Field (1993), for example, found that students preparing to become general educators "rated their competence in adapting instruction for students with disabilities lower than any other skills" (p. 237).

Recognizing that there may be this mismatch between preparation and the changing roles of general and special educators may help the two groups of teachers to learn to work together and accept shared responsibility for the learning of *all* students, finding ways to support each other with their respective areas of expertise. The next chapter takes up this challenging issue of how general education teachers, in particular, can link to other professionals in their building to support them in their efforts to include all students in learning.

Focus and Reflect

- Why do you think it became necessary to enact legislation to assure that students with disabilities had access to a free and appropriate education in the least restrictive environment?

- Do you think most general education teachers have the training and expertise to teach students with mild to moderate disabilities in the general education classroom? Why or why not?

KNOWING AND DOING

Serving Students with Disabilities

Serving a student with a disability begins with the process of identifying her or him as eligible for and in need of special education. Some students begin public schooling having already been identified as having a disability, while others are identified after they enter school and experience problems in learning and/or social adjustment. No matter how well it is conducted, the process of identifying students for special education eligibility, unfortunately, can be a negative labeling experience for some students. In particular, pre-adolescents and adolescents want to be like other students. If they know they are different from others in a way they perceive as stigmatizing, they will not want others, especially their peers, to see this difference. Nonetheless, the structure of IDEA is such that identification and classification of disabilities is necessary to guarantee appropriate educational services for students with disabilities.

Identifying Students as Eligible for Special Education   The process of determining whether students are eligible for special education services involves two steps. First, the student must be identified as having a disability by virtue of meeting eligibility criteria for one of 13 possible disability classifications. Second, the disability must be shown to interfere with the student's ability to receive an appropriate education; that is, the student must be shown to need special education and related services in order to perform at a satisfactory level. Not every student who has a disability requires special services. For example, a student may have a physical disability that does not impair her or his ability to learn in the general education classroom. This student may require adjustments or accommodations, such as wheelchair accessibility or tape-recorded reading materials, but may not require the services of a special education teacher. Keep in mind that *all* students with disabilities are protected by Section 504 of the Rehabilitation Act, which entitles them to reasonable accommodations by public agencies, including schools (Turnbull & Turnbull, 2000).

The student who ultimately will be eligible for, and is shown to need, special education usually has been referred first to a child-study team in the school building to explore some simple adaptations that could possibly alleviate the particular problem or concern. This team, typically composed of two or three general education teachers and a special education teacher, is not required by law to function in this manner; rather, it has evolved through the years as a balance against the tendency to make more formal referrals of students than is necessary (Algozzine, Christenson, & Ysseldyke, 1982). In many cases, however, the child-study team will determine that simple procedures will not be sufficient and that a formal special education eligibility evaluation is warranted. The school district will then seek written permission from the student's parents for this evaluation. Only when this written permission is obtained does the evaluation proceed.

The purpose of the evaluation is to determine, in an unbiased way, whether the student is eligible for and in need of special education. Eligibility is determined by comparing the results of a nondiscriminatory assessment of the student's learning and/or behavioral characteristics with the specific disability classification criteria that exist in the state in which the student's school is located. Disabilities have been defined by classification systems developed over the years by organizations such as the American Psychiatric Association, via its *Diagnostic and Statistical Manual of Mental Disorders* (DSM-IV), the American Association on Mental Retardation, the World Health Organization, and others. Currently, IDEA specifies 11 disabilities as eligibility classifications for special education and related services [20 U.S.C. § 1401 (3)(A)(i) and 20 U.S.C. § 1401 (3)(B)]:

- Mental retardation
- Hearing impairments (including deafness)
- Speech or language impairments
- Visual impairments (including blindness)
- Emotional disturbance
- Orthopedic impairments
- Autism
- Traumatic brain injury
- Other health impairments
- Specific learning disabilities
- Developmental delay (for ages 3 through 9 only)

Though not specified per se in the legislation, IDEA's regulations call for eligibility under two additional classifications: deaf-blindness and multiple disabilities (U.S. Department of Education, 2000). A student with a disability is eligible for special education and related services if she or he (1) meets her or his particular state's criteria for one of these 13 classifications and

(2) ". . . by reason thereof needs special education and related services" [20 U.S.C. § 1401 (3)(A)(ii)].

Disabilities that occur most often in the school-age population are referred to as "high-incidence disabilities." These include specific learning disabilities, speech and language impairments, mental retardation, and emotional disturbance. These disabilities account for over 90 percent of all students identified as eligible for special education in the United States (U.S. Department of Education, 2000), and are most often mild. Adjectives like mild, moderate, and severe are used to describe the degree of severity of the disability. Students with low-incidence disabilities, which include autism, deaf-blindness, orthopedic impairment, multiple disabilities, hearing impairment, visual impairment, traumatic brain injury, and other health impairments, are likely to have moderate to severe levels of disability (McDonnell, McLaughlin, & Morison, 1997).

Although IDEA specifies disability classifications and, in its attendant regulations, provides definitions, most of these definitions are fraught with ambiguities and have generated considerable debate within the various subfields of special education, particularly learning disabilities, mental retardation, and emotional disturbance (Heward, 2000). Consequently, classifications of disabilities across the United States are not necessarily uniform and, as such, can vary from state to state. States and local districts may adopt different classifications or names for categories and even different specific criteria for eligibility as long as there is no violation of federal law. This can mean that a student who is identified as disabled and qualifying for special services in one location may not meet the criteria established in another location (McDonnell, McLaughlin, & Morison, 1997). Variations occur most often in eligibility determinations for students with mild disabilities.

A Perspective on the Characteristics of Students with Special Learning Needs   Characteristics of a particular disability serve as the behavioral indicators that a learning or behavioral problem exists. A middle-school student with a learning disability may, for example, experience difficulty organizing the material needed to study for an upcoming biology test. Thus, difficulty with study skills tends to be a characteristic of learning disabilities for many secondary school students.

We should keep in mind, though, that it is difficult to generalize about the characteristics of students with disabilities. Students with disabilities, like the general school-age population, are a heterogeneous group; any one individual student with a particular disability may evidence a few or many of the characteristics associated with that disability. The problem with dependence upon a laundry list of characteristics imputed to a given disability is the likelihood that such a listing can (and often does) seduce us into assuming that the next student with that disability whom we meet will necessarily display those characteristics. And, thus, we expect to see those characteristics when in fact they are not a part of this particular student's learning or behavioral repertoire.

For example, because problems in reading are often (but not always) experienced by students with learning disabilities, the student with this disability who is new to a classroom will necessarily have reading problems, right? Maybe. Odds are that she or he probably will. However, it is also possible that the student performs *above* grade level in reading, while

---

■ *Scenario Revisited*

To help teachers like Suzanne Kiper and her colleagues, administrators and special services personnel at Hilltop Middle School organized a series of workshops to talk about ways they could be more effective in meeting the letter and the spirit of the laws governing inclusion of students with disabilities. These workshops were scheduled throughout the school year on Wednesday afternoons that the district earmarked for teacher collaboration time, dismissing students an hour earlier than usual. Though a number of parents, and even some Hilltop teachers, balked, Ms. Kiper and most of her colleagues welcomed this extra time to work together and learn how to be more effective in including students with disabilities.

It soon became apparent that, given willing and creative collaboration on the part of teachers, most students did well in Suzanne's math classes, even in pre-algebra. There were a few students who posed real dilemmas, however. "How can we help these kids master the general education curriculum *and* meet their IEP goals?" she asked Wanda Williams, the special education resource teacher, one morning as they walked through the school's front door.

Ms. Willliams, who had recently earned her master's degree from a top-notch university special education department, and had been a special education teacher for 13 years, said that she was free after school. "Let's get together and talk about it."

---

experiencing great difficulty with mathematics concepts and operations. Rather than making assumptions about how students will learn and behave on the basis of the labels we use to obtain services for them, it is more efficient to learn about the student's needs directly from the student and from other professionals who may be providing support services to the student. In fact, teachers report that what they find most helpful in addressing the needs of students with disabilities is being able to ask questions of trained support personnel about the characteristics and learning needs of specific students in their classrooms (Roach, 1995).

While there is always a danger of overgeneralizing about the needs of one student based on the needs of similar students, it is helpful to be aware of the kinds of learning problems experienced by many students with and without disabilities. Many of these learning difficulties, which were listed in Chapter 1, Teaching and Academic Diversity, can be anticipated and addressed in planning for courses, units, and lessons. Planning for instruction that is organized and explicit can help address the diverse learning needs of many students with disabilities.

Special Education in the Least Restrictive Environment   As noted earlier, the least restrictive environment is one that provides the most freedom from social restrictiveness for a student, as well as the most opportunities for interactions with nondisabled peers (Kochhar, West, & Taymans, 1996). While educators are obliged to determine the least restrictive environment for students, their primary concern must be the identification of educational goals that will address the needs of individual learners. Thus, "the degree of integration into general education is intertwined with determinations of what the educational goals should be and whether specialized services can be effectively provided in general education environments" (McDonnell, McLaughlin, & Morison, 1997, p. 60). Here, perhaps, is the crux of the issue: Can the individual student with disabilities meet the demands of the general education curriculum in a general education classroom with specialized support services? and Can those services be provided in an effective manner to the student in a general education classroom setting? If the answer to both questions is "yes," then as educators we have set the stage for what IDEA requires in terms of an appropriate education in the least restrictive environment.

Historically, most general and special educators have agreed that a range of options in learning environments is in the best interests of students with disabilities (Fuchs & Fuchs, 1994; Reynolds, 1989). The least restrictive option is full-time placement in a general education classroom with effective consultation between general and special education teachers. Additionally, or alternatively, a student may be in general education classrooms and spend part of the school day, or *alternate* school days, in a special education classroom, often called a learning center or resource room. Some students may only be placed with nondisabled peers for nonacademic periods such as physical education. The most restrictive environments for students with disabilities are school-based special education classrooms, in which the student is placed full-time, and residential or full-day programs housed in private school facilities.

It has traditionally been the case that students with mild and moderate disabilities are served in both general and special education settings, with general educators providing instruction in the general education classroom and special educators providing specialized instruction in learning centers or resource rooms. Increasingly, particularly at the elementary level, general educators will instruct a class while a special educator (or more often a special education paraprofessional) works with one or more students with disabilities in the same classroom. This arrangement, termed "cooperative teaching," or "co-teaching" (Bauwens & Hourcade, 1995), is advantageous in that it enables the student with disabilities to have the best of both worlds: specialized instruction in the general education classroom. Its obvious disadvantage is that it places more demands on the special educator's use of time. If the special educator devotes most of her or his time to small-group instruction in the resource room or learning center, then co-teaching, sometimes inappropriately, is left to a special education paraprofessional.

Regardless of the specific instructional arrangements, general and special education teachers must work together effectively to assure the success of these students. Glatthorn (1990) has noted, however, that these two groups of teachers have different "frames of reference," or ways of viewing teaching and learning (p. 29). Special education teachers tend to focus more on individualizing learning and on the acquisition of learning and coping skills, while general education teachers usually focus on academic content and the learning of the whole class (Glatthorn, 1990). Teachers need to be aware of their different orientations and act responsibly by meeting one another halfway. Such awareness better prepares them to communicate and cooperate on a regular basis to adequately support the learning of students with disabilities.

The Individualized Education Program If, through a fair and comprehensive evaluation, it is determined that a student is eligible for and needs special education services, the results of this evaluation are used to develop an individualized education program for the student, and then to determine appropriate placement. In no case, however, are these decisions to be made on the basis of a single test. Rather, a variety of formal and informal instruments are given and interpreted by the appropriate specialists, including school psychologists, special educators, reading and mathematics teachers, and so forth.

As noted earlier, students with disabilities are a heterogeneous group. The learning needs of one student with learning disabilities are not necessarily the same as or even similar to those of another student with learning disabilities. It is the intent of special education policies that these individual differences be taken into account during the development of an individualized education program (IEP). IEPs for students with disabilities were first mandated in 1975 by P. L. 94–142. IDEA's 1997 amendments elaborated considerably on the IEP's original requirements. IEPs vary in format from school district to school district, but all must be written plans and, by law, include the following nine elements (National Association of State Directors of Special Education, 1997; Turnbull & Turnbull, 2000):

1. Present level of educational performance, including the way(s) the student's disability affects progress or involvement in the general education curriculum;
2. Annual goals, including short-term objectives or benchmarks, that meet the student's needs arising from the disability;
3. Special education, related services, and supplementary aids and services to be provided, as well as any necessary program modifications or personnel supports to enable the student to: (a) advance appropriately toward annual goals, (b) be involved and progress in the general education curriculum, and (c) participate in extracurricular and other nonacademic activities;
4. An explanation of the extent to which the student will *not* participate with nondisabled peers in the general education classroom(s);
5. Any modifications necessary for participation in state- and district-wide assessments or, if the student will not participate, an explanation as to why the assessment is not appropriate and a description of the student's alternate assessment;
6. Projected dates when services will begin, and the anticipated frequency, duration, and location of those services;
7. A written statement of transition needs and services, for students age 14 and older, that focuses on the student's course of study (e.g., Advanced Placement courses, vocational education, etc.), and specifies interagency responsibilities and necessary linkages (e.g., with job support agencies in the community);
8. Beginning at least one year prior to the student's reaching the age of majority (usually 18), a statement that the student has been informed of her or his rights under IDEA and that those rights will transfer from the parent or guardian when the student is of majority age; and
9. A statement of the ways in which the student's progress toward annual goals will be measured, and how and when parents will be informed of this progress.

IDEA's 1997 amendments also specify the composition of the team that develops the IEP. In fact, the IEP team is a continuation of the team that has conducted the evaluation (Turnbull & Turnbull, 2000). At a minimum, the team must consist of [20 U.S.C. § 1414(d)(1)(B)]:

- The student's parents;
- At least one general education teacher if the student is or may be participating in the general education classroom;
- At least one special education teacher;
- A representative of the school who is informed about the general education curriculum, and knowledgeable about special education and the availability of resources;
- An individual qualified to interpret the educational implications of the evaluation results;
- At the discretion of the parents or the school, other individuals with knowledge and expertise (such as a language specialist, for example); and
- The student, when appropriate.

The process by which a team develops an IEP is intended to ensure that the individual learning needs of each student are addressed, that services are not provided simply on the basis of a disability category or the general characteristics of students in that category. Once again, it is important to emphasize that differences exist among students with disabilities, even among those identified with the same or similar disabilities. IEPs should not only specify goals and services for students but they should also indicate any curricular or instructional adaptations or accommodations needed for the student to progress satisfactorily.

We would be remiss not to acknowledge that most special educators report that the worst part of the job is its sometimes overwhelming paperwork demands (Kozleski, Mainzer, & Deshler, 2000). Effective district and building leadership, along with technological resources, promise to reduce these demands at least to a manageable level (Kozleski, Mainzer, & Deshler, 2000; McIntire, 2000). Yet, the paperwork involved in developing IEPs may tempt some teachers to use computerized data banks to identify goals or other elements of the IEP (Wang & Reynolds, 1995). Similarly, for teachers who participate in many IEP conferences, the process may become routinized (McDonnell, McLaughlin, & Morison, 1997). Where IEPs are influenced by these factors, there is the danger that they do not serve their intended purposes. Where the IEP process resists such influences, effective leadership and productive working relationships among staff are typically evident.

Functional Assessments and Behavioral Intervention Plans   Most controversial among the changes brought about by IDEA's 1997 amendments are the so-called "discipline provisions," which ensure that a student's behavior does not disqualify her or him from the right to an appropriate education, thus subverting the zero-reject principle. When a nondisabled student seriously violates school rules concerning weapons or drugs, for example, most schools expel that student. In 1988, however, the U.S. Supreme Court ruled that two students, identified as eligible for and receiving special education services by virtue of emotional disabilities, could *not* be expelled for their disruptive behavior because the behavior directly resulted from the disability.

This ruling, *Honig v. Doe,* created the policy, later codified by IDEA's 1997 amendments, whereby schools cannot expel students for behavior that manifests from their disabilities (Turnbull & Turnbull, 2000). Students with disabilities for whom it is determined that the misbehavior did *not* manifest from the disability can be disciplined in the same manner as nondisabled students as long as special education and related services continue to be delivered to her or him. The question of whether or not the behavior is the result of the disability is resolved by the IEP team through a process called "manifestation determination." Essentially, the team examines the student's behaviors and studies any possible linkages between those behaviors and the disability. It then renders a judgment as to the relationship between the behavior and the disability. In nearly every case, manifest determination is just that: a judgment; and it is not realistic to expect concrete "proof" as to the potential linkage between the behavior and the disability (Katsiyannis & Maag, 2001).

Suspension, expulsion, and any other means of removing the student from the current placement constitute a "change in placement" in the eyes of IDEA's 1997 amendments. Whenever such a placement change is made or contemplated, the IEP team must conduct a functional assessment, which is a series of procedures used to determine the parameters of the challenging behavior and why it is occurring. This assessment must be done no later than 10 days subsequent (and preferably prior) to any disciplinary action (e.g., a suspension) taken by the school (National Association of State Directors of Special Education, 1997).

The functional assessment is a series of procedures conducted by the IEP team (usually led by the special educator and/or the school psychologist) in order to determine the parameters of the challenging behavior and why it is occurring. These procedures involve measuring relevant dimensions of the behavior, such as its frequency or duration, and doing an analysis of environmental conditions or events that maintain the behavior (Chandler & Dahlquist, 2002). Then, a hypothesis about the relationship between the environment and the behavior is formed (Foster-Johnson & Dunlap, 1993). For example, a behavior like destroying classroom property may *function* as a means for the student to avoid or escape certain demands of the classroom. Though general educators may contribute key information to a functional assessment, they normally do not need to be involved in a primary way in the process.

Based on the findings of the functional assessment, a behavior intervention plan is developed by the IEP team. The goal is to minimize or eliminate the challenging behavior and replace it with one that is more appropriate. The replacement behavior should serve the same function as the challenging behavior (Maag, 2000). Thus, the student who desires an escape from particular classroom demands might be helped to develop more effective strategies to deal with those demands. These strategies become part of the behavior intervention plan that, along with the results of the functional assessment, are appended to the student's IEP. Again, general educators play an important role in supporting implementation of the plan.

Standards-Based Reform in the Education of Students with Disabilities

In December, 2001, Congress enacted the No Child Left Behind Act, a complete overhaul of the 1965 Elementary and Secondary Education Act, requiring that all students, grades three through eight, be tested annually using statewide assessments. The law's main intent is to identify schools that fail to improve in ensuring that their students are proficient in reading and mathematics. This legislation is the latest in a series of federal laws attempting to create standards to which schools are to be held accountable.

As a result of this standards-based reform movement, students with disabilities are not only to be included in the general education classroom and curriculum but may also be held to the standards set for all students and measured by standardized tests. IDEA's 1997 amendments attempted to ensure that students with disabilities were among the beneficiaries of reform by requiring that IEPs describe any modifications needed to allow such students to participate in state- and district-wide assessments or, if students will not participate, an explanation as to why the assessment is not appropriate and a description of alternate assessments. Even as states include many students with disabilities in this testing, they are uncertain how to include them in reforms. Do the same standards apply to students both with and without disabilities? Do the standards define appropriate expectations for all students with disabilities? Or do they define what is appropriate for some students? Will the emphasis on testing tend to narrow a curriculum that, for students with disabilities, might need to be richer? Parents, as well as teachers and school administrators, have a stake in these questions along with students. For now, policy debates will continue with respect to these issues.

At a more practical level, the individualized education program, as mentioned, must specify the extent to which the student will participate in the general education curriculum. This is where decisions about meeting district and state standards should be made and documented. Despite the current uncertainty, a graduated model of testing accommodations can help address some of the issues that arise from the inclusion of students with disabilities in district- and statewide testing. For example, such a graduated model has been presented by Pochowski (2000), and includes four levels:

1. Participation in district/state assessments as is
2. Participation in district/state assessments with accommodations (e.g., items read to the student)
3. Participation in district/state assessments with modifications (e.g., out-of-level testing, such as the use of a lower grade-level test)
4. Participation in alternate assessments (e.g., portfolio assessment; see Thompson, Quenemoen, Thurlow, & Ysseldyke, 2001)

As is the case with other inclusive practices, close working relationships between general and special educators is vital to the successful use of test accommodations and modifications.

Grading Policies   In addition to test accommodations, decisions need to be made concerning grading policies. Giving grades to students with disabilities within the general education curriculum can be a thorny issue, owing in part to the fact that neither IDEA nor any of its precursor laws had anything to say about grading policies. Grades are often a matter of personal standards of individual teachers, combined with standardized criteria contained in various curricula and instructional materials. In essence, however, to reflect how a student with disabilities is performing in relation to curricular standards accurately and meaningfully requires the same efforts at adaptation and accommodation that are used with instructional materials and delivery (Salend & Duhaney, 2002).

Surprisingly few resources exist to address the practical concerns of grading. Perhaps the most promising practice in this regard has been developed by Bursuck and his colleagues (Bursuck, Munk, & Olson, 1999; Munk & Bursuck, 2001). To help general and special educators work out effective grading policies for students with disabilities, Munk and Bursuck (2001) developed and evaluated the personalized grading plan (PGP). PGPs provide a vehicle for teachers to work together toward consensus on how to reflect the performance of students with disabilities. Three types of adaptations are considered in arriving at grading decisions: (1) supplementing letter and number grades with written documentation, portfolio assessment, authentic assessment, and so on; (2) using alternatives to letter and number grades, such as pass/fail grades or qualitative statements about performance; and (3) altering performance criteria by varying the weights of certain performance items or the grading of effort and performance separately (Munk & Bursuck, 2001). Any one or, more often, a combination of these adaptations are agreed upon by the teachers involved. The PGP is then developed, including a brief rationale for adaptations; a description of any adaptations; related instructional adaptations; roles of the general educator, special educator, student, and her or his parent(s); and signatures (Munk & Bursuck, 2001).

▪ *Scenario Revisited*

Suzanne and Wanda got together that afternoon. Though they had been acquainted, the two teachers really did not know each other very well. But now they were getting to know one another and really hitting it off. Time flew and they realized they would need to meet again to discuss some of Suzanne's students. They agreed to meet again the next day after school. It wasn't long before they were meeting regularly—laughing, fretting, problem-solving, and planning for Suzanne's kids.

As the year progressed, Suzanne Kiper was learning more and more about what inclusion was supposed to mean for students with disabilities in her classroom. She and Wanda had looked at each student individually and determined which components of the math curriculum needed modification. Wanda showed Suzanne a variety of cutting-edge resources, such as the work by the Center for Applied Special Technology (see Web site URL at the end of this chapter) in universal curriculum design. Wanda also knew special education law backward and forward, and she made sure all of Suzanne's students with disabilities were included in the statewide math assessments and had appropriate testing accommodations.

The collaborative relationship that Suzanne and Wanda developed benefited each teacher in addition to Suzanne's students. Suzanne learned about curriculum and testing modifications, and she gained confidence as Wanda demystified the law. Wanda learned about important and difficult content areas such as algebra, and how to accommodate students with disabilities in such subjects. And of course the prime beneficiaries of the work of these teachers were the students at Hilltop who learned about mathematics just as those with a stake in IDEA had hoped and intended.

FIGURE 11.3
Expanded Graphic
Organizer

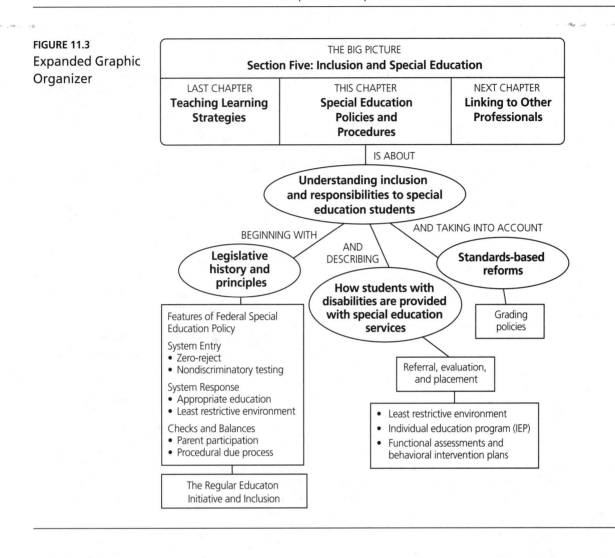

SUMMARY

Legislation, judicial decisions, and professional practice have all contributed to assuring that students with disabilities are included in public education. Inclusion presupposes not only access to a free and appropriate education but also support for students in achieving educational goals.

Successful inclusion depends on the attitudes, judgments, and expertise of teachers in both general and special education to help students achieve those goals. The next chapter discusses how teachers can work together to meet this challenge.

MAKING CONNECTIONS:
*Special Education Policies
and Procedures*

1. *Here are the big ideas to get you started:*
   ▪ It is not unfair to employ different methods of grading for different students. In fact, it would be unfair to use one particular form

of grading for everyone if that method is ineffective in achieving your purpose(s) for grading. Salend and Duhaney (2002) identified no fewer than 11 specific purposes of grading: achievement, progress, effort, comparison, instructional planning, program effectiveness, motivation, communication, educational and career planning, eligibility, and accountability (p. 9).

2. *Try this:*
   ▪ Look at the list of grading purposes above, and decide what purpose(s) your particular method of grading serves.
   ▪ Examine and reflect on whether your method really does achieve its ostensible intent. For example, if one of the purposes is "effort," ask what it is you mean by effort, whether student effort is really reflected in the grading procedure, and whether you can discriminate between high and low effort.

3. *Next steps:*
   ▪ Consult with a colleague, asking her or his impressions of your grading purpose(s) and procedures.
   ▪ Together, examine the 11 purposes of grading and determine which are pertinent to your classrooms.
   ▪ Commit to modifying at least one method of assigning grades to see if you can be more effective in achieving your purpose(s).

WEB SITES

http://www.ed.gov/offices/OSERS/OSEP/index.html U.S. Office of Special Education Programs, the federal agency that oversees the implementation of IDEA. Among a variety of links are the text of both IDEA and its regulations.

http://www.cec.sped.org/idea/ideaqa.html The Council for Exceptional Children (CEC), the major professional organization for special education, sponsors a very useful Web site. This particular link provides a helpful series of questions and answers concerning IDEA.

http://www.cast.org/udl/index.cfm The Center for Applied Special Technology has been the leader in applications of Universal Design for Learning (UDL) principles in the adaptation of curriculum to accommodate the needs and learning characteristics of students with disabilities. This link provides general information about CAST and UDL principles.

SUGGESTED READINGS

Bauwens, J., & Hourcade, J. J. (1995). *Cooperative teaching.* Austin, TX: Pro-Ed. This is an older yet no less informative text on how to teach cooperatively or "co-teach." The book contains a variety of useful tools for implementing the most effective and practical way to bring special education supports into the general education classroom.

Foster-Johnson, L., & Dunlap, G. (1993). Using functional assessment to develop effective, individualized interventions for challenging behaviors. *Teaching Exceptional Children, 25*(3) 44–50. This article provides an outstanding, "hands-on" guide to developing and interpreting functional behavioral assessments, and using the results to design and implement effective interventions.

Fuchs, D., & Fuchs, L. (1994). Inclusive schools movement and the radicalization of special education reform. *Exceptional Children, 60,* 294–309. In this article, the complexities of the inclusion issue are discussed in a straightforward, comprehensive manner. The inclusion movement is placed in the broader context of reforms in education, generally, and special education, specifically.

Rea, P., McLaughlin, V., & Walther-Thomas, C. (2002). Outcomes for students with learning disabilities in inclusive and pullout programs. *Exceptional Children, 68,* 203–222. One of the few assessments of inclusion's effectiveness using "hard data," this article reports the findings of a study comparing inclusion (special education provided in the general education classroom) and "pull-out" (special education provided in the special education resource classroom) programs. The results showed the inclusion program to be more effective on a variety of measures, including achievement and behavior problems.

Salend, S., & Duhaney, L. (2002). Grading students in inclusive settings. *Teaching Exceptional Children, 34*(3), 8–15. The authors provide a comprehensive overview of grading practices that teachers should find particularly helpful.

Turnbull, H. R., & Turnbull, A. P. (2000). *Free appropriate public education.* Denver: Love Publishing. Easily the best and most comprehensive treatment of IDEA and other laws relevant to the practice of special education.

REFERENCES

Algozzine, B., Christenson, S., & Ysseldyke, J. (1982). An analysis of the incidence of special class placement: The masses are burgeoning. *Journal of Special Education, 17,* 141–147.

Bauwens, J., & Hourcade, J. J. (1995). *Cooperative teaching.* Austin, TX: Pro-Ed.

Board of Education v. Rowley, 458, U.S. 176 (1982).

Brown, L., Schwarz, P., Udvari-Solner, A., Kampschroer, E. F., Johnson, F., Jorgensen, J., & Gruenewald, L. (1991). How much time should students with severe disabilities spend in regular classrooms and elsewhere? *Journal of the Association for Persons with Severe Handicaps, 16,* 39–47.

Brown v. Board of Education, 347 U.S. 483 (1954).

Bursuck, W. D., Munk, D. D., & Olson, M. (1999). The fairness of report card grading adaptations: What do students with and without learning disabilities think? *Remedial and Special Education, 20*(2), 84–92.

Chandler, L. K., & Dahlquist, C. M. (2002). *Functional assessment.* Upper Saddle River, NJ: Merrill-Prentice Hall.

Choate, J. S. (2000). *Successful inclusive teaching.* Boston: Allyn & Bacon.

Diana v. State Board of Education (California), No. C-70–37 (N.D. Cal. 1973).

Feiman-Nemser, S., & Floden, R. E. (1986). The cultures of teaching. In M. C. Wittrock (Ed.), *Handbook of research on teaching,* 3rd edition (pp. 505–526). New York: Macmillan.

Foster-Johnson, L., & Dunlap, G. (1993). Using functional assessment to develop effective, individualized interventions for challenging behaviors. *Teaching Exceptional Children, 25*(3) 44–50.

Fuchs, D., & Fuchs, L. (1994). Inclusive schools movement and the radicalization of special education reform. *Exceptional Children, 60,* 294–309.

Glatthorn, A. A. (1990). Cooperative professional development: Facilitating the growth of the special education teacher and the classroom teacher. *Remedial and Special Education, 11*(3), 29–34.

Goodlad, J. I. (1984). *A place called school.* New York: McGraw Hill.

Goodlad, J. I., & Field, S. (1993). Teachers for renewing schools. In J. I. Goodlad & T. C. Lovitt (Eds.), *Integrating general and special education.* New York: Macmillan.

Goodlad, J. I., & Lovitt, T. C. (Eds.) (1993). *Integrating general and special education.* New York: Macmillan.

Heward, W. L. (2000). *Exceptional children.* Upper Saddle River, NJ: Merrill-Prentice Hall.

Honig v. Doe, 484 U.S. 305 (1988).

Johnson, L. J., Pugach, M. C., & Hammitte, D. J. (1988). Barriers to effective special education consultation. *Remedial and Special Education, 9*(6), 41–47.

Katsiyannis, A., & Maag, J. (2001). Manifestation determination as a golden fleece. *Exceptional Children, 68,* 85–96.

Kauffman, J. M., & Hallahan, D. P. (1995). *The illusion of full inclusion.* Austin, TX: Pro-Ed.

Knowlton, H. E. (1985, October). P. L. 94–142's implementation: An evolutionary perspective. Paper presented at the Annual Meeting of the Kansas Federation of the Council for Exceptional Children, Kansas City, KS.

Kochhar, C. A., West, L. L., & Taymans, J. M. (1996). *Handbook for successful inclusion.* Gaithersburg, MD: Aspen Publishers.

Kozleski, E., Mainzer, R., & Deshler, D. D. (2000). *Bright futures for exceptional learners: An agenda to achieve quality conditions for teaching and learning.* Reston, VA: Council for Exceptional Children.

Larry P. v. Riles, 502 F. 2d 963 (9th Cir. 1974).

LaVor, M. (1976). Federal legislation for exceptional persons: A history. In F. Weintraub, A. Abeson, & J. Ballard (Eds.), *Public policy and the education of exceptional children,* pp. 96–102. Reston, VA: Council for Exceptional Children.

Lloyd, J. W., Singh, N. N., & Repp, A. C. (1991). *The regular education initiative: Alternative perspectives on concepts, issues, and models.* Sycamore, IL: Sycamore Publishing.

Lovitt, T.C. (1993). Recurring issues in special and general education. In J. I. Goodlad & T. C. Lovitt (Eds.), *Integrating general and special education* (pp. 49–71). New York: Macmillan.

Maag, J. (2000). *Behavior management.* San Diego: Singular.

McDonnell, L. M., McLaughlin, M. J., & Morison, P. (Eds.) (1997). *Educating one & all—Students with disabilities and standards-based reform.* Washington, DC: National Academy Press.

McIntire, J. C. (2000). Bright futures? *Journal of Special Education Leadership, 13*(2), 48–51.

Munk, D. D., & Bursuck, W. D. (2001). Preliminary findings on personalized grading plans for middle school students with learning disabilities. *Exceptional Children, 67,* 211–234.

Mills v. District of Columbia Board of Education, 348 F. Supp. 886 (D.DC 1972).

National Association of State Directors of Special Education (1990). *Education of the Handicapped Act Amendments of 1990 (P. L. 101–476): Summary of major changes in Parts A through H of the Act.* Washington, D C: Author.

National Association of State Directors of Special Education (1997). *Comparison of key issues: Current law and 1997 IDEA Amendments.* Washington, DC: Author.

Pennsylvania Association for Retarded Children v. Commonwealth of Pennsylvania, 343 F. Supp. 279 (E.D. Pa. 1972).

Pochowski, A. (2000). *Participation of students with disabilities in district assessments.* Unpublished manuscript.

Reynolds, M. C. (1989). An historical perspective: The delivery of special education to mildly disabled and at-risk students. *Remedial and Special Education, 10*(6), 7–11.

Roach, V. (1995). Supporting inclusion: Beyond the rhetoric. *Phi Delta Kappan, 77*(4), 295–299.

Russ, S., Chiang, B., Rylance, B. J., & Bongers, J. (2001). Caseload in special education: An integration of research findings. *Exceptional Children, 67,* 161–172.

Salend, S., & Duhaney, L. (2002). Grading students in inclusive settings. *Teaching Exceptional Children, 34*(3), 8–15.

Schloss, P. J., Smith, M. A., & Schloss, C. N. (1990). *Instructional methods for adolescents with learning and behavior problems.* Boston: Allyn & Bacon.

Showers, B. (1990). Aiming for superior classroom instruction for all children: A comprehensive staff development model. *Remedial and Special Education, 11*(2), 35–39.

Skrtic, T., Guba, E., & Knowlton, H. E. (1985). *Interorganizational special education programming in rural areas.* (Contract No. 400–81–0017). Washington, DC: National Institute of Education.

Thompson, S., Quenemoen, R., Thurlow, M., & Ysseldyke, J. (2001). *Alternate assessments for students with disabilities.* Arlington, VA: Council for Exceptional Children.

Turnbull, H. R., & Turnbull, A. P. (2000). *Free appropriate public education.* Denver: Love Publishing.

U.S. Department of Education. (1983). *A nation at risk.* Washington, DC: Author.

U.S. Department of Education. (2000). *Twenty-second annual report to Congress on the implementation of the Individuals with Disabilities Education Act.* Washington, DC: Author.

Vaughn, S., & Schumm, J. S. (1995). Responsible inclusion for students with learning disabilities. *Journal of Learning Disabilities, 28,* 264–270, 290.

Wang, M. C., & Reynolds, M. C. (Eds.) (1995). *Making a difference for students at risk: Trends and alternatives.* Thousand Oaks, CA: Corwin Press.

Will, M. (1986). Educating children with learning problems: A shared responsibility. *Exceptional Children, 52,* 411–416.

Wyatt v. Stickney, 325 F. Supp. 781 (M.D. Ala. 1971).

Zettel, J., & Ballard, J. (1982). The Education for All Handicapped Children Act of 1975 (P. L. 94–142): Its history, origins, and concepts. In J. Ballard, B. A. Ramirez, and F. J. Weintraub (Eds.), *Special education in America: Its legal and governmental foundations* (pp. 11–22). Reston, VA: Council for Exceptional Children.

12 Linking to Other Professionals

Suzanne M. Robinson

Critical Self-Test Questions

- What does the general education teacher need to know about special education to work effectively with students with special needs in his or her classroom?
- What support should the general education teacher expect from special education and other support teachers?
- How can general and special education teachers work together within the general education classroom?
- How might collaboration among varied professionals enhance education for all students, not just those with special needs?

Including all students in learning becomes particularly challenging in the case of students with disabilities. Many of these students, when they are mainstreamed into general education classrooms, require specialized accommodations or modifications in materials, instruction, and assessments. General education teachers often do not feel adequately prepared to make these accommodations and modifications (Goodlad & Field, 1993). The planning and teaching approaches described in earlier chapters can go a long way toward addressing the needs for explicit instruction for many students with disabilities, especially those with learning disabilities. Addressing the needs of all mainstreamed students with disabilities, however, may require the additional support of other professionals. In this chapter we discuss ways you might effectively work with other professionals in your school or district to utilize their expertise in teaching students with special learning needs.

FOUNDATIONS AND PRINCIPLES

In the past, special education practices often emphasized teaching remedial or basic skills and providing an alternative or life-skills curriculum. Frequently, this instruction differed significantly from the general education curriculum and was delivered outside the general education classroom in a resource room or self-contained program. Students with special needs were exposed to the general education curriculum when "mainstreamed." However, many teachers did not differentiate instruction for students with

FIGURE 12.1
Graphic Organizer

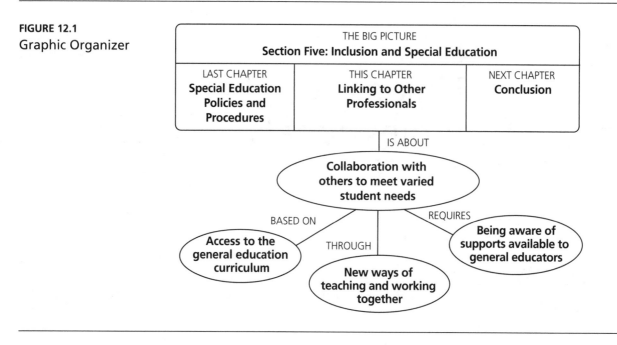

special needs, and thus mastery of the curriculum was often low for these students and their progress slow. In the name of "fairness," students with special needs were either held to a different standard ("just expect less"), or they were held to the same standard as other students but without any specialized instruction. Coordination between a special education program and the mainstream environment was often not considered critical nor planned for.

The relationship between special and general education has been redefined with the emergence of a philosophy of inclusion (Thousand & Villa, 1995). Students with special needs are valued members of the school community and should be a *part of*, rather than *apart from*, the educational and extra-curricular experiences available to their nondisabled peers. This means most students with disabilities should be taught the same knowledge as their nondisabled peers. They should have access to tools that facilitate learning, have instruction that is planned, delivered, and monitored for

▪ Scenario

Ms. Davis, a high school history teacher with ten years of experience, has seen quite a change in the composition of her classes over the last decade. When she began teaching, she seldom had students with special education needs in her classes. As a matter of fact, she had had little contact with the special education teachers and had little knowledge of the special education program (or any other support program) at the high school or in the district. Now, however, she has quite a few students with IEPs (individualized educational programs) in her classes. While she believes that all of her students should have opportunities to succeed, and she tries to find ways to assist and accommodate various student learning styles, she finds the diversity in her classes somewhat daunting. What supports should be available to her and how can she access them?

effectiveness, and have access to the entire learning community (Chard, Vaughn, & Thurlow, 2000). For educators, it means that they need to communicate effectively and frequently with others, share decision making in assessment and instruction, and participate in flexible teaching situations to achieve these desired outcomes.

Focus and Reflect

How might the culture of a classroom have an impact on a student with disabilities?

No one educational professional has the necessary expertise to meet all the educational needs of all the students who may arrive in their classroom. In the past, various education professionals have addressed different student needs in different places with little coordination among them. In the current context of inclusion, this is no longer possible. Collaboration among professionals is critical for inclusion to succeed. And because most students with disabilities will participate in district and statewide assessments, proof of successful delivery of these programs will be evident by the same measures that districts and states use to measure the success of other students. Collaboration among professionals and with students and their families is essential. This chapter will address what linking with other professionals might look like and how it can be accomplished successfully.

KNOWING AND DOING

Most students with special needs will attend general education classrooms. It is important to remember that students with disabilities also have many individual strengths. For example, a student who has difficulty understanding written text, and so reads laboriously, might also have strong auditory comprehension, or be very proficient in mathematics. A student with emotional and behavioral issues, who on occasion exhibits inappropriate classroom behavior and noncompliance, may also, when motivated, express himself movingly in writing. Students with special needs are, by definition, those who often find learning hard and slow, or those for whom the traditional practices of schooling have been marginally effective, thus causing some level of failure. These students can be complicated students for teachers to teach, and collaboration among professionals becomes essential to address their learning needs. Students with special needs in general education classrooms include those with learning disabilities, emotional and behavioral issues, mild cognitive delays, sensory and physical impairments, traumatic brain injuries, attention deficit hyperactivity disorder, pervasive developmental disorders, as well as specific neurological or genetic disorders. Students with severe cognitive delays also attend general education classrooms when there is an appropriate match between the general education curriculum, functional and life-skills curriculum, and an individual student's individual education program (IEP). For students with severe cognitive delays, the goals and expected performance outcomes often are substantially different than those for their classroom peers. Often paraprofessionals support the general education teacher in providing similar but modified curriculum opportunities.

Students with Special Needs in the General Education Classroom

Changes in the Individuals with Disabilities Education Act (IDEA) in 1997 place more emphasis on providing students with disabilities access to the

■ *Scenario Revisited*

Marjorie Miller and her son Trent arrive for Trent's IEP meeting at the start of the fall semester. Ms. Miller is feeling anxious, because the start of the new school year always brings hopes and worries about Trent's future. If he is successful this year, will attendance at the state university be in Trent's future in a few years? If he is less than successful, will this result in Trent's lowered self-esteem and potential noncompliant, or worse, behavior? What will the future hold? Trent is also feeling anxious. IEP meetings are hard for him because he feels all adult attention is focused on what he hasn't done well in the past. He would like to be in regular classes with his friends. He knows that

the reading will be difficult for him, and his track record on homework completion is not good. However, he'd like a chance to try. He feels he has matured and will put forth the effort and be more responsible. Ms. Davis, the history teacher, and Ms. Rutledge, the special education teacher, along with the assistant principal, the counselor, and the transition coordinator enter the conference room, and greet the Millers. Ms. Rutledge begins the IEP meeting by asking Trent, "How did school go for you last year? What are your goals for this year?"

And so, planning Trent's future, at least for this year, begins.

curriculum in the general education classroom. Supplementary aids and services as well as special education and related services are to be provided to ensure *access* is meaningful. The new emphasis is intended to produce attention to the accommodations and adjustments necessary for children and youth with disabilities and to any special services which may be necessary (Committee on Labor and Human Resources, 1977). The IEP required by law for any student receiving special education support must contain a statement about how the child will "be involved and progress in the general curriculum . . . and participate in extracurricular and other nonacademic activities; and . . . be educated and participate with other children with disabilities and nondisabled children. . . ." [Section 614(d)(1)(A)(iii)]. Further, students with disabilities are to participate in state or district-wide assessments, and a statement must be included in their IEP about appropriate accommodations and modifications to which they are entitled to ensure meaningful assessment like their nondisabled peers.

A general educator must be on the IEP team. His or her role is to help determine adjustments in instruction, as well as appropriate supplementary aids and services and positive behavioral interventions, so that students can master the curriculum. It is expected that general education teachers will participate in IEP meetings and contribute ideas about how to make the curriculum and general education classroom more accessible to the student. Further, it is expected that, in collaboration with special educators and other support service providers, the effort of general education teachers to accommodate for a student with disabilities will be in good faith, and that this effort will result in positive outcomes for students.

General education teachers are very important to the program planning and IEP development that occurs yearly for all students with disabilities. A general education teacher has unique knowledge about the curriculum and areas where students might stumble. The general education teacher can

Focus and Reflect
What knowledge might a general education teacher have about the curriculum that other IEP team members might not?

help identify appropriate accommodations or modifications that will assist the student needing support but that will also not impede the learning of other students in the class. The general education teacher can also help determine what accommodations would be appropriate on state assessments. All of these recommendations can be included in the IEP. If the general education teacher does not participate in program planning and IEP development, the accommodations recommended may not reflect the content and context of the general education classroom. Because the IEP addresses how student learning will be supported in the general education environment, as well as through specialized services (e.g., learning centers, vocational programs, work/study environments, etc.), the general education teacher is critical in the process.

Meeting Responsibilities to Students with Disabilities or Students with Learning Problems

It is the responsibility of any teacher to help all students learn. When a teacher notices that a student is struggling with learning the content being taught or is unable to learn specific skills, this should be a signal to try different strategies to reach the student. Teaching is much more than delivering content; teaching is facilitating students' success. This is a teacher's responsibility. So any student who is struggling needs more precise instruction and appropriate accommodations or modifications. For a student with disabilities, these instructional strategies and accommodations or modifications may be specified in his or her IEP, delineating the school environment that has been identified to facilitate his or her success. General education teachers, as well as special education personnel, are obligated to follow these and other recommendations of an IEP.

In using teaching strategies to reach students, teachers must use effective, research-based practices consistently and with fidelity. Consistent use means that the instructional practice is used with enough frequency to have the expected impact. Research-based instructional practices have specified steps that were followed in the research and contributed to producing the positive effect. Teachers who use these research-based practices need to follow the same steps used by the teachers during the research (i.e., fidelity to the treatment protocol). For example, if you had a serious illness, you would want your doctor to follow the best treatment protocol exactly. You would not want the doctor to leave out any steps or any part of the treatment found by research to be effective. The same principle applies when using research-based instructional practices with students for whom learning is difficult.

Special Educators and Support Service Providers   Special educators are advocates for students for whom the traditional educational model has not been a good fit. In this capacity, it is the responsibility of special educators and other support service providers to push the general education environment to address these students' needs. Special educators are also charged with responsibility to support students with disabilities through personalized planning and, often, intensive instruction in needed skills. In addition, these educators support general education teachers by providing: (a) information about students and the potential impact of specific disabilities on their learning; and (b) assistance in developing and providing appropriate

■ *Scenario Revisited*

By the end of Trent Miller's IEP meeting, it was decided that Trent would be in Ms. Davis' American history class, as well as tenth-grade English, geometry, biology, and some elective classes. He would need some support and accommodations in history, English, and biology. As they talked about support and accommodations, Ms. Rutledge reminded the group that there were a number of students with IEPs who would be in this section of American history. It was decided that this class would provide an excellent opportunity for the two teachers to work together, with Ms. Rutledge providing special education support to the class. For English and biology, Ms. Rutledge planned to meet with the teachers and report back to the group on appropriate accommodations.

After the IEP meeting, the teachers talked briefly and shared some concerns that they had about teaching together. While they were friendly as colleagues, they did not know each other well and were not sure about how the collaboration would work. Ms. Davis was reluctant to share instructional responsibility with someone without expertise in the social sciences.

Ms. Rutledge was worried that she might find herself relegated to the role of assistant.

Ruth Davis and Nancy Rutledge decided to attend a district workshop on inclusion, collaboration, and co-teaching so that they would be better informed about how to work together effectively. It was enlightening for both teachers. The workshop was informative about school reform initiatives in general. It also included specifics about the ways in which general educators with a variety of support staff can meet the needs of "hard-to-teach, slow-to-learn" students. There were presentations on strategies for planning instruction that accommodates diverse learners, as well as instructional techniques for organizing content clearly. Information was provided on problem-solving strategies, and substantial information was presented on how collaboration in a classroom in the form of co-teaching should work. Ms. Davis and Ms. Rutledge planned together using many of the strategies that they learned, and discussed how teaching the history class together would address the needs of Trent and a number of other students (possibly most) in the class.

---

instruction, accommodations, and modifications. Special educators and other support service providers are available to provide information and assistance in meeting the needs of any unsuccessful student.

Schools should have a number of ways to support teachers in getting the advice and assistance they need to develop a plan to reach a particular student. A student assistance team (SAT) is one way this is often done. The student assistance team is made up of experienced teachers from the school with a variety of expertise. Any teacher can bring a concern about a student to the team and get assistance in developing a plan for this student. While this could be done for any student, concerns about students with learning difficulties are often brought before an SAT. Some of these students will be referred further to a multidisciplinary team (MDT) for a more in-depth assessment of their learning problems and consultation with professionals having expertise in specialized areas, such as learning disabilities, speech-language disorders, attention deficit disorder, social work, and so on. Some of these students will be diagnosed as having an identifiable disability and will receive an IEP and special education support. Most students with disabilities are identified prior to high school, so the MDT on the secondary level is primarily for planning a student's program and developing the IEP.

Another way that schools can support teachers is through the development and implementation of schoolwide strategies to address the needs of students with challenging behaviors. As you have read in earlier chapters, positive behavioral support (PBS) is an effective, research-based strategy that can be used to help students who engage in inappropriate behaviors learn more positive ways to achieve their goals. PBS shifts classroom management out of negative power struggles between teacher and student and into a context of understanding behavioral intent—Why is the student engaging in this behavior? Functional assessments, described in Chapter 11, can help identify behavioral intent so that positive, alternative behaviors can be taught to students. For some students, instruction in appropriate behavior and social skills can be accomplished as part of the process of establishing principles within the classroom learning community. Other students may need additional instruction and practice in developing appropriate behaviors, and this instruction and practice may be provided in a resource center. However, PBS is most effective for all students when it is developed, implemented, and supported throughout a school so that appropriate behaviors are consistently reinforced and inappropriate behaviors are dealt with proactively (Positive Behavioral Support, 1999).

New Ways of Teaching and Working Together

Differentiating instruction for students with varied learning needs is a challenging task for most teachers and daunting for many. However, it is not the responsibility of any one teacher to meet the needs of *all* students, even if diverse groups of students are receiving instruction in a classroom together. Schools and districts should utilize special education and other support services to assist teachers in making appropriate accommodations and modifications.

Accommodating diverse learners must be a schoolwide effort utilizing the varied personnel in schools to support student learning. These include the principal, the general education teacher, the special education teacher, the district-based support staff (e.g., social worker, speech and language pathologist, physical therapist, etc.), the psychologist, paraeducators, the media specialist, as well as the student. Personnel in all areas of the educational enterprise are having their responsibilities redefined to ensure that their primary task is assisting students in meeting high standards of academic proficiency and promoting a supportive learning environment that ensures all students the best possible opportunity for a productive future. To that end, there is a shift in the responsibilities of everyone within schools and districts (Thousand & Villa, 1995). However, in some schools, some or many of these personnel roles have calcified into ways of working that are grounded in past practice and are not as responsive to student needs as they could be. In these schools, traditional ways of working often get in the way of the redefined professional linkages that can better support student learning. Table 12.1 (adapted from Thousand & Villa, 1995) provides examples of how traditional personnel responsibilities are being redefined.

As the roles of educators change, it is important to recognize that change takes time and is often accomplished in steps. For example, if cooperative learning is used in the classroom to help students learn together, it may take a while for a teacher and his or her students to learn how to make

Focus and Reflect

- Have you been in schools where some staff roles have remained traditional and some have been redefined? What staff was involved and in what ways did roles remain traditional? In what ways were some roles redefined?
- How can redefined roles and responsibilities help school personnel support each other in ways that traditional roles do not?

TABLE 12.1 Changing Job Responsibilities of School Personnel

JOB TITLE	TRADITIONAL RESPONSIBILITIES	REDEFINED RESPONSIBILITIES
General Education Teacher	Refers students who do not "fit" into the traditional program for diagnosis, remediation, and possible removal. Teaches children who "fit" within the standard curriculum.	Shares responsibility with special educators and other support personnel for teaching all assigned children. Seeks support of special educators and other support personnel for students experiencing difficulty in learning. Collaboratively plans and teaches with other members of the staff and community to meet the needs of all learners. Recruits and trains students to be tutors and social supports for one another.
Special Education Teacher	Provides instruction to students eligible for services in resource rooms, special classes, and special schools.	Collaborates with general educators and other support personnel to meet the needs of all learners. Team-teaches with regular educators in general education classes. Recruits and trains students to be peer tutors and social supports for one another.
General Education Administrator	Manages the general education program. Cedes responsibility for special programs to special education administrators, although special programs are "housed" within general education facilities.	Manages the general education programs for all students. Articulates the vision and provides emotional support to staff as they experience the change process. Participates as a member of collaborative problem-solving teams that invent solutions to barriers inhibiting the successful inclusion and education of any child. Secures resources to enable staff to meet the needs of all children.
Paraeducator	Works in special education programs. If working in general education classrooms, stays in close proximity to and works only with student(s) eligible for special services.	Provides services to a variety of students in general education settings. Facilitates natural peer supports within general education settings.
Student	Primarily works independently and competes with other students for "best" performance. Acts as a passive recipient of learning.	Often works with other students in cooperative learning arrangements. Is actively involved in instruction, advocacy, and decision making for self and others.
Psychologist	Tests, diagnoses, assigns labels, and determines eligibility for students' admission to special programs.	Collaborates with teachers to define problems. Creatively designs interventions. Team-teaches. Provides social skills training to classes of students. Conducts authentic assessments. Trains students to be conflict mediators, peer tutors, and supports for one another.

JOB TITLE	TRADITIONAL RESPONSIBILITIES	REDEFINED RESPONSIBILITIES
Library Media Specialist	Manages routine library tasks: purchasing, cataloguing, and tracking materials. Library materials and staff generally isolated from daily curriculum objectives.	Manages library by collaborating with teachers and students in order to provide access to curriculum enhancement materials. Provides consultation and technical assistance to teachers and students in the areas of research, skill acquisition, and curriculum development. Uses flexible library access scheduling, collaborative planning, and research and materials knowledge to advance the learning of diverse groups of students.
Support Staff (social worker, speech & language pathologist, physical therapist)	Diagnoses, labels, and provides direct services to students in settings other than classroom. Provides support only to students eligible for a particular program.	Assesses and provides direct services to students within general education classrooms and community settings. Supports students not eligible for special education. Trains classroom teachers, instructional assistants, volunteers, and students to carry out support services. Shares responsibility to meet the needs of all students.

it work, as you read in Chapter 5, Course Planning: Establishing a Classroom Learning Community. Or, in another example, if two teachers decide they want to co-teach a course, they may find they have to work at the arrangement, resolving any conflicts or disagreements with regular and effective communication and problem solving.

Understanding Supports Available to General Educators

Differentiating instruction within a class is not easy, nor is coordinating curriculum and instruction among different classes. Therefore, linking with other professionals in the school and among programs is critical to success. Linking with other professionals can occur in a variety of ways. Indeed, schools that are most responsive in accommodating students with a variety of learning or behavioral needs have multiple strategies in place to link professionals (Newmann & Wehlage, 1995). Specialized instruction, collaborative consultation, collaborative problem solving, co-planning, and co-teaching are the primary ways that professionals in special education and support roles collaborate to address the needs of individual students (Robinson, 1991). However, when practice is most responsive, strategies for professional collaboration change or adjust as the needs of the students and their families change, and as resources (human and institutional) change.

Specialized Instruction   At some times, most students with special needs will require more intensive instruction than peers without disabilities. An analogy in athletics might help in understanding this concept, because most of us have experienced or observed differences among people in athletic ability and proficiency. If two students, one with and one without athletic ability, were taught a new skill like serving a tennis ball, instruction in how to serve would be fundamentally the same for both athletes. Instruction for both would include a description of the components of the movement, demonstration, and practice. Instruction for the student with athletic ability might require breaking the movement into a few steps, providing a few demonstrations, and then letting that student begin to practice. The instructor's feedback on the practice attempts might include variations on "Good serve!" For the student with less athletic ability, it might be appropriate for the instructor to devote more time to describing the initial throw, or how to time the throw with the swing of the racquet. This athlete might require more opportunities to practice and might need to see many more demonstrations. The feedback might have to be very precise for this student to help her understand how to improve her throw and timing.

This same difference in the instructional needs of individual learners is observed in classrooms where content like math or history is taught. For some students, at some times, instructional goals may need to be more focused or clearly articulated, or instructional increments leading to mastery may need to be smaller. A student may need more practice before he is confident to use the skill on his own, or teacher feedback may need to be more detailed or focused. This type of specialized or intensive instruction could be provided in the general education classroom by a general educator, special educator, paraeducator, or some combination of these teachers. It could also occur in a different setting at a different time. Like the less able athlete, the student might require extra practice at other than the designated class time, or some individualized instruction or tutoring. Specialized instruction requires the classroom teacher to provide alternate paths to mastery, accommodating various learning needs by differentiating instruction for various subgroups in the class.

Sometimes students with special needs require specialized instruction to help them master the general education curriculum. This might mean providing instruction in useful learning strategies that students had not acquired in prior years or developed naturally with maturity. For example, some students may not use effective strategies or techniques to read and understand textbooks. Other students may not have developed organizational techniques useful for writing research reports or themes. Students may also lack prerequisite skills like math facts, which either need to be learned or accommodated for (e.g., using a calculator to do more complex calculations). Specialized instruction to help students overcome these learning limitations might be so different from what is needed by other students in a general education classroom that it entails providing instruction at a different time or place than the scheduled class time. This specialized instruction is often provided in a learning center or in an elective class. When specialized instruction occurs outside the classroom context, it is very important that teachers in the two classes coordinate instruction. Sometimes, teachers may realize that one student's learning needs reflect those of other students, in which case specialized instruction may be offered in the general education classroom to all students who would profit from it.

Collaborative Consultation "Collaborative consultation" is a term used to describe an interactive and ongoing process where individuals with different expertise, knowledge, or experience voluntarily work together to create solutions to identified concerns. It differs from what is commonly thought of as "consultation" (conferring with an expert for a limited amount of time or during a single session). Collaborative consultation entails sharing responsibility for finding effective solutions. It also involves understanding that many solutions require adaptations and adjustments over time. The collaborative consultation process requires a belief among participating educators that a "best" solution will often evolve from contributions from more than one individual. No one individual is considered "the expert," and it is not assumed that any one individual must have the "answer." While individuals are recognized for their expertise in particular areas, all participants' contributions are valued, though their contributions may not be equivalent.

The process of collaborative consultation can look different in different contexts. For example, a classroom teacher may consult with a special education teacher about how to develop and implement a behavior management system, instructional modifications, or other practices with which he or she is not familiar. Or, teachers might learn about a new instructional technique (e.g., learning strategies, cooperative learning) and then decide to work together within a coaching structure to improve implementation of the new strategy. It could entail teachers conferring on a regular basis about particular students, or it could include one teacher asking another for assistance or advice (e.g., how to format a test so that it is more user-friendly). Regardless of what the interaction between teachers includes, underlying that interaction are beliefs that: (1) maintaining an ongoing and interactive relationship with colleagues is important; (2) valuing and sharing expertise, knowledge, and experience increases one's own skills; (3) working together will be mutually beneficial; and (4) sharing problems or concerns that emerge leads to effective solutions for problems that would otherwise not be addressed (Friend & Cook, 1995; Robinson, 1991). When linkages among professionals include collaborative consultation, school personnel are truly more than the sum of their parts.

Collaborative Problem Solving   As previously stated, teachers with different expertise must collaborate if they want to succeed in creating learning environments where students with varied learning needs will successfully master the general education curriculum. Collaborative problem solving is not separate from collaborative consultation, but rather is a component of collaboration that warrants further specification of strategies that are effective. Often problems or needs of students, when viewed by one teacher alone, seem intractable. When analyzed by a collaborative problem-solving team comprised of individuals with varied expertise, solutions to seemingly intractable problems are found. Collaboration may occur in a variety of ways among general education teachers and teachers with expertise in educating students with learning disabilities, behavior disorders, mental retardation, or other developmental or neurological disabilities, along with other support personnel (psychologists, speech language teachers, art teachers, librarians, etc.).

First, general education teachers might request information about particular students, and their abilities and disabilities and ask for suggestions on how to support them in the general education classroom. Or, special educators could provide information to classroom teachers before or as instruction begins. A proactive approach often prevents problems before they occur and might include a meeting, as well as written suggestions about accommodations or modifications that are appropriate. Figure 12.2 is an example of a communication tool that might be used by general and special education teachers.

For some students, more in-depth planning around particular needs or concerns may be required. A problem-solving meeting could be held with the general education teacher, a special education teacher, and any other

FIGURE 12.2 Student Modifications Plan

Teacher's Name _____ Class _____

Students: _____ _____

_____ _____

✔ If Appropriate

Recommendations for Modifications:

_____ Students need organizational help from teacher.

_____ Daily assignments will be shortened.

_____ Extra time given to complete assignments.

_____ Alternative assignments given.

_____ Materials on lower difficulty level.

_____ Adapt worksheets, packets.

_____ Special seating arrangments.

_____ Disciplinary intervention needed
      (contracts, Level System, etc.).

_____ Teacher and/or peer class notes given
      (NCR paper available).

_____ Teacher monitoring/motivation is needed.

_____ Individual assistance before _____, during _____,
      or after _____ school.
         (Times checked are parent approved.)

_____ Students are on same grading system as other students.

_____ Individualized grading systems.

_____ Students are on a credit/no credit (K/NK) system.

_____ Students should be graded more on daily work,
      notebook checks, and less on tests
         (i.e., 60% daily, 25% notebook, and 15% tests).

_____ Grade checks with Learning Center.

Assignments/Study Guides

_____ Record page numbers for questions

_____ Use of cue cards

_____ Use of calculators

_____ Buddies to check/correct answers

Tests/Quizzes

_____ Take tests in Learning Center
      (if scheduled one day in advance).

_____ Verbal review of test with adult before test time.

_____ Use of notes during tests.

_____ Use of teacher-completed study guide.

_____ Open book tests.

_____ Read test to students.

_____ Tests finished in Learning Center
      (if students ask and schedule with L.C.).

_____ Takes regular tests in regular classroom

_____ Modification of test questions
      (word banks, fewer choices on multiple
      choice, color coding on matching).

Source: Developed by Tamara Demuth, Nancy Meyers, Julie Franklin, and Christi Weldon of Blue Valley Middle School, 1996.

appropriate participants. Others who might attend are the student, the student's parents, the counselor, other general educators, or other specialists. These meetings should be focused on solutions as teachers meet and collaboratively problem-solve around the needs of a particular student. A specific, personalized plan is developed on how to assist a student to be successful in a particular setting. A validated 13-step process used with the worksheet shown in Figure 12.3 and detailed in the manual developed by Knackendoffel, Robinson, Deshler, and Schumaker (1992), could be used to structure such a meeting. The steps of the problem-solving process are as follows: (1) Define the problem; (2) gather specific details about the problem; (3) explain problem-solving process and state its usefulness; (4) identify alternative solutions; (5) summarize solutions; (6) analyze possible consequences; (7) rate each solution; (8) select the best solution; (9) determine satisfaction with chosen solution; (10) state support for decision; (11) develop a plan of action; (12) develop a monitoring system and specify criteria for success; and (13) schedule next appointment to refine the plan. This process is particularly appropriate as a means of coordinating support efforts by multiple teachers and others, and ensuring that all appropriate and available expertise is consulted in developing an appropriate plan for an individual student. A step-by-step strategy and protocol for meeting ensures that problem-solving time is productive and that it results in potential solutions and plans to implement them.

Co-Planning for Curriculum Access   Planning processes like the ones elaborated on in previous chapters can be helpful for collaborative planning teams made up of teachers with shared students. It is appropriate for a general education teacher to meet with special education and support personnel when course planning begins to consider the learning needs of special education students. Often, the only planning that occurs collaboratively is about the particular accommodations certain students may need to be successful. While it is appropriate to address individual problems as they arise, a more proactive strategy is to plan instruction with the knowledge that in any class there will always be students for whom learning is difficult. If the goal is to truly transform the learning environment, planning for diverse learners should start at the course level among teachers with varied expertise.

As you have seen in earlier chapters, teachers should ask themselves the following questions as they plan for instruction: What are the BIG IDEAS to be taught during the course and how are they related? What are the desired knowledge outcomes, skill outcomes, or performance outcomes, as well as mastery standards? Only after teachers clarify where they are headed and where they want to end up should they move to individual unit planning. At this point the questions to guide collaborative planning should start with: What are the big ideas for this unit and how do they connect and contribute to understanding the objectives of the course? What are the knowledge outcomes, skill outcomes, mastery or potential performance outcomes for the unit? What resources might we use? What instructional techniques and activities might we use? What accommodations might be needed for particular students?

FIGURE 12.3 Problem-Solving Worksheet

Problem-Solving Team Members: _____ Role: _____

_____ _____

_____ _____

Student: _____ Date: _____

Problem:

[ ]

Details:

_____

_____

_____

_____

Alternative Solutions: _____ Ratings:

_____ ___ ___ ___

_____ ___ ___ ___

_____ ___ ___ ___

Solution to Be Tried First:

_____

_____

_____

Implementation Steps: _____ When _____ Who _____

_____ _____ _____

_____ _____ _____

How Will the Plan Be Monitored?:

_____

_____

_____

What Are the Criteria for Success?:

_____

_____

_____

Date and Time of Next Appointment: _____

Source: Reprinted by permission of Knackendoffel, Robinson, Deshler, & Schumaker (1992).

Focus and Reflect

Identify a concept or skill you would teach in your content area or to an elementary class. Describe both an accommodation and a modification you could make at each of the four levels of instruction identified in Table 12.2.

Accommodations should be considered in the context of overall planning. Researchers have found that if accommodations are planned only when it becomes evident that students are not succeeding, the accommodation of choice is often just to expect less of the student (Garnett, 1996; Vaughn & Schumm, 1996). However, accommodations or modifications can be planned for and made at every stage of the instructional process. Accommodations change the path to achieving outcomes, while modifications change the task, path, or outcome to a degree that the attained outcome is substantially different than that expected of other students. In Table 12.2, there are examples of accommodations and modifications that may be used at four stages of instruction.

Instructional success is always determined by the answers to the following questions: Is the student progressing in understanding and knowledge acquisition? Has the student overcome areas of need that were impeding progress? Is the student progressing at acceptable rates? If the answer is "no" to any of these questions, then the appropriate response is to alter

TABLE 12.2   Curriculum or Instruction Adaptations

STAGE OF INSTRUCTION	ACCOMMODATIONS (EXAMPLES)	MODIFICATIONS (EXAMPLES)
Initial Instruction	• Clear overheads/graphic organizer • Partners repeat or read to each other • Teacher uses signals • Study guide/guided notes • Highlighted text • Teacher position/proximity to particular students	• Different study guide (partially filled out) • Different text • Introduce different but related skill
Guided Practice	• Notated/highlighted/more structured assignment or activity • Teacher/student model • Partners do/check • Partners tutor • Frequent checks by teacher • Alter pace	• Different assignment or activity on same skill or content • Different assignment or activity on related skill or content • Physical guidance by teacher/paraeducator/peer
Independent Practice	• Slower transition from guided practice • More structure	• Do less of same task • Different task • Teach parent/sibling to coach • Do with a partner
Evaluation	• Test under different conditions (more time, different location, test read to student) • Same rubric or standard but different tasks • Portfolio • Mastery standard, but vary time allowed to mastery • Evaluation based on more than curriculum mastery	• Evaluation of different objectives/different outcomes

instructional practices or reanalyze identified student outcomes and the match between desired outcomes and instructional practice.

Co-Teaching   Co-teaching (collaborative teaching or team teaching) is an instructional arrangement that entails two teachers with different expertise sharing instructional responsibility for a general education class that serves a heterogeneous group of students, some of whom have IEPs and receive special education support. All special education support might occur in the co-taught class, or some students may receive support during another class time in a special education learning center. Co-teaching is an increasingly popular strategy to address the needs of diverse students in general education classes and it is a direct means of linking professionals. However, if not thoughtfully planned, the general education teacher may fail to utilize the expertise of a special education colleague who may or may not have similar content expertise. Co-teaching also will not be effective if the special educator assumes a support role that is passive and includes little more than monitoring. In poorly planned co-taught classrooms, the special educator often complains of feeling like an "aide."

Planning an effective co-teaching program should include: (a) time and scheduling commitments (presence); (b) schoolwide program planning and designated planning time at the course, unit, and lesson level (planning); (c) instruction that utilizes two teachers and differing expertise (presenting); (d) opportunities for teachers to confer about how working together is going (processing); and (e) specific problem solving about individual students (problem solving) (Bauwens & Hourcade, 1994).

Presence means that co-teaching requires a time commitment from both teachers that is a part of each teacher's daily schedule. Administrators must support this commitment and not pull out one of the teachers to be an emergency substitute elsewhere during the co-taught class. And neither teacher should regard their co-teacher as someone to provide "cover" for them so that he or she can make phone calls or take care of other business.

Planning must occur on many levels. It must be determined what classes will be co-taught (where is the student need and what core subjects should be covered?) and which teachers will participate in co-teaching teams. Students and their parents should be assured that the collaborative teaching program will be continued at the next grade level. Schools should cooperatively plan for a well-articulated collaborative teaching program through the grades. Teachers must plan how they will work together. Figure 12.4 is an example agenda that co-teaching teams can use to facilitate a conversation about how two individuals will work together. Instructional planning time must be allocated for the co-teaching teams, though it does not have to occur daily. However, proactive planning (discussed earlier in this chapter and in previous chapters) is critical to anticipate learning problems and to ensure that different strengths of teachers are used to advantage.

Presentation strategies must be considered that utilize the expertise of both teachers and ensure that they both are engaged in the teaching process. Bauwens and Hourcade (1995) have defined three ways in which teachers might share instructional responsibility. **Team teaching** occurs when the two teachers share responsibility in delivering knowledge instruction, or when one teacher "shadows" the other to facilitate knowledge acquisition by students. An example of "shadowing" is when one teacher provides an

Five P's of Co-Teaching
Presence
Planning
Presenting
Processing
Problem-solving

FIGURE 12.4   Agenda for Cooperative Teaching Discussion: Getting to Know One Another

Think about . . .

Philosophy/beliefs/attitudes about teaching and learning

- Beliefs about the purpose of schooling
- Beliefs about disability
- Comfort level with individuals with disabilities
- Beliefs about inclusion

Theoretical orientation toward teaching

- Educational approaches knowledgeable about (e.g., behavioral, constructivist, direct instruction, etc.)
- Educational approaches most comfortable using

Preferred classroom procedures

Procedures for . . .

- Managing behavior
- Work completion
- Class participation
- Material management
- Grading
- Homework
- "Helping" students
- Transitions
- Parent communication

Talk about . . .

Procedural considerations for cooperative teaching

Scheduling cooperative teaching

- Frequency
- Duration

Teaching roles and responsibilities including . . .

- Content presentation
- Developing supplemental learning activities
- Material modifications
- Developing study guides/graphic organizers
- Providing complementary instruction in study strategies/learning strategies
- Other

Ongoing planning for cooperative teaching

Instructional considerations

- Curricular focus (critical knowledge, concepts, and skills)
- Scope and sequence of instruction
- Pacing of instruction
- Instructional delivery approaches

Evaluation considerations

- How will you know if the program is successful?
- What will you measure?

analogy or concrete example of a concept after an initial presentation by the other teacher. Another example is when one teacher provides a graphic organizer or visual representation of information while the other teacher is lecturing, or one teacher monitors student note taking or asks questions about, elaborates on, clarifies, or summarizes information as needed. One teacher may be more knowledgeable than the other about creating **supportive learning** activities and may take responsibility for creating activities that provide varied practice opportunities for students. The development of such activities requires considerable thought and time so that they are interesting for students and meaningful in facilitating knowledge acquisition or deepening understanding of content and its applications. It is easier to facilitate student activity when there are two adults monitoring, answering questions, and providing needed reteaching or redirection. Another way that teachers may differentiate teaching responsibilities is for one to plan for content presentation, and the other to plan a **complementary** strategy or study skills instruction. Learning strategies or study skills are often taught in learning center programs, but it is also appropriate to teach them in the context of content instruction as well. Figure 12.5 paints a picture of how these different ways of co-teaching or team teaching might occur in a classroom and how one way of working together might transition to another, with both teachers engaged.

Teachers who work together must have opportunities to *process* and share with each other the concerns and successes that are occurring in the instructional setting. It is inevitable when two professionals work closely together in the same classroom that differences in opinions will arise. When not addressed, differences often fester and can cause a breakdown in the collaborative partnership that is detrimental to the teaching relationship and to students in the class (Reeve & Hallahan, 1994).

Finally, *problem-solving* about unmet student needs and less-than-desirable achievement is crucial to program success. The goal of co-teaching is to provide meaningful access to the curriculum and facilitate achievement for all students. When results fall short of that goal, teachers must identify alternative instructional strategies or supports to assist students in accomplishing what is desired. Effective solutions often must be fine-tuned or modified before success is realized.

Linking to Other Professionals   Expertise to support student success can be found within a school building, and colleagues with special expertise include special education teachers, transition specialists, counselors, media specialists, nurses, and administrators. Within a school district, other professionals who can help support student success include special education and curriculum-area coordinators, inclusion facilitators, assistive technology teams, psychologists, speech/language therapists, and occupational therapists. At the community, state, and national level, teachers can access technical assistance teams, mental health providers, community assistance boards and agencies, advocacy and professional organizations, and journals. And finally, the Internet provides ready access and resources to teachers.

Focus and Reflect

- What conflicts might arise between two teachers who are unaccustomed to sharing instructional responsibility?
- What might occur in a co-teaching relationship if either teacher (special education or general education) does not contribute fully to the partnership?

FIGURE 12.5
Team Teaching

At this point in instruction, one teacher is presenting information to the class, while the other teacher is mapping the information (or modeling note taking, leading students through a graphic organizer, etc.)

At this point in instruction, the teachers decide to create smaller groups. They could provide different instruction for different types of learners, or the same instruction over the same content in a more intensive manner.

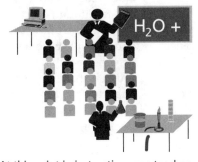

At this point in instruction, one teacher is presenting, while the other teacher is interjecting clarifications, questions, directions, or just monitoring student activity.

The teachers then decide to group students for practice or performance activities. Some groups work fairly independently under the supervision of one teacher, while one group receives more direction from a teacher.

It becomes evident that students could benefit from strategy instruction that complements learning the content. Students move from one group to the other as appropriate.

At this point in instruction, some students are working independently, some are working with a partner, and others are receiving intensive instruction. This is an example of how differentiated and leveled instruction might look.

▪ *Scenario Revisited*

Ms. Davis and Ms. Rutledge started their first co-teaching experience with excitement. As they began to plan together, each became excited about potential instructional activities that were possible when there were two teachers in the classroom. Ms. Davis was relieved that she could plan on regular support and ideas from a colleague on how to meet the needs of a challenging group of students. And the challenging students that she was thinking about included many more than those being served by special education! What a difference from past years when, not knowing that support was accessible to her, going it alone was the only perceived option. Under those conditions, she had avoided teaching classes that might have too many students with varied needs.

Trent and his mother were also approaching the new school year with more excitement than they had in the last few years. Trent felt that,

finally, he was not going to be singled out and kept apart from his friends and classmates. Because of Trent's resolve to "do better," his mother began to think about how a better year might lead to college, or some other postsecondary option as a possibility in the future. While this year needed to be tackled first, the future did look brighter.

Ms. Rutledge started the year on the run. Not only was she co-teaching for the first time, she was also teaching a strategies class, meeting with *many* teachers about necessary accommodations, and facilitating eighteen IEPs. She thought about how the role of the special education teacher had certainly become more complex over the fifteen years that she had been teaching. She found it challenging but also rewarding as opportunities unfolded for students who had been excluded in the past.

FIGURE 12.6

Expanded Graphic Organizer

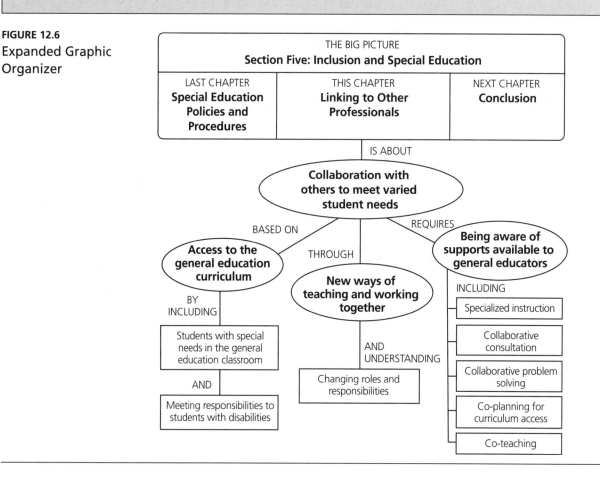

SUMMARY

What should educators and the community want for all children? We should want all children to achieve to their highest potential and participate productively and happily in their, and our, community. Educators and schools can either hinder or help in reaching that goal. To help make the best scenario a reality, it is clear that professionals must work together in a variety of ways. General educators must believe in their ethical responsibility to educate all students and know their legal responsibilities in assisting in the education of students with identified disabilities.

However, there should be many supports available to general education teachers. Special educators, along with administrators and other support personnel, have the responsibility to coordinate and provide their general education colleagues with easy access to such supports. Effectively linking professionals to meet the needs of *all* students is a new way of working that uses both effective instructional strategies and the cumulative expertise of education professionals to achieve the highest standards of learning for all within the general education curriculum.

MAKING CONNECTIONS:
Linking to Other Professionals in Secondary Schools

1. *Here are the big ideas to get you started:*
   - Both special education teachers and general education teachers have a role to play in educating secondary students with special learning needs. General education teachers need to be involved in the selection and the implementation of adaptations and accommodations in the general education classroom to better serve all students—those with and without special needs. There are many students who find it difficult to learn and who are difficult to teach. However, you do not have to have all the answers. There are many ways to get assistance.

2. *Try this:*
Here are some things for you to think about in planning for linking to other professionals in a building, district, and region:
   - Identify all the people in a middle-school or high school building with which you are familiar who could provide assistance and support in educating students with disabilities.
   - Talk to special education teachers or other special services personnel from a middle school or high school and ask them to explain

to you the range of services and supports available in their building for students with disabilities and how teachers can initiate assistance when needed.
   - Ask a special education teacher how a teacher might get assistance in providing accommodations or modifications when they do not have the needed knowledge or skills, or how they might go about modifying materials or procedures.

3. *Next steps:*
   - If possible, sit in on an IEP meeting to observe the discussion and begin to think about how you might contribute to this kind of planning for a student.
   - If you have the opportunity during a field experience or student teaching assignment, ask your cooperating teacher for a list of students whom you may be observing or with whom you may be working. Ask the teacher to go through the list and describe the instructional needs of each student whom you will be teaching. Inquire about students who have IEPs or individual plans that might contain information that you should use to guide your planning and teaching. Ask also for information about the types of accommodations, modifications, or other instructional considerations that may be needed for each student.

WEB SITES

http://www.ed.gov/offices/OSERS/IDEA From the U.S. Office of Special Education Programs, this site provides links for information about IDEA '97 Amendments and Final Regulations.

http://powerof2.org Site for OSEP-sponsored project to assist educators in successfully including children with special needs in the general education classroom.

http://ldonline.org Site of LD Online, featuring information and resources about learning disabilities.

http://www.cast.org/udl Site of the Center for Applied Special Technology with links to sites with information about Universal Design for Learning (UDL) principles and applications.

REFERENCES

Bauwens, J., & Hourcade, J. J. (1995). *Cooperative teaching: Rebuilding the schoolhouse for all students.* Austin, TX: Pro-Ed.

Chard, D., Vaughn, S., & Thurlow, M. (2000, April 5–8). *Providing access to the general education curriculum.* Presentation at Council for Exceptional Children International Conference, Vancouver, Canada.

Committee on Labor and Human Resources. (1997, May 9). *Report [to accompany S.717].* Washington, DC: Government Printing Office.

Friend, M., & Cook, L. (1995). *Interactions: Collaboration skills for school professionals.* White Plains, NY: Longman.

Garnett, K. (1996). *Thinking about inclusion and learning disabilities: A teacher's guide.* Reston, VA: Council for Exceptional Children.

Goodlad, J. I., & Field, S. (1993). Teachers for renewing schools. In J. I. Goodlad & T. C. Lovitt (Eds.), *Integrating general and special education* (pp. 229–252). New York: Merrill.

Knackendoffel, A., Robinson, S., Deshler, D., & Schumaker, J. (1992). *Collaborative problem solving.* Lawrence, KS: Edge Enterprises.

National Information Center for Children & Youth Services (June, 1998). *News Digest,* Volume 26.

Newmann, F. M., & Wehlage, G. G. (1995). *Successful school restructuring: A report to the public and educators.* Madison, WI: Center for Education Research.

Positive Behavioral Support. (Winter, 1999). *Research connections in special education.* (ERIC/OSEP Special Project). Reston, VA: The Council for Exceptional Children.

Reeve, P., & Hallahan, D. (1994). Practical questions about collaboration between general and special educators. *Focus on Exceptional Children, 26* (7), 1–11.

Robinson, S. (1991). Collaborative Consultation. In B. Y. L. Wong (Ed.), *Learning about learning disabilities.* San Diego: Academic Press.

Thousand, J. S., & Villa, R. A. (1995). Managing complex change toward inclusive schooling. In R. A. Villa & J. S. Thousand (Eds.), *Creating an inclusive school* (pp. 51–79). Alexandria, VA: Association for Supervision and Curriculum Development

Vaughn, S., & Schumm, J. (1996). Classroom ecologies: Classroom interactions and implications for inclusion of students with learning disabilities. In D. L. Speece & B. K. Keogh (Eds.), *Research on classroom ecologies: Implications for inclusion of children with learning disabilities* (pp. 107–124). Mahwah, NJ: Lawrence Erlbaum Associates.

Conclusion
Models of Integrated Organizers

Throughout this text we have emphasized the importance of thinking about inclusive teaching in a a new way—within a new paradigm. This paradigm is based on the seven principles we set out in the introduction to this text:

1. Diversity among students in secondary schools must be regarded as representing the norm, rather than the exception.
2. A new way to think about inclusive teaching to accommodate academic diversity among students is for teachers to focus on *making connections* between themselves and students, between students and students and, most importantly, between students and the content they must learn.
3. Making connections can be realized by *selecting critical content*.
4. Making connections can be realized by *building a learning community* in the classroom.
5. Making connections depends on learning about and understanding what students already know.
6. Making connections can be realized by *enhancing instruction* through teaching routines to compensate for the learning problems of students.
7. Making connections can be realized by *teaching students how to learn*.

Chapter 1 established that a first step in addressing diversity is to view it as the norm and to understand and accept the differences that learners bring with them into your classroom. In Chapter 2, we discussed how standards-based reform has prompted a focus on having all students meet higher standards. Getting from establishing standards to having all students meet those standards, however, presents many challenges. Curriculum, materials, and assessments must be aligned with the standards. Moreover, teachers, faced with students with diverse learning needs, have to have a range of methods at hand to address those learning needs so that all students have an equal opportunity to learn. While we cannot expect that all students will reach exactly the same level of achievement, we should expect that all groups of students—regardless of race, ethnicity, gender, learning disability, or socioeconomic status—should have similar patterns of achievement. That must be our goal if standards-based reform is to be equitable.

In Chapter 3 we discussed why you, as the teacher, are also the curriculum maker responsible for translating content standards into clearly defined critical outcomes that all students will be expected to learn.

In Chapters 4, 5, and 6 we discussed how to translate curricular goals into course-planning decisions that will determine specific learning goals, as well as what kind of learning community you will establish in your classroom. The learning community is shaped by how you involve the particular students you have in your classroom in learning—what their prior knowledge and experience is, what engages them in learning, what they know about how to learn. Knowing your students and letting them get to know you and each other helps to build a learning community that can support student learning in ways that one teacher, working alone, simply cannot.

The process of making connections continues as you use planning and teaching routines to organize content to make it more learner-friendly. These planning and teaching routines can also, as discussed in Chapters 7, 8, and 9, provide a way for you to be explicit about the content that students will need to learn and also the routines and strategies you and they will be using to learn the content. By developing or sharing your plans with students, you can provide an opportunity for students to tell you and each other what they know and understand already and what they are interested in learning and understanding. Lilia Bartolome (1994) has argued that this "legitimizes and treats as valuable student language and cultural experiences usually ignored in classrooms" (p. 188).

In Chapter 10, we discussed learning strategies and how teaching students such strategies can help them become independent learners. Some teachers may be reluctant to take the time to teach students how to learn, because in secondary schools there is so much content to be covered. Each teacher must thoughtfully consider whether the students they have in their classroom have the tools needed to learn the content they must learn. Will students learn more effectively if time is taken to teach them how to learn? This is an important question to consider as you plan to teach your course.

In Chapter 11, we discussed some of the issues to consider when you have students with identified special needs in your classroom. And in Chapter 12 we described how other professionals can help and support you as you work to address those needs.

The challenge now is to put all the pieces together in preparing to teach inclusively and strategically. And the challenge rests not only in understanding and implementing the methods described in this text, but, most importantly, understanding that you cannot do it all at once. Begin with the basics and build.

While you should not expect to master immediately all the ideas presented in this text, we do want to give you a snapshot of what the whole process can look like when a teacher builds a learning community through planning a course, units, and lessons incorporating content enhancement routines and learning strategies to help students organize, understand, and remember information and ideas.

PUTTING IT ALL TOGETHER

To illustrate how all the elements of the pedagogies for diversity discussed in this book can be brought together, we will look at how one teacher might plan a course in The Ancient and Medieval World for seventh-grade social studies.

SMARTER Planning

The **SMARTER** steps that capture the linear process of making decisions that lead to more inclusive practice in the classroom:

- **S**hape the Critical Questions
- **M**ap the Critical Content
- **A**nalyze for Learning Difficulties
- **R**each Enhancement Decisions
- **T**each Strategically
- **E**valuate Mastery
- **R**evisit Outcomes

Because the first step in the SMARTER planning process is to select critical ideas, a careful examination of the textbook and the relevant standards is in order. For example, looking at the California Standards for World History and Geography for grade 7, we see that much of the emphasis is on analyzing the geographic, political, economic, religious, and social structures of civilizations prospering during the period 500–1789 AD, so a place to begin is to select at least one important aspect of each civilization in each of these areas.

It is important to be selective, because there is obviously an enormous amount of information and many ideas that could be learned. It is not realistic to anticipate that 7th graders, most of whom probably know very little about world history, can take in and remember this wealth of information, so you must think in terms of the important basics you want them to learn and remember. If you and your students are successful in establishing a basic understanding of the important features of world history, students will have a good foundation on which to build future learning.

Mapping the content can be a helpful way to sort out the critical information. While mapping the critical content is the second step in SMARTER, it may be done in tandem with selecting the content. You may be able to see relationships and connections more clearly if you map them rather than just list them. Figure C.1 shows how our course on The Ancient and Medieval World might be mapped.

You will note in this map that provision is made for identifying the important concepts to be learned in the course, as well as unit topics. This can be another helpful part of selecting critical content, by sketching it out in a map or on an organizer.

Another element in the standards is important developments like the rise of world religions, feudalism, the Reformation, the Renaissance, the scientific revolution, and the beginnings of modern democratic ideas. These topics will involve many concepts that may be difficult for students to understand. Here is where you may want to think about structuring your course differently than your textbook. For example, a text might include the Reformation as one chapter in a larger unit on events in Europe (see, for example, Armento, Nash, Salter, & Wixson, 1991). You may decide that the Reformation is too important and too complicated to be looked at that quickly. As part of your planning to select critical content and to enhance instruction and learning of that content, you could make the Reformation the focus of a whole unit of instruction. Using a unit organizer, you can organize this content more clearly for students and set out important supporting information. Figures C.2a and 2b show how a unit on the Reformation might be organized.

You can then take your planning to a greater level of detail in a Lesson Organizer. A good way to approach the Reformation may be to look at major figures who founded Protestant churches. For example, a lesson on Martin Luther (see Figure C.3) can highlight important ideas of the Reformation as well as the impact of his actions throughout Europe.

In planning to teach abstract ideas in this course, it becomes particularly important to consider what might be difficult for seventh-grade students to learn about these topics (**A**nalyze for learning difficulties) and what content enhancement devices and routines you might wish to use to support student learning (**R**each enhancement decisions). One way to enhance

FIGURE C.1 Course Map

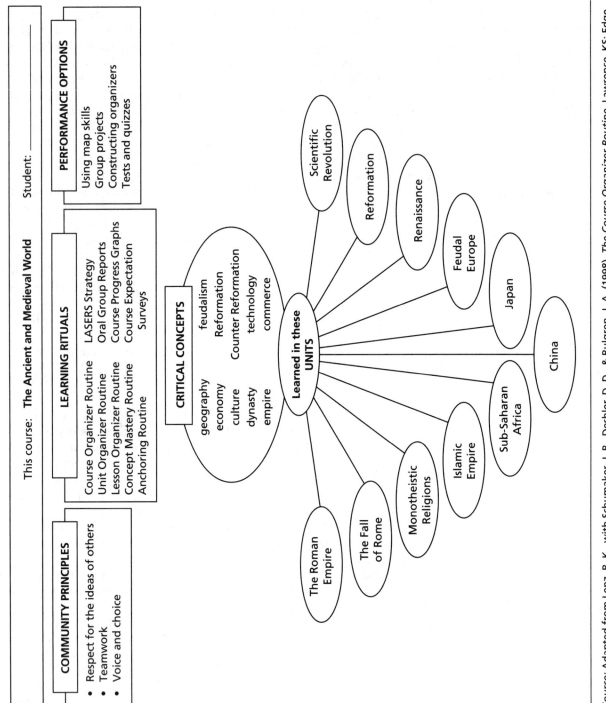

This course: **The Ancient and Medieval World**   Student: _____

COMMUNITY PRINCIPLES

• Respect for the ideas of others
• Teamwork
• Voice and choice

LEARNING RITUALS

Course Organizer Routine   LASERS Strategy
Unit Organizer Routine   Oral Group Reports
Lesson Organizer Routine   Course Progress Graphs
Concept Mastery Routine   Course Expectation
Anchoring Routine   Surveys

PERFORMANCE OPTIONS

Using map skills
Group projects
Constructing organizers
Tests and quizzes

CRITICAL CONCEPTS

geography   feudalism
economy   Reformation
culture   Counter Reformation
dynasty   technology
empire   commerce

Learned in these UNITS

The Roman Empire
The Fall of Rome
Monotheistic Religions
Islamic Empire
Sub-Saharan Africa
China
Japan
Feudal Europe
Renaissance
Reformation
Scientific Revolution

Source: Adapted from Lenz, B. K., with Schumaker, J. B., Deshler, D. D., & Bulgren, J. A. (1998). *The Course Organizer Routine.* Lawrence, KS: Edge Enterprises; and Armento, B. J., Nash, G. B., Salter, C. L., and Wixson, K. K. (1991). *Across the centuries.* Boston: Houghton Mifflin, pp. vi–vii.

FIGURE C.2A The Unit Organizer

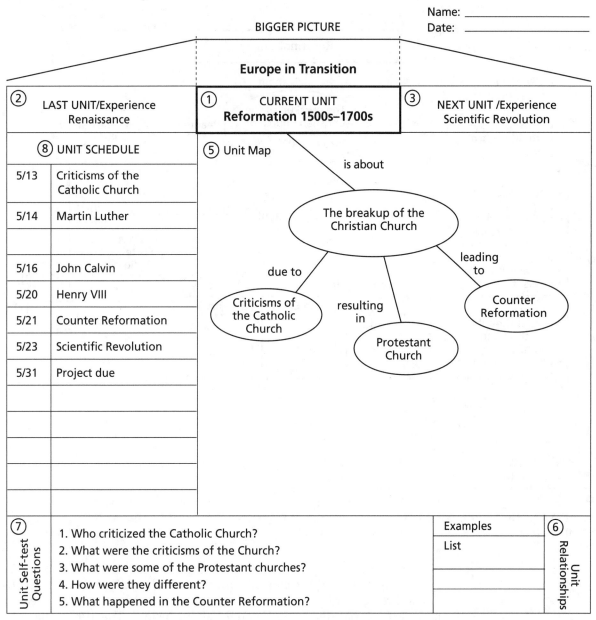

Source: Adapted by C. Spriggs & P. Hamilton from Lenz, B. K., with Bulgren, J. A., Schumaker, J. B., Deshler, D. D., & Boudah, D. A. (1994). *The Unit Organizer Routine.* Lawrence, KS: Edge Enterprises.

instruction and compensate for the lack of prior knowledge among students may be to "anchor" new learning to an event or idea they will understand. In our course on The Ancient and Medieval World, we could use an anchoring routine to help students better understand the significance of the Reformation by anchoring it to the idea of divorce. (See Figure C.4.)

The next step in SMARTER is teaching strategically. Having identified the important information and relationships you want to teach, it is important

FIGURE C.2B The Unit Organizer

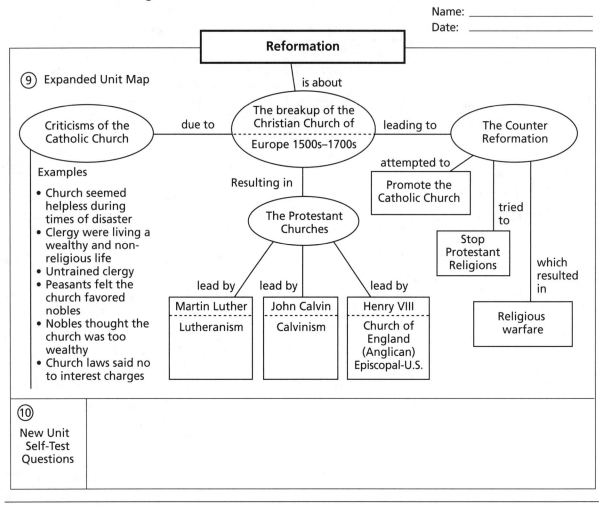

Source: Adapted by C. Spriggs & P. Hamilton from Lenz, B. K., with Bulgren, J. A., Schumaker, J. B., Deshler, D. D., & Boudah, D. A. (1994). *The Unit Organizer Routine.* Lawrence, KS: Edge Enterprises.

to develop the mind-set that this information should be shared with students throughout the course. Let your students see how you, as a learner more expert than they, have thought about history. This can be the kind of compelling pedagogy McNeil (2000) observed and described in an exemplary teacher, whose student exclaimed "He let us see his mind at work" (p. 119).

Another element in teaching strategically is to help students see the value of using strategies to learn more effectively. A strategy that might be taught to students in a social studies class is the LASERS Review Strategy (Lenz, 1993). This strategy can provide a systematic way for students to approach information in a textbook, and it can also help them to construct their own unit and lesson organizers as a learning activity.

Before, during, or after content planning is done, thought may be given to how to establish a true learning community in your course. This is where

FIGURE C.3   Lesson Organizer

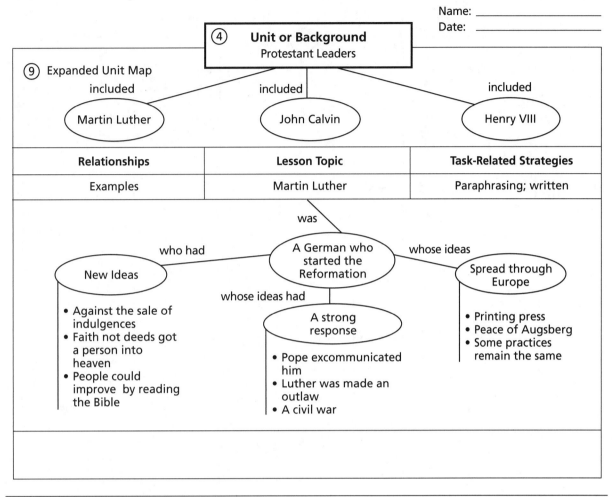

Source: Adapted by C. Spriggs & P. Hamilton from Lenz, B. K., with Marrs, R. W., Schumaker, J. B., Deshler, D. D., & Boudah, D. A. (1993). *The Lesson Organizer Routine.* Lawrence, KS: Edge Enterprises.

the important community principles, learning rituals, and performance options may be identified and made explicit for students. While you can begin identifying what these principles, rituals, and options might be, it is important to remember that your students should be given an opportunity to express their ideas about these features of the learning community so that they have some sense of ownership in the course.

In Figure C.1 you can see that respect for the ideas of others is listed as an important principle. This becomes particularly important in a course where the ideas under study have been ones that mankind has debated and fought about over the years. You will also notice that the content enhancement teaching routines discussed have been listed among the learning rituals for the course. This helps students see that these ways of learning are important and will be used regularly in the course. Identifying the importance of teaching routines up front helps students see that they are worth

FIGURE C.4 Anchoring

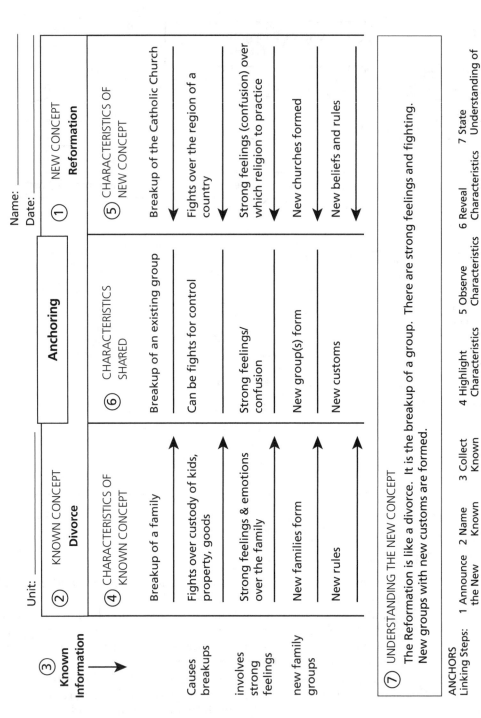

Source: Adapted by C. Spriggs & P. Hamilton. From *The Concept Anchoring Routine*, by J. A. Bulgren, J. B. Schumaker, and D.D. Deshler, 1994. Lawrence, KS: Edge Enterprises. Copyright 1994 by Edge Enterprises.

330

■ *The LASERS Review Strategy*

List key words (without notes). Think about what you have learned in the unit. Using small pieces of paper, list a key word or idea (using no more than 2 or 3 words) on each piece of paper. Don't use your notes. Try to remember what you have learned.

Arrange content into a map. Once you have listed the key words on the pieces of paper, arrange the key words into a diagram on a large sheet of paper (or several sheets of paper). The diagram should show how the information in the unit might be organized to show relationships. To help you draw a good diagram, use the ZAP steps:

1. *Zone into 3 or more levels* to ask yourself what this unit is about, what the main parts of the unit are about, and what each part is about. Repeat these steps until you have a unit title and 3 levels or "zones" of information.

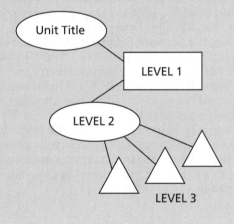

2. *Analyze relationships.* Once you think you have diagrammed the information in the unit, look at your levels and groups and think about how each group of information is related. Ask yourself, "Why do all these pieces of paper go in this group?" and "How are the groups related?" and "What are the relationships between the pieces of information in this group?"
3. *Place line labels.* After you have decided what you think the relationships are between the groups of information, draw lines between the pieces of paper and label the lines to show the relationships.

Share with a partner. When your diagram is completed, pair up with someone else who has completed a unit diagram and compare and contrast the two diagrams.

Evaluate (with notes). Begin working on your own again, and open your notes and examine your Unit Organizer. Consider changes.

Revise (with notes). After you have evaluated your diagram, use your notes and study guide to revise your diagram. Make sure you have three or more levels of information and that the important relationships between the levels of information are written on the diagram.

Self-Test. Ask yourself questions about the information in your diagram. Use the unit self-test questions.

learning to understand and use. Another learning ritual identified in this course map is expectation surveys and feedback. This can tell students you care about how learning is going for them in the course, and you intend to provide ways for students to communicate with you about their interests, progress, and learning difficulties. Finally, listing the performance options allows students to see that they will have a variety of opportunities to show you what they have learned. Identifying performance options can also be another way to indicate to students what is important in the course. For example, indicating that map skills will be used tells students that this will be an important skill they will be practicing and using throughout the course.

The final two steps in SMARTER prompt you to evaluate mastery and revisit outcomes. This has long been an important part of teaching and only becomes more so in an era of standards-based reform. Are all students learning the critical information? Are your instructional methods supporting the learning of all students? Are students helping each other learn? Are patterns of achievement equitable among all groups of students—rich and poor, White and non-White, for example? These are challenging goals that are not easily achieved in a week or a month or even a year. But they are the goals we must set ourselves and continually work toward if we are ever to hope to include all students in learning.

Strategic teaching is instruction that:

- *Is informed,* telling students about the routines or methods that will be used to promote their learning.
- *Is explicit,* being clear with students about the goals and expected outcomes of instruction. Explicit instruction also involves reminding students when teaching routines are being used and then guiding them to effectively participate in use of the routines to succeed in learning.
- *Develops learning partnerships* that show respect for the experiences, beliefs, and values of students by developing lessons that build on what students know and allowing students to have a voice in determining how information will be explored and learned.
- *Communicates the value of using strategies,* helping students learn the connection between learning content and using good strategies by making sure students see that using strategies increases their learning.

REFERENCES

Armento, B. J., Nash, G. B., Salter, C. L., and Wixson, K. K. (1991). *Across the centuries.* Boston: Houghton Mifflin.

Bartolome, L. I. (1994). Beyond the methods fetish: Toward a humanizing pedagogy. *Harvard Educational Review,* 63(2), pp. 173–194.

Bulgren, J. A., Schumaker, J. B., & Deshler, D. D. (1994). *The anchoring routine.* Lawrence, KS: Edge Enterprises.

California State Board of Education Standards—Grade 7—World History and Geography. *http://www.csun.edu/~hcbio027/k12standards/standards/Grade7.html.*

Hamilton, P., & Spriggs, C. (1995–1996). Example Set of Content Enhancement Routines. Turlock Junior High School, Turlock, CA. Unpublished.

Lenz, B. K., with Schumaker, J. B., Deshler, D. D., & Bulgren, J. A. (1998). *The course organizer routine.* Lawrence, KS: Edge Enterprises.

Lenz, B. K., with Bulgren, J. A., Schumaker, J. B., Deshler, D. D., & Boudah, D. A. (1994). *The unit organizer routine.* Lawrence, KS: Edge Enterprises.

Lenz, B. K., Marrs, R. W., Schumaker, J. B., & Deshler, D. D. (1993). *The lesson organizer routine.* Lawrence, KS: Edge Enterprises.

Lenz, B. K. (1993). *The LASERS review strategy.* Lawrence, KS: Center for Research on Learning.

McNeil, L. M. (2000). *Contradictions of school reform—Educational costs of standardized testing,* New York: Routledge.

A Learner-Centered Psychological Principles

A Framework for School Redesign and Reform

The following list prepared by the Learner-Centered Principles Work Group of the American Psychological Association's Board of Educational Affairs (1997) was developed in response to the growing need to blend learning theory with efforts to reform and redesign schools. This list of 14 principles represents one of the best efforts to summarize some of the more critical aspects of our knowledge of learning.

SUMMARY OF LEARNER-CENTERED PSYCHOLOGICAL PRINCIPLES

Cognitive and Metacognitive Factors:

Nature of the learning process
Goals of the learning process
Construction of knowledge
Strategic thinking
Thinking about thinking
Context of learning

Motivational and Affective Factors:

Motivational and emotional influences of learning
Intrinsic motivation to learn
Effects of motivation on effort

Developmental and Social Factors:

Developmental influences on learning
Social influences on learning

Individual Differences Factors:

Individual differences in learning
Learning and diversity
Standards and assessment

COGNITIVE AND METACOGNITIVE FACTORS

1. *Nature of the learning process.* The learning of complex subject matter is most effective when it is an intentional process of constructing meaning from information and experience.

2. *Goals of the learning process.* The successful learner, over time and with support and instructional guidance, can create meaningful, coherent representations of knowledge. The strategic nature of learning requires students to be goal directed. To construct useful representations of knowledge and to acquire the thinking and learning strategies necessary for continued learning success across the life span, students must generate and pursue personally relevant goals.

3. *Construction of knowledge.* The successful learner can link new information with existing knowledge in meaningful ways. Knowledge widens and deepens as students continue to build links between new information and experiences and their existing knowledge base. However, unless new knowledge becomes integrated with the learner's prior knowledge and understanding, this knowledge remains isolated, cannot be used effectively in new tasks, and does not transfer readily to new situations.

4. *Strategic thinking.* The successful learner can create and use a repertoire of thinking and reasoning strategies to achieve complex learning goals. They understand and use a variety of strategies to help them reach learning and performance goals and to apply their knowledge in novel situations. They also continue to expand their repertoire of strategies by reflecting on the methods they use to see which ones work well for them, by receiving guided instructions and feedback, and by observing or interacting with appropriate models.

5. *Thinking about thinking.* Higher order strategies for selecting and monitoring mental operations facilitate creative and critical thinking. Successful learners can reflect on how they think and learn, set reasonable learning or performance goals, select potentially appropriate learning strategies or methods, and monitor their progress toward these goals. In addition, successful learners know what to do if a problem occurs or if they are not making sufficient or timely progress toward a goal. They can generate alternative methods to reach their goal (or reassess the appropriateness and utility of their goal).

6. *Context of learning.* Learning is influenced by environmental factors, including culture, technology, and instructional practices. Cultural or group influences on students can affect many educationally relevant variables, such as motivation, orientation toward learning, and new ways of thinking. Technologies and instructional practices must be appropriate for a learner's levels of prior knowledge, cognitive abilities, and their learning and thinking strategies. The classroom environment, particularly whether it is nurturing or not, can also have a significant impact on student learning.

MOTIVATIONAL AND AFFECTIVE FACTORS

7. *Motivational and emotional influences on learning.* What and how much is learned is influenced by the learner's motivation. Motivation to learn, in turn, is influenced by the individual's emotional stress, beliefs, interests, goals, and habits of thinking. Positive emotions, such as curiosity, generally enhance motivation and facilitate learning and performance. Mild anxiety can also enhance learning and performance by focusing the learner's attention on a particular task. However, intense negative emotions (e.g., anxiety, panic, rage, insecurity) and related thoughts (e.g., worrying about competence, ruminating about failure, fearing punishment, ridicule, or stigmatizing labels) generally detract from motivation, interfere with learning, and contribute to low performance.

8. *Intrinsic motivation to learn.* The learner's creativity, higher-order thinking, and natural curiosity all contribute to motivation to learn. Intrinsic motivation is stimulated by tasks of optimal novelty and difficulty, relevant to personal interests, and providing for personal choice and control.

9. *Effects of motivation on effort.* Acquisition of complex knowledge and skills requires extended learner effort and guided practice. Without learner's motivation to learn, the willingness to exert is unlikely without coercion. Educators need to be concerned with facilitating motivation by using strategies that enhance learner effort and commitment to learning and to achieving high standards of comprehension and understanding. Effective strategies include purposeful learning activities, guided by practices that enhance positive emotions and intrinsic motivation to learn and methods that increase learner's perceptions that a task is interesting and personally relevant.

DEVELOPMENTAL AND SOCIAL FACTORS

10. *Developmental influences on learning.* As individuals develop they encounter different opportunities and experience different constraints for learning. Learning is most effective when differential development across physical, intellectual, emotional, and social domains is taken into account. Because individual development varies across domains, achievement in different instructional domains may vary.

11. *Social influences on learning.* Learning is influenced by social interactions, interpersonal relations, and communication with others. Learning can be enhanced when the learner has an opportunity to interact and to collaborate with others on instructional tasks. Learning settings that allow for social interactions and respect diversity encourage flexible thinking and social competence. Quality personal relationships that provide stability, trust, and caring can increase a learner's sense of belonging, self-respect, and self-acceptance and provide a positive climate for learning. Family factors that interfere with optimal learning include negative beliefs about competence in a particular subject, high levels of test anxiety, negative sex role expectations, and undue pressure to perform well. Positive learning climates can also help to establish the context for healthier levels of thinking, feeling, and behaving. Such contexts help learners to feel safe to share ideas, actively participate in the learning process, and create a sense of community.

INDIVIDUAL DIFFERENCES FACTORS

12. *Individual differences in learning.* Learners have different strategies, approaches, and capabilities for learning that are a function of prior experience and heredity.

13. *Learning and diversity.* Learning is most effective when differences in learner's linguistic, cultural, and social backgrounds are taken into account.

14. *Standards and assessment.* Setting appropriately high and challenging standards and assessing the learner and learning process, including diagnostic process and outcome assessment, are integral parts of the learning process.

Source: From *Learner-Centered Psychological Principles: A Framework for School Redesign and Reform.* Revision prepared by a Work Group of the American Psychological Association's Board of Educational Affairs, 1997. Copyright 1997 by the American Psychological Association. Reprinted with permission.

B Using SMARTER to Enhance Instruction

Margaret E. King-Sears
Jean F. Mooney

SMARTER FOR SOCIAL STUDIES

Shape the Critical Questions

Sylvia Hernandez teaches ninth grade history in a suburban school district in which the local school system has targeted these critical outcomes for the year:

- Understand democratic republic, citizen, common good, and so on, to help learners construct the meaning of ideals that U.S. citizens hold in common;
- Understand class, race, equal access, and so on; help learners ask how to live in communities characterized by both unity and diversity and how to close the gap between ideals and reality; and
- Understand government structures in local, state, and federal systems in the United States.

One of the course questions is: How do government structures vary and how are they the same at local, state, and national levels? Ms. Hernandez's current unit is on government structures, and one of the unit outcomes she sets forth is: *Students will analyze varied government structures and describe what impact the structures have on diverse communities.*

Map the Critical Content

The unit organizer Sylvia Hernandez develops focuses first on the terms that will be used to discuss the government structures. The unit progresses from providing a rich background and understanding of the terms to the use of multiple terms that she expects to see used when students write about, discuss, and compare and contrast varied government structures.

Analyze for Learning Difficulties

Ms. Hernandez realizes that students must not only know words and definitions, but also be able to talk about important ideas and relate the words and ideas to each other. However, she wants to ascertain whether they already know this information, so part of her pretest is to have students respond to queries about the main ideas and relationships in the content for this unit. VanSledright (1995) describes how social studies instruction can be fragmented and unconnected for students, and so having students respond in the pretest to items about vocabulary, big ideas, *and* relationships helps Ms. Hernandez to know more about her students' knowledge base in advance. Students' scores from the pretest confirm that the students can list vocabulary and define some terms, but they are not clear on big ideas and relationships among terms. In particular, students are "fuzzy" on the concept of federalism—few define it correctly, and no one can relate it in a meaningful way to their community. She decides to use a Concept Anchoring Routine (Bulgren, Schumaker, & Deshler, 1994) to teach federalism.

Reach Enhancement Decisions

To introduce the concept of federalism, Ms. Hernandez "anchors" the concept to something the students are already familiar with: decision making in their school. Each student has a Concept Anchoring graphic, and she uses an overhead of the same graphic (see Figure B.1) to introduce the new concept (federalism) and link it to the known

FIGURE B.1 The Teaching Device: The Anchoring Table

Name: _____

Date: _____

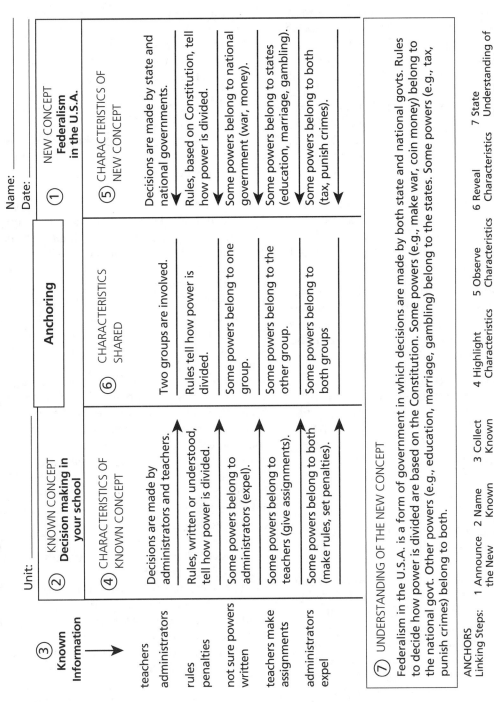

Unit: _____

③ Known Information →	② KNOWN CONCEPT **Decision making in your school**	**Anchoring**	① NEW CONCEPT **Federalism in the U.S.A.**
	④ CHARACTERISTICS OF KNOWN CONCEPT	⑥ CHARACTERISTICS SHARED	⑤ CHARACTERISTICS OF NEW CONCEPT

Known Information →

teachers
administrators

rules
penalties

not sure powers
written

teachers make
assignments

administrators
expel

④ CHARACTERISTICS OF KNOWN CONCEPT

Decisions are made by administrators and teachers. ↑

Rules, written or understood, tell how power is divided. ↑

Some powers belong to administrators (expel). ↑

Some powers belong to teachers (give assignments). ↑

Some powers belong to both (make rules, set penalties). ↑

⑥ CHARACTERISTICS SHARED

Two groups are involved.

Rules tell how power is divided.

Some powers belong to one group.

Some powers belong to the other group.

Some powers belong to both groups

⑤ CHARACTERISTICS OF NEW CONCEPT

Decisions are made by state and national governments.

Rules, based on Constitution, tell how power is divided. ↓

Some powers belong to national government (war, money). ↓

Some powers belong to states (education, marriage, gambling). ↓

Some powers belong to both (tax, punish crimes). ↓

⑦ UNDERSTANDING OF THE NEW CONCEPT

Federalism in the U.S.A. is a form of government in which decisions are made by both state and national govts. Rules to decide how power is divided are based on the Constitution. Some powers (e.g., make war, coin money) belong to the national govt. Other powers (e.g., education, marriage, gambling) belong to the states. Some powers (e.g., tax, punish crimes) belong to both.

ANCHORS
Linking Steps:

| 1 Announce the New Concept | 2 Name Known Concept | 3 Collect Known Information | 4 Highlight Characteristics of Known Concept | 5 Observe Characteristics of New Concept | 6 Reveal Characteristics Shared | 7 State Understanding of New Concept |

Source: From The Concept Anchoring Routine (p. 35) by J. A. Bulgren, J. B. Schumaker, & D. D. Deshler, 1994, Lawrence, KS: Edge Enterprises. Copyright 1994 by Edge Enterprises. Reprinted with permission.

concept (decision making at our school). Then, to tap into students' background knowledge about decision making at their school, she elicits from the students what they already know about how decisions are made at their school. Note that in Figure B.1, the flow of the dialogue with the students follows the numbered sections on the graphic itself. After eliciting students' background knowledge on the familiar concept, Ms. Hernandez then uses the students' words to begin filling in the characteristics of the known concept (4 on the graphic). Discussion and dialogue with the students at this point is intended to clarify what they know, as well as misconceptions. Although Ms. Hernandez fills in the graphic with the students, she has filled one out beforehand for two key reasons:

1. She knows the critical characteristics that need to be emphasized for federalism; and
2. She has already matched federalism's characteristics to school decision-making characteristics.

Once the students have been actively involved in providing the known information about decision making at their school, she puts it on the graphic. She can then "fill in the blanks" with the characteristics omitted that she knows they will eventually link to federalism.

Teach Strategically

This process of using the Concept Anchoring Routine enables Ms. Hernandez to actively involve students, elicit background knowledge, clarify misconceptions, and discuss real-life analogies for the characteristics of federalism and for federalism as a concept. The likelihood that students will remember the new concept and its characteristics is significantly enhanced because the meaning is linked to something they already understand and live with—decision making at their school. Although it does take time to use the concept anchoring routine—remember, Ms. Hernandez has much to teach the students this year—she realizes there will be multiple benefits throughout this unit and subsequent units because she:

- established, at the beginning of the year, a graphic routine that will be useful in teaching new concepts;

- identified concepts that will be abstract for students with varied background knowledge to understand;
- has planned in advance for analogies to link familiar concepts to new abstract concepts, providing the students with an "anchor" for understanding the new concept; and
- will continue to use the graphic routine throughout subsequent units so that students become familiar with the routine.

Kameenui and Carnine (1998) refer to what Ms. Hernandez is doing as planning and presenting instruction using "big ideas" instead of multiple—and often disconnected—themes, using conspicuous instead of implicit strategies, and explicitly drawing upon students' background knowledge. After grounding the students with the familiar known concept, Ms. Hernandez makes links to federalism (5 on the graphic). She takes the time to involve students in the linkages, and, again, fills in the gaps when they do not know the information. Then together they complete section 6 on the graphic (Characteristics Shared). Finally, the new concept is defined by combining numbers 1 and 5. Using this type of map enables students to build knowledge structures—or schemas—linked to relevant and meaningful information. VanSickle and Hoge (1991) maintain that *without* such a foundation, critical thinking will not occur and cannot be learned.

The teaching steps Ms. Hernandez has used are identified by a mnemonic: ANCHORS (for Announce, Name, Collect, Highlight, Observe, Reveal, State; refer to Figure B.1). She explicitly teaches ANCHORS at the beginning of the school year. By the end of the first grading period, students anticipate use of the graphic when new abstract concepts are introduced. Ms. Hernandez is getting to a point where she can provide the new and the known concept and have students work in small groups to consolidate information on the known concept. Furthermore, students use the graphic routines to study for tests and review previously learned and new content.

Note that if teachers use the graphic device only once (to present one concept only), then the importance of the device will not be conveyed to students. The process of developing students' higher-order thinking skills is only maximized when the ANCHORS process is both explicitly taught and used in class and across content in the course (when the content lends itself to linking unfamiliar to more familiar experiences). The value of using such graphic routines is that students learn how to:

- develop content for the graphic;
- use the process to guide them with similar content;
- realize when this graphic is the appropriate one to use; and
- use it to study for and remember information.

In other words, a graphic device has become a strategy through the teacher's explicit use of Cue-Do-Review. It evolves into a classroom routine when students know how to use it, when to use it, why to use it, and how to evaluate its benefits.

Evaluate Mastery

Ms. Hernandez follows up on information gained in the pretest by using what Espin and Tindal (1998) call "perception probes." Perception probes can be used quickly and frequently during a unit of instruction to provide an idea of how well students are learning. The perception probe has three parts: (1) listing important words, (2) telling important ideas, and (3) relating the words and ideas. Ms. Hernandez uses the prescribed directions for perception probes (see Figure B.2); she sets aside 10 minutes at the beginning of class on two days during the week. Students have three minutes to list the most important words they can think of related to the content they are studying, and then they have three minutes to write three important ideas related to the content. Then students pair up and have two minutes to describe how the words and ideas relate to each other; some students write a short paragraph, others draw an illustration, and others reconstruct the concept anchoring graphic.

In addition to using the perception probes, Ms. Hernandez monitors student progress by looking at how homogeneous groups of students within heterogeneous classrooms are doing. For example, she needs to confirm that Joan, who is representative of the *high*-achievers in the class, is making progress similar to Samuel (the representative *a*verage achiever), Kirsten (the representa-

tive *low* achiever), and Douglas (a student with *o*ther identified learning challenges—he is receiving special education services for a learning disability in reading). She uses brief curriculum-based measurements for term definitions or identification that differentiate expectations for HALO students: Joan is expected to write all definitions from memory when responding to a prompt question; Samuel is expected to write all definitions from memory without a prompt question; and both Kirsten and Douglas are expected to match the correct term to the correct definition.

She also uses feedback sessions with individuals and groups of students, who appear to be "on the edge" of being able to apply their understanding, so that she can stretch their knowledge. Note that Joan's knowledge may be stretched to a different level (e.g., researching and describing how federal court decisions impact state regulations) than Kirsten's knowledge (e.g., Kirsten may be researching and describing how a recent city ordinance impacts her neighborhood), but *all* students are expected to be challenged and to learn meaningful, complex information.

Revisit Outcomes: Reevaluate Planning and Teaching Decisions

Ms. Hernandez notes what went well and what she wants to refine or omit after the unit is completed. First, she decides the perception probes were far better than meeting with students one-on-one. Ms. Hernandez really likes the engagement that the perception probes promoted, but she needs to refine the process in two ways:

1. Some students did very well during the role-playing of "good" and "not so good" (e.g., examples and nonexamples) in sharing sessions, but some students seemed to talk "around" the topic instead of getting more specific and talking about the content in depth.

2. Some students did not talk about the content, or took too long to get into pairs, or return to their desks after perception probes. Ms. Hernandez decides to randomly award bonus points to pairs who are on task the entire time. She expects this will increase the on-task behavior for all groups when they realize they have a chance

FIGURE B.2 Perception Probe Used by Sylvia Hernandez in Social Studies

Pretend that you have to tell a friend what you have learned in class today. You would want to tell your friend about the most important ideas discussed. You also would want to tell your friend why these words and ideas are important to remember.

IMPORTANT WORDS

List the words you think are most important to help your friend understand the material discussed in class today. You may list new words you learned for the first time in this unit, or you may list words we have talked about in previous classes. List as many important words as you can remember.

IMPORTANT IDEAS

Tell your friend three important ideas that were discussed today. You may write a phrase or a complete sentence, but be sure to provide your friend with enough information for them to know what you mean.

1.

2.

3.

PUTTING IT ALL TOGETHER

Tell how the words and ideas you listed above are related to one another. You may write a short paragraph or you may draw a sketch that shows how these ideas and words are connected. Use as many words and ideas from your lists as you like. If you need more room, use the back of this page.

Source: From "Curriculum-based measurement for secondary students," by C. A. Espin and G. Tindal, 1998. In M. R. Shinn (Ed.), *Advanced applications of curriculum-based measurements* (p. 240). New York: Guilford Press. Copyright 1998 by Guilford Press. Reprinted with permission.

to earn bonus points, and she anticipates there will be times when she is able to award bonus points to all pairs of students.

The feedback sessions have gone very well, but they are extremely time-consuming. Ms. Hernandez knows this is a balancing act: weighing the pros of students "getting" the information more independently, more quickly, and in more depth against the con of how time-consuming the process is. Keeping the feedback sessions at their current frequency and length (she found she spent 3 to 5 minutes with most students, and 8 to 12 minutes with other students) seems unreasonable for her, yet *not doing* them also does not seem feasible if she wants students to become more independent, move on to higher-order thinking, reinforce their problem-solving skills, and so on. She considers several solutions.

One solution is to develop a feedback system of rules for evaluating examples and nonexamples that she could explain to the whole class at the same time, and then use with groups or individual students as needed. With such feedback, Ms. Hernandez can minimize the amount of time she spends explaining, showing examples, and telling why items students are using are nonexamples. Another solution is to send students to each other for feedback. For example, she already knows that Douglas grasps some very complex content, even if he does have problems getting information from reading. Some students, who are considered "high-achievers," would benefit from Douglas's feedback, and this would also provide an opportunity for students to recognize each other's strengths in different areas. A third solution is to solicit volunteers (maybe parents? senior citizens?) who could assist at key times in the classroom. This would involve training the volunteers on the content information and feedback areas. Moreover, Ms. Hernandez would need to oversee their feedback sessions to ensure they were providing respectful, accurate, and "not too helpful" feedback (Ms. Hernandez knows it is not easy to learn how to provide "scaffolded," or step-by-step, feedback). From these solutions, she decides to try the first two, and meanwhile she will let her team members and administrator know she may be looking for volunteers in the future.

Scores on the unit post-test verify that using the Concept Anchoring Routine was a good idea. Ms. Hernandez sees that, before some students responded to questions on federalism, they wrote the analogy to decision making in their school in the column next to their short answer response. Other students defined federalism without needing to write cues for themselves. She is encouraged by the performance of students on the test and the depth of their understanding of the new abstract concept. Furthermore, the way the students were involved in discussing federalism during the unit was invigorating and satisfying for her. On several occasions, the students continued to make analogies between federalism and other familiar concepts—like decision making at home!

The re-use of the Concept Anchoring Routine also provides opportunities for her to conduct reviews of previously learned information, as well as embed the teaching of a strategy into the course. The reviews are critical for diverse learners, as well as the explicit instruction in the strategy (Carnine, Bean, Miller, & Zigmond, 1994). Carnine et al. recommend that reviews be sufficient, distributed, cumulative, and varied.

SMARTER FOR ENGLISH

Shape the Critical Questions

Alvin Frazier teaches eleventh-grade English, and exploring elements of literature is one of the outcomes his school district has designated for the course. A course question Mr. Frazier has developed is, Why is it important to recognize differences in writing purposes?

Map the Critical Content

One of the first quarter's outcomes is: Compare plot and theme by identifying two ways they are alike and two ways they are different.

Analyze for Learning Difficulties

On the pretest Mr. Frazier gives at the beginning of the school year, some of the items listed include identifying and describing each of the elements of literature. Students are asked to glean each of the elements from a brief passage on the pretest. Assignments Mr. Frazier has used in the past require students to be proficient and independent when:

- listening to and comprehending a lecture;
- answering questions during a discussion;
- completing an assignment or practice exercise;
- writing a paper and defending a position;
- reading a book and planning a report; and
- studying for a test.

Reach Enhancement Decisions

The class profile from the pretest results are all over the place. Some students are very adept at identifying, describing, and selecting all of the elements of literature from a brief passage. Other students identify some elements, and some students have difficulty reading the passage in its entirety. Mr. Frazier is hesitant to teach to the "average" students—primarily because he is finding it difficult to pinpoint an average he feels comfortable with, and because he is concerned about boring some students while overwhelming others. After thinking about it over the weekend, he decides to provide choices for students in selecting the literature they will read and devising how they want to show what they have learned.

He plans for three levels of literature for the students to read, one literature audiotape for a select group to listen to, and one current videotape for students to view. From the varied sources that students can select, the task remains the same: They must compare literature elements so that two similarities and two differences are identified. Prior to students selecting the literature they will read, Mr. Frazier uses a Concept Comparison Routine (Bulgren, Lenz, Deshler, & Schumaker, 1995) to distinguish plots from themes (see Figure B.3).

Teach Strategically

By teaching students the Concept Comparison Routine and how to use it, Mr. Frazier increases the probability that students will learn and use it on their own. Mr. Frazier cannot afford to leave to chance that students will implicitly recognize, learn, and use enhancements like the comparison routine. The value of initially taking the time to be explicit about how to use, when to use, why to use enhancements is offset by the future independence students acquire to promote their own higher-order thinking and develop their own strategies, after having accumulated strong foundations in key strategies.

Evaluate Mastery

Ultimately, students in this course are required to do a creative writing assignment in which each element of literature is developed. Mr. Frazier emphasizes the writing process as more than the technical process of grammar, punctuation, text organization, syntax, tone, and usage. He challenges students to understand their writing as a powerful means to reveal, develop, refine, and communicate their ideas to others (McDiarmid, Ball, & Anderson, 1989).

Students can demonstrate their mastery of literature elements in a variety of ways. Some students elect to write a play together, others elect to work in small groups to develop a set of stories that follows a family through historical events (in conjunction with a history course they are taking), and others decide to write stories on their own. Regardless of the format selected, for each student the grading rubric remains the same: Each element of literature must be identified, described, and distinguished from other elements. For students who work in groups, they must also rate themselves and their teammates on key aspects of teamwork skills.

Revisit Outcomes: Reevaluate Planning and Teaching Decisions

Mr. Frazier is pleased with the progress each student has made. Some students had difficulty with reading comprehension, but they were able to demonstrate competence with elements of literature through their selection of a format for receiving (e.g., listening to an audiotape) and expressing the information. From the range of literature sources Mr. Frazier made available, some students selected very challenging literature to read. For several of those students, he would not have matched them to such challenging literature. However, he coached them through the reading selections and found they were motivated to read the literature they had selected.

FIGURE B.3 Comparison Table

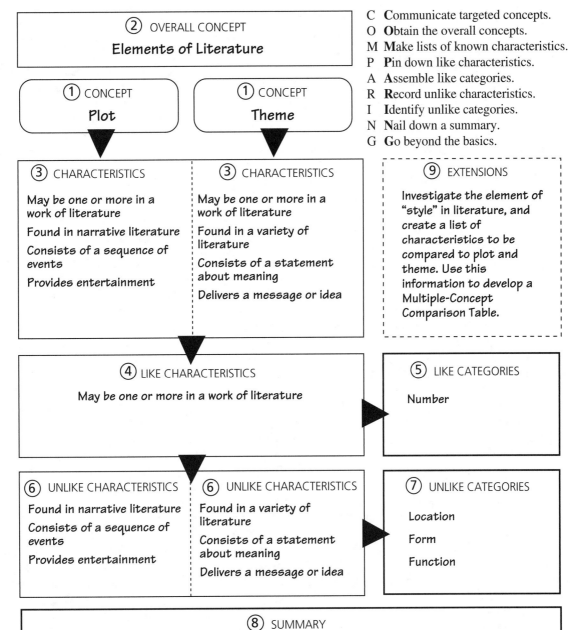

C **C**ommunicate targeted concepts.
O **O**btain the overall concepts.
M **M**ake lists of known characteristics.
P **P**in down like characteristics.
A **A**ssemble like categories.
R **R**ecord unlike characteristics.
I **I**dentify unlike categories.
N **N**ail down a summary.
G **G**o beyond the basics.

② OVERALL CONCEPT
Elements of Literature

① CONCEPT
Plot

① CONCEPT
Theme

③ CHARACTERISTICS

May be one or more in a work of literature

Found in narrative literature

Consists of a sequence of events

Provides entertainment

③ CHARACTERISTICS

May be one or more in a work of literature

Found in a variety of literature

Consists of a statement about meaning

Delivers a message or idea

⑨ EXTENSIONS

Investigate the element of "style" in literature, and create a list of characteristics to be compared to plot and theme. Use this information to develop a Multiple-Concept Comparison Table.

④ LIKE CHARACTERISTICS

May be one or more in a work of literature

⑤ LIKE CATEGORIES

Number

⑥ UNLIKE CHARACTERISTICS

Found in narrative literature

Consists of a sequence of events

Provides entertainment

⑥ UNLIKE CHARACTERISTICS

Found in a variety of literature

Consists of a statement about meaning

Delivers a message or idea

⑦ UNLIKE CATEGORIES

Location

Form

Function

⑧ SUMMARY
Two elements of literature are plot and theme. They are alike in terms of number (there may be more than one plot or theme in a piece of literature). They are different in their location in literature, the form they take, and the function they serve.

For the students who undertook to do a dual project for both the literature and history classes, the results were impressive to both Mr. Frazier and the history teacher. The teachers decided to plan for such joint projects again in the future to promote an interdisciplinary perspective for students. The history teacher also wants to learn how to use the concept comparison graphic, as some content in history is very suitable for comparison structures like that.

One area that Mr. Frazier wants to improve next time is to distribute the scoring rubric for the literature projects well enough in advance to link earlier on the real-life connections with literature. He also wants to link up with the special education teacher and reading teacher to see if instruction they provide related to vocabulary and fluency with reading could overlap with his instruction.

Variations

- Interdisciplinary instruction consists of using the same concepts and ideas across subjects so that students make connections between the same or similar topics within and among subjects. Students are frequently able to study content in more depth when it appears across subject areas for instruction.

- Student selection of literature and ways of demonstrating their knowledge provide voice and choice that increase students' motivation. Furthermore, students who have choices may select more challenging tasks and higher goals than their teachers would have selected for them, resulting in increased achievement (Fuchs, Fuchs, & Deno, 1985; Maher, 1981).

- Representing new content by anchoring it to items that students find meaningful is essential. For example, McDiarmid et al. (1989) suggest that teachers compare characters, events, or themes in content to similar elements in other media, such as films, television, books, or real life.

SMARTER FOR MATHEMATICS

The following story illustrates the SMARTER approach to a course rather than one unit of instruction. As you read it, note the way the teach-

ers began by identifying the BIG IDEAS in the content of the seventh-grade math curriculum, and how they sequenced instructional units, made decisions about instructional practice, and used specific teaching routines to give all students access to the concepts and processes being taught.

In addition, this story shows the careful cultivation of a partnership between teachers and students. It is also the story of an effective collaboration that involved co-planning and co-teaching between a content teacher, Ms. Lerner, and a support teacher, Ms. Vaughn, a special education teacher. The focus is on the course rather than individual units.

Shape the Critical Questions

Ms. Lerner and Ms. Vaughn began with the SMARTER planning approach to keep themselves focused on the curriculum *and* the students. By proceeding toward their goals this way, they took control of the curriculum. Because few of the students could read or understand the complex textbook, which was written way beyond tenth-grade reading level, they collected the books, put them in the closet, and designed the course themselves, using the text as a guide and not a directive. They surveyed the content of this pre-algebra course and determined that they would complete all units of study using instructional practices that would give all students access to the concepts, processes, and strategies that contribute to competency in math. The National Council of Teachers of Mathematics (NCTM) standards and Massachusetts Curriculum Frameworks were uppermost in their minds because the school district was committed to high standards and their students faced the state assessment in math in the eighth grade.

Ms. Lerner and Ms. Vaughn planned the course together using the Course Organizer Routine described in Chapter 4. The course paraphrase and big ideas allowed Ms. Lerner and Ms. Vaughn to give students a complete picture of the journey from September to June. They created a large poster, shown in Figure B.4, with the course paraphrase and course questions.

Developing the course questions was a major challenge. Ms. Lerner and Ms. Vaughn moved from a version of the questions that focused on many discrete skills related to pre-algebra in the

FIGURE B.4   Course Paraphrase and Course Questions

Pre-algebra

is about

developing problem-solving strategies that use mathematics
as a tool to help us understand the world.

Pre-algebra Course Questions

1. What are the skills and behaviors necessary for success in a classroom?

2. What are some ways you use math in your life?

3. What are good strategies to use when solving a problem?

4. How can you use fractions, decimals, and percents to understand and describe events in your life?

5. In what ways can you use your understanding of probability to make intelligent decisions?

6. What is the role of a variable in helping you solve problems in everyday life?

7. How can graphs help you describe and understand real world situations?

8. Why is proportional thinking necessary for understanding many kinds of relationships in life?

Source: Gorman & Lysaght, 1996. Used with permission.

first year to one that reflected broader clusters of skills and then to the poster version that connects the course to the context of students' lives.

Map the Critical Content

Ms. Lerner and Ms. Vaughn considered the course organizer a "lifesaver" in the beginning of their work together. Developing the big-idea questions helped them to develop a focus that shaped subsequent decisions and gave Ms. Vaughn an opportunity to become a "content partner" from the beginning. They knew the questions were not perfect, but believed they would improve them as the year went on. The course map (see Figure B.5) was invaluable in helping them select and sequence the content

and create important connections across the units of study.

The course map also allowed them to manipulate the units to suit the needs of the class. In their first year together, they designated probability and percents as the first unit, as in the text book.

In their second year, they placed integers and variables first to convince students that they were not in "Dummy Math." Because the other seventh graders would not work on variables and percents until Thanksgiving time, the teachers were confident that students in this very diverse group would have achieved mastery of integers by then and could become tutors in "Y Block," the last period of the day, designed to give students opportunities to:

FIGURE B.5 Course Map

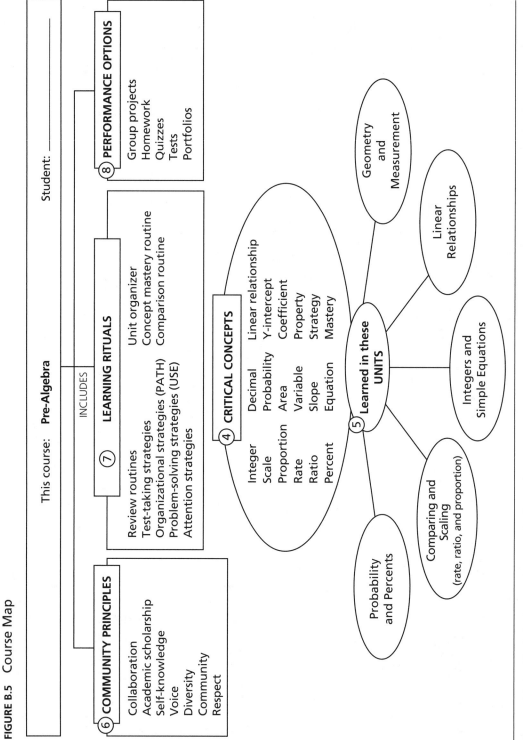

This course: **Pre-Algebra**

Student: _____

INCLUDES

⑦ **LEARNING RITUALS**

Review routines
Test-taking strategies
Organizational strategies (PATH)
Problem-solving strategies (USE)
Attention strategies

Unit organizer
Concept mastery routine
Comparison routine

⑧ **PERFORMANCE OPTIONS**

Group projects
Homework
Quizzes
Tests
Portfolios

⑥ **COMMUNITY PRINCIPLES**

Collaboration
Academic scholarship
Self-knowledge
Voice
Diversity
Community
Respect

④ **CRITICAL CONCEPTS**

Integer
Scale
Proportion
Rate
Ratio
Percent

Decimal
Probability
Area
Variable
Slope
Equation

Linear relationship
Y-intercept
Coefficient
Property
Strategy
Mastery

⑤ **Learned in these UNITS**

Geometry and Measurement

Linear Relationships

Integers and Simple Equations

Comparing and Scaling
(rate, ratio, and proportion)

Probability and Percents

346

Source: Adapted by J. A. Gorman & K. Lysaght, from *The Course Organizer Routine,* by Lenz, B.K., with Schumaker, J. B., Deshler, D. D., & Bulgren, J.A. 1998, Lawrence, KS: Edge Enterprises. Copyright 1998 by Edge Enterprises. Used with permission.

- seek assistance from peers and teachers on content they needed help with;
- participate in more structured tutorial sessions on specific content;
- increase proficiency in new content areas they were learning;
- focus on learning a strategy that could help them be more independent;
- conference with teachers about their performance;
- work on independent projects;
- work on group projects; or
- do make-up work after an absence.

"Y Block" opportunities worked well for the students and the teachers. Tutoring provided Ms. Lerner's students with even more independent practice in the content and an opportunity to be math "experts." These opportunities proved to be empowering for students and promoted their sense of responsibility and ownership for their learning.

Although Ms. Lerner and Ms. Vaughn used a rather unconventional rationale for sequencing the content of the course, they recognized the fact that developing self-efficacy in math early in the year had potential for engaging the students in the content and improving motivation. To them, it was worth a try. The other problem they faced was that students who have experienced chronic failure in math are sometimes suspicious of sudden success. When they become successful they often assume they are in a "low-track" class. Parents are convinced of it. Turning these beliefs around required deliberative action. Therefore, for the fall open house in the second year, Ms. Lerner photocopied the course questions and course maps for parents of students in all of her classes. She explained to the parents that the content of the course was the same for each group.

Analyze for Learning Difficulties

After Ms. Lerner and Ms. Vaughn had identified and sequenced the critical content they looked at the dimensions of the curriculum that would be difficult for students. They targeted five major areas that would require particular care: (1) knowledge and skill gaps, (2) the language of mathematics, (3) connecting new learning to prior knowledge, (4) strategic approaches to learning, and (5) assignment completion.

Knowledge gaps and skill gaps   Because many of the students were below grade level in math achievement, skill gaps and knowledge gaps were to be expected. The teachers also knew that students tend to lose skills during the summer, so there was a great need to devise an approach to identifying what students knew and a process for filling the gaps.

The language of mathematics   Because of the number of students with English as a second language and students with language disorders, the teachers knew vocabulary and language complexity could be a barrier to learning for many students. In order to mediate the content in each unit, they would need to enhance the development of key concepts to ensure that students understood their meaning. The level of abstraction needed to be considered when selecting important concepts to teach with enhancements.

Connecting new learning to prior knowledge
Given the math histories of this group of students, the teachers recognized the development of strong content schemas in math would require helping the students identify relationships between what they already knew and what they would be learning. They would need to provide instruction incorporating explicit information about relationships in content components and about connections of unit concepts to the real world.

Strategic approaches to learning   Students who have not experienced success in math may not be strategic in their approaches to learning. That is, they do not have reliable cognitive and metacognitive strategies required to meet the demands of the school curriculum. Therefore, students would need to be taught specific strategies for computing, checking, and solving problems, as well as organizing materials.

Assignment completion   Because homework provides students with an important form of independent practice, the teachers set a goal for a high rate of completion for homework and group projects. This, the teachers knew, would require a great deal of work on their part.

Reach Enhancement Decisions

The following decisions were made to address each of the five areas that Ms. Lerner and Ms.

Vaughn predicted would be difficult for students.

Knowledge gaps and skill gaps Ms. Lerner and Ms. Vaughn wanted to assess the students' current knowledge of math. Although they had access to the results of the math achievement tests taken at the end of sixth grade, they also knew that some students might not have retained the information since last year. To get a current picture of what each student could do in math, they devised an assessment based on the sixth- and seventh-grade math curriculum. The results showed that one third of the class had developed automaticity with math facts; about two thirds had mastered basic operations and six students were able to solve word problems with 85 percent accuracy. To fill in the gaps, they decided to recruit the assistance of parents, student teachers, and eighth graders recommended by teachers to tutor during Y block. Each student had an individual mastery plan. The teachers kept mastery tests in bins at the back of the classroom so that students could independently check their own mastery of specific skills and determine their readiness to take a "checkout test." It took some time, but all students completed their individual mastery plans and kept up with the seventh-grade curriculum. By the time the third marking period started, the students had a very clear idea of what they could do in math and what they would be learning. Although not all skill gaps were closed, the "catch up" effort resulted in considerable improvement. They celebrated success with a pizza party.

Connecting new learning to prior knowledge The Unit Organizer became an indispensable tool for planning and presenting an overview of content so that students knew exactly where they were and what they would be doing and learning. Students kept the organizer for the current unit in a sheet protector in their math notebooks. Following the completion of a "challenge question" that began each class period, they turned immediately to the Unit Organizer. Ms. Lerner asserted that the Unit Organizer was the best behavior management tool she had ever used because it focused students so much on the content. For example, as soon as the Unit Organizer went up on the screen, everyone flipped to the appropriate place in their notebooks. The Unit Organizer became another classroom routine that "grounded" the students and prepared them to think about math. The unit map kept the components of the content and their relationships to the topic concrete and visible. The expanded unit map allowed the students to track their progress through the unit and add new information as they reviewed at the end of the class period. Halfway through the year, the teachers began to notice that students had become very adept at identifying appropriate phrases to use as line connectors between the individual components and the overall topic. In place of self-test questions, Ms. Lerner and Ms. Vaughn used examples of problems students needed to be able to solve. Most students discovered the value of being able to self-check before a test to make sure they could do each example problem correctly.

Strategic approaches to learning Because the students in this class were not active or independent in their learning, the teachers taught specific cognitive and metacognitive learning strategies, some published and well-known in math and others invented for the group. They developed a mnemonic technique to help them remember key information, like types of angles, by composing lyrics to the tune of "Yankee Doodle":

The Angle Song
(sung to the tune of "Yankee Doodle")
– – – –
When two rays meet up
And a common endpoint share
They form an angle with degrees.
Measure it if you dare.

Greater than 90 is obtuse
90's right and fine
Less than 90 is acute
One eighty's a straight line.

Use a protractor, that's the tool
If angles you must measure
Be sure to read the right number
Or you will have no pleasure.

Greater than 90 is obtuse
90's right and fine
Less than 90 is acute
One eighty's a straight line.

Source: Gorman & Lysaght, 1996. Used with permission

Teach Strategically

Before the formation of the partnership with Ms. Vaughn, Ms. Lerner had no prior experience with approaches to enhancing math instruction for students. Ms. Vaughn had three years of experience working with teachers in social studies, English, science, and math. Her experiences were sufficient to make her realize the power of the teaching routines, like the Unit Organizer, to give all students access to the curriculum. She realized that the conversion of a teaching routine to a learning strategy depended on giving students concrete information about the usefulness of a device, the specific thinking processes needed to complete it (linking steps), and an opportunity to reflect on what they learned while using the device (Cue-Do-Review). Ms. Lerner and Ms. Vaughn gave careful attention to explaining the value of each device, involving the students in their construction and rewarding students who developed a diagram on their own. They also encouraged students to reflect on the teaching and learning process. Halfway through the year, the teachers asked the students for feedback on the use of the Unit Organizer. One student's reflection shows her level of understanding of the device and its usefulness to her as a learner. She wrote:

> I think the unit organizer is very helpful because it helps me to know where we are at and it lets me know ahead of time when there will be quizzes or tests in that particular unit. The only thing that I don't think is needed is the questions on the bottom because we do so much reviewing in the unit that it isn't needed.

Evaluate Mastery

All students were very much involved in monitoring their progress throughout the course. Midway through the course, the teachers asked students to set goals for themselves based on their progress. Work samples, team projects, teamwork behaviors, and other items were placed in a portfolio. Each student reflected on their portfolio work during and at the end of the course. Responsibility for progress was shared between the teachers and the students, promoting motivation, ownership, and accountability for learning.

To check the effectiveness of their planning and instructing, Ms. Lerner and Ms. Vaughn identified representative students in the high, average, low, and other groups (HALO)(King-Sears & Cummings, 1996). They discovered the following:

- **H**igh-achieving student—Janine demonstrated the greatest competency in math at the beginning of the year. Being a quiet person and reluctant to seek recognition, she went unnoticed for some time. However, when doing concept diagrams and other routines to enhance student's understanding, Janine was able to achieve a high level of critical thinking. Her progress through the year remained steady at the highest level of achievement in the group. However, there was a significant change for the better in her ability to engage in group problem solving, and she began to volunteer to tutor, design math games, be a team captain in Math Jeopardy, and to demonstrate novel ways of solving problems.
- **A**verage-achieving student—In the beginning of the year, Marco professed a profound dislike of math and did not see any reason for learning it. He expected to do poorly. The effort to fill in knowledge and skill gaps really paid off for him, however. He was very pleased with his achievement and began to put in more effort. As the class progressed through the curriculum, his homework completion rate went from less than 50 percent in September to 87 percent in May. His scores on tests were consistently in the 90s. At the end of the second quarter, when the students were calculating their own grades, he grinned and said, "I guess doing homework does help."
- **L**ow-achieving student—Walt had a serious language learning disability that made learning concepts very difficult for him. He had not been in a general education math class since he had repeated first grade. His improvement was slow but steady. The use of direct instruction and the achievement of mastery before independent practice reduced his frustration and increased his confidence, as well as his accuracy in calculation. The speech/language pathologist provided some reinforcement on

concepts and strategies, and she helped him with the written work (e.g., his reflections). Otherwise, he was able to maintain his work in the group very well. His quarterly grades went from 78 in the first quarter to 89 in the final quarter.

- **Other student**—Lisette was a student who made limited progress. Although she seemed to grasp concepts readily, her attendance was very erratic. She transferred into the school in October. It wasn't until after Christmas that the counselor was contacted by the Division of Social Services with a request for an after-school program. Lisette's mother had been unable to work for the prior 6 months because of complications with diabetes. The family had been living in a series of homeless shelters, and the children frequently changed schools. The social worker was trying to stabilize the situation and keep Lisette in her current school placement. He indicated a significant improvement in her attitude about school and hoped the teachers would continue to support her progress. Ms. Lerner and Ms. Vaughn hoped so, too. They encouraged her to attend Y block and provided a great deal of support. Despite these efforts, however, Lisette continued to miss school, which seriously affected her achievement.

Being able to maintain Walt in the solid B range for most of the year was a sweet victory for Ms. Lerner and Ms. Vaughn. Walt's parents were thrilled, and his success made them feel that, under the right instructional conditions, their son *could* experience academic success. They began to press the principal to create a co-taught math class for the eighth grade. When they recommended that Janine and five other students be placed in an accelerated program for the following year, three of them decided against it because they were reluctant to give up the pride that goes with being a superstar. They had become very aware of what they needed to do to perform well; they also recognized what the teachers had done that made it possible. When it came to Lisette, Ms. Lerner and Ms. Vaughn felt helpless. They were angry that the social service system lost sight of her for weeks at a time. Their

calls were not returned and the school's resources were limited. There had to be some way to save students with good ability and poor life circumstances.

Revisit Outcomes: Reevaluate Planning and Teaching Decisions

Both teachers benefited greatly from their co-teaching; Ms. Lerner learned new techniques to complement her content knowledge in math and Ms. Vaughn learned more about the math content itself. At the end of the year, when Ms. Lerner and Ms. Vaughn reviewed the effectiveness of the specific instructional approaches they chose, they were ecstatic over the level of mastery attained by the students and were optimistic it would last over the summer. The students really wanted to experience success in eighth-grade math. Each student felt he or she had changed in attitude, motivation, and efficacy, all very important to success in school. The teachers provided their diverse group of learners with skills, strategies, and values that could be built upon in their remaining school years—and beyond.

Variations

- A class like that of Ms. Lerner and Ms. Vaughn could be divided and each half blended in with more heterogeneous groups of students. The presence of higher-achievers would provide a broader range of cognitive modeling and competence for lower-achieving students. In that context, teachers would need to accommodate the discrepancy between the level of discourse of the group and the language competence of the students with limited English or language disorders. The addition of the direct intervention of the speech/language pathologist in the content class could provide support necessary to mediate learning and language.
- The use of technology to provide additional practice on computation and to provide interesting simulations for problem solving would be appropriate and motivating for the students. As students transition to high school, the challenges of the math curriculum technology will be increasingly important.

SMARTER FOR SCIENCE

Shape the Critical Questions

Nate Levin teaches sixth-grade science in an urban middle school. He was a geology major in college and just loves teaching earth science. He has been part of a study group of teachers in the sixth-grade cluster working on improving instruction in science and social studies. Now that the state competency tests include both subjects, they are feeling pressure to help students gain higher levels of achievement. He and Lelia Igric, a science teacher in one of the other sixth-grade clusters, have just started collaborating. Because the preparation of demonstrations and interactive activities requires a great deal of time, they see numerous benefits to a division of labor. At the moment, Mr. Levin and Ms. Igric are beginning a chapter on volcanoes. They expected students' interest to be relatively high, because most of them studied this topic in elementary school and have seen documentaries on television. Activating prior knowledge has not been a problem with the earthquake and volcano chapters in the past. These chapters are part of a unit called Dynamic Earth. The purpose of this unit is to give students an understanding of the ways in which the earth's surface is changing. The chapter on volcanoes was preceded by chapters on the movement of the earth's crust and one on earthquakes. It was followed by chapters on plate tectonics, rocks and minerals, weathering and soil formation, and erosion and deposition.

For the chapter on volcanoes, they identify the following outcomes:

- How are volcanoes formed?
- What kinds of volcanoes are found on earth?
- Where are they located?
- What is the effect of volcanic eruptions on people's lives?

Map the Critical Content

Mr. Levin and Ms. Igric constructed a concept map of the volcano component in the chapter (see Figure B.6). They were careful to include line labels to help the students remember the connections between the specific topics in the chapter. The teachers had provided the students with a Unit Organizer so the content on the volcano component would be recorded on the Expanded Unit Organizer. The students had become very responsible about keeping the Unit Organizer in their notebooks, because they began to realize the value of the device for clarifying relationships and keeping them focused on their progress through the unit. The volcano map corresponded exactly to the presentation of material in the textbook. This was the third unit they had enhanced with a unit organizer, so for the next unit they intended to give the students an opportunity to map chapters on their own to earn bonus points. The teachers were curious to know which students would accept the challenge.

FIGURE B.6
Volcanoes

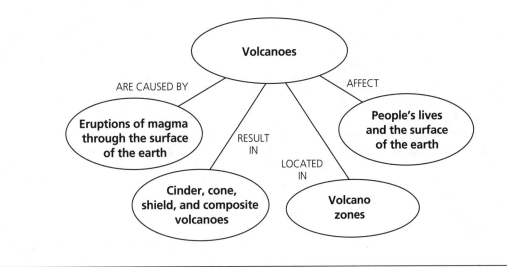

Analyze for Learning Difficulties

Mr. Levin and Ms. Igric believed they were beginning to see some benefits to using the Unit Organizer. Reading in the new textbook was not going well, however. Until they started to work with the study group, they had not realized that science and social studies had such a heavy vocabulary load—at least as much as the first year of a foreign language. Although the book identified some of the important new vocabulary, some students were confused by concepts like "depression," which they thought belonged in social studies and meant a time of unemployment. Clearly, key concepts would need to be clarified, including the comparison of economic depression and a depression caused by movement on or under the surface of the earth.

An even larger problem for students was reading and note taking on the text. Many students for whom English is a second language did not even bother to take the book home. The teachers analyzed their textbook, using the Checklist for Considerate Text Characteristics developed by Deshler, Schumaker, & McKnight (1997) (see Appendix D). Based on this analysis, they decided that the book had good chapter introductions and illustrations. Major headings were written in blue and subheadings in green. There was considerable information density, however. Also, the "Guide for Reading the Chapter" listed on the first page of the chapter was different from the guide for reading that accompanied the main headings. Students found the text confusing. A reading teacher had used a readability formula on all of the sixth-grade books and had found that the science text ranged from a sixth- to eighth-grade level. This was much better than the old textbook, which had reading levels from fifth to ninth grade. The reading teacher pointed out that to reduce the readability level publishers often shortened sentences, thereby eliminating important "connecting" words like conjunctions that help to create coherence (Armbruster & Anderson, 1988). This made the text not particularly "user-friendly." Mr. Levin and Ms. Igric realized they would need to come up with some way to support students as they read the textbook in order to reduce frustration and improve comprehension.

Reach Enhancement Decisions

Mr. Levin and Ms. Igric believed the content maps were working well, and they would make sure to provide students with maps to keep in their notebooks for each component of the chapter. The teachers identified specific concepts they would emphasize with the use of a concept diagram. The key concepts they identified were volcanic eruption and volcano and earthquake zone, both critical concepts to understanding the nature and extent of volcanic activity on planet Earth. The teachers also determined that they would use a comparison diagram to help students clarify the three types of volcanoes.

The decision about ways to help students deal with the reading demands of the chapter was more difficult. Mr. Levin and Ms. Igric had recently learned about the Chapter Survey Routine (Deshler et al., 1997) but had not attempted it. Completing the checklist on the readability of the textbook, however, made them aware that enhancing the students' skills in reading expository texts was critical to their survival in high school. The teachers decided to use the Chapter Survey Routine for the volcano content so that students could experience the value of a combined prereading and postreading strategy.

Teach Strategically

Because the students had already used unit organizers and concept and comparison diagrams in two previous units, the teachers used the Cue-Do-Review routine to provide the rationale for using the device, guiding the students through the linking steps, and reviewing the content they had analyzed. The real challenge came in introducing the Chapter Survey Routine to the students, because of the wide range of reading levels among students in the cluster. On the first day, the teachers provided a rationale for previewing material to be read and using an organized format for lifting information out of a textbook. The teachers guided the students slowly through the completion of the first page of the worksheet, making sure to model the thinking involved in predicting content, identifying relationships between and among the chapters and the unit, and summarizing the introduction. That took a whole period.

Mr. Levin and Ms. Igric noticed that the language of volcanoes was beginning to be heard in the discourse in the classroom. They pointed out the value of knowing ahead of time what they would be reading and to be alert to key information when they encountered it in their reading. The students worked with fourteen pages of text. When they finished, the teachers reemphasized the purpose of the device and the value of previewing and summarizing the chapter. The teachers estimated the amount of time it would take to complete the component on volcanoes and set a date for two quizzes and the chapter test. This information was recorded on the Unit Organizer.

Evaluate Mastery

The results of the quizzes and chapter test were very good. The mean score on the test was 84, which was a full 11 points higher than on the earthquake chapter. Prior to the chapter test, the teachers gave the students time to work in groups to develop questions on index cards and hand in the ones they thought were the best. It was not difficult to incorporate the content of the questions into their own format for the test. When the teachers returned the tests to the students, they encouraged discussion on the value of the Unit Organizer to their test preparation. There were some performances the teachers were pleased to share in the teachers' room. For example, a student from Martinique, with limited proficiency in English, did a particularly outstanding job. The ESL teacher learned that his grandfather had lived near Mount Pelée on the island of Martinique, where several relatives had died in the 1902 volcanic eruption. She helped the youngster search the Internet for information on Martinique and the story of the disaster that wiped out a town of 30,000 people.

Mr. Levin and Ms. Igric computed the mean scores for each of their classes on the earthquake chapter and the one on volcanoes. The differences between scores for the earthquake and volcano chapters were close to being statistically significant. The teachers were very pleased and believed that with practice the students would become better able to read their textbooks and organize and remember information well enough to be able to think and write about it critically.

The greatest difference in performance appeared to be with students who scored in the bottom quartile in the first two units and who were not achieving well in other classes but had done well on the test in this unit. Mr. Levin and Ms. Igric talked to two of them about what they thought of the test, and to congratulate them on doing so well! Both students agreed the test was easy because, as one student said, "I could still see it in my head." The teachers decided it was well worth the extra effort to use teaching routines not only because students performed better, but also because they were developing strategies for learning more efficiently.

Revisit Outcomes: Reevaluate Planning and Teaching Decisions

When reflecting on the volcano chapter, Mr. Levin and Ms. Igric felt very good about the planning they had done. They realized that deciding exactly what concepts would be difficult, and preparing concept and comparison diagrams ahead of time, helped them to be very clear when facilitating discussion and answering students' questions. The teachers had blank diagrams and transparencies ready. They were a little concerned about the fact that students had begun to ask them to do a concept diagram for terms like "obsidian rock," a type of igneous rock from fast-cooling lava. Mr. Levin and Ms. Igric decided it would be a good idea to teach the students a vocabulary strategy to accommodate their need to remember the definition of terms used in text.

The teachers also recognized the power of the Unit Organizer in keeping the students focused on the most important material. The teachers had been completing the Unit Organizer with the students, including the self-test questions, but had not revisited the questions after each chapter nor given the students the opportunity to add or revise questions. Mr. Levin and Ms. Igric decided they needed to build a stronger connection between the unit questions and chapter questions. Their strongest resolve, however, was focused on talking to students more. Interviewing two low-achievers following the chapter test had proved to be very useful for their own reflection on their work, and they noticed both students had started to talk to them and to classmates more often. Perhaps there was no cause-effect relationship, but both teachers suspected that there was. In any event, they planned to target other students to monitor. Mr. Levin and Ms. Igric looked forward to sharing their experience with the study group.

Variations The topic of volcanoes would be ideal for integrating with language arts. The text suggested reading a Native American legend from the Lakota tribe called "Tunkashila," which means "grandfather rock." It is a lovely story about the spirits that tried to live on the sun and eventually came to earth. Students could search for myths and legends that contain explanations of natural phenomena. They could create myths and legends to be read by younger children studying volcanoes (Tiedt & Tiedt, 1995).

REFERENCES

Armbruster, B. B., & Anderson, T. H. (1988). On selecting "considerate" content area textbooks. *Remedial and Special Education, 9*(1), 47–52.

Bulgren, J. A., Schumaker, J. B., & Deshler, D. D. (1993). *The concept mastery routine.* Lawrence, KS: Edge Enterprises.

Bulgren, J. A., Schumaker, J. B., & Deshler, D. D. (1994). *The concept anchoring routine.* Lawrence, KS: Edge Enterprises.

Bulgren, J. A., Lenz, B. K., Deshler, D. D., & Schumaker, J. B. (1995). *The concept comparison routine.* Lawrence, KS: Edge Enterprises.

Carnine, D., Bean, R., Miller, S., & Zigmond, N. (1994). Social studies: Educational tools for diverse learners. *School Psychology Review, 23,* 428–441.

Deshler, D. D., Schumaker, J. B., & McKnight, P. C. (1997). *The survey routine.* Lawrence, KS: The University of Kansas.

Espin, C. A., & Tindal, G. (1998). Curriculum-based measurement for secondary students. In M. R. Shinn (Ed.) *Advanced applications of curriculum-based measurement* (pp. 214–253). New York: Guilford Press.

Fuchs, L. S., Fuchs, D., & Deno, S. L. (1985). Importance of goal ambitiousness and goal mastery to student achievement. *Exceptional Children, 57,* 392–404.

Gorman, J. A., & Lysaght, K. (1996). *Accommodating diversity in a general education math class in a middle school.* Presentation at Boston College, School of Education.

Kameenui, E. J., & Carnine, D. W. (1998). *Effective teaching strategies that accommodate diverse learners.* Columbus, OH: Merrill.

King-Sears, M. E., & Cummings, C. S. (1996). Inclusive practices of classroom teachers. *Remedial and Special Education, 17,* 217–225.

Maher, C. A. (1981). Effects of involving conduct problem adolescents on goal setting: An exploratory investigation. *Psychology in the School, 18,* 471–474.

McDiarmid, G. W., Ball, D. L., & Anderson, C. W. (1989). Why staying one chapter ahead doesn't really work: Subject-specific pedagogy. In M. C. Reynolds (Ed.) *Knowledge base for the beginning teacher* (pp. 193–206). Elmsford, NY: Pergamon Press.

Tiedt, P. L., & Tiedt, I. M. (1995). *Multicultural teaching: A handbook of activities, information and resources.* Boston: Allyn & Bacon.

VanSickle, R. L., & Hoge, J. D. (1991). Higher cognitive thinking skills in social studies: Concepts and critiques. *Theory and Research in Social Education, 19,* 152–172.

VanSledright, B. A. (1995). "I don't remember—The ideas are all jumbled in my head": 8th graders' reconstruction of colonial American history. *Journal of Curriculum and Supervision, 10,* 317–345.

Zentall, S. S. (1990). Fact-retrieval automatization and math problem-solving: Learning disabled, attention disordered and normal adolescents. *Journal of Educational Psychology, 82,* 856–865.

Zentall, S. S. (1993). Research on the educational implications of attention deficit hyperactivity disorder. *Exceptional Children, 60,* 143–153.

Zentall, S. S., & Smith, Y. N. (1993). Mathematical performance and behavior of children with hyperactivity with and without coexisting aggression. *Behavioral Research and Therapy, 31,* 701–710.

Zentall, S. S., Smith, Y. N., Lee, Y. B., & Wieczorek, C. (1994). Mathematical outcomes of attention-deficit hyperactivity disorder. *Journal of Learning Disabilities, 27,* 510–519.

C The Strategic Instruction Model

The Strategic Instruction Model (SIM) offers an integrated approach to addressing the challenges teachers face in today's classrooms and a framework for working toward meeting school reform goals and state standards. SIM encompasses teacher-focused interventions directed at how teachers think about, adapt, and present their critical content in a "learner-friendly" fashion and student-focused interventions designed to provide the skills and strategies students need to learn the content.

TEACHER-FOCUSED INTERVENTIONS: CONTENT ENHANCEMENT

Content Enhancement is a way of teaching an academically diverse group of students in which four conditions prevail:

1. Both group and individual needs are valued and met.
2. The integrity of the content is maintained.
3. Critical features of the content are selected and transformed in a way that promotes learning for all students.
4. Instruction is carried out in a partnership with students.

Some Content Enhancement Routines help teachers think about and organize content and then present it in such a way that students can see the organization. Other routines help teachers explain text, topics, and details. A third group of routines helps teach complex concepts so that students gain a deep understanding and develop a shared vocabulary for talking about important

information. A final group of routines helps students to complete their work in the classroom.

All of the routines promote direct, explicit instruction. This type of instruction helps students who are struggling, but it also facilitates problem-solving and critical-thinking skills for students who are doing well in class.

The teaching routines described in this appendix have been successfully field-tested in general education classrooms characterized by significant academic diversity. Students judged to be at-risk for academic school failure were in each class; all of the routines were field-tested in classes that contained students judged to have learning disabilities. The research took place in public schools, primarily in middle- and high-school settings, and the routines were field-tested by teachers. Research has demonstrated that consistent and explicit instruction and use of each routine are key ingredients for instructional success.

The routines were designed for use during group instruction to help a teacher provide instruction more sensitive to the learning needs of individuals in the group. A combination of instructional models has been successfully tested with general education teachers and special education teachers working individually and collaboratively. All of the routines are taught using a standard set of instructional procedures. These procedures define the necessary instructional conditions needed, regardless of where the routine is used.

Planning and Leading Learning

The Course Organizer Routine is used to plan courses around essential learning and critical concepts. The teacher uses the routine to introduce the course and the rituals that will be used throughout the course. The teacher then uses this framework throughout the year to maintain the big ideas and rituals. Research shows that use of the Course Organizer Routine helps teachers and students keep the big ideas in mind and focuses their attention on understanding important relationships. Teachers using the routine spent more time introducing major course ideas, concepts, themes, and routines to students than did comparison teachers who did not learn the routine. Students with learning disabilities (LD) answered correctly an average of three "big idea" course questions at the beginning of the year. The students with LD in the class that used the Course Organizer answered correctly an average of eight "big idea" questions by the end of the course, while the students with LD in the class that did not use the Course Organizer answered only an average of four "big idea" questions correctly.

The Unit Organizer Routine is used to plan units and then introduce and maintain the big ideas in units and show how units, critical information, and concepts are related. Research results showed that when the teachers used the Unit Organizer Routine, understanding and retention of the information by low-achieving students, students with learning disabilities, and average-achieving students improved substantially over baseline, as reflected in unit test scores and in scores on unit content maps and explanations of these maps. The students of teachers who used the Unit Organizer Routine regularly and consistently scored an average of 15 percentage points higher on unit tests than students of teachers who used it only irregularly.

The Lesson Organizer Routine is used to plan lessons and then introduce and connect ideas to the unit and the course. Research has shown that regular, explicit, and flexible use of the Lesson Organizer Routine by secondary classroom teachers can have a significant influence on student learning. Studies showed that use of the routine increased student learning and performance. Research results showed that the students of teachers who used the Lesson Organizer Routine regularly and consistently scored an average of 15 percentage points higher on unit tests than students of teachers who used it irregularly.

Explaining Text, Topics, and Details

The Clarifying Routine is used to explore related details about a topic and their importance to the topic. Using this routine, teachers can help students master the meaning of targeted words and phrases. Research has shown that students benefit from the use of this routine. Studies in upper-elementary and middle-school general education classes composed of highly diverse student populations, including students with learning disabilities and those for whom English is a second language, have shown that students benefit from teacher use of the routine. When the teacher used the Clarifying Routine, high socioeconomic-level students improved their number of correct answers by an average of 14 percent, middle socioeconomic-level students by an average of 30 percent, and low socioeconomic-level students by an average of 20 percent.

The Framing Routine is used to transform abstract main ideas and key topics into a concrete representation that helps students think and talk about the key topic and essential related information. Research results have consistently demonstrated that the routine can facilitate subject-matter learning, as well as the development of literacy and thinking skills. In a study focusing on written products of 35 eighth-grade students, the students who were taught with the Framing Routine wrote an average of 102 words more per product than did the students who were in the comparison group.

The Survey Routine provides a way for students to gain an overview of a reading assignment when they are have difficulty reading and sorting out information from inconsiderate text. Research has shown that students with LD and other low-achieving students, as well as average and high-achieving students, answered an average of 10 percent to 15 percent more test questions correctly when the Survey Routine was used than when the Survey Routine was not used.

Teaching Concepts

The Concept Anchoring Routine is used to introduce and anchor a new concept to a concept that is already familiar to students. In research studies in secondary science and social studies classes, high-achieving, average-achieving, and low-achieving students (including those with learning disabilities) who had been taught with the Anchoring Routine answered more test questions correctly than those who had not received instruction using the routine. Students with LD taught with the Anchoring Routine scored an average of 25 percentage points higher than those who were not taught with the routine. Low-achieving, average-achieving, and high-achieving students taught with the Anchoring Routine scored an average of 27, 19, and 7 percentage points higher than groups that were not taught with the routine.

The Concept Comparison Routine is used to help students compare and contrast key concepts. Research with students enrolled in general secondary science and social studies classes showed that students correctly answered substantially more test questions related to information that had been presented using the routine than test questions related to information presented using traditional teaching methods. Students with LD and other low-achieving students using the routine correctly answered an average of 71.2 percent (LD) and 86.4 percent (students with no learning disability [NLD]), respectively, of test questions associated with information presented, compared to 56.7 percent (LD) and 62.6 percent (NLD) of questions associated with information presented through traditional means. The experimental study involved 107 students.

The Concept Mastery Routine is used to define, summarize, and explain a major concept and where it fits within a larger body of knowledge. Research shows that use of the routine benefits secondary-level students in several ways. First, students taught using the routine scored significantly better on tests designed to assess concept acquisition. Second, students scored significantly better on regularly scheduled, teacher-made or commercial unit tests during the enhancement condition than during baseline. Gains by students with LD (from a mean score of 60 percent to 71 percent) were comparable to those of their NLD peers (from a mean score of 72 percent to 87 percent) on these regular tests. The percentage of students with LD who passed increased from 57 percent to 75 percent; the percentage of NLD students who passed increased from 68 percent to 97 percent. Third, the students using the routine took better notes during the enhancement condition than before.

Increasing Performance

The Quality Assignment Routine is used to plan, present, and engage students in quality assignments and then evaluate assignments with students. From the research study, characteristics of good assignments and the important elements for the routine were learned through surveys completed by teachers and students and from focus groups with teachers and students. All of the characteristics and elements were deemed important through the survey results. Research study results showed the following: Prior to the study, teachers were observed to include an average of 50.5 percent of the planning behaviors based on the validated assignment characteristics, 32.8 percent of the presentation behaviors based on the validated explanation factors, and 8.2 percent of the evaluation procedures. After the intervention, participants used an average of 96.1 percent of the planning behaviors, 89.3 percent of the presentation behaviors, and 93.8 percent of the evaluation procedures. In contrast, a group of comparison teachers used an average of 45 percent of the planning behaviors, 26 percent of the assignment presentation behaviors, and 10 percent of the evaluation procedures at the end of the study. Teachers who received the training in the use of the routine and their students were significantly more satisfied with assignments.

The Question Exploration Routine is a package of instructional methods that teachers can use to help a diverse student population understand a body of content information by carefully answering a "critical question" to arrive at a main idea answer. Research results showed that students who were taught a lesson using the Question Exploration Routine earned an average test score of 70 percent while students who were taught the lesson with traditional methods scored an average of 48 percent.

The Recall Enhancement Routine focuses on procedures teachers can use to help students remember information. Performance of the students in a post-test-only comparison group study indicated that the performance of students was related to the teacher's use of the routine. Students with or without disabilities in the classes of teachers who used the routine performed significantly better on test items that could best be addressed through the creation of the types of Recall Devices that their teachers had presented than did the students in the comparison classes. The recall performance of both the LD and the NLD students in the experimental group was higher by 29.10 and 20.5 points on reviewed facts, respectively, than the performance of similar students in the control group.

The Vocabulary LINCing Routine is designed to facilitate student use of two powerful tools, an auditory memory device and a visual memory device, that will help them learn and remember the meaning of complex terms. Research results showed that students, including those with LD, improved their performance by an average of 19 percentage points on vocabulary tests.

STUDENT-FOCUSED INTERVENTIONS: LEARNING STRATEGIES CURRICULUM

The Learning Strategies Curriculum has the necessary breadth and depth to provide a well-designed scope and sequence of strategy instruction. The curriculum is divided into strands, or categories of skills.

One strand addresses how students acquire information. It includes strategies for (a) learning how to paraphrase critical information, (b) picturing information to promote understanding and remembering, (c) asking questions and making predictions about text information, and (d) identifying unknown words in text.

A second strand relates to how students study information once they acquire it. It includes strategies for learning new vocabulary, as well as strategies for developing mnemonics and other devices to aid memorization of facts. These strategies help prepare students for tests.

A third strand concerns how students express themselves. It includes strategies to help students write sentences and paragraphs, monitor their work for errors, and confidently approach and take tests.

No single strategy is a panacea. For example, there are reading strategies that help students figure out what a word is, comprehend what they're reading, acquire vocabulary, and understand the structure of text. All of these strategies are essential for a well-integrated, balanced reading program. Likewise, an array of strategies in other areas is necessary for student success.

The learning strategies listed here have been successfully field-tested with students judged to be at-risk for academic school failure; additionally, all of the strategies have been field-tested with students judged to have learning disabilities. The research took place in public schools, primarily in middle- and high-school settings, and the strategies were field-tested by teachers. Research has demonstrated that consistent, intensive, explicit instruction and support are key ingredients for instructional success. A combination of instructional models, involving general education teachers and special education teachers working individually and collaboratively, has been successfully tested. All of the strategies are taught using a standard set of instructional procedures. These procedures define the necessary instructional conditions needed, regardless of where the instruction occurs.

Strategies Related to Reading

Word Identification Strategy provides challenged readers with a functional and efficient strategy to successfully decode and identify unknown words in their reading materials. The strategy is based on the premise that most words in the English language can be pronounced by identifying prefixes, suffixes, and stems, and by following three short syllabication rules. In the research study, students made an average of 20 errors in a passage of 400 words prior to learning this strategy. Having learned the Word Identification Strategy, students reduced their errors to an average of three per 400 words. Reading comprehension increased from 40 percent on the pretest to 70 percent on grade-level passages.

Visual Imagery Strategy is a reading comprehension strategy for creating mental movies of narrative passages. Students visualize the scenery, characters, and action, and describe the scenes to themselves. Research results showed that students who demonstrated a 35 percent comprehension and recall rate prior to learning the strategy improved to an 86 percent comprehension and recall rate after learning the strategy.

Self-Questioning Strategy helps students create their own motivation for reading. Students create questions in their minds, predict the answers to those questions, search for the answers to those questions as they read, and paraphrase the answers to themselves. Research results have shown average gains of 40 percentage points in reading comprehension on grade-level materials after students learned the strategy.

Paraphrasing Strategy is designed to help students focus on the most important information in a passage. Students read short passages of materials, identify the main idea and details, and rephrase the content in their own words. Using grade-level materials, students performed at a 48 percent comprehension rate prior to learning the strategy. During the post-test, these students comprehended 84 percent of the material.

Strategies Related to Storing and Remembering Information

The FIRST-Letter Mnemonic Strategy is a strategy for independently studying large bodies of information that need to be mastered. Specifically, students identify lists of information that are important to learn, generate an appropriate title or label for each set of information, select a mnemonic device for each set of information, create study cards, and use the study cards to learn the information. Research results showed that students who learned the FIRST-Letter Mnemonic Strategy received test grades that increased from an average of 51 percent to 85 percent.

The Paired Associates Strategy is designed to help students learn pairs of informational items like names and events, places and events, or names and accomplishments. Students identify pairs of items, create mnemonic devices, create study cards, and use the study cards to learn the information. Research has shown that before students learned this strategy, they answered correctly only an average of 8 percent of test questions related to paired information when the paired information was identified for them. After they mastered the strategy, they answered correctly an average of 85 percent of the questions about paired information that was identified for them. When given reading passages to study on their own, they answered an average of 22 percent of test questions correctly before instruction in the strategy versus 76 percent after mastering the strategy.

The LINCS Vocabulary Strategy helps students learn the meaning of new vocabulary words using powerful memory-enhancement techniques. Strategy steps cue students to focus on critical elements of the concept, to use visual imagery, associations with prior knowledge, and key-word mnemonic devices to create a study card, and to study the card to enhance comprehension and recall of the concept. Research results showed that in the social studies class where the LINCS Strategy was taught to the students, the students with LD performed at a mean of 53 percent in the pretest and at a mean of 77 percent correct answers after learning the LINCS Strategy. In the control class where students did not learn the LINCS Strategy, the mean percentage of correct answers decreased from the pretest to the post-test.

Strategies Related to Expressing Information

The Sentence Writing Strategy program comprises two parts: (1) Fundamentals in the Sentence Writing Strategy, and (2) Proficiency in the Sentence Writing Strategy. Together these components constitute a strategy for recognizing and writing 14 sentence patterns with four types of sentences: simple, compound, complex, and compound-complex. The program consists of two products: an instructor's manual and a student lessons manual. The instructor's manual features a systematic sequence of instructional procedures; the student lessons manual features exercises that correspond to instructional procedures. Research results showed that students wrote an average of 65 percent complete sentences on the pretest and an average of 88 percent complete sentences on the post-test.

The Paragraph Writing Strategy is a strategy for organizing ideas related to a topic, planning the point of view and verb tense to be used in the paragraph, planning the sequence in which ideas will be expressed, and writing a variety of topic, detail, and "clincher" sentences. The program consists of two products: an instructor's manual and a student lessons manual. The instructor's manual features a systematic sequence of instructional procedures; the student lessons manual features exercises that correspond to the instructional procedures. Research results showed that the students earned an average of 40 percent of the points available when writing a paragraph on the pretest and a 71 percent average of the points when writing a paragraph on the post-test.

The Error Monitoring Strategy can be used by students to independently detect and correct errors in their written work to increase the overall quality of their final product. Instruction stresses the importance of proofreading written work for content and mechanical errors and eliminating those errors before work is submitted. This strategy also includes the development of personal strategies to avoid future errors. Research results demonstrated that students who mastered this strategy dramatically increased their ability to find and correct errors in their written products. Prior to instruction, they were making one error in every four words. Following instruction, they made only one error in every 20 words.

The InSPECT Strategy can be used by students to detect and correct spelling errors in their documents, either by using a computerized spell-checker or a hand-held spelling device. Research results showed that students corrected 41 percent of the errors in their compositions prior to being trained in the InSPECT Strategy and corrected 75 percent of the errors in their composition after receiving training in InSPECT.

Strategies Related to Demonstrating Competence

The Assignment Completion Strategy is designed to enable students to complete and hand in assignments on time. The package consists of two books: the instructor's manual, which provides step-by-step instruction for teaching this strategy, and the Quality Quest Planner, a spiral-bound notebook designed specifically for student use with the strategy. Each instructor's manual comes with one Quality Quest Planner and contains the materials needed to teach the strategy, including blank copies of the forms used with the planner. The planner contains sufficient forms for recording, scheduling, and evaluating assignments for an entire academic year. Performance results in general education classes showed that the number of students who simply turned in their assignments before learning the Assignment Completion Strategy was 43 percent with the percentage increasing to 77 percent after students learned the strategy. Prior to learning the strategy, the number of students who did

the assignment correctly was 45 percent. After learning the strategy, the number increased to 73 percent. Students who did not hand in the assignments were interviewed to discover their reasons for not turning in the assigned work. The major reason they gave was that they did not understand how to do the assignment.

Strategic Tutoring describes a new vision of the tutoring process in which the tutor not only helps the student complete and understand the immediate assignment but also teaches the student the strategies required to complete similar tasks independently in the future. Research results showed that the students in strategic tutoring improved their achievement test scores in reading comprehension, written expression, and basic math skills. On average, their grade-level achievement scores increased by 10 months during a four-month instructional period. In contrast, the students in the comparison group without the strategic tutoring instruction experienced a mean gain of only 3.5 months during the same period.

The Test-Taking Strategy is designed to be used while taking classroom tests. Students allocate time and priority to each section of the test, carefully read and focus on important elements in the test instructions, recall information by accessing mnemonic devices, systematically and quickly progress through a test, make well-informed guesses, check their work, and take control of the testing situation. The emphasis is on teaching adolescents and adults who struggle with learning. Research results in which students were taught the Test Taking Strategy produced an average 10 point increase on tests for participating students.

Strategies Related to Social Interaction

The Self Advocacy Strategy can be used by students when preparing for and participating in any type of conference, including an education and transition planning conference (i.e., IEP or ITP conference). Strategy steps provide students with both a way of getting organized before a conference and with effective communication techniques to use during the conference. When students learned the Self Advocacy Strategy, 86 percent of the goals they most valued were found in their IEPs. The students who had not learned the Self Advocacy Strategy had only 13 percent of their desired goals in their IEPs.

SLANT: A Starter Strategy for Class Participation is a simple, easy-to-teach strategy designed to help students learn how to use appropriate posture, "track the talker," activate their thinking, and contribute information.

Surface Counseling details a set of relationship-building skills necessary for establishing a trusting, cooperative relationship between an adult and a youth, and a problem-solving strategy that youths can learn to use by themselves. Materials include study guide questions, model dialogues, and role-playing activities. This is useful for an adult who has daily contact with children and adolescents. Research results showed that teachers who had not been trained in Surface Counseling used an average of 23 percent of the surface-counseling skills to counsel students on a problem. After being trained in Surface Counseling, the teachers performed an average of 93 percent of the surface-counseling components in counseling sessions. They also reported an increased feeling of confidence and competence in counseling sessions.

Cooperative Thinking Strategies

The THINK Strategy is used by students working together in teams to systematically solve problems. The research studies in which this strategy was used developed school improvement goals in which problem solving, reasoning, and communicating were major targeted areas. Results showed that the mean percentage of points earned by the groups before instruction was the same for experimental and comparison groups at 34 percent. However, at the end of the school year, the mean percentage score for the experimental groups was 84 percent and for the comparison groups 39 percent.

The LEARN Strategy was designed to enable students to work in teams to learn together. Each step promotes creative cooperation; students think together to generate ideas to help them learn. Research results indicated that students in the experimental classes performed a significantly higher percentage of study behaviors than comparison students in their cooperative study groups at the end of the school year. Experimental group pretest scores averaged 18 percent with post-test scores averaging 70 percent. The comparison group pretest score average was 27 percent with the post-test score average 35 percent.

The BUILD Strategy is a strategy students can use to work together to resolve a controversial issue. The purpose of the strategy is to enable students to work together to make decisions using a process similar to a debate. Research results showed that the average score from the observational measure and products written by students as they discussed the issue for the experimental students was 21.4 percent on the pretest and 80.1 percent after learning the BUILD Strategy. The comparison group that did not learn the BUILD Strategy scored 15.1 percent on the pretest and 19.6 percent on the post-test.

SCORE Skills: Social Skills for Cooperative Groups describes a set of social skills that are fundamental to effective groups. Students learn to share ideas, compliment others, offer help or encouragement, recommend changes nicely, and exercise self-control. Results showed the mean percentage of cooperative skills used by students in cooperative groups in class before learning SCORE was 25 percent and 78 percent after learning SCORE Skills. The students in the comparison group that had no instruction in SCORE had average scores of 25 percent and 28 percent for the cooperative skills they used in the cooperative groups.

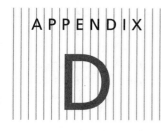

APPENDIX

D Checklist for Considerate Text Characteristics

Textbook Title: _____

Check each questions with a **yes** or **no**.

	YES	NO	
T			1. Does the title reflect the main idea/topic of the chapter?
R			2. Does the table of contents show relationships or organizational patterns between the unit and the current chapter?
			3. Are the headings listed in the table of contents or is there an expanded table of contents?
			4. Does the table of contents show a clear arrangement of ideas by use of one of the most common relationship structures? Check the structure used:
			5. Is there a clear relationship or structure of ideas between the current chapter and the immediately preceding and the following chapters?
I			6. Is there a clearly identified introduction to the chapter?
			7. Does the introduction specify chapter goals/objectives for reading?
			8. Does the introduction provide an overview of the chapter?
			9. Does the introduction specify the relationship or organization of ideas/events in the chapter through use of one of the most common relationship structures? Check structure used:
			10. Does the introduction state the rationale/relevance of the chapter content?

Question 4:
_____ Order _____ Explanation
_____ Process _____ Comparison
_____ Causality _____ Deliberation
_____ Problem/Solution

Question 7:
Are the goals/objectives: _____ Explicit (stated/listed)?
_____ Implied (embedded)?

Question 9:
_____ Order _____ Explanation
_____ Process _____ Comparison
_____ Causality _____ Deliberation
_____ Problem/Solution

Question 10:
_____ Are the rationales/relevance statement:
_____ Explicit?
_____ Implied ?

	YES	NO	
			11. Does the introduction: _____ review previously studied relevant material/information? _____ relate it to the topic of the current chapter? _____ explicitly state the relationship? _____ imply the relationship?
M			12. Do titles of main headings and subheadings clearly reflect the main idea structure of information presented? 13. Do subheadings follow a clear sequence of information directly related to the main headings? 14. Does the author use **size, shape, color, and/or placement** to distinguish types of headings? 15. Are new/key vocabulary highlighted in the text? _____ In bold print or italics? _____ Listed at end of chapter, bottom of page, or margin? 16. Does the text provide _____ A definition of key terms? _____ A pronunciation guide for key terms? 17. Do graphics enhance the most important information contained in the chapter and/or related directly to headings? 18. Do graphics depict information in a succinct, easy-to-read format with instructions provided for interpretation or use of charts and graphs?
S			19. Is there a clearly identified summary? 20. Does the summary synthesize chapter contents? 21. Does the summary review chapter goals/objectives? 22. Does the summary focus student attention on the most important concepts, ideas, and information? 23. Are there chapter review/study questions? 24. Are chapter review questions based on the critical key concepts and ideas? 25. Is there a good balance among main idea, detail/fact, and critical thinking (applications, analysis, synthesis) questions?

Total number of questions answered "YES" _____

The higher the score, the more considerate and "user-friendly" the textbook. The more considerate a textbook, the more likely that students will be able to use it independently. The more inconsiderate a textbook, the more teacher facilitation and intervention will be required.

TRIMS

Strategies for Enhancing Text Problem Areas

Possible Problem Area	Teacher Strategies

Title
☐ Students are unable to paraphrase title because it contains:
a) unknown vocabulary
b) concepts not previously defined or studied
	✔ Assist students in paraphrasing title by eliciting or providing synonyms for unknown vocabulary in the title.
	✔ Have students change title to a question and find answer to the question in chapter introduction.
	✔ Assist students in dividing concept vocabulary into "word parts" to paraphrase definition of concept, e.g.:
	    humanism = human + ism
	    human = mankind
	    ism = system of belief
	✔ Paraphrase title for students to provide a general definition of the title/chapter topic.

Relationship ☐ Students are unable to determine the relationship of information due to a) unknown vocabulary and/or concepts in the chapter or unit titles b) lack of understanding of and/or inexperience in identifying relationship structures	✔ Provide practice in identifying relationships—use preceding chapters (familiar materials) as a basis for identifying relationships. ✔ Provide examples of the 3 most common relationship structures used in text; elicit "real life" examples of the specific relationship; cite examples in text; have students find additional examples. ✔ Name the relationship for students and provide text examples for them.
☐ The order of chapters in the text does not match the order assigned by the teacher.	✔ Direct students to analyze the order and relationship of assigned chapters. ✔ Explain the relationship of chapters assigned by the teacher. ✔ Compare order selected by teacher to order in the text.
Introduction ☐ There is no introduction.	✔ Introduce the chapter to students. ✔ Provide a rationale for the importance of the chapter content. ✔ Review previously learned material and establish a link to chapter content.
☐ Introduction does not provide any goals/objectives for the chapter.	✔ Provide students with goals/objectives for reading. ✔ Continue with the survey, then have students use chapter summary, review questions, headings, etc., to develop goals/objectives for their reading.

Possible Problem Area	Teacher Strategies
Introduction (cont.) ☐ Introduction does not explicitly state, but rather embeds, chapter goals/objectives.	✔ Change the introductory sentences with implicit statements of goals/objectives to explicit statements and list on chalkboard. ✔ Provide students with vocabulary usually employed in goal/objective statements (e.g., *should, will*). ✔ Assist students in identifying goals/objectives embedded in the introduction's implicit statement.
Main Parts and Terms ☐ Students cannot differentiate main headings from subheadings and sub/subheadings.	✔ Direct students to examine the **size, shape, color,** and **placement** of headings to help identify types of headings. ✔ Teach students the outline notations, symbols, and patterns. ✔ Guide students through the outlining process.
☐ Students cannot diagram the headings into content map form.	✔ Guide students through the mapping process. ✔ Provide a content map.
☐ Students have difficulty changing headings into questions.	✔ Guide students through the process of formulating questions. ✔ Provide students with a list of questions and have them match them to appropriate headings.
☐ Students cannot find key terms in the chapter. ☐ Students cannot find definitions of key terms.	✔ Direct students to look for: words highlighted in bold print, words footnoted at bottom of each page, words noted in margins a list at the end of the chapter, a glossary. ✔ Identify key terms and list on chalkboard.
☐ Students' limited background knowledge/experience makes understanding of key terms/concepts difficult.	✔ Pre-teach vocabulary critical to understanding key concepts in the chapter. ✔ Have students create vocabulary cards with terms on one side and definitions on the reverse side. For ESL students, both languages may be used to facilitate understanding. Use cards to create concept/content maps, as a self-testing tool, etc.
☐ Students cannot relate enrichment features to appropriate headings.	✔ Guide students through process.

Possible Problem Area	Teacher Strategies
Summary	
☐ The chapter does not contain a summary.	✔ Check introduction and review questions for summary information. ✔ Using the information gained through the survey process (*intro, headings, review questions, etc.*) have students write their own summaries. ✔ Summarize the chapter for students.
☐ Students have difficulty paraphrasing the summary because it is too long or summary statements are embedded in the text.	✔ Segment the summary to focus students on smaller units of information. ✔ Identify words in the text that cue a summary. ✔ Summarize the chapter for students.
☐ No review/study questions are provided.	✔ Provide students with review/study questions. ✔ Guide students through process of formulating review questions based on what they have learned from their survey of the title, headings, introductions, etc.
☐ The review/study questions do not review the most important ideas in the chapter.	✔ Identify types of information targeted by questions. ✔ Provide questions reviewing most important information in the chapter. ✔ Guide students in formulating appropriate questions.

Source: From *The Survey Routine,* by D. D. Deshler, J. B. Schumaker, and P. C. McKnight, 1997, Lawrence: University of Kansas Center for Research on Learning. Copyright 1997. Reprinted with permission.

Glossary

Academically diverse class   A class with significant academic diversity is characterized by students achieving in the average, above-average, and below-average range of academic performance, as measured by teacher, school district, or state academic standards. This diversity in performance may be attributed to the interaction between individual differences among teachers and students in, but not limited to, learning needs, emotional needs, culture, gender, life experiences, life situations, age, sexual orientation, physical abilities, cognitive abilities, behavior, skills, strategies, language proficiency, beliefs, goals, personal characteristics, and values.

Accommodation   An adjustment in what a student is expected to do relative to what most students are doing but that does not change the content or proficiency level of the content. For example, a student who listens to the chapter recorded on a tape is gaining the same content and is responsible for the same learning as other students, but his or her access to the content information is accommodated by using a chapter-on-tape.

Adaptation   An alteration in instructional content expectations that changes the expectation from what other/most students may be required to do; for example, most students are expected to become proficient in solving word problems with mixed fractions with unlike denominators. An adaptation for one student might be that he or she solves word problems with simple fractions with the same denominators, using concrete objects.

Algorithm   A procedure for solving a mathematical problem in a finite number of steps that frequently involves repetition of an operation; a step-by-step procedure for solving a problem or accomplishing some end.

Anticipatory set   An anticipatory set is a "hook" to gain students' attention, giving them an opportunity to think about their previous learning as well as their personal knowledge as a way to set the stage for new or expanded knowledge development.

Assessment   A mechanism that allows teachers to make judgments about student progress, thinking, and accomplishments. It is a process that teachers also use to evaluate their curricular and instructional practices.

Attention Deficit Hyperactivity Disorder (ADHD)   A disorder characterized by (1) hyperactivity, (2) impulsivity, and/or (3) inattention. Symptoms must be present in more than one setting, persist for longer than six months, and not be attributable to other disorders, and onset must occur before age seven.

Challenge question   A question within a lesson intended to provoke discussion among students so that they might relate lesson content to their own experiences and prior knowledge.

Cognitive delay   A condition in which an individual has significant limitations in cognitive ability and adaptive behaviors that interfere with learning. Also referred to as mental retardation.

Cognitive strategies   Strategies that emphasize the importance of how an individual processes information or thinks when learning.

Community principles   Norms in the classroom that represent shared ideas about the purposes of the community, how the community will work together to achieve their goals, and how community members will relate to one another to assure that everyone is included and engaged in the work of the community.

Concept A category or class into which events, ideas, or subjects can be grouped; all members (or examples) of a concept must possess a set of critical characteristics (e.g., characteristics that are present in examples of the concept).

Concept mapping A concept map is a visual representation of relationships between ideas. It can be used as a teacher planning tool and for instruction and assessment. It can also become a way for students to organize course material.

Constructivism A theory that focuses on an inquiry approach to the collection, interpretation, and use of knowledge by an individual.

Content Enhancement An approach to planning for and teaching content to diverse groups of students. It involves making decisions about what content to teach, manipulating and translating that content into easy-to-understand formats, and presenting it in memorable ways.

Co-teaching The collaboration that occurs when two professionals (e.g., a general educator and a special educator) share responsibility for a variety of pedagogical and instructional practices, including planning for instruction, presenting content, and monitoring the progress of heterogeneous groups of students.

Controlled materials Materials that are selected for practicing a strategy based on a student's current instructional level. By practicing the strategy in easier materials, students can build confidence and fluency in performing strategy steps.

Course vision The big idea of a course; a description expressed in one concise sentence or as a theme or metaphor describing what a course is about.

Cue-Do-Review Sequence An instructional process that promotes the explicit instruction needed for strategic teaching.

Curriculum-based assessment Short-term and long-term brief assessments, typically formative in nature, that provide teachers and students with evidence (usually directly observable evidence) to note how well a student is progressing before and during an instructional unit (short-term) or throughout a course (long-term).

Curriculum-based measurement Long-term brief assessments that teachers use to note student progress within a course.

Effective strategies Strategies that enable a learner to complete a task with accuracy.

Efficient strategies Strategies that enable a learner to complete a task in a timely manner.

Emotional/behavior disorder Students who have significantly inappropriate behavior are referred to as having "conduct disorders," "emotional disabilities," "behavioral disorders," "serious emotional disturbances," or "emotional and behavioral disorders" and can receive special education services. They exhibit behavior that has two common elements that are instructionally relevant: (1) they demonstrate behavior that is noticeably different from that expected in school or the community, and (2) they are in need of remediation. In each instance, the student is exhibiting some form of behavior that is judged to be different from that which is expected in the classroom. The best way to approach a student with a "conduct disorder" and a student with a "behavioral disorder" is to operationally define exactly what it is that each student does that is discrepant with the expected standard. Once it has been expressed in terms of behaviors that can be directly observed, the task of remediation becomes clearer. A student's verbally abusive behavior can be addressed, whereas it is difficult to directly identify or remediate a student's "conduct disorder," since that term may refer to a variety of behaviors of widely different magnitudes. The most effective and efficient approach is to pinpoint the specific behavioral problem and apply research-based instruction to remediate it.

Formative assessment Assessment that occurs during instruction, not usually graded, but used for feedback purposes.

Generalization Ensuring that a newly learned strategy is applied across settings, contexts, and time. Some instructional programs recommend that generalization be taught as a specific instructional phase so that students practice applying and adapting the strategy to new materials and settings.

Guided practice Practice activities that occur when a student is progressing from low proficiency on a skill or knowledge area toward 80 to 85 percent proficiency.

Heuristics Of or relating to exploratory problem-solving techniques that utilize self-educating techniques (as the evaluation of feedback) to improve performance; providing aid or direction in the solving of a problem.

Higher-order thinking Thinking that goes beyond the recall of facts. This includes cause-and-effect thinking, developing analogies to make associations, and making informed judgments.

Integrated curriculum An integrated curriculum is organized so that students encounter the same concepts or skills across disciplines.

Independent practice Practice activities that occur once a student has demonstrated 85 percent proficiency on a skill or knowledge area and is moving from about 80 percent proficiency toward 100 percent proficiency.

Individualized educational program (IEP) Document prepared by a multidisciplinary team or annual review team specifying a student's level of functioning and needs, the instructional goals and objectives for the student and how they will be evaluated, the nature and extent of special education and related services the student will receive, the type of assistive technology needed, guidelines for participation in local and state assessments, transition goals for students age 14 and older, and the initiation and duration of the services. Each student's IEP is updated annually.

Learning disabilities Learning disabilities is a general term that refers to a heterogeneous group of disorders manifested by significant difficulties in the acquisition and use of listening, speaking, reading, writing, reasoning, or mathematical skills. These disorders are intrinsic to the individual, presumed to be due to central nervous system dysfunction, and may occur across the life span. Problems in self-regulatory behaviors, social perception, and social interaction may exist with learning disabilities but do not, by themselves, constitute a learning disability. Although learning disabilities may occur concomitantly with other disabilities (e.g., sensory impairment, mental retardation, serious emotional disturbance), or with extrinsic influences (such as cultural differences, insufficient or inappro-

priate instruction), they are not the result of those conditions or influences. (National Joint Committee on Learning Disabilities, 1988. Retrieved 1/13/03 from *http://www.nifl.gov/ nifl/ld/archive/insert.htm#national*, where other definitions of Learning Disabilities are also available.)

Learning Express-Ways A communication system designed to improve and enhance the way a teacher gets to know students in an academically diverse class.

Lesson organizer A visual device; graphically frames the content of the lesson for students in order that they may see the main ideas of the lesson, as well as how those main ideas relate to prior content knowledge; functions as an alternative instructional planning approach.

Lesson plans and delivery Ways to facilitate higher-level thinking and collaboration among students and teachers in academically diverse environments to include all individuals in the learning process.

Learning rituals A practice to enhance and support learning that is valued and considered to be important and about which there is a shared understanding. A ritual is reenacted regularly.

Learning strategies An individual's approach to a task, including how to approach and do the task and evaluate performance of the task. Also, teacher-taught techniques and ways for students to approach learning tasks.

Linking steps Procedures used with a content enhancement routine to present content to students in an interactive way.

Maintenance Periodically checking to see if a strategy is being used appropriately.

Mastery of a strategy In order to master a given strategy, a student should be able to accurately perform the steps of the strategy (usually with 80 percent accuracy) fluently.

Metacognition Knowing that allows one to plan, monitor, and evaluate one's own thinking.

Metacognitive strategies Strategies used to provide feedback on one's own learning. Examples of metacognitive strategies include making predictions, checking progress, monitoring performance, and evaluating work.

Mnemonics Techniques or devices for increasing the initial learning and long-term retention of important information. These devices include the keyword method, pegwords that rhyme with a number to be remembered, acronyms, and acrostics.

Modeling Demonstrating the steps of a strategy while "thinking aloud" so learners can observe the cognitive processes involved in learning the strategy, as well as the overt behaviors involved in using the strategy.

Modification Sometimes used as a synonym for adaptation, and sometimes used as a synonym for accommodation; an adjustment, variation, or difference in what a student is expected to do or learn, or how a student is expected to demonstrate knowledge in which the knowledge form may or may not be the same content and conceptual level as other students in the class.

Multidisciplinary team (MDT) In education, a group made up of a student's classroom teacher, specialists, administrators, and parents. The group determines whether the student is eligible for special education services and prepares an individualized education plan for him or her.

Multiple intelligences A theoretical construct developed by Howard Gardner in the 1980s, describing the many ways in which individuals can solve problems, develop products, or express reasoning and thinking about content and real world experiences.

Nonnegotiable issues Aspects of classroom activities and expectations that teachers believe are so important to student learning that teachers are unwilling or unable to alter or eliminate them.

Open-ended response items Questions or tasks that can be used with a variety of writing activities and can be easily framed within a curriculum integration or interdisciplinary teaching model. The activities are designed to engage students in a process in which they illustrate or express understanding of content knowledge, integrated concepts or skills, and solve complex problems.

Paradigm A pattern or example.

Pedagogy The art and science of teaching.

Performance-based assessment Tasks that measure how students construct and apply their understanding of course content and conceptual knowledge. For example, in labs,

dramatic performances, music recitals, social studies projects, and so on.

Personal biographer Storyteller who weaves aspects of a fellow classmate's background into an interesting report that is shared with classmates.

Personal practical theories Systematic theories or beliefs held by a teacher based on classroom experiences and personal experiences that occur outside the school setting.

Portfolio assessment A systematic collection of student work that documents that the student has made progress toward meeting goals or expectations.

Rational-linear model A traditional instructional daily plan that reflects four basic elements: objectives, materials, procedures, and assessment.

Rules A generally prevailing quality, state, or standard of judgment; a regulating principle; for example, the general rule that when a three-letter word has a consonant-vowel-consonant pattern the vowel sound is short.

Scaffolded instruction Interactions between teachers and students that promote movement in a stepwise fashion, from basic to more complex knowledge and skills; for example, a teacher may be interacting with a student through a dialogue within which the student moves from recall and understanding of terms toward synthesis and evaluation of situations in which the terms are used.

Schema A diagrammatic presentation, such as a figure, drawing, or a diagram to portray a systematic arrangement of information.

Self-management A process by which students may self-record (e.g., Was I on task or not?), self-evaluate (e.g., How well did I do?) and/or self-reinforce (e.g., I've done enough good work that I've earned for myself . . .) their behaviors; self-management is usually taught to the student and used with some sort of checklist, rating scale, and/or goal-setting sheet.

Self-regulation A process by which students learn how to control their behaviors by increasing awareness of thinking, acting, and evaluating their behaviors toward improvements.

Strategic teaching Instruction that shows students how to compensate for their lack of skills or strategies to learn information independently. Strategic teaching is explicit and interactive and leads to the development of a partnership in learning between teacher and students.

Student feedback Giving students an opportunity to provide information to teachers about how learning is going in the classroom.

Summative assessment Assessment that occurs at the end of instructional units or courses that are used for grading purposes.

System Organization, pattern, or procedure that typically depicts a "sameness" that can be used with other items within a category or class of items; for example, some students may develop or teachers may instruct students on organization frameworks, such as an outline, that can be used repeatedly on additional or novel items.

Teaching routine A set of instructional procedures teachers use to guide the delivery of large chunks of information in a lesson. These procedures are based on a teaching device, such as a graphic organizer, that helps students organize, understand, and remember content.

Traumatic brain injury (TBI) An injury to the brain caused by an external physical force, resulting in total or partial disability or psychosocial impairment, or both, that adversely affects educational performance. The term applies to open or closed head injuries resulting in impairments in one or more areas, such as cognition; language; memory; attention; reasoning; abstract thinking; judgment; problem-solving; sensory, perceptual, and motor abilities; psychosocial behavior; physical functions; information processing; and speech. The term does not apply to brain injuries that are congenital or degenerative, or to brain injuries induced by birth trauma. The definition of "traumatic brain injury" does include an acquired injury to the brain caused by the external physical force of near-drowning.

Voice Expression of ideas, knowledge, talent, cultural background, and other aspects of one's unique identity.

Zone of proximal development A term coined by L. Vygotsky to describe child development as determined by individual problem solving ability, both actual and potential.

Index